Women and Politics in a Global World

THIRD EDITION

Sarah L. Henderson
Oregon State University

Alana S. Jeydel
American River College

New York   Oxford

OXFORD UNIVERSITY PRESS

Oxford University Press is a department of the University of Oxford.
It furthers the University's objective of excellence in research,
scholarship, and education by publishing worldwide.

Oxford New York
Auckland Cape Town Dar es Salaam Hong Kong Karachi
Kuala Lumpur Madrid Melbourne Mexico City Nairobi
New Delhi Shanghai Taipei Toronto

With offices in
Argentina Austria Brazil Chile Czech Republic France Greece
Guatemala Hungary Italy Japan Poland Portugal Singapore
South Korea Switzerland Thailand Turkey Ukraine Vietnam

For titles covered by Section 112 of the US Higher Education
Opportunity Act, please visit www.oup.com/us/he for the
latest information about pricing and alternate formats.

Published by Oxford University Press
198 Madison Avenue, New York, New York 10016
http://www.oup.com

Library of Congress Cataloging-in-Publication Data

Henderson, Sarah, 1971–
    Women and politics in a global world / Sarah L. Henderson Oregon State University,
Alana S. Jeydel, American River College.—Third edition.
        pages cm
Includes bibliographical references and index.
ISBN 978-0-19-989966-1   1. Women—Political activity—Cross-cultural studies.
2. Women—Government policy.   I. Title.
HQ1236.H45   2014
320.082—dc23   2013003851

*This book is dedicated to all who work
tirelessly to achieve equality of opportunity for all.*

BRIEF CONTENTS

☙

CONTENTS

PREFACE

Mao Tse-tung used the slogan "women hold up half the sky" to promote the equality of women as part of his larger goal to restructure Chinese society radically under his vision of communism. Since then, the phrase has been adopted by a myriad of organizations around the world to highlight the fact that even though women make up half of the population, their interests—political, economic, social, and personal—are often vastly underrepresented and undervalued. While they may hold up half the sky, women are not consistently rewarded or acknowledged for their work. Across countries, women make up a disproportionate share of the illiterate, the poor, the displaced, the elderly, the underpaid, the underemployed, and the underrepresented. Even though women have gained visibility and influence in a wide array of political and economic arenas, they are still far from equal to the position and status of men in society. However, beginning in the post–World War II era, an explosion of women's activism occurred globally, with the goals of equality, liberation, and better living conditions, not just for women, but for their families as well. This activism increased in the late 1960s, 1970s, and 1980s as a second wave of women's activism continued to highlight women's often separate and unequal status around the world. *Women and Politics in a Global World* is written to serve as a central text for courses that address women and politics. We provide an overview of the ways in which women participate in politics, discuss some of the key policy issues that impact women, and define some of the critical transnational issues that confront women in the international community. This book is global in its coverage, and it compares women's impact on politics and politics' impact on women from a cross-national, comparative perspective.

We decided to write this book because as political scientists, we both teach classes that address women's issues and politics from a comparative perspective. We found that while a vast literature on women and politics exists, past research tended to focus on the experiences of women in a single country. Alternatively, past comparative literature on women and politics tended to look at the experiences of women in a single region, such as Western Europe, Latin America, or

Asia. The few books that did offer a comparison of women's activism across continents either were outdated or were edited volumes of case studies, which also did
not quite match our needs. We never found that single text that pulled together all
of the themes we wanted to emphasize and described the experiences of women
not just from a particular country or region but from countries across the globe.

This comparative approach comes with inherent dangers. Is sisterhood really
global? Can we really generalize about women's interests, given that women come
from such vastly different economic, social, and cultural backgrounds? A white,
wealthy, college-educated American woman seemingly has little in common with
an illiterate Nigerian woman who was born into, and will in all likelihood die in,
poverty, yet we discuss the condition of both in this book. Even within countries,
vast disparities are found between how women define and advocate their interests;
American women's gender identities, for example, often coexist with equally important ethnic, racial, religious, and class differences. Further, how can we compare
the impact of women on policy and politics when there is such wide variation around
the globe with respect to types of political regimes? France and Zimbabwe both
claim to be democracies, yet any observer would agree that there are significant
differences in how politics functions in these two countries.

Despite these concerns, we argue that a global comparison is not only possible
but necessary. Certainly, a white, wealthy, college-educated woman in the United
States faces different challenges than an illiterate woman in Nigeria does, and
while these women probably have many concerns that they do not share, there is a
set of core issues around which women have organized. In their study of women's
political engagement in 43 different countries, Barbara Nelson and Najma
Chowdury found that women around the world mobilized around four sets of
common issues: ensuring their personal safety, security, and autonomy; providing
reproductive rights and maternal and child health programs; equalizing access to
public resources, such as education, employment, health care, and credit; and remaking the political and legal rules of the game to ensure women's access to political institutions and positions of authority.[1] In other words, women face common
barriers, even though the specifics of those barriers may differ substantially from
country to country. Also, cross-nationally, in broad ways, women have responded
to these challenges similarly by organizing and advocating for greater roles for
women in determining the direction of their lives. Of course there are numerous
differences among women across nations and even within nations. But we find
that women have many common experiences (being raped during war being but
one example) and common ways of addressing issues they care about (mobilizing
in a social movement, for example). We feel it is possible, and advantageous, to
identify and discuss broad themes and experiences that women share across cultures and political contexts.

At the same time, we recognize that while sisterhood may be global, that does
not mean that all women face identical situations or consistently respond in identical ways. Class, ethnic, religious, and cultural differences, for example, all intersect to enrich the variety of women's responses to issues that are important to
them. A variety of scholars have tried to capture the complexity of women's diverse

interests while simultaneously identifying larger commonalities. For example, Maxine Molyneux distinguishes between strategic and practical gender interests as a way to understand the varied ways in which women organize. While strategic gender interests are more explicitly feminist in orientation in that they seek ultimately to change the relations between the sexes to overcome women's subordination, practical gender interests "are usually a response to an immediate perceived need and they do not entail a strategic goal such as women's emancipation or gender equality."[2] Scholars who studied women's activism in Latin America and the Caribbean used this distinction to classify groups as "feminine" in orientation versus "feminist"; that is, "feminine" groups do not question the gender roles that men and women play in everyday life, but actually use these gendered roles as a justification for their activism. In contrast, feminist groups explicitly target issues that would change the relationship between the sexes.[3] Thus, for example, women in both the United States and Brazil may mobilize over the issue of improved access to contraception, but they may be drawn into that activism for different reasons and may use different mobilization techniques and strategies that resonate with local cultures, customs, and needs. Some of these techniques may more overtly challenge existing patterns of gender relations, while others may reinforce them. These distinctions between practical and strategic gender interests and feminine versus feminist organizations are just a few illustrations of how women around the world can care about similar issues while expressing these concerns in very different ways. Commonalities among women can coexist with marked social differences, and thinking about women's activism in this way further explores how gender interacts with other social cleavages and dispels the idea that women's interests are unified and undifferentiated, without dismissing women's broad commonalities altogether.

Further, larger structural factors, such as a country's levels of economic development and social modernization, also affect the nature and impact of women's activism and the design of woman-friendly policy. In the previous few decades, a wealth of research based on survey data drawn from citizens from countries all over the world indicated that there are significant differences in the cultural views and attitudes of people living in agrarian, industrial, and postindustrial societies. This is because economic modernization creates systematic (and predictable) social change in terms of people's values. In particular, Ronald Inglehart argues that there is a rising and clearly distinct emphasis in postindustrial societies on self-expression, subjective well-being, and quality-of-life concerns rather than material concerns of basic security and survival.[4]

In terms of cultural attitudes about gender relations, drawing from survey data from over 70 countries, Ronald Inglehart and Pippa Norris find that citizens of richer postindustrial societies are consistently more likely to support gender equality than are those in agrarian or industrial societies. As they point out, when people are no longer "restricted by widespread fears and insecurities based on life-threatening challenges, then women and men gradually develop greater willingness to adopt interchangeable roles within the family and workforce."[5] Also, postindustrial societies are characterized by significantly large generational divides (which are not very large in other societies), in which younger respondents are even more likely to support gender equality than their parents or grandparents are. However, in their work only 20 countries are considered postindustrial, 58 are industrial, and 97 are agrarian; thus, while this culture shift is significant, it is most noticeable in a minority of countries.[6] Our larger point, however, is that, certainly, these differences in broad levels of modernization and cultural attitudes, norms, and customs will manifest themselves in terms of how women participate in politics as well as in the design and implementation of policy issues that affect women. Thus, when we compare the condition and status of women in Nigeria with women in the United States, we are aware of the socioeconomic backdrops that inform people's values, interests, and identities.

In this book, we try to maintain the delicate balance between stressing the broad commonalities that women share while acknowledging the very real and substantial differences that separate them by carefully choosing which countries we discuss in each chapter. Thus, we try to avoid the "everything but the kitchen sink" approach to examples—bombarding the reader with a host of statistics and random examples from multiple countries that may bear little relation to one another. Each chapter expressly indicates which countries we are comparing and explains why those particular cases were selected. We carefully thought about which countries might illustrate broader theoretical points and when a global comparison would illuminate women's commonalities and when it would superficially impose "a woman's view" rather than "women's views." As a result, while the chapters in Part I tend to draw from the experiences of women around the world, the chapters in Part II focus on policy issues that impact women in the developed world and the chapters in Part III focus primarily on transnational issues that affect women in the developing world. Our aim in pursuing this strategy was to combine a global scope of inquiry with an appreciation for the limitations of such an approach.

Other obstacles to this type of study arise in addition to the thorny issue of defining women's interests. As political scientists we bring certain assumptions and methodologies to this research. As political scientists we have been trained to study the state as a key actor in the lives of its citizens. We also discuss the state quite frequently, since the book addresses women's impact on government institutions and policies and these institutions' impact on women. By "state" we are referring to the various institutions within a country's governing apparatus, such as the legislature, the bureaucracy, and other related policymaking and policy-implementing bodies, as well as the people who are employed by these institutions. Thus, we tend to ask questions that involve finding out more about the relationship between the state and its citizens (in this case, women) versus the role and impact of women in families or clans or villages. We also tend toward more macro-level analysis than other disciplines do. For example, an anthropologist might be more likely to study the role and impact of women in a specific town or village rather than in one country, in several countries, or even around the world.

We also had to think carefully about whether we wanted to present an analytical or a normative work. That is, should we simply present the condition and status of women, or should we take a position on what the condition and status should be?

We decided to take the following normative position: When women's access to political and economic power is increased, women and society as a whole benefit. We echo the principals of the Beijing Declaration and Platform for Action, announced at the United Nations Fourth World Conference on Women (1995), which maintains that "women's empowerment and their full participation on the basis of equality in all spheres of society, including their participation in the decision-making process and access to power, are fundamental for the achievement of equality, development, and peace," as is helping women shape "their lives in accordance with their own aspirations."[7] Thus, this book does advocate for women's equality, without confusing equality with "sameness." By women's equality, we mean that one sex is not superior to the other, nor should one sex have categorical control of the rights and opportunities of the other. Further, we assume that women's condition is socially constructed and historically shaped rather than preordained by God or nature.[8] Thus, while we may discuss the role of women and/or organizations that view women as separate and unequal, we do not endorse this view.

At the same time, we try to avoid presenting women's impact and concerns from an overly narrow feminist perspective only. Feminism as an ideology is quite diverse; it includes liberal feminism, radical feminism, Marxist-socialist feminism, global feminism, black feminism, ecofeminism, and gender feminism. These strands of thought differ in their assessments of the nature and source of women's oppression as well as the strategies needed to overcome it. For example, liberal feminism, the oldest and probably most influential strand of feminist thought, focuses on the importance of increasing women's autonomy through working within the existing political system and structures to allow women equal access to opportunities and resources. In contrast, radical feminists argue that liberal feminists have been co-opted by the male hierarchy since their goal is to reform the system rather than replace it. A third perspective, global feminism, critiques liberal feminism because it evolved out of a specific Western tradition of Enlightenment values that is overly focused on the individual, which does not mesh well with other cultures' focus on community, rather than individualist, values. And conservative critics charge that feminism as a whole is out of touch with mainstream society, which values marriage, motherhood, and family.[9]

While the book does advocate the promotion of women's equality, it does not take a particular position on which strategy should be used to achieve that goal, although it does present a range of differing positions on improving women's status. Many of these strategies differ on how to resolve the tension between *sex* and *gender*, words that are often used interchangeably in the popular press and media. The word *sex* refers to physical and biological differences between men and women. Men and women differ most obviously in their contribution to human reproduction; for example, only women can give birth and breastfeed. In contrast, *gender* refers to "socially determined attributes, including male and female roles."[10] For example, women's roles in raising children after birth are socially defined gender roles, not physically defined biological functions. Women's inequality in society cannot be attributed to sex differences alone; rather, "it is how society interprets differences and values one quality over another that has the greatest impact on women's lives."[11]

Women activists have pursued various strategies in their quest for women's equality, and they reflect differing attitudes about addressing what one scholar has termed the "paradox of gender equality"—that is, resolving demands of gender equality with biological differences between men and women.[12] Some advocates for women's equality have argued that the best way to ensure equality is to treat men and women the same by passing gender-neutral legislation. Thus, differences must be eliminated in laws and policies in order to foster equality. Others argue that treating men and women the same, given their biological and gendered differences, amounts to unfairness. According to proponents of this view, the solution lies in designing laws and policy that account for these differences by treating men and women differently, but fairly. Throughout this book we discuss this tension and show how it has been manifested in women's battles for greater political, economic, and human rights.

The book is divided into three parts. Part I, "Women Impacting Politics," contains three chapters, all of which provide a different perspective on how women in developing and developed societies participate and achieve representation in the political arena. The first part of the book gives the reader a clear analysis of the impact of women on politics in a variety of political settings around the world. Chapter 1 looks at women's participation in political institutions. It covers women's impact in institutions such as legislatures, parliaments, executive branches, and bureaucracies. The increase in the number of women in public office has shaped irrevocably the way these institutions work and the policies they produce. Chapter 2 covers women's involvement in and impact on interest groups and social movements. These organizations play a crucial role in expressing the demands of citizens to their state. Women's involvement in such groups has made a crucial difference in the actions that many states have taken regarding women's issues and concerns. Chapter 3 deals with women's roles in revolutionary movements. Lacking stable channels of participation toward the state, women have been crucial forces in revolutions, although they have not always been rewarded consistently for their efforts with policies that substantially improve their lives.

Part II, "Gendering Public Policy," moves from the topic of women's influence on politics to the ways in which public policy shapes women's lives in advanced industrialized nations. The three chapters explore the tension that exists between the quest for policy that creates gender equality (such as equal pay or anti-discrimination legislation) and the battle for policy that acknowledges the differences that exist between the sexes. Chapter 4 examines employment policy in the advanced industrialized world and its impact on women's lives. How have states attempted to ensure women's equality, and how have they designed policies to reflect that commitment? Chapter 5 explores the politics of difference. In other words, states also write gender-specific legislation, acknowledging the innate differences between men and women. Specifically, this chapter delves into how states have legislated balancing the needs of production (work) with reproduction (family care). Chapter 6 examines how states address issues of privacy by looking at ways that different countries have resolved the issue of abortion.

Part III, "Participation and Protest in the Global Community," explores a variety of women's issues that, although of global concern, tend to be concentrated in the countries of the developing world. This part is different than the first two; instead of long chapters we have chosen to write shorter chapters on a variety of issues that address critical and compelling global issues affecting women in countries on nearly every continent. Chapter 7 surveys how the international community has addressed gender issues and concerns. Chapter 8 examines the role of women in the global economy. We then turn to women and health care in Chapter 9. Chapter 10 examines women and education. Chapter 11 addresses the issue of sexual violence during war. Finally, Chapter 12 discusses women's lack of physical autonomy in issues such as female genital mutilation.

NEW TO THIS EDITION

For the third edition we decided to make several key changes. First we updated the data and many of the text boxes in all the chapters to reflect any recent relevant changes to the political landscape. Second, many of the chapters have new opening stories to reflect how the general issue and/or theme addressed in a particular chapter continues to be relevant in today's world. Third, all of the chapters have been reworked to reflect what has changed in the world since the last edition. For example, Chapter 2, on social movements, has a new text box on Arab women fighting for changes to nationality laws. Chapter 3, on revolutions, addresses gender and the Arab Spring, the Burmese democratization movement led by Nobel laureate Aug San Suu Kyi, and the controversial outcome of the 2009 presidential elections in Iran. Chapter 3 also has new text boxes on Aung San Suu Kyi and women terrorists. Chapter 4, on women and equal opportunity law, provides a picture of how the recent economic downturn has impacted women in terms of income and retirement. In Chapter 5, on women, work, and family, we have removed France as a case study and expanded the sections on Germany and Sweden to explain more fully what has changed in these countries since the last edition. Further, Chapter 5 adds a text box on the "cult of mom" politics, talking about how women have recently used motherhood as "street cred" in elections. Chapter 6 has more information on the issue of reproductive rights as a whole and we have added text boxes on fertility tourism and the debate over the distribution of contraception in public schools in New York. Chapter 7 (and 10 on education) spends more time talking about the Millennium Development Goals, since we are approaching the 2015 deadline, as well as new approaches to measuring women's inequality. And it has a new text box on the impact of the book *Half the Sky*. Chapter 8 pays more attention to the effects of the 2008 world financial crisis on women. Chapter 10, on education, has a new text box on Elizabeth Scharpf, whose organization provides sanitary pads to girls in developing countries, because lack of pads is a key reason girls do not attend school. Chapter 11, on sexual violence during war, is updated and expanded and looks at recent decisions and cases before the International Criminal Court. Finally, Chapter 12, on physical autonomy, looks in more detail at current controversies in

Egypt regarding virginity testing and stoning cases in Iran and adds a text box on the nongovernmental organization Tostan and its work in Africa to end female genital cutting. At the end of each chapter, we added more sources to the "For More Information" section so students can learn more about these issues as well as the people and organizations working for critical change. This section also includes citations for memoirs and documentaries that may provide an alternative narrative for students. In other words, we have made an effort to weed out whatever seems not as relevant and have woven in new trends, themes, and developments that have changed how we think about women and politics.

Throughout the book we discuss a number of dilemmas that women have faced as they have battled for greater representation in political and economic institutions. As we shall see, countries differ dramatically in terms of the degree to which women have access to the state and are able to influence state policy. While there is not one correct way to resolve the demands for women's equality, we hope we have provided enough information for you to think about various women's issues with your professor and your classmates so that you can continue to ponder your position on these issues long after the course has ended.

ACKNOWLEDGMENTS

We would like to acknowledge all those who supported us in the research and writing of this book. First and foremost, we would like to thank each other for providing the support, patience, and love necessary to write and revise this book while also raising small children. At different times, one of us would provide the critical push necessary, without which this book would never have seen the light of day. Alana would like to thank the Center for the Humanities at Oregon State University, which deserves special thanks for providing her with the resources needed to work on this project when it was just starting. Sarah would also like to thank her husband, Doug, for supporting her throughout the long process of researching and writing all three editions, and her graduate assistant, Mika Yasua, for tirelessly hunting down data and finding relevant news stories and media resources to help make this book up to date and relevant. We would also like to thank the following reviewers for their thoughtful comments: Michelle Kaufman, Johns Hopkins University and North Carolina State University; Karen M. Kedrowski, Winthrop University; Kristen Abatsis McHenry, University of Massachusetts Dartmouth; Mary K. Meyer McAleese, Eckerd College; Jody Neathery-Castro, University of Nebraska-Omaha; Brett O'Bannon, DePauw University; Erica Townsend-Bell, University of Iowa; and Alisa Von Hagel, Northern Illinois University and Benedictine University. Finally, we would like to thank Jennifer Carpenter and Maegan Sherlock at Oxford University Press for believing in and supporting this project.

Sarah L. Henderson
Alana S. Jeydel

PART I

Women Impacting Politics

In this part we look at various ways in which women seek to impact the state. Drawing from countries in the developed as well as the developing world, we discuss women's involvement in institutionalized and noninstitutionalized forms of political activism. In other words, we look at women's participation in activities ranging from voting and running for office to participating in interest groups, social movements, and revolutionary movements. To what degree does women's involvement in politics and movements matter, and what barriers still stand in the way of their further involvement?

While women seek to influence the state in a variety of ways, certain common themes unite these chapters. One theme that runs through the chapters is that while women have fought for and attained access to positions of power in elected governments, social movements, and revolutionary struggles, such access is not widespread, uniform, or far-reaching. Women are still marginalized in most governments and movements. They are often relegated to positions that deal with "women's issues" instead of issues like foreign policy and finances. Even in revolutionary movements that profess radical aims in terms of the redistribution of power, women's rights are often put off or ignored altogether, and women are often expected to fulfill the traditional female role of nurturer and caretaker in the movement. Further, multiple barriers still exist that bar or deter women from attaining leadership positions, and many women still attain positions of power via their roles as wives, mothers, or sisters of important male leaders or political dynasties.

Another theme that unites the chapters is the gendered nature of women's activism. That is, women's varied socially constructed roles and relationships are a constant subtext in their motivations to act. Women are often pulled into activism when their socially defined roles are threatened, and they have drawn on their status as mothers and caretakers to fight for issues, such as those involving food, shelter, health, and children, which are perceived to be of immediate concern to them. In addition, women are able to exploit societal expectations about their affinity for "women's issues" to push for specific political outcomes, such as policy or regime change.

However, the ways in which women around the world define and express their gender interests vary widely. As we discussed in the preface, while women from disparate cultures often share broad, common concerns that unite them, cultural, socioeconomic, ethnic, religious, and racial differences often shape how women identify with and mobilize around these broad issues. In the chapters in this part, we try to emphasize these broad commonalities while also explaining how socioeconomic and cultural differences can manifest themselves at the local and national levels. Further, we stress that women are not necessarily united simply by the biological commonality of their sex or the status of their gender and that women can define and express their interests in diametrically opposed ways.

As we shall also see, not all women are motivated to activism out of gender concerns, and in fact, some subordinate these concerns in the face of other, larger causes, such as national self-determination, independence, and greater levels of social justice for all. Some women are conflicted by the question of "double militancy," or allegiance to two simultaneous issues (such as feminism and democracy), while others consciously choose to prioritize alternative issues. Regardless, all too often, primarily male political elites are often ready and willing to take advantage of women's contributions, while denying them substantial access to avenues of power upon achieving political victory.

Yet, as we shall see, the presence of women in political institutions and movements does matter. The increased visibility of women in a variety of political activities has led to increased attention to women's issues, the creation of women's bureaus and commissions, and the design and implementation of policy that impacts the status of women. This is not to say that women's views are always integrated or that women are consistently successful in achieving their political goals; however, having women in positions of power and influence has made a substantial impact.

This part provides a comparative analysis of women's involvement in various forms of political activism and expression. Specifically, we look at three areas of women's involvement in politics: at the institutional level, through struggles to get elected and/or appointed to government institutions, as well as women's voting behavior; at the noninstitutional level, through involvement in social movements and interest groups; and at the level of participation in movements whose aim is the overthrow of the government and the institution of a new, totally restructured government. Thus Chapter 1 covers women and institutional politics, Chapter 2 covers women in social movements, and Chapter 3 covers women in revolutionary movements.

The chapters highlight the impact that women have had on politics while also demonstrating the barriers and obstacles that remain in their way even in the twenty-first century. In Chapter 1, "Women and Institutional Politics," we provide a comparative overview of women's representation in political institutions and their voting behavior. While the number of female elected officials has increased greatly in the past 20 years, there are still a number of countries where female representation is scant to nonexistent. Further, there appears to be a political "glass ceiling"; women are not moving up the rungs of the political ladder and are often relegated to "women's issues" departments, committees, and bureaus. Also, many barriers still exist to women's participation in politics, both cultural barriers and structural barriers. Finally, women worldwide are less likely to get involved in politics than men are—this means they are less likely to vote, run for office, and get involved in politics in general. Nonetheless, we see that women's involvement in politics does matter. Elected female officials are more likely than their male counterparts to introduce, lobby, and vote for legislation of immediate concern to women and their families. Further, in some countries, women's voting behavior has at times been decisive in election results, such that many now often talk about a gender gap. In short, women clearly have impacted institutional politics, but in most countries there is still vast room for improvement in women's representation and in addressing issues of direct consequence to women's lives.

In Chapter 2, "Women and Noninstitutional Politics," we examine women's involvement in and impact on social movements and interest groups worldwide. We see that women's movements and organizations are important players in politics around the world. From women taking over oil plants in Nigeria to Christian women fighting to limit or curtail access to abortion in the United States, women have been involved in and have impacted a wide spectrum of movements. Socially and culturally, women's groups have changed the way society perceives women, have motivated women to get more involved in grassroots politics, and have often changed the way women view themselves. Institutionally, women's groups have impacted governments by encouraging them to pass legislation directed toward women's issues and to create women's bureaus and ministries, and they have made politicians aware of the usefulness of a woman's bloc of votes. But women also have become involved in religious fundamentalist and nationalist movements that often seek to roll back or prevent any advances that women have made. Their participation in such movements perplexes many scholars—why would women wish to maintain or return to a time when they had fewer rights and were subservient to men? We conclude the chapter with a discussion of this intriguing question. In sum, women have impacted the state in a multitude of ways via their involvement in social movements; however, this involvement is not without its contradictions, as recent years have seen a spate of religious fundamentalist and nationalist movements attracting women to their ranks.

Chapter 3, "Women and Revolutionary Movements," examines women's involvement in and impact on revolutionary struggles. In this chapter we see that despite the radical goals of most revolutionary movements, the key activists in the struggles often hold very orthodox views regarding the role of women in society and in the movement. And while some revolutionary leaders speak the rhetoric of women's rights, in practice they are more concerned with class struggle and often place women's rights on the back burner to be dealt with at some nebulous later date. Thus, it is rare that women occupy important leadership positions in revolutionary movements or the government, should the movement be successful. We do see, however, that women have played an active and important role in numerous revolutionary struggles—as messengers, fighters, and more. In sum, while revolutionary movements are not consistently revolutionary in their views of women, women have certainly impacted the course and outcome of many revolutions through the ages.

Women have had an important impact on the politics of many states in both advanced industrial and developing nations. Women are increasingly running for and winning access to political office. They are participating more frequently in the political process by utilizing their right to vote (where they have it) and by organizing around issues of interest to them. They are mobilizing in increasing numbers in revolutionary movements. In sum, their presence in institutions and movements does matter. Nonetheless, the number of women involved in politics as compared to men is still comparatively low in most countries and abysmally low in others. Further, there appears to be a glass ceiling in both political institutions and revolutionary movements, whereby women can advance only so far on the leadership ladder. This is caused, in part, by lingering societal norms about the "appropriateness" of women's involvement in politics, as well as by persistent gendered divisions of labor that keep women from exercising their full range of talents. Until societies view women as politically capable and are willing to redistribute the division of labor between men and women, women's impact on politics will continue to be hampered and countries will not experience the rich rewards that come from politically empowering their entire adult population.

1

Women and Institutional Politics

In November 2002, Yvonne Khamati, a candidate for the Kenyan legislature, was beaten up, allegedly by supporters of one of her rivals.[1] Khamati noted, "The threat had been made on me since early October. The aspirant had been threatening to undress me in public if I did not step down for him, but I have resisted. . . . I fear the threat itself more than the actual act."[2] This violent act was not an anomaly in the 2002 Kenyan elections. It was reported that in early December 2002, women who were waiting to hear a candidate for the Langata constituency of Nairobi were assaulted by a gang of youths who supported the opposition. Further, a parliamentary candidate and her children were attacked on the campaign trail, and another female candidate's convoy was stoned as she campaigned among her constituency.[3] And while violent attacks against candidates in Kenya are not limited to women, they are certainly a tactic used to try to prevent women in particular from seeking political office. In the 2002 elections in Kenya, 130 women expressed an interest in running for office, but ultimately only 44 did.[4] Kenya's legislature has one of the worst records in Africa regarding female representation. In the 2007 Assembly only 22 out of 224 members were women. A patriarchal culture, a lack of funding, and Kenya's electoral system are just a few of the variables that stand in the way of women's decision to run for and ultimately win office.

The Kenyan case is one example of a pervasive problem—women's underrepresentation in institutional politics. As of 2012, worldwide, women comprised just over 19.6 percent of members of legislatures.[5] There are also only 17 elected female heads of state and government.[6] However, despite these discouraging general statistics, women's representation in political institutions varies substantially from region to region and is improving. Women constitute over 42 percent of members of parliament in the Nordic countries and at least 30 percent of members of lower houses of legislatures in 30 countries located primarily in Europe and Africa.[7] Further, although on average women comprise 19.8 percent of legislators in sub-Saharan African countries, countries such as Rwanda, Mozambique, and South Africa have high percentages of women legislators. In fact, Rwanda has the highest

5

percentage of any nation; 56.3 percent of the members of the lower house are women.[8] In comparison, in the U.S. Congress (as of 2012) women comprised almost 17 percent of representatives and 17 percent of senators, placing it 78th out of 189 countries in terms of its representation of women.[9] Women are also increasingly visible as heads of legislatures, members of cabinets and bureaucracies, and executives. These increases are a largely recent phenomenon. For example, of the 32 women who have served as heads of state in the twentieth century, 24 were in power in the 1990s.[10]

But, as the Kenyan case suggests, there is still vast room for improvement. In a wide array of countries women's presence in government is scant. In the newly independent states of the former Soviet Union and in the former members of the Eastern bloc the number of women in political positions has dropped.[11] And women's representation in politics is extremely low in Middle Eastern countries. In Arab states, women comprise just over 11.7 percent of elected officials.[12] On a positive note, women recently won the right to vote and stand for elections in Saudi Arabia (granted in September 2012 to begin in 2015 for local elections); Qatar in 1999 and Kuwait in 2005; women in Oman could stand for elections beginning in 1997; in 2002 all Omani citizens received the right to vote; and finally, in 2006 the United Arab Emirates began the slow path toward democracy with the creation of an elective body in which 15 percent of the candidates and eligible voters were women.[13] But overall, while women's legislative representation is higher, at its current growth levels, women legislators will not achieve parity with men until the turn of the twenty-second century.[14] What explains women's underrepresentation, and what factors can continue to improve their status?

This chapter examines women and institutional politics. Institutional or formal politics is the realm of politics that takes place in formal governmental institutions, such as parliaments/legislatures and the executive branch, and encompasses political behavior, regulated by the state, which is geared toward electing people to those institutions. We explore women's voting behavior, their paths to political office, the reasons for their underrepresentation in office, and their political behavior once in office. In closing, we discuss a variety of strategies that have been used to improve women's representation in institutional politics.

Why study women and institutional politics? Quite simply, because the decisions made by political institutions have a direct impact on women's lives. Political institutions were created and largely run by men for centuries, and, as a result, many women's concerns have been ignored, forgotten, or inadequately addressed. And since men and women often experience life differently (arguably as a result of socialization and societal constraints on appropriate behavior), it stands to reason that they might have different concerns, views, and modes of behavior that might result in different voting patterns, laws, regulations, and policies. And in fact, this is the case. As we show, a significant gender gap exists in voting patterns, and this gap has been decisive in determining the outcome of elections. Further, women's presence in political office, particularly in legislatures, does matter, as do their voting patterns. When compared with men, women elected officials are often more progressive, more consensus-oriented, and more likely to introduce legislation that directly addresses women's concerns (health care, education, welfare). They also work hard to see that such legislation become law. While there are individual exceptions to all of these generalizations, nonetheless, across countries and contexts, women engage in distinctly different patterns of political behavior.

WOMEN AND VOTING

The Expansion of Suffrage

Beginning in the mid-1800s women worldwide began to organize to demand the right to vote in their countries, and in some countries women are still working to gain this basic political right. In 1861, Sweden introduced limited suffrage for women in local elections. Over 30 years later, in 1893, New Zealand became the first country to grant all women the right to vote at the national level. Australia extended suffrage to women in 1902 and Finland in 1906, with a number of European countries as well as the various republics of the former Soviet Union following suit in the 1910s. By 1930, 42 countries had granted women the right to vote, and in the ensuing three decades, from 1931 to 1960, an additional 86 countries widened suffrage regulations to include women. Finally, an additional 38 countries extended the right to vote after 1960.[15] The end of World War I, World War II, and the ensuing decolonization (and initial democratization) in many countries around the world were some of the factors that created a wave of women's suffrage. Table 1.1 offers a glimpse of when national voting rights were granted to women around the globe. As noted, New Zealand was the first country to expand the suffrage to all women in 1893; over a century later, Qatar, Oman, Kuwait, and, to a limited degree, Saudi Arabia and the United Arab Emirates became the most recent countries to expand suffrage to women.

Winning the right to vote was not easy, often requiring decades of struggle. For instance, in the United States women began agitating for the right to vote in 1848 but only received that right nationally 72 years later, in 1920. Nor did women win the right to vote for particularly noble reasons. For example, U.S. women were granted the right to vote, in part, to counteract the influx (and political influence) of immigrants into the country. Further, some legislators assumed that women would vote as their husbands directed. In other countries, suffrage was gradually extended to all women. For example, while white women won the right to vote in Australia in 1902, Aboriginal women did not gain that right until 1967.[16]

In some countries, women's right to vote is still fragile. In Kuwait, the emir issued a decree in May 1999 granting women full political rights (the right to vote and to run for and hold political office). However, the National Assembly threw out this decree and then subsequently defeated a bill that would have granted women these rights. The issue, however, did not disappear, and on May 16, 2005, parliament granted women the right to vote and run for parliament. The law first went into effect in the 2007 parliamentary elections (see photo 1.1). Other Gulf nations, such as Bahrain, Qatar, and Oman, all had their first elections in recent

Table 1.1 Year Suffrage Granted in National Elections in Selected Countries

COUNTRY	YEAR
New Zealand	1893
Australia	1902
Finland	1906
Germany	1918
Austria	1919
United States	1920
Cuba	1934
France	1944
Japan	1946
Argentina	1951
Bolivia	1952
Nigeria (Southern)	1957
Nigeria (Northern)	1976
Iran	1963
Yemen	1967
Switzerland	1972
Jordan	1974
Zimbabwe	1982
Qatar	1999

SOURCE: United Nations Development Programme, "Women's Political Participation," Human Development Report 2004 (New York: UNDP, 2004), 234–237.

years and allowed women to cast ballots.[17] Saudi Arabia granted women the right to vote and run in local elections only in September 2012, to begin in 2015.

Women's Political Participation

What has been the impact of women's suffrage, and how have women participated in other forms of political activities? Early research on women in the United States indicated that women voted and engaged in political activities (such as helping political parties, attending political rallies, and other such civic activities) at rates lower than men did.[18] Since women gained the right to vote in the United States they have historically lagged behind men in their rates of turnout at election time. For example, in 1964, 72 percent of voting-age men cast a ballot, versus 67 percent of voting-age women.[19] A few explanations were put forth to explain these lower rates of participation. First, some argued that women are politically passive and thus do not participate in political activities. Second, some argued that women's family responsibilities hinder their involvement in politics. Finally, some maintained that women are less likely to be found in those segments of society that are most politically engaged—the highly educated, for example. While this research was limited to the United States (and in terms of voting is no longer valid), we will show that these explanations travel well to other countries.

However, since 1980, women's turnout in U.S. elections has been greater than that of men.[20] In 2000, women led men in turnout 56 percent to 53 percent.[21] Similarly, in 2008, turnout was higher for women (66 percent) than for men (62 percent).[22] And while this difference is not great, it is interesting. It sends a message to elected officials that women are worth targeting because they will vote. In addition, the gender gap in party identification with regard to voting in the United States is significant; since 1980, women have been more likely than men to vote for Democratic Party candidates. In the 2000 presidential election, for example, approximately 54 percent of women voters backed Al Gore, while only 43 percent of men did.[23] In 2004, 55 percent of men voted for George W. Bush, while 48 percent of women voted for him.[24] 2008 witnessed a continuation of this trend, with 56% of women voters favoring Barack Obama and 43% favoring John McCain. The media quickly labeled this emerging gender gap in voting as the "soccer mom" vote. In their depiction, these women are not only behind the wheels of suburban minivans but are also increasingly in control of the fate of presidential elections. As a result, both Republicans and Democrats have become much more attentive to women voters, and the gender gap is an incentive for them to include more women's issues on their party platforms as well as to nominate more women for office.

Interestingly, however, women's rate of participation in campaign activities (working for a candidate, contributing money, attending a political meeting or a campaign rally, trying to persuade someone how to vote, or wearing a political button or displaying a campaign sticker) consistently has remained below that of men since 1952.[25] However, when we expand participation to include involvement in community groups, women's involvement improves. Women are somewhat more likely than men to be members of and actively involved in such groups.[26] And as you will see in the chapter on noninstitutional politics, women are very involved in social movements and interest groups. Research seeking to explain women's lower levels of political participation in the United States has found that while women have as much, if not more, of some of the resources necessary for becoming involved in politics, namely education, they lack other crucial resources, such as personal income and occupations that facilitate political participation and a sense of personal efficacy.[27] Nonetheless, and no matter the explanation, with the exception of voting, women's political participation in the United States remains below that of men.

What about in other countries? What are women's rates of political participation around the globe? Some studies indicate that in advanced industrial nations, traditional gender differences in voting participation have either diminished or reversed.[28] In most countries outside of the advanced industrial world, women's rate of voting is generally below that of men. However, it is important to note that we do not have longitudinal data for many countries. We have limited longitudinal data for a few developing democracies, all of which are at varying levels of economic development: Chile (elections since 1989), Barbados, and Guatemala. And longitudinal data since World War II exist only for eight other democracies (not including the United States), only one of which would be considered a developing

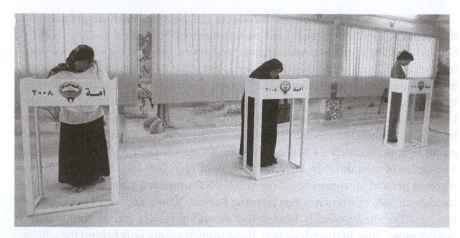

Kuwaiti women, long denied suffrage, vote in parliamentary elections in Kuwait City on May 17, 2008. SOURCE: YASSER AL-ZAYYAT/AFP/Getty Images

nation—India. Of these countries for which we have data, the evidence is inconclusive. In Chile women have voted in greater numbers than men in each election for which we have data (by about 5 percent), and in Barbados women have also voted in greater numbers than men (by about 9 to 10 percent), but in India and Guatemala men have voted in greater numbers than women (by about 10 percent and 14 percent, respectively).[29] In Israel, Arab women display a higher rate of voting than do Arab men, although there is no noticeable difference between Israeli women and men.[30] However, this is not a representative sample of developing nations, and, while limited, evidence does seem to suggest that women vote in lower numbers in most developing nations.

Low voter turnout among women in developing nations is not surprising given the significant discrepancies in adult literacy rates between men and women. Further, men's longer history of political involvement provides them with the basic know-how concerning how to vote. One deterrent to voting is fear—a lack of knowledge about what to do once one enters the polling site. Nigeria is no exception to this rule. One group, the Women's Rights Advancement and Protection Alternative (WRAPA), is working to change this by educating women on how to vote correctly (e.g., how to use the machines).[31] Arab women are also working to overcome this barrier to women's participation. In some tribal communities, Arab women have provided women-only transportation and polling stations in an attempt to increase the number of women voting.[32]

However, even if women may be less likely in many countries to vote, nonetheless the gender gap in party identification is noticeable in many countries, as it is in the United States. Until 1980, the conventional wisdom was that women were more conservative than men. In fact, The Civic Culture, a comparative study of political cultures that was first published in 1963, found that "wherever the consequences of women's suffrage have been studied, it would appear that women differ from men in their political behavior only in being somewhat more frequently apathetic, parochial [and] conservative. . . . Our data, on the whole, confirm the findings reported in the literature."[33] Yet, by the 1980s, scholars were finding signs of gender dealignment in Britain, Germany, the Netherlands, and New Zealand. Drawing from survey data collected from over 70 countries over the course of several decades, Ronald Inglehart and Pippa Norris found that in most nations surveyed, women hold more left-leaning values than men do, favoring active government intervention and public ownership. This left-leaning gender gap is most pronounced among young voters; older voters tend to adhere to pre-1980 expectations about women's more conservative political behavior.[34] Thus, the United States is not singular and is one example of a growing and enduring gender cleavage in voting.

In addition, around the world, women's participation in other forms of traditional political activity—party membership, contact activity, and community organizing—has historically been below that of men. A 1978 17-nation comparative study of political activity found that, even after controlling for levels of education, institutional involvement such as trade union membership, and psychological involvement in politics, women in advanced industrial nations were less active than men were.[35] However, recent research presents a less conclusive picture. One study demonstrated that women's rates of political activity in advanced industrial nations increased in the 1980s and 1990s, and in some cases their participation surpassed that of men.[36] The Inglehart and Norris study found that while there is a gap in traditional forms of political activism, particularly in advanced industrial societies, that gap is narrowing and is very modest. However, particularly in agrarian societies, the gap is more substantial, and men are much more likely to join parties, discuss politics, and work in community organizations than women are.[37]

In sum, while there still seems to be a modest gap in traditional forms of political participation, particularly in developing countries, nonetheless women's participation is increasing. This increase appears to have a few causes. One clear pattern is that the increase in participation is largely found among younger women (those under 25), who are turning out in greater numbers to vote than their male counterparts are.[38] The other causes appear to be changes in social norms and in structural lifestyles, which have removed many barriers that had deterred women's participation.[39] However, it is important to remember that voting is no guarantee of political, social, or economic equality. And further, voting may mean little in authoritarian regimes where voting has no impact on the outcome or in patriarchal states where men may inform their female family members how they should vote. As a woman in Oman commented to a Reuters reporter, "Some [women] . . . follow their male relatives' lead when choosing which candidates to vote for."[40] Finally, voting is but one form of political involvement. As we will show, women increasingly are involving themselves in other forms of nontraditional political participation.

PATHS AND BARRIERS TO POLITICAL OFFICE

In the beginning of this chapter, we gave some statistics to illustrate women's persistent underrepresentation in positions of political leadership. Specifically, as of March 31, 2012, only 19.6 percent of the world's parliamentarians were women (although this was the first time that women exceeded 19 percent and was a 3.3 percent increase from the first edition of this book). Moreover, women comprise only 7.3 percent of the world's heads of state and government (both elected and unelected). In sum, the higher women ascend the ladder of political power, the rarer their representation. Why has the rate of women in political office historically been so low? Cross-national research on this question has produced three general explanations for the persistent lack of women in political office. Women worldwide running for office, no matter which path they have taken, run into some common obstacles or barriers.

The first explanation emphasizes the role of structural barriers, such as levels of political and socioeconomic development, as well as women's representation in professional and managerial occupations. For example, scholars have argued that the degree to which a country is democratic is positively related to women's presence in elected office. That is, newly democratized countries are likely to promote widespread political and civil liberties, increased political party building, and other measures that would increase the involvement of women. However, the evidence to support that claim is inconclusive.[41]

Another study demonstrated that levels of socioeconomic development are significantly associated with the number of female parliamentarians worldwide.[42] In other words, in developing countries, many women are disadvantaged because they are more likely to be illiterate, have inadequate health care, and live in poverty. Further, women in the developing world are less likely to have an independent source of income, making it difficult to accumulate the funds to run for office. In Uganda, for instance, women lack the monetary resources required to dole out beer, small gifts, and contributions to fundraising events, thus making their run for office more arduous in a society accustomed to such offerings during the campaign season.[43] All of these are barriers to running for office.

Further, studies have demonstrated that in established democracies, the presence of women in professional, administrative, and managerial occupations is critical, as these types of careers often provide the experiences, financial resources, social networks, and flexibility needed to compete for elected office.[44] However, since women have traditionally not been well represented in careers that prepare them for politics, they often have difficulty running campaigns that highlight their preparation for political office. Women also often lack the resources (primarily money) required to run a successful campaign. Individuals and political parties often donate to the candidate with the greatest chance of winning, and women are still not seen in many countries as viable candidates. Further, since men traditionally have been in the paid labor force and women relegated to the home, women often do not have the same personal financial resources that men have to contribute to their own campaigns. And while money is critical, women also lack access to the "old boy's network" that has enabled men to have access to political power.

This explanation, however, does not fully explain the variance in women's rates of election to office. Countries that have similar standards of living exhibit major disparities in the proportion of women elected to parliament. For example, in 2012, nearly 25 percent of Canadian parliamentarians were women, while in the United States, that figure was just under 17 percent. The countries in Europe and Africa also demonstrate great disparities in women elected to office, even when they share similar socioeconomic characteristics. Comparatively, in 2012, Rwanda had a very high percentage of women legislators, even though it is one of the world's poorest countries.

In addition, in many postindustrial societies, while women are increasingly well represented in careers, such as law, that serve as a jumping ground for political office, they are not reaping a clear increase in their political representation. For example, while about a third of all lawyers (31.9 percent) in the United States are now women, the United States has not witnessed a similar surge in women's representation in the U.S. House or Senate.[45] Nor has increased funding for female candidates in countries such as the United States led to a dramatic increase of women representatives. Thus, while improving women's socioeconomic status and career opportunities is an important condition for improving their access to political office, it is not in and of itself sufficient.[46]

A second explanation for women's underrepresentation focuses on the role of institutional design and the "rules of the game" as expressed by electoral laws and the use of what are known as positive action policies. Specifically, scholars point to the importance of proportional representation (PR) electoral systems and the adoption of gender quotas, either via internal party rules or mandated through national legislation. A PR system is one in which parliamentary seats are awarded in proportion to the vote received by each party. In addition, voters in a PR system often choose among party lists, which are lists of candidates who would assume seats if the party is elected. In contrast, countries such as the United States use a single-member plurality electoral system, also known as a majoritarian system. That is, the candidate who obtains more votes than any other is elected. The larger difference between the two systems is that a PR system tends to produce a multi-party legislature, in which power is shared among a coalition of varied parties, while a majoritarian system produces a two-party system, in which power usually alternates between two large catchall parties.

PR systems have beneficial ramifications for female candidates; research shows that women are almost twice as likely to be elected under the rules governing a PR system.[47] The Inter-Parliamentary Union reported that in 2007 the 21 chambers that used PR elected an average of 18.3 percent of women to seats versus 13.8 percent of the seats being won by women in chambers that do not use PR (21 such chambers).[48] This is because parties in majoritarian systems are less likely to nominate women, since they are afraid of losing the seat to a male competitor. In contrast, parties in PR systems are more likely to add women to their party lists to make their ticket more diverse and broaden their appeal. Women candidates in PR systems are perceived to be less risky because a woman is part of a larger group of candidates running for office, rather than a sole candidate competing for office.[49]

Other institutional variables, such as the adoption of various quota regulations, have also been critical in promoting women to elected office. Many parties, particularly those of the left, have moved to adopt voluntary internal quotas mandating that women must constitute a minimum proportion of parliamentary candidates or elected representatives within each party. This is usually done by requiring that a certain percentage of female candidates appear on party lists. For example, in 1980, the Green Party in Germany became the first party in Europe to institute a 50 percent quota for women on party lists. Eventually, two other major German parties moved to implement quota systems in their own party rules. Political parties in Scandinavian countries followed the Green Party model several years later; in 1983, the Norwegian Labour Party implemented a 40 percent quota for all elections, and other Norwegian parties soon followed with similar strategies. However, while this is significant, the effects can be limited by several factors. One, given that voluntary quotas are adopted by individual parties within a country, the potential benefits to women can be limited if the practice does not spread to other parties. Second, the effects can be diminished if parties decide to place women at the bottom of party lists, which lessens their chances of making the cut for political representation. In response to this problem, some parties, such as the Greens, also simultaneously adopted what is known as a "zipper" or "zebra" principle; that is, names on the party's nomination list must alternate evenly between men and women.[50] Finally, it is easier to adopt this type of quota system in PR systems than in majoritarian ones, which govern the United States and Great Britain. However, this does not mean it cannot be done. In 1993, in response to an electoral defeat in which they failed to attract sufficient levels of women voters, the British Labour Party agreed that in half of certain categories of targeted seats, local party members would be required to select their candidate from an all-female short list. Although this provision was eventually dropped under legal challenge, the proportion of women at Westminster doubled from 1992 to 1997.[51] Around the world, 101 political parties, representing 50 countries, have instituted voluntary internal quotas.[52]

Other countries have moved to mandate party list quotas by passing legislation that applies to all parties.[53] For example, in the summer of 2000, the French legislature passed parity legislation, a constitutional amendment requiring parties to include 50 percent representation of women in their party lists for local, regional, parliamentary, and European elections.[54] Belgium, Portugal, Spain, and various Latin American countries have instituted legal gender quotas. Further, Finland and Norway have implemented legislation that sets out gender quotas for appointments to public bodies and consultative committees.[55] Alternatively, other countries have implemented legislation that reserves a certain percentage of legislative seats for women (and in some instances, ethnic minority candidates). This system of reserving seats has been used, for example, in Afghanistan, Bangladesh, France, Iraq, Nepal, Pakistan, Serbia, and Tanzania. However, some argue that this is not as effective a mechanism as party quotas, for it can simply be used to sideline or appease women, particularly in countries where the women are appointed, rather than elected. While this system is most often used in countries with more limited democratic rights, a notable exception is India, where a third of seats in local municipal elections are reserved for women.[56] Despite these concerns, a vast array of countries worldwide utilize some form of quotas, and quotas have shown to be the most successful means for getting more women into office.[57] Tables 1.2 through 1.6 provide an overview of the varied use of quota systems around the world.

Political scientist Eileen McDonagh, in her research on female leaders, has found that women are more likely to be elected head of state or government in political systems that combine both traditional and modern features. She maintains:

> Every nation where women have been elected to be head of state or government is one that combines modern guarantees of individual rights and electoral processes with the retention of at least one major traditional feature, such as a monarchy, a state religion, or a constitutional connection between the state and the family as an institution or another ascribed group.[58]

It will be interesting to see if this holds true in the twenty-first century. A third explanation for women's poor electoral performance focuses on the role of cultural barriers. This explanation contends that "ideas about women's role and position in society can enhance or constrain women's ability to seek political power."[59] Thus cultural norms can inhibit women's participation, as the Kenyan case certainly suggests. This explanation has recently found strong support in research done by Paxton and Kunovich, which draws on survey data from 46 countries.[60] Further, Inglehart and Norris found a strong relationship between attitudes toward women's political leadership and the actual proportion of women legislators. In other words, countries with egalitarian cultures, such as Sweden, Finland, and Norway, have more women in power. This egalitarian culture is a reflection of

Table 1.2 Quota Systems for Women's Representation

QUOTA TYPES	TOTAL NUMBER OF COUNTRIES	AVERAGE % OF WOMEN
Constitutional quota for national legislatures	18	25.4
Election law quota regulation, national legislature	49	22.9
Constitutional or legislative quota, subnational level	44	N/A
Political party quota for electoral candidates	50	22.4

SOURCE: International IDEA and Stockholm University, "Global Database of Quotas for Women," 2010 http://www.quotaproject.org/system.cfm (June 4, 2012).

Table 1.3 Constitutional Quotas for National Legislatures

COUNTRY	% WOMEN
Afghanistan	27.7
Argentina	37.4
Bangladesh	18.6
Burundi	32.1
Ecuador	32.3
France	18.9
Haiti	4.2
Iraq	25.2
Kenya	9.8
Nepal	33.2
Pakistan	22.2
Rwanda	56.3
Serbia	21.6
Sierra Leone	13.2
Somalia	6.8
South Sudan	26.5
Tanzania, United Republic of	36
Uganda	34.9

SOURCE: International IDEA and Stockholm University, "Global Database of Quotas for Women," 2010 http://www.quotaproject.org/system.cfm (June 4, 2012).

broader patterns of socioeconomic development and cultural modernization that are affecting many countries, not just northern European ones.[61]

Cultural norms have made it difficult for women to run in a number of ways. One barrier women encounter when running (or deciding to run) for office is that political behavior is seen as masculine because aggression and autonomy are considered requisites. These are not traits commonly associated with women, and thus women are not seen as capable of doing the job if elected (thus people may not vote for them). And, when women do exhibit these traits, they are seen by the electorate as abnormal or deviant, which are not adjectives often ascribed to successful candidates for elective office.

In addition, voters often have trouble overcoming traditional societal norms about appropriate divisions of labor between men and women. Women are associated with parental roles, and men are associated with paid labor. Thus politics is not seen as an appropriate realm for women since it will interfere with their parental responsibilities. In Uganda, female parliamentary candidates confronted cultural prohibitions on their political activity that their male colleagues did not face: "[W]omen candidates . . . faced greater public ridicule than men, were labeled 'unfeminine' and some even risked their marriages and public discrediting by their husbands."[62] In Oman, a female university lecturer told a Reuters reporter that "My husband stopped me from standing for elections."[63] These societal norms are even still prevalent in advanced industrial nations; female candidates with

Table 1.4 Election Law Quota Regulation, National Legislature

COUNTRY	% WOMEN	COUNTRY	% WOMEN
Afghanistan	27.7	Jordan	10.8
Albania	16.4	Korea, Dem. People's Republic of	15.6
Angola	38.6	Korea, Republic of	15.7
Argentina	37.4	Kyrgyzstan	23.3
Armenia	9.2	Macedonia	27.6
Belgium	39.3	Mauritania	22.1
Bolivia	25.4	Mexico	26.2
Bosnia and Herzegovina	16.7	Nepal	33.2
Brazil	8.6	Niger	13.3
Burkina Faso	15.3	Pakistan	21.3
Burundi	32.1	Panama	8.5
China	21.3	Paraguay	12.5
Columbia	12.7	Peru	21.5
Costa Rica	38.6	Poland	23.7
Djibouti	13.8	Portugal	26.5
Dominican Republic	20.8	Senegal	22.7
East Timor	27.7	Serbia	21.6
Ecuador	32.3	Slovenia	32.2
Egypt	2	Spain	36
Eritrea	22.0	Sudan	25.1
France	18.9	Tanzania, United Republic of	36
Guyana	31.3	Tunisia	26.7
Honduras	18	Uganda	34.9
Indonesia	18	Uruguay	15.2
Iraq	25.2	Uzbekistan	22

SOURCE: International IDEA and Stockholm University, "Global Database of Quotas for Women," 2010 http://www.quotaproject.org/system.cfm (June 4, 2012).

children are routinely asked how their election may affect their ability to care for their children, but male candidates with children are almost never asked such questions.

This barrier not only prevents people from voting for women but also prevents many women from running. Women often do not see elective office as an option, either because they also ascribe to this societal norm or because they choose not to come forward as candidates for office. Those who choose to run often face a negative environment. A study conducted by the Inter-Parliamentary Union found that female politicians in many countries identified hostile attitudes toward women's political participation as one of the most important barriers to running for office.

Further, holding political office is not a family-friendly job for either women or men. It is extremely difficult to be a parent and hold elective office. National capitals are often quite far from most people's homes, the hours are unorthodox,

Table 1.5 Constitutional or Legislative Quota, Subnational Level

COUNTRY	COUNTRY
Afghanistan	Macedonia
Albania	Mauritania
Argentina	Mexico
Bangladesh	Namibia
Belgium	Nepal
Bolivia	Pakistan
Bosnia and Herzegovina	Paraguay
Brazil	Peru
Burkina Faso	Philippines
Colombia	Poland
Costa Rica	Portugal
Dominican Republic	Rwanda
Ecuador	Senegal
Eritrea	Serbia
France	Sierra Leone
Greece	Slovenia
Honduras	South Africa
India	Spain
Ireland	Tanzania, United Republic of
Italy	Uganda
Korea, Republic of	Uruguay
Lesotho	Uzbekistan

SOURCE: International IDEA and Stockholm University, "Global Database of Quotas for Women," 2010 http://www.quotaproject.org/system.cfm (June 4, 2012).

Table 1.6 Political Party Quota for Electoral Candidates

COUNTRY	NUMBER OF WOMEN ELECTED	% WOMEN
Algeria	30 of 389	7.7
Argentina	96 of 257	37.4
Australia	37 of 150	24.7
Austria	51 of 183	27.9
Bolivia	33 of 130	25.4
Botswana	5 of 63	7.9
Cameroon	25 of 180	13.9
Canada	76 of 308	24.7
Chile	17 of 120	14.2
Costa Rica	22 of 57	38.6
Cote D'Ivoire	28 of 255	11.0
Croatia	36 of 152	23.7
Cyprus	6 of 56	10.7

Table 1.6 *(continued)*

COUNTRY	NUMBER OF WOMEN ELECTED	% WOMEN
Czech Republic	44 of 200	22.0
El Salvador	22 of 84	26.2
France	109 of 577	18.9
Germany	204 of 622	32.8
Greece	52 of 300	17.3
Guatemala	21 of 158	13.3
Hungary	35 of 386	9.1
Iceland	27 of 63	42.9
Israel	23 of 120	19.2
Italy	134 of 630	21.3
Kenya	22 of 224	9.8
Korea, Republic of	47 of 300	15.7
Lithuania	27 of 141	19.1
Luxembourg	12 of 60	20.0
Mali	15 of 147	10.2
Malta	6 of 69	8.7
Mexico	131 of 500	26.2
Morocco	34 of 395	8.6
Mozambique	98 of 250	39.2
Namibia	19 of 78	24.4
Netherlands	59 of 150	39.3
Nicaragua	37 of 92	40.2
Niger	15 of 113	13.3
Norway	67 of 169	39.6
Paraguay	10 of 80	12.5
Philippines	62 of 280	22.1
Romania	38 of 334	11.4
Slovakia	26 of 150	17.3
Slovenia	29 of 90	32.2
South Africa	178 of 400	44.5
Spain	126 of 350	36.0
Sweden	157 of 349	45.0
Switzerland	57 of 200	28.5
Thailand	79 of 500	15.8
United Kingdom	143 of 650	22.0
Uruguay	15 of 99	15.2
Zimbabwe	32 of 214	15.0
Total countries:		50
Total political parties:		101

SOURCE: International IDEA and Stockholm University, "Global Database of Quotas for Women," 2010 http://www.quotaproject.org/system.cfm (June 4, 2012).

and there are often no onsite day-care options. Given that women are traditionally expected to be the primary caregiver in the family, prevailing cultural norms serve as a significant barrier for women wishing to hold political office.

There is some evidence that cultural values toward women in office are changing. For one, Inglehart and Norris found a significant generational gap in attitudes about women's abilities. Younger, postwar generations are much less likely to believe that men make better leaders than women do. Further, there is a significant emerging gender gap; while men and women of older generations are equally likely to be suspicious of women as leaders, the gap widened substantially across generations, until by the youngest generation the gap has become considerable. Women are much less likely than men to agree with the statement "men make better political leaders than women," and as a result, they may be more likely to raise the issue of women's underrepresentation in office.[64] While changes in cultural attitudes in and of itself are not enough to improve women's access to political power, changing public opinion can also pressure parties and legislatures to institute institutional reforms, such as quotas, which we discussed earlier.

Theory aside, practically, what are the various paths that lead women to political office? There are four general paths that women have tended to take to reach political office. The first is the political family path. Women on this path come from families that have a long history of involvement in electoral politics. For example, a former prime minister of India, Indira Gandhi, was the daughter of Jawaharlal Nehru, the first prime minister of an independent India. In turn, she mentored her two sons in their political careers, and both later served as prime minister. In Asia, every past or present female executive had a male relative who at one point or another held the top executive position in that country.[65] Second, women have assumed office, often temporarily, as a surrogate for a father, husband, or brother who recently died. These women often have little or no political experience, although occasionally they find they enjoy politics and, upon the expiration of the term, run and are elected on their own merits. Mary Bono, for example, served out the term of her husband, U.S. Representative Sonny Bono, who died in a skiing accident. At the end of the term, Representative Bono decided that she enjoyed politics and sought and won election with her own political agenda. Another example is Jean Carnahan, who took her husband's place in the U.S. Senate after he was killed in a plane crash. Later, when a special election was held to fill his seat, she ran but was defeated. Corazon Aquino of the Philippines, Isabel Perón in Argentina, and Mireya Moscoso in Panama all assumed office upon the deaths of their husbands. Violeta Chamorro was elected as president of Nicaragua after the death of her husband, a noted political journalist. And in India, Sonya Gandhi rose to head the Indian National Congress after the death of her husband, Rajiv (son of Indira). However, even though her party won national elections in 2004, she declined the office of prime minister in the face of public opposition (she is Italian by birth, although she became an Indian citizen). Nonetheless, she still heads the Congress Party.

The third path is the party or political insider path, in which women come to office by starting at the bottom of the party/political ladder and working their way to the top over a number of years. In parliamentary systems this may mean decades of dedication to the party, serving whatever roles are needed. Margaret Thatcher, the former prime minister of Great Britain, ascended the political ladder of power after years of dedicated service to the Conservative Party. New Zealand's current prime minister, Helen Clark, also followed the party insider path to power. She notes that she became interested in politics early in life and became "fully committed" while at university in Auckland.[66] She joined the Labour Party in 1971 and slowly moved up through the ranks. In nonparliamentary systems this may mean beginning in local or state-level politics until one has accrued enough political experience to make one look like a savvy, qualified politician.

Finally, women assume office by pursuing a political outsider path. In this scenario, they may emphasize their lack of political experience or connections, and instead run on the platform that they will bring something new to politics and will serve as an alternative to the status quo. This is the least successful path for women seeking political office.

Thus, women worldwide face numerous and often similar obstacles if they seek political office. At the end of this chapter, we will discuss various ways in which women can overcome these obstacles. However, now we address the impact that women elected officials have on politics and whether they are as effective as their male counterparts.

THE IMPACT OF FEMALE LEGISLATORS, BUREAUCRATS, AND EXECUTIVES

How do female politicians behave once they achieve elected office? What types of legislation do they introduce and work on? Are they as effective at legislating and leading as their male counterparts are? Do women executives behave differently than their male counterparts do? And do women bureaucrats tend to emphasize women's issues? Further, if the answer to any of these questions is no, why is this so? First we examine women legislators in the advanced industrial world and then the developing world, and then we turn our attention to female executives and bureaucrats.

Women in Legislatures, Parliaments, and Cabinets

Advanced Industrial Nations

Women have a clear impact in legislatures in the advanced industrial world. There have been many research studies on women in the U.S. Congress and state legislatures, all of which demonstrate that women's presence has a demonstrable impact. Scholars have shown that female legislators tend to hold more liberal views than their male colleagues do.[67] Women are also more likely to make feminist speeches on the floor of the U.S. House of Representatives than their male colleagues are[68] and are more likely to take the lead in advocating for women's issues bills on the Hill.[69] Further, women are also more likely to sponsor or co-sponsor feminist legislation in Congress than their male colleagues are.[70] Similarly, Swers, in her analysis of voting behavior in the 103rd (1993–1995) and 104th (1995–1997) Congresses, found that women are more likely than men to vote for women's issues bills, even when controlling for ideological, partisan, and district factors.[71] And further, she found that gender is more likely to influence a female representative's vote when the bill deals directly with issues that affect women, such as reproductive policy and women's health concerns, rather than on issues that do not affect women as directly, such as education.[72] Frederick found similar patterns in the Senate. He found that when female senators replace male senators, they tend to be more supportive of women's issues than their male predecessors, and when male senators replace female senators, they are less supportive of women's issues than their female predecessors.[73] Thus, at the national level in the United States, the presence of women in Congress does make a difference: women are more likely than their male colleagues to introduce legislation of concern to women, to vote for women's issues bills, and to fight hard for their passage.

At the subnational level in the United States, a study in 1991 by the Center for the American Woman and Politics (CAWP) found that women state legislators have distinct issue priorities from men and are more active on women's rights legislation than male legislators are.[74] For instance, women are more likely to sponsor or co-sponsor feminist legislation than their male colleagues are.[75] And Thomas and Welch found that among state legislators, bills sponsored by women on women's issues are more likely to pass than are bills sponsored by men on men's issues.[76] Further, women actively advocating for women's issues appears to enable their passage.[77] Also, legislative committees in state legislatures that blocked anti-abortion legislation had a greater proportion of women on them than in the chamber at large.[78] Thus, as at the national and subnational levels in the United States, women clearly make a difference to the legislative agenda and output of those legislatures.

There is also evidence that women in Congress and the state legislatures have different, more collaborative, consensus-oriented leadership styles than their male colleagues do.[79] Research has suggested that these differences arise out of the different ways that girls and boys are socialized[80] or that different life experiences compel women to lead differently than men do.[81] As Burrell suggests, "Gender role socialization may predispose women to certain styles of leadership."[82] Further, others find that women state legislators are also influencing the behavior of their male colleagues. Male legislators appear to be "shifting toward the adoption of 'female' types" of leadership.[83] And, male legislators who have had female mentors "indicate stronger motivations to involve people in legislative deliberations and report less dominating, more nurturing traits than men without female mentors."[84] Finally, the CAWP survey of 1991 found that women state legislators are more likely than their male colleagues to bring the citizen into the process by advocating for greater levels of public scrutiny in the legislative process and greater levels of access to underrepresented segments of society.[85]

In gendered institutions like legislatures these differences could decrease the effectiveness of women since their mode of interaction may be seen as aberrant by many male colleagues and thus antithetical to the process of lawmaking.[86] But recent research has shown that female members of the U.S. House of Representatives are as effective as their male colleagues. It does appear, however, that to be effective, women need seniority, membership on influential committees, membership in the majority party, and leadership positions within the party and committee systems.[87] The presence of women in legislatures is important, but it is no panacea. We will see that this holds true worldwide.

Thus, in the United States it appears that women in Congress and state legislatures clearly make a difference and are as effective as their male counterparts. But what is the impact of women in legislatures in other countries? Research on female politicians in other parts of the advanced industrial world and the developing world is not as extensive as that on women in the United States, but some clear trends have been found. In the advanced industrial world many of these trends are consistent with the findings in the United States. But in the developing world we will show that while the presence of women has made a difference, women still face a variety of barriers and are often marginalized by male colleagues, who often relegate them to committee assignments and duties that revolve around issues that have traditionally been of concern to women.

In the remainder of the advanced industrial world, the presence of female legislators appears to have a similar impact as in the United States. Research in Scandinavia has shown that women legislators have been successful in "bringing into the public realm the debate over what political equality of the sexes should be."[88] Bratton and Ray have found that the presence of women in Norwegian local councils had a positive impact on policy outcomes related to child care.[89] Interviews with Norwegian politicians indicate that women legislators introduce women's issues into debate as well as more policies favorable to women.[90] Further, these interviews suggest that women's presence has wrought a change in the way politics is conducted as well as the language used; in meetings and debates male politicians have become more polite, less direct conflict occurs, and men now excuse themselves to go pick up their children from day care.[91] However, these same female politicians indicate that they have conflicting loyalties and demands that make it difficult for them to work as a group to influence politics. Further, many are careful not to be perceived as too feminist, as they fear this may result in negative reactions from colleagues and possibly party sanctions in the form of poor committee assignments.[92] Further, the political system, which was created by men, still continues to serve largely male interests, and while women have been able to effect some changes in the way politics is conducted in Norway, they have not substantially altered the political system.[93] As Bystydzienski notes, "Masculine values continue to be at the foundation of political structures. Masculine images of the politician prevail, and organizational arrangements that appear to be gender-neutral advantage men."[94] Thus institutional barriers still exist that prevent women legislators from having as great an impact as they might under different structural conditions.

Research on women in the British parliament had, in the past, found that women did not attempt to represent women.[95] However, this changed in 1997, when 101 women Labour members of parliament (MPs) returned to parliament, 65 of whom were newly elected. More recent research done on these women does seem to indicate that they have articulated women's concerns in debates, in select committees, and in the Parliamentary Labour Party's women's group and that in the constituency their presence has engendered greater access among women constituents, women's organizations, and women representatives and the articulation of a feminized agenda.[96]

Other recent research on the British parliament has found that women MPs in general, not just those in the Labour Party, do "bring a different set of values to issues affecting women's equality, in the workplace, home, and public sphere."[97] Research conducted on the New Zealand parliament yielded findings similar to those in Britain and the United States. Women MPs in New Zealand are more active in debates on child care and parental leave than their male counterparts are. Further, they make fewer personal attacks than their male colleagues do during debates and do not interrupt as often as their male colleagues do.[98] In these examples, attaining a critical mass of women MPs was a key factor in fostering a distinctly female style of leadership.[99] All of this research indicates that women's presence in legislatures does matter and that if the numbers of women in office continue to increase, there is the potential for women to effect legislative change on women's issues and to influence the conduct of parliamentary debate.

The Developing World

In the developing world, while women have clearly had an impact on politics, they nonetheless still face many barriers. First we will look at their impact. Research on legislatures in Latin America indicates that despite the conservatism of many of these countries, there has been an increase in the number of laws passed that support women's equality as well as changes to political structures that can be tools for women's empowerment, such as women's franchise, quota laws, and the creation of women's ministries. These changes were correlated with increases in the number of female legislators.[100] For example, in Nicaragua, women in the Frente Sandinista de Liberación Nacional (FSLN) party succeeded in persuading the party leadership to implement quotas; currently, a minimum of 30 percent of all party positions must be reserved for women, and this same quota must be applied in the selection of candidates for elections.[101] And these same women fought to make sure that some female candidates were actually placed at the top of the lists, thus ensuring their election.[102]

Women in Latin America have also succeeded in attaining the important party leadership position of speaker of the parliament in a number of countries. The first was in Argentina in 1973; since then women have held this position in eight more countries (six since 1990): Bolivia, Costa Rica, El Salvador, Mexico, Nicaragua, Panama, Peru, and Venezuela. In Costa Rica, since 1994 women have been given high governmental positions such as vice president of the Republic, vice president of Congress, and various cabinet nominations at ministerial and vice ministerial levels.

Further, research on women legislators in Latin America has found that they are as effective in getting all types of legislation passed as their male counterparts, in some cases more so. Research on women in Costa Rica found that female deputies have an 81 percent success rate in getting laws they have submitted to the Legislative Assembly approved, versus a 48 percent success rate for their male counterparts.[103] This is largely because "women spend many more hours in meetings with constituents and in congressional committee meetings than men. . . .

[Men] devote much time to other economic activities such as their professional vocation or personal business."[104]

In the Middle East, women are also trying to impact the political game, although often their biggest impact is simply in getting elected. The number of female elected officials throughout the Middle East is slim (as noted previously), but nonetheless women are attempting to gain access to formal politics. In Iran in 1996, 190 women competed with 3,010 men for 270 seats in the Majlis (the Iranian parliament).[105] And while this number may seem small, it is a remarkable feat in a country that experienced a conservative religious revolution a little over 30 years ago. Thirteen women were elected in 1996, and once elected, these women were active on gender issues. Women were also actively involved as candidates and as voters in the local council elections in Iran in 1999, and they won office in 25 provinces. Further, voters elected at least one female member in 23 cities and at least two women in 48 cities, which means that "a large number of women will be participating in decision making at both city and local council levels in economic, political, social, and cultural issues."[106] In the 2004 parliamentary elections, Iranian women maintained their presence at the national level, winning 12 seats, comprising 4.1 percent of the legislature, but 2008 saw a decline in the number of women elected to 8, and the number remains at that level today.[107]

While the policy impact of these female elected officials is still unclear, the importance of female voters is more visibly significant. When *Zanan*, an influential women's magazine, interviewed the two presidential candidates, Khatami and Nateq-Nouri, in 1996, it asked each candidate about his views on various women's issues. Khatami's answers expressed sympathy while Nateq-Nouri refused to answer.[108] Khatami was ultimately elected, and the majority of women and youth, especially young women, voted for Khatami.[109] Thus the presence of women in elective office and as active voters has signaled to the political establishment in Iran that it must begin to at least be aware of women's concerns, and this is certainly an initial step toward recognition of women's political influence.

However, women still have made few inroads in access to Iran's highest elected office. The Iranian constitution is somewhat ambiguous in its wording regarding the necessary qualifications for presidential candidates. The Arabic word *rajul*, used to define the prerequisite condition for assuming the post of president, can be interpreted to mean both a man and a renowned personality, which technically can also be a woman. A few women activists have used this ambiguity to launch unsuccessful bids to have their candidacy approved by the Guardian Council, the most influential governing body in Iran. In the 1997 presidential elections, 8 women (out of 238 candidates) declared their candidacy, although all were eventually disqualified, with no accompanying reason.[110] In the 2005 Iranian presidential elections, over 1,000 hopefuls, including 93 women, registered, but the Guardian Council ruled that only 6—all men—qualified.[111] This trend continued in 2009, where all women candidates were barred from running. Given that the Guardian Council is currently controlled by conservatives, women may make little progress in their quest for candidacy to Iran's highest elective office in 2013.

Elsewhere in the Middle East women are also leaving their mark on politics. In Israel, women are making strides as candidates and, once elected, as members of parliament. The number of women elected to the Knesset (the Israeli parliament) is now 20 percent, up from 14 percent in 2009, and these women matter. One study of Israeli female politicians found that they were more active than their male colleagues and sometimes even more successful in their legislative efforts.[112] However, female members of parliament in Israel do not focus their attention on women's issues; instead, their interest tends "toward the national flag more than toward the feminist banner."[113] As Wadie Abunassar, a political analyst at the University of Tel Aviv stated, "They [women] have not made a difference in governance. . . . [T]hey mainly focus on the Israeli-Palestinian issue and have neglected the bread and butter, everyday issues ordinary women face."[114] Nonetheless, the presence of active, successful female politicians is important, for it signals to society that women are capable legislators. This, in turn, may lead more women to decide to run for office and eventually build a critical mass of female legislators. Another impact that engaged female voters and politicians have had on the Knesset is the creation of a subcommittee on women's affairs, an entity that may not have been seen as necessary if women were not playing an active role in Israeli politics.

We now turn to countries in Asia. Although India has produced some very prominent female politicians, such as Indira and Sonia Gandhi, nonetheless, most women politicians do not focus on women's issues. Research on women in the Indian parliament has shown that they do not have women's issues high on their list of priorities.[115] Given their low numbers—as of 2012, women comprise only 11 percent of parliamentarians in the lower house—this is not surprising.[116] As previously noted, research has pointed to the fact that women often must reach a critical mass before they are not only able to effect change for women but are also interested in effecting change for women. However, trends at the local level in India may generate some change. In 1993, the Indian parliament mandated a 33 percent women's quota in rural and urban local councils, or Panchayat, creating space for over 1 million female politicians. However, efforts to introduce a 33 percent quota in the national legislature stalled in 1996 and 1998. Male politicians opposed the law, arguing that women should stay at home where they "belonged." In addition, they claimed that the bill would benefit only middle-class city women.[117] However, the issue of women's representation in India is bound to recur, partly as the effects of increased women's representation at the local level trickle up to impact national politics.

In the Kashmir region of India, one woman in particular is having an impact on politics. Mehbooba Mufti is the vice president of the region's ruling People's Democratic Party (PDP). In the region's first election in October 2002, the PDP won 16 of the state assembly's 87 seats, making it the third strongest party and a coalition partner in the government. Some political analysts believed that Mufti would be the coalition's choice as chief minister "because of her common touch and widespread popularity."[118] And in 2011 she was elected by the opposition party, the PDP, for a second 3-year term as their president. In an area torn by strife, where many women have lost a male relative to the insurgency that has been ongoing between Pakistan and India over control of Kashmir, Mufti is seen by the people of the region as someone who may be able to begin a dialogue with the separatist militants and bring some peace to the region.[119] While her ultimate impact is still unknown, traditional gendered beliefs in women as more peaceful, consensual communicators may have helped contribute to her rise to power and her subsequent election.

Research on women politicians in other parts of Asia is scant. However, we do know that women occupy a significant proportion of seats in a number of legislatures. Nepal leads with 33.2 percent of its legislature made up of women. It is followed by the Democratic Republic of East Timor (32.3 percent), Afghanistan (27.7 percent in lower house, 28 percent in upper house), Iraq (25.2 percent), Laos (25 percent), Vietnam (24.4 percent), Kazakhstan (24.3 percent), Singapore (23.5 percent), Kyrgyzstan (23.3 percent), the Philippines (22.9 percent in the lower house and 3 percent in the upper house), Pakistan (22.5 percent in its lower house, 17 percent in its upper house), Uzbekistan (22 percent), China (21.3 percent), Cambodia (20.3 percent), and Bangladesh (19.7 percent).[120] The remaining countries in Asia all have female legislative representation at 19 percent (Tajikistan) or below.[121] Given the wide variety in levels of political freedoms in these countries, it is important to put these figures into context. For example, while one of five legislators in China is a woman, given the authoritarian nature of the political system, one must question whether this figure constitutes significant representation of women's political power or any real "progress" for women's equality. In sum, while political representation can signal the advancement of women's interests, it is no guarantee of success.

Finally, let us look at the African continent. Here there is less research quantifying women's impact on political institutions. We do know that women occupy a significant number of seats in the lower houses of legislatures in 25 African nations, ranging from 15.0 percent for Zimbabwe to 56.3 percent for Rwanda. However, in 29 other African nations, the number of women in the lower houses of legislatures is fairly low, ranging from 3 percent in Comoros to 13.9 percent in Cameroon, with a majority in the 9 to 14 percent range.[122] This, combined with other factors, including the tendency of academics studying women in Africa to focus on topics other than female politicians, has resulted in limited data concerning the impact of women in African legislatures.

However, many point to the experiences of South Africa as a model for promoting more women to formal politics. Women were always extremely active in the African National Congress (ANC), the main opposition force to apartheid rule in South Africa and currently the dominant political party in the postapartheid era. They were a critical force in drafting the new South African Constitution, which includes many clauses guaranteeing the rights of women, and have introduced legislation to benefit women.[123] In turn, the ANC has often promoted the position and status of women in words as well as in deeds. The commitment of the government to the cause of women's emancipation can be heard in President Nelson Mandela's remarks in May 1994: "Freedom cannot be achieved unless the women have been emancipated from all forms of oppression."[124] And it can be seen in its actions, too. In South Africa's first democratic elections in 1994, the ANC adopted a 30 percent quota for women on their party lists. As a result, women's representation increased from below 3 percent to 27 percent. In the 1999 elections, the ANC adopted internal party rules in which women were placed in every third position on the national party list, so that women would not be pushed to the bottom of lists and thus in effect denied political office. These proactive policies have generated results; of the 119 women elected to parliament in 1999, 96 (80 percent) were from the ANC.[125] And as of 2012, women make up 42.3 percent of elected representatives to the National Assembly, the lower house of parliament. The ANC has pushed through legislation to increase women's representation at the local level as well; the Municipal Structures Act of 1998 specifies that political parties should ensure that women make up at least half of their party lists in local elections, although there is no penalty if this rule is not followed.[126]

This increased representation at all levels also helped women rise to increased positions of power within the government. Gwen Mahlangu-Nkabinde was elected as speaker of the National Assembly in 2008 (this position has been held by a woman since South Africa became a democracy in 1994), a position she held until the 2009 elections. Nomaindia Mfeketo was elected deputy speaker of the National Assembly in May 2009; also, as of 2010, 41 percent of cabinet ministers were women. Further, the government has established various bodies within the administration to monitor the position and status of women in South Africa. In 1996, the government established a Joint Committee on the Improvement of the Quality of Life and Status of Women in the parliament, as well as the Office on the Status of Women in the executive branch the following year.[127] As a result of this critical mass of numbers, women have taken steps to advance the cause of women, as has the government itself.[128]

Despite these gains, throughout the developing world women in politics still face barriers in politics, even once elected. Women legislators in India noted that within the political parties women are rarely found in leadership positions.[129]

And even fewer women are found in government cabinets, although this is changing. Worldwide in 1997, women made up 20 percent or more of cabinet members in only 15 countries.[130] By 2001, women made up 20 percent or more of cabinet members in 36 countries.[131] And as of 2010 (most recent numbers), women account for 30 percent or more of ministers in 30 countries, although on average they hold only 16 percent of ministerial posts worldwide.[132] Some of this increased representation is because of quota laws. For example, in 2000, a quota law passed in Colombia mandated that at least 30 percent of appointed positions in the executive branch be filled by women. When President Alvaro Uribe took office in 2002, 6 women were appointed to his 13-member cabinet and received powerful portfolios such as the Ministry of Defense.[133] However, the Colombian example is the exception, not the rule; as with committee assignments, women ministers around the world are primarily concentrated in social areas (14 percent), not in legal (9.4 percent), economic (4.1 percent), political (3.4 percent), or executive (3.9 percent) areas.[134]

Further, female legislators are still often assigned to committees and roles that "fit" their gender—committees that deal with reproduction, social welfare, and motherhood, for example.[135] While many women have a genuine interest in the issues these committees deal with, these are not the "power" committees that influence the direction of the country or serve as stepping-stones to positions of greater authority in government. In addition, while the creation of women's ministries and subcommittees is important in the struggle for women to bring attention to issues that directly affect their everyday lives, women's ministries do not always receive the status and resources necessary for them to impact politics.[136] Thus, in the developing world, while women have been active in institutional politics at all levels of government, they are often concentrated in the least influential positions and have had a tough time moving up the ranks to more influential government positions.[137] To create a pool of qualified women candidates, more women will need to hold cabinet positions (and party and committee positions) of greater political importance if they are going to attempt the next step to executive office.

Further, social and cultural barriers in the developing world still inhibit women's actions in running for office and once elected. In many countries, the lack of a critical mass of women legislators makes it difficult for them to form alliances with other women on key issues. Women who do choose to run and are elected note that there are many ongoing difficulties once elected. When women first entered the South African parliament there were no restrooms for women. And while this structural issue has been addressed, women legislators still have a difficult time balancing family life with a work environment that includes late hours and lots of travel.[138] Women politicians worldwide often comment on the difficulty of balancing a demanding career with the demands of their families. Since women are still mainly responsible for care of the family, they are faced with demands that male legislators often do not have to consider.

A final barrier that women politicians face is that of balancing their concerns over gender issues and identities with the predominantly male world of politics. For example, they are often conflicted over conforming to male patterns of leadership behavior. Female legislators in Latin America noted the contradiction present in the traits required to be an effective MP: "the characteristics of good parliamentary practice remain male; long, unsociable work hours, aggressive in debate and a tendency to dominate."[139] To be successful, women must adopt these characteristics, which are perceived as male, while also remaining "feminine" in the eyes of their culture. Further, as Tripp found in Uganda, existing parliamentary practice makes it difficult for women to realize their interests since parliamentary rules of procedure, as they were written and currently stand, entrench particular male interests.[140] Women do manage to get these rules to work for them and do manage to "win" at times, "but rarely can they make the rules or make the rules work on their own terms."[141] Thus, while women have made great strides in legislatures, and their presence clearly affects the proceedings and output of these legislative bodies, there are still barriers to be overcome.

Women as Executives

As of June 2012, there were 20 female presidents and prime ministers out of 193 rulers (see Table 1.7). This is an increase from 14 in 2008. Women rule in other capacities (as queen, for example); however, we do not discuss them as they exercise little political power. The world's first female prime minister was Siramavo Bandaranaike of Ceylon (now Sri Lanka), who was elected in 1960; a small but increasing number of female leaders have followed in her footsteps in the ensuing decades (see photo 1.2).

What has been the impact of female rulers on the politics and policies of their countries? This question does not have a clear answer. First, not all prime ministers and presidents are created equal. In parliamentary systems, for example, the position of president, the head of state, is largely ceremonial, while the prime minister, as head of government, wields most of the consequential executive powers. This is the situation in Ireland's parliamentary system, where the president's role is more symbolic, while in the United States, for example, the president is vested with a substantial measure of authority. Thus, while it is important that women have attained these presidential positions, their impact on governmental policymaking is minimal, particularly if they have assumed the presidency in a parliamentary system. Further, because of their small numbers, very little research has been done on female executives. And given the nature of the job—one is theoretically required to act in the interests of the entire country, not in those of

Table 1.7 Current Female Leaders

NAME	POSITION, COUNTRY, AND DURATION
Angela Merkel	Federal Chancellor of Germany since November 22, 2005
Ellen Johnson-Sirleaf	President of Liberia since January 16, 2006
Portia Simpson Miller	Prime Minister of Jamaica since March 30, 2006
Pratibha Patil	President of India since July 25, 2007
Cristina Fernández de Kirchner	President of Argentina since December 10, 2007
Sheikh Hasena Wajed	Prime Minister of Bangladesh since January 6, 2009
Johanna Sigurdardottir	Prime Minister of Iceland since February 1, 2009
Dalia Grybauskaite	President of Lithuania since July 12, 2009
Laura Chinchilla	President of Costa Rica since May 8, 2010
Kamla Persad-Bissessar	Prime Minister of Trinidad and Tobago since May 26, 2010
Julia Gillard	Prime Minister of Australia since June 24, 2010
Iveta Radicova	Prime Minister of Slovakia since July 8, 2010
Dilma Rousseff	President of Brazil since January 1, 2011
Atifete Jahjaga	President of Kosovo since April 7, 2011
Yingluck Shinawatra	Prime Minister of Thailand since August 8, 2011
Helle Thorning-Schmidt	Prime Minister of Denmark since October 3, 2011
Eveline Widmer-Schlumpf	President of Switzerland since January 1, 2012
Monique Ohsan-Bellepeau	President of Mauritius since March 31, 2012
Slavica Djukic Dejanovic	President of Serbia since April 4, 2012
Joyce Banda	President of Malawi since April 7, 2012

Argentine President Cristina Fernandez de Kirchner (R) and Brazilian President Dilma Rousseff (L) chat after the LXIII Mercosur presidential summit in Mendoza on June 29, 2012.
SOURCE: JUAN MABROMATA/AFP/Getty Images

Michelle Bachelet

Michelle Bachelet was born on September 29, 1959; on January 25, 2006, she became the first female president of Chile and the first female president in Latin America not elected on the basis of her husband's name. Bachelet served as Chilean President until 2010. She rose through the ranks, following the party-insider path. She was Chile's Minister of Health in 2000 and later became the first woman ever in Latin America to hold the position of Minister of Defense. Michelle's father was arrested and tortured because of his opposition to the regime of Augusto Pinochet, the brutal leader of Chile from 1973 to 1990. He died in prison soon after in 1974. Michelle and her mother were also arrested in 1975 for their opposition to the regime and held at a torture center. She and her mother left Chile and lived in exile in Germany and Australia. While in exile, Michelle finished her medical education and became a pediatrician. She has also studied military strategy in both Chile and the United States. Bachelet's election was heralded by many as an exciting step forward for women, especially in the developing world. While president she focused on fixing the troubled economy and is credited with increasing spending on pension reform and social protection programs for women and children, and tripling the number of free early child-care centers for low-income families. In February 2011, Bachelet was appointed Executive Director for the newly created UN Women. Bachelet's election on her own merit, and not on that of a male in her family, and ascendance to a top position in a key international organization offers some hope that some of the barriers to women holding higher political offices are beginning to crumble.

a subset of the population—a leader needs to have a broad-based agenda. Particularly, women leaders may not want to appear to be overly concerned with women's issues lest they be branded as too soft or unable to handle important military and foreign policy decisions (see the text box "Michelle Bachelet"). Therefore, it is difficult to discern a difference in leadership styles or issue concerns. For example, Margaret Thatcher, former prime minister of Great Britain, showed absolutely no interest in women's issues and in fact distanced herself from them. In contrast, when Gro Harlem Bruntland became prime minister of Norway for her first term in 1986, she announced her intent to represent women's concerns as a route to promoting social justice.[142]

Thus, we simply do not have enough data to know whether female leaders have affected politics in ways that differentiate them from male leaders. However, we can argue that it is important to have female executives because their presence shows their citizens and the world that women can get elected and can lead the country on a broad range of issues, not just women's issues. This may open the doors to women's leadership roles in a host of other areas. However, to get more women elected as executives, more women need to be elected to parliaments and appointed to cabinet posts. Women need political experience to be serious contenders for executive office worldwide. So how can more women get elected to legislatures and other positions of political power? We now turn to this question.

ADVANCING WOMEN'S EQUALITY

Advocates have been working to advance women's political equality for well over a century. What are some ways that women can increase their political representation? Simply increasing the number of women in parliament is not a magic bullet. The increased presence of women in institutional politics does not necessarily translate into concern for women's issues. Even when women politicians are interested in women's issues, they may have vastly differing opinions about what those issues should be or how they should be resolved. However, increasing women's presence is a start to ameliorating some of the inequalities that govern women's lives. A variety of strategies have been proposed; some entail implementing specific policy solutions, while other proposals involve fostering large-scale social change.

As we discussed earlier, quotas, whether encoded in constitutions, mandated by law, or adopted voluntarily by political parties when composing party lists, have been a promising way to get more women elected. Currently, 14 countries have constitutional quotas for national parliaments, 33 countries have legislated quotas for national legislatures, and 17 countries have adopted quotas for women's representation in subnational legislative bodies. In 62 countries, parties have established internal guidelines governing women's representation in party lists.[143] As we have discussed in greater detail in earlier sections, this has been one proven method of increasing women's presence in legislatures around the world.

Quotas, however, are no panacea. They do not necessarily translate to political power. For example, they can be used to marginalize women by symbolically supporting their progress without substantively improving their position in political power. Thus, for example, while some hailed the Argentine government when it became one of the first in Latin America to institute a quota law for women, others argued that it was a simple way for the government to show its support of women as political actors without actually addressing a women's agenda.[144] Quota laws do not necessarily combat the male culture of many parties. Even if parties have quotas on the books, they can still marginalize women by placing them at the bottom of lists, thus meeting the requirement of quota laws but not honoring the spirit of them, which is to increase women's representation. As we discussed earlier, the adoption of "zipper" laws, which prevent parties from relegating women to the bottom of party lists, has helped combat this problem.

Nor are all women convinced that quotas further women's quest for greater acceptance as equal political players. For example, the passage of parity legislation in France, which mandated women's equal representation on party lists, was met with resistance from many prominent women, who argued that "the reform would undermine the concept of universalism in political representation and therefore open the door to demands from other specific groups based on race, religion, or sexual preference."[145] Other French women argued quotas are "insulting and unnecessary."[146] Overall, however, the quota law does have overwhelming public support in France.[147]

One other method for increasing the number of women legislators is to adopt a preference vote system combined with a party-list PR electoral system. In such a system, voters are presented with a list of candidates from their political party and may choose up to a certain number of the candidates from the list (no matter where the candidate is on the list—top, middle, or bottom). Further, PR rules entail that the party's share of seats in parliament is approximately equivalent to the percentage of the electorate that votes for it. This combination system, used in countries such as Belgium, Denmark, Finland, Luxembourg, and Switzerland, has been shown to assist in the election of women to parliament, whereas winner-take-all systems, like that in the United States, hinder the election of women.[148] Also, PR systems, even without the preference vote system, are more advantageous to women than the winner-take-all, majoritarian system of the United States. Thus, changing the political "rules of the game," either via adopting quota laws or via adopting an alternative electoral system, has been a proven method of improving women's political representation.

Finally, political parties and political elites matter. Women are more likely to run for office when they are recruited by political party leaders, and when women run they are as likely as male candidates to win (predominantly in advanced industrial nations). A study by the Center for American Women and Politics in 2009 argued that parties play a critical role in many women's decision to run for office.[149]

However, institutional changes can go only so far. While quotas have been a very significant tool for women's advancement, advocates argue that their impact is limited in the absence of broader cultural change in which society becomes more accepting of women as political leaders. If the public is more broadly sympathetic to getting more women into public office, they may be more likely to vote for women. In addition, politicians and parties may feel more pressure to intro-duce reforms and be willing to enforce them.[150] For example, while the Nordic countries are often cited for their impressive levels of women's representation, this is in part because of quota laws but also is a manifestation of these societies' strong egalitarian cultures.

Changing societal norms and values is a slow process; it often emerges via generational change rather than over the course of a few months or years. Often, these changes are caused by broader shifts wrought by the processes of economic and social modernization. However, fostering a change in social values can be further reinforced through education. Educating children from a young age that women are not only capable of serving in government but also do an effective job at it is one important step.

Educating the public would also require the media to change the way they report on female candidates and elected officials and the types of questions they ask them. For instance, the media often focus on the clothing and physical attributes of female candidates and officials, often, although not always, to the detriment of dis-cussing their policy positions. This tendency is not singular to mainstream media: even media that are supposedly dedicated to women's issues and concerns note such facts. For instance, in an article posted on the Women's eNews site regarding Argentine presidential candidate Elisa Carrio, the author, in a section entitled "From Glamour Queen to No-Frill Politician," noted that "The chain-smoking, cake-eating, plain-dressing lady is now known affectionately by some as Lilita and by others as 'La Gorda' (the fat woman)."[151] It is hard to imagine many articles about male candi-dates making such observations. The media also tend to ask women questions about how they will balance home and elective office, a question they do not ask of male candidates. These are just a few ways that the populace could be educated regarding the suitability of women as candidates/elected officials.

CONCLUSION

Women's involvement in politics at all levels does matter, from voting to running for office. In many countries women legislators behave differently than their male colleagues and actively work for the passage of bills that will assist women. Even where women legislators are not focused on women's issues, their presence is important because it signals to society that women belong in the political, public realm, thus expanding the range of careers and lifestyles open to women. Further, given that female legislators can be as effective as their male colleagues, their presence helps dispel any myths regarding women's political abilities. The impact of women executives is a bit more difficult to gauge, but as with women legislators, their presence also has positive impacts on how society views women and their appropriate roles. However, even though increasing numbers of women are getting elected to office worldwide, their committee assignments are often to the "caring" committees, not the power committees, and they are rarely included in cabinets and other power positions within political parties. Without such power positions, women will have trouble impacting the direction of their country on issues like foreign policy, and, ultimately, politics will still be a man's world. And unfortunately, in most countries, but particularly in developing nations, the women who run for any office (or are able to run) are often from the upper class. Thus, it is not clear if their presence will alter the way society views lower-class women or if it will clear the obstacles, such as lack of monetary resources or child care, to their involvement in politics. This dilemma highlights the need for institutional and procedural political reform in many countries, as well as broad-based cultural change in the way society views women. While each of these reforms is necessary, none in and of itself is a sufficient means for increasing the number of women involved in politics. Improving women's representation in and impact on institutional politics involves engendering change at multiple levels over the course of multiple decades.

FOR MORE INFORMATION

"Are Quotas for Women in Politics a Good Idea?", *Atlantic*, January 11, 2012 (http://www
    .theatlantic.com/international/archive/2012/01/are-quotas-for-women-in-politics-a-
    good-idea/251237/)
Aspen Institute Council of Women World Leaders (http://www.womenworldleaders.org)
Center for American Women and Politics (http://www.cawp.rutgers.edu/education_
    training/trainingresources/index.php). This site has a database of resources for women
    interested in running for office.
Current Women Leaders (http://www.guide2womenleaders.com/Current-Women-Leaders
    .htm)
Database on Gender and the Empowerment of Women in the Arab Region (http://www
    .guide2womenleaders.com/Current-Women-Leaders.htm)
Elect Women magazine and website (http://electwomen.com). This website was started by
    one-time candidate turned political consultant, Kathy Groob. It has resources, articles,
    and information about women running for office.
Game Change: This film follows John McCain's 2008 presidential bid and his selection of
    Sarah Palin as his vice presidential running mate.
Global Database of Quotas for Women (http://www.guide2womenleaders.com/Current-
    Women-Leaders.htm)
Inter-Parliamentary Union Women and Parliaments Database (http://www.ipu.org/wmn-e/
    world.htm)
The Delegate: This film follows one of the first female delegates to the Republican National
    Convention in 1972, 21-year-old Cathy Swajian. It provides an insider's look at the
    presidential selection process and the role of women in presidential politics.
Fourteen Women: This documentary, narrated by Annette Bening, looks at the 14 women
    who served in the 109th Congress in the United States.
Our Times: This documentary looks at the role of women in Iranian politics; in particular it
    follows a group of women who ran in the 2002 elections and one woman's unsuccessful
    bid for the presidency.
Recall Florida: This nonfiction movie follows former Attorney General Janet Reno in her
    2002 bid for the Democratic Party nomination for Florida's governor.
Why Is Kofi Anan Not a Woman: Gender and Leadership at the United Nations: This docu-
    mentary looks at the lack of female leadership both at the head of the United Nations,
    where a woman has never held the position of secretary general, and at its lower levels.

2

Women and Noninstitutional Politics

In July 2002 a group of about 200 Nigerian women took over a multinational plant of Chevron-Texaco in Escravos, Nigeria, and held 1,200 employees hostage for approximately 9 days. Armed with only food and cooking pots, these women seized a boat used to transport workers to the island terminal and, upon arrival, stormed the plant.[1] The women demanded that Chevron-Texaco create more jobs for their unemployed sons and invest in their communities. After 5 days of occupation the women agreed to allow about 400 workers to leave but threatened to strip naked in front of the men should any of the remaining captive workers try to escape. Discussing this strategy, a representative of the women stated, "Our weapon is our nakedness."[2] This is because in many Nigerian tribes any display of nudity by wives, mothers, or grandmothers is considered a damning protest and shames all those who are exposed to it. After the women occupied the plant for 9 days, which halted oil production, Chevron executives agreed to their demands to hire more than two dozen villagers and to build schools, water systems, a town hall, and other amenities. Further, the action by these women prompted similar occupations across Nigeria, and other women seized four other oil plants during the Escravos siege.

This story illuminates important concepts and themes in the study of women's roles in noninstitutional politics. Why did these women join together to challenge authority? Why did they choose the tactics they did? And why did the executives grant their demands? Or, to pose these questions differently: When/why do social movements and interest groups form? Why do people join such groups? What strategies and tactics do social movements and interest groups employ, and why? Under what conditions do social movements and interest groups attain their demands? And, finally, how have social movements and interest groups impacted government, society, and people's lives?

Since World War II, the world has witnessed an increase in women's mobilization, not only in the industrialized nations but also in countries in the developing world. Increased social activism in the 1960s in numerous countries gave birth to a variety of groups and movements pushing for more equitable distribution of power and access. Out of this context, women's activism increased in size and magnitude, as women converged into more clearly articulated feminist movements in the industrialized Western countries that pushed for increased political and economic rights as well as long-term structural changes in gendered divisions of labor. At the same time, women in the Southern Hemisphere also became increasingly active in a wide array of women's issues, some of which overlapped with their fellow activists in the industrialized West and some of which took on local and regional flavor. This activism has been stimulated further by a growing international women's movement, which in turn has been facilitated by global events such as the UN Decade for Women (1975–1985), as well as a variety of international conferences devoted to women's issues in Kenya (1985), Cairo (1994), and Beijing (1995). Finally, women have become increasingly active in political movements that are neither feminist in orientation nor concerned with issues that have traditionally been considered important to women. In fact, sometimes they join movements whose goal is to act collectively against the interests of other women.

Drawing from examples around the world, this chapter looks at the role of women in noninstitutional politics. Noninstitutional politics, or informal politics, encompasses any political activity that does not take place directly within formal political institutions. Thus, actions such as voting and running for and serving in political office are not considered in this chapter because they are activities that take place directly within formal political institutions. We will examine why women's movements and interest groups form, why women join such groups, the strategies and tactics they use, and their impact on themselves, the public, and the state. In discussing women's movements in comparative perspective, we will cast a broad net and will discuss women's activism in women's movements rather than a unified women's movement.[3] In addition, we will address the issue of "women in movement," or women's activism in other social movements, where men predominate in leadership roles and decision making.

Women's activism in social movements is often gendered—that is, their reasons for joining and their strategies and tactics often are based in, and also challenge, traditional societal expectations about women's appropriate roles in society. Women have drawn on their status as mothers and caretakers to justify their actions, and they have sometimes exploited these roles, in ways that men cannot, to attain their demands. However, the ways in which women around the world use their gender vary widely, and what may be a successful tactic in the industrialized West may not resonate with women in the countries of the Southern Hemisphere. The impact of women's activism has been substantial; women have lobbied successfully for legislative changes, have advocated for the creation of administrative offices to address women's issues, and have used their experiences to jump into positions of political leadership in institutionalized politics. However, it is also important to remember that women are not necessarily united simply by the biological commonality of their sex or the status of their gender and that women can define and express their interests in diametrically opposed ways.

DEFINING SOCIAL MOVEMENTS, INTEREST GROUPS, AND WOMEN'S MOVEMENTS

What is a social movement? A social movement is a group of people with a common interest who work together either to change a policy of government and/or to change how society perceives something (e.g., gay activists trying to alter how society views gays and those afflicted with AIDS). It is often made up of various organizations all working on the same topic, such as the environment, but often on different issues within that topic. For example, within the environmental movement, some groups may focus on clean air, others on clean water, and others on the issue of land conservation. Nor do all social movements utilize similar tactics; some may opt to lobby the government, while others may choose more militant strategies such as spiking trees to halt logging. In addition, some of these groups may be organized formally with an executive director, chapters throughout the country, paid lobbyists, and thousands of dues-paying members. In contrast, others may be much more informal in structure, with no clear leadership or organized chapters. Membership size is indeterminate because individuals do not pay dues or may not even need to formally join in order to be a member. In other words, the organizations that participate in social movements are incredibly diverse, often sharing few commonalities beyond their common issue.

Sometimes the groups that make up a social movement are called social movement organizations (SMOs) and other times they are referred to as interest groups, which are organizations that attempt to influence government but are not part of the government they are trying to influence.[4] As you can see, an interest group is quite similar to an SMO. However, while many SMOs can be called interest groups, not all interest groups are part of a social movement and thus cannot be called SMOs. For example, the American Association of Retired Persons (AARP) is an interest group but not a social movement organization because it is not part of a social movement, in the sense that we cannot say there is a retiree movement in the same way that we refer to the environmental movement or the women's movement. In contrast, the National Organization for Women (NOW) can be considered both a social movement organization and an interest group because it is part of the women's movement and attempts to influence the government with its organizational activities.

Defining a "women's movement" can be difficult, contested terrain, particularly if one is trying to generalize across a wide array of examples of women's mobilization. How can we produce a definition of women's movements that can apply to radical feminist activists in Great Britain and the Nigerian women discussed at the beginning of this chapter? Women's organizations represent a diversity of interests, ideologies, and goals, mediated by competing class, ethnic, religious, cultural, and racial identities. For example, some women's movements and organizations, like the Lesbian Avengers, who use civil disobedience to highlight what they see as a patriarchal, unjust society, are quite radical in their ideology and tactics. Others, like many women's organizations in Latin America, do not claim to be feminist or interested in changing their roles in the social order. Rather, they wish to see services for their families improved and are more conservative in their ideology and tactics. Can we discuss these movements and organizations in the same breath? The answer is both no and yes.

We cannot argue that there is a worldwide "women's movement." Cultural, religious, ethnic, and class differences result in varied interests, concerns, and needs for all people worldwide, and to expect half the world's population to feel identically about these things is unrealistic and naïve. Even within countries, these barriers create a diversity of often-clashing interests. For instance, in the United States some conservative, Christian women are fighting to protect what they perceive to be the rights of a developing fetus. This movement is at odds with the traditional Western feminist movement, which has framed the issue as maintaining women's right to choose whether or not to carry a pregnancy to full term. These two groups of women within a single country do not see themselves as part of a common women's movement. These differences in interests and concerns can widen even further as we make observations about women's mobilization over a large range of countries that differ drastically in terms of levels of economic and social development, as well as cultural and religious traditions.

One way of acknowledging this problem is to distinguish more clearly between the various strands of women's activism in noninstitutionalized politics. Women's activism is not always feminist in orientation. While feminist organizations explicitly challenge the patriarchy by critiquing the gender-based domination of men over women, women's organizations often mobilize over issues considered important to women but may not go so far as to challenge broader societal or structural impediments to women's equality. Further, it is important to recognize that sometimes women organize collectively against other women; for example, as we discussed, women have mobilized on both sides of the abortion issue. To encompass these varied motivations, Karen Beckwith has defined women's movements as ones that are characterized

> by the primacy of women's gendered experiences, women's issues, and women's leadership and decision making. The relationship of women to these movements is direct and immediate; movement definition, issue articulation, and issue resolution are specific to women, developed and organized by them with reference to their gender identity.[5]

This definition allows us to encompass a wide variety of women's activism and acknowledges that how women define their issues will vary across continents and contexts. At the same time, it distinguishes between women's movements and the broader phenomena of "women in movement," in which women's activism is channeled into alternative causes, such as nationalist or religious movements. Certainly, often women's activism in these other movements is gendered, in that their biological or social status as women affects their participation. However, they are not necessarily mobilized because of their identities as women. Thus, when we discuss "women's movements" in this chapter, we are referring to women who are active in a variety of feminist and women's issues, which we distinguish from the more general phenomenon of women in movement, which will be addressed at the end of the chapter.[6]

Given these differences, we write about women's movements that often share broadly defined interests and utilize similar tactics rather than a global women's movement united identically around specific concerns. What commonalities can we emphasize, without obscuring the differences that separate women? Many of the issues around which women mobilize are common across cultures: to be seen as a human being, not as property; a desire for fair employment opportunities; the right to reproductive choice; widened access to health care and education; the right to vote and participate in politics; and more.[7] Second, as you will see in this chapter, across cultures women's movements form and women join them for similar reasons, no matter the goal. Third, women's movements, like all social movements, make use of a variety of tactics to achieve their desired ends. However, one tactic that is used widely by all women across cultures, and that is not available to men, is the tactic of emphasizing their gender and the rights and responsibilities that come with it. That is, women often draw their legitimacy and authority from their roles as wives, mothers, caretakers, and sometimes even sexual objects to justify their activism. As we shall see, across the world and across class, culture, religion, and ethnicity, women who are fighting for everything from educational opportunities for their children to clean water and air, equal pay, and ample food to feed their families all emphasize a common thread—that is, they are women and as such have certain responsibilities that they feel only women can fulfill. Further, as we saw with the example of women in Nigeria, they may use their bodies to emphasize their point.

Finally, women's movements across the globe have impacted their societies and the world's perception of women. Despite many societies' efforts to portray women as the weaker sex, incapable of voicing their demands and in need of protection by their male relatives (and the state), women have disproved this through action. This change in the world's view of women is a result of women's past and present mobilization, and while the extent of the change may vary across cultures, it is undeniably an important commonality among women's movements.

WHY DO WOMEN'S MOVEMENTS AND ORGANIZATIONS FORM?

Women's movements and organizations often, although not always, form for reasons that are similar to those that are found in the formation of other movements and organizations. The reasons for social movement and interest group formation often fall into three general models. The first model is a psychological model, which has a few variants but in general argues that drastic disruptions in society such as war, economic depressions, and industrialization often lead to feelings of confusion and alienation among individuals. Individuals react to this psychological distress by forming groups in attempts to return society to "normal."[8] In contrast, proponents of the resource mobilization model maintain that movements emerge when resources in society, such as people, money, office space, and a communications network of individuals with a shared history or concern, are plentiful; people are willing to join and lead the movement; and some elite allies, such as government officials, church leaders, and corporations, are interested in building alliances with the movement.[9] The third model, the political process/political opportunity model, acknowledges the critical role of resources, leaders, and occasionally elite assistance in explaining movement emergence. However, it also maintains that these factors are not sufficient; the other crucial variable for formation is favorable political conditions.[10]

Using the psychological model, we can try to understand why the women's movement in the United States developed from emerging women's consciousness in the post–World War II era to feminist mobilization in the 1970s. During the war, women became accustomed to working outside of the home and in workplaces that provided day-care and training programs. The number of women holding college degrees also increased during the war. But when the war ended, many of these women were fired to make room for the returning soldiers. Women who had worked during World War II saw men with similar training and education receive the jobs and benefits they once had received, at their expense. Other scholars point to the role of the civil rights era several decades later in increasing women's sense of alienation and anger at their position in society—that is, women activists who had mobilized to fight for racial equality were awakened to their own unequal status in society. According to the psychological model, this led to feelings of anger and frustration among women, who then ultimately mobilized for change. However, this model lacks explanatory power because it leads one to assume that women just spontaneously organized, without leadership or assistance, in a political environment that was not particularly open to the issue of women's rights.

We can also apply the resource mobilization approach, which emphasizes the role of monetary and human resources as well as elite allies to explain women's mobilization in the decades following World War II. The economy in the United States after the war and into the 1960s was rapidly expanding; thus, individuals had excess resources in terms of money and time. In addition, a number of women working in government and corporate America had encountered numerous instances of discrimination and had the training and education to serve in leadership positions in a movement. Further, in 1961, President Kennedy created the President's Commission on the Status of Women, whose mission was to examine the legal status of women in the United States (although with the hopes of pinpointing potential minor changes in women's rights policy formulation, thus negating the need for the Equal Rights Amendment). The commission was composed of numerous women from the government sector, and it spawned the creation of similar state-level commissions in all 50 states. These national and state commissions created a communications network of women who were able to discuss their shared history and experiences of discrimination. Finally, the publication in 1963 of Betty Friedan's *Feminine Mystique*, a book that highlighted the condition of middle-class women, sparked a sense of outrage among women, many of whom had previously been unable to identify their sense of grievance.[11] Calling it "the problem with no name," Friedan detailed the unhappiness of middle-class women who were educated and raised to become housewives and mothers rather than individuals with a capacity to work and earn incomes outside of the home.[12] When taken all together, ample resources, a communications network, potential leaders, some elite facilitation (even if unwitting), and a sense of outrage fostered the emergence of a women's movement in the 1960s. This explanation is far more satisfactory than the psychological model, but it still appears to leave out an important variable—the political situation at the time.

Political process theory, which points to the role of the larger political context, can also be used to explain the emergence of the U.S. women's movement. First, the U.S. political system, in which power is divided among a variety of branches as well as between federal, state, and local authorities, is generally open to citizen pressure. Citizens can lobby Congress and can write letters to, call, and e-mail their representatives; they can also pressure the president and the executive branch; and groups can file legal proceedings in federal courts in an attempt to challenge federal law. Further, individuals and groups can stage sit-ins, protests, and marches without fear of arrest, assuming they follow basic laws, such as obtaining a permit and so forth. Thus, the women's movement had a variety of access points through which members could advocate their interests. Second, the political situation in the middle to late 1960s and early 1970s was favorable to the emergence of social movements in general, and the women's movement in particular. The successes of the civil rights movement had, to a certain degree, paved the way for other progressive movements, such as the student movement, the environmental movement, and, of course, the women's movement. Further, the Kennedy, Johnson, and Nixon administrations were somewhat amenable to the issue of increasing citizens' rights, especially since they were involved in fighting a war in Vietnam, whose ostensible purpose was to liberate a people from a political system that denied them their rights. Finally, the Watergate scandal, in which President Nixon was found to have used campaign funds to pay individuals to break into Democratic Party National Headquarters at the Watergate Hotel, led to the defeat of many incumbent representatives in the House. Voters were disgusted with government and its members in general, even those who were not associated with the Nixon administration. The new representatives, most of whom were elected by slim margins, were eager to increase their winning margins in the next election and thus were wooing potential voters. Women fit the bill for many of these Democratic members. Thus, American political institutions and the political context of the middle to late 1960s and early 1970s were conducive to the formation of a women's movement. The additional factors of women's rising sense of frustration, as well as their increased resources, arguably led to the emergence of a women's movement in the United States.

Let us now return to our example discussed in the beginning of the chapter: How can we explain the mobilization of the women in Nigeria? To begin with, it appears that these women were frustrated with Chevron. As one activist told a reporter, "Chevron has long been neglecting the Ugborodo community in all areas of life. They have not shown concern at all to involve our people in employment and provision of social amenities."[13] Thus, a key element of the psychological model was present. Resources were also present: a majority of the women who occupied the Escravos plant were from the same tribe, the Itsekiri, which served as a communications network among a people with similar histories, experiences, and concerns. Further, there were other, more intangible resources available to these women. Reports indicate that their men were very supportive of their actions[14] and that while the local Nigerian authorities were not encouraging their actions, they supported their demands.[15] And finally, the political situation was conducive to their siege. While local government authorities did not condone their actions, they were not going to interfere in the occupation. Thus, the system was open to their protest. Further, Chevron was willing to work with them. As Dick Filgate, an executive of parent company Chevron Texaco stated, "We now have a different philosophy, and that is do more with communities."[16] As a result, the political and corporate climate was amenable to their protest, thus facilitating the maintenance of the movement. Overall, we can see that all three models contribute to an understanding of the emergence of this social movement. We now turn to another question: Why do women join women's movements and organizations?

WHY DO WOMEN JOIN WOMEN'S MOVEMENTS AND ORGANIZATIONS?

Women join women's organizations and movements for a variety of reasons, many of which are similar to the reasons that individuals join any SMO. Often, a trauma or disaster has impacted their lives directly. Sometimes they are integrated into activism through their varied networks of friends and family, who encourage them to join. Alternatively, they get something out of membership, whether it is a sense of camaraderie, contribution to a higher cause or good, or a material benefit. Many of these motivations act upon a person in tandem; no one reason is often enough to explain why a woman joins a women's movement. Women's gender identity is also relevant to explaining why women join women's movements; in the following examples, we will see that women's gender, their varied socially constructed roles, and their relationships are a constant subtext in their motivations to act. Women are often pulled into activism to meet practical gender needs when their socially defined roles are threatened, as well as in response to strategic gender concerns that arise out of their frustration from their subordinate social status as women (see photo 2.1).

Much research has shown that a common thread that explains why women join movements, even in the face of political repression, is that some trauma or disaster has occurred in their life and has in a sense "woken them up" to the need to take action. In El Salvador, the Farabundo Marti National Liberation Front (the FMLN), a guerrilla organization dedicated to overthrowing the government and creating a more just and equitable society, engaged in violent conflict with an authoritarian and repressive government. The government was responsible for arresting, detaining, torturing, and killing thousands of El Salvadoran men. In this climate, women formed the organization Co-Madres to pressure the government of El Salvador to explain and discover the whereabouts of their missing relatives. Many of the women in this organization had a "disappeared," assassinated, or

Libyan women gather to protest for more women's rights and celebrate the revolution against Moammar Gadhafi's regime. SOURCE: AP Photo/Alexandre Meneghini

jailed relative.[17] It was this traumatic event that encouraged many, who had no history of political activity, to act despite the very real possibility that they might be arrested and/or jailed, heckled, and physically abused by the government for their actions.

An example from the United States also serves to illustrate this point. The founder of Mothers Against Drunk Driving (MADD) began this organization after her daughter was killed by a drunk driver with a history of arrests for drunk driving. The trauma of her daughter's death, coupled with her frustration that someone with such a deplorable driving record still had his driver's license, prompted her to take action. Many other members of MADD have a family member or friend who was killed or seriously injured by a drunk driver. Thus a traumatic, disastrous event in one's life might encourage one to take action by joining a group.

Another motivation to join women's movements appears to be encouragement from others. Recruitment by friends, relatives, or other organizations such as one's church/temple/synagogue is a commonly cited explanation for joining a movement or organization. Women also join women's movements and organizations for the solidarity benefits (feelings of camaraderie) that come from such organizations. In the 1960s, in the women's movement in the United States, women joined consciousness-raising groups in which women gathered informally and discussed issues in their lives and sought solutions to their problems through their shared experiences. An example from Uganda illustrates that such motivations are not limited to the advanced industrial world. One scholar studying the women's movement in Uganda asked women why they had joined women's organizations.

Their reasons included "that they wanted to socialize, gain new ideas, and meet like-minded people."[18] Thus, solidarity benefits are often important factors in women's decisions regarding whether or not to join an organization.

Another common motivation appears to be the desire to do good (purposive benefits). Many of the women in the Co-Madres in El Salvador argued that they owed it to the next generation to work for change so that the horrors they had experienced would not be repeated in the future.[19] Material benefits are also often cited as a reason for joining women's movements and organizations. Women worldwide have joined movements to protest prices and rents, the loss of day-care centers, and the cost of water and electricity.[20] In Uganda, for example, research has found that women are joining women's movements so that they may improve their standard of living.[21] Thus, another motivation for women in joining a women's movement is the pursuit of material gain (or protecting what material benefits they have).

Finally, a common subtext for all of these examples is the role that women's gendered identities play in informing their activism. For example, many women organize to meet what are known as "practical gender interests."[22] Practical gender interests are those interests that are traditionally considered within women's realm of concern, such as issues concerning the family, children, and almost anything related to caring for them (e.g., access to food, water, shelter, health, education). Women are motivated to join organizations that fight for improvements in these areas because they feel they have a legitimate right to do so. And while stereotypes of women often impede their advancement and claims, sometimes their role as mothers gives them the authority and legitimacy to demand that the state take care of concerns that are considered "women's issues."[23] Women in the developing world, who may mobilize more frequently around practical gender interests, often embrace these categories as identities that legitimate their political activity. In a sense, women who accept the gendered division of labor have a certain legitimacy in demanding rights that pertain to their role. Further, motherhood provides a common identity for many women that can cut across race, ethnicity, and nationality.[24] Thus, many women join women's organizations to improve areas of life considered within their realm of concern and expertise as women.

For example, women joined the Co-Madres, in part, to respond to some trauma, but also because their experience of the trauma had a gendered dimension. As mothers, they were responsible for the welfare and care of their children, and they were mobilized to action in ways that men (and fathers) were not. Similarly, women in the developing world who mobilize to protest prices and rents are doing so out of a desire to improve their material conditions, but also because as women, they are traditionally responsible for care of the household and their family's immediate living conditions, which have come under threat. Thus, while women join movements for similar reasons as do men, often their gender identities further define which issues mobilize them, and often, it is when their practical gender needs and roles have been threatened. However, women who mobilize to meet practical gender needs often do not explicitly challenge larger gendered divisions of labor and women's subordinate position in society.

In contrast, "strategic gender interests" are "those fundamental issues related to women's . . . subordination and gender inequities. Strategic gender interests are long-term, usually not material, and are often related to structural changes in society regarding women's status and equity. They include legislation for equal rights, reproductive choice, and increased participation in decision-making."[25]

In other words, they arise out of a recognition of women's subordinate position in society, and women who are mobilized out of a concern for strategic gender interests often explicitly challenge gendered divisions of labor, power, and control, as well as traditionally defined norms and roles. For example, activism on issues such as women's legal rights, equal wages, and women's control over their bodies often uses a rhetoric that challenges societal norms about women's appropriate roles in society, rather than reinforcing them. Women's mobilization to advance strategic gender interests is more common among Western feminists, who are often trying to escape classification as mothers and wives. While women in the developing world do mobilize around strategic gender interests, more often their interests are defined by immediate needs that draw on traditional expectations of the appropriate division of labor between men's and women's interests.

We have thus far examined why women's movements emerge and the various reasons why women might join such movements. Now we turn to the strategies and tactics that women's movements utilize. Do these differ from the strategies and tactics available to other social movements? Do women have strategies and tactics available to them because they are women?

STRATEGIES AND TACTICS

Tactics are the tools a social movement uses to achieve its ends, and often movements use a variety of tactics in their quest to attain their goals. Some tactics are conventional and include such things as writing letters to public officials and meeting with public officials to express one's views. Other tactics are militant and include acts of civil disobedience (openly disobeying a law in protest) such as the Nigerian women's occupation of the oil plant in Escravos. There are also violent tactics, such as assassinations, kidnappings, and armed struggle, but these tactics are most often used by revolutionary organizations and will be discussed in the following chapter. Finally, there are tactics that are considered conventional in advanced industrial/democratic societies, such as marches, strikes, and sit-ins, but that in developing and/or authoritarian societies might be considered militant.

Women's movements and organizations have used a bevy of tactics to fight for change, which often depend on factors such as levels of repression/authoritarianism within the state, the resources of the group, the culture of the country in which the women live, and the organizational structure of the group. As noted earlier, across cultures, many women use their gender as a tactic, although varied cultural, political, and social contexts often define the appropriateness or effectiveness of varied strategies. Public attitudes about women differ across cultures, and women in the advanced industrial world may be able to use their gender in ways that women in the developing world cannot. For example, as will be discussed in greater detail later, women in the advanced industrial world can live in lesbian communes to protest nuclear weapons or they can bare their mastectomy scar on the cover of a national magazine to bring attention to breast cancer. Such use of their gender differences as a tactic is not always available to women in developing nations because of culturally accepted norms of appropriate female behavior. More will be said on this later. Let us now examine tactics available to women in authoritarian/repressive states.

Repressive states often arrest and jail dissidents; as a result, movements rarely use such tactics as lobbying or even marches, and instead move underground or use alternative means of political expression. Female activists often use tactics that are only available to them as women; that is, they are able to use gendered expectations about their behavior in order to participate in unorthodox forms of political protest. Women, in many societies, are not seen as a threat. They are often viewed as complacent, apolitical, and solely concerned with their children and home. These assumptions allow them a certain cover, and even provide them with hidden venues in which they can organize. Women active in movements in authoritarian states may gather at a seemingly benign sewing circle or tea party. As Craske notes in her research on women activists in Latin America, "women were able to be invisible simply by being women."[26] Adams shows that women protesting Pinochet's regime in Chile were able to hide subversive artwork under their skirts—something men clearly could not do![27] And women in Uganda, during the internal war to oust dictator Idi Amin, hid weapons of Tanzanian soldiers who were in the country to assist in overthrowing Amin and provided shelter and food for these men. Amin's troops never suspected women of these acts, simply because they were women.[28]

Further, since women worldwide are still primarily responsible for the care of their children and home, they have authority and legitimacy when they fight for improvements in these areas. Or, they may work in caregiving tasks to assist others less fortunate. For instance, they may work in a food cooperative or communal kitchen that provides food to the poor. Men do not have all of these tactical choices—their gender also limits the tactics and strategies they may use (as it does women). When the state does not allow people (men) to gather or form groups, women are still allowed to meet to do traditionally female pastimes because women are assumed not to be political.

Further, women in authoritarian states can conduct silent protest, as the Madres de la Plaza de Mayo (Mothers of the Plaza de Mayo) in Argentina did when they gathered every day in the Plaza de Mayo to bear witness silently to the disappearance of their loved ones, who had been "disappeared" by the state because they were seen as revolutionaries and/or potential threats. The state dared not take action against these women because it risked losing the little legitimacy it had left. How could they justify jailing women who were doing nothing more than silently gathering to mourn for their lost family members? They were being "womanly and true" and violating no culturally held norms of appropriate female behavior. Their femaleness granted their behavior a legitimacy and protection that men did not have. As Craske argues, "It [motherhood] has a significant cultural and political currency and as such lends legitimacy to demands made within this rubric."[29]

However, utilizing motherhood and one's female identity as a tactic also has its limitations. As Craske notes, motherhood is a limited identity for politics because "the tight links between motherhood and social reproduction . . . are evident and for many motherhood remains an apolitical identity. Furthermore, the non-negotiable stance of many motherist demands is anti-politics. The limitations of using motherhood as the basis for female political action is apparent."[30] Thus women cannot rely solely on motherhood as a tactic or issue; doing so may provide the state with an excuse for dismissing women's concerns as nonpolitical and, thus, not important.

Yet, on the other hand, often this is women's safest choice in terms of activism. Safa and Flora argue that women have been forced into focusing on motherhood and their femaleness in authoritarian regimes because traditional avenues of protest have not addressed women's issues meaningfully, and thus women are left with few other tactics when fighting for change in such settings.[31] Women in authoritarian regimes often must utilize certain tactics because they conform to culturally held norms about acceptable gender roles. Women can do things like feed and clothe the poor in an authoritarian system because these are viewed as appropriate pastimes for women. In this sense, it is important to note that even behavior that conforms to "appropriate" female roles is political because it is a tactic that often contributes to the downfall of authoritarian regimes. By providing such services women are demonstrating the inadequacies of the state and in doing so are making a political statement about the need for change.

Women in authoritarian regimes and the developing world do not always emphasize their femaleness and use conventional tactics; in addition, despite their gender, many have suffered at the hands of the state for their participation and tactics. In El Salvador, the Co-Madres have combined accepted modes of female behavior with more confrontational tactics that angered the state. They have utilized conventional, accepted tactics such as distributing fliers at Sunday Mass, but they have also utilized militant tactics such as occupying government offices and staging sit-ins.[32] As a result, women have suffered, as have men, for their actions. Major Roberto D'Aubuisson, the authoritarian leader of El Salvador during most of the 1980s, threatened the Co-Madres with decapitation if they kept up their work. Their office was also bombed in 1980, 1981, 1986, 1987, and 1989. Further, in 1982 three mothers were captured by death squads and detained and tortured. Others have been raped and some assassinated.[33]

Women in industrialized, democratic regimes often have a wider array of tactics available to them because there are more diverse views of acceptable roles for women, but also because the state is more open to a variety of tactics. Costain and Costain note that the women's movement in the United States has used almost every routine and nonroutine method in its attempts to gain political influence.[34] The tactics and strategies chosen, they find, changed depending on the views of the movement. In the 1960s the women's movement viewed political parties as part of the male power structure and so would not work with them and used protest instead. By the 1970s the movement saw a need to embrace all types of tactics; however, as a result of some political gains, by the 1980s, the movement settled on lobbying and electoral politics in order to consolidate their hard-fought victories.[35] Similarly, in their comparative study of women's movements in western Europe and North America, Banaszak, Beckwith, and Rucht found that women's movements have shifted from radical tactics and suspicion of the state in the 1970s to a more moderate, state-involved, and accommodationist stance by the 1990s. In part, this shift in tactics is a tribute to the successes of women's movements; in the wake of the creation of varied policy agencies to address women's issues, many activists have become inside players rather than outside agitators. In addition, however, state structures have also shifted since the 1970s, and the increased significance of international organizations, delegation of power to governments at the local level, and reliance on nonstate actors has changed how women's organizations respond to and seek influence with the state.[36]

Women in advanced industrialized democratic states often utilize their gender as a tactic. But protest by women in these states, even when emphasizing similar female traits as their fellow activists in the developing world, often takes different forms than such protest in authoritarian regimes. In advanced industrialized democracies, women may have a greater variety of tactics available to them to emphasize their gender than women in the developing world do.

For example, worldwide, women are often characterized as the more peaceful sex, who, if in power, would work to prevent and end wars. Throughout the world, there are many examples of women organizing to protest wars, military build-ups, military actions, and armed conflict in general. In the United States in 1983, a group of women built an encampment near the Seneca Army Depot in Seneca, New York, to protest the deployment of nuclear missiles, as well as the patriarchal system that created these instruments of destruction. Daily, they proceeded to the depot to demonstrate peacefully against the deployment of nuclear weapons. Currently, there are still women living near the depot in a communal, nonhierarchical community. Their very presence is a form of peaceful protest against nuclear weapons. Both genders have protested actively against nuclear weapons; however, this group is different in that it is using gender as a tactic. That the group is made up solely of women is a political statement—that women are innately more concerned about preventing destruction and more adept at taking care of the problem. Further, the organizational form of their group is a tactical choice, a political statement. Hierarchy is often associated with patriarchy and male-dominated organizations, so by opting for a communal, all-female, nonhierarchical organization they are rejecting traditional male-defined organizational structures. Finally, while peaceful protest as a tactic does not often inflame public opinion, living as a communal group of women can. These women have unsettled their socially conservative rural New York neighbors with their choice of living arrangements.[37]

These women have chosen on the one hand to embrace a traditionally female characteristic—being peace-loving. At the same time, however, they have chosen a radical way of expressing it—by living only with women. So while these women share something in common with their Latin American sisters—embracing some traditional female characteristics and tactics—they are also radically different from them. It would culturally be very difficult for women in the developing world to use an all-female commune as a tactic to protest the politics of their country. Thus, we can see that women in industrialized democratic regimes have a wider array of tactics available to them, even when emphasizing a cultural norm that would be viewed as acceptable in the developing world.

The experiences of breast cancer activists also illustrate the use of gendered tactics in advanced industrialized democracies. Breast cancer activists have also emphasized their differences from men in fighting for increased funding for breast cancer research. Since breast cancer primarily affects women, this is not so odd. However, while many of the tactics of the movement have been fairly traditional—walks for the cure, bicycle tours to increase public awareness of toxic sites that may contribute to breast cancer, lobbying, and electoral politics—some have not. In May 1993, a breast cancer survivor and activist appeared on the cover of the *New York Times Magazine* with half of her white dress cut away to reveal a mastectomy scar.[38] This act was controversial in many ways; breasts are a defining feature of women, and to show a cancer survivor with a scar where a breast formerly existed publicly displayed some of the physical repercussions of breast cancer. The picture emphasized the physical differences between men and women, showing that breast cancer is something that primarily afflicts women. But breast cancer also has a psychological impact on women since breasts are seen by society as an essential characteristic of what it is to be a woman. Once again, this is a tactic that is not as available to women in authoritarian and/or developing nations, where censorship of the press or notions of female modesty prevent such radical tactics.

Finally, in Love Canal, New York, a group of women discovered that the cause of the increasing rates of cancer among their children was the existence of a toxic waste site underneath their town. These women decided to confront the corporation responsible for the toxic waste and get them to clean up this site. This group of women emphasized their femaleness even as they became adept, somewhat radical, political actors. Kaplan, in her research on this movement, notes that they presented themselves to the corporation and to the world as helpless mothers trying to protect their children and that this approach was a key element in their stock of tactics.[39] The corporations responsible for the toxic waste had a tough time presenting their side in the face of this strategy. But it must be noted that these women did not simply sit around and proclaim their helplessness; they also utilized radical tactics. They burned effigies of authorities, they took mock coffins to the state capital, and they even took hostages (albeit for a short period, and it was not premeditated). But all along they emphasized that they were women who were doing the socially acceptable thing—protecting their children and families as good mothers ought to. So while women in authoritarian or developing nations may not always have such tactics available to them (though in some instances they do), they do share a tactic with women activists in the advanced industrial world—many of the women organizing in these economically, socially, and politically different societies are emphasizing their femaleness and claiming it as a source of legitimation for behavior that might not otherwise be tolerated or acknowledged by the state.

Explicitly feminist movements that seek to ameliorate women's subordinate status in society are often torn over whether explicitly to utilize strategies that draw on (and sometimes exploit) conventional norms and expectations about women's appropriate spheres of activism. For example, the feminist movement in the United States chose strategies emphasizing women's similarities to men and lobbied for the passage of laws that highlighted their equality with men. They drew primarily on classical liberalism, values embodied in the Declaration of Independence, which emphasized the importance of self-determination and individual rights. Historically, many discriminatory laws against women were grounded in the belief that women were inherently different (and often inferior) to men and that women and men should occupy separate spheres of influence, with women designated as caretakers of the home and hearth and men as breadwinners. In response to these traditional beliefs, many liberal feminists argued that equality between men and women is possible only when laws require men and women to be treated equally. Their focus was on achieving equality under the law and on pushing for equal rights as citizens to education, jobs, or political office as well as equal protection from violence or unfair treatment.[40] Thus, they were hesitant to pursue strategies that magnified women's differences or exploited their traditional roles because they wanted to emphasize the lack of differences between men and women as part of their overall strategy for improving the position and status of women. As we shall discuss in further detail in Chapter 4, this strand of the feminist movement in the United States and Europe has sued companies and governments for violations of laws that grant them equal opportunity and access in employment, education, credit, housing, and more. For example, in the United States the women's movement has often used Equal Employment Opportunity laws as a tactic for gaining equality in employment.[41] Feminist organizations have also used tactics common to a variety of social movements and interest groups, such as lobbying, launching letter-writing campaigns, forming political action committees to funnel money to candidates, volunteering for campaigns, mobilizing voters, and organizing marches.

In sum, women's movements and organizations have utilized a variety of tactics in their quest for their goals. Women both in the developing world and in advanced industrial nations find that using their gender as a tactic is useful because it often legitimates their actions and their cause. However, local political and social contexts often define which tactics will resonate with society. While not all women's movements use their gender as a strategy, until the burdens of raising children and caring for the home are shared more equitably in all parts of the world, gendered tactics will likely continue to be used by women's groups in a variety of contexts.

THE IMPACT OF WOMEN'S MOVEMENTS

We have looked at why women's movements and organizations form, why women join them, and what strategies and tactics they use, but what, if any, are the impacts of women's movements? Inarguably, women's movements worldwide have been successful in changing laws that impact the condition and status of women. As we shall discuss in greater detail in Part II, some of this legislation directly affects women's status by mandating equal pay, education, and job opportunities; increased political participation and representation; liberalized divorce, contraception, and abortion rights; increased maternity leave benefits; and the criminalization of violence against women. Further, women's activism has changed legislation that often impacts women indirectly (see the box "Women Win Nationality Laws"). Women's movements have successfully lobbied for increased gun control, higher levels of education funding, and better access to a wide array of social services.

Second, the efforts of women's movements have led to the creation of ministries and bureaus that address women's issues. Also known as "women's policy machineries," these agencies mushroomed in the industrialized countries in the 1970s and 1980s (although in the United States, the President's Commission on the Status of Women was created in 1961).[42] For instance, Ireland created the Commission on the Status of Women in 1972, and Norway, the Netherlands, Australia, and France followed suit in the ensuing 3 years. This change is, in part,

---

Women Win Nationality Laws

2010 and 2011 were watershed years in many Arab countries as the people rose up and overthrew entrenched dictatorships, but they were also crucial years because, after a decade of organizing by women, nationality laws were passed in numerous Arab countries. For a decade women's rights groups in many Arab countries advocated and fought to win the passage of nationality laws. Key among these groups was the Collective for Research and Training on Development-Action, which receives assistance from the Global Fund for Women. Traditionally, in almost all Arab countries, if a woman married a man of a different nationality, then their children did not have the citizenship of the mother's homeland (though if a man married a foreign woman, the children *did* have citizenship). Passage of these laws means that today, women can pass their citizenship on to their children. Being able to pass citizenship on to one's children means those children will have access to education, health care, and employment. Palestine was the first Arab country to pass a nationality law, followed by Libya, Tunisia, Yemen, Algeria, and Egypt. The United Arab Emirates now allows the children of women who marry foreigners to apply for citizenship at age 18. And Saudi Arabia has said that it will grant citizenship to children of Saudi women married to foreigners as long as the children meet other citizenship requirements. While Lebanon, Bahrain, Jordan, Kuwait, Oman, and Syria still do not have nationality laws, the passage of the laws in the countries above was an important victory for women's rights movements in the Arab world.

a result of feminist movements' pursuit of alliances with political parties, primarily of the left, to push for policy reform.[43] Further, particularly in industrialized nations, pressure from feminist-oriented women's movements led to the increased presence of "femocrats," a term used to refer to "both feminists employed as administrators and bureaucrats in positions of power and to women politicians advocating gender equality policies."[44] These newly emerged femocrats worked in the newly formed women's policy machineries, ranging from equal opportunity commissions and councils to departments and ministries for women, to integrate gender concerns into national policy agendas. This also granted feminist activists further access to institutional politics.[45]

This change is no longer restricted to industrialized nations; worldwide, this shift in discourse has resulted in the creation of women's ministries and bureaus and the introduction and passage of more laws having a positive impact on women. For example, the United Nations has its own policy machinery devoted to women's agendas; the Commission on the Status of Women and its administrative arm, the Division for the Advancement of Women, have lobbied national governments tirelessly to establish similar structures to assess the progress of women's status. In fact, the United Nations estimates that nearly three quarters of all states have established some form of national machinery for the advancement of women, particularly in the wake of the fourth World Conference of Women, held in 1995 in Beijing.[46] The United Nations' efforts to advance women could not have happened in the absence of women's mobilization; as Enloe notes, "Part of the success of the emergent second wave of feminism has been to put women's lives and feminist questions onto the formal agendas of the foreign policy establishments of dozens of state regimes and international agencies."[47] We will discuss this phenomenon in greater depth in Chapter 7, which discusses international responses to fostering women's equality.

Also, as we discussed in greater detail in Chapter 1, women's movements and organizations have forced public officials to pay more attention to women's issues, women's organizations, and women voters. As Costain notes, in the late 1960s and early 1970s, politicians in the United States became aware of the potential electoral impact of women and made serious efforts to attract women's support.[48] This phenomenon is not limited to the United States; political parties around the world have made an increased effort to organize women's sections within their party structures and have also integrated women into party lists at election time. Despite this, increased women's activism in women's movements has not led to a significant trend toward forming women's political parties, although there are a few exceptions. For example, in Russia, women have mobilized twice to form political parties that are primarily run and staffed by women and address issues that are considered important to women.[49] Nonetheless, for the most part, women's movements have tended to work with preexisting parties rather than form a new political party devoted explicitly to women's issues.

However, these strategies of cooperation with the state have not always augured well for women's movements. Sometimes states respond to women's movements with "symbolic reform," policies that are supposed to address certain problems but fail to solve these problems, partly because governments refuse to imbue them with anything beyond rhetorical force.[50] For example, many constitutions contain wording that recognizes men's and women's formal equality, without establishing clear mechanisms to measure, monitor, or enforce this pledge. Further, in some countries, the impact of mobilization has been kept to a minimum because the state has co-opted women's organizations. Following the Cuban Revolution, the government mobilized women into state-sponsored women's organizations under the umbrella of the Federation of Cuban Women. Similarly, many authoritarian states in Africa do not wish to have their power challenged, so women's groups, since they represent a challenge to their power, are often funded by and sponsored by the state in order to keep the organizations as apolitical as possible.[51] As a result of this state sponsorship, these organizations lose their ability and leverage to place demands on it. Alternatively, sometimes a movement accepts the aid of the state and finds its goals placed on the back burner or diluted by the state. For instance, in Kuwait in the 1970s, the Arab Women's Development Society (AWDS) was able to pressure the all-male National Assembly to discuss an equal rights bill.[52] However, the state disbanded the AWDS in 1980 and was hesitant to license any women's organizations that did not have a religious purpose. Thus the impact of women's organizations can be seriously curtailed in states where groups must receive permission from the state to form.

This phenomenon is not limited to countries in the developing world; advanced industrialized democracies can co-opt women's movements in more subtle ways, and some scholars argue that women's movements in western Europe and the United States moved from "an early radicalism, autonomy, and challenge to the state in the 1970s, to a more moderate, state-involved, and accommodationist stance by the 1990s," using rhetoric that would have been "unthinkable" in the 1970s. Drawing on the example of women's mobilization over day-care issues in the United States, the authors traced the transformation of a movement that once pushed for collectively run child-care centers free of state intervention into one that did not seriously oppose radical (and potentially punitive) welfare reform in the 1990s.[53] In sum, working more closely with the state, either through increased integration with political parties or women's policy machineries, has brought benefits in the form of increased legislation as well as passage of symbolic and material reforms. However, as women's movements move to a more legitimized "insider status," they have also, in many instances, moderated their demands and, in some instances, been used as a tool for the state.

Third, women's movements have also left a trail of motivated, skilled, and politically active women in their wake who have impacted politics and society in multiple ways. One way these women have impacted politics and society is that globally, participation in movements and organizations has "encouraged the development of citizenship and political subjectivity" among the women involved.[54] These women may go on to lead other movements, run for political office, or just remain aware of and involved in politics. Women's participation in movements also often alters how they see themselves. In some instances, while women may have joined an organization because they felt it was their duty as mothers to protect their children and the family, through their participation they discovered a new identity—one of a political being.[55] Further, women's mobilization has encouraged other marginalized groups in society to fight for change.[56] For example, in the United States, the peace movement adopted feminist ideological frames and organizational structures built on feminist processes, and also adapted some of the tactical innovations of women's movements. In addition, women became increasingly prominent in leadership positions.[57]

Finally, women's movements have had a broad transformational effect, altering the way society views women. In many countries, women's mobilization has made a previously unseen, invisible population highly visible. When women fight for their rights and/or the rights of their family, they emerge from the woodwork and become political actors. While this is no guarantee of success, nonetheless the impact is notable. It is easy for a government to ignore a population that is complacent and quiet, but it must respond in some way to a movement that is increasingly organized and vocal. Further, public opinion polls demonstrate that societies are more supportive of gender equality than in previous decades. While this change is more significant in postindustrial societies than in industrial and agrarian societies, and is also dependent on larger processes of socioeconomic modernization, nonetheless the rise of women's movements played a role in this broader process of attitudinal transformation.[58] And the proliferation of women's and gender studies programs indicates the spreading influence of the women's movement and the issues it has raised and continues to raise. There are over

2011 Nobel Peace Prize winners Tawakkol Karman of Yemen, left, Liberian peace activist Leymah Gbowee, center, and Liberian president Ellen Johnson Sirleaf display their prizes for their work organizing women in the developing world to protest for their rights as women.
SOURCE: AP Photo/John McConnico

700 such academic programs, located primarily in the United States, Canada, and Europe, but also in developing countries in Latin America (Brazil, Chile, Colombia, Costa Rica), Africa (South Africa, Uganda), eastern Europe and the countries of the former Soviet Union (Ukraine, Russia, Belarus, Croatia), Asia (China, India, Thailand, Korea), and the Middle East (Egypt, Lebanon).[59] In sum, women's movements have brought women into the public sphere, a sphere previously inhabited primarily by men, and have altered their own and society's perception of them (see photo 2.2).

THE RISE OF EXTREMIST NATIONALIST AND RELIGIOUS FUNDAMENTALIST MOVEMENTS

Not all women who join social movements are motivated by women's issues. Further, they may join movements that, as a byproduct of their larger goals, often seek to impose a vision of women's roles that seems antithetical to the rhetoric of equality for women. Extremist nationalist and religious fundamentalist movements, while not primarily composed of women, attract a small but critical female constituency. Both types of movements have often emerged in societies undergoing wide-ranging social and economic changes, which have altered men's and women's traditional division of labor in society. Both movements often advocate returning to a past in which these traditional roles are restored and, in some instances, further entrenched. How can we explain why women would become involved in movements whose primary aim is often to return them to traditional divisions of labor where they know their "appropriate" role? To answer that question, we will discuss how extremist nationalist movements and religious fundamentalist movements view women, outline women's involvement in these types of movements, and then explore some explanations for their involvement.

A nationalist movement is a group of people who often feel that they have some important commonalities that unite them and make them distinct from the rest of society. This may include, but is not limited to, a common history, language, religion, and/or ethnicity. Further, they believe that as a result they should form their own sovereign nation or force the state to incorporate them more equally into society/government. Nationalist movements are often not concerned with women's issues, as independence from their "oppressor" or a more significant political role for their group is the main goal. While nationalist movements have often been channeled into peaceful demands for independence, autonomy, and democracy, they can also morph into extreme right-wing, xenophobic movements. For example, the rise of the National Front (FN) in France (which is actually a political party, although it refers to itself as a movement), the savage war in the former Yugoslavia, and the horrific genocide in Rwanda were motivated by extreme forms of nationalist fervor, which drew on and inflamed ethnic and racial divisions within society.

In these instances, women are often portrayed as the symbolic and physical reproducer of the nation. Women are expected to embrace their role as mother and find total fulfillment in that role. For example, the FN, an extreme far-right

French party founded by Jean-Marie Le Pen in 1972, focuses on women as part of its larger obsession with the growing population of non-European immigrants in France, the rapidly declining birth rate in France, and the perceived moral decay of society in the face of rampant individualism. As Le Pen explained in *Le Pen Without Mask*,

> One has artificially turned women away from their natural function by offering them an illusory integration into the working world presented by pernicious ideologists as a token of dignity and liberation. . . . Deflected from their intrinsic social role, millions of women have found themselves pushed into a less and less open sector, contributing to the development of unemployment and—but is it really by chance?—serving against their will to create a new proletariat, easily to exploit—and manipulate—by political organizations whose aim is to destroy national harmony by constantly arousing totally artificial confrontations.[60]

In this view, women's true mission is to return to a traditional and subordinate role in the household, where they will find a higher sense of purpose than that provided by economic modernization.

To remedy the problems created by society's moral decay, the FN promotes a social order that glorifies the traditional nuclear family and "is based on the difference of the sexes—the men direct and command, in public as well as in private life. The women must obey and submit themselves to their biological destiny, that is, to have babies and raise them."[61] To better organize women to the cause, the FN founded a women's organization, the National Circle of European Women, whose stated objective is to "defend the French family, women and fundamental values of our society."[62] In addition, the FN has proposed a number of pronatalist policies, such as providing stay-at-home mothers with a monthly paid wage to take care of their children (and also to liberate jobs for unemployed men). Alternatively, they have proposed introducing "family-based voting," in which more electoral weight is given to families with children (parents should have as many extra votes as they have children below voting age).[63] Given their priorities, they are also vehemently opposed to the legalization of abortion. In sum, women are seen not as individuals but as the critical reproductive element within the family unit. They are heralded as both the symbol of the regeneration of society (if they live up to these traditional, familial roles) as well as the potential enemy of this same process (if they defy the previously described "ideal").

Worldwide, religious fundamentalist movements are often formed in reaction to what they see as an increasing level of moral decay in society, often brought on by encroaching modernization and Westernization.[64] By forming such groups the members hope to encourage government to roll back or stop any further changes that would exacerbate this decay, which, in their eyes, is partially caused by a rhetoric of women's rights that encourages women to abandon their traditional roles. And particularly in the developing world, women's movements are perceived as Western imports that are not truly reflective of the culture of their society and, in some sense, are the catalyst for this moral decay. While Muslim fundamentalist movements in countries such as Iran, Afghanistan, and Nigeria have garnered a significant amount of media attention, Hindu fundamentalist movements are a significant force in India, and Christian fundamentalist movements from a variety of denominations continue to play a strong role in U.S. politics and society.

While there are numerous differences between countries in the developing world and those in the advanced industrial world, religious movements in both are seeking a similar solution—a return to "traditional female virtues and morality."[65] Similar to the rhetoric of extremist nationalist movements, this often entails the return or maintenance of what fundamentalists view as a more moral and traditional society and family structure, where the woman's main role is as mother, wife, and caretaker of the home and where male authority is paramount. In developing countries, some fundamentalist movements have moved to impose dress codes, ban divorce, allow for honor killings of women who have dishonored the family, prevent women from leaving the home without a male family member as escort, and more. In industrialized democracies, religious movements usually have proposed less extreme measures for women, focusing on the incorporation of religious values into a society that is overly secularized.

The Islamist movement in Turkey provides an interesting example of a conservative, right-wing movement that organizes within the parameters of a secular, democratic state. Turkey has been torn between secularism and Islam since the foundation of the republic in 1923, partially because this split for much of Turkey's history has been portrayed as a struggle between modernism and Westernization and traditionalism and the Ottoman past. Women have often been caught in the middle of this struggle because both sides want to claim them as symbols of either Westernized progress or the embodiment of Islamic values. Turkey's first president, Mustafa Kemal Ataturk, launched Turkey on a path toward Westernized modernization, and as part of that goal he targeted the veil as a symbol of woman's oppression and unveiling as a sign of her emancipation. The government, often through state-sponsored women's organizations, sponsored unveiling campaigns in an effort to publicize Turkey's embrace of Western, modern, secular customs.[66] Considered by the government to be symbols of backwardness, veils were banned from public spaces, such as government offices, although women could wear them in private. In addition, women benefited from other reforms, such as suffrage, liberalized divorce laws, and other Westernized policies. The overall goal was not so much to eradicate Islam from society but to confine it to the private sphere in an effort to push Turkey closer to European standards of living.

However, Islamists, male and female, wanted to reclaim women's bodies for their own version of an ideal society, and since the 1970s there has been a revival of Islamist movements in Turkey through political organizations such as the National Order, National Salvation, Welfare, and Virtue parties. These parties at different times united religiously conservative Sunni Muslims, small businessmen, and others who had waited to benefit from Turkey's modernization policies but failed to do so.[67] Also, they channeled citizens' dissatisfaction with secularization, which was equated with a rejection of Turkish heritage. While the various strands of the Islamist movement attracted predominantly men in the 1970s, as we shall see, women became increasingly drawn to protest activities in the 1980s and participated frequently in veiling protests.

So what roles do women play in extremist nationalist and religious fundamentalist movements? Let us first turn to our example of the French FN, where women have been recruited primarily in supporting roles. When the FN first emerged as a movement in the 1970s, women candidates were few and far between. However, the FN has tried to recruit a few token women to prominent political positions, particularly at the local level, to appeal to women voters and to soften its image. Women candidates are highlighted as "family women," and they are often used specifically to propagate the antifeminist rhetoric of the FN. For example, Marie-France Stirbois, a prominent FN member, has pledged to "liberate women from feminism" and to replace feminism with femininity. She also discourages the concept of equality between men and women, arguing that it "humiliates women."[68] Thus, women in the FN are useful because they are able, as women speaking to other women, to promote a more compelling critique of feminism than the male leadership, who may not engender the same kind of legitimacy advancing similar rhetoric.

Primarily, however, women are more visible in the movement as wives to male leaders in order to emphasize the FN's focus on the traditional nuclear family. At times, these wives have been recruited to political office to serve as surrogates for the values of their spouses. And often female family members are recruited to various supporting roles in the organization to perform the "helping tasks" needed to make things run smoothly. They also carry out the movement's charitable activities, such as organizing collections for the nation's poor, organizing summer camps for children, and other "feminine" activities. However, despite its rhetoric of women's central force in society, nonetheless the FN still places women's interests behind more "important" issues, like immigration or security; out of the 426 pages of the movement's program, the chapter on the family (women don't merit a separate entry) is restricted to 14 pages.[69]

Women's involvement in religious fundamentalist movements, both in the developing world and the advanced industrial world, has increased greatly in the past few decades. In Turkey, women mobilized in response to a 1982 decision to ban the veil at university campuses. Veiled women became increasingly militant and staged sit-ins, demonstrations, and fasts. They also, through their voting power, helped sweep the conservative Welfare Party to electoral victory in 1994. Many Islamist women adopted a vision of the "ideal" Turkish woman by emphasizing the piety and obedience of the Prophet's daughter, Fatimah, rather than focusing on women's submission to patriarchy. For example, for Cihan Aktas, a prominent Islamist woman writer, the ideal Muslim woman represents "the intelligent, brave, chaste, productive and virtuous woman" who submits to Islam, while simultaneously rejecting traditional interpretations that minimize women's participation.[70] In a sense, they are advancing an "equal, but different" version of womanhood.

So why would women join these movements? While the supporters of the FN are disproportionately male, a small (but increasing) percentage of women have thrown their support behind them. In fact, in 2002, 14 percent of women cast their votes for Le Pen in his bid for the presidency.[71] Women tend to respond to the FN for the same reasons that men do; that is, they fear how immigration, crime, and unemployment will affect their lives, although some women also respond to the rhetoric of the defense of the traditional family.[72]

In the instance of religious fundamentalist movements, some join in reaction to the growth of feminist ideologies, which conservative religious women see as threatening their culture and/or position in society, or as imposed by the West or by women not in touch with the mainstream. However, other women see their adherence to Islamist values and dress codes as a choice that should not be taken as an automatic rejection of women's equality. In Muslim countries that have a dress code, and even in those that do not, many Muslim women argue that they prefer to wear conservative dress, especially in the workplace (in countries such as Egypt where they are allowed to work) because it forces men to look at them only as colleagues, to focus on what they have to offer intellectually, as opposed to physically. Writing of her own choice to wear the headscarf, Merve Kavakci, a former representative of the right-wing Virtue Party in Turkey's parliament, argued that "Mainstream Islamic tradition considers the headscarf an obligation for Muslim women because it conceals their physical allure. By covering themselves, Muslim women can be recognized not only for their religious beliefs but for their contributions to society as well; they can be judged for their intellect and not just their appearance." Further, she maintained, the headscarf is an important part of women's identity and should be a choice; simplistic interpretations of the *hijab* as a symbol of oppression reveal a "deep and growing misunderstanding between Muslim women and the rest of the world."[73]

Further, some common themes emerge between the two types of movements. As we mentioned previously, both are responses to larger processes wrought by economic and social modernization and globalization, which often have altered radically men's and women's roles in society. For both types of movements, while it is tempting to assume that women have been forced into wanting a return to traditional family structures by strong-willed, patriarchal men in their lives, that explanation is too simplistic and insulting to women. The fact is that there are women who prefer traditional roles. They feel that motherhood and taking care of the family confers a certain status upon them as well as a level of safety and security. Further, these movements do not just push a negative agenda for women; rather, they seek to legitimize and uphold the role of mother and caregiver. This can have a powerful appeal to women homemakers and mothers who feel their work is undervalued in societies in which more women are working outside the home and gaining increased levels of public visibility and power.[74] In sum, many women join these movements because they believe that their status and lives are better under more traditional codes of conduct and conceptions of rights. Further, many women are not responding primarily to the messages regarding women's roles in the household, but to the larger goals advanced by the movements. In France, women, like men, are attracted to the FN because of their affinity for the authoritarian, nationalist, and racist rhetoric of the party. In Turkey, women, are, in part, trying to establish an alternative between the secularism of the West and the more severe fundamentalism of the Middle East.

CONCLUSION

In this chapter, we have read about women who have occupied oil refineries, held silent vigils in honor of their disappeared sons, set up communes to promote peace, spread breast cancer awareness, lobbied for tougher drunk-driving laws, and pushed for a variety of antidiscrimination laws mandating equality between the sexes. As we have seen, it is more useful to look at women's activism in women's movements, broadly defined, than to impose a narrow definition on what constitutes a "legitimate" woman's issue. While women do not mobilize over identical issues or express their interests in uniform ways, nonetheless, women do tend to organize over similar concerns, many of which are not expressly feminist in orientation, but are often seen as important to women. Women have used their multiple roles of wives, mothers, and caretakers as a strategy to grant legitimacy to their demands.

Women's groups have clearly had an impact on both society and politics. They have lobbied successfully for the passage of numerous items of legislation that have directly and indirectly impacted women's status. They have pushed for the creation of women's policy machineries and have built alliances with sympathetic "femocrats," politicians, and political parties. They have created an active base of women who go on to influence and sometimes lead other movements, who remain active in and aware of politics, and who may run for political office. Finally, they have changed the way society perceives women, and they have often changed the way women view themselves (see the box "Guerrilla Girls Take on the Art World").

Yet, it is important to recognize that women are not united simply through their common sex or gender status. Not all women agree on what constitutes "progress" and "equality" for women, and as a result, women have been active in movements that seem to work against women's collective interests. Their participation in these movements poses interesting questions for scholars—why would women wish to maintain or return to a time when they had fewer rights and were subservient to men? Many such women feel that feminism is either imposed by the West or out of touch with the mainstream or believe that societies that esteem and protect the role of mother and wife are preferable to those in which the sexes are considered equal. In the former, they feel that they have a status and level of safety that they would not or do not have in the latter.

Women's movements and organizations will continue to be a powerful force worldwide. In particular, since 1985, in the wake of the third United Nations conference on women in Nairobi, Kenya, women's activism has become increasingly transnational, crossing borders and cultures. Globalization has both united women, by highlighting the commonalities that the process of global economic restructuring has wrought,[75] and increased the divide between the winners and losers of this process. On the one hand, some scholars have theorized that with the increasing trend toward supranationalism, women will be facing conditions that are increasingly similar. In turn, this will encourage the homogenization of women's movements.[76] The challenge for the future is to continue to forge stronger links between women across cultures, without obliterating their differences. And

Guerrilla Girls Take on the Art World

In 1985 a group of women decided that patriarchy in the art world had gone on long enough. When the Museum of Modern Art held an exhibition in 1984 titled "International Survey of Painting and Sculpture" and of the 169 artists chosen, all were white and less than 10 percent were women, some female artists decided that enough was enough. Thus, in April 1985, the Guerrilla Girls emerged. The movement was made up of woman artists who assumed the names of dead women artists and wore gorilla masks to hide their identities. The masks and assumed names were used so that the world would focus on the women's message, not on their personalities or looks. Using unconventional tactics, between 1985 and 2000 over 100 women artists anonymously produced posters, books, billboards, and public actions to bring attention to their cause. They used humor to show that feminists could be funny, too; they protested in front of the Guggenheim; and they took part in various panels where they came dressed in high heels and their telltale gorilla masks and passed out pamphlets that sarcastically poked fun at the male art establishment. In one such pamphlet they facetiously commented that "I'm a Guerrilla Girl and I think the art world is perfect. . . . [W]omen artists make fully one whole third of what male artists make, so what's there to be mad about?"[i] By the 1990s the art world had become more accepting of female artists, partly in response to the tactics of the Guerrilla Girls. This success forced the movement to reexamine its purpose. For some, the mask, which had initially been empowering, was now a burden and had "become a projection of racist fantasies and a perpetuation of the sexual allure of the veiled woman."[ii] Nonetheless, the Guerrilla Girls continued on and still exist today, although their work and focus have changed with the times. Today they have an official website, www.guerrillagirls.com, and three of the members have formed Guerrilla Girls on Tour, which dramatizes women's history and the patriarchy that persists in all realms, including politics and the family, as well as the art world.

---

[i]"How and Why Did the Guerrilla Girls Alter the Art World Establishment in New York City, 1985–1995?," Introduction, http://womhist.alexanderstreet.com/ggirls/intro.htm, March 6, 2009, p. 4.
[ii]Ibid.

as power increasingly devolves to supranational institutions, global women's movements will have to respond with new strategies, tactics, and goals to keep pace with an ever-changing international structure.

FOR MORE INFORMATION

Pambazuka News: Weekly Forum for Social Justice in Africa: Social Movements, http://www.pambazuka.org/en/category/socialmovements

Social Movements and Culture: A Resource Site, culturalpolitics.net/social_movements

Women and Social Movements in the United States 1600–2000, http://womhist.alexanderstreet.com

Beyond Beijing—This is a documentary film about the 1995 Beijing Conference and the numerous women's nongovernmental organizations that attended; produced by Women Make Movies.

Butterfly—This film looks at 24-year-old Julia "Butterfly" Hill, who sat in a tree for 2 years to protest the clear-cutting of redwood trees in California.

Not for Ourselves Alone: The Story of Stanton and Anthony—This film looks at the life and history of the two women who started the women's suffrage movement in the United States.

The Righteous Babes—This documentary film looks at the impact of the "third wave" of feminism on such female rock artists as Ani DiFranco and Queen Latifah; produced by Women Make Movies.

Union Maids—This film looks at the role of women in the United States in the labor and leftist movements of the 1930s and 1940s.

Welfare Warriors—This film looks at a grassroots movement of women on welfare who protested the 1996 Clinton welfare reform bill.

The Women of Hezbollah—This film looks at the lives of two women members of Hezbollah.

3

Women and Revolutionary Movements

Samara Ibrahim, a young woman originally from Upper Egypt, was one of the thousands of protesters participating in the sit-in in Tahrir Square in Cairo on March 9, 2011. In the face of organized and determined popular protest, President Mubarak, Egypt's longstanding autocratic president, had resigned the previous month, handing power over to a military junta known as the Supreme Council of Armed Forces (SCAF). However, protests continued in the Square, as Egyptian citizens demanded not only the collapse of the old regime (of which the junta was a part) but a transition to a new and, they hoped, democratic political system. That night, military police used force to evacuate the Square, violently dispersing protesters. Samira and 17 other women at the demonstration were allegedly beaten, given electric shocks, strip-searched, and then forced into receiving a "virginity test," which involves an inspection of the hymen, on the assumption that it can be torn only as a result of sexual intercourse. An unnamed general was quoted by CNN defending these actions, stating that the female protesters "were not like your daughter or mine. We didn't want them to say we had sexually assaulted or raped them, so we wanted to prove they weren't virgins in the first place."[1] Only Samira Ibrahim reported this violation, challenging the authority of the SCAF by suing her abusers. (A military court eventually exonerated the military doctor who had allegedly performed the forced virginity tests.) This wasn't the only incidence of gendered tactics used by the military to discourage women from protesting. Months later, in December 2011, a video, which went viral on YouTube, showed Army officers dragging a woman (known only as "blue bra woman") by her black robe, worn by many Muslim women, revealing her blue bra and chest and torso. Then she was repeatedly kicked and clubbed. That incident prompted a march by 10,000 women through Cairo. (Would it have prompted as much protest if the woman had "merely" been beaten and kicked but not exposed?) Yet, on June 8, 2012, about 50 women held a march demanding an end to sexual harassment in Cairo before being assaulted and molested by a mob of hundreds of men, who quickly overwhelmed the male supporters who had turned out to protect the female protesters.[2] It seems that many would prefer women to stay home during times of political upheaval.

All of these anecdotes tell us something about the role that gender plays in revolutions. Women were at the frontlines of Egyptian protests, as they were in many other protest movements across the countries swept up in the Arab Spring. They organized and participated in protests, smuggled arms (sometimes beneath their burqas), got information to international media outlets, nursed the sick and injured, and prepared food for the protesters. But in a conservative Muslim society, security forces cannily used strategies to deliberately humiliate women and discourage them from protesting. In Egypt's deeply patriarchal society, where more than 90 percent of married women report that they have been circumcised (the practice was banned in 2008), many believe women shouldn't be protesting at all. For many, a woman who sleeps outside the home (in this case, in the tents that had been set up in Tahrir Square) has loose morals. And undressing a woman to show her chest and torso in public is taboo.[3] Although women helped foment the revolution, it isn't clear whether the revolution is going to benefit women, a topic we will return to later in this chapter.

This chapter explains how women interact with the causes, processes, and outcomes of revolutions and revolutionary movements in Europe, eastern Europe, Asia, Latin America, and the Middle East. We assess how participation in this form of noninstitutionalized politics has changed women's lives, both in positive and negative ways. How do women interact with the origins, processes, and outcomes of revolution? Do they respond similarly to men in why and how they participate in revolutionary movements? Are they affected in the same ways by the new regime? The answer to all of these questions is, not surprisingly, a resounding "no."

Throughout history, women have been recruited to revolutionary movements to fight for profoundly new societies. Women have responded to the revolutionary call, fighting for women's rights, but more frequently for what they perceive to be larger struggles involving issues of class or national self-determination. While women may not have been motivated by concerns of gender equality, the ways in which they participate are rarely gender neutral. While women have masterminded complicated assassination plots, served as soldiers and tacticians, and died for their cause on the battlefield, in prison, or strapped to a bomb, more frequently, women have fulfilled critical, but often unacknowledged, supporting roles. Further, many have succeeded in their revolutionary tasks by exploiting traditional societal expectations about women's supposedly apolitical status. Gender matters, particularly given that as we march further into the twenty-first century, women have increasingly filled the ranks of guerrilla movements in Latin America, Asia, and the Middle East.

However, despite women's multifaceted and emphatic participation in altering the distribution of power, it is unclear to what degree they have benefited from such movements. Revolutionary leaders are adept at promising rewards for women in return for their support; they are much less successful in (and committed to) working to ensure that these benefits actually materialize under the new order. Disappointingly, the effects of revolution have rarely been as radically progressive for women as originally promised. While revolution has significantly changed the way that women live their lives, it is often in unanticipated ways or in ways that rarely live up to the promises issued. There is something of a "glass ceiling" for women in that they are allowed to reap the benefits of radical change, but only to a certain degree. Often, men are able to maintain crucial positions of economic, social, and political power, leaving women to serve as symbols of progress, but often, in reality, to act as maidservants to the new postrevolutionary regime. Part of this is because women themselves are often willing to sacrifice "women's" issues to a perceived "more important" cause, such as national self-determination and identity. Thus, revolutions have been something of a double-edged sword for women.

DEFINING REVOLUTIONS

Revolutions involve more than just a change in political leadership. Most scholars agree that a revolution entails a large-scale alteration, not only in terms of who governs but also in terms of dominant cultural mores and values. This change is often implemented rapidly, over the course of months, years, or perhaps decades, but not centuries.[4] For example, the French Revolution was radical in its impact, not only because it brought new people into the hallways of political power in the space of a few years but also because it seriously weakened the power of the aristocracy and ushered in a new class of ruling elite that espoused the values of classical liberalism, popularly expressed as "liberty, fraternity, and equality."

When explaining why revolutions happen, some scholars have focused on the role of psychological factors, such as people's perceptions of deprivation; people revolt when their expectations for a better life are not met, particularly when their position in society is improving, but not as quickly as another group's in society.[5] In contrast, structuralist explanations have tended to focus on the actions of the state in explaining breakdown. In this view, revolutions occur (often in societies undergoing rapid modernization) when social and economic institutions develop faster than political institutions, and the state is unable to absorb citizens' competing demands, which leads to political disintegration. Other theories have posited that states fall apart in response to international pressures, combined with fragmentation among the political elite. The conjuncture of these two factors creates a political opening that allows disenfranchised citizens, such as peasants, to mobilize in opposition.[6] Demographic theories have focused on the problems that arise when sustained population growth outpaces economic growth, thus undermining stability.[7] While these theories differ in their approaches, nonetheless they all tend to underplay the role of individual leaders and instead focus on broader, societal-level changes that provide openings for a variety of players to act on their frustration.

Yet, until the 1980s, researching revolutions felt like entering a museum; when studying examples of widespread and far-reaching political breakdown, one would study a select grouping of historical events. Revolutions were perceived to be something of a rarity; scholars tended to focus on the "great" revolutions, studying every nook and cranny of political upheaval in England (1640), France (1789),

Russia (1917), and China (1949). The field was sometimes widened to include events such as the Mexican (1910) and Cuban (1959) revolutions.[8]

However, world events caught up with standard definitions and demonstrated that scholars needed to broaden both what they considered to be a revolution and the nature of the underlying conflict. As the text box entitled "Revolutionary Movements in Advanced Industrialized Democracies" discusses, in the late 1960s and early 1970s, the political stability of Western democracies was rocked by a variety of radical left-wing terrorist movements that often recruited from a growing pool of disillusioned middle-class youth. And more recently, throughout the final two decades of the twentieth century, in a phenomenon termed the "third wave" (following two previous eras of significant, widespread democratic surges), authoritarian regimes collapsed in countries in almost every continent of the globe. In the 1980s and 1990s, military regimes disintegrated in Latin America, "people power" succeeded in toppling corrupt governments in the Philippines and Haiti, communism collapsed in eastern Europe and the former Soviet Union, the apartheid regime stepped aside in South Africa, and prodemocracy movements challenged dictatorships in China, Indonesia, and Burma. It seemed as if this "third wave" of democratization had peaked during the first decade of the 21st century, until the self-immolation of a street vendor in Tunisia in December 2010 sparked a wave of protests and regime change in Tunisia, Egypt, Libya, and Yemen, major uprisings in Bahrain and Syria, and protests in almost every country of the Middle East and North Africa. Collectively called the Arab Spring, this wave of protests has produced a variety of outcomes, none of which can be termed solidly democratic (or positive for women). In Burma, one of the world's most repressive states, the military junta released Nobel Peace Prize winner Aung San Suu Kyi from house arrest as part of a larger set of political reforms launched in 2010 and 2011, causing many to speculate that democratic change may be on the horizon for this pariah state. Later on in this chapter, we will address the status of this potential "fourth wave" of democratization.

Revolutionary Movements in Advanced Industrialized Democracies

Many of the movements and activists mentioned in this chapter hail from countries either in the developing world or from what used to be known as the second world, those countries that fell within the Soviet sphere of influence. We often don't think of revolutionary movements agitating in relatively stable, wealthy democracies. After all, a hallmark of a stable democracy is its ability to absorb competing interests through the more institutionalized political processes of elections, lobbying, interest group politics, and social movement activities that practice mostly legal forms of protest. Further, what helps make stable democracies endure is a political culture in which almost all citizens choose to cooperate within the rules of democratic politics or, at the very least, choose not to defect. Many students born in the post–Vietnam War/post–Cold War era are surprised to learn that countries such as the United States, Germany, Italy, and Japan were rocked by the activities of small underground terrorist organizations such as the Weather Underground (United States), Red Army Faction (Germany), Red Brigades (Italy), and Japanese Red Army in the late 1960s and throughout the 1970s and 1980s. Other groups, such as the Black Panther Party in the United States, flitted between radical left-wing, but legal, protest activity and advocating armed uprising against legal authority. In all movements, women held important leadership positions, although for most, gender was not an important rallying cry; rather, the enemy was usually the capitalist system, Western imperialism, and the people who enforced these systems at home and abroad.

The damage inflicted by these relatively small groups was significant. In its 6 short years, the Weather Underground, which was founded in 1969 by disillusioned members of Students for a Democratic Society (SDS), organized riots, detonated bombs in a number of public spaces, and facilitated a jailbreak of famed LSD advocate Timothy Leary. Tired of the supposed futility of nonviolent protest to the Vietnam War and inspired by the militancy of the Black Panther Party, the Weather Underground believed in the potential of urban guerrilla actions to fundamentally reset the priorities of the U.S. military, and in 1970, they issued a "Declaration of a State of War" against the U.S. government. As Naomi Jaffe, a former member, explained,

> We felt that doing nothing in a period of repressive violence is itself a form of violence. That's really the part that I think is the hardest for people to understand. If you sit in your house, live your white life and go to your white job, and allow the country that you live in to murder people and to commit genocide, and you sit there and you don't do anything about it, that's violence.[i]

However, after the United States reached a peace accord in Vietnam in 1973, the group gradually disintegrated, as some leaders were arrested, others turned themselves in, and some refocused their militancy on other issues. Their legacy was briefly unearthed during the 2008 U.S. presidential elections when vice presidential candidate Sarah Palin accused Barack Obama of "palling around" with terrorists because of Obama's alleged relationship with a former member of the Underground.

While the Weather Underground primarily targeted buildings, rather than people, with their bombs, other radical groups in other countries were not as discriminating. For example, the German Red Army Faction (RAF, also known as the Baader Meinhof Gang), which operated from the late 1960s to 1998, was responsible for 34 deaths and numerous injuries from bombings, kidnappings, and other forms of armed protest over almost 30 years of activity. Their armed resistance reached a peak in autumn 1977 when, in response to the convictions of members of their group, part of the RAF tried to free their imprisoned comrades and kidnap a prominent German businessman, killing three policemen and the driver in the process. Eventually, the businessman was also executed, in the wake of an audacious hijacking attempt. Like the Weather Underground, members of the RAF cited their disillusionment with capitalist society. In addition, members felt alienated from what they perceived to be a conservative, pro-order political culture that echoed totalitarian currents from the Nazi era. This two-decades-long spasm of violence transfixed the world and shattered Germans' vision of their society as a democratic and orderly one. The RAF continued its sporadic campaign of terror into the 1990s, assassinating the head of the Treuhandanstalt, the trust in charge of privatizing East Germany's state-owned assets (and bringing capitalism to the former socialist state). Finally, in 1998, a letter faxed to the Reuters news agency, signed "RAF," announced the dissolution of the group.

Communist-inspired terrorist groups also shattered the stability of Japan and Italy throughout the 1970s and 1980s. The Japanese Red Army, whose stated goal was to overthrow the Japanese government and start a world revolution, conducted numerous hijackings, kidnappings, and hostage takings and launched a series of 17 bombs in buildings belonging to large corporations. In Italy, the Red Brigades, in their efforts to create a revolutionary state through armed struggle and to remove Italy from NATO, kidnapped and murdered a former prime minister, in addition to conducting several high-profile political kidnappings.

Young women became increasingly active in these terrorist cells and, in almost all of these movements, assumed leadership positions. Bernadine Dohrn of the Weather Underground, Gudrun Ensslin and Ulrike Meinhof of the RAF, and Fusako Shigenobu of the Japanese Red Army were all key public faces and behind-the-scenes organizers of their respective organizations. Their female status was often a source of great fascination to the public, in part because they completely upended gender expectations about "appropriate behavior" for middle-class, college-educated women. Dohrn, for example, had been a cheerleader in high school, something perceived as American as apple pie, before becoming radicalized in college and law school. Ensslin was a pastor's daughter pursuing her Ph.D., and Meinhof was the daughter of an art historian and a teacher, and herself was studying at university when she became much more polarized in her political beliefs. Media coverage of the women often mentioned their attractive physical appearance, as if this was somehow unexpected or noteworthy about their terrorism (male terrorists were rarely described in any fashion). Further, Ensslin and Meinhof had both married and had children before pursuing a life underground as terrorists. They had decided to leave their children behind, which was seen as "unwomanly" and "unnatural," even though this was a common decision made by male activists who chose political violence over their children. Further, these women's recruitment to political violence was often portrayed as being an outgrowth of a "love connection" with a male member, rather than a carefully considered political choice.

Although there was a gendered component to how the public perceived these women, the activists themselves rarely pursued a gendered political agenda. Certainly, given that they were active in radical, Marxist-inspired movements, they were well versed in the Marxist critique of women's subjugation. And women active in the Weather Underground connected the battle against sexism with their violent activities, arguing that "the struggle against sexism demands the destruction of the American state, and . . . the immediate personal nature of sexism requires struggle against men who enforce that oppression as well as its institutions."[11] Yet, for the most part, women active in these movements subjugated their gender concerns to their larger struggle against what they perceived to be an oppressive state.

Has the evolution of time and world events (such as the collapse of communism in the former Soviet Union and Eastern Europe) changed these women's views? Many of the women of the Weather Underground went underground themselves, although almost all eventually resurfaced, either when they voluntarily turned themselves in or were arrested. Dohrn, a former leader once on the FBI's Ten Most Wanted List, eventually turned herself in and served a commuted sentence; she currently teaches law at Northwestern University and heads a nonprofit organization that advocates for the reform of the juvenile court system. Ensslin and Meinhof both committed suicide in the 1970s under suspicious circumstances in prison while awaiting trial for their participation in terrorist attacks. And Shigenobu, founder and leader of the Japanese Red Army, was arrested in 2000 after spending over 25 years in hiding. She vowed to continue her revolutionary goals from prison, although this time by establishing a political party rather than from the barrel of a gun. Although media attention has shifted to covering female suicide bombers in the Middle East, Chechnya, and Russia, it is important to recognize that women from all classes and all backgrounds and from many different countries have been recruited to political violence and will probably continue to respond to armed revolutionary calls in a wide array of contexts.

[i] As quoted in the documentary film *The Weather Underground,* produced by Carrie Lozano, directed by Bill Siegel and Sam Green, New Video Group, 2003, DVD.
[ii] "Women of the Weather Underground," *Ms. Magazine,* February 1974, p. 105.

While many countries were moving toward implementing Western-style political and economic systems, other areas of the world were gripped by movements that questioned or rejected these same values. In Latin America, guerrilla movements that challenged the benefits of globalization and integration continued to spring up in Mexico, Colombia, and Brazil as the promise of better lives failed to materialize for many citizens. Fundamentalist movements grew in pace and popularity in the Middle East and Africa, as the rhetoric of political inclusion failed to encompass varied demands for political, cultural, and religious self-determination. Many of these movements incorporated a powerful anti-Western theme to accompany their ideological message. For example, in 1979, Islamic-inspired forces overthrew the corrupt Western-allied government of the Pahlavi family and replaced it with an Islamic theocracy. In 1987, Palestinians launched an "intifada" (uprising) against Israeli occupation that waxed and waned over the following decades, with no foreseeable end to an increasingly polarized conflict. Several years later, in 1992, Algeria was gripped by a deadly revolt when a general election won by an Islamist party was annulled.[9] In addition, ethnicity became an increasingly compelling rallying cry for the world's dispossessed, as conflicts over class diminished in the wake of the Cold War. Civil war and ethnic genocide in Bosnia, Kosovo, the Sudan, Rwanda, and the Congo were the horrifying accompaniment to the more positive democratization developments elsewhere in the world. While the events of the Arab Spring were greeted with initial optimism that democracy would take root in formerly autocratic societies, ensuing initial election results have demonstrated that the path out of autocracy will not be an easy one, nor a preordained result.

In addition, new actors became critical players in revolutionary movements. Specifically, since the 1970s, women have been recruited in rapidly multiplying numbers to guerrilla and revolutionary movements in countries such as Nicaragua, El Salvador, Mexico, and Iran. Women are also increasingly recruited as suicide bombers in the Middle East and in the Chechen conflict. And they were on the front lines of protests throughout the events of the Arab Spring, countering the stereotype of Muslim women as veiled ciphers, silent and submissive. Despite this increasing participation of women, nonetheless, one observation remains constant: while revolutions have been waged in the name of many different ideologies, such as liberalism, communism, and various forms of nationalism, they have never been waged exclusively in the name of feminism.

In response to changing events, one could currently say that "a revolution is an effort to transform the political institutions and the justifications for political authority in a society, accompanied by formal or informal mass mobilization and noninstitutionalized actions that undermine existing authorities."[10] This definition can cover disparate events that all share a core set of characteristics: (1) They are efforts to change the political regime by drawing on a competing vision of justice and a just society; (2) They involve a substantial amount of both formal and informal means of citizen mobilization; and (3) They encompass efforts to change politics through noninstitutionalized means, such as the use of mass demonstrations, protests, strikes, riots, and more violent forms of political expression. This definition allows us to unite a diverse array of events—ranging from the "classic" revolutions such as the French Revolution and the democratic transitions in countries all over the world to the chaotic periods of state breakdown in Africa and guerrilla movements that spring up in Latin America and the Middle East as well as the most recent events of the Arab Spring. At the same time, it allows us to exclude protests and movements that seek to work within the system or through the ballot box. As we shall see, however, this means that it becomes harder to distinguish clearly the social movement activity in authoritarian or semi-authoritarian countries described in the previous chapter, for example, from the revolutionary activity outlined in this chapter. Protest strategies and tactics have expanded and a wider range of actors have been critical in revolutions. And in the third wave of democratization, revolutions morphed from violent upheavals into primarily peaceful transfers of power. Thus, for the purposes of our discussion in this chapter, revolutionary activity proceeds along a continuum of activities rather than belonging in a discrete category.

WHY DO WOMEN JOIN REVOLUTIONARY MOVEMENTS?

While this chapter discusses the myriad ways that women participate in and are affected by revolutionary movements, it is important to recognize that women have been and still are a minority in these movements. While women have become increasingly active in guerrilla struggles, particularly in Latin American countries, nonetheless, in only a few cases do women represent even a third of the participants in revolutionary movements.[11] Why is there a gender imbalance in this area of political participation? As in other areas of women's participation in political and economic institutions, there are serious barriers and impediments to women's inclusion.

As we have seen, across contexts, women occupy a subordinate position in almost all realms of the public sphere because of their duties in the private realm. In other words, many women are simply too busy with their domestic responsibilities of raising children and tending to the household to organize. This sometimes extends to the direct family of revolutionary leaders. A wife often shares her husband's political beliefs but remains out of the political limelight, caring for the family. For example, Joshua Nkomo, head of the Zimbabwe African People's

Union, which fought for the overthrow of white rule in the former Rhodesia, commented:

> My marriage was the best thing I ever did in my whole life. In the thirty-four years of our marriage we have spent less than half the time together, but we have had a perfect understanding all the time. My wife has always borne the main responsibility for such property as we have owned: more, she has kept our family together, because all of us have always been confident that she would be there whatever happened.[12]

Further, in his memoir covering his participation in South Africa's struggle for justice, Nelson Mandela talks eloquently of the sacrifices his wife made so that he could pursue his political activities. While Winnie Mandela also emerged as a prominent opposition leader, nonetheless, she was also responsible for caring for the children, the house, and other family obligations.[13] Many women participated in revolutions by staying out of them or by occupying supporting positions; because they took full responsibility for activities in the household, their spouses or partners could engage fully in the struggle.

In addition, many women have less access to education and, as a result, receive less exposure to revolutionary ideas and plans. Women's lesser integration into the workforce also diminishes their opportunities to become exposed to revolutionary ideas of change. However, joining the workforce in and of itself often is not a sufficient catalyst for change. Class issues further complicate women's participation. Middle- and upper-class women often encounter fewer barriers to participation than do working-class women, who often have little education, meager incomes, few marketable skills, and sometimes sole responsibility for the domestic sphere. Even though their levels of deprivation and exploitation may be higher, they have less opportunity to voice their frustration. In this sense, women's experiences in revolutionary movements mirror men's in that revolutionaries often come from the middle and upper classes. Greater levels of economic independence, more education, and potential access to day care have all helped wealthier women organize for other women (and men) who are less advantaged.[14] In sum, despite women's desire to participate in movements of political change, they often cannot participate in the same ways that men do.

For the women who do answer a revolutionary call for action, what prompts them to get involved? Is it for the benefits that could potentially accrue to them as women, or are they motivated by other concerns that override gender identity? The following sections discuss three types of revolutionary movements—Marxist, liberal and democratization movements, and religious fundamentalist movements—and explain what they offer women and why women have responded to them. Because Marxist movements have most explicitly targeted women and women's equality as a revolutionary goal, we shall start our discussion there.

Marxist Revolutionary Movements
Overcoming the contradictions of capitalism and freeing the workers are the primary goals for socialist revolutionaries. In peasant-based, agrarian societies, such

as those in Latin America, Marxist revolutionaries sought to rectify the unequal distribution of land, which helped maintain the power of a small, privileged land-holding elite over a relatively landless and powerless peasantry. However, Marxist-inspired ideologies also directly addressed and critiqued women's status within the larger framework of capitalism. Many Marxist theorists argued that women are doubly burdened—as workers they are exploited by capitalists, and as wives and mothers they are further exploited, for they are still responsible for the cooking, sewing, childrearing, and cleaning. Marxists argued that marriage is, in fact, often a form of prostitution, as women marry out of economic necessity rather than choice and "earn their keep" by performing essential domestic and sexual tasks. This double burden of production and reproduction further prevents them from entering the public realm in positions of power on an equal footing with men. This Marxist critique of class and gender relations was used widely among revolutionaries in the Soviet Union, China, Cuba, and Vietnam and, more recently, in guerrilla movements in Columbia, Nicaragua, El Salvador, Peru, and the Chiapas region of Mexico. As we shall see, many of these more recent movements also incorporated strong nationalist ideologies; fighting economic injustice often was combined with a rhetoric of national self-determination, and imperial powers, such as the United States, were condemned for their overbearing role in directing domestic politics.

Marxists theorists proposed a variety of solutions to the "woman question." For example, the Bolsheviks in Russia painted a Marxist utopia in which household cares would be transformed to the public sphere. Paid workers would assume the duties that wives had once fulfilled, and communal dining rooms, laundries, and child-care centers would ensure that women could be freed to enter the public sphere, unburdened by duties at home. Marriage, even, would become superfluous, and men and women would come together and separate as they wished, no longer shackled together because of economic dependency.[15] In China, Mao Tse-tung supported women's right to vote and run for office, to hold land on equal terms with men, to reject forced marriages, and to initiate divorce proceedings.[16] In Chiapas, Mexico, on the first day of the 1994 rebellion, the Zapatistas distributed pamphlets listing their demands, many of which related to issues of gender equality. Known as the Revolutionary Women's Law, the list included an affirmation of a woman's right to an education and primary health care. In addition, it affirmed a woman's right to choose how many children to have and when to have them, to choose her spouse without forceful intervention, and to live free from violence both in and out of her home.[17] In Peru, Shining Path designed different outreach messages for women, tapping into women's frustration over poor access to the labor market, increased cost of basic consumer goods, and, in rural areas, public shaming of violent and abusive men/husbands.[18] Across contexts, many Marxist-inspired movements offered a postrevolutionary society that included increased political opportunities for women, increased access to professional opportunities (which would thus make women less economically dependent on men), and a variety of social reforms (increased access to higher education, better health care, increased maternity benefits, and day care) to make this possible.

In practice, Marxist-inspired revolutionaries turned to women, actively recruit-ing them by acknowledging their importance to the struggle. Lenin claimed that "there can be no socialist revolution, unless a vast section of the toiling women takes an important part in it . . . and the success of a revolution depends on the extent to which women take part in it."[19] Mao echoed these sentiments when he said that "women have an urgent need for revolution. . . . [T]hey are a force that will decide the success or failure of the revolution."[20] Further, he argued, man could not be free unless woman was liberated. Fidel Castro declared the quest to end women's subor-dination within the household as a "revolution within the revolution."[21] Abimael Guzman, the leader of the Peruvian guerrilla movement Shining Path, was fond of quoting Lenin directly regarding his policy toward women. And Daniel Ortega, the leader of the Sandinista Front (FSLN), which eventually overthrew the corrupt Samoza regime in Nicaragua, proclaimed that "the FSLN commits itself to guaran-teeing women's rights and to struggle energetically against the residual sexism inher-ited from our past."[22] Revolutionary leaders, most of them male, who borrowed their inspiration from Marx, certainly knew the rhetoric of gender equality. Later on, we will discuss whether women responded to this call to gendered revolution and how willing male revolutionaries were to implement gender equality in practice.

Despite the explicit critique of women's position in society, Marxism has never been the panacea for women that leaders have claimed. Ultimately, the enemy to defeat, according to Marxist theory, is the capitalist system and the bour-geois class. Thus, despite the rhetoric of gender equality, women have often been recruited in the name of overall class struggle, rather than the battle of the sexes. Women's liberation was part of a more important cause, the rights of the worker, and women were to identify as workers first, rather than as women with separate agendas, identities, and reactions to revolutionary policy. Despite the gendered critique of the capitalist system, the struggle for workers' rights was preeminent, and once that was won, Marxists argued, gendered oppression, much like the state, would simply wither away. Thus, while Marxism is one of the few revolutionary ideologies to critique women's position in society explicitly, nonetheless the demands of class struggle usually trumped gender concerns.

There are a few signs that this may be changing as Marxist-inspired revolu-tionary movements unfold in the wake of national and international women's movements. For example, Lisa, an activist in the Zapatista Front for National Liberation (FZLN), connected gender concerns with the larger struggle for in-creased autonomy. Putting the Zapatista movement in context with other Latin America guerrilla movements, she explained:

> I think it [the FZLN-led struggle] has learned from the earlier processes and it
> has gone beyond them. Obviously as a woman I am very interested in taking on
> women's struggles. [In FZLN meetings] we have begun to talk about the fact that
> one cannot be a Zapatista and an oppressor. And it is incongruent to be a revolu-
> tionary and to block women's liberation.[23]

It is hard to tell whether this quote represents one individual's thought process or is indicative of a larger change in the way that Marxist-inspired revolutionaries interpret class and gender relations. Another interviewee had a different perception of the FZLN's commitment to gender issues. In her view:

> What I think is that the FZLN is not a feminist movement but rather a movement that is military, hierarchical, and authoritarian. Not all of them have gender consciousness but some of them do. The FZLN is not against working with women, but I think that it has been a little careless about work with women. The topic of women is always treated as less important than other topics. But it does try to break with the patriarchal system.[24]

While the second participant presents a less rosy view of the FZLN's integration of gender interests, she does acknowledge that the FZLN is making an effort to balance gender with other issues. Nonetheless, Marxist revolutionary ideology, of all the revolutionary ideologies discussed here, most explicitly critiques the status of women and seeks to rectify imbalances with proactive policies.

Liberal/Democratization Movements

Democracy's third wave refers to a major surge of political transformation that started in 1974 with the collapse of the military regime in Portugal, before spreading through the rest of Southern Europe, Latin America in the 1980s, Eastern Europe and the Former Soviet Union in the late 1980s and early 1990s, as well as sub-Saharan Africa and other regions before petering out by 2005. In that 30-year period, the number of countries that moved from authoritarian systems to ones that are nominally democratic, governed by relatively free and fair elections, more than tripled, and they inspired a number of governments and international actors to actively work to promote (or impose) democracy in countries ruled by autocratic leaders. The opposition to authoritarian regimes in these countries often grounded their grievances in the rhetoric of classical liberalism. Classical liberalism, a political and economic philosophy that emerged in seventeenth- and eighteenth-century Europe, focuses on establishing an array of individual rights and liberties to counteract the actions of an often too-powerful state. Revolutionary movements that profess the ideology of classical liberalism focus on the need for greater political inclusion as a way to wean power away from traditional elites and stress themes such as democratic government, individual liberty, and laissez-faire economic growth. While Marxists saw the division of wealth as the obstacle to equality, liberals identified the lack of political freedom and an authoritarian political system as the main impediment to progress. John Locke, Jean-Jacques Rousseau, Adam Smith, Benjamin Franklin, and Thomas Jefferson all came to be identified with a wide variety of ideas associated with classical liberalism, and liberalism was the inspiration for revolutionary movements in America, France, and the more recent democratization movements of the third wave. Although many believe the momentum of the third wave has subsided, the recent reformist wave in Burma, marked by the release of democracy activist Aung San Suu Kyi from house arrest in 2010 as well as the organization of semicompetitive elections in 2012, is another example of liberal-inspired opposition (read the profile of Aung San Suu Kyi on the next page). The recent events of the Arab Spring have been hailed by some analysts as the start of a fourth wave of democratization, though, as we shall discuss toward the end of the chapter, prospects for genuine democracy in the region remain unclear. Nor do we know what will transpire in Iraq and Afghanistan, two countries where Western-style democracy based on the tenets of liberalism has been imposed by external forces, but has worked extremely imperfectly due to economic collapse, corruption, perceptions of illegitimacy, lack of basic security, and ethnic diversity and lack of a national identity.

Women in Motion: Aung San Suu Kyi

Myanmar, also known as Burma, has long been considered a pariah state, isolated from the rest of the world because of its abysmal human rights record. Until 2011, the country had spent nearly a half-century under a military junta that suppressed almost all dissent and whose power was unrivaled, despite a host of international condemnations and sanctions. However, the first general election in 20 years was held in 2010, and a nominally civilian government was installed in March 2011. Although the military still wields the power, these changes have raised hopes that Burmese politics may gradually be moving toward democracy, or at least to a softer authoritarian state with democratic elements.

The leader of Burma's democracy movement is Aung San Suu Kyi, an icon of Burma's struggle against the military junta. She was awarded the Nobel Peace Prize in 1991 in recognition for her campaign for peaceful, nonviolent change as leader of the National League of Democracy. Until the 2010 election, she had been living under house arrest for 15 of the previous 21 years. As part of a larger set of incremental reforms, the political junta released her from custody, and in 2011, she stood as a candidate in a by-election for the Burmese legislature, winning by a landslide. In May 2011, Suu Kyi set off on a world tour (part of which involved delivering her Nobel acceptance speech, two decades after winning the award), making it the first time she had left her country since 1988.

Suu Kyi was born in 1945, the daughter of General Aung San, who negotiated Burma's independence in 1947. However, 6 months before the actual transfer of power from the British to the Burmese, he was assassinated by rivals. Suu Kyi's mother gained prominence as a political figure in her own right in the newly formed Burmese government, and was appointed Burmese ambassador to India and Nepal. As a result, Suu Kyi spent much of her adolescence in India. It was during this time that the military junta seized control in Burma, implementing a regime that included such human rights abuses as the forcible relocation of civilians and the widespread use of forced labor, including children. After finishing high school in India, Suu Kyi continued her education at Oxford University, where she received a B.A. in philosophy, politics, and economics. She then moved to New York City, where she worked at the United Nations, before returning to England and marrying Michael Aris, a British scholar of Tibetan culture, with whom she had two sons. She then earned a Ph.D. at the School of Oriental and African Studies in London.

Her life took an unexpected turn in 1988, when she returned to Burma to care for her mother, who had suffered a stroke. Her trip coincided with a period of rising protest against the military government, and she felt compelled to get involved. She soon became the secretary general of the National League for Democracy

(NLD), the main opposition force. As she told a crowd of supporters, "I could not, as my father's daughter, remain indifferent to all that was going on."[i] To suppress the protests, the military launched a bloody crackdown, killing an estimated 2,000 protesters. When her mother died at the end of 1989, she stayed on to continue her campaign to end military rule. In retaliation, the military regime placed her under house arrest, for "endangering the state," but offered her her freedom if she would leave the country. She refused, dramatically changing the arc of her life. She would not leave Burma again (for fear of not being allowed back into the country) until 2011.

In 1990, the year following the crackdown, the military called for a general election, the nation's first in 30 years. The junta was confident that in the face of the previous year's brutal suppression, the voters would rubber-stamp their rule. But Suu Kyi's NLD won a landslide victory (although she was barred from running for office), winning 80 percent of the seats. The military invalidated the elections and extended Suu Kyi's period of house arrest. The next two decades proceeded as a political battle of cat and mouse between Suu Kyi, her party, the NLD, and the military junta. Although she spent much of this time under house arrest or under extremely constricted mobility, she served as a potent, peaceful symbol of opposition that placed the brutal methods of the ruling regime in sharp, unflattering contrast. In 1991, she was awarded the Nobel Peace Prize, and although she was not able to travel to receive it, it validated her struggle at the international level and helped bring international attention to this poverty-stricken, resource-rich, oppressively governed country.

After decades of sanctions and international condemnation, in 2010, the junta slowly began to implement incremental reform, promising a controlled transition from military rule to a civilian democracy. These reforms include semicompetitive general elections, held in 2010, the appointment of a civilian (but former general) to the presidency, and the release of Suu Kyi and noninterference into her growing political activities in Burmese politics. At the same time, the military is not planning on removing itself from office any time soon; the 2008 constitution reserves a quarter of the seats in Burma's parliament for the military, as well as three key ministerial posts—interior, defense, and border affairs. Yet, this is the most significant political opening in Burma since the military took control in 1962, and past experience of authoritarian regimes, such as those in the USSR, Latin America, and Southern Europe, indicate that it is often hard for regimes to control reform and stay in power once the political doors have been opened. It is hoped that Burma will follow in these countries' trajectories, where military rule was replaced by electoral democracy.

Despite Suu Kyi's wishes to see democracy develop in Burma, she is adamantly opposed to any kind of Arab Spring-style uprising to hasten the pace of change. Inspired by relatively peaceful democratic transitions, such as South Africa's defeat of apartheid, she hopes to see change delivered through negotiation, rather than the barrel of a gun. Echoing some of the sentiments of other nonviolent activists such as Czechoslovakia's Vaclav Havel, she notes that "What has to be done is a revolution of the spirit."[ii] In particular, no longer living in fear is a necessary change in mental state and a precondition for democracy. As she wrote in *Freedom from Fear*:

> Within a system which denies the existence of basic human rights, fear tends to be the order of the day. Fear of imprisonment, fear of torture, fear of death, fear of losing friends, family, property or means of livelihood, fear of poverty,

fear of isolation, fear of failure. A most insidious form of fear is that which mas-
querades as common sense or even wisdom, condemning as foolish, reckless,
insignificant or futile the small, daily acts of courage which help to preserve
man's self-respect and inherent human dignity. It is not easy for a people con-
ditioned by fear under the iron rule of the principle that might is right to free
themselves from the enervating miasma of fear. Yet even under the most
crushing state machinery courage rises up again and again, for fear is not the
natural state of civilized man.[iii]

To Suu Kyi, fear affects the oppressor as well, for it is not power that corrupts
but fear, specifically the fear of losing power, that corrupts those who use it. Similar
to other female activists in democratization movements, the larger goal is freedom
for all, rather than a specific gendered vision of freedom.

Suu Kyi has paid a high personal price for her unswerving commitment to democracy in Burma. She has sacrificed her physical health after decades under
house arrest, which often involved minimal amenities. In 2008, a cyclone ripped off
the roof of her house and destroyed the electricity, a situation that was not remedied until the following year. She also sacrificed the life she had built in London as
an academic, wife, and mother when she left in 1988, not to return until 2011. Her
husband, Michael Aris, was allowed to visit only a few times, and after a Christmas
visit in 1995, the Burmese dictatorship refused to grant any further entry visas. He
was diagnosed with prostate cancer in 1997, which was later found to be terminal,
and the regime continued to refuse to grant him a visa, offering instead to allow
Suu Kyi to leave. She chose to stay in Burma, fearing that by leaving, the regime
would not allow her back in, and Aris died on his 53rd birthday in 1999, not having
seen his wife in 4 years, and having seen her only five times since she was placed
under house arrest in 1989. Similarly, Suu Kyi was separated from her two sons this
entire time, and they were not allowed to visit her in Burma until 2011.

In this most recent thaw, she remains cautiously optimistic, although recognizing that "we are at the beginning of a road," one that will not necessarily lead in a
straight line to democracy. But she is optimistic enough that, after 24 years, she left
Burma, confident that this time the reformist leaders would allow her to return.[iv]

---

[i]Profile: "Aung San Suu Kyi," Al Jazeera English, http://www.aljazeera.com/news/asia-pacific/
2009/05/2009514339158749.html
[ii]Ian MacKinnon, "Aung San Suu Kyi sees signs of political change in Burma," *The Telegraph*,
Sept. 18, 2011. http://www.telegraph.co.uk/news/worldnews/asia/burmamyanmar/8772004/
Aung-San-Suu-Kyi-sees-signs-of-political-change-in-Burma.html
[iii]Aung San Suu Kyi, "Freedom from Fear," http://www.mro.org/mr/archive/26-2/articles/
freedomfear.html
[iv]BBC News, "Profile: Aung San Suu Kyi," http://www.bbc.co.uk/news/world-asia-pacific-
11685977.

However, revolutionary movements that espouse liberal ideologies rarely
focus specifically on women's rights (or the lack of) as a critical problem to be
rectified. Rather, revolutionary leaders have tended to pitch their rhetoric to
women as citizens, rather than as women with specific gendered interests. For
example, some revolutionary movements that fought for greater political inclusion, such as the French Revolution, sought broader changes within the political
system in an attempt to wean power away from traditional elites, such as the

monarchy and the nobility. Thus, they appealed to women as citizens to support the larger goals of "liberty, equality, and fraternity." They did not address the reasons that might make it problematic for women to participate equally with men in the political realm. Two hundred years later, when democratization movements were sweeping communist regimes from power across eastern Europe, the leaders of these movements were appealing to all citizens to unite to topple authoritarianism, rather than targeting women in particular and communism's failure to address women's inequality. However, many feminists active in women's movements, particularly in the West, have used liberal ideology to fight for greater women's rights by arguing that women, like men, should be valued as individual, autonomous agents deserving of equal rights, rather than targeted as justified cases for discrimination. Thus, liberalism has been something of a double-edged sword for women; on the one hand, it has been used to justify women's equality in the sense that it supports equality for all citizens, but on the other hand, liberal-inspired movements fighting for greater political inclusion have tended to blur the distinction between genders in the search for a widened space for political participation for all citizens, thus obscuring the reasons why women may be unable to participate equally.

In practice, leaders of liberal movements could be ambivalent, even hostile, about the gains of women's participation. In the French Revolution, the male leadership always treated women gingerly, despite women's enthusiastic participation. Overall, women were tolerated only as long as their help and activity were necessary. When they were not perceived as necessary, they were excluded from participating in the newly formed clubs and political organizations.[25] Robespierre, one of the leaders of the Revolution, thought women's involvement in political debate "unnatural" and "sterile."[26] The Republican Convention outlawed women's clubs at the height of the Revolution, perceiving them as dangerous and counterproductive.

Unfortunately, the passage of time (and the greater awareness of women's rights) did not necessarily ameliorate the tension between supporting gender equity and the larger political struggle of increased citizenship rights for all. Women participated actively in mass demonstrations and protests against communist regimes in eastern Europe and the former Soviet Union. Many joined in the hopes of installing a new, liberal, democratic regime. In fact, women made up half the membership of Solidarity, the trade-union-turned-opposition-movement in Poland.[27] Yet, as we shall see, women's concerns were virtually ignored in the aftermath of the overthrow of the communist system.

In fact, many women would not have been interested in, and would have even been alienated by, promises for gender equality in the democratization movements that felled communist regimes across eastern Europe and the former Soviet Union. In part, the authoritarian communist systems they were trying to topple had enforced a strong rhetoric of gender equality, and many women were uninterested in lining up behind a rhetoric that now seemed dated and insincere. Under communism, women were told they were equal to men and that the communist state would provide them with advantages that would afford them higher standards of living than experienced by their counterparts trapped in the capitalist West. Reality was very much at odds with the official myth, however, as the rhetoric of women's equality under communism translated into long workdays on the job followed by equally weighty responsibilities in the home. Furthermore, the heightened, yet essentially symbolic, political status of women in communist regimes simply loaded them down further as they faced a triple burden of work, home, and public life. Consequently, many women, particularly those old enough to remember the communist era, did not respond, and would not have responded, to a Western liberal feminist rhetoric of equality, for it seemed to echo the empty promises of the Soviet past. Shana Penn, who interviewed many women who had been active in the Polish movement against communism, found that many felt that the communists had not really succeeded in solving the various conflicting demands on women's lives; rather, they had profoundly silenced discussion about it. In fact, most of her interviewees "forthrightly declared that they were not feminists and had no intention of adopting another ideology when they had just discarded one."[28]

In addition, many women who grew up in the drab uniformity of the communist period reacted positively to the promise of a new consumerist culture of postcommunist society. Many women initially embraced makeup, high heels, and tight clothing as a welcome change from the drab uniformity of the Soviet era. Thus, Western feminist concerns about social pressures on women to conform to narrow standards of beauty fell on deaf ears. Moreover, one mobilizing factor for the women's movement in the West—a woman's right to choose to have an abortion—did not exist in countries of the former Soviet Union and eastern Europe. Women during much of the Soviet era could choose to terminate their pregnancies with an abortion, and most were forced to do so in the absence of other forms of reliable contraception. Furthermore, women across the eastern bloc enjoyed relatively generous maternity leave benefits. Thus, many of the issues that mobilized women in the West either did not exist or were subverted by Soviet ideology, thus making it difficult for a new wave of female activists to appropriate the rhetoric of feminist principles of liberation and equality.[29]

Finally, women participants saw the goal of overthrowing the previous regime as more important than ensuring their rights as women. Commenting on her own role in the opposition to communist rule in Poland, Joanna Szczesna noted the discrimination against women in society. However, she said, "I considered feminism a needless luxury in those days. I'd rather get involved in activities protesting the use of physical violence by the police than in a struggle for the equal distribution of a policeman's blows." She went on to add, "It happened that once in my life, I put out a lot of fires, but please believe me, it was not because of gender discrimination that I didn't become a fireperson. I didn't become one because I didn't want to be one."[30] In the democratization movements that swept communist governments from power across eastern Europe and the former Soviet Union, neither male revolutionary leaders nor female participants were interested in appealing to women along gender concerns. As we shall see, some women soon regretted their rejection of women's issues as important ones once they saw their economic, social, and political status slide under the newly minted democratic regimes.

Religious Fundamentalist Movements

A third type of revolutionary movements has been formed in the name of establishing a theocracy, a form of government in which religion and government are intertwined. In a theocracy, some, if not all, civic leaders are identical with leaders of the dominant religion, government policies are identical to or are strongly influenced by religious principles, and often the leader claims to rule on behalf of God or some alternative religious authority. The main qualification is that there is little or no distinction between religious and government authority. While many Western countries contain small Christian movements that push for a greater role for the church in determining state policy, and while the Vatican City is an example of a Christian theocracy, recently, many revolutionary theocratic movements have been centered on various tenets of Islam. In addition, these movements have melded a powerful vision of an alternative society guided by religious precepts with another potent ideology, nationalism, often defined with an anti-Western bent. Revolutionary movements have been successful in establishing theocracies in Iran under the Ayatollah Khomeini and in Afghanistan under the Taliban. There are also strong Islamic revolutionary movements in Algeria and Bahrain, and the Kingdom of Saudi Arabia is a theocracy. Currently in Arab Spring countries such as Tunisia, Egypt, and Libya, it is unclear what kind of regimes will replace the ones that collapsed. In all three countries, there is a strong Islamic presence pushing for a future political system that incorporates Islamic theology and ideals, which all present a separate and unequal legal status for women.

There is widespread discussion about the position and status of women in Muslim societies. It is important to remember that countries that are predominantly Muslim vary extensively in their political systems and their design of public policy toward women, ranging from democratic and secular Turkey to the semi-authoritarian clerical rule of Iran, which has enforced Islamic law, to the Kingdom of Saudi Arabia, where women are still not permitted to even drive, and represent about 15 percent of the labor force. This chapter is not meant to address the very complicated and complex issue of Islam and women's rights. As with all religions, there is a host of contradictory evidence about how Islam defines a woman's role, position, and status in society. However, in this section, we will discuss women's participation in movements that seek the imposition of an Islamic state, for many argue that countries such as Iran, which have moved to implement Shari'a, or Islamic legal code, proscribe a role for women that is not only different from that of men but also inferior.[31] Shari'a, as it has been interpreted and implemented in various countries, has tended to minimize women's rights in areas such as marriage, divorce, child custody, inheritance, access to higher education, employment, and political office.[32]

The Iranian Revolution (1979) provides an interesting example of women's mobilization in support of a regime that promised to radically alter (and, as some would argue, reverse) women's recently gained political, economic, and social opportunities. In 1979, the world's attention was riveted on Iran. A broad alliance of liberal, leftist, and religious groups ousted Shah Mohammed Reza Pahlavi, who had been in power since 1941. While the Shah had implemented a variety of Western economic and social reforms to modernize Iran, his rule primarily benefited a small, wealthy elite.

Further, he was widely perceived to be a stooge for the Western powers, primarily the United States. In the face of widespread protests in which millions of citizens filled the streets, the Shah fled the country in January. However, in the wake of his abdication, the alliance of opposition forces further fragmented, leading to the eventual rise of the Ayatollah Khomeini, an Islamic fundamentalist who had spent the previous 14 years in exile in Iraq and France because of his opposition to the Pahlavi regime. On April 1, less than 3 months after the toppling of the Shah, a referendum led to the proclamation of the Islamic Republic of Iran, with the Ayatollah Khomeini as Supreme Leader.[33] As we shall discuss in greater depth later in this chapter, Khomeini moved to implement a variety of changes that would bring women's status in line with Islamic law, which is unfavorable to women with regard to marriage, divorce, and inheritance. Yet, many women supported Khomeini and mobilized extensively to support his rule. Why would women support a leader who expressly argued for their diminished rights?

As in other movements, many women did not respond to a revolutionary call for action out of a desire to change their own gendered status; many were temporarily united in their opposition to the rule of the Shah. While still in exile in France, the Ayatollah presented a vision of an Islamic state in which the political and social rights of women would be guaranteed and women would gain true freedom, dignity, and respect. In addition to endorsing women's political rights, Khomeini declared that "democracy is incorporated in the Quran and people are free to express their opinions and to conduct their acts. Under the Islamic government, which is a democratic government, freedom of expression, opinion, and pen will be guaranteed for everyone."[34] In part, Khomeini's vision of Iran was attractive to women because his rhetoric presented a rosier picture for citizens than what eventually ensued after the installation of an Islamic government. In addition, however, after attaining power, Khomeini announced several jihads—one against illiteracy, another to rebuild the country, and a third against foreign invasion and the possibility of a coup. Millions of women joined up, not for religious reasons, but because they believed in the goal of rebuilding the country in the wake of a tumultuous revolution.[35]

Further, women responded to the gendered elements of an Islamic state, such as wearing the veil, as a vehicle to express their frustration at the failures of corrupt, Westernized elites who were perceived to have sold their country's national interests to an all-powerful, decadent West. Reclaiming their country from their rulers also entailed embracing an alternative to Westernization. In this sense, gender motivations were important to the revolution in that women took to wearing the veil as a symbol of opposition to the decadence of the Pahlavi regime, and the middle- and upper-class, Westernized woman came to embody the corruption of the old system.[36] As Valentine Moghadam notes, "the idea that women had 'lost honour' during the Pahlavi era was a widespread one."[37] Other women initially embraced an Islamic dress code, such as the veil, because they were tired of constant and public sexual harassment as a result of their Western clothing. Adopting Islamic cultural customs was a way of reclaiming national pride and heritage that they felt had been subverted under Pahlavi's rule. Later in this chapter, we will discuss how the revolutionary regime impacted women once the leadership implemented Islamic law and made issues that had once been a matter of choice compulsory.

In sum, several themes resonate across all three types of revolutions. One common theme is that few women joined revolutionary movements in order to fight specifically for greater levels of gender equality (or inequality). Even in Marxist-inspired revolutions, which most directly addressed women's issues, few if any women saw their actions as connected to feminism.[38] For example, based on inter-views with over 200 women who were active in the guerrilla movements in Nicara-gua, El Salvador, and Chiapas, only one woman had joined out of a desire for increased gender justice.[39] Women joined guerrilla movements in Latin America for other reasons not related to women's rights. Similar to the men, they wanted to end the dictatorship, end the exploitation of the poor or the indigenous, or create a more just country for their children.[40] Further, the example of Leila Khaled, a Palestinian who was part of a team that hijacked a TWA flight in 1969 and who, the following year, led an attempted hijacking, further illustrates many revolutionary women's priorities. She explained her motivations in the following way:

> We wanted to put the Palestinian question in front of international opinion. All the time we were being dealt with as refugees who only needed human aid. That was unjust. Nobody had heard our screams and suffering. All we got from the world was more tents and old clothes. After 1967, we were obliged to explain to the world that the Palestinians had a cause.[41]

Throughout history, many women, like her, have been motivated by causes such as nationalism, self-determination, and greater political autonomy for all, rather than gender equality.

However, many women in various movements have been recruited out of what Maxine Molyneux terms practical (as opposed to strategic) gender interests. That is, they have organized to meet immediate needs that arise out of issues that are tradition-ally perceived as being important to women and mothers. For example, as the ones primarily responsible for gathering food, making meals, and overseeing the house-hold, women often became involved because their abilities to perform their gendered duties at home were threatened. The most notable expression of women's participation in the French Revolution was expressed by a women's march to Versailles to petition King Louis XVI for change; they were upset about the lack of food, which dramatically affected their ability to feed their families. Many women joined Latin American move-ments to alleviate the sense of fear they felt for the well-being of their families.[42]

Yet, there has been an undeniable increase in the number of women active in underground movements. Revolutionary movements in the eighteenth and nine-teenth centuries and the first half of the twentieth century tended to produce a few high-profile female revolutionaries; however, women were not systematically in-corporated into the rank-and-file opposition. For example, female revolutionaries such as Alexandra Kollantai in the Soviet Union, Vilma Espin of Cuba, and Nguyen Thi Binh in Vietnam were the exception, not the rule. However, increasingly, women have made up the ranks of soldiers in various guerrilla movements across Latin America. For example, while some estimate that 5 percent of the Cuban revolutionary movement was female, women's participation in Latin American guerrilla movements from the 1970s onward ranged from 20 to 30 percent.[43]

In Peru, an estimated 35 percent of leaders of Shining Path were women, primarily at the underground cell level.[44] We should treat these numbers with some caution since they have been contested; actual visitors to guerrilla camps reported having seen few female combatants.[45] While we don't know how many women joined the protests that launched the Arab Spring across the Middle East, in footage and in action, they are readily visible. Whatever the numbers, it is true that significantly more women are involved in revolutionary movements than in previous decades.

What explains this dramatic increase? Various scholars have posited a number of factors that have converged to facilitate women's increased participation. With regard to the Latin American context, Ilya Luciak argued that part of this increase is due to the rise of the international feminist movement.[46] Karen Kampwirth, in her research on Nicaraguan, Salvadoran, and Mexican women, attributed women's increased presence to four related trends. First, the economic changes after World War II in Latin America increased land tenure inequality. This forced many women to move to the cities, where they were exposed to new organizing opportunities that had not been available in the countryside. In addition, the emergence of liberation theology in Latin America, which stressed social justice and human rights issues, meant that the church was much more active in organizing activists, and women in particular. This opened up new opportunities that helped women gain organizational experience, which in turn facilitated their transition to more revolutionary political movements. Third, Kampwirth noted that many guerrilla movements in Latin America switched organizational strategies from the "Cuban model," which emphasized mobilizing a small cadre of tightly trained revolutionaries, to one that involved mass mobilization and the need to recruit as many people as possible. Finally, she argued that women became recruited for a variety of personal factors, such as early childhood experiences of resistance, participation in preexisting networks, higher levels of education, and youth, which contributed to high levels of participation.[47] Although these findings are specific to Latin America, overall, larger forces such as increased levels of economic development, female education and literacy, global declines in fertility, and larger socioeconomic changes wrought by modernization have all fed into lowering the barriers of entry for women in all regions of the world. As the Internet and social networking rise in significance, some of the mobility barriers that have hindered women, particularly in Islamic societies, have also declined as well. All of these factors point to the fact that women's involvement in revolutionary movements has increased dramatically in scope. However, we still do not know if this increase in women's mobilization will result in an increased focus on practical or strategic gender interests.

REVOLUTIONARY STRATEGIES AND TACTICS

Once women are recruited to revolutionary movements, do they contribute to the cause differently than their male counterparts do? History is not lacking examples of exceptional women who rose to prominence in a "man's world" of revolutionary combat. For example, in the French Revolution, Theroigne de Mericourt fought for the right to form a women's battalion to fight.[48] In Russia,

Vera Figner was born into the privileges of the aristocracy in 1852 but by the age of 32 had become one of Russia's most vocal revolutionaries. She was a member of the Executive Committee of the People's Will Party, an underground organization that masterminded the successful plot to assassinate Tsar Alexander II. She was eventually sentenced to life imprisonment for her involvement.[49] Speaking of her own experiences in the Cuban Revolution, Haydee Santamaria professed that "I believe it takes a great effort to be violent, to go to war. But one has to be violent and to go to war when there is good reason. . . . It is painful to kill, but if it is necessary, you must do it."[50] In the long struggle for Vietnamese independence and the subsequent battle against American involvement in Vietnam, Nguyen Thi Dinh fought with the Viet Minh forces against the French while still a teenager. After her release from imprisonment, she went on to help lead various armed insurrections against the French- and American-supported governments.[51] Another Vietnamese woman, Nguyen Thi Binh, eventually became a member of the Central Committee for the National Front for the Liberation of Vietnam and played a major role in the signing of the Paris Peace Accords on Vietnam, which ended the war in 1973 (although only Henry Kissinger and Le Duc Tho received the Nobel Peace Prize and were named *Time* magazine's Men of the Year for their roles in the process).[52]

More often, however, women did not assume prominent leadership positions but instead worked in critical (but often undervalued) secondary roles and engaged in tasks such as weapons transport, intelligence gathering, or recruitment. Often they performed these activities precisely because tacticians counted on their opponent's gendered expectations about "appropriate" areas of activity for women (which did not include joining revolutionary movements). As a result, women were crucial as decoys and as on-the-ground agents because they often attracted less suspicion. For example, in the Cuban Revolution, in Castro's first attempt to overthrow the Batista regime, two women went by train to Santiago carrying weapons in a suitcase and a flower box. One of his mistresses typed and mimeographed copies of a manifesto written by Castro. Women also stored weapons, smuggled messages, and played vital roles as arms runners in the name of the Cuban Revolution.[53] Vilma Espin, Cuban revolutionary and sister-in-law to Fidel Castro, would smuggle political pamphlets into Santiago. As she explained, "It seemed easier for us because we could carry papers in our skirts."[54] In more recent guerrilla struggles in Latin America, women continued this trend, participating in supporting roles, such as keeping safe houses, acting as messengers and decoys, and transporting weaponry and communications equipment in the guise of going to the market.[55]

In the anticommunist struggle in Poland, when many prominent men were arrested in the wake of the imposition of martial law in 1981, women single-handedly started the underground paper and, after 1989, created the first free press, *Gazeta Wyborcza*.[56] Polish women would smuggle dissident pamphlets in their heavy shopping bags; this was not questioned because authorities were used to seeing women haul around heavy shopping bags and assumed that women were too occupied with feeding their families to express political opinions.[57]

In the Iranian Revolution, women were critical to the Ayatollah Khomeini's rise to power. Millions of women ignored night curfew and took to the streets when the Ayatollah called on them to attend public demonstrations. Their presence at the front lines of the demonstration kept them relatively peaceful, as soldiers were hesitant to fire on fellow Muslim women to protect a corrupt, Westernized regime.[58]

There has also been an increase in the number of women engaged in terrorism across the globe (read more in the following profile on "Black Widows"). For example, between 1985 and 2010, female bombers committed over 257 suicide attacks (which represents about a quarter of the total number) on behalf of a variety of terrorist organizations. In the increasing wave of violence subsuming the Middle East, terrorists are recruiting women because border guards are still not accustomed to viewing women as potential terrorists. Palestinian women, who are often draped in bulkier, less form-fitting garb, can carry the necessary explosives under their clothes without arousing suspicion. In fact, explosives can be strapped to a woman's midsection to mimic a late-term pregnancy, which can incite stereotypes about women and mothers' inherent peacefulness. Terrorist organizations further exploit cultural norms against invasively searching or touching women, particularly in conservative societies. Also, because many men are still socialized to protect women as the "weaker sex," using female recruits provides terrorist organizations with a comparative advantage, particularly the element of surprise. This strategy also can damage the psychological well-being and morale of the soldiers opposing them. The requirement to shoot people that soldiers ordinarily are trained to protect can have a much more harmful psychological impact than killing adult men. Women are often seen as nurturers, not destroyers, and this norm is increasingly exploited in a violent, conflict-ridden world.[59]

Black Widows

In August 2012, Sheikh Said Afandi, a moderate Sufi cleric, was giving a sermon to some of his followers in his home. Aminat Kurbanova entered under the guise of a follower and proceeded to detonate her vest, killing Afandi and six other people. The attack was the third in 2 months against prominent Muslim clerics who were working to promote moderate versions of Islam in southern Russia, where the conflict in Chechnya and now neighboring Dagestan has dragged on for nearly two decades, and appears to be widening in its scope and deepening in intensity, as al Qaeda has expanded into this region. This latest bombing was significant because it marked the first time an ethnic Russian woman became a suicide bomber rather than a Chechen woman.

The problem of female terrorists is particularly acute in Russia; more than 50 percent of the country's suicide attacks have been committed by women, compared with about 25 to 30 percent globally. Over the past decade, these attacks have included the attack on the Nord-Ost Moscow theater (129 killed); an assassination attempt against Chechen President Akhmad Kadyrov (14 killed); a suicide attack on a train in Southern Russia (46 killed); a dual suicide attack at a rock concert at Tushina airfield in Moscow (16 killed); the destruction of two Russian airliners in 2004 (more than 90 killed); the attack on a school in Beslan in North Ossetia (334 killed); the Moscow Metro bombings (39 killed); and the Moscow airport bombing (37 killed).

These women quickly became known as "black widows"; the media claimed that these women were drawn to terrorism after their Chechen husbands, and often other relatives as well, had been killed by Russian forces.[i]

Why and how do Chechen women become recruited into terrorism? Is it true that they are all seeking revenge? It is true that a critical recruiting factor is relationship; the best predictor that a woman will engage in terrorist violence is if she is related by blood or marriage to a known insurgent. For example, Kurbanova, the terrorist mentioned in the opening story, had two previous husbands who were militants, and her third husband was also an Islamist militant, according to police. The two female bombers who struck the Moscow subway station were also married to militant Islamists from Dagestan, one of whom had been killed. Yet, we should not rush to play along with the media label that portrays Black Widows as loyal wives seeking justice: many of these terrorists are also a product of a sophisticated process of indoctrination. The recruitment process usually does begin when a loved one collaborates with insurgents and then is killed or persecuted by Russian forces. When the family becomes ostracized by other members of the community, the alternative, radicalized Islamist one steps in to provide support. As one expert commented: "The community that welcomes you after that is the Islamist one. There you find self-respect. You are called a sister. You go to pray with them, socialize with them, and you integrate into these groups based around Islam."[ii] Extremists then turn these women to the ends of terrorism. In this context, some or many of these women may be converted believers in the cause, and in search of respect from this new Islamist community. Alternatively, in Muslim societies such as Chechnya or Dagestan, rape can be used as a method of coercion, for once a girl or woman is raped, only an act of martyrdom can eradicate her shame.[iii] And sometimes women are recruited through the age-old system of networking; they become enmeshed through their relationship to a friend, relative, or spouse. Terrorist organizations, in turn, value successful suicide missions by women. Not only are they often successful because of the element of surprise (people still don't expect women to be terrorists), but their attacks also speed the flow of new recruits and money. As one terrorism specialist hypothesized: "The women come forward and shame the men into participating. They appeal to masculinity, to the manly urge to protect women, and that fills up their [the terrorist organizations'] ranks and their coffers."[iv] This increased use of women as terrorists, not only in Russia but in other conflicts as well, means that governments will have to rethink and adjust their antiterrorism strategies if they want to be successful in dealing with the shifting nature of terrorism.

---

[i]Daniel McLaughlin, "Bombing Shocks Russians: Muscovites Aghast at 'Black Widow' Attacks," *The Vancouver Sun*, July 7, 2003, p. A5.
[ii]As quoted in Simon Shuster, "Russia's 'Black Widows': Terrorism or Revenge?" *Time*, April 7, 2010, http://www.time.com/time/world/article/0,8599,1978178,00.html
[iii]Mia Bloom, "Bombshells: Women and Terror," *Gender Issues* (2011) 28: 1–21.
[iv]As quoted in Simon Shuster, "Russia's 'Black Widows': Terrorism or Revenge?" *Time*, April 7, 2010, http://www.time.com/time/world/article/0,8599,1978178,00.html

Women often become the symbols of revolutionary movements, and leaders manipulate the image of the self-sacrificing woman to rally and mobilize support. In Vietnam, women were used prominently in propaganda posters, not only to rally citizens behind the concept of the nurturing mother but also to exemplify the bravery of the Vietnamese, the totality of national mobilization, and the extent of sacrifice demanded by the struggle. Women were also used by the Vietnamese to mock the weakness of the enemy; one popular and ubiquitous cartoon portrayed a small Vietnamese woman holding a rifle on a much taller and bulkier U.S. pilot as she marched him off to a POW camp.[60] In this scenario, even the powerful United States could be brought to its knees by the determination of an organized resistance movement, even one populated by women giving selflessly to the cause.

Yet, even as women have used gender stereotypes to their advantage in one area of revolutionary activity, they have fulfilled them in others. In addition to their roles as fighters, women still found time to fulfill their traditional roles as caretakers, even in guerrilla camps, serving in less visible roles as cooks, health providers, and sex providers/workers.[61] These roles often were endorsed enthusiastically by leaders who were equally comfortable talking about gender equality in theory. Castro, in a letter to Celia Sanchez, commented that "Your absence has left a real vacuum. Even when a woman goes around the mountains with a rifle in hand, she always makes our men tidier, more decent, gentlemanly—and even braver. . . . But what would your poor father say?"[62] Che Guevara, another famed guerrilla warrior, found women valuable because they would do the tasks and chores that men spurned in favor of more traditionally male roles of active combat.[63] Although he considered women to be indispensable to the revolutionary struggle, nonetheless, as he wrote in *Guerrilla Warfare*, women were valuable for their specific "female" traits:

> The woman can also perform her habitual tasks of peacetime; it is very pleasing to a soldier subjected to the extremely hard conditions of this life to be able to look forward to a seasoned meal which tastes like something. One of the great misfortunes of the [Cuban] war was eating cold, sticky, tasteless mess. Furthermore, it is easier to keep her in these tasks; one of the problems in guerilla bands is that they [men] are constantly trying to get out of these tasks.[64]

While Guevara may have spoken the rhetoric of gender equality, he was also capable of making breathtakingly stereotypical assumptions about the "appropriate" gendered division of labor.

He was not alone; male leaders often spoke the rhetoric of equality, even gender equality, while simultaneously maintaining traditional views of appropriately gendered divisions of labor within the movement. Despite an increasing acceptance of women as colleagues in the struggle, women active in Latin American guerrilla movements in the latter half of the twentieth century still met resistance from their male colleagues. For example, men were hostile to women leaders and resisted taking orders from them.[65] In the Nicaraguan struggle, when Monaca Baltodana, a high-ranking commander in charge of the final push to take Managua, went to negotiate, a guard refused to speak with her because she was a woman.[66] Nicaraguan activists faced resistance within their own party cadres; the Association of

Nicaraguan Women (AMNLAE), the women's arm of the Sandinista National Liberation Front (FSLN), pushed the leadership to include women in the draft. However, FSLN leadership resisted this push, arguing that women were needed at home to care for their children.[67] Speaking of her own experiences working with the revolutionary movement in Nicaragua, Margaret Randall observed that "only one, perhaps two, have the slightest interest in or respect for the feminist agenda. I do not know if any of them understands a feminist agenda as something beyond the proverbial 'equal rights for women.'"[68] Revolutionary actions rarely matched the discourse of gender equality in movements.

And finally, some movements actively worked to oppress women, despite theoretical commitments to human rights. In 2011, the Columbia Police released a damning report on the treatment of women with the FARC, the main guerilla movement. Based on testimony from 112 women who had deserted that year, in addition to various documents and files seized in army operations, the report details a litany of horrors, such as forced sexual obligations, forced abortions, and the spread of sexually transmitted diseases. In addition, young girls between 13 and 15 were targeted for recruitment because they (or their bodies) were "considered necessary to maintain the discipline of the FARC." About half of the women who deserted did so to search for their children, to whom they gave birth in the jungle but were subsequently forced to give away. Further, up to 90 percent of the women had been forced to have at least one abortion, in part due to male soldiers' refusal to use a condom. For many of these women, an additional traumatic aspect of their treatment was the complicity of female leadership at the top in allowing and encouraging these practices.[69]

Across many revolutionary movements, the few women who were included in leadership circles often did little to overturn these attitudes and practices because they felt that sexism was not an issue in the struggle. When Fidel Castro created the Federation of Cuban Women and appointed Vilma Espin, part of the inner circle of leadership, to head it, she objected vehemently. As she commented, "Why do we have to have a women's organization? I have never been discriminated against. I had my career as a chemical engineer. I never suffered."[70] Drawing from the experience of women revolutionaries in Cuba, Nicaragua, and El Salvador, Karen Kampwirth argued that high-powered women did not see sexism as much "because the advantage of their prestige overrode the disadvantage of their sex."[71] Certainly, in the case of Columbia's FARC, women leaders actively worked to further disempower women lower in the chain of command.

Nonetheless, Kampwirth notes that while sexism still did exist within revolutionary struggles, for women these struggles still offered unprecedented opportunities. Many women experienced more equal treatment than they had before. Further, male leaders for the most part were not ideological feminists but pragmatic strategists. They needed more participants, and to exclude women just because they were women would have been inefficient.[72] Thus, while conditions for women may not have matched the rhetoric of equality, these revolutions nonetheless presented women with opportunities and, as we shall see, transformed the women as a result of their experiences.

THE REVOLUTION'S IMPACT ON WOMEN

How did women benefit politically, economically, and socially from the various revolutions we have covered? Did the transition open up opportunities for women, and did these opportunities eventually erode as the new political system consolidated its authority? Revolutions, which often result in a totally transformed state, seemingly offer a window of opportunity in which women can take advantage of the opening of political space to fight for increased benefits and representation.[73] After all, old structures and ideologies are swept aside, political authority is weakened, and women have an opportunity to take advantage of these uncertainties. Women potentially have easier access to political roles, and women's activities can expand as the boundaries between "men's work" and "women's work" blur. As Barbara Jancar concludes, "because the new order has not yet been established the real possibility of change still exists."[74] Or, as Nikki Craske maintains, "moments of revolution and periods of transition provide opportunities and open up the political system when changes can be made that are positive to women." However, she goes on to add that "once the system begins to consolidate the opportunities for change decrease and in some situations women's positions erode."[75] Let's turn to our various revolutionary movements to see if these general observations hold for our cases.

Marxist Revolutionary Movements

Marxist-inspired revolutions explicitly promise greater levels of political participation to women, through increased suffrage, through the creation of state-facilitated organizations to represent women's interests, or through women's increased elevation to elected office, often through the use of quotas. Yet, while women increasingly have become recruited to the cause of foot soldier in revolutionary struggles, they have rarely received political promotions for their loyalty, and they remain excluded from top leadership positions. Their participation in the revolutionary struggle often represents the zenith of their influence in formal mechanisms of power. Once a new regime comes to power, women historically have been marginalized or pushed off into gender-specific positions, heading departments of women's affairs or formulating policy for women, children, and the family, which are positions that are accorded relatively little political power or significance. They are rarely allowed into other areas of policymaking. For example, Alexandra Kollantai, a Bolshevik feminist, theorist, and politician, was initially on the Central Committee of the Bolshevik Party and on the Central Executive Committee of the Petrograd Soviet. However, under the Soviet regime, she was put in charge of the "women's section" of the party, a position that eventually was taken from her.[76] Similarly, despite the fact that many in Castro's closest circle were women, once he assumed power, most of the women who had participated in the guerrilla struggle disappeared from public view.[77] Castro then created the Federation of Cuban Women and appointed his sister-in-law, Vilma Espin, to head the organization. Although she had been part of Castro's inner circle, her appointment was perceived (particularly by her) as a political demotion, since women's issues were not considered to be as important as key policy areas such as foreign policy, defense, or other pressing national issues.[78] In Latin American countries, women's organizations, which had been formed to harness women's support for the revolution, fought against efforts by the state to co-opt them in the wake of the revolution, as newly formed postrevolutionary parties saw them as a conduit to potential voters.[79] Further, postrevolutionary regimes were suspicious of autonomous women's organizations and tried to contain women's activism by organizing them into state-sponsored groups, thus limiting their independence.[80]

Economically, women often are enlisted in larger projects of economic modernization instigated by the revolutionary regime. This was particularly the case in the Soviet Union, China, and Cuba. Women's entry into the workforce was facilitated through legislation, such as maternity leave or child care, which ensured greater access to employment possibilities. Women initially benefited from the potential economic gains and resulting independence that financial wealth brought. In addition, women benefited in less direct ways. The need for a better educated, more skilled labor force led to dedicated drives to educate women in order to meet the demands of industrialization.

However, familial relations within the household often remained embedded in more traditional settings. The result is that women ended up doubly burdened, working full-time outside of the house as well as within, by taking care of the cooking, housework, and childrearing. Often, the habit of using women's unpaid labor to fuel greater change became the convenient fallback strategy.[81] In analyzing the impact of guerrilla struggles in Latin America, scholars such as Craske concluded that while postrevolutionary regimes were able to make improvements in women's lives, they failed to address gender inequalities in the private sphere. Women still had to do all or most of the work in the home, which limited the ability of revolutionary regimes to foster gender equality.[82]

Finally, postrevolutionary Marxist regimes usually implement a wide array of policies that have an impact on women's social status. They often pass wide-ranging legislation that redistributes power among families. Women are often granted new rights, such as suffrage, the right to divorce, child support, or abortion. However, these initial gains for women are often rolled back or reversed as governments attempt to consolidate power and appease old political enemies. Often, radical and far-reaching social policies are scaled back in the face of larger political, economic, and social needs. For example, women's opportunities in the Soviet Union were scaled back as Stalin reprioritized Soviet goals. In the initial heady months following the Bolshevik rise to power, the new Soviet administration pushed through a variety of social reforms. It removed legal restrictions to divorce; secularized marriage; established paternal responsibilities for all children, whether born under wedlock or not; legalized abortion; recognized unregistered marriages; and enforced men's alimony obligations. In short, the Soviets envisioned a radical redistribution of power in an area usually shrouded in privacy—the household. Just over a decade later, many of these policies were being cut back or reversed altogether. Women's political organizations, the Zhenotdel, were abolished in 1930. By 1936, abortion was outlawed. By the end of World War II divorce was nearly impossible, and unregistered marriages were no longer legally recognized. Womanhood and motherhood were glorified.[83]

Similarly, leaders of the Chinese Revolution, another Marxist revolution that directly appealed to women, implemented radical reforms at first, only to back off as they faced looming obligations during World War II. Initially, women's feet were finally unbound and such basic rights as the right to mobility were ensured. The communists also enacted legislation backing free-choice marriages and access to divorce. But the party also had to continuously compromise on the "woman question," and women within the Communist Party and at large acquiesced to these compromises.[84] In Vietnam, in the wake of independence, the new government outlawed polygamy, although they did not work particularly hard at enforcing the law, making it an important step for women on paper but a toothless idea in practice.[85]

In the more recent guerrilla struggles in Latin America, women responded more vociferously to the new governments' weak commitments to gender issues. In Latin America, Kampwirth argues, an unintended legacy of the revolutionary struggle was that it radicalized women and helped create a feminist consciousness and sowed the seeds of a feminist movement. This trend developed after the overthrow of various authoritarian regimes, when women guerrillas were expected to return to "normal" gender relations after the conclusion of the war. Many women were transformed personally by their participation in the movement and gained new skills and confidence in their abilities. In particular, Kampwirth argues that what she terms "mid-prestige" women formed the bulk of this unanticipated feminist movement. That is, these women were members of the rank and file who had experienced some authority in carrying out their duties but were not important enough to overcome the culture of machismo. Nor were they so powerless in the movement that they didn't develop important skills. In other words, their work was important enough that they got the opportunity to make decisions and develop some authority, but they were not important enough to carve out spheres of political influence after the revolution ended, and as a result, they became more aware of issues of sexism.[86] For example, Letty Mendez, member of the Farabundo Marti Front for National Liberation (FMLN) of El Salvador and later head of the women's secretariat of the FMLN, commented:

> We did not have a gender consciousness, before and during the war, but unconsciously we hoped that with change in society and from the class struggle, there was going to be a situation of equality for women. Unconsciously that was the feeling. . . . They [the men on the left] always said that this [the women's] struggle was secondary; always they said the problem was capitalism and I think we believed that because we didn't know the depth of our situation.[87]

This activist subsequently developed a gendered consciousness after her participation.

Further, an independent women's movement may be a necessary outgrowth of revolutionary movements. Because of the new government's tendency to scale back on promises in various Latin American regimes, Craske argues that independent women's organizations are necessary as an alternative to the regime's plans for women. As she points out, "even the most 'women-friendly' regimes seem to harbour an antipathy towards feminism, particularly among the male leadership; consequently an independent, grassroots movement is needed to promote this particular perspective."[88] One unintended consequence of the revolution has been increased autonomous women's organization around women's and feminist issues.

In closing, in many postrevolutionary Marxist states, while women's political, economic, and social situation did improve as a result of proactive policy, women's activism in the revolutionary struggle did not neatly translate into participation in the new, postrevolutionary state, and policy was rarely as emancipatory as promised.

Liberal/Democratization Movements

In liberal-inspired revolutions, women are often promised change in their capacity as citizens, not specifically as women. Their rhetoric often stresses increased political, economic, and/or social participation for all. Therefore, in democratization movements, particularly those that occurred in the countries of the former communist bloc, women benefited, as did men, from the opportunity to participate in meaningful democratic elections. However, after these revolutions women in these same countries lost their previously high levels of political representation. While under communism, women were often allotted quotas in legislatures, the installation of new, quota-free legislative systems led to their representational decimation in elections. While their previous levels of political representation under communism were essentially symbolic, given that legislatures served as rubber stamps for state policy, nonetheless the new reality of women's lack of political voice in the legislative arena was sobering to many female activists. This was particularly evident in Poland, for example, when the fledgling, male-dominated parliament proposed a ban on abortion. When the women's section of Solidarity, the opposition-movement-turned-leading-party, objected to the bill, they were shut down.[89] Sidelined by the power of the Catholic Church, women were unable to register much impact with their opposition to a further change in legislation, which replaced the word fetus with "conceived child."[90] While the previous communist regimes often failed to acknowledge their failures in advancing gender equality, the male-dominated regimes that replaced them simply ignored or overrode women's concerns.[91]

In Russia, some Soviet-era women's organizations eventually responded to this by forming their own political party, Women of Russia. Although the party enjoyed some initial electoral success in 1995, it soon faded from political prominence. More recently, the Russian social movement Committee of Soldiers' Mothers organized more formally into a political party to advocate more forcefully for the end of the war in Chechnya. However, after forming into the United People's Party of Soldiers' Mothers in 2004, the organization soon fizzled out, failing to attract a significant number of votes in national elections.[92] Not all democratization movements registered such a negative political impact on women; as we discussed in Chapter 1, the South African transition resulted in significant levels of female representation in the legislature. However, for postcommunist transitions, women must also confront the baggage of communism's rhetoric of women's equality and its subsequent delegitimation in the new democratic era.

Women in liberal/democratization movements also struggled to navigate stormy economic waters in the wake of the previous regime's collapse. Particularly after the collapse of communism in eastern Europe and the former Soviet Union, women bore the brunt of the costs of economic transition. The economic impact of revolution was particularly harrowing because reforming former communist economies into capitalist ones involved a series of structural reforms that proved much more problematic than attempting to make underdeveloped economies more competitive. While the former communist regimes prided themselves on full employment and relatively equal divisions of wealth, the new democratic regimes had to implement reforms that led to massive joblessness, underemployment, and burgeoning poverty rates for large segments of the population. Initially, women were on the front lines of the unemployed; they were the first fired and last to be rehired and were further ghettoized into low-paid jobs with few opportunities for advancement.[93] While more recent analyses indicate that women's economic position, particularly in eastern European countries that have entered the European Union, has improved from the initial chaotic years of reform, nonetheless women face substantial hurdles in the labor market. The reduction in cradle-to-grave social benefits, such as maternity leave, child-care subsidies, family benefits, and pensions, that impact women have significantly complicated their efforts to combine work and family responsibilities.[94]

Liberal and democratization movements also have curtailed more progressive policies regarding women's status. In the wake of the French Revolution, women's rights were curtailed as Napoleon sought to return France to a more traditional, less tumultuous path. Women were enshrined in their roles as traditional wives and mothers, and with the Napoleonic Code of 1804, women found themselves legally and socially to be more powerless than before the Revolution.[95] In the wake of the collapse of communism in eastern Europe, as we mentioned previously, the Polish government quickly moved to place further restrictions on abortion, despite women's protests, although this also sparked the beginnings of a postcommunist feminist movement.[96] In Russia, in the wake of severe economic dislocation, many women chose not to have children, causing the birth rate among the Russian population to decline rapidly. Male politicians quickly responded with a nationalist rhetoric, urging women to fulfill their "natural" responsibilities, and some proposed banning access to contraception or restricting access to abortion as a potential solution. President Putin eventually resorted to providing cash incentives to encourage women to have a third child, rather than address some of the reasons why women might hesitate to have larger families. Further, across many postcommunist countries, women lost their cradle-to-grade social benefits as governments attempted to scale back and meet "more important" targets, such as economic growth or increased employment. Yet, women were initially ambivalent about the changes in their social status. Many, exhausted from years of communist propaganda that stressed women's invincibility on all fronts, initially embraced a pronatalist rhetoric that sought to return women to the sanctity of hearth and home, which would potentially scale back their enormous workload. However, as the reality of the implications of lessened social benefits became more obvious, women began to organize, either in social movements or in political parties, as in Russia.

In sum, women's political, economic, and social trajectory varied, depending on whether they were in countries that were moving out of communist-inspired, authoritarian governments. For countries of the former Soviet Union and Soviet bloc, the transition to nominally democratic states gave women more opportunities for meaningful political representation (in that elections were truly competitive) but often reduced their formal political presence. If times were hard economically, they bore the brunt of the costs of transition, as women do in many societies. And social policy tended to be less progressive. In noncommunist authoritarian regimes making the transition to democracy, such as in Latin America and sub-Saharan Africa, for example, the gendered nature of the shift was not as obvious. Because there was no former Marxist-inspired rhetorical emphasis on women, the lack of such emphasis in the posttransition regime was less startling. Thus, while women's condition does often improve in liberal/democratization movements, many times it is dependent on, and a byproduct of, overall levels of socioeconomic recovery and growth in these countries, and it may not proceed at the same pace and scope as men's.

Religious Fundamentalist Movements

We now turn to revolutionary movements, such as the ones that came to power in Iran, that are built around explicit ideologies that return women to traditional roles in the household and negate women's presence in the public sphere. In the wake of the Iranian revolution, the various forces that united to uproot the Shah fragmented, and the fundamentalist faction gained control of the postrevolutionary regime. The new Islamic political system fused elements of an Islamic theocracy with modern democratic elements. A network of unelected institutions is controlled by the highly powerful conservative Supreme Leader. In addition, the unelected 12-member Guardian Council reviews all bills passed by parliament and has the power to veto them if it considers them inconsistent with the constitution and Islamic law. The council can also bar candidates from standing in elections to the three elected institutions—parliament (known as the Majlis), the presidency, and the Assembly of Experts. Since the 1990s Iranian politics has been characterized by continued wrangling between these elected and unelected institutions as a reformist president—and, at times, parliament—struggled against the conservative establishment.

Within this new political system, women maintained their political rights, such as their right to vote and run for office. Although women's formal political representation in the Majlis before the revolution was greater (there were about 22 female deputies), in the repressive context of the Pahlavi regime, that figure was more symbolic than real. After the revolution, the number of women parliamentarians continued to drop; they made up about 1.5 percent of the seats in the Majlis in the first three postrevolutionary parliamentary elections.[97] However, women's issues and the presence of women in public spaces became more prominent following the end of the Iran–Iraq War (1980–1988), which had mobilized much of both countries' material and human resources. Women's political representation in ensuing elections since the 1990s has hovered between 3 and 4 percent. Despite their minimal representation, the increased presence of women was felt in policy; two female representatives presented a motion in January 1993 to create the Special Commission of Women's Affairs. Although this proposal failed, women continued to push for change. In the fifth Majlis, another deputy argued that "I believe that half of the deputies should be made up of thoughtful and specialist women who are aware of women's sufferings. In countries where women's rights are respected, a growing number of women are elected to the parliaments."[98] Women's voices still tend to be marginalized, and if they are taken into account, they are circumscribed to advocating primarily on women's issues.

Part of this marginalization may be due to the role that the Guardian Council plays in vetting candidates for elections. Often controlled by conservatives, it has assiduously weeded out many liberal voices, including those of women. Yet, to avoid charges of complete fraud and political repression, the Council often allows a small percentage of reformers to contest elections. Perhaps the same is true of women; in the past few elections, about 10 percent of the candidates have been women. We don't know if women are more likely than men to be weeded out by the Guardian Council; however, it does seem as if a small percentage are allowed to contest elections, but like liberals, not enough to rock the political system. Nor has the Guardian Council interpreted Islamic law to allow women to contest the highest elected office, the presidency. Women have signed up to run since 1997, but no woman has been approved to run, in part, many speculate, over an interpretation of the word *rejale*, a qualification that some claim means "religious and political men" as opposed to "religious and political personalities," which is gender neutral. The Guardian Council claims that its choice has nothing to do with the candidate's sex but rather is due to the fact that female candidates lack "general competence." For the highly contested 2009 Presidential elections, 42 women were among the 475 people who submitted applications to run for the presidency; apparently, none passed muster. Nor have women been appointed to significant cabinet posts; the exception is Massoumeh Ebtekar, who was appointed by a reformist president in the 1990s to the position of vice president as well as the head of the Department of the Environment.[99]

Women exert what political power they do have as voters, and they have been increasingly targeted in hotly contested elections. In the historic 2009 elections, which many charge were falsified to return a victory to ultraconservative incumbent Mahmoud Ahmadinejad, opposing candidate Mehdi Karroubi declared he would consider women for six of his cabinet posts, including the ministries of Foreign Affairs and Islamic Guidance and Culture. Another candidate, Mohsen Rezai, told *Time* magazine that he would consider a woman as Minister of Foreign Affairs to serve as "Hillary Clinton's Iranian counterpart." And the supposed winner of the elections, Hossein Mousavi, raised hopes, and eyebrows, by campaigning with his wife, Dr. Zahra Rahnavard, the first woman university chancellor in postrevolutionary Iran, at his side (an unusual strategy in Iran, where officials occupy the public stage without their wives). In a political system where symbols and symbolism play a prominent role, many interpreted this as a sign that should Mousavi win the Presidency, women would be more welcome in the public arena of Iran's affairs.[100]

Further, Iranian women have maintained a political presence in civil society. The women's press continued to serve as a discussion forum for secular women and addressed critical contemporary political and social issues. For example, in the "Necessity for the Reform of Laws Concerning Divorce, Polygyny and Child Custody," published in the magazine *Payam-e Hajar*, the author presented an analysis of Quranic verse to demonstrate that women's equality and Islamic values are not inherently contradictory. Many other articles have tried to demonstrate how Islam favors the equality of men and women.[101] In 1996 some women activists launched the One Million Signatures Campaign in support of changing discriminatory laws against women in Iran in order to conform with what they view as true Islamic principles. Specifically, they wished to secure equal rights in marriage and inheritance, an end to polygamy, and stricter punishments for honor killings and other forms of violence. While the movement has been targeted for persecution domestically, it has been successful at the international level in calling attention to women's lesser legal status in Iran. It is important not to overstate the condition of women's political rights in postrevolutionary Iran; however, women have been able to maintain alternative spaces of expression in a regime that is hostile to a Western definition of women's equality.

Women's economic status did change significantly after 1979. In the initial wake of the Iranian Revolution, women were dismissed from administrative positions and encouraged to assume their suitable positions of influence in the home, where they were to focus on their familial roles as mothers and caretakers. In addition, given the high levels of unemployment among men, the government did not want to encourage women's participation in the labor force. As a result, the government introduced a variety of policies to reduce the number of women in the labor market, such as offering early retirement and the option of transferring their salaries to their husbands if they chose to leave their jobs. The effects of these policies, however, are unclear.[102] The government has struggled to resolve its dual aims of reducing women's participation in the paid workforce and maintaining its gendered ideology, which requires separate facilities for men and women in many spheres of life. If, for example, women are not to be seen or touched by men who are not kin (as Ayatollah Sanei, a powerful member of the leadership, proclaimed), then this requires the hiring of female teachers, doctors, and so forth.[103] As a result, the government has effectively removed women in more visible, high-level jobs, particularly in the public sector, while maintaining their participation in domains exclusive to women. Thus, while women's employment is low (about 30.5 percent of women are integrated into the paid labor force), nonetheless the government has had to compromise on its initial goal to dramatically decrease the percentage of women in paid employment.

Women's social status in society was radically altered in postrevolutionary Iran, when women were governed under the jurisdiction of Shari'a law. Officials imposed an Islamic dress code and made covering of the hair and body compulsory, first for active women and then for the entire female population. Women's access to higher education was limited. The implications of Shari'a law were manifested most radically in family law. The husband was declared the head of the household, and the wife was obliged to submit to her husband. Her failure to comply can result in sanctions, or even divorce. Overall, men were given overwhelming privileges in matters of marriage, divorce, child custody, and so on. Further, the minimum age of marriage for girls was lowered to 9 years of age.[104] Although the government introduced some moderate reforms to divorce law in the early 1990s (legislation passed that granted women wages for housework in the event of divorce), under President Ahmadinejad, parliament approved a new amendment to a controversial law in the civil code that allows men to have as many sexual partners as they want—all sanctioned by Shari'a law under the term "temporary marriage." Simply put, women have a lesser and unequal status within the Iranian legal system. Read more about one woman's efforts to change this in the profile of Shirin Ebadi below.

Women in Motion: Shirin Ebadi

"With a correct interpretation of Islam, we can have equal rights for women."[1] Shirin Ebadi, an Iranian lawyer and human rights activist, has a fascinating life story that bridges Iran before and after the revolution. Raised in a middle-class family, Ebadi was the first female judge in her country, until the Iranian revolution derailed her career plans. An initial supporter of the revolution, Ebadi became one of its early victims as the regime soon implemented a system that was punitive to women. Yet, rather than emigrate to the West, as many of her friends and colleagues did, Ebadi chose to stay in Iran and has since devoted her career to working within the repressive laws of the regime to bring about change. In 2003, she became Iran's first Nobel Peace Prize winner in recognition of her campaigns for increased rights for Iranian women and children and greater levels of democracy, an award the Iranian government deemed "not very important." Respected internationally, Ebadi has faced increasing levels of harassment at home, as her work places her increasingly at odds with a regime controlled by conservative clerics.

Shirin Ebadi was raised during the Westernized reign of the Shah and benefited from many of his modernizing reforms, which opened up education and career opportunities for women. After receiving her law degree from Tehran University, she became the first woman judge to preside over Tehran's legislative court in 1975. However, larger political events—namely, the Iranian revolution of 1979—soon stopped her promising legal career in its tracks. A practicing Muslim, Ebadi was initially attracted to the aims of the revolutionaries. Like many other Iranian women, Ebadi was alienated from the Shah's corrupt regime, which was increasingly propped up by military aid and assistance from the United States, and initially welcomed the nationalist Islamic rhetoric of the revolutionaries. However, after the overthrow of the Shah, she soon became one of the revolution's victims; the regime of the Ayatollah Khomeini soon decided that Islam forbade women to serve as judges, and she and other female judges were dismissed and given clerical duties. In fact, they made Ebadi serve as a clerk in the court she had once presided over. Frustrated by the lack of professional opportunities, Ebadi took early retirement, focused on raising her two daughters, and became an independent scholar, writing out of her home.

In the wake of the election of reformist president Mohammad Khatami, Ebadi applied for a lawyer's license and set up a private practice in 1992. Since starting her practice, Ebadi has also taken on various child abuse cases and has worked to improve the rights of girls and women in a system in which they legally have fewer rights than do boys and men. For example, Ebadi represented the family of an 11-year-old girl who was raped and killed. Although three men were eventually found guilty of the crime, Iran's laws proclaim that a woman's life is worth half that of a man's. As a result, the bizarre outcome of the guilty verdict was the following: the girl's family was required to come up with thousands of dollars for the "blood money," or the price of a human life, for the execution of their daughter's killers. The family of the victim soon sank further into poverty as a result of this verdict; they eventually sold their house and most of their possessions before moving into a tent outside the local courthouse during the trial. Further efforts to sell their kidneys to raise money ended in failure. After 7 years of legal efforts, Ebadi succeeded, in addition to raising an enormous amount of public awareness and unprecedented media coverage on the issue, in forcing the state to pay one third of the sum required, an extremely unusual concession given the conservativeness of the regime.[ii] Further, Ebadi has defended a number of pro-Western liberal and dissident figures that have fallen afoul of the regime. In 2008, she took on the defense of seven Bahai leaders accused of spying for Israel.

Perhaps what is most interesting about her work is her approach, which seeks to work within the rules of the Islamic system rather than import solely Westernized models of law, justice, and gender equality. She has always worked from the premise that Islam and democratic principles are not mutually exclusive belief sets. As she wrote in her autobiography, *Iran Awakening*:

> In the last 23 years, from the day I was stripped of my judgeship to the years of doing battle in the revolutionary courts of Tehran, I had repeated one refrain: an interpretation of Islam that is in harmony with equality and democracy is an authentic expression of faith. It is not religion that binds women, but the selective dictates of those who wish them cloistered. That belief, along with the conviction that change in Iran must come peacefully and from within, has underpinned my work.[iii]

Further, in interviews, Ebadi has referred to herself as a "traditional Iranian woman" whose duty is to take care of the housework and the children, work that she enjoys after her often psychologically rough and bruising work as an attorney. In sum, equality between men and women can be accomplished in many ways and in ways that may draw on, rather than repudiate, traditional and/or Islamic values.

Her work, while praised by international human rights agencies, has won her few friends in the ruling regime in Iran, and as her international reputation has increased, she has faced increasing levels of political repression at home, a reflection of Iran's larger deterioration in its human rights record. In 2008, the Iranian news agency criticized Ebadi for defending homosexuals, appearing in public abroad without an Islamic headscarf, questioning Islamic punishments, and defending CIA agents. In addition, the Iranian police have shut down the office of one of her human rights groups, citing irregular paperwork. In 2009, proregime "demonstrators" attacked her home and office, accusing her of being insufficiently critical of Israel's actions in Gaza and their effects on children. Despite the increased levels of harassment, Ebadi initially vowed to continue her work in her fight to demonstrate that Islam, women's rights, and democracy can be mutually compatible concepts. In a February 2009 interview, she noted that "I don't feel secure, but this will not cause me to leave the country or to stop my activities. The Iranian government knows very well that as long as I am alive, I will do my duty."[iv] However, in June 2009, while she was abroad, the Iranian government rigged the presidential elections to ensure a victory for ultraconservative incumbent Mahmoud Ahmadinejad. Security forces brutally suppressed widespread popular protest, and two of the candidates were later placed under indefinite house arrest. She fled to the United Kingdom, after decades of staunchly holding her moral ground in her home city of Tehran. In retaliation, Ebadi alleges that the Iranian authorities seized her Nobel medal (a charge the authorities deny), together with other belongings from her safe deposit box, and detained her sister, who is not politically active but still lives in Iran. Yet, she continues to advocate for increased human rights in Iran, most recently protesting to the United Nations the August 2012 decision by 36 Iranian universities to ban women from 77 courses across a wide array of disciplines.[v] Exiled, but not silenced, Shirin Ebadi continues her work from afar to improve the human rights of all Iran's citizens, but particularly its women.

[i] Radio Free Europe/Radio Liberty, "Interview: Iranian Peace Prize Laureate Shirin Ebadi on Women's Rights," March 15, 2006, http://www.rferl.org/content/article/1066743.html.

[ii] Dan De Luce, "Iran Girl's Murder Spurs Debate over Blood Money," Women's e-News, December 1, 2003, http://womensenews.org/story/the-world/031201/iran-girls-murder-spurs-debate-over-blood-money#.URwMm6wTzSg

[iii] Shirin Ebadi with Azadeh Moaveni, *Iran Awakening: A Memoir of Revolution and Hope*, Random House, 2006, p. 204.

[iv] Mike Shuster, "Iran Cracks Down on Human Rights Activists." NPR, February 18, 2009. http://www.npr.org/templates/story/story.php?storyId=100780499

[v] Robert Tait, "Anger as Iran Bans Women from Universities," *The Telegraph*, August 20, 2012, http://www.telegraph.co.uk/news/worldnews/middleeast/iran/9487761/Anger-as-Iran-bans-women-from-universities.html.

At the same time, the postrevolutionary leadership in Iran became more pragmatic in its treatment of women. The government also readopted family planning and birth control in 1989, after discouraging it in the previous decade. A high birth rate, combined with a depressed economy, threatened the leadership's ability to build a just Islamic society that could provide for its citizens. As a result, some religious leaders reasoned that the Prophet allowed Muslims to practice contraception during times of economic hardship. The result was a successful, government-sponsored family planning program. Further, the government, partially in response to its family-planning policies, has increased efforts to improve the low female literacy rate. Although this has been accompanied by sex segregation, veiling, and enforced religious education, nonetheless women's literacy has increased more rapidly than has men's.[105] Further, women continued to seek access to higher education, and in 1998–99, for the first time since women entered the University of Tehran in 1939, 52 percent of the admitted students were women, although they remain barred from certain areas of study.[106] In fact, women have been so success-ful that they outnumbered men by three to two in passing the 2012 university entrance exam, and Iran currently has the highest ratio of female to male under-graduates in the world. Fearing the social side effects of rising educational standards among women, such as declining birth and marriage rates, universities moved in the summer of 2012 to exclude women from a broad range of studies, including English literature, English translation, hotel management, archaeology, nuclear physics, computer science, electrical engineering, industrial engineering, and business management.[107] At this point, it is unclear whether we can continue to celebrate to the same degree women's achievements in the Iranian higher educa-tion system.

While it is important not to overstate the liberalism of the Iranian leadership since 1979, nonetheless, it has been much more pragmatic in its policies toward women than initially feared. This has also opened a small space for Iranian women activists, who may support the regime but reject its vision of women's status in Islamic society. They have been able to use a woman-centered interpretation of Islamic text to push for incremental reforms within a system that, in its early years, was much more fundamentalist in its approach to women's issues.

In sum, the political, economic, and social impact of successful revolutionary movements has been mixed for women. However, Marxist-inspired movements have historically directly addressed the lesser condition and status of women by trying, perhaps imperfectly, to address this lesser status with proactive policy. This has not been the case with liberal/democratization movements, which have tended to see women as citizens who are in theory equal to men. As a result, they have not been as effective in dealing with the frequent reality of women's secondary status. And finally, religious fundamentalist revolutionaries have consistently put into place a system that often severely curtails women's rights in both the public and the private realm, although this policy shift has sometimes been initially actively supported by women themselves. However, as the work of Shirin Ebadi illustrates (see the text box entitled "Women in Motion: Shirin Ebadi"), reform that works in favor of women can be implemented, often incrementally, even in more repressive societies.

The Arab Spring

On December 16, 2010, a 26-year-old Tunisian named Mohamed Bouazizi set himself on fire after local authorities stopped him from selling vegetables, his only source of financial support. This incident sparked massive protests against Presi-dent Zine al-Abidine Ben Ali's corrupt and autocratic regime, and by January 2011, Ali stepped down from power after 23 years at the helm of the Tunisian state. These protests soon spread to other countries of the Middle East. In February, President Hosni Mubarak, who had ruled Egypt for 23 years, was toppled after 18 days of intense protest in Tahrir Square in Cairo. The Libyan regime was the next to face extreme pressure; February protests against the rule of Muammar Gaddafi quickly slid into armed conflict, rebel forces took the capital city of Tripoli in August, and Gaddafi was captured and killed in October. President Ali Abdullah Saleh of Yemen was another leader who was challenged and deposed; in November, after 33 years of rule, he handed over power to his deputy after months of protest. Political leaders in Bahrain, Algeria, and Oman have all faced popular opposition and pressure for reform. And in Syria, the regime of Bashar al-Assad has maintained power, but at the price of killing 15,000 protesting citizens since protests erupted in March 2011.[108] In varying degrees, protest spread in 2011 and 2012 across almost all countries in the Middle East. This is the most significant level of regime change in one region since the heyday of the third wave, in which autocratic regimes were toppled in countries in almost every region of the world.

However, in the countries within the Middle East that have deposed long-serving strongmen, it is unclear what political direction they will take in the near future. Despite optimism that democracy would quickly flower once old regimes had been removed, the past year has demonstrated that democracy is only one possible political outcome, and it may be highly unlikely. Until the events of the Arab Spring, the Middle East had the dubious honor of being the most autocratic region in the world. In other words, according to nonprofit organizations such as Freedom House, which collects data on civil rights and political liberties in countries around the world, countries within the Middle East, particularly Arab countries, performed the worst of any region in terms of respecting political rights, civil liberties, and guaranteeing relatively free and fair elections. While some speculate that the popularity of political Islam is one culprit, others posit that the region's Arab culture and common (though not universal) economic model of resource dependence on oil and gas also discourage democratic norms and practices. Regardless, the unfolding events of the past year in countries such as Tunisia, Egypt, and Libya, where initial elections have been held to choose delegates to draft a new constitution, tell us that while protesters were united in what they *didn't* want in their now-deposed leaders, it is less clear what voters in these countries *do* want for a future political system. In countries such as Tunisia and Egypt, for example, Islamist groups have dominated postrevolution politics. Will some or all of these countries take the path of liberal/democratization movements, religious fundamentalist movements, or some alternative in between? We don't know yet, but what we can say is that the position and status of women in the new regimes is potentially under threat.

As the story at the beginning of this chapter noted, women were a significant presence in the events of the Arab Spring; they joined in the protests, led public demonstrations, blogged and launched social media campaigns, covered the protests as journalists, smuggled weapons, and cared for the wounded. Tawakkol Karman, who was instrumental in organizing the protests in Yemen that eventually led to president Ali Abdullah Saleh's relinquishment of power, was awarded the Nobel Prize in 2011, the first Arab woman to receive such an honor. When accepting the award, she praised others who struggle "to win their rights in a society dominated by the supremacy of men." Unfortunately, however, women are finding that it is easier to overthrow dictators than to change longstanding cultural norms that consider women to be separate, and often unequal, beings. As one

Although women were at the frontlines of protest during the events of the Arab Spring, it is unclear whether they will benefit from regime change. SOURCE: Sipa via AP Images.

protester from the Egyptian movement recounted, "During the 18 days against Mubarak there were no women and men. It was just Egyptians in danger . . . But that changed after Mubarak stepped down. We were back to face the reality of where we are as Egyptian women. We're not a priority even with fellow revolutionaries. They're just thinking of the political change but no one is thinking of setting the rules for basic rights including women's rights. I think because even the activists don't really consider women's rights part of the larger concept of human rights, which is a huge issue."[109]

Many women are concerned about what the new regimes hold in store for them because of the high levels of popular support for Islamist parties in countries such as Egypt and Tunisia. As the opening story to this chapter illustrated, in Egypt, women quickly became targets of harassment, particularly after the decampment of Mubarak from the presidency. At the political level, women have been excluded from major decision-making bodies since the fall of the Mubarak regime, and the now-dissolved parliament, which was formed after the revolution, had fewer women in it than under the Mubarak regime. Women's representation dropped from 12 percent to 2 percent, and a Mubarak-era quota that allocated 64 seats to women was abandoned. The victory of the Muslim Brotherhood in the initial parliamentary elections (which were later annulled) and the presidential elections in July 2012 raised further concerns. Although some argue that the Muslim Brotherhood is similar to European Christian Democrats in that the members are socially conservative with religious roots but ultimately respectful of others' rights, this may be wishful thinking. The now-dissolved Islamist-dominated parliament, in its short operating life, reduced the marriage age for women to 14 years and restricted a woman's right to end abusive and unhappy marriages. There have been increased calls for women to dress modestly in public, as well as increased efforts to "Islamify" public spaces.

In Tunisia, a country where women have enjoyed relatively progressive marriage and divorce laws and access to birth control and abortion since the 1950s, recent debates over Tunisia's draft constitution have raised concerns among women's rights advocates. Leaders of Ennahda, the country's Islamist party, and also the dominant postrevolutionary political force, have tried to stress their similarities with European Christian Democrats, and openly vowed that Shari'a, or Islamic law, would not be the basis of the country's constitution. Yet, in August 2012, thousands of women took to the streets in protest when a new constitutional clause was proposed that describes a woman as "complementary to the man in the family and an associate to the man in the development of the country." The original 1956 constitution simply held women and men as equals. As in Egypt, women are increasingly under pressure to wear the hijab, or headscarf. However, women do seem to be faring better overall in Tunisia. Thanks to electoral rules requiring favorable placement of women on party lists, women won 23 percent of the parliamentary seats, which at least normalizes the presence of women in politics. In addition, Ennahda formed a coalition with liberal parties, and the coalition has focused on economic recovery and human rights, while avoiding more divisive cultural wars. Given that women constitute nearly a third of Tunisia's workforce, if nothing else, economic reality will encourage a pragmatic approach to women.

And in Libya, the post-Gaddafi regime has created mixed results for women. The head of the interim government worried many women's rights advocates when he vowed in 2011 that all laws that contradict Shari'a would be annulled, using restrictions on polygamy as an example. The results of the elections for the 200-member national congress in the summer of 2012 also sent mixed signals about the direction of Libyan politics. One the one hand, a coalition of secular parties won just under half of the seats, compared to the party associated with the Muslim Brotherhood, which came in second. Yet, all political parties agree that Shari'a should be a main source of legislation for drafting the country's new constitution. At the government handover ceremony in August 2012, a female presenter was removed after an Islamist parliamentarian complained that she was not wearing a hijab. But Libyan women have not been completely politically marginalized. More than 600 women ran as candidates in the parliamentary elections, and 33 women won seats, a not-insignificant force. The Health Minister in the interim regime is a woman, who left her life in Ireland to help build a new regime. She remains optimistic; although she notes the conservative, patriarchal, and traditional nature of Libyan society and the relatively small presence of women in government, she thinks women "want to play a bigger role. With more encouragement, and when women see other women doing well in politics, a lot more will come forward." Let's hope that prediction holds true, and that further impediments are not put in women's paths to achieving the kind of roles they want to play in post-Gaddafi Libya. Like the situation in Tunisia, at this point, it seems as if the concerns over ensuring some economic recovery are more important to the leadership than adversely changing women's legal and social status.

Why has it been hard for women to translate their efforts to overthrow the old regimes into longer-term political, economic, and social gains in the new regimes? The "winners" of the revolution have tended to be Islamist parties rather than liberal parties. Although not all advocate a fusion of church and state and an automatic secondary status for women, nonetheless they are all socially conservative, as are most Arab societies. Patriarchal customs run deep. It also doesn't help that in many of the pre-Arab Spring regimes, the women's rights agenda was closely associated with the now-discredited rulers. In Egypt, President Mubarak's wife ran a state-affiliated women's NGO; Tunisia's despised first lady was president of the Arab Women's Organization, sponsored by the Arab League; and the spouses of Syria's and Jordan's leaders are active on women's issues. Supporting women's rights can somehow get caught up in also being against the new political systems being built in countries such as Tunisia, Egypt, and Libya. It certainly makes it hard for Western-style women's organizations to develop a rhetoric that resonates with post-Arab Spring politics, although they will need to if women's rights begin to erode. And like other postrevolutionary societies we have studied in this chapter, women's claims are often lost in the larger battle to overthrow political regimes that have failed to benefit all citizens, men as well as women. Although countries that were part of the Arab Spring may not yet fall neatly into our typology of Marxist, liberal, and fundamentalist revolutionary movements, one thing is clear: there is no guarantee that many of the women who were active on the front lines of protest will be able to turn their engagement into longer-term economic, social, and political gains. One analyst, commenting on the political status of the region asked, "is the Arab Spring bad for women?" She answers her own question, noting that "overthrowing male dominance could be harder than overthrowing a dictator."[110]

CONCLUSION

Throughout history, revolutionary leaders pushing for the radical redistribution of power—political, economic, and social—have targeted women as enemies, victims, allies, and saviors. As wives, lovers, and relatives of imperfect political leaders, they have been reviled for their tainted pasts and supposed excesses under corrupt and bloated prerevolutionary political regimes. They have been recruited to revolutionary movements to fight for profoundly new societies, with greater women's rights dangled in front as an ideological carrot. They have been enshrined as the symbol of a brighter and better future under a new and more enlightened leadership. In conclusion, were women included or excluded from the unmaking of the old regime and the remaking of the new one? Were women manipulated or transformed by their participation in revolutionary movements? Perhaps the answer lies in the nature of women's exclusion and inclusion in revolutionary origins, processes, and outcomes, rather than the presence or absence of their influence.

As events past and current demonstrate, women have participated actively in radical processes of political change. Women, however, often join causes not because they are fighting for greater rights and access for their sex, but because they identify with a larger cause. Thus, often women willingly surrender specific gender concerns to larger, more encompassing political struggles. On the one hand, some women have assumed traditional "male" roles and have made bombs, masterminded plots, and led troops into battle with equal zeal. However, the high-profile female revolutionary is the exception, not the rule, and women rarely hold positions of power within the movement, instead serving as crucial assistants. Further, women have assumed traditionally female, nurturing roles as helpers in revolutions by raising money, giving shelter, teaching, and nursing. Revolutionary leaders, in turn, have been ambivalent about women's participation in the movement. On the one hand, they have exploited society's traditional visions of women's femininity by assigning women difficult and dangerous decoy assignments. However, many leaders are hesitant to put their revolutionary rhetoric of equality into practice; they rarely appoint women to true leadership positions and save the most visible and high-ranking jobs for their male colleagues.

Once a new regime takes control, women often are pushed out of or denied real leadership positions. While a movement headed by a woman makes great material for the newsroom, the actual incidences of female leadership are relatively few. Loyal foot soldiers, women rarely make the transition into political office, and thus have a muffled impact on the design of the new state. The few women who do make the cut are often designated to token "female" positions of power and are appointed to various committees in charge of women's and children's affairs.

It is important not to overlook the numerous organizations, social programs, and economic opportunities that have been designed for women, and sometimes by women. But at the same time, it is important to acknowledge that rhetoric toward women's greater participation has always outpaced the reality of programs offered. Part of this is because women themselves have often not been united on what it means to be a woman in revolutionary times. A large part, however, also is because for women to gain or advance in society, another social group, often men, has to lose something in return—a position of power, a job, a certain status in society or the family. Throughout history, people have been willing to offer women reforms until another group loses. Acknowledging that women's gains may end up costing another segment something (but is still worth it) is a revolutionary idea whose time is yet to come.

FOR MORE INFORMATION

Video and Multimedia

Aung San Suu Kyi, BBC Reith Lecture 1.1. (2011). YouTube. http://www.youtube.com/watch?v=fFLiCb359Rs. The Burmese pro-democracy leader Aung San Suu Kyi explores what freedom means in the first of the 2011 BBC Reith Lecture series, "Securing Freedom."

"Aung San Suu Kyi records message for US Congress." (2011). *BBC*. http://www.bbc.co.uk/news/world-asia-pacific-13884748. In June 2011, Aung San Suu Kyi addressed the U.S.

Congress for the first time, via video message, and appealed to the United States to support the fight for democracy in Burma.

"For Neda." (2010). HBO. http://www.youtube.com/watch?v=F48SinuEHIk. This is an HBO documentary on Neda Agha-Soltan, a victim of Iran's violent crackdown on postelection protests on June 20, 2009, and a symbol in the larger Iranian struggle for democratic freedoms.

"A Death in Tehran." (2009). Tehran Bureau. www.pbs.org/wgbh/pages/frontline/tehranbureau/deathintehran/. A PBS documentary that covers the death of Neda Agha-Soltan from Tehran Bureau, an independent news source on Iran and the Iranian diaspora.

"Women of the Revolution." (2012). Women's World. Press TV. http://www.youtube.com/watch?v=AK_yKc9eG3M. This episode of Women's World, a UK news show on women's rights, features the Nobel Peace Prize winner Tawakkol Karman from Yemen and other women to examine and profile each Arab Spring revolution and its female support and participation.

"Guerrilla Girls of the PKK—Turkey." (2007). Journeyman Pictures. YouTube. http://www.youtube.com/watch?v=pRsw5s28jxY. This rare 25-minute documentary features the lives of guerrilla women of the PKK, the Kurdistan Workers' Party, who live in the mountains in northern Iraq.

"United Red Army." (2007). This is a somewhat fictionalized account of the leaders of Japan's leftist paramilitary group, the United Red Army.

"Children of the Revolution." (2010). This is a documentary film about Ulrike Meinhof and Fusako Shigenobu, leaders of the German Red Army Faction and the Japanese Red Army, which were profiled in the text box entitled "Revolutionary Movements in Advanced Industrialized Democracies" earlier in this chapter.

Readings

Gioconda Belli. (2003). *The Country Under My Skin: A Memoir of Love and War.* New York: Anchor. A first-person account of one woman's journey from upper-class wife and mother to armed revolutionary in Nicaragua's Sandinista movement.

Mia Bloom. (2011). *Bombshell: Women and Terrorism.* Philadelphia: University of Pennsylvania Press. http://www.upenn.edu/pennpress/book/14946.html. Bloom explains how female involvement in terrorism is not confined to suicide bombing and is not limited to the Middle East.

Jung Chang. (1992). *Wild Swans: Three Daughters of China.* New York: Anchor. An autobiographical family history of three generations of women who survived China's tumultuous century of political upheaval and revolution, from the collapse of the Imperial order to the fallout from Mao's cultural revolution.

Angela Y. Davis. (1989). *Angela Davis: An Autobiography.* New York: International Publishers. This book covers the life and early career of left-wing activist and scholar Angela Davis, including her association with the Black Panther Party and the Communist Party of America.

Bernadine Dohrn, Bill Ayers, and Jeff Jones, eds. (2006). *Sing a Battle Song: The Revolutionary Poetry, Statements, and Communiques of the Weather Underground, 1970–1974.* New York: Seven Stories Press. A collection of three complete and unedited publications by the Weathermen during their most active period underground.

Slavenkac Drakuli. (1993). *How We Survived Communism and Even Laughed.* New York: Harper Perennial. A series of essays portraying the daily struggles women faced in communist eastern Europe.

Shirin Ebadi with Azadeh Moaveni. (2007). *Iran Awakening: One Woman's Journey to Reclaim Her Life and Country.* New York: Random House Trade Paperbacks. A first-hand account of the 2003 Nobel Peace Prize laureate's life and work in Iran both before and after the revolution.

Barbara Alpern Engel and Clifford N. Rosenthal, eds. (1987). *Five Sisters: Women Against the Tsar.* New York: Routledge. The memoirs of five young anarchist women who participated in Russia's underground revolutionary movements in the 1870s.

Pardis Mahdavi. (2009). "'But What If Someone Sees Me?' Women, Risk, and the After-shocks of Iran's Sexual Revolution." *Journal of Middle East Women's Studies* 5(2):1–22. This article discusses women's conceptions of social risk, their vulnerability to HIV/STIs, and their access to testing and treatment centers through fieldwork involving participant observations, in-depth interviews, and focus groups with women, health providers, and policymakers in Iran.

Rigoberta Menchu, Elisabeth Burgos-Debray, and Ann Wright. (1984). *I, Rigoberta Menchu: An Indian Woman in Guatemala.* New York: Verso. The life story of a Quiche Indian woman and her family's struggle to survive the repressive military dictatorship in Guatemala.

Alifa Rifaat. "Distant View of a Minaret." A short story by an Egyptian writer detailing what it means to be a woman living in a traditional Muslim society.

Organizations and Websites

Change for Equality. www.we-change.org/english/. The One Million Signatures Campaign aims to collect 1 million signatures on a petition addressed to the Iranian Parliament asking for the revision of current laws that discriminate against women.

International Campaign for Human Rights in Iran. http://www.iranhumanrights.org. This organization gathers support for Iranian human rights activists and defenders who are advocating for their civil, political, social, and economic rights within the framework of international treaties and standards that define Iran's obligations.

Iran Amnesty International. www.amnesty.org/en/region/iran. This is the Iran website of Amnesty International, an international organization that campaigns to end grave abuses of human rights.

Nobel Women's Initiative. http://nobelwomensinitiative.org/. The Nobel Women's Initiative uses the prestige of the Nobel Peace Prize and women Peace Laureates to increase the power and visibility of women's groups working globally for peace, justice, and equality.

RAWA (Revolutionary Association of the Women of Afghanistan). www.rawa.org. RAWA was established in Kabul, Afghanistan, in 1977 as an independent political/social organization of Afghan women fighting for human rights and for social justice in Afghanistan.

PART II

Gendering Public Policy

In the previous part, the three chapters focused primarily on ways in which women try to influence the state. As we have seen, they have gained access to political institutions by running for office, by participating in social movements and interest groups, and through joining revolutionary movements in the hopes of bringing about radical change. Despite the myriad of ways in which women are active in both institutionalized and noninstitutionalized forms of political activism, common themes link all forms of women's activities. Certainly, women's participation in institutionalized and noninstitutionalized politics has had an impact. Yet, while women have played an important role in gaining access to formal positions of political power, that access is not widespread, uniform, or far-reaching. Nonetheless, as we saw with their activities in social movements, women are often able to use their gender to their advantage by successfully exploiting traditional expectations of women's and, particularly, mothers' "appropriate" spheres of activity. However, even in revolutionary movements, which profess radical aims in terms of redistributing power, women's rights are often sacrificed to larger, "more important" revolutionary goals, and revolution's impact on women is never as significant as promised by charismatic leaders. In sum, while the increased presence of women in all levels of activity has resulted in more women-friendly policies, it has come as a result of a long and protracted struggle for influence, and the push for women's equality is a slow, trickle-up process that is still met with great resistance.

We now turn to look at the other side of the equation, moving from an examination of women's influences on the state to looking at the impact of state structures and policies on women. One of the key themes that cut across the chapters of this part is that of "the activist state." Often, we don't think of states as actors, with specific interests, agendas, and concerns. Rather, we view the state as an arena in which interests battle for influence and control. Yet, it is the various institutions and organizations within the state that are in charge of making and enacting policies, and these policies are often shaped to further specific state goals, interests, and targets. For example, when the U.S. government issues policies on affirmative action, they are not only regulating terms of employment but are also pushing a certain vision of an equitable, diverse society. When the French government bans headscarves from public schools, they are, on the one hand, designing school policy. But this policy also is a statement about the French government's views on the separation of religion and state and the methods by which Muslim minorities should integrate into French society. Thus, by looking more closely at policy, we can learn a lot about state visions of "ideal societies" and the policies they pursue to bring the real closer to the ideal.

In the following three chapters, we examine how states have designed policies that impact the position and status of women in society. We assess the degree to which states have sought "to advance women's status and condition as a group . . . and/or to strike down gender-based hierarchies."[1] Primarily in the 1970s, many states started "feminizing the state" by founding offices, advisory councils, and administrative bureaucracies to deal specifically with gender concerns. Further, bureaucrats sympathetic to women's issues, also known as "femocrats," began to fill various positions within the emerging policy machinery. In addition, as a result of pressure coming from women voters, activists, and bureaucrats, states began to embed gender issues in national policy agendas by adopting legislation that addressed women's inequality in such areas as political representation, equal employment, family law, education, health care, and reproductive choice. This has led a number of scholars to define this trend as "state feminism" as a way of describing this institutionalization of policies that promote women's status and strike down gender hierarchies.[2] The chapters in this part explore this trend toward state feminism by looking at three policy areas within advanced industrialized nations: equal employment, reconciliation (balancing the demands of work and family), and reproductive choice. Thus Chapter 4 deals with issues of equality in the public realm, Chapter 5 addresses bridging the public and the private divide, and Chapter 6 addresses the challenge of passing policy to govern issues of privacy that are contested areas of government intervention.

As we shall see, across all our policy issues, states have responded to the problem of gender inequalities with varying levels of commitment. They have issued symbolic statements, encoded new rights into the constitution, passed legislation, issued plans and reports, and installed government machineries. But some countries are more dedicated to rectifying gender imbalances than others and demonstrate varying levels of commitment to enforcing existing legislation. In addition, some states are more proactive than others in implementing policy that not only protects women from discriminatory practices but also actively attempts to redress past imbalances with affirmative policies. Throughout the three chapters, we will see that states are somewhat contradictory in their policies. Often, they advance the rhetoric of gender equality but then do not put policy in place that can realistically assist women in achieving that equality. Alternatively, they advance the rhetoric of gender equality while simultaneously enacting policies that actively discourage women from achieving equality. Issuing the rhetoric of gender equality has become almost required of advanced industrialized nations; achieving that equality has been a much more uneven process.

Another important theme that runs throughout all the chapters of this part is the intentions of the state. Policies tell us something about how various governments view women's appropriate position in society, and state policies often send subtle (and sometimes not-so-subtle) messages through the enactment of specific policies, which legitimize or challenge existing social and economic inequalities. Rhetorical support for women's equality that is not accompanied by strict enforcement mechanisms can indicate that a state does not see women's equality as a policy priority. Policies that encourage women to leave the workforce to become mothers can tell us something about how states view women's participation in the workforce. Sometimes states send contradictory, mixed messages about the ideal position of women in society by designing policies to strengthen traditional family values while simultaneously enacting other programs that try to ensure women's economic equality.

The following chapters demonstrate the difficulties states have in matching their rhetoric of gender equality with significant results. In Chapter 4, "Women and Employment," we provide a comparative overview of equal employment policies in Japan, the United States, and the European Union. Our three case studies demonstrate varying levels of commitment to ensuring women's equality in the workforce. Further, equal employment policy can go only so far in correcting women's subordinate position in the labor market. In all countries, women occupy a separate and unequal status. Women's pay for positions of equal value still lags behind that for men. Women are persistently marginalized in workforces; there is both a "glass ceiling" that keeps women from attaining a large share of top management positions as well as a "sticky floor" that relegates many women to low-paying jobs and positions of borderline poverty. In short, passing legislation to ensure equality has been easier than ensuring that that equality will automatically follow from activist policy. Much of this is because equal employment policy does not address the inequalities in the division of labor outside of the workforce.

Chapter 5, "Women, Work, and Family," acknowledges that equal employment policies that address equality issues in the public realm often ignore the fundamental causes that affect men's and women's unequal position in work, politics, and public society. This is particularly true in the areas of balancing production (work) with reproduction (family care). Because women are biologically responsible for activities related to pregnancy and childbirth and still take care of many of the "nurturing" responsibilities of childrearing, they often are unable to compete equally for competitive jobs or perform to their fullest potential. In response, states have enacted legislation that provides various benefits, such as parental leave and child-care provisions, to help citizens manage the competing demands of public and private life. In this chapter, we compare the varying policy approaches of the United States, Germany, and Sweden with regard to parental leave and child care. As we shall see, the design of these policies can either enforce existing gendered divisions of labor or help redefine them, for example, by encouraging men to become more active in parenting.

Chapter 6, "Abortion Politics," addresses the state's increasing involvement in enacting policies that limit or expand women's reproductive choices. Drawing from our case studies of Ireland, the United States, and the Netherlands, we explore the varying outcomes of the abortion debate. While Ireland has implemented one of the most conservative laws in Europe in terms of restricting access to abortion services, the United States has designed relatively liberal laws that have been challenged repeatedly in all political arenas. As a result, abortion practices have been restricted significantly in the decades following legalization. In contrast, the Netherlands has implemented a liberal policy that has not been challenged significantly since it was approved in the 1980s.

You may notice that all of the case studies are from advanced industrialized nations and may wonder why we are not covering the countries of the developing world in this chapter. After all, women in these countries also face employment discrimination, juggle work with child-care responsibilities, and struggle to control their fertility. There are several answers to this question, which we also addressed in the preface. First, there is a wide disjunction between state policy and state action in developing countries. One of the enduring characteristics of developing countries is the weak state. That is, governments exist, but they are often too weak and fragmented to design and then effectively implement policy. They lack what is known as "capacity." In effect, laws that exist on paper often are not enforced in reality. Thus, we felt that comparing government action in these policy areas would tend to overemphasize similarities while obscuring very critical differences in terms of policy implementation and impact. In addition, as we have argued elsewhere, while these issues are of concern to women everywhere, the ways in which women vocalize and act on that concern often differ as a result of economic, cultural, ethnic, racial, and religious differences. For example, while women around the world have mobilized over issues of reproductive choice, many women in the Southern Hemisphere still face enormous health risks in even bearing children, while women in the Northern Hemisphere may be more concerned about access to abortion services. Again, trying to generalize across these policy issues would obscure interesting differences in women's responses and make facile generalizations about their commonalities. However, the final part of the book will discuss many of the issues that affect women in the developing world. Thus, the reader will still get an opportunity to learn about how women in the Southern Hemisphere are affected by a variety of issues.

4

Women and Employment

Joseph Ackermann, the chief executive of Deutsche Bank, commented recently, in a debate over whether Germany should set quotas for the number of women on company boards (as France, Norway. and Spain have done), that appointing women to the currently female-less executive board would make it "prettier and more colorful."[1] When Gretchen Swan, a part-time employee, was asked by her employer to take on a few more hours of work, she accepted, but she asked for something in return—benefits, including a pension.[2] In Great Britain, Citigroup recently paid £1.4 million (about $2.8 million) to a former employee, Julie Brower, "whose track record had been described by her manager as 'had cancer, been a pain, now pregnant,'" and Deutsche Bank paid £500,000 to Kate Swinburne, "who was described, among other things, as 'hotty totty.'"[3] In Scotland, male government workers recently lodged discrimination complaints because of a dress code that insists that men wear ties at all times, whereas women have no dress code and can show up to work in T-shirts.[4] All of these stories indicate that women and men are still not treated equally in the workforce and that, despite numerous gains, (primarily) women face different, unequal, and at times hostile working conditions. Cultural attitudes about women's abilities, gendered divisions of labor within the workforce, and lack of government enforcement of existing legislation are just a few of the variables that stand in the way of women's equal treatment in paid employment.

The economic emergence of women has been one of the most significant developments in the post–World War II era. Between 1970 and 2010, women's participation in the workforce in Organisation for Economic Co-operation and Development (OECD) countries increased from nearly 45 percent to 65 percent.[5] Yet, in country after country, women earn substantially less than men.[6] Part of the problem is that women are often segregated into low-paying "female" professions such as secretarial work, sales, teaching, and other service-oriented and caregiver industries. Further, women are less likely to ascend to positions of power and authority and are passed over for promotions more frequently than equally qualified male counterparts are. In addition, women are often clustered in part-time or temporary jobs that offer less financial reward and fewer opportunities for advancement. Nor are working conditions ideal for women. For many decades, employers could discriminate against women because of their reproductive capabilities, and sexual harassment was often a byproduct of a predominantly male working environment. By the end of women's lives, these disadvantages take their toll on working women, and, upon retirement, women make up the vast majority of the elderly poor.

How have governments tried to address these inequities in the workforce? The increase in the number of women in the workforce, the emergence of feminist movements in the 1970s, the creation of women's policy machineries, and the increasing numbers of female politicians led many governments to pass equal employment policies to address the barriers that prevented women from participating in employment in the same way that men did. These laws have focused on establishing a more level playing field by mandating equal treatment and equal opportunities for women at work and by criminalizing forms of discrimination such as sexual harassment. The rationale for many of these policies has stressed a liberal, gender-neutral rhetoric. That is, the assumption is that the pathway to better employment conditions lies in stressing women's legal equality with men.

As we shall see, although important, equal employment policies are limited in their impact, for while they can address direct barriers that operate in the job market, they do not address the indirect obstacles, such as gender inequities involved in family life or socialization to gendered divisions of labor, that affect women's abilities to perform equally to men on the job.[7] As one scholar commented, "The design of equal employment policies still needs to recognize that inequities in wage labor are actually a product of forces outside of the labor market."[8] As a result, state activism regarding equal employment legislation has not "solved" the problem of sex discrimination in the workplace. However, equal employment legislation does legitimate the problem of discrimination, demonstrates to society at large that the problem will not be tolerated by the government, and penalizes firms and individuals who engage in blatant acts of prejudicial behavior. It is a necessary tool in the battle for women's equality; however, equal employment legislation in and of itself will not result in economic equality for women.

In this chapter we look an array of equal employment policies that address the following issues: pay; hiring, promotion, and firing; sexual harassment; and retirement income. We use Japan, the United States, and the European Union (EU) as case studies of how states have designed and implemented policy to further women's status in the workforce. Japan has made the least progress in advancing gender equality in the workforce, having implemented equal employment legislation that is merely symbolic in its support for women's equality because it lacks critical enforcement mechanisms. In contrast, the United States has been more successful in implementing a variety of policies to encourage equal employment practices. While government support for this was initially symbolic, a well-mobilized women's movement actively lobbied the state to enforce its own regulations. The EU provides an interesting example of policy design and implementation at the supra-national level, which has, in turn, affected individual policies adopted by member countries. While the EU has been hospitable to women's demands and lobbying, nonetheless it has been more adept at urging nations to pass equal employment legislation than pressuring them to enforce it. Across our cases, we find that many states are better at advancing the rhetoric of gender equality in the workforce than they are at designing and enforcing policy to ensure a more equitable employment outcome for women.

THE DEBATE OVER EQUAL EMPLOYMENT POLICIES

One of the most significant demographic trends of the post–World War II era has been the massive influx of women into the paid workforce. As we mentioned pre-viously, in OECD countries in 2010, on average 65 percent of women were em-ployed. Certainly, that broad average masks a number of differences between the 34 member states of the OECD; for example, in Turkey, 30 percent of women were working, in comparison to a high of 77 percent for women in Iceland. However, most countries are somewhere between these two endpoints: 2 OECD countries have a female labor participation rate in the 40- to 49-percent range (Greece and Mexico), 11 are in the 50- to 59-percent range, 14 are in the 60- to 69-percent range, 7 are in the 70- to 79-percent range, and none have female labor participa-tion rates at or over 80 percent. These figures, in general, are an improvement from the early 2000s, but most all are below the participation rate of men.[9]

Despite this increase in women's participation, women have often had a sepa-rate and unequal experience in the paid labor force. Despite their increasing par-ticipation, there are significant employment gaps between men and women. Women are less likely to be employed than men are and are more likely to make less money and advance less quickly when in the workforce; as a result, women are at a higher risk of poverty throughout their lives.[10] For many years, particularly before the passage of antidiscriminatory legislation, these problems could be par-tially attributed to blatant acts of discrimination. Companies openly refused to hire women, paid them less for identical jobs, and fired them when they got preg-nant, often under the rationale that women were less competent, capable, or able to perform their work responsibilities.

Equal employment was one of the early mobilizing issues for feminist move-ments, and it became one of the earliest targeted areas for state activism in advanc-ing gender equality in the 1960s, 1970s, and 1980s. Equal pay laws were often the first to be enacted, followed by equal treatment laws that criminalized direct dis-crimination against women in hiring, promotion, and firing.[11] Yet, legislation out-lawing direct discrimination did not immediately solve women's problems in the workforce. While women continued to experience direct discrimination (even though it was illegal), the larger problem consisted of designing policy to combat less obvious forms of indirect discrimination.

For example, the vast inequalities between men's and women's salaries are often attributed to women's occupational segregation in careers that are less highly valued and mimic women's "caring" and "nurturing" functions in the household. Various nations' economies are literally divided between "women's jobs" and "men's jobs" women are overrepresented in low-paying professions, such as teaching, secretarial work, sales, and domestic services, while men predominate in more remunerative careers, such as management, administration, policy, and industry. The most recent United Nations (UN) report on the world's women in 2010 finds that at least three quarters of women's employment is in the services in the developed regions of the world (with the exception of Eastern Europe, at 66 percent), Latin America, and the Caribbean.[12] In the member countries of the EU 52 percent of all employed women are concentrated in the services sector, while men are disproportionately employed in agriculture and industry, which are "male" areas of employment that tend to be more financially rewarding.[13] As of 2010, in the United States, women made up 91.1 percent of the nation's nurses, 81.8 percent of its elementary and middle school teachers, and 80.8 percent of its social workers.[14] In contrast, 98 percent of the nation's firefighters, 74 percent of its physicians, and 97 percent of its construction workers were male.[15] Women also tend to be overrepresented in low-skilled, low-wage jobs, such as low-tech assembly line workers, and in jobs such as clerks, service workers, and shop assistants. In addition, women are much more likely to work part-time than are men, in part because they still assume primary responsibility for child care, elder care, and housework. For example, in Japan as of 2009, 62 percent of the part-time workforce was female.[16] In the Netherlands that number was 75 percent, and in the EU in 2010, 41 percent of working women worked part-time.[17] As a result, women become segregated in jobs that are more disposable and, hence, are less well paid. This matters because, as the opening story about Gretchen Swan indicates, part-time workers often do not receive the benefits that their full-time counterparts receive. And as the UN argues in "The World's Women 2010":

> The costs of part-time employment can be great . . . [it] is associated with lower income—with a long-term impact on pensions—and does not carry the same social benefits as full-time employment. Career advancement . . . is often jeopardized because the image persists that they are not serious about their jobs and careers. The types of part-time jobs available and the conditions of work are all a concern. Thus . . . it reinforces the male breadwinner model, relegating women to a secondary role in the labour market.[18]

All of these factors mean that women enter their retirement years in a much more financially precarious situation than men do.

Further, worldwide, a glass ceiling keeps women from ascending the corporate ladder to important management positions. For example, in the United States, women account for 16.1 percent of board directors (only Norway with 40.1%, Sweden with 27.3%, and Finland with 24.5% rank above the United States; all other countries have fewer than 16% female board directors), 4.0 percent of chief executives of Fortune 1000 companies, and only 3.8 percent of chief executives of Fortune 500 companies.[19] As we shall discuss in greater detail in the next chapter, women who have children tend to take more time off from work, often at times when they are in the midst of climbing the career ladder, and thus tend to miss out on critical opportunities that could launch them into higher management positions. A study of American graduate managers found that women returning after a break of 3 years or more lost an average of 37 percent of their earnings.[20] In addition, indirect social barriers continue to impede women's progress. Women for many decades have been shut out of the "old boy's network" and all of the accompanying activities, such as informal lunches, golf games, and trips that mix business and pleasure. As we shall see, it is harder to devise strategies to counter these forms of "indirect" discrimination because they are not a product of blatant, illegal hiring practices but rather emerge from a variety of societal norms that steer women into occupations, career paths, and work networks that do not advance them as quickly as men.

What are the arguments in support of equal employment policies? Some advocates for women's equal treatment in the workforce frame the issue as one of fairness; as human beings men and women share a common humanity and should treat each other, and be treated by business, government, and social institutions, equally. Second, potential differences in ability are because of socialization patterns, rather than as a result of biological sex, and thus are not valid reasons for discrimination. Women's increased presence in higher education and advanced study demonstrates that, when given the opportunity, women can excel as frequently as men can. Third, discrimination is bad for a nation's economy, for it does not tap the full potential of a nation's citizenry. For example, evidence indicates that hiring women makes good business sense; *The Economist* reports that research results from the United States, the United Kingdom, and Scandinavia demonstrate a strong correlation between shareholder returns and the proportion of women in high-level executive positions. There are a variety of explanations for this; some posit that women tend to be better at team building and communications, which indirectly can increase profits. Others maintain that a homogeneous white male executive culture stifles the diversity needed to generate new, innovative ideas.[21] On a more general level, the World Bank notes, "It [gender equality] strengthens countries' abilities to grow, to reduce poverty, and to govern effectively. Promoting gender equality is thus an important part of a development strategy that seeks to enable all people—women and men alike—to escape poverty and improve their standard of living."[22]

However, while many agree on the need for equal employment policies, there is less agreement on potential policy solutions to rectify women's unequal status. States have faced numerous dilemmas in designing equal employment policies. For example, how should equal employment be promoted? Should states simply outlaw discriminatory practices, or should they more proactively ensure that women have equal opportunity to compete in the paid labor force, such as through the use of affirmative action policies? And to what degree should states attempt to correct for gender imbalances in the division of labor in the household, in which women carry the burden of childrearing and family care? While the next chapter addresses the latter question, in this chapter we address the former ones. Similarly, advocates for women's equality in the workforce also differ on which policies should be implemented under the rubric of equal employment. Does "equal employment" mean that men and women should have similar employment profiles in lifetime work patterns—that is, comparable occupational distributions, job status, salaries, and promotions? Extending this logic, many advocates for women's equality pursue strategies that tend to emphasize men's and women's innate commonalities, rather than their differences, and target abolishing laws that distinguish between men and women based on sex.

However, not all proponents of women's advancement believe that focusing on treating women in the workforce equally is an appropriate strategy. For example, "difference feminists" such as Carol Gilligan argue that men and women are developmentally different.[23] Women's ways of knowing and thinking, and their caring abilities, should be preserved and honored, and difference feminists argue that gender-neutral legislation may dilute differences that should be honored and preserved. Difference feminists argue that policies should not try to treat women and men equally in certain areas, but instead should compensate women for the ways their biology makes them different from men, particularly with regard to their reproductive roles. Further, women's socially constructed roles as nurturers and caretakers further hinder their abilities to participate equally in the workforce, which also should be taken into account. In this view, gender-neutral laws are detrimental since they merely perpetuate and exacerbate inequalities in the household. Difference feminists advocate for differential treatment in the workforce through the passage of protective legislation, specific maternity leave benefits, or affirmative action policies to redress past imbalances. Let us now turn to how states have attempted to rectify inequalities in men's and women's experiences in the workforce.

POLICY AREAS

Equality in the workplace encompasses a number of topics, among them equal pay; equal treatment in hiring, promotion, and firing; the right to a harassment-free working environment; and equality in retirement benefits. We will now examine each of these four issues in greater depth in our three case studies—Japan, the United States, and the EU.

Japan has made the least progress in advancing gender equality in the workforce, implementing equal employment legislation that is merely symbolic in its support for women's equality in that it lacks critical enforcement mechanisms. This can be attributed to a variety of factors. For one, Japanese society is, compared to other advanced industrial nations, more accepting of traditional gendered divisions of labor. Women are expected to leave the labor force after marriage, and particularly after having children. In addition, Japan's small women's movement mobilized much later on employment issues and has struggled to gain access to important decision makers in the Japanese state. As a result, the movement has used Japan's participation in international treaties as a pressure point to facilitate domestic reform. In turn, the government has been unwilling to offer more than symbolic policies, which are stronger on rhetorical support for women's equality and much weaker on enforcement mechanisms that could advance that equality. In sum, as Joyce Gelb has argued, legislation to improve women's equality "has produced only limited gains in employment opportunity for a small number of Japanese women and, arguably, has created even worse conditions for many."[24] Larger contextual factors, such as Japan's ongoing economic woes and declining birth rate, have created a backlash against further implementation of equal employment policy.

In contrast, the United States has implemented a variety of policies to encourage equal employment practices. While government support for this was initially symbolic, a well-mobilized women's movement actively lobbied the state to enforce its own regulations. Further, the U.S. system of litigation, in which claimants can sue for substantial monetary damages, has encouraged a number of government agencies and businesses to address the issue of equal employment with proactive policies. While the government has tended to design policy that is gender neutral, it has also introduced various affirmative action policies to promote women, which is still a controversial issue in the United States. Yet, as we shall see, the impact of equal employment policy has been limited in that women still face substantial barriers in breaking the glass ceiling in a number of professions.

Finally, the case of the EU illustrates efforts to resolve gender inequalities at the supranational level. The EU is an intergovernmental and supranational union of 25 member states (and 4 candidate countries). Although the EU is not intended to replace the nation-state, its member states have set up common institutions to which they delegate some of their sovereignty so that decisions on specific matters of joint interest can be made democratically at the European level. While enforcement issues are problematic (as they are with all international organizations), the member nations have transferred more sovereignty to the EU than to any other regional organization. Thus, the EU provides an interesting point of comparison with our other two case studies; although it does not act as a traditional nation-state, it has significant and growing influence on the politics of the various countries of Europe.

The EU repeatedly has advanced a progressive rhetoric regarding equal employment. It has placed pressure on member countries to institutionalize equal opportunity policies, particularly in Mediterranean countries, which lagged behind other member countries in designing policy. However, member states have responded to various directives to improve their legislation with mixed levels of enthusiasm. And while the European Parliament and the European Commission have been hospitable to women's demands and lobbying, nonetheless the EU has been more adept at urging nations to pass equal employment legislation than at pressuring them to enforce it.[25] That said, the EU law is supreme and prevails over national law when a conflict emerges. The European Court of Justice has issued (as of 2010) over 200 binding judgments regarding equality.[26] We now turn to how our three cases have designed and implemented a range of policies related to equal employment.

Equal Pay

Over the years all advanced industrial nations have enacted legislation designed to eradicate the differentials in pay between men and women, which are substantial. The short-term and long-term impact of this pay gap on women, families, and countries is significant. For example, women's low income increases the incidence of poverty, which often has a female face. In the United States, women's advocates argue that if women received the same pay as men "who work the same number of hours, have the same education, union status, are the same age, and live in the same region of the country, then these women's annual family income would rise by $4,000 and poverty rates would be cut in half."[27] Other issues, such as women's over representation in part-time labor and time taken off from work to raise a family, compound this problem. As Britain's Equal Opportunity Commission noted, "taking time off work to bring up children, the average gender-pay gap and the large number of women working in part-time or low-paid jobs all contributed to their poverty."[28] Further, women live longer than men and are increasingly swelling the ranks of the elderly. Since many women who worked did not earn as much as men throughout their lives, their savings and pension benefits tended to be much lower. Thus, the pay gap between men's and women's salaries is a significant policy issue for states. We now turn to how states have tried to legislate equal pay and the effectiveness of their policies.

Japan

Japan's approach to addressing equal pay has lagged behind that of other industrialized countries. While the Japanese Diet adopted weak equal employment legislation in the 1980s, it did not specifically address the issue of equal pay for equal, or comparable, work. As we shall see, compared to other countries, women's mobilization in Japan has been lower, and much of the pressure to reform Japan's equal employment laws came from external, international pressure. Finally, the government has not been committed to passing and enforcing legislation relating to a wide array of workforce issues that might advance women's equality.

Technically, the Labor Standards Act of 1946 required equal wages for women and men. However, because the equal pay clause applied only to the same type of labor, employers often paid women less by segregating them into separate jobs than men.[29] The passage of the 1985 Equal Employment Opportunity Law (EEOL) prohibited gender discrimination in training, pension allocation, and employee dismissal but did not specifically address the issue of equal pay. Thus, Japanese policy mandating equal pay for equal work is somewhat murky; although the EEOL does not mention equal pay for equal work, it is the most visible policy that addresses the broader issues of gender equality in employment.

The passage of the equal employment legislation occurred much later in Japan than in other countries and evolved from a combination of international and domestic pressures. While there are organized women's groups in Japan, they did not mobilize as early as those in the United States and Europe. Further, the Japanese government was slower to respond to their demands and established relevant women's political machinery much later. In contrast to the U.S. feminist movement, which had developed a well-honed strategy to promote equal opportunity legislation by the 1970s, in contrast, in Japan, the small feminist movement was relatively quiescent until its participation in the 1975 UN Decade for Women. Their participation in this event exposed them to international women's networks and new rhetorical frames and strategies, which in turn acted as a mobilizing force. In addition, the Decade for Women resulted in the establishment of women's political machinery in the Japanese bureaucracy, creating an access point through which women's advocates could lobby for change. Finally, in 1985, Japan ratified the UN Convention on the Elimination of All Forms of Discrimination Against Women (CEDAW), which requires the eradication of all legal, political, social, and cultural structures that prevent women from enjoying full equality with men. According to the provisions of the treaty, the Japanese government is legally obligated to aim for actual, not just formal, equality between men and women. This gave advocates of antidiscriminatory legislation a further weapon; given that government officials had committed themselves to enacting certain policies, activists could now pressure them to honor their commitments. Thus, in Japan, pressure for change came from international influences, which women's organizations exploited for further leverage.

Because of Japan's international obligations, the government was required to take positive action to achieve gender equality, and a coalition of progressive social scientists, sympathetic bureaucrats, and feminist organizations successfully lobbied for the passage of the EEOL in 1985, which prohibits discrimination in hiring and firing, promotion, and pension benefits. Further amendments passed in 1997 provided additional refinements to the law. In 2000, the government adopted the "Basic Plan for Gender Equality," and a Gender Equality Bureau was created within the Cabinet Office. As a result, while Japan has moved to remedy issues of discrimination, the EEOL does not address directly the specific issue of pay equity and the Gender Equality Bureau does not appear to have helped decrease the pay gap between men and women. Current research shows that women in Japan are the highest percentage of part-time workers (62 percent in 2009) and often earn as much as 30 percent less than their male counterparts.[30] In addition, women in Japan make up the majority of the working poor (13.39 percent women vs. 9.85 percent men).[31] In sum, the government's commitment to pay equity has been primarily symbolic in that it has expressed support for women's equality but has failed to give the legislation substantial "teeth" by supporting it with enforcement mechanisms.

The United States
In contrast, in the United States, women's organizations mobilized in the 1960s on the issue of equal pay. The government responded with a series of policy reforms, which initially served a symbolic function because government agencies were unwilling to enforce the legislation. However, increased pressure from women's movements helped encourage government agencies to enforce existing legislation, creating opportunities for women's progress.

Equal pay for women became a contentious issue in the United States in the early 1960s. Although there were a few government initiatives to address the issue of discrimination, equal pay legislation was not passed at the federal level until 1963, when President Kennedy signed into law the Equal Pay Act, which provides for equal pay for equal work. Although advocates of the bill, such as the Women's Bureau, had wanted the wording to be equal pay for work of comparable worth, they acquiesced to the present wording to get the bill passed. The act "provides that when an employer has men and women doing the same or substantially the same job (that is requiring the same or substantially the same skill, effort, and responsibility) at the same location and under similar working conditions, the employees must receive equal pay."[32] However, employers could still base pay differentials on factors such as seniority, merit, and measures related to the quantity and quality of the work. This continued to hurt women who often were segregated in low-prestige jobs, which continued to reinforce pay inequities between men and women.

Improvement upon the Equal Pay Act came the following year, with the passage of the Civil Rights Act of 1964. The initial intent of this act was to end discrimination based on race or religion. However, Representative Howard Smith (D-VA), an opponent of the law, proposed an amendment that he was sure would lead to the act's failure; he added sex to the list of groups protected by the legislation. Much to his chagrin, the amendment passed and so did the act. Thus women attained additional rights in an odd fashion. However, even some women's groups, including the President's Commission on the Status of Women, the Women's Bureau, and the American Association of University Women, also opposed the inclusion of sex in the wording of the act, fearing that protective legislation barring women from certain occupations would then be declared unconstitutional.

Title VII of the Civil Rights Act, among other things, prohibits discrimination on the basis of race, color, sex, religion, or national origin in determining wages. The act is in many ways stronger than the Equal Pay Act because of its enforcement measures. It created the Equal Employment Opportunity Commission (EEOC) to handle complaints, and those found violating its provisions could be subjected to judicially issued cease-and-desist orders.

However, the impact of the law in its initial decade was limited. First, coverage of legislation was not universal; it did not (and still does not) provide equal opportunity and nondiscrimination protections in pay and benefits for part-time workers.[33] Further, for many years, the EEOC did not respond to complaints. It ignored claims until the National Organization for Women (NOW) formed in the 1970s (in part, in reaction to this lack of enforcement) and actively pursued the enforcement of the Equal Pay Act and Title VII.

Women's groups have drawn on strategies used by the civil rights movement and have used the courts actively since the 1960s to advance their interests. One landmark Supreme Court decision, *Frontiero v. Richardson*, established the precedent that preferential treatment given to military men in pay and benefits was unconstitutional. In 1970, Sharon Cohen, then Lt. Sharon Frontiero, opened up her paycheck at Maxwell Air Force Base in Alabama to find that she had not received the expected increase in housing allowance or medical benefits for her new husband. At the time, federal law treated men and women in the military differently. It stipulated that male servicemen could receive an increase in pay for housing costs and health benefits for their wives; however, the same was not the case for women unless they could prove that their husband relied on them for more than half their support. In 1973, the Court ruled that such discrepancies were unconstitutional. While this case specifically pertained to the U.S. military, the decision has been used as precedent in cases arguing for equal pay and benefits for women in the private sector as well. In 2008, in a blow to women's ability to sue for pay discrimination, the Supreme Court ruled in *Ledbetter v. Goodyear* that employees have 180 days from the first act of pay discrimination to sue, not 180 days from the first discovery of pay discrimination. Lilly Ledbetter had been working for Goodyear for almost 20 years before she discovered that she had been discriminated against (see the text box entitled "Lilly Ledbetter"). As one journalist noted regarding this decision, "The Supreme Court's rulings strayed from years of precedent. And it now guarantees corporations the freedom to discriminate with impunity, while restricting access to the civil court system for many ordinary Americans who often have no other legal recourse."[34] However, in a historic move in 2009, the U.S. Congress passed the Lilly Ledbetter Fair Pay Act. This act amends the Civil Rights Act to allow employees 180 days to sue from the discovery of pay discrimination. President Obama signed the bill into law immediately. This bill is certainly a step in the right direction, but in itself it will not end pay discrimination. Pay discrimination lawsuits are costly and emotionally draining, so many employees who suspect pay discrimination will never seek recourse. And 2011–12 witnessed two further setbacks for women. The first occurred in June 2011, when the Supreme Court stopped a class-action lawsuit that female workers had brought against Wal-Mart alleging unequal pay and promotion. The women may pursue cases on their own, but individual cases, as noted above, are costly and draining. The second setback came in June 2012, when the Senate blocked a bill that built on the Lilly Ledbetter Fair Pay Act. The new bill would have made it easier for women to litigate cases regarding pay equity. What might be helpful is pay transparency. In public universities, government jobs, and much of the nonprofit world, salaries are public information. Transporting this transparency to the private sector would help alleviate some pay discrimination.

In sum, while U.S. government action on equal employment issues was initially symbolic, in that it professed support for equal pay, pressure from women's groups eventually led the state to enforce the laws more actively. Women's groups have pursued a predominantly gender-neutral strategy that assumes women and men experience the workforce in similar ways. Later on, we will discuss whether these efforts helped promote equal pay for equal work.

Lilly Ledbetter

In 1979 Lilly Ledbetter began working at the Alabama Goodyear Tire and Rubber Company. Immediately before her retirement in 1998 a colleague slipped an anonymous note into her mailbox. The note informed her that while she had been earning $3,727 a month, male colleagues doing the same job were earning anywhere from $4,286 to $5,236 per month. Ledbetter filed a complaint with the Equal Employment Opportunity Commission (she had filed earlier complaints with them regarding sexual harassment in the workplace and her supervisor had been reassigned) soon after she found out about the pay discrepancies. Ledbetter also sued Goodyear for pay discrimination. Goodyear countered that she was not a good worker, despite her Top Performance Award in 1996. Ledbetter was awarded $3.3 million by a jury, but that amount was later reduced to approximately $300,000. Ledbetter appealed her case to the Supreme Court, who heard it in 2007. The Supreme Court, in a 5–4 decision, ruled against Ledbetter. They argued that anyone filing for pay discrimination had to file his or her complaint within 180 days of his or her *first* paycheck. The Supreme Court decision created quite a public outcry from women's groups and other citizens because the decision effectively meant that any employee, male or female, would have to know of discrimination within 6 months of a new job. Such knowledge is rare: most employees of private companies are told not to discuss their pay with colleagues, so discovering pay discrimination is difficult to impossible and often emerges only from anonymous tips like the one Ledbetter received. Soon after the Supreme Court decision, the U.S. House of Representatives passed the Lilly Ledbetter Fair Pay Act. This act changes the Civil Rights Act so that employees can sue employers for pay discrimination within 180 days of receiving *any* discriminatory paycheck. The bill was filibustered in the Senate, however, and eventually died. In 2009, the bill was reintroduced and passed the House on January 9 and the Senate on January 22. Soon thereafter President Obama signed the bill into law; it was the first piece of legislation he signed as president.

The European Union

The EU integrated equal employment concerns into its early treaties and has continued to support increased gender equality at all levels with its current policy of gender main streaming, which involves the integration of equal opportunity rules into other areas of policymaking. In addition, various branches of the EU, such as the European Commission, the European Parliament, and the European Court of Justice, have been responsive to women's mobilization at the national and supranational levels. Yet, many individual member countries were slow to respond with legislation, although they increasingly have recognized, primarily through rhetorical support, the importance of equal rights for women. Nonetheless, as noted earlier, EU law is supreme over national law and the European Court of Justice has issued a number of rulings on gender equality.

Article 119 in the Treaty of Rome (1957), the founding treaty of the European Community (which became the EU in 1993), provides that women and men should receive equal pay for equal work. In the treaty's words, "Equal pay without discrimination based on sex means: (a) that pay for the same work at piece rates shall be calculated on the basis of the same unit of measurement; (b) that pay for work at time rates shall be the same for the same job."[35] This clause was inserted largely because of French pressure: France had already passed equal pay legislation and wanted to ensure that other member states were required to adhere to a similar standard. However, the initial commitment of member states to equal pay was lukewarm; according to the European Parliament, they showed "little enthusiasm for implementing this provision."[36] Thus, Article 119 was essentially symbolic; it existed on paper but was not implemented in practice.

However, beginning in 1975 a number of directives were adopted in an attempt to force the issue. A directive is a legally binding joint decision made by the Council of the EU or the Parliament that sets common objectives for member countries. Failure to comply with appropriate legislation or regulations can result in sanctions placed by the European Court of Justice. In 1975, the European Council passed Equal Pay Directive 75/117, which broadened the definition of *pay* and *equal work*. Specifically, the Council clarified that equal work did not have to mean the same work, but rather "work to which equal value is attributed." By including "equal value" in the wording, the Council was prohibiting indirect discrimination, such as prejudicial job classification schemes. Further, the directive ordered member states to pass necessary legislation to implement the principle of equal pay for equal work or value and directed states to report on their application of the directive. However, the directive did not define what was meant by "work of equal value," thus limiting the impact of the potential policy.[37] The European Parliament has also issued resolutions backing various commission communications on eradicating pay inequalities.[38]

Further, the EU has taken action on other factors that indirectly address equal pay. Further directives issued in the 1970s broadened the principle of equal treatment for men and women.[39] In the 1980s and 1990s, frustrated with the slow pace of reform, the European Commission, the EU's bureaucratic arm, issued four Action Programmes to foster equal opportunity for women in the workforce, which, although not binding, placed pressure on member countries to act more proactively in advancing equal employment policies.[40] And as we shall discuss in greater detail in the following section, in 1999, the Treaty of Amsterdam inserted into the EU treaty the principles of equality and nondiscrimination based on sex or sexual orientation. Finally, the EU Social Charter now guarantees equal rights to part-time workers, and the European Court of Justice has ruled that "unfair treatment of part-time workers can constitute indirect sex-discrimination against women."[41] While these policies do not directly discuss equal pay, they do address issues of discrimination, which often lead to inequality in salaries. In 2006, the EU came out with the "Roadmap for equality between women and men" (2006–2010). In this roadmap the EU outlined six priority areas covering such topics as equal economic independence for women and men and the reconciliation of private and professional life. The goal of the roadmap was to modernize existing EU gender equity legislation. Building on this roadmap, the Council of the EU adopted the European Pact for Gender Equality for the period 2011 to 2020. This pact seeks to encourage member states to adopt policies to close gender gaps in employment and pay, among other areas. Finally, in 2010, the European Commission adopted the Women's Charter. In this Charter, the Commission outlined five priority areas, such as equal pay for equal work and equal economic independence. In this charter the Commission committed itself to working with member states to explore ways to achieve gender equality in these priority areas. Continued pressure from varied offices of women's policy machinery within the EU, such as the Committee on Women's Rights and Gender Equality of the European Parliament and the Equality for Women and Men unit of the European Commission, keeps women's issues on the EU agenda. However, while women's groups are able to access the EU policy machinery by participating in hearings, writing policy briefs, and so forth, it has been harder to translate advocacy into policy gains at the national level. And while the Council of the EU and the European Commission have issued roadmaps and pacts committing the EU to gender equality, there is only so much the EU can do, as ultimately each state in the EU is sovereign. We see that the issue of equal pay in the EU and its member states has received a great deal of legislative attention over the past 30 years, though enthusiasm from the member states is sometimes lacking.

Impact

How has all of this legislation affected women? Given the vast increase in women's activism, government policy, and corporate efforts to remedy women's often second-class status in the workforce, one might think that the pay gap between men and women is a relic of the past. However, the data indicate otherwise. In no advanced industrial nation do women earn the same as men, even for work in similar or identical occupations.

Equal pay legislation has not been able single-handedly to close the pay gap between men's and women's salaries. This is particularly true in Japan, where working women still earn only 70.6 percent of the average man's pay.[42] In the United States, according to research done by the General Accounting Office, in 1979 female full-time wage and salary workers earned only 63 percent of their male counterparts' pay; by 2000 this gap had decreased to 76 percent.[43] And in 2010 in the United States, women still earned 23 percent less than their male counterparts, according to a report by the American Association of University Women.[44] Finally, in the EU, men still earn 17 percent more than women.[45] These figures, however, mask large differences between employment patterns in the private and public sectors; while women earned 89 percent of men's salaries in the public sector, the pay differential was 78 percent in the private sector.[46]

Some might argue that the pay gap does not mean that women do not have pay equity. They note that the figures used to measure pay inequalities are averages across all work categories and do not take into account important intervening variables, such as years of employment and experience. Yet, even when age, educational background, and years worked are taken into account, there is still a disparity between men and women. A recent report by the American Association of University Women found that even when accounting for "college major, occupation, industry, sector, hours worked, workplace flexibility, experience, educational attainment, enrollment status, GPA, institution, selectivity, age, race/ethnicity, region, marital status, and number of children," the pay gap persists.[47] They found that the difference in earnings between men and woman was 5 percent 1 year after graduation and 12 percent 10 years after graduation.[48] This may sound small, but over time this means that "the lifetime wage gap for a woman who did not finish high school is $300,000, while the lifetime wage gap for a woman with at least a bachelor's degree is $723,000."[49] Across the OECD countries the gap between men and women in identical jobs is 18 percent, which is an improvement from 40 years ago, but the gap has stopped narrowing in recent years.[50] The 2003 study of EU member nations echoed these findings: even in identical occupations, women made less than their male counterparts, even controlling for years of employment and experience.[51] And a 2007 survey in Great Britain of 42,000 managers found that the gap between male and female managers had widened to 12.2 percent from 11.8 percent in 2005 and from 20 percent to 23 percent among directors.[52] Thus, the pay gap between men and women, while diminishing, is still significant, despite legislative efforts to correct for it. While it is impossible to determine the degree to which antidiscrimination legislation has helped close this gap, nonetheless, it has helped change some of the more obvious prejudicial employment policies against women.

Part of the problem lies in the fact that the persistence of the gender pay gap also can be attributed to indirect discrimination. An EU study linked the pay gap to the pervasive problem of gender segregation in the workforce, women's concentration in low-paying sectors and occupations, and the added responsibilities that women shoulder in childbearing and childrearing.[53] And an article in the *Japan Times* argues that "seniority systems at most companies, especially large-scale ones, ensure that men are promoted more often than and receive extra allowances for dependents and housing. These fringe benefits, including higher bonuses, are often significantly less for women."[54] Further, women working part-time suffer even greater pay discrimination. As discussed earlier, women make up a majority of part-time workers in Japan, the United States, and Europe and often are not paid as well as their full-time female or male colleagues are. Can broader policies that address equality in hiring, promotion, and firing address some of these deeper problems that lead to women's unequal status in the labor market?

Equality in Hiring, Promotion, and Firing

For decades, women have been "the last hired and the first fired." Deemed "the weaker sex," women were "protected" from certain occupations because of supposed limitations on their physical capabilities or because the job could potentially interfere with their reproductive health. In fact, it was only recently that Belgium repealed nineteenth-century restrictions on women working at night.[55] Such protective legislation kept women from being hired for many jobs and from advancing if hired. Further, many women remained unhired or were fired after announcing their pregnancies; they were perceived as a threat to profits, and employers assumed that they would "naturally" choose to leave the workforce to devote themselves to motherhood. And while most protective legislation such as this no longer exists, certain barriers still keep women from being hired and promoted. Even when women embark on a career path, they rarely advance far. A glass ceiling still keeps women from achieving the highest positions, with the accompanying prestige, power, and pay. States have responded with legislation that bars employers from discriminating against women. Further, some have more proactively implemented affirmative action policies to promote women's advancement. We now turn to our three case studies: How has each designed policies to combat discrimination, and what has been the impact of these policies?

Japan

As we discussed in the previous section, the UN Convention to End Discrimination Against Women created the international pressure that prompted the Japanese Diet to pass the EEOL in 1985. For the first time, Japanese law prohibited discrimination in termination of employment and encouraged equal treatment in recruitment, hiring, job assignment, and promotion. However, the law, as originally written, was essentially toothless; there were no sanctions for employers who refused to comply.[56] The law "only required that employers 'endeavor' to treat men and women the same in terms of hiring and promotion."[57] Nor were courts given the power to mediate by issuing orders to cease and desist or award punitive damages. And the law did not establish an administrative agency, such as the U.S. EEOC, to enforce compliance. Rather, the Ministry of Labor's Women's Bureau was charged with establishing "administrative guidelines" and "ministerial ordinances" to clarify the legislation. Finally, the legislation established a cumbersome, three-step system of mediation (as opposed to litigation) to attempt to resolve disputes. The final third step involved the Equal Opportunity Mediation Commission (EOMC), which would handle the dispute only if one party requested mediation and both parties agreed to it. Yet, at most, mediation bodies could provide only advice, guidance, and recommendations, rather than legal resolution. The law was further amended in 1997 to, among other things, simplify the mediation process and provide for the publication of the names of companies violating the EEOL provisions and the nature of the violation. Nonetheless, 23 years later, the law still lacks significant enforcement mechanisms.[58] In addition to the EEOL, the Japanese Diet passed amendments to the Labor Standards Law, which abolished various protective measures for women related to overtime, late night, and hazardous work.[59] Thus, while the government has become more proactive in making symbolic efforts to advance women's equality, the lack of enforcement mechanisms severely weakens the impact of the law.

The United States

In the United States, until legislation deemed otherwise, employers were permitted to refuse to hire women in a variety of positions, many of them the higher-paying, managerial ones. It was not uncommon for newspaper advertisements to specify "men only." Women were often paid less than men even for identical work.[60] The United States began addressing the issue of equality in hiring, firing, and promotion with Title VII of the Civil Rights Act of 1964 as amended in 1972. Title VII states that discrimination on the basis of race, color, religion, sex, or national origin is unlawful in hiring or firing; determining wages (as discussed previously); providing fringe benefits; classifying, referring, assigning, or promoting employees; and more. Most lawsuits concerning discrimination are brought under the auspices of this act. In 1978, the act was further amended; the Pregnancy

Discrimination Act declared that classifications based on pregnancy and pregnancy-related disabilities fell within the meaning of "sex" under Title VII.

However, the language of Title VII was open for interpretation. While the law banned discrimination of the basis of an individual's race, color, religion, sex, or national origin, it also specified an important exception, known as the Bona Fide Occupational Qualification (BFOQ), which allowed employers to take factors such as sex into account where it was deemed "a bona fide occupational qualification reasonably necessary to the normal operation of that particular business enterprise."[61] This clause often pulled the courts into the debate, for the wording is open to interpretation. For example, in 1977, the Supreme Court ruled in *Dothard v. Rawlinson* that an Alabama state penitentiary could refuse to hire women as prison guards because, they maintained, women might not be able to maintain order as effectively as men because women were at risk of assault from inmates "deprived of a normal heterosexual environment."[62] On the other hand, the courts have also found that other employers' policies did not meet BFOQ guidelines and were thus discriminatory. For example, the courts have repeatedly found that employers cannot bar women from holding positions that required lifting more than a certain weight. In addition, men have successfully used the BFOQ clause to take on airlines that pursued a policy of hiring only female flight attendants. The BFOQ clause has been important because courts have often ruled against companies' discriminatory policies under the rationale that limits are often based on stereotypes of women's (and men's) abilities, rather than on factual evidence.

Further, a series of executive orders addressing equality in hiring, firing, and promotion became quite controversial because they sought not only to bar discrimination but to also remedy past inequalities by taking proactive measures to increase women and minority representation. Executive Order 11246 prohibited discrimination regarding race in hiring, firing, and promotion by contractors and subcontractors with federal or federally funded contracts (this encompasses a massive number of businesses and places of higher learning). This executive order was amended in 1967 by Executive Order 11375 to include sex. These executive orders are often referred to as affirmative action because of the wording of Executive Order 11375, part of which states that "The contractor will take affirmative action to ensure that employees are employed and are treated during employment, without regard to their race, color, religion, sex or national origin."[63] Many people have come to see affirmative action as preferential treatment for women at the expense of men and have been able to frame the policy of affirmative action as one of reverse discrimination. In their interpretation, businesses and places of higher learning use quotas to ensure the promotion of minorities and women, despite their supposedly inferior qualifications. The Supreme Court has ruled repeatedly (most recently in the summer of 2003 in a lawsuit against the University of Michigan) that quotas are unconstitutional but that race and sex can be taken into account in hiring and admittance decisions. However, in February 2012 the Supreme Court announced it would take up the issue again and should hear the case in late October or early November 2012. The decision by the Court to take up the issue again so soon has some supporters of affirmative action concerned that this may be its death knell.

A final piece of legislation that might have assisted women in the United States with their claims of equality was the Equal Rights Amendment (ERA). The text of the ERA is as follows: "Equality of rights under the law shall not be denied or abridged by the United States or by any state on account of sex. The Congress shall have the power to enforce, by appropriate legislation, the provisions of this article. This amendment shall take effect two years after the date of ratification."[64] Depending on the design of resulting policy, and the government's willingness to enforce these policies, the ERA potentially also could have been used as an equalizing force in employment. In fact, the ERA passed Congress in 1972 and was sent to the states in search of ratification by three fourths of the states. However, by 1982 the ERA failed to attain ratification by the requisite number of states and thus did not become an amendment to the U.S. Constitution. Thus, in the United States, litigation has been a successful method of punishing some discriminatory hiring practices; however, more proactive policies, such as affirmative action and constitutional amendments, have been much more controversial.

The European Union

The EU, as previously discussed, has attempted to integrate equal employment policy into its laws and treaties from its inception. However, the member states have not been too eager to follow its lead. Throughout the 1970s, the European Community continued to issue directives related to equal opportunity employment issues. As we mentioned in the previous section, a 1976 directive broadened the principle of equal employment for men and women to cover the issues of equal access to employment, which included promotion, as well as job training, and barred discrimination on grounds of sex, particularly with regard to marital and family status.[65] Further, the directive allowed for positive action measures (which in the United States are known as affirmative action policies) to address gender inequalities in the labor force. However, the directive did not contain clear implementation directions for member states, which weakened its force. In addition, the affirmative action measures were only recommendations and thus were not binding on member nations.

The 1997 Amsterdam Treaty (which took effect on May 1, 1999) extended the EU's abilities to take action to foster gender equality beyond the issue of equal pay for equal work. The treaty's broader purpose was to update and clarify the conditions of the Maastricht Treaty (which created the EU), prepare for EU enlargement, and clarify the powers of the European Parliament and the Council of Ministers on a range of issues, including social policy.[66] In terms of fostering gender equality, Article 13 empowered the Council of Ministers, the executive branch of the EU, to take "appropriate action" to combat discrimination based on sex, racial or ethnic origin, religion or belief, disability, age, or sexual orientation. The Council of Ministers and, to some extent, the European Parliament are vested with the power to design and adopt legislation that goes beyond ensuring equal pay, but also encompasses equal treatment and equal opportunities.[67]

In addition, the European Court of Justice, the judicial branch of the EU, has grown more proactive in enforcing the directives and advancing women's equality through its decisions in important cases. Initially, the Court was relatively conservative in its approach, issuing two judgments that in essence ruled that affirmative action hiring policies, such as quotas, were contrary to European equal opportunities legislation.[68] However, in the wake of the Amsterdam Treaty, and its expanded definition of gender equality, the court has pursued a more proactive strategy and has recognized that member states can take action to improve women's ability to compete in the labor market so that women with the same qualifications as men can receive preference for promotion in areas in which they are underrepresented.

Thus, equality in hiring, firing, and promotion is protected in various EU treaties, directives, and decisions of the European Court of Justice. Yet, because of the relative youth of the EU, continuously evolving policies, and changes in leadership style of the European Commission, it is important not to overemphasize the presence of directives, legislation, and court rulings. Certainly, directives oblige all member states to adopt or amend existing legislation to ensure compliance with EU rules. And the rhetorical leadership of the EU on various equal employment policies sets an important example to member nations and can provide further pressure on member countries to implement national-level legislation to meet EU standards. This can also encourage women's organizations at the national level to lobby their governments for prompt legislative initiative, as well as the formation of transnational networks of women's activists. For example, the founding of the European Women's Lobby in 1990 was in response to support from the European Commission and the Committee on Women's Rights of the European Parliament.[69] However, implementation of policy at the national level will be the key challenge.

Impact

What has been the impact of all of this legislation on women? In Japan, despite the EEOL, women still lag behind men in promotions and hiring. While in 1985 women held just 6.6 percent of all management jobs in Japanese companies, that number had risen to less than 10 percent by 2011, even though women make up nearly half of Japan's workforce.[70] This is in part because of holes in the legislation. For example, the law fails to guard against indirect discrimination. Many companies initially responded to the EEOL by establishing a dual career-track system for men and women, with men hired in managerial track positions and women relegated to clerical positions. While managerial positions involve complex judgment, involuntary transfers, and unlimited access to promotion, the clerical track, although often full-time, involves less time and commitment and thus fewer opportunities for advancement.[71] Given that many Japanese companies operate on an informal policy of "lifelong employment," which offers high job security, demands high worker commitment, and involves extensive worker training, this dual model often places women in a long-term disadvantageous position from which they are unable to extricate themselves.[72] Further, the lack of strong enforcement measures limits the impact of the EEOL. The Equal Opportunity Mediation Commission can only recommend and encourage parties to resolve their differences, but businesses are under no legal obligation to follow the advice of the commission. In addition, the worst the Ministry of Labor can do is publish names of violators, which it has never done.[73] Instead, it has taken a cautious route and has attempted to appeal to employers' goodwill in complying with the law rather than fighting for greater enforcement mechanisms.[74]

This has not stopped a few women from attempting to fight for more equitable working conditions. Indirectly, the passage of the EEOL, which heightened women's awareness of discrimination issues, led a few to pursue litigation through other means, such as Article 14 of the Constitution, which provides for equality between the sexes, or Article 4 of the Labor Standards Act, which prohibits gender-based discrimination at work.[75] In 1995, four women who worked at Sumitomo Metal Industries Ltd. filed a lawsuit claiming that the company uses a sexually discriminatory employment system that in practice kept women's wages much lower than men's in similar jobs with similar qualifications.[76] Nine and a half years later, the Osaka District Court ruled in their favor and ordered the company to pay compensation. Sumitomo appealed the ruling but ultimately reached a settlement with the government.[77] The increased use of lawsuits, even if not under the auspices of the EEOL, points to the greater consciousness surrounding issues of employment.

However, women are still blocked by a very thick glass ceiling. As noted above, less than 10 percent of senior management positions in Japan are held by women. And the Japanese government's White Paper on Equal Gender Participation found that 67.7 percent of Japanese women believe that men are given preferential treatment at work.[78] Women's underrepresentation, in part, can be attributed to pervasive cultural attitudes about women and work: women seeking jobs in Japan are described by employers as "too ambitious" and/or "uncooperative" and "too proud to listen to their colleagues' advice."[79] This is coupled with the persistent social belief that "women should be the primary caregivers for children and sick or elderly family members."[80] Given these impediments, women will need more than symbolic policy to change their unequal position in the labor market in Japan.

In the United States, while Title VII and affirmative action policies both have aided women in their quest for equality in hiring, firing, and promotion, their impact is limited. Women slowly are increasing their numbers among the top employees of companies and among chief executive officers. Since 1992, the number of female CEOs of large nonprofit organizations has increased significantly.[81] And women have clearly increased their numbers among the middle to upper ranks of companies. However, as of June 2012, only 19 Fortune 500 companies had female chief executive officers or presidents, an increase from the past few years, but still a paucity.[82] And a survey conducted by the General Accountability Office found that "women who are full time managers are paid less and advance less often than male managers."[83]

The state of hiring and promotion practices in the EU is also quite poor. In the EU member states, according to the European Parliament, women are still found in the basic career grades and "women eligible for promotion are less likely than men to actually get promoted."[84] The UN reports that in 14 of 27 EU countries there is "no woman CEO in the top 50 publicly quoted companies."[85] Further, according to the European Trade Union Confederation, women remain sequestered in a narrow range of occupations (one in six women works in health and social services) and primarily at the bottom of the ladder.[86] As the EU noted of its own performance, "despite all the efforts of the past decades, complete equality of opportunity has not yet been achieved. . . . In other words, there is still work to be done in the EU to implement equal opportunities in practice."[87] One step that has been taken is quotas. Increasingly, European government are adopting quotas for the number of women required to be in boardrooms. Countries that have adopted quotas, to date, include Norway, France, Spain, the Netherlands, Iceland, Italy, and Belgium. In France, the number of board seats held by women increased from 7.2 percent in 2004 to 20.1 percent in 2011.[88]

Further, as the EU expands to encompass candidate countries in eastern Europe, its abilities to enforce its rulings will be tested to the limit, as these countries will have to bring their equal opportunity legislation (which is often nonexistent) into line with European standards. Discrimination in hiring is still blatant in eastern Europe, even though some of these nations have recently been admitted to the EU. Employment advertisements, for instance, still ask for such things as "attractive female receptionist" or "girl under 25," and sometimes women must promise not to get pregnant for 5 years.[89] For those nations that have recently been admitted to the EU, these practices will need to end because EU legislation prohibits them.

However, EU policy has affected some countries' domestic policies on equal employment dramatically, which probably could not have changed in the absence of EU pressure. For example, the EU did have an impact on Irish women's equal access to employment. As Julia O'Connor found,

> The Community has brought about changes in employment practices which might otherwise have taken decades to achieve. Irish women have the Community to thank for the removal of the marriage bar in employment, the introduction of maternity leave, greater opportunities to train at a skilled trade, protection against dismissal upon pregnancy, the disappearance of advertisements specifying the sex of an applicant for a job and greater equality in the social welfare code.[90]

In this example, the presence of EU directives pushed an individual member country to change its policies to align with European standards.

Sexual Harassment

A third crucial issue for women in the workplace is that of sexual harassment. Sexual harassment is not a new problem; however, it was not seen as an issue for many years because of women's limited participation in the workforce. Further, for many years, it was treated as an unpleasant working condition to be tolerated. However, beginning in the 1960s and 1970s, women's movements raised the consciousness of many women, and many began to question patriarchy and its attendant trappings. By the 1980s women began to believe that sexual harassment was not something they had to accept and slowly began to work toward changing laws as well as attitudes. Men are certainly subject to sexual harassment as well; however, since it predominantly affects women, women will be our focus here.

Before delving into the topic of sexual harassment it would be helpful to have a working definition of it. What is sexual harassment? One definition, used by the U.S. Equal Employment Opportunity Commission, states that sexual harassment includes

> unwelcome sexual advances, requests for sexual favors, and other verbal or physical conduct of a sexual nature when submission to or rejection of this conduct explicitly or implicitly affects an individual's employment, unreasonably interferes with an individual's work performance, or creates an intimidating, hostile, or offensive work environment.[91]

One problem with sexual harassment has been deciding what actions constitute it. This definition helps but still leaves some people confused. Do dirty jokes told around the water cooler at the workplace constitute sexual harassment? What about statements made regarding one's appearance? The story at the beginning of the chapter about the employee who was called a "hotty totty" by her employer appears today to be a fairly straightforward example of harassment, but other examples are not so clear-cut. However, we adopt the preceding definition because it offers a fairly comprehensive definition that can guide the discussion of this issue.

Another complication is that harassment can be hard to prove, since it often happens in the privacy of someone's office, rather than in public, in front of witnesses. This can make it difficult for women to come forward, as illustrated by the Anita Hill and Clarence Thomas hearings. In 1991 Clarence Thomas was nominated to the U.S. Supreme Court. During the confirmation process allegations arose by his former aide, attorney Anita Hill, that Thomas had sexually harassed her when they worked together at the Department of Education and later at the Equal Employment Opportunity Commission during the early 1980s. Hill underwent grueling cross-examination by the Senate Judiciary Committee, which was made up of all men (see photo 4.1). They queried her as to why it took so long for her to say something about this harassment and whether she had invented the incidents. Ultimately, the Judiciary Committee confirmed Thomas. The topic of sexual harassment stayed in the public's mind when Paula Jones charged that President Clinton had sexually harassed her when he was governor of Arkansas.

And, as the story at the beginning of the chapter illustrates, the problem is certainly not confined to the United States. What laws have been passed to assist women in their quest to end this form of discrimination, and what has been their impact?

Japan

The concept of sexual harassment is still relatively new to Japanese workers and the EEOL, as it was originally written, said nothing specifically about sexual harassment. But U.S. attention to the matter in the late 1980s brought the issue more attention in Japan. Interestingly, the Japanese language does not even have a word for sexual harassment—the word used, *seku-hara,* has been derived from the

Anita Hill testifies before the Senate Judiciary Committee on charges that she was sexually harassed by her former boss, Clarence Thomas, while working for him at the Equal Employment Opportunity Commission. Thomas, at the time a nominee for the Supreme Court, was ultimately confirmed to the Court in a contentious 52–48 vote by the U.S. Senate.
SOURCE: AP Photo.

English term. The term first emerged in Japan in 1989 when the media was covering Japan's first hostile work environment sexual harassment case, the Fukuoka case.[92] The Fukuoka District Court found in favor of the employee and fined the harasser and the company (approximately $15,700 in U.S. dollars).[93] Other early cases also brought attention to the matter in Japan, and by 2000, 100 cases had been filed and 10 heard by the highest court in Japan.[94] While the EEOL says nothing specific about sexual harassment, the 1997 amendments to the EEOL make employers responsible for the prevention of sexual harassment. Yet, as we discussed previously, the amendments (and the original law) lack significant punitive measures to enforce compliance. The Ministry of Labor can publicize the names of companies that violate the conditions of the EEOL.[95] In addition, women can use the cumbersome mediation process specified in the EEOL. Thus, as in other areas, the policies are primarily symbolic and lack "teeth" that could enforce new standards of equal employment. Instead, the policies rely on the Ministry's abilities to cajole good behavior out of companies. That said, women do file cases, and in 2008, 8,140 women had brought claims of harassment, a drastic increase from the 100 claims brought in 2000.[96]

The United States
In the United States, sexual harassment is considered to be a form of gender discrimination that is covered under Title VII of the Civil Rights Act of 1964 as well

as under Title IX of the Education Act of 1972. According to the EEOC, sexual harassment includes instances of quid pro quo (e.g., requiring the provision of sexual favors as a term or condition of one's employment) as well as the creation of a hostile working environment. As in many countries, it is often difficult to prove harassment; in the United States, the plaintiff must show that

> (1) she was subjected to unwelcome sexual conduct; (2) these were based on her sex; (3) they were sufficiently pervasive or severe to create an abusive or hostile work environment; and (4) the employer knew or should have known of the harassment and failed to take prompt and appropriate remedial action.[97]

The courts have used a "reasonableness" standard to determine what defines an unwelcome sexual advance and a hostile work environment. That is, under similar circumstances, would a "reasonable person" have identified the behavior as unwelcome? As one can imagine, this does allow for a wide degree of latitude in terms of what constitutes "reasonable." However, the federal courts in the United States have made it clear that companies are financially liable for the actions of their employees. As a result, many employers conduct extensive training and educational outreach with their employees in hopes of halting the problem. Much of this is because of the efforts of the women's movement; NOW and other women's groups litigated and lobbied extensively in the 1970s (and beyond) and as a result were successful in expanding the interpretation of Title VII. Thus, the U.S. system of litigation, the state's willingness to enforce the law, and active women's mobilization have forced many companies and institutions to take the issue of sexual harassment seriously.

The European Union

European countries have been much slower in addressing sexual harassment. However, studies conducted in the 1980s in individual member countries indicated that the problem was severe, and another report published in 1988 revealed that no member state had an express legal prohibition against sexual harassment. In fact, in only two countries—the United Kingdom and Ireland—did courts accept the argument that sexual harassment constituted discrimination. However, the European Commission was divided on whether they needed to issue a directive, which would be legally binding on member states, to address the issue. Some members argued that the 1976 directive on equal treatment, which banned sex discrimination, could be used to sanction harassment. Finally, in 1991, the Commission adopted a recommendation (which is not legally binding) on the protection of the dignity of women and men at work and added it to a code of practice on measures to combat harassment. In essence, the commission urged member states to take the matter of sexual harassment seriously, without providing the clarity or enforcement mechanisms that could have made it an effective Europe-wide policy tool. As a result, while member states responded with various legislative acts addressing harassment, the acts are often weak or unclear or put an undue burden on the woman to prove her case.[98] Thus, while initial efforts heightened awareness of sexual harassment as a problem and led to initial legislation to address the issue, nonetheless most national-level policies lack strong sanctions against offenders.

The EU raised the issue again when it amended the 1976 directive on equal treatment in 2002. Currently, "binding legislation defines sexual harassment and outlaws it as a form of discrimination based on sex. It bans any form of unwanted sexual behavior that creates an intimidating or degrading environment and also urges employers to take preventive action against all forms of discrimination and to compile regular equality reports for staff."[99] Under the conditions of the amended directive, when an employee files a sexual harassment claim with an employer, that employer is required to prove that it has done all it could to prevent sexual harassment. Further, employers are financially liable when sexual harassment allegations have been shown to be true. Finally, the directive gives courts a freer hand when awarding financial compensation to victims of sexual harassment. Member states had until 2005 to comply. France was one of the first to comply and did so by making sexual harassment a criminal offense, the only nation in the world to do so. However, not all women's equality advocates support this move. Some argue that the criminalization of sexual harassment in France will make it harder for women to bring charges. They argue that a civil law approach, where one uses a lawsuit to threaten a firm, is more successful in getting firms to take the issue seriously. Finally, women in France whose sexual harassment charges against men fail can be hit with a defamation lawsuit by the men and then forced to pay damages.

Impact

What has been the impact of these laws on women's lives? In Japan it appears that sexual harassment is still widespread. A 1997 survey by the Ministry of Labor reported that "62 percent of women claimed to have experienced at least one act of sexual harassment."[100] On a positive note, another survey indicates that some of the more extreme forms of sexual harassment may be on the wane in government workplaces. Female government workers reported a decline in their bosses pressuring them to have a sexual relationship—from 17 percent in 1997 to 2.2 percent by 2000.[101] And, as noted earlier, there has been a large increase in the number of women reporting sexual harassment in the workplace since the EEOL revisions went into effect in 1999.[102] Further, as in other areas of equal employment policy, women's disenchantment with the EEOL's mediation process has led women to use other antidiscrimination legislation to press sexual harassment suits. From 1989 to 1997, women brought forward 58 lawsuits related to sexual harassment charges. Thus, the weakness of the EEOL in many ways spurred women on to exploit alternative venues of leverage. While fewer women are coming forward than in, say, the United States, nonetheless it marks a very small but significant cultural shift in the acceptability of harassment on the job. Consciousness of sexual harassment as unacceptable is growing in Japan, and this emerging consciousness is crucial to its eradication.

In the United States the number of sexual harassment claims to the EEOC more than doubled between 1990 and 1996, from about 6,000 to 15,000.[103] While this may be because of the existence of laws allowing women to sue their employers, it also may be, in part, because of the media attention paid to the topic in the 1990s. The Clarence Thomas confirmation hearings were televised, and the allegations by Paula Jones against President Clinton received a great deal of media attention. Some speculate that after these nationally televised events regarding sexual harassment, the number of cases brought to the EEOC increased dramatically.

The EEOC has also been willing to enforce legislation criminalizing harassment and has charged a number of large corporations with sexual harassment. One of the largest suits it brought was against the Mitsubishi Corporation, alleging sexual harassment against more than 350 women. The suit was settled in June 1998 and Mitsubishi was ordered to pay the plaintiffs over $34 million, end sexual harassment in the workplace, and make sure that no retaliation against these women occurred. A team of monitors was established to ensure that Mitsubishi complied. The EEOC has also successfully led a case against the largest lettuce grower in the United States on behalf of female migrant workers who alleged they had been sexually harassed. The company, while not admitting to any wrongdoing, agreed to pay $1.85 million, fire one manager, reprimand another, and train and monitor all other supervisors and employees. This is an important victory because migrant women have few resources to battle sexual harassment. They often do not know the law, fear losing their jobs, and lack the language fluency to act on harassment. The deck is stacked against them even more so than it is for middle-class women.

The number of sexual harassment cases heard in U.S. federal courts had been increasing until recently, when numbers dropped significantly (according to the EEOC, 11,364 cases were brought in 2011, down from about 15,000 in the mid-2000s). The cause of this drop is unclear, though various pundits allege that this may be due to the economic downturn—no one wants to risk losing his or her job in a poor economy. The Supreme Court has handed down numerous rulings on the topic beginning in the mid-1980s. The first rulings dealt with what behaviors constituted unlawful sexual harassment. More recently, the Court has begun handing down decisions regarding legal responsibility for sexual harassment. In one of the first cases addressing sexual harassment, *Meritor Savings Bank v. Vinson* (1986), the Supreme Court recognized as unlawful both types of sexual harassment defined in the EEOC guidelines. This decision and others, as well as the fact that the Supreme Court is hearing sexual harassment cases, are significant indicators that the courts take the issue of harassment seriously. The Supreme Court can pick and choose which cases it hears, and if it is choosing to hear sexual harassment cases and upholding EEOC guidelines, then this indicates that it views such cases as involving important legal questions, thus granting legitimacy to women's claims.

While sexual harassment persists in the United States, some improvements have occurred. Women are stepping forward to charge their employers with sexual harassment, the EEOC is successfully waging battles against these employers, the Supreme Court has upheld the EEOC guidelines and handed down decisions that assist women alleging sexual harassment, and companies are creating their own guidelines and holding training sessions to educate their employees on the topic. However, sexual harassment does persist, as the recent highly publicized downfalls of Hewlett Packard CEO Mark Hurd (he allegedly touched, propositioned, and pressed a contract employee to spend the night with him) and Republican presidential candidate Herman Cain (he allegedly made inappropriate comments to female employees), demonstrate. The laws and the legal decisions have assisted women and scared corporations who do not wish to suffer large monetary losses because of the behavior of some of their employees. It will very likely take time and more education to further decrease the incidence of sexual harassment.

The EU only recently has devoted concerted attention to policy pertaining to sexual harassment, and, as a result, policies still differ significantly at the national level. And sexual harassment is rampant in Europe. One survey indicates that up to 50 percent of European women have experienced some type of sexual harassment (ranging from sexual remarks to assault or rape).[104] However, national estimates vary widely, from 11 percent in Denmark to 54 percent in the United Kingdom to 81 percent in Austria.[105] This discrepancy is largely because of a lack of an agreed-upon idea of what constitutes sexual harassment. In some of the southern European countries women feel sexual harassment is an unfortunate but enduring part of the work environment that must be tolerated. Further, many men do not see their behavior as inappropriate. This is different than in northern Europe, where sexual harassment is recognized more widely and is not condoned by women (or men). So, sexual harassment persists throughout Europe, although in varying degrees from country to country. The attitude of the country and the legal recourse available have influenced whether or not women have filed suit against harassers and how successful these suits have been. The stories at the beginning of this chapter indicate that women in Europe are bringing suit against their employers for sexual harassment and winning. The EU directive discussed earlier adopts a common definition, which should assist women in identifying what it is and in bringing suit against employers. A common EU policy, accompanied by a public relations campaign designed to educate the populace about the policy, should further assist women by making lawsuits easier to wage and, it is hoped, decreasing the prevalence of sexual harassment in the workplace.

Retirement Income

We now move on to examine our final area of policy in which women have strived to attain equality—retirement income. Retirement income usually refers to income that people receive from the state after they retire, such as Social Security in the United States, pensions that an employer provides to its workers, and any money that people may have saved over their lifetime. Retirement income is of crucial concern to all people, but especially to women, in part because women tend to live longer than men and thus need income for a longer period of time than men do. However, for a variety of reasons that we shall discuss in this section, women earn much less than men in retirement income. For example, on average, women's government pensions in Europe are significantly less than men's—the gap between what women and men receive ranges from a low of 16 percent in the

United Kingdom to a high of 45 percent in Austria.[106] And in the United States, as of 2010, women's average annual social security income was $11,794 compared to $15,231 for men (and neither number is enough to live on) and made up 49 percent of unmarried elderly women's income versus 32 percent for unmarried elderly men.[107] The result is the feminization of poverty among the elderly. While this is a critical issue for women, there have been fewer efforts to design policy to address this issue. Thus, this final section diverges from the previous ones in the sense that we discuss why retirement is a gender issue rather than discuss the design and impact of policy reforms in our three case studies.

Why is retirement income a women's issue? For one, women who do work often work fewer years than men because they assume the tasks of child care and care of elderly relatives, and the amount of retirement income that a person receives from the government depends on the number of years that he or she has participated in the workforce. Thus, women have usually paid less into the government system and get less back upon retirement. As the European Institute for Women's Health finds, "In Italy . . . only 20 percent of women have a 30-year contribution record compared to 60 percent of men."[108] In Australia, for the year 2000, men averaged 38 years in the workforce while women averaged only 20, and these numbers have not improved for women over the past few years.[109] In countries such as Japan, women's participation in the workforce is perceived as a reason to potentially deny women their benefits, for they have shunned the more valued occupations of wife and mother. For example, a former prime minister of Japan noted in public that women who did not bear children were not worthy of public (government) pensions. He said: "The government takes care of women who have given birth to a lot of children as a way to thank them for their hard work. . . . It is wrong for women who haven't had a single child to ask for taxpayer money when they get old, after having enjoyed their *freedom and fun* [emphasis added]."[110]

The effects of private pension plans on women are similar to government pension plans. A person's retirement income from a private pension plan with an employer often depends on the number of years that he or she has been with a specific employer. Because women move in and out of the workforce more frequently than men do (often because of family commitments), they often don't stay long enough in a job to become eligible. Further, women are still relegated to lower-paying jobs than men, and even when they have jobs similar to those of men their income is often less. This means that they often pay less into public and private pension plans and get less back. Finally, many service sector, retail, and part-time jobs—jobs primarily occupied by women—offer no pension plan. In the Netherlands, "of women working part-time and in low paid jobs, more than one-third (37 percent) are not in occupational pension schemes."[111]

The laws governing spousal pension rights in the circumstance of marriage, divorce, and death also often work against women, particularly those who spent their working years caring for their families rather than in the paid labor force. They have accrued little if any retirement income over the course of their lives and thus are often almost entirely dependent on their husband's income. Yet, for example, in the United States, if a couple has been married for less than 10 years and they divorce, the ex-wife receives none of her husband's Social Security benefits upon his retirement. Alternatively, if the husband dies, the wife is under 60, and there are no children under the age of 18, the wife receives none of her husband's benefits until she turns 60. Further, with regard to private pension plans in the United States, for many years a man could waive his wife's survivor benefit without her consent. On the positive side, this bolstered a couple's monthly income when the husband retired. However, when the husband died the payments ceased. This was not a problem if the wife died before the husband, but since women often outlive men, this left a great number of women with no retirement income in old age. Thus, women are often placed in a precarious financial situation upon divorce or the death of their husband. Inequality in the distribution of bereavement benefits isn't solely a problem confronting women. In the United Kingdom, until recently men whose wives died were not entitled to a widower benefit; only women could receive benefits when their husbands died. However, the United Kingdom has changed its pension system so that now, should a man outlive his wife, he can receive widower's benefits.

Since women often live longer than men, retirement benefits, particularly those provided by the government, are of crucial importance to their lives. For example, in the United States women rely heavily on Social Security for their retirement benefits, as stated earlier in the chapter. And, "In 2010, 48 percent of elderly unmarried females receiving Social Security benefits relied on Social Security for 90 percent or more of their income."[112] Yet, because women receive substantially less in benefits than men do, the result is the feminization of poverty among the elderly. In the United Kingdom, one in four pensioner women lives in poverty.[113] According to a report by the Economic and Social Research Council in the United Kingdom, these inequalities are the result, in part, of gendered divisions of labor at home: "mothers who take career breaks to bring up their children are seven times as likely to face hardship and poverty when they reach their 60s than single women."[114] The United States and the United Kingdom are just two examples in a larger trend affecting all European countries, where, in general, older women are more likely than men to rely on social assistance for their needs.[115]

In contrast to our other equal employment policy issues, there have been fewer concentrated efforts to address this imbalance, in part because the inequality in retirement benefits is often the result of indirect forms of discrimination. However, there are a few examples of policy reform that may have a limited impact on women's economic status in their retirement years. In Europe, the European Court of Justice has taken a positive step to improve the lot of part-time workers. They have ruled that part-time workers must be included in private pension schemes on a pro-rata basis. But this still leaves many women without pension plans and so, as the story at the beginning of the chapter regarding Gretchen Swan indicates, women often do not receive pension benefits and must fight for them. The U.S. Retirement Equity Act of 1984 was designed to help widows win more spousal benefits from private pension plans. It "made it mandatory for workers with private pension plans to get the written consent of their spouses in order to waive their survivor benefit."[116] The act also helped divorced women because it requires private pension plans to honor state court orders that divide pension plans in settlements. However, these isolated acts tend to respond to specific issues rather than broadly address issues of gender inequality. As a result, the issue of retirement income is of ongoing concern for women, with few legislative changes in sight.

ADVANCING WOMEN'S EQUALITY

In this chapter we have surveyed the current status of women in their search for equality and examined some of the legal remedies that have been enacted in hopes of attaining equality between the sexes. Despite improvement in women's working conditions, there is still much room for improvement in all of the areas we have discussed. What are some further suggested reforms? We will briefly examine this question in light of each of the broad areas we have covered in this chapter.

As we discussed earlier, many women are paid less than men because they are segregated into predominantly "female" professions. As a result, they work in different positions than men, and it is thus hard to prove overt discrimination in pay scales when women are paid less for their work. As a result, some women's groups have stressed the importance of "comparable worth," a proposal to pay different job titles the same based on their value. For instance, in a law firm a legal secretary is of vital importance to the firm, and in the contracting industry a carpenter is also vital. However, carpenters make significantly more money than legal secretaries even though both jobs may be of comparable importance to their respective employers. As a result, one change that women have fought for is making comparable worth the benchmark for pay. Companies would have to rate the importance of certain jobs; all jobs rated a "5," for example, no matter the description, would receive comparable pay. In this scenario, while factors such as years of experience and performance reviews would impact salary, the gendered divisions with regard to pay inequality would be lessened. However, while women's groups in most advanced industrial nations have lobbied for comparable worth policies, they have been unable to make much legislative progress on the issue.

In our three case studies, women's groups have worked on a variety of specific policy proposals to further the cause of fair pay. In Japan, women's groups have lobbied for the abolition of the "two-track" personnel administration system found in most corporations, in which women form the overwhelming majority of general-track (as opposed to management-track) jobs, which tend to be lower-paying and do not lead to promotions to management positions. Abolition of this system would assist women in gaining equality in the workplace. Further, women's groups advocate the continued use of affirmative action policies in hiring and promotion decisions to assist women in achieving equality in the workplace. In the past, affirmative action unquestionably has assisted women in gaining greater access to a variety of jobs and entrance into institutions of higher learning. Finally, the EU and its member states continue to work toward improving gender equality in pay and hiring and promotion. One improvement for women would be making the European Charter on Human Rights legally binding, which would provide the EU with more tools for ending discrimination. There are fewer solutions to the ongoing problem of sexual harassment. While many companies are taking necessary steps by educating their workers about what constitutes sexual harassment and methods of communication, broader cultural norms are slower to change. While the U.S. system of litigation has encouraged companies to move more rapidly on implementing harassment policies, there has been less progress on this matter in Europe, where there is less agreement on what constitutes harassment and fewer legislative efforts to combat it.

In terms of retirement benefits, advocates have pushed for a variety of reforms. For example, greater protections for part-time workers in the United States would improve the pay and benefits of part-time workers, the majority of whom are women. Other countries have moved to implement changes that would reward women for their years off from work for raising children. For example, Germany has reformed its pension system to grant women a 3-year pension credit if they are the primary caretakers of their children (and thus not employed in the paid labor force). While this amount is more symbolic than significant, it nonetheless acknowledges the contribution of women who are not consistently working outside the home. Further, private pension accounts (worldwide) could be made more female-friendly by shortening the time one has to work until becoming vested. And all retirement schemes would greatly benefit women if women were paid the same as their male colleagues. The pay differential is one of the biggest contributors to women's poverty in their later years.

CONCLUSION

Despite the strides made with equal employment policies, this chapter also illustrates the limits of equal employment policies in many countries. These policies do not address the fundamental inequalities between men and women outside the workforce; women's caretaking and nurturing responsibilities have a dramatic effect on their abilities to compete in the realm of work, as we shall see in the next chapter. Further, laws can only go so far in ameliorating women's separate and unequal status in the absence of significant cultural change about the acceptability of discriminatory practices. Education is one key to this cultural change, as well as an educational system in which the topic of equality is at the heart of its curriculum and in which women's achievements and contributions are a regular part of the curriculum, not just during Women's History Month in March. Until more cultural change occurs, women will still be fighting an uphill battle for equality. Laws and their enforcement are important, and additional legal changes could assist women in their quest for equality. But societal change must come as well. And while this may be slow in coming, the rewards to individuals and society will be worth the time and effort.

FOR MORE INFORMATION

The European Commission: Employment, Social Affairs, and Inclusion, http://ec.europa.eu/social/home.jsp?langId=en

The International Labour Organization, http://www.ilo.org/public/english/region/eurpro/geneva/what/events/malta/equal.htm

The United States Equal Employment Opportunity Commission, http://www.eeoc.gov

The World Economic Forum—The Global Gender Gap, http://www.weforum.org/en/initiatives/gcp/Gender%20Gap/GenderGap

Cairo 678—This 2011 film is a fictional account of sexual harassment in Egypt. Following the stories of three fictional women, this film found its influences in the realities of life for women in Egypt.

Clarence Thomas and Anita Hill: Public Hearing, Private Pain—This 1992 film looks at the intersection of gender, race, and sexual harassment.

Egypt: Will the Revolution Free Women from Sexual Harassment?—This 2012 documentary examines the question of whether the recent revolution will free women in Egypt from sexual harassment.

Elechek—This film, made in Kyrgyzstan in 2006, looks at the life of a woman whose husband has decided to take a younger second wife. The film addresses the difficulties and abuses that women face, often as a result of a lack of economic opportunities.

Made in Dagenham—This 2010 film covers a pivotal moment in the movement for equal pay in Europe in the 1960s. The story centers around a group of female workers at Ford Motor Company's plant in Dagenham, England, who staged a strike to protest working conditions and inequalities in pay.

North Country—This 2005 film is a fictionalized account based on the first major successful sexual harassment case in the United States.

Women and Public Policy: The Actors and the Issues—This film discusses the role that women have played in the public policy that affects their lives.

Women's Happiness or Men's Dignity—This film, made in Armenia in 2006, looks at the lives of two women, a divorcee and a widow, and their very different views on the appropriate roles of men and women in the economy and the family.

5

Women, Work, and Family

Many women plan to combine career and family in some way. But is the ubiquitous phrase "work–life balance" a myth? Or can women "have it all" if they just choose to do so and work to achieve that? When Marissa Mayer, the new chief executive of Yahoo, and one of the few powerful women in the high-tech industry, was asked about taking maternity leave when her first baby was due in October 2012, she blithely replied that her leave would be "a few weeks long, and I'll work through it" because she likes "to stay in the rhythm of things." To her, perhaps maternity leave is an outdated notion for high-achieving women such as herself who have demanding jobs. A "maternity pause" is what she sees in her future if she is also going to simultaneously lead Yahoo.[1] Sheryl Sandberg, the chief operating officer of Facebook, and mother of two young children, urges more women to occupy powerful positions in the business and political realms. However, they currently don't, due, in part, because of how they react to motherhood. When women have children, they "lean back," and pave their path out of leadership positions for good. Instead, she argues, they need to "lean into their careers and to be really dedicated to staying in the work force." In this view, women can be their own worst enemies, and sabotage themselves, often when they choose to have children.[2] In contrast, in the summer of 2012, the *Atlantic Monthly* ran a cover story by Anne-Marie Slaughter called "Why Women Still Can't Have it All." Slaughter, a well-known Princeton professor and former top aide to U.S. Secretary of State Hilary Rodham Clinton, tells of how, 18 months into her foreign-policy dream job, she decided to quit and move home. Before her service in government, she spent her career as a law professor and then as the dean of Princeton's Woodrow Wilson School of Public and International Affairs, demanding jobs in their own right. Yet, after nearly 2 years of juggling weeks in Washington and weekends in Princeton, with two teenagers at home, Slaughter concluded that "juggling high-level government work with the needs of two teenage boys was not possible," even with a supportive, helpful husband. She found it unexpectedly hard to do the kind of job she wanted to do as a high government official and be the kind of parent she wanted to be. As someone who had believed that she could have it all (and for many years had successfully achieved that), she admitted that "we're not actually helping by just repeating this mantra. For those of us who have managed to do it, we need to admit that we are the exception and not the rule. We need to stop congratulating ourselves and focus on the reality for most women."[3]

These three women, who all represent a narrow slice of women (highly educated and very well off to extremely wealthy) have inadvertently opened up a firestorm of commentary on whether women can successfully achieve work–life balance. Is it progress for high-profile women to willingly forgo their right to a maternity leave? Or, by making maternity leave yet another victim of our always-on culture, does it send the message that taking time off is only for the uncommitted? Is it progress when women executives work the same 80-hour work weeks that male executives do, and, when children are born, subcontract out child-care responsibilities to day care or nannies so they can "keep their foot on the pedal"? And is a woman's decision to step down from a powerful position to prioritize family an empowering answer? And if so, why did it prompt, in addition to letters of support, responses of vitriol, anger, even betrayal (often from other women) at this one woman's choice? Which of these three women's experiences and opinions intrigues you, and why? Granted, most women will not be in charge of Fortune 500 companies, or high-powered advisors to the government; many women work out of choice but also financial necessity. They don't have the same financial means to help them devise solutions to answer to both a newborn and a boss. Particularly for these women, what are the costs and benefits of juggling work and family?

The previous chapter discussed how states often become involved in public policy to ensure that men and women are treated equally in the workforce. However, women's biological differences (in that only women can become pregnant and give birth), combined with gendered expectations that women will care for and raise children in their early years and beyond, as well as assume much of the care of the household, often affect their abilities to interact on an equal basis in the paid labor force. Thus, childbearing and childrearing have serious ramifications for women's equality in the workforce; women with children often work less, advance much more slowly, and accumulate fewer earnings and hence less in retirement benefits. As a result, granting formal equality in the work sphere often does not translate into actual equality, since women's responsibilities in the home affect their abilities to compete at work. Thus, many feminists maintain that policies that increase work opportunities for women, without targeting the division of labor between men and women in responsibilities at home, will yield, at best, a flawed form of gender equality.[4]

States have responded to this dilemma to balance the demands of production and reproduction with activist public policies, such as parental leave, family allowances, or subsidized child care, which help women (and men) reconcile work and family life. However, not all states respond in the same ways, and they have designed various policies depending on their beliefs about the "appropriate" role of the welfare state in society and which societal issues should be considered public or private responsibility.[5] For example, some states, such as the United States, the United Kingdom, and Australia, are oriented around an ideology that stresses the primacy of the market and the privacy of the family, which often leads to policies in which government intervention is minimal in the economy and family life. Many European states are more interventionist and try to moderate the harmful consequences of the market through transferring money and benefits, such as pensions, insurance, and welfare payments, to citizens. Finally, nations such as those in Scandinavia have an even more proactive model of state intervention in order to achieve greater levels of economic and social equality, providing cash benefits as well as a wide array of social services to its population. Each one of these approaches to the welfare state has implications for women.[6]

These differing concepts of the welfare state intersect with state attitudes toward the "ideal" family and "appropriate" gender and family relations, and governments enact policies that can reinforce, alter, or transform existing gender relations. Some governments enact policies that encourage strict divisions of labor, with the husband as earner and the wife as carer; for example, if only women can claim state-funded maternity leave, then there isn't much incentive for men to stay home. In contrast, other governments have enacted policies that have helped redistribute responsibilities and roles within the home, so that both men and women can be workers as well as carers if they choose. Many Scandinavian countries do this, for example, by granting paid paternity leave to fathers on a "use it or lose it" basis.[7] Often, states send mixed messages regarding their attitudes about managing the balance between women's productive and reproductive roles. They are inconsistent on what aspect of women they value more, and there is a tension between ensuring women's full participation in their domestic and work responsibilities. In turn, women (and men) also struggle to make choices about whether and how to achieve a "work–life balance" that reflects their authentic selves. There are no easy answers; historically, however, parents' responses to this struggle have been gendered in that men "win the bread" and women nurture, and states can do much to nudge people's responses to either break down gender stereotypes of reinforce them.

In this chapter, we ask how different states have legislated the politics of sex and gender difference with regard to motherhood. We will address these issues by comparing and contrasting what are known as reconciliation policies of various advanced industrialized countries in three areas: parental leave, family allowances, and child care. We discuss three different approaches to balancing the demands of work and parenting: the pro-family noninterventionist approach of the United States, the traditional breadwinner model exemplified by Germany, and the egalitarian model of Sweden. These three cases give very different policy solutions to the state's role in facilitating work–life balance and also facilitating changing norms about gendered divisions of labor.

THE DEBATE OVER RECONCILIATION POLICIES

Reconciliation policies refer to a group of measures that help parents balance the competing needs of work and family life, particularly those with children aged 5 and younger, when the demands of childrearing are particularly intense. The most common reconciliation policies are parental leave, family allowances, and early child education and care. In an ideal situation, these three policies work together seamlessly to support parents through a significant period of the children's lives.

Parental leave laws allow parents to take time off to care for their infant or young child from the time just before or at birth as well as an amount of time following the birth. They are important to new parents because they offer job protection for a period of weeks, months, or years around the birth of a child, allowing the parent to return to the same (or a comparable) job at the end of the leave period. Also, most parental leave laws offer financial support during that leave, given that most parents cannot afford to take time off from work unless they are paid some level of compensation. Many countries (88) also provide a wide array of child and family cash and tax benefits to defray the costs of childrearing.[8] The benefits are usually relatively small (often less than 10 percent of average wages), but they are nonetheless a vital part of family income. Finally, many states partially or fully fund early childhood education and care until the child is ready to enter compulsory education, or the formal education that starts either at kindergarten or first grade in most countries. While these are not the only policies that governments enact to facilitate work–life balance (for example, almost 100 countries provide for breastfeeding breaks for nursing mothers), they are the most significant in terms of spending commitments and impact on families.[9]

Why do states design reconciliation policies? Welfare state activism regarding family policy preceded the rise of the women's movement, and states historically have been motivated by a variety of reasons, many of which are not related to advancing gender equality, to assist families. For one, there is a potential health benefit; these policies generally help improve the health of the mother as well as the child, and can reduce problems such as child mortality. These policies, by offering some sort of financial assistance (direct or indirect), also help lessen social and economic inequality, particularly the incidence of childhood poverty. Thus, states design reconciliation policies to help promote social cohesion. In addition, many states want to encourage women to have children. Despite concerns about the "population bomb," for the global north, a larger concern might be the underpopulation bomb. That is, women in highly industrialized nations are having fewer and fewer children, at a rate well below replacement levels. This is a demographic crisis with huge repercussions for countries' economies. Fewer babies mean fewer future workers, which means less economic productivity and fewer financial resources to support a rapidly aging population. In fact, the graying of the labor force in many countries, who all plan to retire and claim health and social security benefits, is one of the most critical crises facing industrialized nations. Although this crisis is particularly severe now, pronatalist impulses have driven generous reconciliation benefits since their inception in the nineteenth century. In sum, historically reconciliation policies were paternalistic in intent and designed to protect mothers.

However, the dramatic increase of women's participation in the labor force in the decades following World War II shifted the parameters of the debate over reconciliation policies toward helping mothers work. In particular, women, who had previously left the workforce upon marrying or having children, were returning to work after getting married and having children, a trend that continues into the present. Part of this is because of the satisfaction women receive from employment, and part is because of the increasing difficulties that families face in surviving on one income. In addition, states themselves, who were facing a labor shortage in the 1960s and 1970s, saw women as a potential underutilized resource, and a sometimes preferable alternative to relying on immigration, for example, to fill labor shortages. They wanted to design policies to help nudge into the labor force women who may have stayed out after having children.

At the same time that women were entering the workforce, feminist movements emerged in many OECD countries and lobbied for policies to address gender inequities in the workforce. In addition, more women were filling the ranks of government bureaucracies and advocating for more female-friendly policies. In response to these trends, governments were also establishing special commissions, departments, and other bureaus to deal specifically with the condition and status of women in society. There was increasing pressure on states to help women balance the demands of production and reproduction.

Why should states create policy to help women balance these two parts of their lives? Historically, employers refused to hire women, or fired them once they became pregnant. However, currently there are numerous laws in place in all of the OECD countries to protect women's equal treatment at the workplace. Shouldn't this be enough to protect women? Many feel the answer is "no" for a number of reasons. For one, even though discrimination on the basis of sex is illegal, many employers still treat women, particularly women of childbearing age, differently than male colleagues. Employers have an interest in ensuring smooth and uninterrupted periods of work from their workforce in order to facilitate the continued stability of their businesses. Women are still sometimes perceived as a potential business "risk" in that they may need substantial time off to give birth to and care for children. In countries where employers, rather than the state, are responsible for paying benefits, having to provide maternity benefits is also perceived to be a greater financial burden that can be avoided by employing men. Alternatively, businesses underpay women to make up the cost of employing someone who may need more time off or additional benefits. It is only recently that many businesses have realized that, in fact, guaranteed maternity leave increases job continuity rather than the reverse; prospective parents are less likely to quit if they know that their jobs will be waiting for them, and they are more motivated to retain their skills and knowledge specific to their employer. Also, businesses are beginning to accept that in avoiding female employees, they also miss out on tapping some of the most talented people in the application pool. And that by not promoting women to more powerful positions, they may also be missing out on potential gains that could come from tapping the entire pool of employees. For example, Google recently increased the length of its maternity leave, as well as the level of financial benefits that accrue with it, to ensure that fewer women leave their workforce, taking their skills (and abilities to help generate profits) with them.

Secondly, many argue that women can't truly be equal at work given their biological and gendered roles as mothers. Only women can become pregnant and give birth, and thus childbearing and the early development stage affect them differently. Despite endless images from popular culture of Hollywood stars giving birth before "regaining their bodies" and former lives within weeks of their child's birth, the reality for many women is that pregnancy, birth, and the early years of a child's life, in addition to being immensely rewarding, can also take a tremendous toll on their bodies, time, and abilities to balance competing demands. The 9-month process of pregnancy often affects women's health; they may be tired, they may be sick as a result of the increased hormones coursing through their bodies, or in some cases they are put on bed rest. In addition, childbirth often requires substantial periods of rest and recovery for the mother, particularly if she underwent a cesarean section. In the early months of a child's life, babies need to be fed frequently, and many women breastfeed, meaning that they must be in close proximity to their newborns (although in many countries, the breast pump has helped alleviate this issue for some women). Women simply must perform a larger portion of the responsibilities associated with these activities because of their sex, although certainly, many women also freely want to be closely engaged in the care and development of their babies, temporarily free from the demands of work. But the responsibilities of parenthood do not end after the initial few months of a child's life; infants and toddlers cannot care for themselves. Traditional gender roles replace biological ones; women carry, often by choice, a "double burden." Not only are they responsible for a variety of duties at work, but they are also responsible for many of the childrearing and child-care activities at home. If a child becomes sick, it is often the mother who takes time off from work to shuttle the child to the doctor, to home, and to bed.

"Mom-in-Chief": The "Cult of Mom" Politics

It is not uncommon for politicians to have families. In fact, it is somewhat expected, particularly in the United States, when campaigns inevitably pit candidates wanting to play the "family values" card. It helps to have an intact, preferably photogenic family in tow, complete with a loving and supportive spouse (see photo 5.1, for example). It is taken for granted that a male politician would of course work outside the home even if he has children, and that his political career is important enough to continue pursuing it while raising a family. And journalists and the public don't really question whether pursuing the career will in some way disadvantage the family, or vice versa. For women in politics, however, juggling work and family prompts criticism and doubt as to whether women are up for the job of running for and occupying office. For example, Alaska Governor Sarah Palin's bid for the vice presidency of the United States in the 2008 race was extremely controversial; as a working mother of five children, Palin reignited a fiery debate about the issue of women, family, and the workplace in unexpected and unusual ways. For one, many female politicians have entered politics when their children are either older or out of the house completely. Palin, mother of five, had, at the time of her nomination, an infant son diagnosed with Down syndrome. In addition, during the campaign, it was revealed that her 17-year-old daughter was expecting a child with her boyfriend. Many questioned whether a woman, no matter how talented at multitasking, could successfully serve in such a high-powered office with a small infant with special needs and also tend to the needs of her other four children, one of whom was expecting a baby of her own at a fairly young age. But what was particularly interesting about the public debate was how traditional left-wing and right-wing views flip-flopped. Palin, a Republican candidate who represented the social conservative, religious wing of the party, had a life narrative that seemed to contradict the stated platform of her own party. Traditionally, the Republican Party and Republican voters have been more leery of the qualifications of working mothers running for office. Surveys conducted by the Pew Research Center found that Republicans were far less likely to support a female candidate who is the mother of young children than were Democrats and were more likely to believe that it was "bad for society" when mothers of young children work outside the home. Yet, Republicans swarmed to her defense, while many Democrats questioned her ability to be both mother of five and serve in such a high-powered position. Supporters of Palin decried the sexism behind the critique; would opponents really have had a problem with her profile if she had been a father, rather than a mother, of five? And women, many of whom were mothers themselves, had strongly held views that polarized them on Palin's candidacy. While Palin was a controversial candidate for women as well as men for many reasons; her personal life history added even more fuel to an already combustible mix of political positions, statements, and actions. More recently, Illinois Attorney General Lisa Madigan, who is contemplating a run for the governorship, also came under attack for considering such a move while mother to a 4-year-old and a 7-year-old. Reporters asked how she was going to manage to raise her children and be governor at the same time. Male politicians who are fathers rarely get asked this question; 2012 GOP vice presidential candidate Paul Ryan, father of three children under 10, was not queried on his fitness for office, given his parental status. And male politicians are often praised for being forward-thinking if they take a weekend off from a campaign, or make time to have breakfast with their children, while female politicians are criticized for doing the same thing.

However, women's increasing candidacy for office also raises, but does not answer, uncomfortable questions about gender equality. Men and women are biologically different, and despite the greater involvement of fathers in traditional "women's activities," studies show that the reality is that parenting and household maintenance is still primarily women's work. Women still shoulder the heavier burden of child care, housework, and other important caretaking responsibilities. As columnist Lisa Belkin asked, given this reality, "[D]o such obligations make women less suited than men for certain professions or roles? . . . [W]hen do someone's family commitments rule her out as a strong candidate for a highly responsible position?"[ii] In other words, can female politicians transcend gender when we are still enmeshed in a reality so unequally structured by it?

Politicians who are also women and mothers themselves often play the "mother" card. Palin described herself on the campaign trail as "just a hockey mom," a traditional, family-first kind of woman. Palin also coined the term "mama grizzly," a term she uses to refer to a conservative woman with "common sense," who "rises up" to protect her children when she sees them endangered (in her view, by bad policies in Washington, D.C.). This breed of female politician is fearless, female, and therefore scary. She will take on any foe and, the implication is, rip him or her to shreds. In ensuing political campaigns, other Republican women, such as Sharron Angle of Nevada and Michele Bachmann of Minnesota, took on this moniker, basing their skills as a political predator on the fact of their "mom-ness," "because moms kind of just know when there's something wrong."[iii] It's not just Republican women who play the "mom" card; Nancy Pelosi, the first female Speaker of the House and the highest-ranking woman to achieve elected office in the United States, has referred to her journey from "kitchen to Congress," playing up an "I'm just a mom at heart" image. At the Democratic National Convention of 2012, featured speakers Michelle Obama, Elizabeth Warren, and Debbie Wasserman Schultz, all of whom have very prominent political profiles, downplayed their professional accomplishments and instead focused on the centrality of being a mom as the most important work of their lives (Fig. 5.1). This focus seems to obscure the fact that women are very effective as politicians; in fact, a recent study of the performance of male and female politicians nationally found that female politicians are more successful in winning additional funding for their districts, sponsoring more bills, and attracting more co-sponsors than their male colleagues.[iv] And most female politicians, to succeed in what has traditionally been a "man's world" of politics, have had to pursue unusual trajectories to realize their aspirations. Palin was back at work as governor of Alaska 3 days after giving birth to her fifth child, as was New York Senator Kirsten Gillibrand. Is it really progress for women, and all working parents, that now women, like men, can also take relatively short breaks from the labor market? Or is this a sign of the relative inflexibility of many careers when it comes to the demands of parenting and work? Alternatively, if this represents these women's authentic choices, is this a positive development, or does it demonstrate that women still have to adapt to "men's game rules" to compete?

President Barack Obama, First Lady Michelle Obama, and their daughters, Sasha and Malia, sit for a family portrait in the Oval Office. During her speech at the Democratic National Convention on September 4, 2012, Mrs. Obama stated that her most important title is "mom-in-chief." SOURCE: Rex Features via AP Images.

What do you think? Is there a time when a person's family situation makes him or her ineligible for a job that involves significant levels of responsibility, even if he or she freely chooses that option?

iLisa Belkin, "Palin Talk," *The New York Times*, Oct. 5, 2008. www.nytimes.com/2008/10/05/magazine/05wwln-lede-t.html?_r=1
iiChristina Bielazska-DuVernay. "Sarah Palin, Working Mother." *Business Week*, Sept. 9, 2008. http://www.businessweek.com/managing/content/sep2008/ca2008099_703240.htm
iiiLisa Miller, "Hear Them Growl," *The Daily Beast*, Sept. 27, 2010. http://www.thedailybeast.com/newsweek/2010/09/27/what-does-mama-grizzly-really-mean.html
ivTony Dokoupil, "Why Female Politicians are More Effective," *The Daily Beast*, Jan. 22, 2011, http://www.thedailybeast.com/newsweek/2011/01/22/why-female-politicians-are-more-effective.html

Given these differences, and in the absence of proactive reconciliation policies, women who work outside the home have a separate and unequal working experience. Many choose to work part-time (or are unable to work full-time) in order to balance their varied responsibilities. In fact, many more women than men are employed in part-time labor. In OECD countries, around 25 percent of women work part-time but only 6 percent of men do so.[10] Many do not advance in their careers as quickly as men or fathers do because the demands of their home lives have taken a toll on their abilities to advance professionally. As a result, women make less money, retire with less money, and are more dependent on "breadwinners" to survive, or, if they are single parents, are more likely to fall into poverty. Despite formal mechanisms that legislate against discrimination, inequalities in the home often translate into inequalities in the workforce.[11] As states have become increasingly committed to advancing gender equality, they have responded to this issue by designing more generous reconciliation policies.

Advocates for women's equality have also weighed in with a number of opinions about how states (along with employers) should help women (and men) balance productive and reproductive responsibilities. Many point out that this will be difficult to achieve without changing gender inequalities in the household division of labor. Yet, many disagree about the appropriate solution to resolving the tension between productive and reproductive responsibilities. Should advocates for women's rights support "special treatment" for women or equal treatment for women in the workplace? Historically, as women joined the workforce, states began to pass protective labor legislation based on women's reproductive capacities. Convinced that women needed special treatment, policymakers excluded women from a variety of jobs that might be considered hazardous to their health, allowed them to be paid less than men, or placed them in menial positions. In practice, protective legislation often enforced inequalities between men and women. Women were ghettoized into jobs that were considered women's work, which translated into less-desirable jobs with little to no opportunity for advancement. Underneath the veneer of progressive rhetoric, much protective legislation codified a belief that women's appropriate place was at home, raising children, or in temporary jobs that could withstand a revolving workforce.[12]

As a result, advocates for increased attention to the issues of childrearing faced a dilemma. One the one hand, women's abilities to bear children do make them different, but should legislation then be passed to treat them separately, with explicit maternity benefits? States had historically used women's biological "destiny" as a reason to deny them equal treatment in access to education, employment, and social benefits, and women experience a burden that is substantially different from that of men. Thus, some activists argued for the need to highlight women's biological singularities, for to ignore that in policy design simply creates an extremely uneven playing field in the workplace.

Other women's rights advocates argue that the work involved in raising children is undervalued (most mothers who work in the home are not paid for raising their children). Further, they question the prevailing model of women's participation in the workforce, which often merely pushes them to adapt to a "male" model that values competition and defines "success" in overly narrow, materialistic terms. Working to ensure women's participation in this system merely forces them to adapt to already established "male" rules of the game, rather than transforming them into more humane conditions for all. Some argue that parents (primarily women) who choose to raise their children should receive a yearly allowance or income, thus elevating and highlighting the work of those who choose to define their careers as raising their children. Yet others point out that this solution glorifies the traditional view of motherhood without necessarily challenging the traditional division of labor between men as breadwinners and women as caregivers. In sum, ensuring that women's differences, whether a result of biology or gendered expectations, do not result in inequality at work is a challenge, and there is no agreement on how this should be acknowledged and remedied in public policy and about which "ideal" family model the state should promote.

Let's now turn to our reconciliation policies. Drawing from the cases of the United States, Germany, and Sweden, we will compare three different policy approaches to resolving the tension between production and reproduction. The potential effects of these policies can not only enable women to make choices about their lives but can also help ensure equality, not only in the public sphere but in the private realm as well.

POLICY AREAS

Parental Leave Policies and Family Allowances

Historically, parental leave has really been known, formally or informally, as maternity leave, because women give birth and have often been the ones who have taken on the significant care responsibilities after the birth of the child. The first programs were implemented in Germany and Sweden at the end of the nineteenth century, and leave ranged from 4 to 12 weeks, with a small lump-sum payment or flat-rate benefits and no job protection. Maternity leave policies spread across the continent in the first half of the twentieth century, and by the start of World War II, all major Western European countries offered paid maternity leave. These policies were paternalistic in intent; they were designed to help improve the health of the child and mother, and were part of larger, pronatalist campaigns to encourage women to have babies, as well as to maintain the family unit. However, in the post–World War II era, states expanded their maternity policies in scope and shifted their rhetorical approach. The length of leave was expanded, cash benefits were increased, and the intent of the policy shifted from protecting women as mothers to ensuring their rights as workers by legalizing job-protected time away from work.[13] Countries have become increasingly flexible in defining who is eligible for leave. In the 1980s and 1990s, as feminist movements pushed for, among other things, the redistribution of responsibilities within the home, some states began enacting policies that encouraged male as well as female participation in the task of childrearing by granting parental leaves, paternity leaves, and family leaves. Parental leaves are gender-neutral, job-protected leaves from employment that follow the same guidelines as maternity leaves or offer additional time off to care for an infant, toddler, or sick child. In this scenario, either men or women may share the leave or choose which one of them will use it. In some countries, part of the parental leave is reserved for fathers on a "use it or lose it" basis to encourage fathers to play a more active parenting role. In contrast, other countries provide specific paternity leaves, which are job-protected leaves for fathers. The conditions behind the leave are similar to maternity and parental leave, but specifically target men to encourage them to be more engaged in family life. However, they are usually much briefer than maternity leaves, supplement maternity leaves, are more likely to be unpaid, and are usually important for families in which a second child is born. In this scenario, for example, the father may take time off to care for the elder child as well as provide help to the mother and the newborn. Finally, family leaves are granted to care for an ill child or to meet parental obligations, such as parent–teacher meetings, once the child is no longer covered by various maternity/parental leave policies. Later in this chapter, we will see how these different kinds of leaves have been implemented in our case studies, and why it might matter if the law is designed as maternity, paternity, or gender-neutral leave.

What do countries currently grant to mothers and fathers of newborns? The World Health Organization (WHO) collects data on its 167 member states, and all of them have some legislation on maternity protection. Leave provisions consist of three key aspects: duration, level of financial benefits, and the source of the funding (public vs. private or some combination). Leave duration is calculated to be the minimum time considered necessary for the rest and recuperation of the parent, as well as the minimum time deemed essential for the health of the newborn. States define this period of time differently, with some states legislating a few weeks' worth of leave, while other states provide several months, even up to a year, of leave. WHO currently recommends a mandated leave of at least 14 weeks, and over the past two decades, an increasing number of nations have met that target. For example, globally, over half (51 percent) of countries provide a maternity leave benefit of at least 14 weeks. One fifth of countries mandate 18 or more weeks of leave, while about one third of countries (35 percent) provide 12 to 13 weeks. Only 14 percent of countries provide less than 12 weeks of maternity leave. There is a geographical component to the duration of leave; it tends to be more generous in developed economies, such as the European Union countries, and Eastern European and Commonwealth of Independent States (CIS) countries. Leave is shorter in developing economies, particularly in Africa, Asia and the Pacific, and the Middle East, in part because of the financial resources of governments as well as social norms that may discourage women's entry into the paid workforce (if women aren't likely to work outside of the home for pay, then there is no need for paid leave).[14]

The amount and duration of paid leave is also a critical component; many families cannot survive without some level of income replacement. The International Labour Organization (ILO) recommends that the cash benefit paid during maternity leave should be at least two thirds of a mother's previous earnings for a minimum of 14 weeks. Globally, 42 percent of the 152 countries studied by WHO meet this standard. In fact, over a third (34 percent) of countries go over this standard by providing 100 percent of previous earnings for at least 14 weeks. Over half (59 percent) of the countries pay less than the recommended amount or for less time. While the majority of countries have some sort of wage replacement payout scheme, others issue a flat monthly benefit, which might be set at the national minimum wage, regardless of the women's previous earnings. Only four countries in the world do not mandate paid maternity leave: the United States, Lesotho, Papua New Guinea, and Swaziland.

A final component of leave is the source of benefits. Who should cover the cost of leave—the government or the employer? Once again, the ILO has weighed in, arguing that employers should not be individually liable for the cost of maternity benefits. In many countries, benefits are paid for by the state, through national social security agencies. This is because relying on employers to cover the costs of maternity leave is problematic. As mentioned previously, this added cost often discourages firms from recruiting women and may be a factor in explaining why women's wages are lower than men's; firms are trying to find a way to recoup the "loss" of potentially paying out maternity benefits. In over half (53 percent) of the 167 countries surveyed, governments provide cash benefits through national social security schemes. In just over a quarter (26 percent) of countries, benefits are paid solely by the employer. In one in five countries (17 percent), the costs are shared between social security systems and employers. Table 5.1 provides a summary of how OECD countries have resolved the issue of childbirth-related leave. It is important to remember that even in countries with generous provisions, not all women are covered. Home workers are frequently excluded, as are women employed in small enterprises. In sum, how countries define leave is critical. Vital issues to consider are whether leave is paid or unpaid, levels of payments as well as duration of benefits, and the beneficiaries of the leave.

Table 5.1 Parental Leave Policies in OECD Countries, 2010

COUNTRY	DURATION OF CHILDBIRTH-RELATED LEAVE	% OF WAGE REPLACED
Australia	1 year parental	Up to 18 weeks at national minimum wage
Austria	16 weeks maternity; 8 weeks before/8 weeks after birth (mandated)	100% of wages
Belgium	15 weeks maternity	82% first 30 days; 75% up to a ceiling for remaining period
Canada	17 weeks maternity	55% for 15 weeks up to a ceiling
Czech Republic	28 weeks maternity	69%
Denmark	18 weeks maternity including 4 weeks prebirth	100%
Finland	105 working days	70% up to a ceiling plus 40% of additional amount, plus 25% of additional amount
France	16 weeks for first two children; 26 weeks for third child	100% up to a ceiling
Germany	14 weeks maternity including 6 weeks before birth	100%
Greece	119 days	100%
Hungary	24 weeks maternity	70%
Iceland	3 months	80%
Ireland	26 weeks paid (plus 16 weeks unpaid)	80% up to a ceiling
Italy	5 months maternity including 1 month prebirth	80%
Japan	14 weeks (6 prebirth and 8 postbirth)	60%
Korea, South	90 days	100%
Luxembourg	16 weeks maternity	100%
Mexico	12 weeks maternity (6 weeks prebirth)	100%
Netherlands	16 weeks maternity	100% up to a ceiling
New Zealand	14 weeks	100% up to a ceiling
Norway	36 (or 46) weeks	100% (or 80% for 46 weeks)
Poland	20 weeks	100%
Portugal	120 (or 150) days	100% (or 80% for 150 days)
Spain	16 weeks maternity	100%
Sweden	420 days	80%
Switzerland	14 weeks maternity	80% up to a ceiling
Turkey	16 weeks maternity	66-2/3%
United Kingdom	52 weeks	6 weeks at 90%, lower of 90%; flat rate for weeks 7–39; weeks 40–52 unpaid
United States	12 weeks family leave, includes maternity	Unpaid

SOURCE: International Labour Organization, "Maternity at Work: A Review of National Legislation," 2nd edition. (Geneva: ILO, 2010).

There are other ways that states can help parents balance work and family in the early years of childrearing. Family allowances are a monthly (more or less) cash payment to parents. Allowances vary, depending on family size, family income, and employment status. In some countries, child and family allowances are provided to all families, regardless of income, while others base eligibility and benefit levels on income. Allowances are often further supplemented by birth grants (a lump sum granted at the birth of the child), prenatal and breastfeeding allowances, school grants, childrearing or child-care allowances, adoption bene-fits, supplements for single parents, and so on. Unlike most other OECD coun-tries, the United States provides no form of family allowances to defray the costs of childrearing.[15] Rather, the government provides tax benefits to parents for having children. Nonetheless, all of these benefits and services can help ease the financial burdens of childrearing.

Let's look more closely at how these policies work the United States, Germany, and Sweden, and their impact on women.

Pro-family/Noninterventionist Model: The United States

The United States is exceptional in its treatment of parents; along with three other countries (all of which are relatively poor), it does not have any form of paid maternity leave, and of the OECD countries, it has the least generous maternity or family leave policy in terms of time off from work. Until 1993, when the Family Medical Leave Act (FMLA) was passed, the United States did not have a federal policy defining and granting parental leave. The policy that did pass is extremely limited. The act applies only to employers with 50 or more employees. The em-ployee also has to have worked for at least 1,250 hours during the previous 12 months at the company. In addition, although employees are allowed to take 12 weeks off a year to care for a newborn, newly adopted, or foster child; a child, spouse, or parent with a serious health condition; or a serious health condition of the employee, the leave is unpaid. As a result, many people cannot afford to take the time off. Further, employees may be required to first use up accrued sick leave or vacation time to cover part or the complete duration of the leave. Finally, em-ployers may deny leave to an employee within the highest-paid 10 percent of its workforce, if letting the worker take leave would create a problem for the firm. With all of these adjustments and further specifications, an estimated 40 percent of workers are not covered by the act.[16] Nor does the law cover care for grandpar-ents, grandchildren, in-laws, or domestic partners. Even with these limited provi-sions, the bill was vetoed twice by President George H. W. Bush. Upon its passage (for the third time) by Congress, it became President Clinton's first signed piece of legislation in 1993.[17]

In 1985, when Congresswoman Patricia Schroeder (D-CO) introduced the nation's first family leave bill (and the first version of what was to become the FMLA), 135 countries had already established maternity leave benefit programs, and of those, all but 10 provided for some form of paid leave.[18] This policy inaction is not for lack of trying; since 1942, various government agencies have attempted to implement a family leave policy. The U.S. Department of Labor originally proposed a 14-week leave, in which women could take the 6 weeks preceding and the 8 weeks following the birth of a child. However, in the 1960s and 1970s the United States did not follow in the footsteps of its European counterparts, which substantially redesigned their national policies toward working mothers. Rather, policy evolved at the state level. However, even in the 1980s, states were slow to enact legislation; by 1987, only 9 states had a maternity leave law in place, and by 1989, another 14 states had added provisions for maternity (3 states) or parental (11 states) leave. All of these policies granted unpaid leave only.[19] In fact, unless an individual company offers paid leave, claiming temporary disability benefits is currently one of the few ways that women can receive financial remuneration during their leave. In 2004, California made history when it became first state in the nation to provide its workforce with 6 weeks of paid family leave (55 percent of earnings, up to $959 a week). New Jersey enacted a paid leave law in 2008 that also provides for 6 weeks away from the job (66 percent of earnings, with a maximum weekly benefit of $546). In 2007, Washington state passed legislation that would provide a full-time worker with $250 per week for up to 5 weeks to care for a newborn or newly adopted child, but implementation of that legislation has been put on hold.[20]

In the absence of federal legislation, some businesses began to offer leave options. According to one study of 279 U.S. businesses, in the late 1950s, only 5 percent of companies offered leave; however, by 1985, over half offered it. Nonetheless, this increase was not because companies voluntarily decided to help women and men balance family responsibilities with work. Rather, most implemented leave policies in response to a 1972 EEOC ruling that stated that companies that offered leave for temporary disability also had to allow leave for maternity. Although this requirement was later overturned by the Supreme Court (but was then subsequently voted into law by Congress in 1978), nonetheless many companies in the early to mid-1970s implemented leave policies out of fear of lawsuits or as a result of the negative publicity generated by lawsuits.[21] However, paid leave in the private sector is not a widespread phenomenon; U.S. government survey data estimate that only 10 percent of private-sector employees have access to it.[22] Further, as we discussed earlier, delegating the design and implementation of parental leave to private businesses is seen as an imperfect solution, for it simply encourages businesses to avoid hiring women, or to pass on the additional costs of paying for leave to its workers.

When the FMLA was finally passed in 1993, it was not touted as a feminist bill; in fact, neither political party was willing to frame it as a "pro-woman" issue. Instead, the Democratic Party claimed it as a "pro-labor" measure, while the Republicans who helped pass it used the legislation to bolster their image as a "pro-family" party.[23] (In fact, Henry Hyde, a Republican, switched his vote to supporting the bill because he thought that it would discourage women from having an abortion.[24]) In the end, both labor and families ended up with the least generous benefits of any country in the OECD, and, some would argue, the world. Further, women's groups argued over the conditions and framing of FMLA; some advocated for wording that would grant women leave, while others wanted to make the language gender-neutral and applicable to either men or women. The battle over whether leave should be defined as "special treatment" for women versus "equal treatment" for everyone was eventually won by the "equal treatment" advocates, who argued that benefits should go to all workers, and not just parents, and certainly not just women. While this may have seemed like a reasonable strategy in the wake of charged arguments about affirmative action, it ended up creating less advantageous benefits for women than policies created by states, such as California, that offered a specific maternity leave policy.[25]

Why has the United States tended to lag behind other countries in this area, especially in an era when "family values" are omnipresent in political debate? For one, the United States has long exemplified a political culture that is suspicious of an interventionist state, or what is more often framed in the press as "big government." In addition, it embraces an individualist culture and touts a free market rhetoric, which also emphasizes the negative aspects of an interventionist state. Thus, when President George H. W. Bush vetoed the FMLA for the second time in 1992, he commented that "I want to strongly reiterate that I have always supported employer policies to give time off for a child's birth or adoption or for family illness and believe it is important that employers offer these benefits. I object, however, to the Federal Government mandating leave policies for America's employers and workforce."[26] Similarly, Bob Dole, in the first presidential debate against President Bill Clinton in 1996, declared his opposition to the FMLA; he also argued that Congress should not have used the "long arm of the federal government" to pass FMLA to make employers offer leave.[27] Both Bush and Dole offered a variety of other incentives that would encourage businesses to grant leave, while stopping short of mandating it; both echoed suspicion of an overreaching federal government and worried about the effects of federal governments "tampering" with business practices.

A second potential answer lies in the nature of the decentralized American system, in which much policy is left in the hands of individual states. Finally, unions, which have been a driving force in advocating for greater levels of worker benefits, are relatively weak in the United States, compared to other European countries. As a result, another pressure point that had been utilized by other countries was not really an option for U.S. workers.[28] The result is that the United States has a very limited family policy, and pervasive cultural values that emphasize individualism and limited government interference in family matters further enforce America's singular approach to reconciliation policies.

Traditional Breadwinner Model: Germany

Germany takes a different approach to maternity and family leave. Until recently, the German model of benefits was one that encouraged a two-parent, one-earner family and reinforced a traditional division of labor between men and women in the household. Several trends led the government to reform its policies. For one, reunification, in which East and West Germany merged into a united Germany, required merging two different benefits models (and cultures) into one. This highlighted the significant differences between the two groups of German women who were both parents and workers outside of the home. Secondly, many German women are choosing to focus on their careers and not to have children, a trend that is of great concern to the German government. As a result, Germany is in the process of redesigning its policies away from its traditional model to one that encourages more flexibility for working women as well as increased gender equality.

Germany was the trailblazer for the concept of the modern "welfare state"; Otto von Bismarck was the mastermind behind Germany's fledgling social insurance system, which laid out the framework for a variety of benefits for the unemployed, the sick, and, for our purposes, the pregnant. However, in the post–World War II era, two systems of benefits evolved. East Germany (GDR) adopted a Soviet-style system of benefits that encouraged women's full-time employment in the workforce with generous leave benefits. Thus, in the 1980s, the GDR had a nearly 90 percent female labor force participation rate, and women were also entitled to 26 weeks of leave with a 90- to 100-percent wage replacement rate. In 1986, 3 years before the collapse of the GDR, East German women were granted an additional 7 months of paid leave. They were also given one day of additional leave per month for housework, a reduced work week for having two or more children, and additional weeks of leave to care for sick children. The model, though generous, did not challenge the division of labor in the household by designing policy to encourage fathers to participate in child care or housework. When Germany unified in 1990, West German policy replaced that of the East.

The West German policies were designed to preserve the traditional nuclear family, with a male breadwinner and an "at-home" mother caring for the children. Maternity leaves were paid, job-protected leaves for 14 weeks. After reunification, parental leave was extended to cover the child's first 3 years, although this leave was accompanied by a much smaller financial benefit. Both mothers and fathers who work in firms that have more than 15 employees are entitled to this parental leave. In addition, the German government offers a childrearing allowance (*Erziehungsgeld*). This allowance, about $300 a month, subsidizes the child's care needs during the first 2 years of a child's life. However, it requires that one parent (in practice, overwhelmingly the mother) be designated the full-time caregiver or work part-time.[29] This is just one part of a larger, more complex system of child benefits (*Kindergeld*) that are distributed until the child turns 18.

As we shall discuss later in the chapter, these benefits are generous, but they do not encourage women to balance work and family. In practice, leave defined in this way encouraged primarily women to take 3 years off from work, and then to return to work part-time afterward. This was in part because of social norms, but also because women tended to already be the lower income earner; it made financial sense in most families. As a result, women tended not to advance as far in their careers, or didn't work outside the home at all (and until 1977, they officially needed their husband's permission to work). For example, by 1990, before unification, the female labor participation rate in West Germany was about 58 percent, while in the East it was near 90 percent.[30] By 2010, 66 percent of German women worked, but that number plunged to 32 percent for women with children under 3. Only 14 percent of women with one child resume work full-time and only

6 percent of those with two. German women don't seem to be embracing this future; Germany has one of Europe's lowest birthrates of 1.38 children per woman, and one in three German women enters her mid-40s without children.[31] Due to these results, many argue that the German model reinforced a family model of a male breadwinner and female caregiver.[32] Later on, we'll see why that is the case and some of the reforms the German government has implemented recently to change this model.

Egalitarian Model: Sweden

Finally, in contrast to the other two models, Sweden has designed a series of policy initiatives to encourage an egalitarian model of childrearing. First, the Swedish model is based on the presumption that children will be better off both economically and developmentally if they bond early with both parents in a family that is financially stable. Second, Sweden encourages a "dual breadwinner" model, in which pay equity between men and women is a major goal. To help achieve this, Sweden designed a parental leave policy to encourage men to take more time off from work.

Sweden's approach to maternity and parental leave policy evolved in part out of the Great Depression, when birthrates were considered to be dangerously low. Two academics, Alva and Gunnar Myrdal, in their book *Crisis in the Population Question*, urged increased government intervention to improve the well-being of families, and hence their desire to bear children. In the 1960s, the government also had to respond to the pressing problem of a looming labor shortage. Women were seen as a potential untapped source. The result was a policy that encouraged society as a whole to display a commitment to both family life and economic engagement.

Currently, Sweden has a complex policy that includes stipulations for maternity leave, parental leave, and several provisions specifically addressed to fathers that total up to 480 days of paid leave (up to 80 percent) however parents want, up to the child's eighth birthday. It is policies such as these that have made Sweden the poster child of family leave policies, and particularly those that help advance gender equality. Sweden began its journey away from looking solely at women as carers in the 1970s, when it became the first country to replace maternity leave with parental leave (available to either mothers or fathers). The parent on leave got almost a full salary for a year before returning to a guaranteed job, and both could work 6-hour days until their children entered school. Both female employment rates and birthrates surged. The only problem was that men rarely took the leave; either because of socialization, preference, or economic necessity, it made more sense for the mother to care for the baby. Up through the early 1990s, the share of fathers on leave was stalled at 6 percent. In 1995, the Swedish government introduced "daddy leave." Fathers weren't forced to stay home, but the family lost 1 month of parental leave benefits if he did not. Within a few years, more than 8 in 10 men took leave. In 2002, the government added a second nontransferable father month on a "use it or lose it" basis; those months are nontransferable to the mother.

This slightly increased already high take-up rates and also encouraged many men to extend their leave, taking more than the 2-month minimum.[33] Parents are further assisted by a number of additional benefits. Working parents (and grand-parents) may take a certain number of days per year on paid leave to care for a sick child (and grandchild). Finally, Sweden grants parents a monthly cash allowance to any family with one or more children under the age of 16. In 2012, this amount equaled about $160.[34]

As we shall discuss, in combination with their early childhood education and care system, the Swedish model promotes a more egalitarian division of labor between men and women rather than reinforcing traditional gendered divisions of labor. Fathers needed a policy "nudge" to spend more time at home; but when given this nudge, they took advantage of it. Bengt Westerberg, the deputy prime minister who phased in the first month of paternity leave in 1995, commented, "I always thought if we made it easier for women to work, families would eventually choose a more equal division of parental leave by themselves. But I gradually became convinced that there wasn't all that much choice . . . The only way to achieve equality in society is to achieve equality in the home. Getting fathers to share the parental leave is an essential part of that."[35]

As the photo demonstrates, fathers in countries beyond Sweden also see the value of staying home with their newborns.

Fathers with babies and young children attend a meeting of the European Union Committee on Women's Rights and Gender Equality to support paternity leave legislation at the European Parliament in Brussels on February 23, 2010. SOURCE: AP Photo/Thierry Charlier.

Impact

All of these policies tell us something about how states view the challenge of balancing public and private responsibilities for parenting and the "appropriate" division of labor within the household. Of all of our case studies, the United States has provided the most minimal intervention in terms of facilitating parents' abilities to manage work and family, despite the recurring invocation of family values in political discourse. In particular, the lack of accompanying financial benefits makes it difficult for poor and lower-income families to take advantage of the FMLA. Further, it is virtually impossible for a household headed by a single parent to use FMLA, given the difficulty of going without pay for 3 months. In contrast, the other countries we looked at provide much more generous support to enable families of all income levels to take time off from work. This, along with some of the other benefits discussed, has a significant impact on minimizing the incidence of child poverty.

Yet, often, policies can be deceiving. A policy that is generous but targets only mothers, either formally or informally, may not in the end advance gender equality at home or at work. For example, what are we to make of generous maternity leave benefits, such as Germany's? Certainly, they can help ease women's responsibilities at work and acknowledge that giving birth to a child, and then raising that child, is a difficult, time-consuming process that is also extremely valuable to society. However, policies can also be interpreted as a statement about where women "should" be spending the majority of their time once they have children. Thus, Germany has a generous leave policy because historically, women have not been expected to return to work or to return to a full-time position, and the assumption has been that the man will continue to be the primary breadwinner. German women were more likely to live the old mantra of *Kinder, Küche, Kirche*.

A maternity leave policy that allows a woman a significant amount of time off from work may help her balance the varied competing demands placed upon her, but it may not advance her long-term economic interests. For example, on the one hand, studies demonstrate that granting leave has encouraged women to return to work after the birth of their child.[36] Presumably, this is because they know that their job will still be available to them. Thus, despite business fears that mandating leave would result in increased complications because of a constantly changing workforce, in fact, most employees did not use up their full leave time and returned to work when they were ready. However, women with children who do work are still less likely to advance as quickly as men, even men who also have children. Women who have children earn significantly less than men, while men actually receive a pay boost after they have children. This can be for a variety of reasons; traditional gender roles often place pressure on men to be even more productive after the birth of a child to provide for their families, while it is more socially acceptable for women to ease out of a grueling work schedule. Alternatively, when women have children, employers see them as an employment risk, while they interpret the same development as a sign of stability and commitment from a male employee. Regardless, while maternity leave policies have helped women stay active in the workforce, either as part-time or full-time employees, they have not necessarily helped women earn more at the workplace vis-à-vis men or advance in other ways in their careers. This is part of the same point that Sheryl Sandberg, Chief Operating Officer at Facebook, was making in the opening story in this chapter.

In fact, research shows that the more generous the leave policy, then the less likely it is that women will return to full-time work.[37] In contrast, parental leave systems that do not exceed 6 months or a year in length are generally associated with either no effect or slight increases in the relative earnings of mothers.[38] Certainly, we are not arguing that progress for women is solely exemplified by their abilities to work full-time outside of the home; many women choose different work paths to meet their personal wants and needs, and many freely choose to scale back work responsibilities in the face of family needs. However, there are ramifications for women who choose to work part-time or to leave the paid work-force completely. This often lessens their financial independence, increasing their reliance on a male "breadwinner" model of family relations, as well as their dependence on the state. While women may be choosing to work less, the side effect of this decision is less economic power within the household, which can have serious implications if the family unit dissolves or is reconfigured. Further, it has serious ramifications for the level of women's pension benefits when they retire. Thus, it is important to evaluate varying parental leave plans carefully and to think about the long-term ramifications of each system for reinforcing or reconfiguring family dynamics.

Some of this impact could be lessened by radically restructuring the division of labor within families. You may have noticed the overwhelming focus on women in this chapter, even though many countries are now implementing paternity, pa-rental, and family leave policies. According to the ILO, at least 48 countries have legislated leave provisions for fathers or leave that can be used by fathers as mater-nity leave. There is enormous variation, however, in how countries define this leave, and whether it is paid. For example, the Kingdom of Saudi Arabia grants 1 day of paid paternity leave, and many African, Asian, Latin American, and CIS countries grant around a week's worth of leave, plus or minus a few days. In many European Union countries, there has been a much larger effort to reserve a sub-stantial amount of time for the father. For example, Germany now reserves 2 months of leave for fathers; Norway grants 10 weeks; Iceland is the leader at 3 months.[39] Yet, granting men leave, even paid leave, isn't always a sufficient "nudge." Men have been slow to take full advantage of the leave opportunities available to them. The reasons for this are multifaceted; when given the option of who should take leave, couples may fall back on traditional societal norms in which it is more accepted for women to take time off. Men in particular may have difficulty diverging from a work culture that values men as breadwinners and not as nurturers. Also, given that, on average, men make a much higher salary than women, it may be more difficult for families to absorb the costs of paternity leave unless the benefits are quite generous. However, research has demonstrated that policy design matters; men are much more likely to take advantage of leave bene-fits when they are framed as paternity leave benefits rather than the more neutral "parental leave."[40] Further, policies such as Sweden's "use it or lose it" scheme have also encouraged fathers to take leave when previously they abstained. This increased equality at home has had an obvious impact; a study published by the Swedish Institute of Labor Market Policy Evaluation showed that a mother's future earnings increase on average 7 percent for every month the father takes leave.

These findings point to the limitations of designing "gender-neutral" policies in a context of extreme gender imbalances. Sometimes more proactive policies are necessary to change longstanding habits. Regardless, unless fathers use their benefits or find alternative ways to be more involved in parenting, the unequal distribution of labor that pervades the household will continue to affect women's abilities to participate successfully in the workforce.

Early Childhood Education and Care

After parental leave ends, many parents who work outside the home need to find care for their children until they reach school age. Child care has become increasingly important in the wake of significant demographic and attitudinal shifts: women's entrance into the workforce, the need to keep women in the labor market at a time when skilled labor is at a premium, an increase in single-parent households, as well as the importance attached to good educational services for young children have all led to a marked increase in demand for state services.[41] Historically, day care for children grew out of the charitable movement to help poor and working-class mothers. In the wake of World War II, governments began to take over the costs and responsibilities for providing day care in the wake of the large influx of female workers into economic activity.[42] States rapidly increased their commitment to providing day care in the 1970s, partly in response to the critical mass of women in the labor force as well as their demands for more services. Currently, all OECD countries provide universal, publicly funded education for children starting at the age of 5 to 7, and most provide some form of publicly funded and publicly delivered day care to lessen the financial burdens on parents. As one can see in Table 5.2, however, the countries differ substantially with regard to the scope of the state's commitment to providing early care and education. In addition, across all countries, despite the strides countries have made in providing day care, demand in many countries outstrips supply. While there is adequate day care in many countries for children ages 3 to 6, providing good care for infants and toddlers is still a challenge for almost all OECD countries. And entering primary school is no guarantee that parents will be able to return to work full-time; many countries still send children home for lunch, and many primary schools in Germany end at 12:30 p.m. The result is that many women choose to opt out of the labor market or work part-time until their children are old enough to stay in care full-time. This tends to lessen women's abilities to advance their careers, which in turn has consequences for their short-term and long-term financial autonomy.

We shall discuss three approaches to the state provision of child care. The United States provides minimal coverage, assuming relatively little responsibility for the task of day care. In this scenario, the government leaves it to the private sector and to individual parents to provide day care, and the financial burden of

Table 5.2 Early Care and Education

COUNTRY	PUBLIC ECEC SPENDING AS A % OF GDP	PUBLIC SPENDING PER CHILD ($) 0- TO 2-YEAR-OLDS	3- TO 5-YEAR-OLDS	NET CHILD-CARE COSTS AS A % OF FAMILY INCOME DUAL EARNERS	SOLE PARENTS
Austria	—	—	—	15	17
Belgium	0.79	2,333	4,698	4	4
Canada	—	—	4,052	22	30
Denmark	1.17	6,376	3,743	8	9
Finland	0.94	7,118	2,420	7	7
France	1.00	2,858	4,679	11	10
Germany	0.38	860	3,538	8	8
Greece	—	—	—	5	5
Iceland	1.18	5,733	4,589	15	11
Ireland	—	—	—	29	45
Italy	0.61	1,558	4,626	—	—
Netherlands	0.47	1,092	5,881	12	9
Norway	0.77	6,425	4,127	8	−2 yet 8
Portugal	0.40	—	3,293	4	4
Sweden	0.98	5,928	3,627	6	6
Switzerland	0.23	1,129	2,525	30	18
United Kingdom	0.58	3,563	4,255	33	23
United States	0.35	794	4,660	19	37

SOURCE: Christopher J. Ruhm, "Policies to Assist Parents with Young Children" *Work and Family*, Vol. 21, no. 2, fall 2011, p. 51.

day care falls primarily on the parents' shoulders. Other countries, such as Germany, are more proactive in providing publicly funded day care. However, often this coverage does not start until age 3 or is provided in such a way to encourage male full-time employment and female part-time employment. A third group of countries, exemplified by Sweden, have attempted to provide comprehensive day care so that either parent may enter the workforce with the greatest freedom possible.

Pro-family/Noninterventionist Model: The United States
The United States stands alone in its record of support for working mothers. While the government subsidizes the cost of day care in most OECD countries, in the United States parents are responsible for covering the majority of the costs. Further, while in many OECD countries the coverage of the programs is

universal and all children are eligible regardless of the parents' income or employment status, the United States provides federally funded day care for neglected, abused, and/or low-income children only as well as a part-day educational kindergarten program for middle- and upper-class children ages 5 and 6. Britain and Canada also subscribe to a model that conflates federally funded day care with welfare programs.[43] The only system of benefits that the United States does offer for parents with children in day care is a variety of indirect tax credits. The Internal Revenue Service offers a tax credit for between 20 and 35 percent of parents' expenses, although the amount (as of 2010) is capped at $6,000.[44] In sum, the expectation is that the state should intervene only in the event of market or family breakdown. Otherwise, families and individuals are expected to support and care for themselves. For those who cannot provide for themselves, the state has provided a minimum safety net.

In the United States, federal funding for child care has been used to respond to perceived emergency situations and pressing social problems. The first federal investment in child care was made during the 1930s, during the years of the Great Depression, as a way to provide jobs for the unemployed and to provide child-care assistance to poor families. However, as the economy improved, the program was canceled.[45] The U.S. entrance into World War II, which generated an enormous demand for female labor, once again brought the issue of publicly funded day care to the fore of the political arena, and for a brief period during World War II, child-care services were subsidized with public tax dollars. From 1942 to 1946, the federal government financed a preschool program for children of working mothers in "war impact areas." This wartime federally funded child-care service expanded to more than 3,000 centers in 47 states. While congressmen initially were reluctant to fund the program, they were eventually persuaded by the practical problems presented by women's influx into the labor market as men left to fight the war in Europe. Despite widespread protest from mothers, federal policymakers moved to terminate the program at the war's end.[46]

The rise of the feminist movement in the late 1960s rekindled the issue, and in the 1970s, local feminist groups were active in building community day-care centers, run cooperatively by parents. In addition, the National Organization for Women fought for the passage of the Comprehensive Child Development Act of 1971, which would have provided federal funding for day-care centers, open to all parents, on a sliding fee basis. Although Congress passed the bill with bipartisan support, President Nixon vetoed the measure.[47] Similar to the rhetoric used two decades later by President Bush to veto the FMLA, Nixon expressed symbolic support for working parents but stopped short of offering federal financial support. Arguing that the government's intervention should be kept to a minimum, he vetoed the legislation on the grounds that "for the Federal Government to plunge headlong financially into supporting child development would commit the vast moral authority of the National Government to the side of communal approaches to child rearing over against [sic] the family centered approach."[48] Since then, there has been no similar attempt to mandate federal support for comprehensive child-care policies.

In the United States, the limited discussion over the provision of federally funded day care for all was replaced by a policy strategy in which public child-care funds became entangled with debates over welfare reform. Publicly subsidized day care became framed as part of a broader policy package to cure welfare "dependency." This approach to federal day-care funding was reintroduced in 1962 through the Aid to Families with Dependent Children (AFDC) program, but was available only for a limited number of families with working mothers whose children were identified as "at risk" and in danger of neglect.[49] The creation of early childhood education programs in the mid-1960s, such as Head Start, furthered the focus on assisting very-low-income families. In 1996, Congress passed a radical welfare reform bill, and the Temporary Assistance for Needy Families (TANF) program replaced AFDC. TANF stressed, among other things, ending poor families' reliance on federal assistance by making eligibility for cash aid dependent on participation in the workforce. Thus, at least for poor women, the government designed a policy explicitly to encourage them to work more in an effort to reverse their perceived "unproductivity" under the previous system. Although in 2012, about 19 percent of TANF dollars were allocated for child-care support, demand vastly outstrips supply of actual services. The increased work requirements, combined with inadequate child-care assistance, often encourage the proliferation of poor mothers who work.[50] Further, single mothers (except in the state of Wisconsin) currently lose some of their benefits if they cannot identify the father of their children.[51]

In short, the United States follows a model in which managing work and child care is relegated to the private domain and parents are left to purchase child-care services on the private market. Publicly funded day care has become intertwined with various welfare reform programs. While this approach has less of an impact on middle- and upper-class women who can afford to pay for care, this approach to family policy has been particularly difficult for low-income families and has compounded the incidence of child poverty.

Pro-family/Breadwinner Model: Germany

Other child-care systems encourage a division of labor with the man as breadwinner and the woman as caretaker, at least for the first years of a child's life. This type of system couples generous maternity leave provisions and cash benefits with limited publicly subsidized child-care support, particularly for day care for children from birth up to age 3. For example, in Austria, only 11 percent of children in this age range are in part-time or full-time day care, but that number changes to over 80 percent by the time the child is 4. Germany, Greece, and Switzerland also have low rates of early care, particularly in the first 3 years. This system indirectly discourages women's full-time return to work until the child is of school age.

Let's now turn to exploring more fully the Germany system, which until recently has been a good exemplar of this approach. In line with Germany's pro–single breadwinner family policy, publicly subsidized day-care options, particularly for parents with children from birth to age 3, are extremely limited, although there are growing state levels of support for child-care programs for children from the ages of 3 to 6. Rather, the German state is more willing to give financial assistance to those taking on the task of child or elder care in the family, as opposed to investing in expanded social services (such as access to day care).

In the German "breadwinner" model, the work involved in childrearing is considered an alternative to paid employment, and, as we discussed earlier, parents on leave from work (primarily women) may receive a stipend (*Erziehungsgeld*) for the first few years of a child's life. The allowance that a parent may receive for the care of a child is more symbolic than real; it does not fully cover the costs of raising a child, nor does it equal a salary. However, it is intended as a symbolic recognition for the work of child care and childrearing.[52] In the government's own words, "bringing up a child is a great responsibility," and "Children are a wonderful gift, but they do cost money."[53] Further, to lessen the long-term impact that loss of wages can have on pension plans, the German government grants a pension credit to mothers who spend up to 3 years at home rearing a child. The value of the credit is equal to up to 3 years of work at average wages.[54]

Why did this type of male breadwinner model emerge in Germany in the postwar era? For one, German political culture, particularly in its attitudes about the family, has always been conservative. The rise of center-right Christian Democratic parties in the postwar years further cemented the emphasis on the preservation of traditional family structures, defined as a working father, a stay-at-home mother, and children. Further, the government took an anti-woman stance when women did join the workforce in increasing numbers. In public campaigns, the family ministry portrayed working mothers as greedy "double earners" who were pursuing their selfish personal aspirations at the expense of fulfilling their family obligations. The government also pursued a policy of relying on foreign "guest workers" to fill the demand for labor rather than encouraging women into the workforce.[55]

Nor did the West German feminist movement focus on child-care provision as a means to advance women's equality. Rather, women's and feminist organizations focused on women's increased access to part-time employment so that they could continue to meet their care responsibilities in the home but also achieve some level of economic independence in the workforce. The issue was framed as one in which the government should provide sufficient levels of material support so that mothers would not be forced to work out of economic necessity. The result of this framing was that for the most part, feminist organizations did not challenge women's traditional roles in the family and home.[56] The few radical feminist organizations that did mobilize on issues of day care as a means to advance women's autonomy found little public support, since they were deeply suspicious of a paternalistic, authoritarian state and thus advocated for collective child care.

This suspicion of the state kept them from working with potential allies within key government policy agencies. In addition, German feminists chose to focus on abortion and the right to choose *not* to become a mother and *not* to have children. Thus, the women's movement overall was fractured between the "new maternalists," who did not directly challenge women's traditional roles, and in fact pushed for society to place more value on them, and the more radical feminists, who questioned the entire family structure and whether women could truly emancipate themselves and simultaneously continue to bear children.[57]

The return of a center-left governing coalition, increased pressure from women, as well as demographic pressures resulting from reunification in 1990 prompted the state to revisit the issue of publicly subsidized child care, where demand vastly outstripped supply. The merging of two welfare systems—the East German one, with a much more extensive and comprehensive system of day care for children from birth to age 6, with the West's much less extensive one— highlighted the realities of an increasingly active female workforce, which was out of step with Germany's "breadwinner" model of welfare policy. In 1996, the government moved to extend day-care options to accommodate funding for half-day preschool for children between the ages of 3 and 6, although this still did not fully ease the burden of dual-career couples who worked full-time. Further reform was implemented in 2004, when the ruling leftist coalition partners, the Social Democratic and Green parties, pushed through new legislation to increase full-time day-care offerings for children under 3 years of age. (In the former West Germany, the situation was particularly dire: only 3 percent of children younger than 3 had spaces in day care in comparison to 37 percent of children in the former East Germany).[58] However, it took the election of a female Prime Minister, Christian Democrat Angela Merkel, before the issue was seriously revisited. Born and raised in the former East Germany, she was long used to the rhetoric and reality of women's equality, and while she herself did not have children, she has made the improvement of reconciliation policies a domestic priority for her government. She tasked Ursula von der Leyen, former Family Minister and current Labor Minister and mother of seven (!), with this job. In January 2007, the government announced several policy changes to encourage women to return to the workforce sooner, to increase fathers' involvement in child care, and to increase state involvement in early childhood care and early childhood education.[59] More specifically, Ms. Von der Leyen introduced tax credits for private child care, a guaranteed right for all children to a place in a day-care center by August 2013, and her signature measure, "parent money." Similar to the scheme in Sweden, mothers and fathers can now share up to 14 months of generously paid parental leave. If the father does not take at least 2 months, the government pays for only 12. All of these measures are designed to give women incentives to move away from the permitted, barely paid 3-year maternity leave and encourage fathers to share in child care. While it will take time for the effects of these changes to be felt (particularly building up infrastructure for increased child-care spaces), nonetheless, in the short term, the percentage of fathers taking leave at the birth of their children has surged from 3 percent before the reforms were introduced to 21 percent (although about 60 percent took only the minimum 2 months).[60] This is a marked change to Germany's approach since the post–World War II era; one scholar has argued that it "not only reconstructs traditional gender roles, but it also enhances new forms of social inequality among women."[61] In sum, the pre-2007 model of benefits (generous maternity leave combined with little support for day care) kept many women permanently out of the workforce, and for those who continued to work, encouraged them to take a "baby break" for several years or to work part-time for numerous years until returning to work full-time.[62] This, in turn, tended to support a family structure in which one parent serves as the breadwinner while the other provides care and supplementary income. It will be interesting to see if Germany will move closer to the Swedish model over time.

Egalitarian Model: Sweden

A few countries, primarily the Scandinavian countries of Denmark, Finland, and Sweden, as well as France and Belgium, have taken great strides in ensuring that with state support, families can balance work with parenting. All of these countries have implemented a wide array of policies to provide strong coverage for children from birth through age 6. Denmark, Finland, and Sweden even adopted legislation in the 1980s that established day care as a right for all children under the age of 6.[63] In addition, particularly in the Nordic countries, the state has assumed the financial burden of providing these services, rather than relying on fees from parents. How much money is this? In the case of Sweden, it represents almost 1 percent of the country's GDP (compared to a U.S. rate of 0.35%). We now turn to looking at Sweden's system in greater detail. What does this 1 percent provide in terms of benefits?

Sweden is one of the few countries that spends about the same amount on child-care services as on family benefits. Swedish child-care policy is designed with twin aims: "one is to support and encourage children's development and learning, and help them get a good start in life, while the other is to enable parents to combine parenthood with employment or studies."[64] Since the 1970s, the Swedish government has focused increasingly on providing quality child care, with full access to all and financed by public funds in order to improve "the well-being of the young and a desire for greater equality between the sexes."[65]

Initially, Sweden's child-care program was designed to meet the needs of poor, working, and single mothers. However, as women entered the workforce in increasing numbers in the 1960s and feminist groups agitated for increased government support for day-care options, the government moved to update its approach to the provision of day care. In 1968, the government appointed a special commission, the National Commission on Childcare, to compile proposals for an overhaul of the current system. Out of this came the foundations of the Swedish model, which emphasized an integrated system of care for infants and education for small children, with the goal of enabling parents to meet their work needs. As the government explained, "Without such a highly developed childcare system, the changes in family patterns and gender roles that have occurred since the 1970s would not have been possible." Thus, they consciously linked their policy design with a stated goal of advancing women's equality in the labor market and encouraging a more equitable distribution of labor at home.[66] However, in the 1970s, the government's performance often lagged behind its rhetorical commitment, and demand vastly outstripped supply. For example, in 1972, there were 95,000 child-care spaces available and demand for 400,000. Women's groups played a critical role in staging sit-ins and other forms of protest to highlight the gap between the government's symbolic versus real levels of support.[67] Since the 1970s, the state has increasingly emphasized universal coverage so that all parents, working or non-working, can access child-care services and all children, regardless of income, can access education. Reforms from 2001 to 2003 increased both the scope and the scale of coverage. Preschool programs are universal and serve all children under age 7, with priority for children with working mothers, with single mothers, from immigrant or low-income families, or with a disability. In addition, there is a cap on the amount that parents must contribute to the costs of day care. The aim, according to the government, is to "make public childcare a part of the general welfare system, available to all. The basic principle is that all children in Sweden shall have access to childcare and that fees shall be so low that no child is excluded."[68] Further, all families with children qualify for a monthly allowance until the child reaches the age of 16 (or 20 if a student, 23 if attending a school for the mentally retarded).[69]

Why did Sweden design such generous policies, in comparison with some of the other countries we have examined? Like the other countries, political culture, institutional design, political opportunities, and levels of women's mobilization all provide keys to answering this question. For one, the Swedish government made several critical policy decisions. In response to labor shortages in the 1960s, the Swedish government consciously tapped the reserve of married women, who had previously chosen to withdraw from the labor market upon marrying and bearing children. Further, labor unions, which played a much more powerful role in policy formulation, agitated for better day care, partially in response to increased female membership, as well as because they felt that employed women were the "lesser evil" when compared to relying on guest workers (the German strategy). At the same time, Swedish society was more accepting of a dual-income family model that advanced gender equality vis-à-vis the division of labor. This trickled up to political parties, and by the mid-1960s, parties on both the left and the right acknowledged the need for public child care in principle. Finally, the different strands of the women's movement in Sweden were more united around the idea that combining family and full employment were not contradictory aims. In addition, they did not adopt the antistatist rhetoric of the radical German feminists, and thus actively courted allies with key government policy positions, with the end goal of the establishment of state-supported child-care services. In turn, the government was relatively open to the demands of the women's movement. The increasing number of women in decision-making positions in political parties and labor unions facilitated this access.[70]

Impact

Similar to our discussion regarding maternity leave policies, child-care policies also tell us something about how states view the challenge of balancing public and private responsibilities for parenting and the "appropriate" division of labor within the household. In the United States, little attempt is made to encourage women's departure from the workforce, although there is also little attempt to subsidize child care for working parents to facilitate women's increased participation. Rather, the government simply stays out of that arena and looks to the market, rather than the state, for solutions unless it needs to step in and provide a minimal social safety net for the neediest families. In contrast, Germany until recently actively encouraged a "mommy" break through its combination of maternity and child-care policies. Finally, Sweden has moved furthest in its efforts to design policy that encourages full employment for men or women as they balance work responsibilities with childrearing.

Drawing from the data in Table 5.3, there is widespread variation in the number of children who have access to day care in each of the countries studied here. Further, there is widespread variation within countries in children's access to day care from birth up to age 3 and age 3 to 6. Thus, for example, while Germany ranks last in our country case studies in terms of children in care from birth through age 3, that number increases significantly for children ages 3 to 6, and it surpasses both Sweden and the United States in terms of coverage. Sweden has the highest percentage of children in day care from birth through age 3, but not as high a percentage as Germany from ages 3 to 6. And despite the absence of uniform publicly subsidized care for children in the United States, parents are finding ways to piece together day care for their children, although they trail Sweden and

Table 5.3 Early Care and Education Arrangements

	PERCENTAGE OF CHILDREN IN PART- AND FULL-TIME DAY CARE			
COUNTRY	BIRTH TO AGE 3	3	4	5
Austria	11	48	83	93
Belgium	42	100	100	100
Canada	24	16	42	100
Denmark	63	94	93	85
Finland	26	66	70	74
France	43	99	100	100
Germany	14	83	93	93
Greece	18	—	56	86
Iceland	56	94	95	97
Ireland	25	—	47	100
Italy	29	97	100	100
Netherlands	23	—	47	100
Norway	42	87	92	93
Portugal	44	63	81	93
Spain	34	96	97	100
Sweden	45	82	87	88
Switzerland	<10	9	38	97
United Kingdom	40	79	91	100
United States	31	39	58	78

SOURCE: Christopher J. Ruhm, "Policies to Assist Parents with Young Children," *Work and Family*, Vol. 21, no. 2, fall 2011, 50.

Germany's numbers (for ages 3 to 6). However, given the lack of substantial federal funding, day care in the United States is something of a class issue and is more readily available to those who can afford it. Further, there is wide variation in the United States in the quality of child care, and it is highly dependent on parents' abilities to pay for it.

The availability of subsidized child care, in addition to paid maternity leave and family allowances, also helps reduce the incidence of child poverty because these policies are specifically targeted to reduce the often onerous costs of having and raising children. Conversely, the lack of generous reconciliation policies can help exacerbate poverty. In part, the generosity of reconciliation policies tend to tell us about larger approaches of each country's welfare state. For example, the United States has a relatively small welfare state and minimal level of reconciliation policies. Not surprisingly, its lack of intervention is accompanied by high rates of poverty, particularly child poverty. According to the 2010 U.S. Census, 22 percent of all children under 18 live in poverty, representing over a third of the total poor population in the United States. Further, African Americans and Hispanics are disproportionately likely to live in poverty.[71] As a result, poor working parents raise children in poverty, who in turn will perpetuate the cycle, contributing to the fact that the United States has one of the highest levels of income inequality in the industrialized world. In contrast, Sweden has a child poverty rate of 7 percent, and Germany's is 8.3 percent. Their approach to designing reconciliation policies has helped create these low statistics.[72]

What has been the impact on women's employment? Women's advocates have long argued that the availability of child care is strongly linked to women's access to paid employment. Further, promoting maternal employment is important for increasing women's financial autonomy and is also critical in preventing child poverty, particularly in families that are headed by a single parent.[73] Has increased child care, in addition to our other reconciliation policies, kept women in the workforce? In the United States, 67 percent of mothers of children under the age of 15 work. In Germany, 71 percent of mothers work, while the figure for Sweden is 80 percent (the fourth highest figure in OECD countries).[74] While correlation does not equal causality (we cannot determine whether day-care policy and reconciliation policies more broadly are the primary force driving women into or keeping them out of the workforce), we do know that women who live in systems with generous benefits, such as Sweden's, are able to balance work and parenting more readily than those in Germany's, where women tend to take time off during early childrearing years. The experience of the United States is roughly on par with the overall OECD average. Women are not discouraged from joining the workforce, but policy does not do much to help them balance work and life.

What political conditions are conducive to or, alternatively, hinder policies reducing gender inequalities? What determines whether states will promote "equity for breadwinners or parity for caregivers"?[75] The prevailing societal vision of the "ideal family" is critical. In the United States, suspicion of "big government" and care providers outside of the family, plus Americans' individualist values, combine to create a model in which the federal government is hesitant to intervene. Germany's conservative family culture, combined with an acceptance of the welfare state, helped foster policies that reward caregiving activities and support a "male breadwinner" family structure. It is only now trying to move toward a model similar to Sweden's. Sweden's relatively tolerant political culture, combined with an acceptance of a strong welfare state and active state intervention in social policy, helped create more egalitarian policy that also sought to foster more equal divisions of labor within the family.

Second, the nature of the women's movement in each of our countries was also critical. In each of these countries, the prevailing belief system of the feminist lobby has affected which measures groups will push in order to bring about gender equality. For example, some movements have stressed the differences between the sexes and women's special capacities and have fought for policies that acknowledge that. In contrast, other women's movements have tried to frame women's issues as a matter of gender equality and equal rights. These two approaches engender different visions of gender relations. Thus, for example, women's movements in Germany, the United Kingdom, and Norway have tended to take the gender difference argument, pushing for recognition of women's caregiving activities and for benefits that financially reward caregivers. In contrast, equal rights advocates have been influential in the United States, Netherlands, and Sweden, although women's demands have been spun differently in the countries. While the United States has tended to focus on the equality of women at work while pushing for their abilities to be breadwinners as well, women's movements in the Netherlands and Sweden have focused on trying to redistribute tasks of breadwinning and caring so that men do more caring and women have more access to breadwinning than before and both parents perform both careers equally.[76]

The presence or absence of a strong labor movement has also affected the scope and nature of policies that affect balancing productive and reproductive responsibilities. In countries with strong unions and/or collective bargaining, the differences between male and female wages are much smaller for full-time workers. Nonetheless, unions do vary to the degree to which they promote women's interests. Often, this is based on the extent of women's labor market participation, as well as their participation in unions. Women's share of total union membership has increased; in Finland, Sweden, and Denmark, women account for roughly half of union membership.[77]

Finally, parties and the political makeup of governments matter in terms of pushing for policies that encourage balancing production and reproduction. Traditionally, left-wing parties have been much more receptive to implementing policies that encourage female equality, while right-wing parties have been more skeptical, even hostile. Left-wing parties in various countries have introduced child-care services, equal taxation, women's policy machinery within the administration, policies that reduce gender pay differentials, and lower poverty rates among women and children. However, left-wing parties are not the only avenues for women's participation. Women's entry into all parties can make a difference. For example, it was the administration of Christian Democratic Union leader Angela Merkel that passed the most significant reform to Germany's "breadwinner" system.

ADVANCING WOMEN'S EQUALITY

What are some further potential solutions to the dilemma of balancing work and family? What issues are still on the horizon? Women's equality advocates do not all agree on appropriate strategies for advancing women's equality. One of the biggest divisions has been whether to focus on further integrating women into the workforce while simultaneously pushing for a more equitable division of labor in the household or to push states to value the task of childrearing, which often falls on the shoulders of women. Still others advocate combating what they see as an overly materialistic focus on accessing traditionally male institutions of work. But all of these scenarios are fraught with difficulties. Does integrating women into the workforce merely push them to further adopt a flawed, patriarchal approach to work? If a woman willingly chooses to stay at home and engage in caregiving as a career, is the fact that she chose this path more empowering than the critique that this type of family arrangement reinforces traditional divisions of labor in the household and increases her financial dependency? What is the alternative to a rejection of work-centered modern societies and male-dominated work norms? We try to take no position on this. However, we do take the position that women who work are an increasing reality and that currently, the design of a wide array of policies has serious implications for women who also choose to be parents. Despite the improvement in policies, women who work are still penalized (in terms of income and career advancement opportunities) more so than men for having children.

What are ways to ease this tension? Particularly in noninterventionist states such as the United States, advocates have focused primarily on extending the provisions of FMLA and pushing for partially paid leave for parents and secondarily on better levels of federal support for early childhood education. After signing the FMLA, President Clinton hoped to expand leave entitlements for parents by expanding the application of the legislation to companies that employ 25 workers or more (as opposed to the current 50) and by providing some sort of wage replacement, perhaps through focusing on increased coverage of temporary disability Insurance. From 1993 to 1999, almost 20 initiatives were put forth by members of Congress to expand FMLA.[78] However, the dominance of the Republican Party, which is suspicious of increasing government intervention, along with a renewed focus on foreign policy concerns, put the domestic issue of parental leave on the back burner. Many hoped that the issue would be revisited under the Obama administration, but the 2008 global financial crisis and the victory of the Republicans in Congressional elections in 2010 make this unlikely.

For European countries that have more significant levels of federal support for both leave and child-care provisions, emphasis has focused on improving the conditions of the benefits, through increased financial support, longer and more flexible conditions of leave, and/or improved access to and coverage of child care. Advocates have focused on lobbying businesses for increasingly flexible work conditions to meet parental demands. In particular, countries such as Germany have struggled to update and modernize their pro-family/breadwinner structure, which tends to discourage mothers from fully participating in the workforce. As a result, far fewer German women have children than in other European countries, a trend that will have significant implications as the current population continues to age out of the workforce.[79] Further, the German government, in response to Germany's ongoing economic slump, has realized that it needs to harness the productivity of all of its citizens, not just its male ones. Germany is slowly moving toward a more equitable model that does not rely on a male breadwinner and a stay-at-home mother.

In addition, particularly in Europe, governments have shifted the focus away from mothers to fathers. They have targeted policies to nudge men to take on more of the caring responsibilities that mothers have historically taken on. Even though men are increasingly assuming more of the traditionally female tasks within divisions of labor in the household, men still spend more time at work outside the home breadwinning and women still spend more time in the home cleaning and caring. While these divisions are becoming more blurred, many argue that states need to more proactively encourage men to claim a more active role in the home with policies such as paternity leave. Further, as women increase their education and participation (and, we hope, their earnings) in the labor force, it will potentially encourage a more even distribution of labor, as families no longer assume that men will, by default, be the main breadwinner.

In the future, states will have to respond more coherently to the issue of single-parent households. In the post—World War II era, governments had to adjust policy to absorb the relatively new trend of the dual-income family. Since then, countries have had to adjust to further changing demographic trends. Household size has decreased in recent decades, and in all industrialized countries (except the United States), women have been having children later. Fewer individuals have chosen to marry, and a higher percentage of marriages end in divorce. Births outside of marriage have grown, and single-parent households are increasingly common. The rise of same-sex unions across OECD countries has further stretched traditional definitions of the family unit. All of the trends have led to a rapidly changing definition of the family, and states will have to continue to adjust to these changes with new policy.

CONCLUSION

Governments have been motivated by a variety of factors to grant benefits to parents who work outside of the home. Initially, many of these policies were designed not to help women balance work and family life but as part of larger pronatalist campaigns to encourage women to have children. In addition, benefits are part of an effort to redistribute income from childless households to families with children, given the increased financial burden associated with childrearing. Alternatively, states are motivated to supplement the incomes of poor or lower-income families as a means of reducing or preventing poverty, or to increase social cohesion among all families. Other countries want to encourage parents (primarily women) to engage more fully in the task of childrearing, and thus offer incentives for a parent to stay at home with the child rather than return to the workforce. In contrast, other countries are trying to facilitate greater participation in the labor force, and offer generous benefits so that parents can balance work with family life.

How have varied policies relating to parental leave and early and childhood care affected parents' abilities to manage work and family and reduce gender inequalities? Noninterventionist approaches to this dilemma, exemplified by the United States, have enacted minimal gender-neutral policies to ease the tension between work and family but have done little to implement more proactive policies. In contrast, until recently, the German model consisted of policies that, while generous, tended to encourage traditional views about the appropriate division of labor within households. The state tended to adhere to a "male breadwinner" model of social benefits, and mothers were given strong maternity benefits, not because they were to return to the workforce, but because upon becoming pregnant, they were to leave work and engage themselves in caring activities of home and hearth, or *Kinder, Küche, Kirche*. Germany is now moving closer to the framework used by Sweden, a country that has designed policies that help men and women combine careers with family responsibilities by providing generous leave benefits with comprehensive child care. Sweden has gone furthest in designing proactive policy to encourage fathers to contribute to a more equitable distribution of labor in the household.

However, it is important not to overemphasize the effects of trends to ease the tension between parenting and working. Most countries' policies have been reworked and are gender-neutral in language, giving both parents equal rights to take leave or draw benefits. However, gender-neutral policies, even if written with the idea of encouraging fathers to share more equally in the burden of care, still have gender-specific results. Even though states increasingly are legislating on parental, as opposed to maternity, leave, fathers are still hesitant to take advantage of the benefits offered them, and women continue to shoulder the burden of care responsibilities. The European Union is also aware of the problem and has acknowledged that "there is broad agreement on the need to encourage fathers to make use of the opportunities for child care that are available to them. Whilst short-term leave at the time of a child's birth is becoming more popular, longer-term care options seem to be ignored by the vast majority of fathers." While citing a need for a "radical shift in attitudes," the European Union was less aggressive in addressing the means to facilitate this and merely acknowledged that member states had launched "information campaigns" to address the issue.[80] However, this is only the beginning. As one scholar noted: "Mothers have changed the gender balance in breadwinning. Changing the gender balance in caring remains a challenge for parents, work organizations and policy reform."[81]

In closing, the degree to which states provide parental benefits is of enormous significance to women. In the absence of generous benefits, women often end up in low-paid, part-time, and irregular jobs.[82] Yet, talk is cheap; providing the resources, such as publicly funded leave as well as universal day care, is easier to promise than to provide. While states have improved their commitment to public spending to help bridge the divide between private and public divisions of labor, designing policy that encourages the redistribution of that divide is a more elusive task. However, passing policy to do such a thing has been a contentious process. Even in states that have designed policies that provide incentives for men to take a more proactive role in assuming traditional women's duties, men have been slow to respond. Policy in some ways is only the first step; changing people's habitual behavior is the ongoing challenge.

FOR MORE INFORMATION

Video and Multimedia

"Amy Chua/Tiger Mom, 'Didn't Expect this Level of Intensity!'" (2011). Good Morning America, ABC News. http://www.youtube.com/watch?v=GAel_qRfKx8. ABC News interviews Amy Chua on the controversy surrounding her book *Battle Hymn of the Tiger Mother.*

Sheryl Sandberg, "Why we have too few women leaders." http://www.ted.com/talks/sheryl_ sandberg_why_we_have_too_few_women_leaders.html. Facebook COO Sheryl Sandberg looks at why fewer women than men reach the top of their professions and offers three controversial pieces of advice to women.

"Paternity Leave in Sweden." (2008). ABC News.http://abcnews.go.com/Nightline/video/ swedens-paternity-leave-11923331. ABC News looks at what it is like to have paternity leave in Sweden.

Debbie Bain Brickley. (2011). "Integrating Family Planning and Maternal/Child Health Services: Interview." Population Reference Bureau. http://www.prb.org/Journalists/ Webcasts/2011/integrating-family-planning-maternal-child-health.aspx. This 7-minute webcast from Debbie Bain Brickley, senior researcher at UC San Francisco, covers how integrating family planning services with maternal and child health care can enhance the path toward economic growth and development for countries.

"Time With A Newborn: Maternity Leave Policies Around The World." (2011). NPR. http:// www.npr.org/2011/08/09/137062676/time-with-a-newborn-maternity-leave- policies-around-the-world. This interactive map shows how many total days of mater- nity leave are offered by countries around the world.

"Parental Leave: The Swedes are Most Generous." NPR. http://www.npr.org/player/v2/ mediaPlayer.html?action=1&t=1&islist=false&id=139121410&m=139127120. This segment from "All Things Considered" is about Sweden's parental leave law.

Readings

Babies and Bosses—Reconciling Work and Family Life: A Synthesis of Findings for OECD Countries. (2011). OECD. http://www.oecd.org/document/45/0,3746,en_2649_34819_ 39651501_1_1_1_1,00.html. This report reviews work and family reconciliation poli- cies and family outcomes from 13 OECD countries from 2002 to 2005.

"Chinese Population Said Rapidly Aging After 30 Years of Birth Control Policy." (2010). BBC Monitoring International Reports. http://go.galegroup.com/ps/i.do?id=GALE%7 CA236239747&v=2.1&u=s8405248&it=r&p=AONE&sw=w

Doing Better for Families. (2011). OECD. http://www.oecd.org/document/49/0,3746, en_2649_37419_47654961_1_1_1_37419,00.html. Published in 2011, this book con- tinues the examination of *Babies and Bosses* and looks at the different ways in which OECD countries support families.

C. Haub. (2010). Recession Putting Brakes on Increases in Low Birth Rates. *Population Reference Bureau.* http://www.prb.org/Articles/2010/lowfertilitytfr.aspx. This article illustrates the impact of the most recent worldwide recession on total fertility rates in 10 countries.

B. K. Hofer and A. S. Moore. (2010). *The iConnected Parent: Staying Connected to Your College Kids (and Beyond) While Letting Them Grow Up.* New York: Free Press. Today's iConnected parents say they are closer to their kids than their parents were to them. This book questions whether this is good for the kids.

Gretchen Livingston. (2011). "In a Down Economy, Fewer Births." http://www.pewsocial trends.org/files/2011/10/REVISITING-FERTILITY-AND-THE-RECESSION-FINAL.pdf. According to a new analysis of multiple economic and demographic data sources by the Pew Research Center, a sharp decline in fertility rates in the United States that started in 2008 is closely linked to the downturn of the U.S. economy that began about the same time.

G. Livingston and D. Cohn. (2010). "The New Demography of American Motherhood." Pew Research Center. http://pewresearch.org/pubs/1586/changing-demographic-characteristics-american-mothers. This report examines the changing demographic characteristics of U.S. mothers by comparing women who gave birth in 2008 with those who gave birth in 1990.

M. K. Nelson. (2010). *Parenting Out of Control: Anxious Parents in Uncertain Times.* New York: New York University Press. This book explains why today's prosperous and well-educated parents are unable to set realistic boundaries when it comes to raising their children.

Charlotte J. Patterson. (n.d.). "Lesbian & Gay Parenting: Theoretical & Conceptual Examinations Related to Lesbian & Gay Parenting." American Psychological Association. http://www.apa.org/pi/lgbt/resources/parenting.aspx. The publication is provided for the use of clinicians, researchers, students, lawyers, and parents involved in legal and policy issues related to lesbian and gay parenting.

Cecilia Rouse. (n.d.). "The Economics of Workplace Flexibility." White House, Council of Economic Advisors. http://www.whitehouse.gov/blog/2010/03/31/economics-work place-flexibility. This report from the White House presents an economic perspective on flexible workplace policies and practices in the United States.

Annamaria Sundbye and Ariane Hegewisch. (2011). "Maternity, Paternity, and Adoption Leave in the United States." Institute for Women's Policy Research. http://www.iwpr .org/publications/pubs/maternity-paternity-and-adoption-leave-in-the-united-states. A report on the Family and Medical Leave Act (FMLA) passed in 1993 and how it has not been implemented at companies in the United States.

W. Wang. (2011). "For Millennials, Parenthood Trumps Marriage." Pew Social & Demographic Trends. http://www.pewsocialtrends.org/2011/03/09/for-millennials-parent hood-trumps-marriage/. For the Millennial Generation, the social institutions of marriage and parenthood are becoming delinked and differently valued, according to this report from the Pew Research Center.

Organizations and Websites

CafeMom: Moms Connecting About Pregnancy, Babies, Home, Health, and More. http://www.cafemom.com/.

Childstats.gov

"Country comparisons: Total fertility rate." *CIA: The World Factbook*. https://www.cia.gov/library/publications/the-world-factbook/rankorder/2127rank.html.

"Family Database." OECD. http://www.oecd.org/document/4/0,3746,en_2649_34819_37836996_1_1_1_1,00.html.

"Family Support Calculator." OECD. http://www.oecd.org/document/36/0,3746,en_2649_37419_47804068_1_1_1_37419,00.html.

Future of Children (Princeton University and Brookings Institution). www.futureofchildren.org.

Guttmacher Institute. http://www.guttmacher.org. The Guttmacher Institute conducts research, policy analysis, and public education on the advance of sexual and reproductive health and rights.

Institute for Child, Youth and Family Policy (Research Institute of the Heller School at Brandeis University). http://icyfp.brandeis.edu/index.html.

"International Female Labor Force Participation Rates." U.S. Census Bureau. http://www.census.gov/compendia/statab/2012/tables/12s1368.pdf

MomsRising.org

"Motherlode: Adventures in Parenting." *New York Times*. http://parenting.blogs.nytimes.com.

MothersOughttoHaveEqualRights.org

National Association of Mothers' Centers. http://www.motherscenter.org.

"Working Moms: Working Mothers Community | Work It, Mom!" http://www.workitmom.com/.

6

Abortion Politics

very state in America requires that a patient give consent before undergoing medical treatment and that the consent must be "informed." Informed consent usually entails three elements: (1) patients must possess the capacity to make decisions about their care, (2) their participation in these decisions must be voluntary, and (3) they must be provided adequate and appropriate information.[1] Most of you who have been to a doctor have probably signed a consent form for treatment, and maybe you haven't given it much thought as you scribble your signature at the bottom of the page. However, particularly when applied to the battle over abortion, "informed consent" has become extremely murky and contested. Recently, anti-abortion activists have framed their opposition to abortion around their concern for women's health and their desire to make sure that women fully understand what they feel are the potential health risks and emotional complications resulting from having an abortion. For example, the Texas legislature passed a bill in which abortion providers must perform an ultrasound first, show and describe the fetal image to the patient, and play sounds of the fetal heartbeat. Though women who are victims of rape can decline to view the images or hear the heartbeat, they must listen to a description of the ultrasound.[2] Is this "informed consent," or intimidation tactics? In Kansas, the House of Representatives passed a bill that, among other things, required doctors to tell women that abortion causes breast cancer, along with other state-approved health issues, although there is no conclusive evidence to support this assertion. In South Dakota, the Eighth Circuit Court of Appeals upheld a law requiring physicians to advise women seeking an abortion that they face an increased risk of suicide and suicidal thoughts if they obtain the procedure—even though this claim has been contradicted by numerous reviews of scientific and medical evidence.[3] Can consent be informed if the medical information being distributed is highly contested and, in some cases, actually contradicted by an overwhelming amount of research? What about doctors' rights to free speech? And who gets to govern women's reproductive choices, and to what extent? Informed consent is not the only battleground on which the abortion war is waged, and the intensity and scope of the conflict are only expanding; in 2011, a record 92 restrictions on abortion were passed throughout the United States.

We now move to one of the most contentious issues in the realm of women, policy, and politics—legislating the legal rights and freedoms relating to reproduction and reproductive health. A woman's ability to bear children significantly affects her life; yet, she may lack the freedom and/or choice to control when and with whom she will have sex and whether she can do so without fear of infection or unwanted pregnancy. She may have little to no control over the timing and number of her children and may lack the ability to make informed decisions about her reproductive health. Women's interests should be central to the equation of reproductive health, but often their rights in shaping the direction of their reproductive health are subjugated to other interests. Despite United Nations recognition that reproductive rights are a subset of universal human rights, in practice, reproductive rights are a contested set of norms, and many countries have been slow to incorporate a full range of reproductive rights into national law and internationally binding agreements. We look at the most contentious issue—abortion—and compare how states have legislated if, when, and under which conditions women have a right to terminate a pregnancy.

Many women's activists and international organizations devoted to women's health and status believe that the availability of safe and legal abortion is an important reproductive freedom. In practice, the abortion issue has been more successful at raising very complex questions than resolving them. Because women alone can give birth to children, should they then be given full choice as to controlling what happens in their bodies? To what degree should the state regulate women's autonomy in making choices about their bodies? All countries to some degree regulate women's bodies, but they differ in how they weigh demands for women's autonomy with a variety of diverse and often warring interests. On the one hand, many feminists argue that abortion is primarily a woman's issue about personal autonomy and choice over her body. Alternatively, the medical industry has often framed the debate as primarily a potentially dangerous, life-threatening health issue that is best left to medical experts to regulate. Religious figures have couched abortion as a moral conflict and proclaim that all living beings, born as well as unborn, have a right to life. Governments also have a responsibility to regulate the welfare of their citizens, although there is no agreement over how to balance the rights of the mother with the rights of the fetus. Further, because reproduction includes other people, should the rights and interest of others, such as the father, the extended family, and society, be taken into account?

Very few countries have navigated a policy that has pleased all interests. This is partly because the varied sides of the debate share almost no common language. For example, while anti-abortion activists begin by stipulating that the embryo is an unborn child, pro-legalization activists view this initial premise as highly problematic. While abortion foes may see the presence of a fetal heartbeat as evidence of life, abortion legalization supporters may respond that the fetus does not breathe independently until birth. At heart, the debate centers around how society should define personhood, which theoretically grants one an array of inalienable and acquired rights. And this decision is based on interpretations of the meaning of personhood rather than lining up clear "facts."[4]

In this chapter, we look at various ways in which governments have addressed the abortion issue. While nearly all OECD countries have liberalized their policies regulating abortion, the scope of the legislation varies dramatically from country to country, as do governments' commitments to designing and enforcing policy in these areas. We highlight the varied abortion policy outcomes in Ireland, the United States, and the Netherlands. Ireland has one of the most restrictive policies. In contrast, the United States has a confusing mix of abortion policies, which vary tremendously at the state level as a result of intense legal and legislative battles waged between pro- and anti-legalization sides. Finally, in the Netherlands, the abortion debate has largely been resolved on the side of pro-legalization. We find that the strength of the women's movement, prevailing cultural norms, and government institutional design all play a role in determining the outcome of this policy struggle. In closing, we look at various ways to advance women's equality, particularly with this controversial issue of abortion. Not all women's advocates endorse women's "right" to have full access to terminating a pregnancy. We look to see if there are ways to reduce abortions but uphold women's right to reproductive freedom.

THE DEBATE OVER REPRODUCTIVE RIGHTS AND ABORTION

According to the United Nations, reproductive rights rest on the recognition of the basic right of all couples and individuals to decide freely and responsibly the number, spacing, and timing of their children. This involves additional rights, such as access to information and contraception, as well as sexual and reproductive health services. Finally, the United Nations asserts, people have the right to make decisions concerning reproduction free of discrimination, coercion, and violence. As you can see, reproductive rights cover a wide range of issues, from sex education, contraception, pregnancy termination, sexually transmitted infections, and pregnancy-related health care, to forced sterilization, population control methods, and gender-based practices such as female genital mutilation. Thanks to technological and medical innovations, it also includes emerging conflicts over sperm donation and in vitro fertilization. The textbox on fertility tourism delves more deeply into the frontiers of dilemmas of international surrogacy.

At the international level, reproductive rights emerged as a concept within the larger set of human rights in the late 1960s. In 1968, member states at the United Nations International Conference on Human Rights agreed that parents have a basic right to freely determine the number and spacing of their children as well as a right to adequate information and education so they can make this choice. Nearly three decades later, 184 member states adopted the Cairo Programme of Action (1994) at the International Conference on Population and Development. Although nonbinding, the Programme of Action asserted that governments are responsible for meeting individuals' reproductive needs, rather than demographic targets.

It recommended that states provide family planning services as well as access to health-care services that will enable women to go safely through pregnancy and childbirth. Think for a minute about the implications of this: it gives primacy of choice to individuals, rather than religious authorities or governments, on decisions relating to reproduction. And it also implies that governments have responsibilities in terms of providing services, such as access to contraception and additional information to help women and men make these reproductive choices freely and with full information.

Although this program was adopted by the member states, many Latin American and Islamic states expressed formal reservations about the program, and in particular to its concept of reproductive rights and sexual freedom. There was enormous debate over what this program implied in terms of access to abortion. If women are given choice and control over their reproduction, then does this include a tacit support of abortion as one means of control? To accommodate concerns, the Programme of Action supported women's access to methods of regulating fertility "which are not against the law," and this allowed countries where abortion was heavily regulated or outlawed to still sign on. However, the Cairo Conference brought the issue of reproductive rights front and center to the international stage while also highlighting how many countries struggle with defining how and to what extent women can control their reproductive choices, particularly after conception.

Fertility Tourism

How far will some women go to have a baby, and how involved should governments become in regulating their efforts? According to the Centers for Disease Control and Prevention, in 2010, 7.3 million women in the United States between the ages of 15 and 44 were unable to bear children. This is not a distinctly American problem; there are millions of women who want children but are unable to conceive. As more women get an education and join the workforce, they push back the age of childbearing to the point where it becomes more difficult to conceive. Also, single and gay parents have established new types of families in addition to the heterosexual, two-parent nuclear family structure, which is becoming less common. While adoption used to be the most common route for women and men who wanted children but could not biologically conceive them, rapid changes in reproductive technology have led to a dramatic increase in the use of in vitro fertilization (IVF), which involves removing eggs from a woman's ovaries and combining them with sperm in a lab. The strongest embryos are then implanted into a woman's womb. The egg and/or the sperm do not necessarily have to be biologically linked to the parent. The use of IVF alone raises many important moral and ethical issues. Who "owns" the fertilized eggs, particularly if the sperm or eggs were donated? What should be done with eggs that are not implanted? And how many eggs should be implanted at once, given that the more eggs that are implanted, the higher the risk to the mother as well as the fetus(es)? These issues become even more complex with the use of surrogates—women who agree to carry the fertilized egg to term, but then give up the child upon birth to the "parents." Who is the "real mother" in this situation, and does one balance the rights of the surrogate with the rights of the future parent(s)?

As a result, many countries regulate IVF and surrogacy differently. For example, sperm and egg donation is banned completely in Italy and in many Islamic countries. In Turkey, a woman can spend up to 3 years in prison if she goes abroad to receive donated sperm or eggs—a law that is very hard to enforce. Other countries allow patients to use donated sperm, but not samples given anonymously. Britain and Canada allow the use of donated eggs, but not when the provider is paid. And in France all kinds of surrogacy are prohibited.[i] Many women travel to other countries to pursue IVF treatments or hire surrogates in search of less regulated, more available, and often less expensive treatments.

Fertility tourism refers to the practice of traveling to another country for fertility treatments. India is known as the "surrogacy capital of the world." Surrogacy was legalized in India in 2002, and in 2008, the Supreme Court of India upheld the practice of commercial surrogacy, or paying a woman to gestate a fertilized egg. India is an attractive destination for many overseas couples in search of a surrogate; the practice is less stringently regulated than in many other countries, and India has a world-class medical infrastructure and highly trained doctors able to cater to relatively wealthy aspiring parents. For even though surrogacy in India is comparatively inexpensive, Indian clinics still charge between $10,000 and $20,000 for a package deal, which includes fertilization, the surrogate's fee, and delivery of the baby at a hospital. On top of that, clients still pay the costs of flight tickets, medical procedures, and hotels, and some add a monthly food allowance to ensure the surrogate eats well during pregnancy. If they are pleased with the condition of their child, they may tip the surrogate $1,000 to $5,000. All of this is still much less expensive (and less regulated) than the price many couples would pay in their home countries for IVF or surrogacy.

Commercial surrogacy is controversial. Critics dub the practice "wombs for rent," "outsourcing pregnancies," and "baby farms." In this view, relatively wealthy Westerners exploit women in poverty-stricken countries such as India, which represents a staggering 19% of the world's 287,000 women who die in pregnancy or in childbirth. On the other hand, those in favor of commercial surrogacy argue that nobody is forcing these women to become surrogates. Rather, they are paid well for their efforts (potentially $5,000 to $10,000), which gives them a significant boost in being able to improve their own lives as well as the lives of their family.[ii] For example, an American woman writing of her own experience with an Indian surrogate saw this as an opportunity to help her surrogate's growing family. The fee the surrogate received was the equivalent of several years' salary in India, which allowed her husband to buy a taxicab, her brother-in-law to start his own business, and her children to receive an education.[iii] Patients who cross borders in search of less expensive, more available fertility treatment can now choose from more than 100 countries, but is fertility now just another consumer item, to be regulated mostly by the supply-and-demand dynamics of the "invisible hand"? When and how should states step in to regulate this emerging (and lucrative) business?

---

[i]Sarah Elizabeth Richards, "Mother Country," *Slate* online, March 27, 2012, http://www.slate.com/articles/double_x/doublex/2012/03/fertility_tourism_the_perils_of_having_a_baby_abroad_with_assisted_reproduction_technology_.html

[ii]Neeta Lal, "Pitfalls of Surrogacy in India Exposed," *Asia Times*, May 24, 2012, http://www.atimes.com/atimes/South_Asia/NE24Df02.html

[iii]Adrienne Arieff, "Having Twins with a Surrogate–in India," *New York Times*, March 16, 2012, http://parenting.blogs.nytimes.com/2012/03/16/having-twins-with-a-surrogate-in-india/.

Although regulating abortion became a common policy battle in many countries starting in the latter half of the twentieth century, abortion was not always perceived as a contentious or thorny moral issue. Abortion techniques are described in some of the earliest medical texts of China and Egypt; ancient Greeks argued that abortion was an appropriate method for regulating population size. During the Roman Empire, it was used with few if any restrictions; abortion was considered not as a crime but as an "immoral act." The fetus was considered to be part of the "mother's viscera" and thus was within her sphere of influence. Nor were abortion prohibitions part of the indigenous cultural, religious, and legal traditions of most of the non-Western world; rather, they were imported as part of colonial, imperial, or Western influences in the previous two centuries, when legal restrictions increased in the colonial countries themselves.[5] Thus, historically, abortion was practiced in virtually every society, despite the great variation in cultural and moral views about it.

However, with the advent of Christianity, and Catholicism in particular, came a new focus on souls and on humans in general as God's creatures. Nonetheless, it took centuries for the church—and the Catholic Church in particular—to settle the debate about when fetuses became "human," endowed with souls, and thus connected to God. In the twelfth and thirteenth centuries, Pope Innocent considered that the fetus had life, or a soul, only when "quickening" (movement of the fetus) was felt, which occurs around 24 weeks. In the sixteenth century, Popes Sisto V and Gregory XIV argued that the fetus has a life or soul from the beginning of conception. The Catholic Church became more firmly entrenched in this second view when, in 1869, Pope Pius IX further emphasized the idea of the immediate animation of the fetus by accepting the dogma of the Immaculate Conception. Since then, the Catholic Church has espoused the protection of human life since conception, and Catholicism presents a unified and nearly absolute opposition to induced abortion in nearly all circumstances.[6] Religious fundamentalism—Christian or Islamic—is also often associated with curtailing women's full access to reproductive rights, in part because fundamentalists tend to favor traditional roles for women and see women predominantly as wives and reproducers.

For centuries, the state stayed out of regulating reproduction. For example, before the nineteenth century in Great Britain, there were no statutes relating to abortion, and it was not considered a crime to abort a fetus before "quickening."[7] States began to legislate abortion in the nineteenth and early twentieth centuries by criminalizing or recriminalizing it. At the time, abortion was not framed primarily as a religious issue, but by the emerging medical profession as a protective one. Women needed to be protected from nefarious doctors, who were performing dangerous operations on women and deterring them from performing their natural mothering functions. States responded with legislation that began to lay out a framework regulating the conditions under which women were allowed to terminate their pregnancies. The most common allowances for abortion were in cases where carrying the child to term threatened the health and/or life of the mother. In many countries, both the doctors performing the abortion and the women undergoing the medical process were punishable, although different countries pursued this with varying degrees of zeal. In an era when contraception was not widely available, abortion also served as a method of birth control, and criminalizing the process often drove the process underground, or to backstreet alleys.

Although some countries liberalized abortion policy in the early to mid-twentieth century—most notably many communist countries as part of other reforms designed to unlink law from religious influences, improve the status of women, and get women into the workforce—for the most part, abortion did not reappear as a political issue until the 1960s. England was one of the first countries to liberalize its abortion policies; in 1967, it passed the Abortion Act, which decriminalized abortion and broadened women's choices by widening the conditions under which they could have abortions. In the ensuing three decades, abortion policy was challenged, and mostly widened, in every Western industrialized country. Ironically, the medical profession, which in the nineteenth century had been one of the forces to push for criminalization of abortion, a century later played a central role in overturning these same laws.[8]

Abortion debates raged around several issues. First, under what conditions could women have an abortion? Many countries already did provide for abortions in order to save the life of the mother. Additional permissible conditions were to preserve the woman's physical health, in the case of rape or incest, or in the case of fetal impairment. While many countries already granted exceptions in these three areas, movements in the 1960s began to stress new reasons why an abortion might be necessary. While some countries had allowed abortion to preserve the physical health of the mother, supporters of legalized abortion emphasized the need to broaden definitions of what constitutes "health." Advocates introduced the idea that mental health was also a necessary consideration and that many women, while physically able to have a child, would be placed under enormous emotional stress if forced to carry the child to term. In addition, advocates also argued that women should be able to terminate pregnancies for economic or social reasons—that is, lack of financial means to support a child should be a legitimate reason to terminate a pregnancy. In addition, the social stigma attached to young mothers and single mothers meant that women of all ages, but particularly young women, should be granted more choice in whether to carry the fetus to term. Finally, the concept of "abortion on demand" became increasingly common. That is, advocates argued that it is the woman's choice to have an abortion and that there do not have to be "extenuating circumstances."

In addition to debating the reasons why women could terminate the pregnancy, advocates and opponents argued about when women could legally terminate a pregnancy. Even in countries that provided abortion without asking for extenuating circumstances, there was disagreement about how far into the pregnancy the woman exercised control over choice and when the state needed to intervene to protect the rights of the fetus. Many feminists argued that since only women can experience pregnancy, they should then have complete control over deciding the fate of their bodies. However, many countries adopted a version of the trimester system, in which women had a wider latitude of choices in the first 12 to 14 weeks. After the first trimester, many states restricted access to abortion. Particularly in the third trimester, when the fetus is theoretically "viable" (potentially able to survive outside the womb, although often with extensive medical intervention), abortion was restricted to very specific circumstances, such as to save the life of the mother. Thus, models were set up that gave women more choice and control in the first part of the pregnancy, but then followed this with a more assertive role for the state in the second and third trimesters.

Governments have regulated abortion in other ways. Some decreed that women needed first to undergo counseling in order to understand the full range of issues involved and the alternatives to abortion. In other countries, women had to go before a committee to make their case for terminating their pregnancy, even if the decision ultimately was theirs to make. Still others legislated that women could have an abortion, but only after a specified waiting period during which they could reconsider their choice. Alternatively, women had to verbally and in written form request an abortion. Other countries, concerned with the right of the partner who had helped conceive the child, enacted policy in which women had to get permission from their spouse, who presumably had been the partner in conception. For teenagers, governments grappled with whether teens should be vested with the power to make this decision on their own or whether, as minors, they should have to inform their parents of the decision. Additionally, the issue of government funding arose: Should government funds be used to finance such a divisive medical procedure? A refusal to finance abortion could turn it into a class issue, in which wealthy women could afford abortions, while poor women would be forced to forgo them for financial reasons. But would government funding be interpreted as government endorsement of abortion? Finally, access became a big issue. While governments may have legalized abortions, ensuring that women had access to them was a separate issue. For example, while many U.S. states have legalized abortions, fewer doctors can be found to perform them, effectively denying women, particularly poor women without the means or resources to travel, access to the procedure. In sum, abortion is not a "yes/no" issue; rather, it involves a wide array of issues beyond simply deciding the legality of the procedure.

Given this background, what is the current status of abortion worldwide? According to the World Health Organization, abortion is one of the most widely used medical procedures by women; about one in five pregnancies worldwide ends in abortion. Abortion is least prevalent in Western and Northern European countries, where nearly all (94 percent) abortions are safe and legal. In contrast, in the developing world, abortion is more prevalent, in part because contraceptive use is less common. Further, abortion in the developing world is much less safe; over half of all abortions are unsafe, and nearly all (98 percent) of the world's unsafe abortions occur in the developing world. High rates of unsafe abortions are correlated with highly restrictive abortion laws, and the passage of restrictive laws has not stopped women from having abortions—they simply have them in back alleys, performed by untrained, unqualified providers. And women pay the price with their lives; complications from unsafe abortions account for an estimated 13 percent of all maternal deaths worldwide. For this reason alone, advocates from various sides of the abortion debate agree: lowering the abortion rate, particularly the number of unsafe abortions, is a critical goal. And in fact, the number of induced abortions in the past two decades has declined worldwide, although continued progress has stalled since 2003.[9] At the end of this chapter, we'll discuss various ways that countries have lowered their overall abortion rates.

Despite the universality of the practice of abortion, there are wide variations across countries with regard to the legality of the practice, access to the procedure, societies' acceptance of abortion, and the prevailing moral and ethical views concerning its practice. Fifty-eight countries, representing nearly 40 percent of the world's population, permit abortion without restriction as to reason, and the woman makes the decision about whether to terminate a pregnancy. These countries are geographically concentrated in Europe, the former Soviet Union, North America, and northern Asia, although some countries in these regions, such as Poland, Malta, and the Republic of Korea, maintain restrictive laws that run counter to regional trends. Even in countries with few restrictions, many impose a variety of limits that can complicate women's access to the procedure. For example, many countries, such as Belgium and Germany, impose mandatory counseling and waiting periods. In countries such as Japan, Denmark, and Italy, as well as most Eastern European countries, a woman may not have an abortion without first obtaining permission from her spouse or parents.[10] And most countries impose limits on the period during which women can readily access the procedure. In Denmark, for example, a woman can procure an abortion without restriction as to reason during the initial 12 weeks of pregnancy. Subsequently, an abortion can be performed in cases of fetal impairment, on specified socioeconomic grounds, or if the pregnancy is a result of rape or poses a risk to the woman's life or health.

The rest of the world's population faces differing degrees of restrictions. A second category of countries allows abortion if the woman has justifiable grounds related to her physical well-being and overall emotional health. Fifteen countries (about 22 percent of the world's population) allow abortion on socioeconomic grounds. These laws are often interpreted liberally, allowing for such considerations as a woman's economic resources, her age, her marital status, and the number of children she has. In a similar vein, an additional 23 countries (4 percent of the world's population) allow abortion in situations that would preserve a women's mental health, allowing for such factors as psychological stress suffered by a woman who is raped or severe strain caused by social or economic circumstances. In this second group of countries, there is wide variation in how countries define the risk to women's mental and physical health, and whether a woman's socioeconomic position should be included in the assessment. A third group of countries allows abortion in extremely limited circumstances. Thirty-five countries (10 percent of the world's population) allow abortion to preserve the physical health of the mother. The most restrictive laws are those that ban abortion altogether or permit the procedure only to save a woman's life. Sixty-eight nations, representing 26 percent of the world's population and located primarily in the developing world, have enacted these laws. Of these 68 countries, 33 do not permit abortion under any circumstance. Nicaragua joined this group in 2006 when the legislature passed a complete ban on abortion, eliminating the only exception under the previous law, for women whose lives or health were at risk.[11]

Table 6.1 provides an overview of the world's abortion laws as of 2011.

Table 6.1 The World's Abortion Laws, 2011*

TO SAVE THE WOMAN'S LIFE OR PROHIBITED ALTOGETHER

Afghanistan	Gabon	Marshall Islands	Somalia
Andorra	**Guatemala**	Mauritania	**South Sudan**
Angola	Guinea-Bissau	Mauritius	**Sri Lanka**
Antigua & Barbuda	Haiti	**Mexico**	Sudan
Bangladesh	Honduras	Micronesia	Suriname
Bhutan	**Indonesia**	**Myanmar**	**Syria**
Brazil	**Iran**	Nicaragua	**Tanzania**
Brunei Darussalam	Iraq	**Nigeria**	**Timor-Leste**
Central African Republic	**Ireland**	Oman	Tonga
Chile	**Kiribati**	Palau	**Tuvalu**
Congo	Laos	**Panama**	**Uganda**
Cote d'Ivoire	**Lebanon**	**Papua New Guinea**	**United Arab Emirates**
Democratic Republic of	Lesotho	**Paraguay**	**Venezuela**
the Congo	**Libya**	Philippines	**West Bank & Gaza Strip**
Dominica	Madagascar	San Marino	**Yemen**
Dominican Republic	**Malawi**	Sao Tome & Principe	
Egypt	**Mali**	Senegal	
El Salvador	Malta	**Solomon Islands**	

TO PRESERVE PHYSICAL HEALTH (AND TO SAVE THE MOTHER'S LIFE)

Argentina	Costa Rica	Kenya	Poland
Bahamas	Djibouti	Kuwait	Qatar
Benin	Ecuador	Liechtenstein	Republic of Korea
Bolivia	Equatorial Guinea	Maldives	Rwanda
Burkina Faso	Eritrea	Morocco	Saudi Arabia
Burundi	Ethiopia	Mozambique	Togo
Cameroon	Grenada	Niger	Uruguay
Chad	Guinea	Pakistan	Vanuatu
Comoros	Jordan	Peru	Zimbabwe

TO PRESERVE MENTAL HEALTH (AND TO SAVE THE MOTHER'S LIFE AND PHYSICAL HEALTH)

Algeria	Israel	Nauru	Sierra Leone
Botswana	Jamaica	Northern Ireland	Swaziland
Colombia	Liberia	Saint Kitts & Nevis	Thailand
Gambia	Malaysia	Samoa	Trinidad & Tobago
Ghana	Namibia	Seychelles	

Table 6.1 (*Continued*)

FOR SOCIOECONOMIC REASONS (AND TO SAVE THE MOTHER'S LIFE, PHYSICAL HEALTH, AND MENTAL HEALTH)

Australia	Fiji	Iceland	Saint Vincent & Grenadines
Barbados	Finland	India	
Belize	Great Britain	Japan	Taiwan
Cyprus	Hong Kong	Luxembourg	Zambia

WITHOUT RESTRICTION AS TO REASON

Albania	Denmark	Mongolia	Slovak Republic
Armenia	Estonia	Montenegro	Slovenia
Austria	France	Kyrgyzstan	South Africa
Azerbaijan	Former Yugoslav Republic of Macedonia	Latvia	Spain
Bahrain		Lithuania	Sweden
Belarus		Moldova	Switzerland
Belgium	Georgia	Mongolia	Tajikistan
Bosnia-Herzegovina	Germany	Montenegro	Tunisia
Bulgaria	Greece	Nepal	Turkey
Cambodia	Guyana	Netherlands	Turkmenistan
Canada	Hungary	Norway	Ukraine
Cape Verde	Italy	Portugal	United States
China	Kazakhstan	Puerto Rico	Uzbekistan
Croatia	Kosovo	Romania	Vietnam
Cuba	Latvia	Russian Federation	
Czech Republic	Lithuania	Serbia	
Dem. People's Republic of Korea	Moldova	Singapore	

*COUNTRIES IN **BOLD** ALLOW AN EXCEPTION TO SAVE THE MOTHER'S LIFE.

SOURCE: Center for Reproductive Rights, "The World's Abortion Laws 2011," http://worldabortionlaws.com/map/

Around the world, women choose abortion for a variety of reasons. Particularly in the absence of widely available or affordable contraception, many women use abortion as a form of birth control. This is particularly true, for example, for women in sub-Saharan Africa, who often do not have the means to effectively control the timing and sequencing of their pregnancies. Further, women may be motivated to protect the family economy from having to make outlays on education or life course rituals or ceremonies in close succession. In places such as Russia or Eastern Europe, where housing is extremely limited and married couples live in small apartments with their parents, abortion is a choice motivated by a housing shortage. In Western European countries, where contraception is more widely available, women may choose abortion because of concerns over the increased financial and social responsibilities that come with additional children.[12] Also, the demographic profile of women who get an abortion differs geographically. In countries of the West and sub-Saharan Africa, three out of every four abortions are to single women or to women under the age of 20. The majority of these women have borne no children. In contrast, in Eastern Europe, Latin America, and much of Asia, three out of every four abortions are to married women and to women over 20 years of age. In some cultures, bearing a child before marriage is taboo, while in other countries, the concern over the increased responsibilities, financial as well as social, that come with added children predominates. However, making abortion legal, particularly in the developing world, does not always make it open. India has a relatively liberal abortion law, yet an estimated 90 percent of abortions in India are illegal and clandestine and are not performed by qualified medical staff because the priority is not on safety or cost, but rather on secrecy.[13] In Western countries where abortion is legal, it is not so much social mores but lack of access that restricts women from choosing safe methods of abortion.

In the following section, we turn to three case studies of abortion policies in OECD countries. Specifically, we look at the debates over abortion in Ireland, the United States, and the Netherlands. Each case demonstrates a different outcome and illustrates larger lessons about why and how some states have resolved the abortion issue. Ireland is unique in that not only has it not liberalized abortion, but it has also taken further steps to strengthen legal prohibitions against it.[14] In contrast, while the United States has a relatively liberal abortion law, it has been faced with constant legal challenges, with many restrictions implemented in the previous decade at the state level. Finally, we will look at the case of the Netherlands, where abortion policy was resolved relatively quickly and has not been challenged. What explains the varying array of policy outcomes in each country?

IRELAND

The Republic of Ireland is unusual in that unlike most other European Union member states, it has not enacted significant reforms that widen women's access to abortion services. Abortion in Ireland has been a criminal act since 1861, and this act remained intact until an anti-abortion movement successfully mounted a campaign for a constitutional prohibition on abortion in the early 1980s. Since then, the abortion debate has revolved around several issues: Does an Irish woman have a constitutional right to seek an abortion in another country? Can women seek information about abortion in Ireland so they can procure a safe one abroad? Can a woman seek an abortion if there is a real and substantial risk to her life, including a risk of suicide? While other European countries significantly reformed their abortion laws in response to public opinion, women's groups, and other pro-legalization lobbies, there was no similar cultural shift or organizational push in Ireland. Thus, Ireland is unique in that not only has it not legalized abortion except to save the life of the mother, but it has also taken steps to strengthen legal prohibitions against abortion. This is backed by a majority of citizens and has not been strongly opposed by the women's movement, which has not significantly brought the issue of gender into the debate. Rather, the abortion debate has been tentatively gendered over time, with a focus on the mother's right to life and a more empathetic understanding of crisis pregnancies.[15] The minimal changes that have occurred in the politics of abortion in Ireland are due to external pressures from international organizations.

As a former subject of the United Kingdom, Ireland based its abortion laws on the 1861 Offences Against the Person Act. According to the act, performing and procuring an abortion "unlawfully" is a crime, although the act does not specify which abortions are to be considered unlawful.[16] This legislation remained in effect after the country gained its independence. When Great Britain became the first country to decriminalize abortion to any great extent in 1967, Ireland maintained its steadfast position on the criminalization of abortion.[17]

With an overwhelming majority of practicing Catholics, many citizens followed the church's injunctions regarding contraception, divorce, and abortion. The provision of contraceptives in Ireland, for example, was a topic of great controversy. It was not until 1973 that the Supreme Court, basing its decision on a right to marital privacy, ruled that adults be allowed to import and possess contraceptives. Nonetheless, the sale of contraceptives was still illegal until 1979, when Parliament allowed pharmacists to sell contraceptives with a prescription. In 1985, it expanded its categories of people who could sell contraceptives and allowed persons over 18 years of age to buy condoms and spermicides without prescription. These reforms in the contraceptive law were not based on feminist arguments, but were a response, in part, to a rise in the incidence of sexually transmitted infections.[18] Access to contraception widened further in 2011; with little fanfare, it was announced that emergency contraceptives, also known as morning-after pills, would be dispensed at all pharmacies without a prescription. This change was not a result of tireless lobbying from women's groups, but rather a result of the clout of Boots, one of the largest pharmaceutical chains in the United Kingdom and Ireland. Regardless of the initiator, this is a significant development in a country where one had to have a prescription to buy a condom until 1985. Similarly, attitudes about divorce have also been slow to change. This heavily Catholic nation also voted on whether to legalize divorce, rejecting it by a landslide in 1986. Nearly a decade later, voters legalized divorce, but by a margin of only 0.7 percent. Ireland has implemented a variety of family policy reforms much later than other European countries have, and these decisions have been much more divisive.

Irish society grappled with the issue of abortion regulation in the early 1980s, when conservative Catholics, in response to the Irish Supreme Court's decision to legalize contraception, tried to find a way to ban abortion in such a way that it could not be overturned by either the Supreme Court or the European Court of Justice. Given that the Supreme Court had, similar to the United States, based its decision to legalize contraception on a right to privacy, conservative Catholics formed the Society for the Protection of the Unborn Child and worked to avert what they feared would be a repetition of the American path to legalization of abortion through the justification of a right to privacy. They campaigned for a constitutional amendment that would prevent the legalization of abortion. In 1983, the amendment was put before the public in a referendum and was worded as follows: "The state acknowledges the right to life of the unborn and, with due regard to equal right to the life of the mother, guarantees in its laws to respect, and as far as practicable, by its laws to defend and vindicate that right."[19] In sum, the amendment placed the lives of the mother and the unborn child on an equal level, rather than specifying under which conditions the state could place the life of the mother above that of the fetus. The wording of the Irish amendment obligated the state to adopt measures to protect the life of the fetus and, in effect, banned legislators from passing any law to loosen the abortion ban.[20] Women's groups opposed the bill, although they did so by emphasizing the inadequacies of the bill rather than framing it as a woman's right to choose. Thus, their arguments tended to focus on the fact that the amendment made no provisions for exceptions, was a waste of public funds, and would prevent possible future legislation on the issue. Although this helped build opposition to the amendment, it still passed easily, with 66 percent of voters in favor and 33 percent against, although the voter turnout was relatively low, at 50 percent.[21] Thus, abortions were completely prohibited in Ireland, with no explicitly stated exceptions.

Nonetheless, Irish women still found ways to access abortions abroad. England had liberalized its abortion laws in 1967; as a result, many Irish women traveled to England to have a legal and safe procedure. By the 1990s, 4,000 Irish women were traveling to England for abortions each year.[22] Further, in 1990 the European Community defined abortion as a commercial service; thus, as citizens of a member country of the Community, women had a right to access services, including abortion, available in other member states.[23] In addition, various public agencies, such as clinics, student groups at universities, and bookstores in Ireland, distributed information that touched either tangentially on abortion or gave specific information about accessing abortion abroad. Once again, opponents of abortion mobilized, arguing that these services were in violation of the 1983 amendment, and, at the request of the government, the Supreme Court of Ireland banned the provision of these services by family planning groups and student groups, arguing that the government had a duty to defend and vindicate the rights of the unborn. Thus, by the beginning of the 1990s, all information on abortion, even in magazines and books, was illegal. Copies of *Our Bodies, Ourselves*, a woman's health manual, were removed from public libraries, and British editions of fashion magazines, such as *Vogue* or *Elle*, were censored to fulfill Irish abortion regulations.[24]

Opponents of these restrictions, having exhausted national outlets, turned to international organizations to apply pressure on the Irish government. The Irish Supreme Court ruling was brought before the Council of Europe (not be confused with the EU body the European Council), which monitors human rights in its 47 member states in light of the provisions of the Convention for the Protection of Human Rights and Fundamental Freedoms. As a member state and signatory to the Convention, Ireland was accountable to the Council. The Council ruled that the denial of information violated the right to impart and receive information contained in the Convention. Thus, they ruled, Ireland was obligated to change its law to correct this violation.[25] However, like many international organizations, the Council cannot coerce countries to abide by its rulings, and while it sent a strong message to the Irish government, the government did not immediately act on the ruling.

Other events in Ireland continued to generate controversy over the issue of abortion and over the right of women to travel to procure an abortion. The plight of a suicidal 14-year-old girl who had been raped by an older man caught the attention of the public. The parents wished to take their daughter to England for an abortion because the daughter claimed she would kill herself if forced to carry the pregnancy to term. However, the attorney general sought to block the family from leaving the country, arguing that the state had a responsibility to defend the right of the unborn in light of the terms of the 1983 constitutional amendment. However, supporters of the girl's case argued that the amendment also tasked the state with equally valuing the life of the mother. In this situation, they argued, the mother, who was suicidal, should also have her life defended by being granted access to an abortion. The "X case," as it was known in the media, made its way to the Supreme Court in 1992. The Court allowed the family to go to England, arguing that even under the 1983 amendment, an abortion could be legally performed if there was a "real and substantial risk" to a pregnant woman's life, including a risk of suicide (although the girl eventually miscarried).[26] This reading of the amendment opened up a new debate: What did the court mean by "real and substantial risk," and how liberally or conservatively should this be interpreted? The government was not in a hurry to write legislation further defining the parameters of what constituted a "real and substantial risk" (including suicide), and, two decades later, no legislation had been passed to flesh out this court decision.[27] As a result, there are no guidelines for doctors or women to follow, effectively making it impossible for a pregnant woman with a serious health risk to get an abortion in Ireland.

Abortion foes continued to mobilize to close what they perceived to be loopholes in various laws restricting abortion access, focusing on restricting women's abilities to travel abroad to procure an abortion. Women feared that there would be pregnancy tests given to all women leaving the country. The government put the abortion issue to the public once again in a series of referenda. Voters approved amendments guaranteeing rights to travel and to information, which were signed by the president in December 1992; this put Ireland in alignment with the Council of Europe ruling discussed earlier. The voters rejected the third amendment, which narrowly defined when abortions could be considered legal (suicide could not be used as a justification).[28] Thus, women were allowed to access information about abortion in Ireland and to travel abroad to procure an abortion, and the Supreme Court's interpretation of the abortion amendment following the X case held.

Even after the Council of Europe ruling and the results of the referendum, which guaranteed women's right to access of information and travel, the government was still unwilling to design policy quickly to reflect the referendum decisions, and didn't announce proposed legislation to implement the results of the referendum until 1995. Further, the legislation placed restrictions on the information distributed about abortion: it may not advocate or promote abortion, be displayed by notice in a public place, or appear in publications that are distributed without having been solicited by recipients. Organizations and individuals providing information, advice, or counseling on pregnancy may not advocate or promote abortion. They must provide information on all possible options, and they may not make any arrangements for the woman seeking an abortion, among other restrictions. The Supreme Court later upheld these regulations, disappointing both those who thought the laws were too liberal and those who felt the laws were overly restrictive.

In 1997, a case similar to the 1992 X one reopened the issue of abortion. A 13-year-old girl was pregnant as a result of an alleged rape and said that she would kill herself if she could not have an abortion. However, because she was under the medical care of the Eastern Health Board, a state agency, the staff there could not assist in the procurement of an abortion. In addition, the girl's father did not wish her to have an abortion. Similar to its ruling in 1992, the Court upheld the girl's right to have an abortion, reaffirming that suicide constitutes a "real and substantial risk" to the girl's life. The case also brought the issue of crisis pregnancies to public debate once again and highlighted the government's failure to pass legislation clarifying what constitutes a "real and substantial risk" to the mother's life. Instead, the government commissioned a working group to produce a Green Paper on the issue, and in September 1999, the government finally published the results, outlining seven possible legislative options. However, while the paper generated public and political debate on the issue of abortion, it did not prompt the government to formulate or propose legislation detailing under what conditions a woman facing a real and substantial risk to her life may seek to terminate her pregnancy in Ireland.

On March 6, 2002, voters once again went to the polls for a referendum on abortion. Voters were asked to decide on the Protection of Human Life in Pregnancy Bill, which, if passed, would have reversed the 1992 X case ruling, thus making all abortions once again illegal, regardless of circumstances. The bill was defeated by a margin of less than 1 percent (about 10,000 votes), although voter turnout was quite low (43 percent).[29] In other words, the original conditions of the 1992 Supreme Court ruling still apply: abortions are legal if a woman's life is at risk from continued pregnancy, including cases of threatened suicide. But once again the government dodged the task of writing legislation on an issue so clearly divisive, and Prime Minister Bertie Ahern instead announced the establishment of the

Crisis Pregnancy Agency to help women deal with unplanned pregnancies.[30] In March 2005, a spokesperson for the Department of Health reaffirmed the government's decision not to pursue legislation, stating that "the government has no plans to introduce legislation regarding abortion and there is no plan to legislate for the X case."[31] Thus, there has been no significant movement breaking the stalemate. Technically, abortion under very limited circumstances is legal in Ireland; however, few doctors will provide an abortion without stronger legal parameters defining what constitutes a "real and substantial risk" to a woman's life. Meanwhile, women are traveling to Great Britain and other European countries to have the procedure; according to the UK Department of Health, between 1980 and 2011, over 150,000 women living in Ireland traveled to England and Wales to access abortion services.[32] However, this is not an option for low-income women, who may not have the financial reserves to travel to another country for an abortion.

There have been international efforts to highlight the issue of the status of reproductive rights in Ireland. In June 2001, a Dutch organization called Women on Waves docked their 100-foot converted trawler in Dublin. Their mission, in part, was to dispense contraceptives and family planning advice. They were also licensed to use the drug RU-486, which is a pill that induces abortion in the first 2 months of pregnancy (also known as the "abortion pill"). In addition, the ship was also equipped to administer surgical and medical abortions. While Women on Waves did not intend to carry out surgical abortions, the group did plan on administering RU-486 to pregnant Irish women under Dutch law. Because they anchored their ship 12 miles offshore, they were located in international waters and thus were not subject to Irish law.[33] Further, in 2005, the Irish Human Rights Commission, a government commission that monitors Ireland's adherence to the United Nations-sponsored Convention on the Elimination of Discrimination Against Women (CEDAW), criticized the government for not doing enough to combat discrimination against women. It also specifically urged the government to pass legislation specifying the precise circumstances under which an abortion could take place in Ireland.[34]

Twenty years after the X case, in which the Irish Supreme Court ruled that a suicidal pregnant teenager had the right to an abortion, the Irish legislature has yet to write legislation that honors the constitutional amendment, which values equally the life of the fetus and the mother, but also accommodates the Supreme Court ruling, which allows an abortion given a substantial risk to the life of the mother (including a danger of suicide). Once again, pressure from the European Council may be the main impetus for the legislature to take on this task. In 2005, three Irish women (known only as A, B, and C) who had traveled to England to procure an abortion brought suit in the European Court of Human Rights, which adjudicates on human rights issues among the 47 states of the Council of Europe. They argued that the restrictive and unclear Irish laws violated several provisions of the European Convention on Human Rights by jeopardizing their lives and their well-being and violated their human rights. In particular, applicant C unintentionally became pregnant while in remission from cancer, and had further tests for cancer that are normally forbidden when a patient is pregnant. Upon finding she was pregnant, she was unable to find an Irish doctor willing to advise her about the pregnancy's impact on her life and health or the impact of the tests on the fetus. After researching the issue herself, she traveled to England for an abortion, since she was effectively denied a domestic remedy. In 2009, the Court agreed to hear the challenge, and in 2010 handed down its decision. The Court did not find that Ireland's restrictive abortion law violated the European Convention on Human Rights, but it held that in circumstances in which abortion is legal in Ireland (which the Supreme Court had established in theory in 1992), Ireland had failed to adopt legislation and establish an effective and accessible procedure for women to access lawful abortions. The Court ordered Ireland to establish a legislative framework to implement the abortion law and to adopt procedures to ensure women's access to legal abortion services in Ireland. Any court decision at this level is binding on the Irish government. As of August 2012, the government was waiting for a further report from the European Court of Human Rights in its deliberations before deciding how to respond.[35]

In addition to the decades-long ambivalence of the government, there is little indication that Irish society is ready to tackle decisively the issue of abortion, and citizens are still enormously conflicted, more so than in other European countries, about whether and when a woman can terminate her pregnancy. For example, in 1990, two years before the X case, a European Values study found that 65 percent of Irish respondents approved of abortion when the mother's health was at risk; in contrast, 95 percent of Europeans approved of abortion under these circumstances. Support for abortion crumbled in the face of other potential scenarios: only 32 percent approved of an abortion when it was likely that the child would be handicapped, and only 8 percent supported a woman's right to have an abortion when the mother was not married or when a married couple did not want to have more children. Thus, the public's approval of liberalized abortion law was highly dependent on a specific set of circumstances and did not encompass the feminist rhetoric of personal autonomy and a "woman's right to choose."[36] Other data indicate that an even lower percentage of Irish citizens support abortion rights; according to the 2000 World Values Survey data, 51 percent of those surveyed thought that abortion was never justifiable, while only about 3 percent of the population felt that it was always justifiable.[37] These figures also indicate that public tolerance for abortion is substantially lower in Ireland than in other European countries. The government has reflected this ambivalence by attempting to resolve the issue through public referenda and by delaying the implementation of legislation that would clarify the issue.

In addition, the coalition of organizations opposing abortion has been extremely well organized and influential. For example, the Irish Medical Council has been a central player in maintaining a unified stance against substantially liberalizing the practice. The council was established by law in 1978 to register and discipline doctors and provide guidance on professional standards and ethical conduct. It is the main state-sanctioned regulatory agency for the medical profession. Until recently, the council took an express position against any kind of abortion, and its ethical guidelines contained the statement, "The deliberate and intentional destruction of the unborn child is professional misconduct."[38] While the 2004 edition of the *Guide to Ethical Conduct and Behavior* has been updated to reflect the changing nature of abortion policy in Ireland, nonetheless the current language states that "We consider that there is a fundamental difference between abortion carried out with the intention of taking the life of the baby, for example for social reasons, and the unavoidable death of the baby resulting from essential treatment to protect the life of the mother."[39] Thus, while the Medical Council has softened its opposition to abortion, it has been a major force in advocating for a more restrictive policy, unlike medical associations in other countries that have sided with substantially liberalizing abortion laws. The Church has also been a central player in a country where 84 percent of the population checked off the Catholic box in Census 2011. However, according to a variety of surveys, the influence of the Catholic Church has been waning precipitously, particularly in the wake of sex abuse scandals and crises of leadership. According to the World Values Survey, in 2000, the public's level of trust in the Catholic Church, one of the leading forces arguing against liberalization of abortion laws, declined, and only 30 percent of those surveyed thought that churches gave answers to moral problems, compared to 42 percent in 1990.[40] Recent surveys performed in 2012 found a continued decline in the Irish public's religiosity. Attendance at weekly Mass has dropped (although Ireland still has one of the highest rates in Europe); less than half of the respondents queried thought of themselves as religious, a 22-percentage-point drop since the question had been asked 7 years previously, and the proportion of Irish identifying themselves as atheist or not religious nearly doubled. More than 70 percent viewed Catholic Church teachings on sexuality as irrelevant to them or their family.[41] It is unclear whether this will have any effect on the population's views or the church's leadership on the abortion issue in the coming years. Undoubtedly, political tensions resulting from the European Court decision will only rise if the legislature finally attempts to draft policy.

In contrast, the women's movement has struggled in mounting a well-organized opposition along themes that resonate with the public. While there are numerous women's organizations that advocate for liberalizing the abortion laws, they have been unable to generate massive support for widened access to abortion by framing the issue around feminist arguments regarding women's autonomy over their own bodies. Rather, they have tried to soften laws by appealing to a public sense of compassion for women in crisis. Further, because the state is heavily influenced by anti-liberalization forces, the women's movement in Ireland has been more active internationally, working with the organization Women on Waves and advocating for the EU and the Council of Europe to put increased pressure on the Irish government or to bring attention to the situation of women seeking abortions in Ireland.[42]

THE UNITED STATES

While the United States, compared to other countries, has enacted relatively liberal abortion laws, these laws have come under some of the most sustained and vigorous attack of any nation that has legalized abortion. The debate has occupied nearly every branch of the government and civil society, including the legislative, executive, judicial, and bureaucratic bodies at federal, state, and local levels. The issue has become entangled with policies touching on education, welfare, sexuality, science and medical research, licensing of professionals, health care, the military, foreign aid, labor, and taxation. It involves making decisions about limits on protest, the regulation and legalization of funding for and access to medical services, family planning, reporting requirements, advertising, fetal research, parental consent and notification, and spousal consent and notification.[43] The issue continues to divide American politics, holding up judicial nominations and determining nominations for political office at all levels of politics. Mobilization over the debate has intensified significantly since 1992, when a Supreme Court ruling gave individual states more latitude in setting restrictions. While women's organizations have had a substantial impact on abortion policy, that impact has constantly been under attack, and increased restrictions on abortions, particularly at the state level, ensure that while women have a legal right to abortion, in practice, many women, particularly low-income ones, are unable to access abortion services.

Historically, abortions were permitted in America before "quickening." However, in the nineteenth century, many states, at the urging of the American Medical Association, began passing laws prohibiting all or most abortions.[44] Part of this stemmed from the emerging profession's attempts to establish greater authority over the area as well as to professionalize a field still populated with quacks, traditional healers, and semitrained practitioners. By 1900, all but six states had designed legislation that gave doctors discretion in deciding when abortion was necessary (usually to save the life of the mother) and thus legal.[45] This model remained in place up to the early 1960s, and in all but nine states, abortion was permitted only if the woman's life was in danger. Reform was implemented in many states in the 5 years before the landmark 1973 *Roe v. Wade* decision; 18 states reformed or repealed their anti-abortion legislation. In the remaining 32 states and the District of Columbia, laws that criminalized abortion unless performed to save the life or health of the mother remained on the books. The pregnant woman's mental health also became more accepted as a justification for abortion.[46]

However, the 1973 Supreme Court decision, which legalized abortion throughout the United States, tipped off a nationwide debate that continues. It was the culmination of developments in social movements, previous court decisions, and statewide trends. The National Organization for Women, formed in 1966, was one of the early proponents of legalized abortion. Drawing from the experiences of the civil rights movement, which had achieved numerous goals via constitutional litigation through the court system, the women's movement adopted a similar strategy. An early success was the 1965 Supreme Court case *Griswold v. Connecticut*, which legalized contraception for married couples under the argument that the Constitution protected a couple's "right to privacy." Finally, reform of abortion laws at the state level created a momentum that crested with *Roe v. Wade*.

Women in Motion: Margaret Sanger (1884–1966)

"A woman's body belongs to herself alone. It does not belong to the United States of America or any other government on the face of the earth. Enforced motherhood is the most complete denial of a woman's right to life and liberty. Women cannot be on an equal footing with men until they have full and complete control over their reproductive function."[i]

Abortion policies have become such a controversial issue that many forget that the various sides in the debate often have a similar goal—to reduce, if not end, the need for women to terminate their pregnancies. Women's activists often point out that one way to reduce the number of unwanted pregnancies is to increase the availability of contraceptives, as well as education for women, men, and families about family planning options. Women's right to control the timing and number of their children has been affirmed at numerous international conferences. Yet, we forget that for many years, women lacked (and still lack) this basic freedom; the state often restricted women's access to birth control, as well as any information about family planning. In the United States, up until 1965, a Connecticut law prohibited the use of contraception, even by married couples, until the Supreme Court struck it down in *Griswold v. Connecticut*. This right to contraception wasn't extended to unmarried couples until 1972.[ii]

Although hundreds of men and women worked to increase women's access to information about and means to use birth control, Margaret Sanger was the public face and driving force behind the movement to legalize contraception in America. Sanger's public drive was very much influenced by events in her own life; she was deeply influenced by watching the experiences of her devoutly Catholic mother, who endured 18 pregnancies, 11 births, and 7 miscarriages before dying of tuberculosis from the ravages of so many births. Sanger, who wanted a different life for herself and for other women, went to nursing school in the hopes of expanding her own and, by extension, other women's medical knowledge about pregnancy. She was further radicalized by the experiences of working in the slums of New York City's Lower East Side, where she was inundated with requests from mothers desperate for information about and means to prevent (or at least plan) future pregnancies. Further, she saw firsthand the terrible results when women took medical matters into their own hands and resorted to illegal or self-induced abortions, often dying from their efforts. This was at a time in America when buying even a single condom made one a criminal in 30 states.[iii] Sanger also became convinced that poverty was a driving force in constraining women's choices.

In response to her experiences, Sanger launched a variety of newsletters offering information about contraception. At the time, this violated New York state law, and she was arrested and served time in jail in 1913 and 1916 for her efforts to educate women. After a state judge allowed doctors to provide birth control information to married women, Sanger worked tirelessly to found a network of clinics to serve women. Her efforts eventually led to the establishment of the Planned Parenthood Federation of America, as well as Planned Parenthood International.

She then turned her energies to spearheading the effort to create America's first nearly 100 percent reliable oral contraceptive, the birth control pill. She worked tirelessly, lecturing not only in the United States but also in Europe and in Japan, in her efforts to enable women to make their own reproductive choices.

Most of us don't realize how much this tiny pill has transformed society after it was approved by the Food and Drug Administration in 1960; over the following decades, it redistributed power in so many places—the bedroom, the classroom, and the workplace, to name a few. Women, on a mass level, had the ability to choose when and whether to have children, to marry, and to work. Perhaps the pill has helped create the current situation in which women outnumber men in colleges and graduate degrees. In 1931, H. G. Wells wrote the following about Margaret Sanger's crusade to legalize birth control: "The movement she started will grow to be, a hundred years from now, the most influential of all time. When the history of our civilization is written, it will be a biological history, and Margaret Sanger will be its heroine."[iv]

---

[i] As quoted in Nancy Woloch, *Women and the American Experience* (New York: Alfred A. Knopf, 1984), 369.

[ii] Gloria Steinem, "Margaret Sanger," *The Time 100: The Most Important People of the Century*, www.time.com/time/time100/leaders/profile/sanger.html (accessed March 21, 2009).

[iii] "Margaret Sanger: Birth Control of a Nation," *BusinessWeek* (Sept. 13, 2004), www.businessweek.com/magazine/content/04_37/b3899026_mz072.htm (accessed March 21, 2009).

[iv] As quoted in Steinem, "Margaret Sanger."

In *Roe v. Wade*, the Court established the framework for deciding the legality of abortion. There were several larger issues at stake: for example, when does a fetus become a "person," and thus a citizen of the United States deserving of rights and protection of those rights? The Court held that a fetus is not a person and therefore is not entitled to protection under the U.S. Constitution until it reaches the point of viability, or the point at which it is sufficiently developed that it could live and develop in normal conditions outside of the uterus. The Court defined viability as occurring between 24 and 28 weeks of gestation. It then set up a trimester system, which outlined the changing balance between a woman's right to choose to terminate her pregnancy and the state's interest in regulating the procedure. The justices ruled that a woman's decision to have an abortion in the first trimester was a decision to be made by a woman in consultation with her doctor. However, the Court ruled that individual states could regulate abortion in the second trimester in ways that would preserve and protect the woman's health. In the third trimester of pregnancy, which was after fetal viability, the Court ruled that states could regulate or even outlaw abortion unless the procedure was necessary to preserve the life or health of the mother. In the 1973 case *Doe v. Bolton*, the Court defined "health" to include "all factors—physical, emotional, psychological, familial, and the woman's age—relevant to the well-being of the patient."[47] In sum, the Court required states to justify interfering with a woman's decision by showing that it had a "compelling interest" in doing so and that restrictions on abortion before fetal viability were limited to narrowly and precisely defined concerns about maternal health.

Writing for the majority, Justice Blackmun based the Court's decision on the "right to privacy." The Court did not invent this right in 1973; it was drawing on a legacy of court decisions dating back to 1891 that had articulated the boundaries of government intervention in private affairs. A right to privacy had been used to defend people's rights to refuse medical treatment, not to undergo forced sterilization, and to access birth control. However, *Roe v. Wade,* by arguing that a woman's decision to continue her pregnancy was protected under the constitutional provisions of individual autonomy and privacy, extended this right to privacy to encompass a woman's right to choose whether or not to terminate a pregnancy.

This decision had an immediate effect. On the one hand, thousands of women who before might have undergone a dangerous, illegal, and potentially life-threatening medical procedure now had access to legal, safe, and relatively simple methods to terminate a pregnancy. Within a few years following the decision, the mortality rate for women undergoing legal abortions was ten times lower than the rate for women who had illegal abortions. It was also five times lower than that for women undergoing childbirth.[48]

However, rather than settling a nationwide debate, *Roe v. Wade* actually launched and mobilized a divisive struggle between pro-abortion and anti-abortion forces. The anti-abortion forces, who had been a small, relatively disorganized contingency, became much more organized and active after the ruling and began a campaign aimed at reversing *Roe v. Wade* and creating as many legal barriers to abortion as possible. The pro-abortion rights organizations similarly mobilized to protect a woman's right to choose to terminate a pregnancy on her own terms.

This battle has been waged in small and large ways in the various arenas of American politics. In terms of the judicial arena, the Supreme Court has ruled repeatedly on the abortion issue. A significant case in terms of affecting the reach of *Roe v. Wade* was the Webster ruling of July 3, 1989 (*Webster v. Reproductive Health Services*). By a one-vote margin, the Court upheld a Missouri law that barred the use of public funds, employers, or buildings for abortions. As we will discuss later in greater depth, the effect of this was to restrict the availability of abortions, as well as who could access them. In addition, the law required abortion providers to conduct tests to determine whether a fetus was viable at 20 weeks. As a result, in upholding the Missouri law, the Court's decision also weakened the trimester framework outlined in *Roe v. Wade.*

This also signaled the Court's willingness to allow individual states greater latitude in designing abortion policy. In fact, following the *Webster* ruling, many states interpreted this as a green light to pass more restrictive legislation. For example, Pennsylvania soon enacted a law requiring a woman to notify her husband, receive state-prepared information on alternatives to abortion from her physician, and wait an additional 24 hours before obtaining an abortion. Kansas, Mississippi, North Dakota, and Ohio also required the provision of alternative information as well as waiting periods. Louisiana, Utah, and the territory of Guam enacted more punitive abortion bans, narrowing the conditions under which women could seek an abortion. Less than two decades after writing his original opinion in *Roe v. Wade,* Justice Blackmun wrote in his dissent on the *Webster* ruling: "For today, the women of this Nation still retain the liberty to control their destinies. But the signs are evident and very ominous, and a chill wind blows."[49] For the first time, only four justices had voted to uphold *Roe* in its entirety.

The Supreme Court further adjusted the conditions set down by *Roe v. Wade* in its June 1992 ruling, *Planned Parenthood of Southeastern Pennsylvania v. Casey.* The Court upheld a woman's constitutional right to an abortion before viability and ruled that a state may prohibit abortion thereafter only if it provides exceptions for the life and health of the mother. However, the Court also rejected the trimester framework established by *Roe v. Wade* and argued that states have legitimate interests in protecting the health of the woman and the life of the unborn fetus from the outset of pregnancy. In addition, the Court adopted more lenient standards under which to evaluate the constitutionality of state restrictions on abortion. Under this new ruling, the state may regulate abortion throughout pregnancy as long as it does not "unduly burden" a woman's right to choose. An undue burden was defined as a substantial obstacle in the path of a woman seeking to terminate an abortion before fetal viability. For example, in this case, the Court ruled that a Pennsylvania law that had imposed a 24-hour waiting period before attaining an abortion, required a woman to receive alternative information, and mandated that teenagers receive the consent of at least one parent did not constitute an "undue burden." It did, however, find spousal consent to be an undue burden on a woman's right to abortion and struck down that portion of the law.[50]

Once again, taking the lead from the courts, individual states moved to implement more restrictive abortion laws. As of September 1, 2012, 37 states require some kind of parental involvement for minors seeking an abortion; 26 states have enforced mandatory waiting periods; 17 states mandate counseling that includes information one at least one of the following: the purported link between abortion and breast cancer (5 states), the ability of the fetus to feel pain (11 states), and the long-term mental health consequences for the woman (8 states); and 8 states restrict private insurance coverage for abortion unless the woman's life is endangered if she were to carry the pregnancy to term.[51] Many opponents to these tightened regulations argue that they do, in fact, impose an "undue burden" on women.

The U.S. Congress has also gotten involved in the abortion issue. In 1976, Congress passed the first Hyde Amendment, which banned the use of federal Medicaid dollars, essentially health insurance for the poor, and other federal funds for almost all abortions, except when the pregnancy was terminated as a result of rape or incest or endangered the life of the mother. As of September 1, 2012, only 17 states covered abortion under Medicaid for reasons beyond rape, incest, and life endangerment.[52] In later years, other restrictions on the use of federal funds for abortion were placed on other federal spending measures, which covered federal workers, military personnel, women on reservations, and inmates. The effect of the Hyde Amendment was to make abortion unfeasible for many poor women, whose health benefits were covered under Medicaid. While abortion costs $300 to $500 during the first trimester, the fees escalate precipitously after the first 12 weeks. Thus, even though abortion is legal, for many poor women, it is financially out of reach and not an option. The Supreme Court upheld this ban in *Harris v. McRae*

(1980), reasoning that government could distinguish between abortion and "other medical procedures" because "no other procedure involves the purposeful termination of a potential life."[53]

Abortion foes in Congress also lobbied to have their views implemented in U.S. foreign policy. Senator Jesse Helms of North Carolina, in response to the *Roe v. Wade* decision, introduced the "Human Life Amendment" to the Constitution, which would have overturned *Roe v. Wade*. It failed to pass. However, he did insert restrictions on foreign assistance, which prevented the use of federal funds for "abortion as a method of family planning." President Clinton lifted this ban, also known as the Global Gag Rule; in 2000, President George W. Bush reimposed the ban and tied development dollars once again to domestic demands. President Obama, upon assuming office in 2009, lifted the ban, once again freeing up federal funding for international nonprofit organizations that provide a full range of information on women's reproductive choices. Presidents have gotten involved in the abortion debate in other ways. When President Clinton took office in January 1993, he rescinded several of the policies of previous administrations designed to discourage women from obtaining an abortion. The president lifted restrictions on abortion counseling at federally financed family planning clinics and also allowed federal research using fetal tissue from aborted fetuses. He also reversed a 1979 decision and allowed physicians at U.S. military hospitals to resume providing abortions for armed service personnel and their dependents who paid the cost. Finally, the president asked the Department of Health and Human Services to review the ban on the import of RU-486, the French-manufactured "abortion pill," and to rescind it if there was cause to do so.[54]

However, Congress mobilized in response to these steps and soon moved to impose more restrictions on abortions. Congress reinstated the prohibition against physicians at U.S. military hospitals performing abortions for armed services personnel and their dependents who paid for the procedure. They also passed legislation prohibiting federal employees' health insurance from including abortion coverage except in cases of rape, incest, or danger to the life of the mother.[55]

Congress also passed legislation banning certain abortion procedures, specifically the performance of the dilation and extraction procedure for late-term abortions. Although this procedure accounts for only about 0.03 to 0.05 percent of all abortions, abortion opponents were successful in mobilizing support against the procedure. Using extraordinarily graphic images, many of which had been enhanced and altered, and naming the procedure "partial birth abortion," anti-abortion advocates portrayed the practice as a bloody and brutal act of violence on both the mother and the unborn child. Opponents of the ban contended that the procedure, used in only a handful of cases, was both necessary to protect the health of the mother and was safer than the alternative methods. This legislation was approved by wide margins twice and was vetoed twice. Congress was unable to override the veto and waited until a president who was more sympathetic to the legislation took office. In November 2003, President George W. Bush signed into the law the Partial Birth Abortion Ban Act, stating that "at last, the American people and our government have confronted the violence and come to the defense of the innocent child." He went on to state that the "right to life cannot be granted or denied by government, because it does not come from government, it comes from the Creator of life."[56] The following year, three district courts declared the ban unconstitutional because it did not include an exception for the women's health and also because the language defining the procedure was so broad that it could be used to outlaw a range of second-trimester procedures.[57] Appeals to these decisions were filed, and in 2007 the Supreme Court ruled in *Gonzalez v. Carhartt* that the legislative ban does not represent an undue burden on women, and as a result is constitutional. Thus, the Partial Birth Abortion Ban Act stands, and 18 states have laws in effect that prohibit the procedure, of which only 3 apply only to post-viability abortions.[58]

On the other hand, Congress has also acted to protect access to abortion services. In response to the growing militancy and extremism of anti-abortion advocates picketing abortion clinics, Congress passed the Freedom of Access to Clinics Act in 1994. The act establishes federal criminal penalties and civil remedies "for certain violent, threatening, obstructive, and destructive conduct that is intended to injure, intimidate, or interfere with persons seeking to obtain or provide reproductive health services."[59] Despite the legislation, abortion providers are continuously harassed by anti-abortion forces. In a 2000 survey of abortion providers, 80 percent reported that they had been picketed, 28 percent had been picketed and their patients had had physical contact with the protesters, 18 percent had experienced vandalism, 14 percent said the homes of staff members had been picketed, and 15 percent had received bomb threats.[60] Despite the legislation protecting them, women seeking abortions as well as abortion providers face severe verbal and physical harassment. And in some extreme circumstances, they face death: in June 2009, Dr. George Tiller, one of the few remaining doctors in the United States who performed third-trimester abortions, was gunned down in the lobby of his church Sunday morning as he handed out the bulletin.[61]

As a result, even though the United States has, on paper, a relatively liberal abortion law, it is increasingly difficult for many women to access these services. For one, women are discouraged from having abortions in a variety of ways; many states have imposed legislation requiring women to undergo mandatory counseling, endure a waiting period, or acquire parental permission. Further, the various restrictions on the use of federal funds for abortion services essentially place abortion beyond the financial parameters of poor women, who ironically take on the long-term financial burden of raising a child with inadequate resources because they lack the short-term resources to make preventing that pregnancy possible. Finally, despite the legality of abortion, abortions are increasingly difficult to procure because many doctors are no longer willing or able to provide them. Increasingly, abortions are provided at abortion clinics (defined as facilities where half or more of patient visits are for abortion services) rather than at hospitals or doctor's offices. For example, while about 1,500 hospitals performed abortions in 1980, that number fell to about 600 by 2001.[62] Many doctors were intimidated by the constant harassment and violent methods of certain factions of the anti-abortion movement, who were willing to picket doctors at work as well as at their homes.

The abortion debate in America has been waged in all branches of government at both the national and state levels. Here, an anti-abortion protester prays outside the Supreme Court building, where the Court, in a 5–4 ruling, upheld a federal ban on partial birth abortions.
SOURCE: Photo by Jonathan Ernst/Getty Images.

In addition, abortion providers are aging, and newer colleagues are not entering the field; fewer than half (46 percent) of residency training programs in obstetrics and gynecology routinely provide training in first-trimester abortion.[63] The result is a dramatic decrease in the number of facilities where women can go if they want to terminate a pregnancy. In 2008, 87 percent of U.S. counties had no abortion provider; this number goes up to nearly 100 percent in nonmetropolitan areas.[64] At least one in four women having an abortion travels 50 miles or more for it.[65] As a result, even though abortion is legal, it is increasingly less accessible.

In the United States, it is estimated that 22 percent of all pregnancies end in abortion. What is the profile of an "average" woman seeking an abortion? Just over half had used some form of contraception during the month they became pregnant, but had used it inconsistently or incorrectly. The "average" woman is in her 20s, single or in a temporary relationship, already a parent, and poor. In terms of numbers, women in their 20s account for more than half of all abortions (teenagers account for 18 percent); 45 percent are not married and are not living with a partner; 61 percent already have at least one child; and 42 percent have incomes that place them below the federal poverty level for a single woman with no children. The reasons women give for having an abortion reflect their understanding of the responsibilities of parenthood and family life. Three fourths say that they cannot afford a child and that having a baby would interfere with work, school, or the ability to care for dependents and cite current responsibilities for other individuals. Half do not want to be a single parent or are having problems with their husband or partner. At the end of this chapter, we will discuss ways to address one of the key factors that determines the relatively high incidence of abortion in the United States: the high number of unintended pregnancies.

THE NETHERLANDS

The Netherlands represents an interesting case study of abortion politics and policies. One the one hand, the government liberalized its abortion policy later than many other Western European countries did. Abortion was not legalized until 1981, and the legislation did not come into effect until 1984, although in practice abortion services were liberalized a decade before these changes were legalized. In addition, while women have the right to terminate their pregnancy until viability (about 24 weeks), they must receive counseling from their doctor and must undergo a 5-day waiting period. Thus, the Netherlands provides a slightly modified version of "abortion on demand" by involving the medical establishment more thoroughly in a woman's decision than in countries such as the United States. However, since the passage of the Pregnancy Termination Act, abortion has not been challenged seriously by any social group within the Netherlands. In addition, the Netherlands has one of the lowest abortion rates in the world, despite the widespread availability and public financing of the procedure.[66] What accounts for this particular outcome in the Netherlands?

Abortion was criminalized in the Netherlands in 1886. However, the law required proof that the fetus was alive at the time of the abortion as a requirement for conviction; because such proof was difficult to obtain, it was nearly impossible to convict anyone for performing the procedure. This legislation was amended in 1911 to try to further regulate abortions, and in practice, abortions were outlawed except when performed to save the life of the mother.[67] However, few people were convicted under the laws; in 1973, when the abortion debate returned to the public arena, only three people had been convicted.[68]

As in many other countries, challenges to and efforts to revise the criminalization of abortion surfaced in the late 1960s and throughout the 1970s. For one, Dutch society in the 1960s was in the midst of massive attitudinal changes. Traditionally, family planning had been discouraged, for it interfered with the objectives of marriage and supposedly encouraged promiscuity. However, the birth control pill was introduced in 1964, and contraceptives in general became more readily available. In addition, England liberalized its abortion laws in 1968, and Dutch women began to travel there to terminate their pregnancies. Further, there was emerging pressure from women's groups, academics, and the medical industry to update legislation to accommodate current practice. In particular, the medical industry argued that existing legislation did not adequately allow for abortion under conditions of medical necessity and that doctors should be able to decide when an abortion was necessary. Starting in 1967, with the tacit approval of the relevant legal authorities (even though no new legislation had been passed), several university hospitals created "abortion teams" to reach consensus on the conditions under which an abortion would be medically necessary. By 1973, teams were essentially allowing all abortions if the woman requested it, and throughout the 1970s, doctors openly defied the law by opening private clinics providing abortion on demand. In essence, the Dutch government had to address the abortion issue because practice was in direct conflict with legislation.[69]

The government first delved into the issue in 1967, when members of parliament first considered reforming abortion; 3 years later, in 1970, the Cabinet appointed a special commission to study the issue. However, the main obstacle to passing reform lay in the Dutch multiparty, parliamentary system. In parliamentary systems, no one party is usually able to win a majority of seats. As a result, coalition governments are often the only way to build a parliamentary majority. The leadership of the various coalition parties negotiates a pact for each new cabinet, which sets the political agenda for the next 4 years. Party discipline is strict, and adherence to the pact is expected and is relaxed only in the event of individual conscience. This negotiation process can take weeks, even months, to hammer out so that all parties reach agreement.

In addition, this process is complicated by the fact that until 1994, coalition governments always involved the three main religious parties, which had united into a coalition called the Christian Democratic Appeal (CDA). The CDA often served as the critical coalition partner with either of the two major ruling parties, the Liberals and the Social Democrats, and was able to veto abortion reform, even if its larger coalition partner was in favor of such a development. As a result, from 1971 until 1984, the abortion issue was raised but not resolved in the negotiations of coalition pacts. On several occasions, the issue threatened to endanger the life of incumbent cabinets.[70]

Throughout the 1970s, the Dutch government unsuccessfully tried to resolve the issue of abortion. An initial liberalization of the abortion law, which would have permitted the procedure only where pregnancy posed a threat to the woman's physical or mental health, was presented to parliament in June 1972 and was met with strong opposition from both the left, who felt it did not go far enough, and the right, who felt it had gone too far. However, before the parliament could vote on it, the cabinet fell because of an unrelated fiscal policy issue, and the bill died a silent death. The bill was also the last time that the Dutch government tried to contain abortion; afterward, the debate moved on to an issue of who decides when women can get an abortion, as opposed to under what conditions women may get an abortion. In the next coalition government, the relevant parties could not come to an agreement, and legislation foundered once again.[71] However, coalition partners were able to agree not to prosecute clinics that were performing abortions except in cases of medical malpractice.

After a flurry of coalition negotiations, in 1980 the government finally succeeded in introducing abortion legislation to the parliament. In May 1981, the Dutch parliament passed the Pregnancy Termination Act, which repealed the restrictive 1911 regulations. However, it took another 3 years for the legislation to be translated into administrative regulations. Further, the legislation passed with the smallest majority of votes possible, mainly because those who voted against the law felt it was not liberal enough.

The legislation essentially affirmed abortion practices that had been implemented over the previous decade.[72] Currently, abortion is permitted virtually upon request between conception and viability, which the legislature set at 24 weeks, although in practice this was translated into 22 weeks. According to the law, abortion is allowed if the woman is in an "emergency situation," which is to be determined by the woman together with her physician. In practice, this has been loosely interpreted, and abortion is permitted virtually on request. However, the woman must also accept counseling from the physician to ensure that the decision to terminate the pregnancy is taken carefully and that the woman feels that it is her only viable choice. After the initial visit, women must wait for 5 days before undergoing the procedure. After the abortion, a woman must be given access to adequate aftercare, including information on how to prevent unwanted pregnancies in the future. Physicians in a clinic or hospital may perform abortions only with the appropriate permit from the Ministry of Health, Welfare and Sport. Finally, a doctor who has a conscientious objection to providing abortions must immediately inform the woman of this fact, and the doctor may also choose not to perform the procedure. Since November 1984, the government-sponsored national health insurance system has covered the costs of abortion for Dutch women. Despite initial fears, this did not result in an immediate rise in the number of abortions.[73]

In the wake of the law's implementation, there has been relatively little opposition. There has been concern expressed over the fact that technically, a woman cannot seek an abortion (unless her life is endangered) once the fetus is considered viable (which, at the very latest, is 24 weeks). In practice, abortions are allowed after viability only if there are very serious defects, which in effect means that the fetus will die in the womb or shortly after birth (thus, it is not viable).[74] However, in many situations, doctors are unable to detect severe (but not life-threatening) diseases or impairments such as Down syndrome or spina bifida until about week 24, thus eliminating abortion as a legal option.[75] Women who find out after viability that their fetus has severe (but not life-threatening) developmental issues then have to travel abroad to seek a late-term abortion if they choose to terminate the pregnancy.

Yet, for the most part, abortion has been a noncontentious social issue. Why is this? Several significant themes emerge from the Dutch case study. For one, legislation legitimized a decade of abortion practice that was much more liberal than existing law dictated. In some ways, legislation enforced an already evolving social acceptance of the practice, rather than exacerbating existing social cleavages. The main impediment to legislation was not public opinion but, rather, the complexities of the Dutch parliamentary system, which gave disproportionate amounts of power to smaller coalition partners, who could often derail legislative initiative. Further, a key player, the medical industry, which had derailed reform in countries such as Ireland, was a major proponent of reform in the Netherlands.

In addition, the Netherlands has always combined a liberal abortion policy with strong support for contraception programs. The Netherlands has one of the lowest abortion rates in the world, and through much of the 1990s, it had the lowest rate in the world. In 2009, the abortion rate in the Netherlands was 5.5 per 1,000 women; this was no longer the lowest, although it was one of the lowest. Further, 95 percent of abortions are performed within the first 13 weeks of pregnancy.[76] These figures stand in stark contrast to the abortion rate in the United States (19.6 per 1,000 women) and the proportion performed in the first trimester (88 percent), when they are safest for the woman. In the United States, many women would like to have abortions earlier but cite problems with having to raise the money to pay for them (in 2009, a nonhospital abortion with local anesthesia at 10 weeks' gestation cost $451). This is a particular problem for teenagers in the United States, who are more likely than American women in their 20s to delay obtaining the procedure.[77] In contrast, the Netherlands has one of the lowest teen pregnancy rates in Europe; given the strong family planning programs that exist, Dutch women are able to exercise more choice and control over their fertility and, thus, perhaps, do not have to face the decision of whether to abort as often as women in other countries do. As a result, abortion is less frequently used as the "last resort" method of family planning.

The number of abortions performed in the Netherlands rose starting in the 1990s, threatening the Dutch reputation for liberal abortion laws but low abortion rates. In 2003, the rate had risen to 8.7 abortions for every 1,000 women of childbearing age.[78] This rise in abortion rates was most significant among immigrant women and young girls, many of whom are from immigrant families. Of the teenagers seeking to terminate a pregnancy, 60 percent had an ethnic background from traditional immigration countries such as Suriname, the Dutch Antilles, Turkey, Morocco, and countries of Africa, eastern Europe, and Asia. Many of these women came to the Netherlands seeking asylum or as refugees, were raised in different cultural contexts, and also had less knowledge, as newly arrived residents, of Dutch family planning services. Many women seeking abortion in the Netherlands had also traveled from other countries.[79] However, in the following decade, the rate began to decline again and then stabilize, perhaps signaling that increased contraception use is trickling down to these new residents.

GENERAL THEMES

What larger lessons can we learn from the cases of Ireland, the United States, and the Netherlands? What explains the varying outcomes of abortion policies in these three countries? While Ireland has moved to further restrict access to abortion, the United States wrote one of the most liberal laws, although the law has been under sustained attack for the past three and a half decades. Finally, the Netherlands has implemented a law that places some restrictions on woman's full autonomy but has also encountered relatively little resistance. What lessons can we draw from these differing outcomes?

One explanation may lie in prevailing attitudes about the justifiability of abortion. The World Values Survey tracks attitudinal changes among populations in more than 80 countries on a wide array of social, economic, and political issues. One of the questions asked in the 2002 survey delves into people's tolerance for abortion. The question reads: "Please tell me for each of the following statements whether you think it [abortion] can always be justified, never justified, or something in between, using this card" (scale is 1 = never justifiable to 10 = always justifiable).[80]

As demonstrated in Table 6.2, the responses to this question from citizens in Ireland, the Netherlands, and the United States reveal marked differences in the public's acceptance of abortion. In Ireland, just over half of the population feel that abortion is never justified; the United States is in the middle, with less than a third of the population feeling that it is never justifiable; and the Dutch are most tolerant in their attitudes toward abortion, with only 15.3 percent of respondents answering that abortion is never justified. Despite these figures, abortion for most citizens of these three countries is not a black-or-white issue; support for or opposition to the practice is contingent on a variety of extenuating circumstances, as the data indicate. Except for Ireland, the bulk of the citizenry differ, not so much in whether they support or oppose abortion, but under which conditions. Nonetheless, it is true that the citizenry in Ireland is most consistently opposed to liberalizing abortion laws; in the United States, public opinion seems to indicate more tolerance for the practice; and in the Netherlands, citizens are most tolerant, with just over 29 percent of the population placing themselves on the upper third of the ten-point scale of acceptance. Thus, some of the variation in policy outcomes potentially can be explained by variations in public opinion.

In addition, in our varied cases, the venues used for decision making were critical to the outcome of the debates. In Ireland, many of the decisions were made through the use of public referenda, and the government repeatedly distanced itself from the debate by delaying legislating the matter further. Thus, the debate was waged primarily in the court of public opinion, with some assistance from the Irish Supreme Court. Because the government has refused to design or enact policy, this has forced the issue into the broader arena of European politics. In the United States, the relatively open system, with power divided between the varied branches and among federal and state authority, allowed a variety of interest groups to lobby for policy in all possible arenas, thus prolonging the battle. Finally, in the Netherlands, the major policy decisions were left to the prime minister and the legislature, although the Dutch parliamentary system of coalition governments impeded the formulation of abortion policy for quite some time.

In addition, levels of social mobilization differed in our case studies. In particular, women's groups differed in their abilities to "gender" the debate and frame it as a woman's right to personal autonomy and choice with regard to her body. In Ireland, the women's movement for much of the debate was unable to present a unified position on abortion. Further, they had relatively few allies within the government. As a result, they have been hesitant to frame the issue of abortion as a feminist issue, but have instead focused on invoking sympathy and tolerance for

Table 6.2 Acceptance of Abortion in Ireland, Netherlands, and the United States

		COUNTRY/REGION			
		IRELAND	NETHERLANDS	UNITED STATES OF AMERICA	TOTAL
Justifiable: Abortion Never justifiable	Count	498	152	354	1,004
	% Within country/ region	50.7%	15.3%	29.7%	31.7%
2	Count	79	57	84	220
	% Within country/ region	8.0%	5.7%	7.0%	6.9%
3	Count	78	75	74	227
	% Within country/ region	7.9%	7.5%	6.2%	7.2%
4	Count	43	59	66	168
	% Within country/ region	4.4%	5.9%	5.5%	5.3%
5	Count	160	171	184	515
	% Within country/ region	16.3%	17.2%	15.4%	16.3%
6	Count	26	97	145	268
	% Within country/ region	2.6%	9.8%	12.2%	8.5%
7	Count	27	91	69	87
	% Within country/ region	2.7%	9.2%	5.8%	5.9%
8	Count	24	114	85	223
	% Within country/ region	2.4%	11.5%	7.1%	7.0%
9	Count	16	51	34	101
	% Within country/ region	1.6%	5.1%	2.9%	3.2%
Always justifiable	Count	31	127	97	255
	% Within country/ region	3.2%	12.8%	8.1%	8.0%
Total	Count	982	994	1192	3168
	% Within country/ region	100.0%	100.0%	100.0%	100.0%

SOURCE: World Values Survey, "1999–2002 World Values Survey Questionnaire." http://www.worldvaluessurvey.org/statistics/index.html. (April 22, 2006).

women in crisis pregnancies and improving women's access to abortion abroad. They were never able to fully counter the power of the Catholic Church and the medical profession, two potent lobbies in opposition to liberalized abortion policy. In the United States, women's organizations framed abortion as a women's rights issue. However, they were soon countered by an increasingly powerful and well-organized countermovement. Further, abortion became an increasingly partisan issue, with anti-abortion advocates dominating the Republican Party and pro-legalization advocates influential in the Democratic Party. As a result, the debate increasingly has been framed as one that weighs competing rights of women with the status of the fetus. Although the Democratic Party reclaimed the presidency in 2008 and 2012, it is unclear whether the administration will revisit the issue, given its priorities on economic policy and health care. Given the current role of the Republican Party in national politics, it is doubtful that women's organizations in favor of abortion will be able to recapture the framing of the debate. Finally, in the Netherlands, women's groups succeeded in defining abortion as a women's issue and in winning most of their demands on access to services. The increasing presence of women in parliamentary parties, key cabinet positions, and a women's policy agency ready to advocate for abortion helped settle the debate by the 1980s. Further, the medical industry strongly favored reform, and opponents to liberalization did not organize or mobilize effectively.

ADVANCING WOMEN'S EQUALITY

The broader issue of reproductive rights is central to women's equality. Only women are biologically capable of giving birth and nursing, and then they often assume the primary responsibilities for caring for and raising these children. And even though not all women will have children, almost all will be sexually active at some point in their lives. Yet, they often do not have full choice and control over a number of decisions relating to reproduction and reproductive health, such as when and with whom to have sex, the timing and spacing of children, and access to education and other critical resources to make those decisions. This impacts not only their status in the realms of work, politics, and the family, but also their abilities to lead the kinds of lives that they value. Although member nations of the United Nations signed on to the 1994 Cairo Programme of Action, which recognizes that reproductive rights are human rights and therefore inalienable, translating this broad commitment into specific policies has not been an easy task. While the Programme of Action upholds the right of "all couples and individuals to decide freely and responsibly the number, spacing and timing of their children and to have the information and means to do so, and the right to attain the highest standard of sexual and reproductive health," there is wide variation on how countries interpret this commitment, or to which parts they want to commit. In particular, establishing and protecting a woman's access to abortion is perhaps the most highly contested "right"; proponents argue that ensuring safe, legal, and broad access to this practice is critical if one truly believes that women should have the ability to freely choose their own reproductive futures, while opponents maintain that this supposed "right" has to coexist with the equally important right of the fetus to human life. How would both sides advance women's equality, and is there any shared ground between these two positions?

Those who advocate for legalization of abortion and those against actually agree on one key component: both sides would like to see a dramatic reduction in the number of abortions. How can such a reduction be brought about? Outlawing the practice has actually not been an effective strategy; women simply have them done illegally, often at great risk to their health and often their lives. An alternative strategy would be to reduce the number of unplanned and unwanted pregnancies. One way to do that would be to focus on increasing the availability of contraceptives and reproductive health education. The education component is key, advocates argue, because getting people to use contraception is not just a question of availability and access; it's also a matter of convincing women (and men) that using contraception is a wise strategy to prevent pregnancy, and to ensure that if contraception is being used, it is used properly. Many point to the Netherlands, for example, as a country that, through its extensive funding of sex education and responsible contraception programs, also has one of the lowest abortion rates in the world, despite the fact that the procedure is legal, free, and available upon request.

However, widening access to contraception and health education, particularly during adolescence, the period in which many begin to experiment with their sexuality, has not been embraced universally across the political spectrum. Some (often Christian) organizations have objected that it encourages promiscuity and teenage sex rather than abstinence before marriage. Unfortunately, in practice, abstinence-only programs are not particularly effective, particularly in a changing world of lessening social cohesion where communities have less authority to impose social norms such as chastity and abstinence. The text box "Contraception to Teenagers" discusses a pilot program launched in New York City that tries to take a more pragmatic approach to the reality of teenage sexuality and the resulting high pregnancy and abortion rates.

Contraception to Teenagers

According to the New York City Department of Health, in 2011, 7,000 girls got pregnant citywide. Ninety percent of those pregnancies were unplanned. Sixty percent were aborted. Twenty-two hundred girls became mothers by age 17. About 70 percent will drop out of school.[I] These statistics are not unique to New York City; the United States leads the industrialized world in the incidence of teen pregnancy. The U.S. teen birth rate is nearly eight times higher than that of the Netherlands, over five times higher than France's, and over four times higher than Germany's.[II] Teen pregnancy is a problem for a number of reasons; physically, emotionally, and in terms of economic security, most teenagers are not equipped to become parents. Teen pregnancy is costly to society in a number of ways. For one, it accounts for nearly $11 billion per year in costs to U.S. taxpayers for increased health care and foster care, increased incarceration rates among children of teen parents, and lost tax revenue because of lower educational attainment and income among teen mothers. Second, pregnancy and birth are significant contributors to high school dropout rates among girls. Third, the problems associated with teen pregnancy are usually passed down to the next generation; the children of teenage mothers are more likely to have lower school achievement and to drop out of high school, have more health problems, be incarcerated at some time during adolescence, give birth as a teenager, and face unemployment as a young adult.[iii] There are many reasons why governments at the local, state, and national level want to reduce teen pregnancy.

One strategy is to widen publicly funded sex education and contraception programs in the schools, an effective tactic pursued in many other countries. However, this has been controversial in the United States, where sex education programs emphasize abstinence as a strategy much more heavily. However, abstinence is not a particularly effective strategy used on its own; comprehensive research on the decrease in the U.S. teen pregnancy rate between 1988 and 1995 found that about 25 percent of it was due to the decline in the proportion of teenagers having sex, while 75 percent was due to improved contraceptive use.[iv] (In addition, a focus solely on abstinence also tends to drive up the incidence of sexually transmitted infections, as teens think they are not sexually active if they do not have intercourse.)

New York City schools are increasing students' access to contraception through the CATCH (Connecting Adolescents to Comprehensive Health) program. According to state law, students may obtain contraception without telling their parents in community clinics and school-based health centers. The CATCH program distributes contraception in the schools to students, but it also allows parents to choose which types of reproductive services they wish for their children. Alternatively, they can opt out of the program, although just 1 to 2 percent of parents have done so. In addition to birth control pills, students can receive the morning-after pill (which prevents the girl's ovaries from releasing an egg, so that it cannot become fertilized with a sperm). Since its inception in January 2011, the program has already distributed a form of contraception to over 1,000 students. Starting in the fall of 2012, students were also able to get Depo-Provera, a form of birth control that is injected every 3 months. What do you think? Should schools expand access to birth control to all students? Should parents be involved at all in this decision, or to what degree?

---

[i]K. J. Dell'Antonia, "New York Schools Provide Morning After Pills," *New York Times*, September 25, 2012.

[ii]Advocates for Youth, "Adolescent Sexual Health in Europe and the United States."

[iii]Centers for Disease Control and Prevention, "Teen Pregnancy," http://www.cdc.gov/teenpregnancy/

[iv]Cynthia Dailard, "Understanding 'Abstinence': Implications for Individuals, Programs and Policies," *The Guttmacher Report on Public Policy*, December 2003, Volume 6, Number 5. http://www.guttmacher.org/pubs/tgr/06/5/gr060504.html

In sum, while both sides of the debate would, in truth, like to see a reduction in unwanted pregnancies, not all factions would equate this reduction with increasing the availability of contraception and sexual health education. Groups who are leery of increased availability of contraception and health education have lobbied for increased funding for crisis centers and counseling for women to help them manage their conflicted reactions to a pregnancy so that they can come to terms with the ramifications of their pregnancy for their lives. It is unclear whether this solution really upholds a commitment to allowing women "choice" over their reproductive futures.

While many pro-legalization advocates would like to see an overall reduction in the number of abortions, they also support a woman's right to full access to these services, regardless of income, race, and ethnicity. This is particularly the case in the United States, where abortions are legal in theory but not widely available in practice, because few clinics will perform them, fewer doctors are being trained in them, and fewer and fewer federal dollars can be used to fund them. In practice, this puts many hurdles in the way of low-income women, who are often also of color. They may lack the resources to travel to a clinic and to pay for the procedure and any follow-up treatment required. Therefore, advocates have emphasized the importance of state funding for abortion services, so that it is not a medical practice available to predominantly middle-class white women, as well as ensuring that women have access to a facility within a certain geographical range. They also emphasize the importance of contraception being covered in federally funded health-care programs as a way to decrease the use of abortion as a last-resort form of birth control.

However, it is important to recognize that not all women agree that improving access to abortion is the only way to increase women's abilities to make autonomous decisions about their bodies or that abortion is synonymous with advancing women's equality. For example, in the United States, conservative organizations such as Concerned Women for America (CWA) consciously identify themselves as women's organizations that address women's issues from a conservative woman's point of view. The CWA is opposed to abortion and most forms of birth control, lobbies for legislation to limit or fully criminalize abortion, and opposes the use of federal funds for most domestic and international family planning programs. Their position is that abortion and family planning programs ultimately hurt women. First, they argue that abortions are psychologically damaging to women and can lead to "postabortion syndrome," in which women may suffer from something similar to posttraumatic stress disorder. They base their opposition to family planning on the argument that it has negative side effects on women's health. While the CWA does not speak for all women who oppose abortion, it is an example of a woman's group that opposes contraception, abortion, and other family planning services from a "woman's perspective."[81]

CONCLUSION

In the past 40 years, abortion has moved from an issue that was considered to be a private dilemma to one of public controversy. In deciding who ultimately gets to make the final decision, women's groups, governments, religious organizations, and the medical industry have all become key players in advocating what they feel to be the appropriate balance between a woman's right to control her own body and fetal rights to survival.

Abortion is merely one issue in an increasingly contested domain of reproductive rights. Dramatic leaps in technological and medical innovation have further complicated a variety of issues. Better fetal testing blurs the line between parental concerns over raising a child with a significant disability with more blatant eugenic motivations. Improved prenatal care has improved premature babies' chances of survival outside of the womb, even if those chances are heavily dependent on technology rather than internal levels of fetal development. States eventually will have to assess what this will mean for legislation that bases access to abortion on "viability." Strides in stem cell research and alternative conception methods have complicated a host of issues related to women's reproductive abilities and also challenge traditional notions of what constitutes the family. While abortion currently may be one of the more visible issues concerning reproductive rights on which states are expected to legislate, it will not be the last.

FOR MORE INFORMATION

Video and Multimedia

Information on a number of films dealing with the topic of abortion can be found at http://www.abortionfilms.org/?lang=en.

4 Months, 3 Weeks and 2 Days—This Romanian film by director Christian Mungiu that won the top prize at the 2007 Cannes Film Festival tells the story of a student who goes to great lengths to help her friend have a secret abortion.

Eggsploitation—A documentary that explores the health risks facing younger women who provide eggs for other people's fertility problems. For more information, go to http://www.eggsploitation.com/.

I had an Abortion (http://abortionandlife.com/film.html)—A documentary that features 10 women who candidly describe their experiences with procuring an abortion, spanning seven decades, from the years before *Roe v. Wade* to the present day.

Made in India—A feature-length documentary film about the human experiences behind the phenomena of "outsourcing" surrogate mothers to India. For more information, go to http://madeinindiamovie.com/.

Vera Drake—A British film by director Mike Leigh that tells the story of a woman who provides illegal abortions in 1950s England.

Readings

Margaret Atwood, *The Handmaid's Tale*. A novel that explores themes of women in subjugation and the various means by which they gain agency through the prism of science fiction/futuristic projection (New York: Anchor, 1998).

Boston Women's Health Book Collective, *Our Bodies, Ourselves* (Touchstone, 2011). A classic, now updated work looking at women's sexuality and reproductive health.

Susan Wickland, *This Common Secret: My Journey as an Abortion Doctor* (New York: Public Affairs, 2008). A memoir by a doctor who has provided abortions for over 20 years.

Organizations and Websites

Abortion Rights, United Kingdom, http://www.abortionrights.org.uk. A pro-choice organization based in the United Kingdom that also advocates for increased access to abortion in Ireland.

Americans United For Life, http://www.aul.org. An American pro-life public-interest law firm and advocacy group based in Washington, D.C. Since the 1990s, it has focused on promoting anti-abortion legislation at the state level.

Catholics for Choice, http://www.catholicsforchoice.org. A pro-choice, dissenting Catholic organization whose mission is "to serve as a voice for Catholics who believe that the Catholic tradition supports a woman's moral and legal right to follow her conscience in matters of sexuality and reproductive health."

Center for Reproductive Rights, http://reproductiverights.org/. A global reproductive rights organization that uses constitutional and international law to secure women's right to an abortion in over 45 countries.

I Had an Abortion, http://abortionandlife.com/. A project that collects first-person narratives from many women who have chosen to have an abortion.

International Planned Parenthood Federation, http://www.ippf.org/en/What-we-do/Abortion

National Abortion Rights Action League, http://www.prochoiceamerica.org. A nonprofit organization that engages in political action to oppose restrictions on abortion and expand access to abortion.

National Organization for Women, http://www.now.org/issues/abortion. Founded in 1966, NOW is the largest feminist organization in the United States.

National Right to Life Committee, http://www.nrlc.org. The oldest and largest anti-abortion organization in the United States, with affiliates in all 50 states and over 3,000 local chapters nationwide.

Our Bodies, Ourselves, http://www.ourbodiesourselves.org/default.asp. Also known as the Boston Women's Health Book Collective, OBOS is a nonprofit, public interest women's health education, advocacy, and consulting organization. Beginning in 1970 with the publication of the first edition of *Our Bodies, Ourselves*, OBOS has inspired the women's health movement in the United States and globally.

Our Bodies, Ourselves Health Resource Center, http://www.ourbodiesourselves.org/book/default.asp.

Planned Parenthood, information on Ireland, http://www.plannedparenthood.org/issues-action/international/articles/irelands-rights-6470.htm

SAMA: Resource Group for Women and Health, http://samawomenshealth.wordpress.com/. An organization based in New Delhi that works on women's health issues.

UNFPA: United Nations Population Fund, http://www.unfpa.org/rights/rights.htm. An international organization that supports countries in using population data for policies and programs to reduce poverty and to ensure that "every pregnancy is wanted, every birth is safe, every young person is free of HIV/AIDS, and every girl and woman is treated with dignity and respect."

Women on Waves, a Dutch NGO working to prevent unwanted pregnancy and unsafe abortions throughout the world, http://www.womenonwaves.org

The World's Abortion Laws 2012, http://worldabortionlaws.com/. A interactive map giving information on abortion laws in every country in the world.

PART III

Participation and Protest
in the Global Community

I n the previous part, the three chapters focused on ways in which advanced industrialized states have designed policies that impact the position and status of
women in society. We focused on employment policies, reconciliation policies that
help parents balance the demands of production and reproduction, and policies
governing reproductive choice, specifically abortion. We found that while many
states advance the rhetoric of gender equality, ensuring that that equality exists is
a different matter. Providing equal employment opportunities, generous maternity
leave benefits, comprehensive day care, and control over reproductive choice often
butts up against contentious debates about women's and men's "appropriate"
spheres of influence and poses difficult questions about whose interests, and
whose welfare, should truly be at stake.

In this final part, we now turn to exploring a variety of women's issues that, although of global concern, tend to be concentrated in the countries of the developing
world. For many of the world's citizens—men as well as women—dealing with the
varied manifestations of poverty defines their daily lives. Extreme poverty is a constant for much of the world's population—nearly 1.5 billion people survive on less
than $1.25 a day.[1] However, levels of economic deprivation are not the sole indica-
tors of poverty; poverty also encompasses dimensions such as lack of empowerment, opportunity, capacity, and physical security. Thus, economic scarcity is a
problem, not only in and of itself, but also because it often robs people of the abilities to make decisions about the ways they want to live their lives.[2] Further, as we
shall see in the following chapters, while it is a constant for many people, poverty,
and the problems that arise from it, also has a female face. Women participate in and
benefit from the process of socioeconomic development in different and unequal
ways. Not only do these gender inequalities exacerbate the varied facets of poverty,
but the reverse is also true: poverty also exacerbates gender inequalities.

We want to underscore that many of the issues we will discuss in the ensuing
chapters are universal to women all over the world; access to education, stable
employment, adequate political representation, and physical and mental well-
being are important goals that all women share, in all countries. Yet, a variety of

problems—colonial legacies, weak governments, endemic poverty, and some traditional cultural values—ensure that many women in the developing world have a fundamentally different experience from Western women in achieving these goals. For example, while women all over the world struggle to secure their own reproductive health, many women in the developing world face challenges in gaining control and choice over this basic element of their lives that are fundamentally different from those faced by women in advanced industrialized nations. A woman in some sub-Saharan African countries faces a 1 in 16 chance of dying in childbirth, while for a woman in a developed country the risk is 1 in 2,800. The reasons behind this figure are numerous: women's lack of power in the household, lack of government funding of public health care, and endemic poverty all play a role in ensuring that women in the developing world lack access to choices, opportunities, and services to improve their lives. Thus, it is important to underscore that while women are unequal in status in almost all societies, the depth and nature of, the reasons for, and the solutions to that inequality differ substantially in various countries and contexts. Also, within countries in the developing world, not all women live equally impoverished lives; in fact, inequalities between women can be more severe. In the absence of a large middle class in many countries, with severe levels of economic inequality, a small stratum of elite women can sometimes have more in common with their social and economic sisters in the Global North than with impoverished women who may live as little as five blocks from them. Perhaps a constant around the world is that women of privilege can live vastly different lives from the rest of the population, wherever they are.

In addition, although these issues tend to be concentrated in the countries of the developing world, they are still of global significance. The effects of increased globalization and migration, resulting in large immigrant populations in Western countries, as well as greater interdependence among nations, also mean that few problems are entirely "local." Many of the issues discussed in this final part are not constrained by national borders; sweatshop labor, trafficking in women, or HIV/AIDS transmission do not stay contained within the boundaries of nation-states. Nor can the problem always be resolved solely by any one government. Further, many governments in the developing world lack the capacity to tackle these issues on their own and need assistance, technical as well as financial, to address many of the social dimensions related to poverty. Thus, the scope and nature of the problem as well as the nature of the remedy increasingly demand concerted, international, coordinated action. Efforts to ameliorate these problems also extend beyond traditional nation-state borders—international organizations, such as the United Nations, foreign governments, and nonprofit organizations have all become involved in trying to improve the quantity and quality of women's lives in the developing world. In turn, women's organizations, either at the grassroots level or through their participation in transnational networks, have lobbied these same agencies to incorporate gender concerns more thoroughly into their development projects.

In this final part, we look at a variety of issues that affect women globally. You may notice that the chapters in this final part are quite short. They are meant to be. In this final part, we wanted to devote our time and energy to highlighting a variety of issues rather than delving in depth into a select few. As a result, the chapters may not treat topics as deeply as the previous chapters do, but they do provide a telling snapshot of some of the most critical issues facing women around the world.

We start off in Chapter 7 by surveying the wide array of international organizations that are involved in addressing gender issues and concerns before honing in on several critical and compelling global gender issues. In Chapter 8, we address the emerging role of women in the global economy, focusing on the varied ways that economies have increasingly become reliant on women to fuel economic growth, whether as cheap but reliable labor in garment and low-tech industries, or as maids, nannies, and cleaners. Next, in Chapter 9 we discuss the gendered dimensions of women's health, exploring such issues as boy preference, access to reproductive services, and HIV/AIDS. Chapter 10 addresses the education gap between boys and girls, the high price attached to this gap, and the benefits of investing in closing it. We then turn in Chapter 11 to the topic of women and war. Despite, or perhaps because of, the end of the Cold War, regional and civil warfare has increased. While all conflict involves destruction, dislocation, and incalculable levels of human loss, waging war, living through war, and recovering from conflict are gendered. Our final chapter on women and physical autonomy (Chapter 12) addresses the practice of female genital mutilation, virginity testing, and "honor" rapes and killings and the causes and consequences of such practices on women around the world.

In each chapter in this part, we describe how numerous international organizations and development agencies are working to address the various ways in which women experience poverty, as well as the manifestations of poverty, such as the lack of adequate employment, health care, and education, or bitter civil strife over control of economic, political, and social resources. International agencies have made great strides in improving the conditions of many women's lives. However, the international community is better at promising change than delivering on it; international agencies have the power to lobby, pressure, and embarrass national governments, but they do not have the power to coerce. Yet, in countries plagued by weak governments, miniscule budgets, and fragmented societies, international organizations can step into the void to provide support, moral and financial, to women around the world seeking better lives for themselves and their families. In turn, women themselves, as agents, rather than subjects, have increasingly mobilized as activists in community foundations, nongovernmental organizations, and government to proactively participate in change.

7

Gender, Development, and International Organizations

Afghanistan has the dubious honor of topping TrustLaw's index of "The World's Most Dangerous Countries for Women." Looking at risk factors such as health threats, levels of violence (sexual and nonsexual), lack of access to resources, and cultural and religious constraints, this organization paints a grim picture of women's daily lives in places such as Afghanistan, where women have a one in 11 chance of dying in childbirth. Girls and women are disempowered in other areas of their lives as well; 87 percent of women are illiterate, and 70 to 80 percent of girls and women faced forced marriages. The Democratic Republic of the Congo places a close second. Named the rape capital of the world, a recent report in the *American Journal of Public Health* estimated that about 1,150 women are raped every day, or some 420,000 a year, creating a climate of institutionalized sexual violence as a result of years of warfare. Pakistan earns its third-place spot for its myriad cultural, tribal, and religious practices that are harmful to women. More than 1,000 women and girls are victims of "honor killings" every year, and an estimated 90 percent of women in Pakistan face domestic violence. Neighboring India enters the list at number four, earned because of its high rates of female feticide, child marriage, and trafficking and domestic servitude. Somalia rounds out the list of the "top five" due to a myriad of factors such as the country's high maternal mortality rate, widespread practice of female genital mutilation and child marriage, and extremely low levels of female political representation.[1] These are just a few snapshots of women's lives in a variety of countries in the developing world, where powerlessness in the household and in the public sphere and lack of access to social services often translate into economic poverty, poor health, low levels of personal safety, and an overall inability to make choices about one's life.

But the United Nations (UN), in cooperation with other development agencies, national leaders, and nongovernmental organizations (NGOs), is trying to change this. In 2000, a record number of world leaders and development agencies renewed their efforts to integrate gender concerns into development strategies with the Millennium Declaration, a set of ambitious goals to advance development and reduce poverty in all areas of the world by 2015 (read more about living in poverty at the end of this chapter in the text box "What Will $1 a Day Buy"). Leaders pledged to work for eight outcomes. Six of them are as follows: to eradicate extreme poverty and hunger; to achieve universal primary education; to reduce child mortality; to combat HIV/AIDS, malaria, and other diseases; to ensure environmental sustainability; and to develop a global partnership for development by working on issues such as debt relief for the world's poorest countries. Two additional goals specifically target women. Goal Five pledges to improve maternal health, aiming to reduce maternal mortality by three quarters and increase access to reproductive health. Goal Three promises to "promote gender equality and empower women," with a focus on achieving educational parity for girls, equalizing women's representation in parliaments, and increasing the share of women in wage employment in the nonagricultural sector.[2] While these two goals do not encompass all the ways in which girls and women are disenfranchised, they do identify some of the key ways in which girls and women become marginalized in making choices about their lives. In addition, drafters of the Millennium Development Goals stressed how gender inequality hampers levels of human development around the world and how gender equality is critical, not only as a goal in its own right, but also as an essential ingredient for achieving all of the other Millennium Development Goals. Because women play such a strong role in ensuring the well-being of their families and their communities, development agencies argue, they also need to be at the center of any development effort to raise the quantity and quality of life for all the world's citizens. This represents one of the most ambitious international efforts to date to eradicate hunger, poverty, poor health, and other problems related to economic deprivation and to do so by looking at these issues through the prism of gender. However, we are now rapidly approaching the deadline of 2015, and while we'll see in this chapter that there has been significant progress in some targets, such as increasing primary school enrollment rates for girls, there is much slower improvement in other key areas, such as increasing women's political representation and reducing the maternal mortality rate. For many international organizations, it is easier to set targets than to design and implement effective policy to achieve them, which is also often the responsibility of national governments.

This is not the first time that the UN has tried to foster gender equality or to address issues of particular concern to women, although, as we shall see, international approaches to advancing gender equality have shifted substantially over time, as have some of the issues that women confront. The UN, soon after its formation in 1945, made gender equality a central concern and has remained a crucial international player in fostering international dialogue, policies, and laws that foster that equality. It has spearheaded a number of treaties, conferences, and campaigns aimed at bringing increased attention to pervasive gender inequalities, and as the UN family has grown, so has the number of UN-sponsored development agencies devoted to gender and gender equality. In addition, many governments, particularly those of the advanced industrialized nations, have established gender offices within their overall development assistance programs. And a number of other international organizations and nonprofit organizations, from

Amnesty International, Human Rights Watch, the Ford Foundation, and the Global Fund for Women, to the Women's Environment and Development Organization (WEDO), focus on the position and status of women as an integral part of their work. Finally, since the 1970s, a plethora of Southern Hemisphere–based women's NGOs have mobilized to provide better input and feedback into these international efforts, to give women in the developing world a voice in shaping their own futures, and to bring to bear greater levels of domestic pressure to come up with local solutions to global problems. All of these organizations work on a wide array of issues that affect the position and status of women in society, ranging from improving women's access to employment and promoting gendered health initiatives to increasing female literacy rates and ensuring women's physical autonomy and safety. Further, the previous decade has brought new challenges, such as the gendered impact of globalization, international migration, and war. As international organizations and laws have evolved against a constantly shifting backdrop of global events, so too have approaches to address the discrepancy between men's and women's quality of life.

In the following pages, we discuss why international organizations have increasingly focused on gender equality as both a means and an end of development strategies. We cover how they have translated these concerns about gender inequality into programs that can affect the lives of millions of women around the world. We shall see that in response, women themselves have increasingly participated in setting the development agenda, rather than merely being subjects of a process discussed solely among development practitioners. And finally, we assess the impact of some of these efforts to improve both women's lives and their abilities to choose the kinds of lives they value.

THE ARGUMENT FOR GENDER EQUALITY

Why should we care about gender equality or—as is the case in current times—gender inequality? As we have discussed in previous chapters, gender inequalities, although lessening, are still pervasive throughout the world. Yet, as the examples in the beginning of this chapter illustrate, the inequalities often become more severe as one travels to the poorest regions of the world. For example, in many developing countries, women still lack independent rights to own land, manage property, conduct business, or even travel without their husband's consent. Nor do they have equal access to the resources, such as education, information, and financial opportunities, that could help them exercise greater autonomy over their lives. For example, of the world's 775 million adults (15 years or older) who cannot read or write, two thirds (497 million) are women. Even though the size of the global illiterate population is shrinking, the female proportion has remained virtually steady at 63 percent.[3] Discrepancies such as these severely constrain a woman's abilities to make choices about her life, whether it's where to live, whom to marry, how many children to have or not to have children at all, or how to ensure her financial livelihood. This lack of access to critical resources also limits a woman's power to influence decision making in the home and the public realm of politics.

While women and girls shoulder many of the direct costs of these inequalities by often living less healthy, more constrained lives, the indirect costs of women's lesser status hurt everyone. China, Korea, and South Asian countries have excessively high female mortality rates as a result of the social norm of boy preference, leading to 60 to 100 million "missing girls" who could potentially be alive in the absence of a culture of boy preference. In Chapter 9, we'll see how this preference is creating a demographic crisis of unparalleled proportions in China, India, and other parts of Asia that will affect everyone, not just girls. Further, because women often perform many of the nurturing, caring tasks within households—growing, buying, and preparing food; tending livestock; providing heath care to ailing family members, raising children, and ensuring familial survival—they serve as a crucial conduit in terms of fostering the human development of the members of their family. Thus, it is no surprise that mothers' lack of access to critical human resources, such as education, disadvantages their entire families. As we shall see in the following chapters, women with more education are more likely to use contraception and space the births of their children further apart when they have access to knowledge about how to do so. They are more likely to nurture healthier babies who are more likely to be immunized and better fed. Gender discrimination also has an economic cost; countries need to harness women's abilities to promote economic growth and, most importantly, living standards. One study showed that closing the gender gap in education increases a country's growth rate by almost 1 percent a year. And promoting women's political voice has obvious benefits as well. A World Bank study showed that where the influence of women in public life is greater, the level of corruption is lower. Other studies indicate that women in business are less likely to pay bribes to government officials. And giving power to women at the local level in countries such as India led to increases in the provision of public goods, such as water and sanitation, which mattered more to women.[4] In sum, holding on to discriminatory practices against women hurts not only the women themselves but also their families, their communities, and their countries. As the World Bank argued in an influential 2001 report, "gender equality is a core development issue—a development objective in its own right. It strengthens countries' abilities to grow, to reduce poverty, and to govern effectively. Promoting gender equality is thus an important part of a development strategy that seeks to enable all people—women and men alike—to escape poverty and improve their standard of living."[5] The costs of ignoring the existing situation are high, particularly in comparison to the costs of trying to ameliorate the situation by investing more resources in education, public health, and economic planning.

THE STATUS OF GENDER EQUALITY

So how do we get a sense of how the world's women are faring in terms of achieving gender equality? How can we collect data that would allow us to compare how women live their lives in Zambia, India, and Indonesia, for example, in any meaningful way, and how can we track these trends over time to assess the changing magnitude of the problem? There are multiple agencies that now collect data and measure and track the quantity and quality of women's lives around the world. Perhaps the best known is the United Nations Development Program (UNDP), a UN agency that publishes the annual Human Development Report that provides a narrative of the state of the world. This report is based on statistics from 187 countries along a wide array of indices, ranging from health indicators such as life expectancy and child and maternal mortality to social statistics such as access to education and literacy levels and more standard economic data such as gross domestic product (GDP), growth rates, trade flows, and poverty rates.

While the UNDP is best known for its Human Development Index, which attempts to capture and quantify levels of quality of life of citizens from 187 countries, it has also developed the Gender Inequality Index, a composite measure reflecting inequality in achievements between men and women in three dimensions: reproductive health (measured by the maternal mortality ratio and the adolescent fertility rate), empowerment (measured by the share of legislative sets held by each sex and by secondary and higher education attainment levels), and the labor market (measured by women's participation in the workforce). The Index varies between zero (when women and men fare equally) and one (when men or women fare poorly compared to the others in all dimensions). While no country scores a perfect zero, top-ranking countries such as Sweden, the Netherlands, and Denmark come closest to closing gendered gaps in health, empowerment, and labor market participation parity.

The results can reveal illuminating differences between how men and women experience their lives, both within countries as well as between countries. For example, Afghanistan secures its place near the bottom of the ranking system in part because of its horrific maternal mortality ratio and its significant lack of political, economic, and social opportunities for women. When less than 6 percent of young women have at least a secondary education, one wonders how the country can reconstruct itself after years of warfare. Further, sometimes there are significant gaps between a country's Human Development Index ranking, which measures citizens' educational, health, and economic well-being, and its Gender Inequality Index, which hones in on the gaps between men and women. For example, the United States is ranked 4th according to its Human Development Index; citizens live relatively lengthy lives, they are well educated, and they are economically productive. Yet, the United States is ranked 47th in the Gender Inequality Index; maternal mortality and teen pregnancy rates are actually quite high compared to other industrialized nations, and women's political representation is relatively paltry. On the other end of the spectrum, Rwanda, one of the word's lowest-ranking countries with regard to human development (166), scores much better in terms of gender equality. It leads the world in terms of women's political representation (women represent 51% of the parliament), and the gap between men and women with regard to educational access and economic employment is relatively small (although with education, it seems that men and women are equally disempowered with regard to access to secondary school). There are also important regional variations. Gender equality is highest in Europe and Central Asia, followed by Latin America and the Caribbean, the Arab states, South Asia, and sub-Saharan Africa (there are not enough data to rank East Asia and the Pacific). If you take some time to explore Table 7.1, you'll see how important it is to focus on data broken down by sex. Judging from the data, in which countries would you like to be a woman? Which countries would you avoid?

While the UN cautions that indices such as the Gender Inequality Index serve as rough proxies for measuring gender disparities, nonetheless they represent important international efforts to collect and standardize data in order to quantify gaps between men and women and then think about the ramifications of these gaps. As interest in the position and status of women around the world has increased, so too has the number of reports and indices devoted to this topic. The World Economic Forum also has created a Global Gender Gap Index, which ranks countries according to their gender gaps in four areas of inequality: economic participation and opportunity; educational attainment; political empowerment; and health and survival. Similar in concept to the Gender Inequality Index, the Global Gender Gap Index uses 14 variables, some of which are related to (but different from) those used by the UNDP. For example, it uses sex ratio at birth to capture the problem of "missing women," which is prevalent in many countries with a strong son preference. The 2011 report finds that while there has been much progress in closing gendered health and education gaps in countries around the world, economic and political participation rates are still significant to severe.[6] The OECD has created a Social Institutions and Gender Index that, rather than focusing on the outcomes of gender inequality, such as maternal mortality or educational attainment, tries to capture the social institutions, or long-lasting codes of conduct, norms, traditions, and informal and formal laws that contribute to gender inequality. Thus, it measures levels of gender inequality in countries by tracking the status of social institutions relating to family code (such as norms and laws on early marriage, polygamy, parental authority, and inheritance); physical integrity (violence against women, female genital mutilation); son preference (birth ratio); civil liberties (freedom of movement); and ownership rights (access to land, bank loans, and property). For example, the 2012 report highlights discriminatory practices against women and girls around the world; almost three quarters of the 121 countries surveyed have discriminatory inheritance laws and practices, and about half of the women in these countries think that domestic violence can be justified in specific circumstances. Indices such as the Social Institutions and Gender Index highlight the point that countries not only need to change legal frameworks to promote gender equality, but also must address the difficult task of changing mindsets.[7] And finally, the Economist Intelligence Unit's Women's Economic Opportunity Index focuses more on laws and regulations about women's participation in the labor market and social institutions that affect women's economic participation. According to their data, economic opportunities for women still lag behind those of men, and the persistent gap cannot be explained away by schooling and experience. Legal and social restrictions, such as prohibitions against owning property or venturing outside the home without a family member, are some of the more severe impediments to women's abilities to advance.[8] Other agencies, such as the World Bank, also collect data that are disaggregated by sex

Table 7.1 Gender Inequality Index

COUNTRY	GENDER INEQUALITY INDEX (GII) RANK	HUMAN DEVELOPMENT INDEX (HDI) RANK	MATERNAL MORTALITY RATIO (PER 100,000 LIVE BIRTHS)	ADOLESCENT FERTILITY RATE	SEATS IN NATIONAL PARLIAMENT (% FEMALE)	POPULATION WITH AT LEAST SECONDARY EDUCATION (% AGES 25 AND OLDER)		LABOR FORCE PARTICIPATION RATE (%)	
						FEMALE	MALE	FEMALE	MALE
Sweden	1	10	5	6.0	45	87.9	87.1	60.6	69.2
Japan	14	12	6	5.0	13.6	80.0	82.3	47.9	71.8
Bahrain	44	42	19	14.9	15.0	74.4	80.4	32.4	85.0
United States	47	4	24	41.2	16.8	95.3	94.5	58.4	71.9
Cuba	58	51	53	45.2	43.2	73.9	80.4	40.9	66.9
Russian Federation	59	66	39	30.0	11.5	90.6	95.6	57.5	69.2
Algeria	71	96	120	7.3	7.0	36.3	49.3	37.2	79.6
Turkey	77	92	23	39.2	9.1	27.1	46.7	24.0	69.6
Rwanda	82	166	540	38.7	50.9	7.4	8.0	86.7	85.1
Iran	92	88	30	29.5	2.8	39.0	57.2	31.9	73.0
South Africa	94	123	410	59.2	42.7	66.3	68.0	47.0	63.4
India	129	134	230	86.3	10.7	26.6	50.4	32.8	81.1
Pakistan	115	145	260	31.6	21.0	23.5	46.8	21.7	84.9
Haiti	123	158	300	46.4	4.2	22.5	36.3	57.5	82.9
Sierra Leone	137	180	970	143.7	13.2	9.5	20.4	65.4	67.5
Afghanistan	141	172	1400	118.7	27.6	5.8	34.0	33.1	84.5

SOURCE: United Nations Development Programme, *United Nations Human Development Report 2011*, http://hdr.undp.org/en/reports/global/hdr2011/ (accessed July 23, 2012).

and thus provide a sense of how women have a separate and usually unequal political, economic, and social status.[9] While each index focuses on different, if overlapping, conceptions of ways to measure women's empowerment, they all paint a troubling picture of the quantity and quality of women's lives around the world, lives that are often separate and unequal. At the end of this chapter, look through the "For More Information" section if you want to find out more about these indices, reports, or agencies working on the issue of gender inequality.

These data are invaluable not only for research but also for tracking progress and setbacks within countries over time, to compare countries within and across regions, and to hold governments and agencies accountable for implementing programs to improve people's lives. Until the 1970s, many countries, and development agencies, did not collect data on women, particularly in the developing world. As a result, it was extremely hard at first to design effective programs to improve the position and status of women or to pressure states to improve their programs. In the past 30 years, the collection of data on the position and status of women has improved immensely, although in extremely poor and often war-torn countries such as those in sub-Saharan Africa, data collection is not only difficult but also life-threatening at times. These statistics have also been invaluable in terms of tracking the UN's progress toward meeting the Millennium Development Goals. Increasingly, women's groups and activists have used the findings as pressure points on governments that are stronger on rhetoric than action. In short, data collection and measurement are important not just to academics but also to practitioners at the domestic and international levels and activists working to improve the lives of the men and women in countries in every region of the world.

So judging from statistics, what can we say about the position and status of women? As we enter the final few years of the Millennium Development Goals campaign, there is much to celebrate. Gender gaps in primary education have closed in almost all countries, and at the secondary level, these gaps have reversed in many countries, especially in Latin America, the Caribbean, and East Asia. Among developing countries, girls now outnumber boys in secondary schools in 45 countries and there are more young women than men in universities in 60 countries. Women now live longer than men in all parts of the world, and in low-income countries, women now live 20 years longer on average than they did in 1960. Thanks in part to the reduction in fertility in countries such as Bangladesh, Colombia, and Iran, over half a billion women have joined the world's labor force over the past 30 years. But this progress coexists with serious gaps. Females are still more likely to die than males in many low- and middle-income countries. Of the nearly 4 million "missing" women and girls, about two fifths are never born, one sixth die in early childhood, and over one third die in their reproductive years. The number is growing in sub-Saharan Africa, due the difficulties with reducing maternal mortality in the region as well as fully addressing the HIV/AIDS epidemic. And despite the progress made in education, school enrollment for girls still drags behind that for boys in many sub-Saharan African nations and some parts of South Asia. Economically, the influx of women into the workforce has been mixed, for women are more likely than men to work as unpaid family laborers or in the informal sector. Women farmers tend to farm smaller plots and cultivate less profitable crops than men, which helps explain the large wage gap that still exists. In particular, for poor women in poor places, when poverty is combined with other forms of exclusion, such as remoteness, ethnicity, and disability, the gaps become chasms.[10] Further, while the push to meet certain targets toward gender equality and the entire set of Millennium Development Goals has had an enormous impact on people's lives, much of this has been driven by the impressive economic growth in China and India, and it can mask the lack of progress made in regions such as sub-Saharan Africa or other parts of Asia. Women do live longer, are more educated, and have more political representation than they did 30, 20, even 10 years ago—but the gaps will not close without serious efforts to design specific policy fixes for gendered inequalities, and longer-range efforts to change some of the underlying norms and values that govern how men and women live their lives in all countries of the world. As discussed below, books such as Half the Sky compellingly portray the deprivations many of these women face, as well as describe some of the efforts individuals are making to improve the status of women.

Half the Sky

Every few years, a book will come along that is able to put a human face on the often-numbing statistics that summarize human pain and suffering. For disempowered women around the world, that book was *Half the Sky: Turning Oppression into Opportunity for Women Worldwide* (2009). Written by husband-and-wife team Nicholas Kristof and Sheryl WuDunn of the *New York Times*, the book painted verbal pictures of the horror many women and girls face on a daily basis, merely because they were born the wrong sex. Acid attacks, forced prostitution, child marriage, rape, genital mutilation: no atrocity is left uncovered. But the book does more than alert the public to the reality that millions of women and girls are still treated like slaves; it also covers some of the heroic actions of individuals and nonprofit groups trying to make a difference and change the trajectory of many women's lives. In addition, Kristof and WuDunn advocate for increased investments in girls' education and women's widened access to microfinance, or small loans, to unleash their potential. Although the policy suggestions are not new, the vivid descriptions and immediacy of the writing helped catapult the book to the top of bestseller lists. Oprah Winfrey read the book, loved it, and devoted several episodes of her show to covering some of the specific injustices committed against women as well as some of the inspiring work of individuals working to reverse them. As a result, the book's message was spread far beyond the relatively small community of development workers. The authors aimed to recruit readers to join a worldwide movement to end the routine and daily oppression of women, and it looks as if many readers have taken that challenge. The book spawned a website, full of compelling practical strategies used by NGOs and activists to improve women's lives, and a foundation to fund the types of activities suggested in the book. PBS developed a companion documentary to the book, which aired in September 2012. With its delicate mixture of heartbreak and inspiration, Kristof and WuDunn's book has done more than educate millions of readers: it has propelled a movement.

A Zimbabwean woman carries wood to boil water at home in Harare. For many of the world's women, readily accessible fuel, clean drinking water, and other items that could improve their quantity and quality of life are out of reach. SOURCE: ALEXANDER JOE/AFP/ Getty Images.

International Development: Designing Policy to Promote Gender Equality

We now turn to how development organizations have designed programs to improve women's lives. This task is complicated; as you can imagine from reading through some of data already presented, women (and men) are faced with innumerable obstacles to making choices about leading lives they value. And for development specialists and NGO activists, this has set off heated debate over the years. What should be the focus of aid to women—and for that matter the developing world as a whole? Meeting basic needs, such as ensuring food, shelter, and water (see photo 7.1)? Improving access to critical human resources, such as education and health? Focusing on gender-specific issues, such as violence against women or rape as a tool of warfare? Should development agencies fix the symptoms of women's lesser status (economic poverty, poor health, etc.) or design more far-reaching but less focused programs that get to the reasons behind women's lack of empowerment (lack of influence in the household and/or the political sphere, for example)? How should one design a program to address women's lack of power in the private and public realms? And how should one distribute technical and financial assistance? To the governments themselves, or to local NGOs? The answers are not obvious, and development agencies themselves have switched strategies several times in the previous five decades.

In the initial decades of development work, international organizations did not consider gender to be a salient analytical tool. As former colonies made the transition into independent nations in the 1950s, 1960s, and 1970s, international organizations' work expanded exponentially. Many of these countries needed assistance in designing economic and social institutions that would create the income needed to improve the quality of their citizens' lives. The primary task of development agencies was to help stimulate economic growth, and men were assumed to be the breadwinners and women were perceived as homemakers. Thus, the focus was on improving opportunities for wage-earning men, and until the 1970s, development policies, if they targeted women at all, tended to do so in their roles as wives and mothers, and programs focused on improved maternal and child health or on reducing fertility. Not only did this approach assume that women would naturally benefit as income trickled down through the household (which ended up not being the case), but it also often bypassed women without husbands, who didn't even benefit indirectly from development assistance. This basically ignored many of the women in the most vulnerable positions in society— the widowed, divorced, or abandoned. And for those women who were part of a family unit, it tended to reinforce a Western middle-class view that men made the money and women were housewives—a gross oversimplification of the situations of families living in fragile, politically unstable, resource-poor, underdeveloped newly independent nations. In sum, development practitioners at the national and international level largely ignored women, both as participants in development and as subjects of the same process. Women were often absent from the policy-making process, and gender often was ignored when designing policies or assessing their impact. Nor did development agencies collect much data on the position and status of women, so it was hard even to assess the impact of larger economic development programs on women. In fact, some leading development theorists, such as Walter Rostow and Edward Banfield, viewed women as antithetical to development, assuming that their support for traditional values and religion would impede "progress."[11]

The assumption that overall economic growth would naturally trickle down to affect women in positive ways was challenged by Ester Boserup, an anthropologist, in her book *The Role of Woman in Economic Development* (1970). Drawing from her research on rural African economies, Boserup contested the predominant assumption that the development process affected men and women in the same way and argued that development projects actually hurt women in some ways. She maintained that development theory had underestimated the role of women in agricultural production and that development projects redefined the division of labor between the two sexes in ways that deprived women of their previous productive functions, thus retarding the overall process of growth.[12] Development programs, which often encouraged the cultivation of cash crops for export rather than small-scale food production, favored men and squeezed women out of the areas where they had previously been productive. Women often could not hold title to land or get access to credit, two critical inputs that promoted men's advancement in large-scale agricultural business. Nor did extension services target women, despite the fact that they were the ones in many regions in the world who were responsible for growing food. The fact that many extension workers were male exacerbated the problem in cultures where strict norms dictated that male–female interaction outside the immediate family circle is unacceptable. Boserup and others were publishing an emerging body of critical literature that led many development agencies to reassess the assumption that women would inherently benefit from a "trickle-down" version of economic growth as well as assumptions about how women participate in and contribute to predominantly rural economies.

In addition, dedicated female development practitioners lobbied for increased funding and attention to women, arguing that the process of development is not gender-neutral, in process or in impact, and that women participate differently in and benefit unequally from the process of socioeconomic development, and thus need specific programs that address their position and status in society. Inga Thorsson first proposed the idea of using development aid money for women to the Swedish Parliament in 1963, and 6 years later, the Swedish International Development Agency funded two positions in the UN family to ensure a voice for women at the policy level. In the United States, Mildred Marcy of the U.S. Information Agency argued that the issue of women must be included in the legislation revising the U.S. Foreign Assistance Act. Working through her connections in the Senate, Marcy secured support for an amendment to integrate women into U.S.-funded development programs. Known as the Percy Amendment, the legislation dictated that women had to be included specifically in all development projects sponsored by the U.S. Agency for International Development (USAID).[13]

As development agencies began to accept that women do not automatically benefit from overall levels of economic growth, they turned to what became known as a "women in development" (WID) approach. The WID approach arose out of the second wave of feminism that was sweeping across the industrialized North and was based in the ideological tenets of liberal egalitarianism. That is, one could not just assume that women would be positively affected by gender-neutral economic development projects; one had to explicitly include women in the development approach by focusing on harnessing their productive labor and promoting them into the workforce.

These projects tried to integrate women into economic development in a variety of ways. For example, development projects began to focus on income-generating projects for women, such as sewing, embroidery, or handicraft businesses. The idea was to find ways to build on women's income-generating possibilities despite the fact that most of them possessed few skills to compete in the formal labor market. Alternatively, development agencies, under the WID approach, began to fund projects that focused on providing labor-saving technologies, such as grinding mills, pumps, or cooking stoves, in an effort to reduce women's workloads.

This policy focus on explicitly acknowledging women in the development process was buttressed in the 1970s and 1980s by UN-sponsored international conferences that addressed women's issues within the development process. Once again, the change in policy was often in response to women mobilizing on behalf of women, although sympathetic male colleagues were certainly crucial to this policy shift as well. For example, a few women on the UN Commission on the Status of Women, led by Finnish feminist Helvi Sipila, succeeded in getting the General Assembly to pass a resolution calling for the "full integration of women in the total development effort."[14] This then prompted the Assembly to declare 1976–1985 the "Decade for Women: Equality, Development, and Peace."[15] The start of the Decade for Women was marked by the First World Conference on Women, held in Mexico City in 1975. Two further gender-related conferences were held in 1980 in Copenhagen (the Second World Conference on Women) and in 1985 in Nairobi to review the achievements of the previous 10-year campaign, galvanize public interest, raise awareness of women's issues, and adopt international plans of action relating to gender.

These conferences were critical in stimulating a focus on women in development. For example, they brought together hundreds of senior government officials in charge of making policy, which not only increased attention to gender issues but also led governments to create or bolster domestic-level agencies devoted to women's issues. For example, the 1975 Mexico City conference attendees passed a Plan of Action that instructed governments to prepare a report on the status of women in their country, to set up a bureau or office dedicated to women's issues, and to ensure that women were included in their economic planning. As a result, the 1975 UN Year for Women and the International Women's Decade led many countries to establish women's ministries, which in turn created access points for domestic women's movements to lobby, advocate, and work for explicit policies affecting women's status. Major bilateral donors, such as the United States, developed programs that could reach poor women in the developing world. Further, the Mexico City conference led to the creation of gender offices at the international level as well; the UN Voluntary Fund for Women (later known as UNIFEM) and the International Research and Training Institute for the Advancement of Women (INSTRAW) were created to address directly the specific issues facing women in development. The creation of these additional agencies and programs at the domestic and international levels also led to the influx of primarily women to staff, direct, and oversee these programs, helping to create a critical mass of women in development. While not all female employees advocated for or worked for women's programs, nonetheless, enough women did that it made advocacy of women's issues within the institutions themselves much more acceptable.[16] And, as we shall see in the next section, these conferences also formed the base from which evolved an increasingly articulated set of international norms and laws related to gender equality.

Finally, the array of global conferences facilitated the emergence of transnational feminist networks in the 1970s and onward. Each of the conferences was complemented by a major NGO forum, which brought together thousands of women's activists, giving them an opportunity to meet, exchange experiences, and, gradually, over the course of several decades, build important transnational alliances. The initial NGO meetings held before the 1975 Mexico City conference were not promising; while they represented some of the first international gatherings of female activists, sisterhood did not feel global. Instead, the rise of the second wave of feminism in North America and Europe seemed to highlight the differences between women's activism in the industrialized Northern Hemisphere and the economically underdeveloped Southern Hemisphere. Many women from the South rejected Western-style feminism, which they perceived to be hostile to men and the family. Further, women were not united on which issues should be of primary concern to the world's women. While European feminists fought for issues involving women's legal equality and reproductive rights, Southern activists focused on underdevelopment, colonialism, and the exploitation of the global South by an industrialized North as impediments to women's (and men's) progress, rather than patriarchy. However, the increased prevalence of international conferences devoted to women's issues, such as the UN-sponsored conferences in Copenhagen (1980) and Nairobi (1985), helped women from around the world network and identify common areas of concern, such as violence against women, while acknowledging their differences. The rapid growth of a globalized economy also created similar conditions for many women around the world, which further underscored women's common agenda on certain issues. As a result, transnational organizations, such as Development Alternatives with Women for a New Era (DAWN), the Sisterhood Is Global Institute (SIGI), and the Women's Environmental and Development Organization (WEDO), became increasingly active in advocating women's interests at the international level.[17]

Women's grassroots mobilization, combined with the efforts of primarily female development specialists, helped bring further changes in how development agencies tried to foster better development outcomes for the world's women. By the 1980s, women had become increasingly vocal in their critique of the WID approach discussed earlier, arguing for a new "gender and development" (GAD) framework to guide policy endeavors. Many argued that WID, although an important first step in increasing attention to women's roles, nonetheless served primarily as a Band-Aid by treating the symptom of women's poverty without really addressing the illness, diagnosed by some as capitalist development. Others maintained that while a WID approach was an improvement, in that it recognized that women deserved additional policy focus beyond family planning services controlling their fertility, it also treated women as an untapped source of development, with free time that could be diverted into paid labor. But activists pointed out that a WID approach simply ignored all of women's unpaid labor, which often kept them busy from morning until night, day after day. They called for a deeper gender analysis, one that viewed women's and men's roles as socially constructed, not biologically determined. Without acknowledging larger gender power relations that held women back, they argued, development projects focused on increasing women's access to the economic sphere, for example, would just increase their already substantial amount of labor within the household. They also urged development agencies to recognize the diversity of women's experiences and that factors such as class, age, marital status, religion, and ethnicity or race affect women's issues. In sum, while a WID approach focused on meeting women's "practical" gender needs—that is, steps that would improve women's lives within their existing roles—some activists stressed the importance of meeting women's "strategic gender needs" by increasing their abilities to take on new roles and ultimately empowering them to make choices and to transform them into desired actions and outcomes.[18] Proponents of a GAD approach urged development programs to challenge gender roles by training women in "male" skills, working for women's ownership rights to land and housing, and providing child-care and transport facilities that suited women's specific needs.

As in the previous two decades, this evolution in policy in part was facilitated by women's networking at a variety of international conferences, which were all accompanied by NGO forums. The UN held another major Conference on Women, in Beijing, China, in 1995, to assess progress in achieving women's equality worldwide. The term "gender mainstreaming" came into widespread use among development policymakers with the adoption of the Platform for Action. Gender mainstreaming as a strategy sought to avoid the segregation of women into "gender projects" by integrating gender into all development projects, such as increased literacy, better access to health care, or improved public services. As the UN argued, "gender mainstreaming entails bringing the perceptions, experience, knowledge and interests of women as well as men to bear on policy-making, planning, and decision-making."[19] For example, a program sponsored by the UN Development Fund for Women (UNIFEM) worked with governments to design gender-responsive budgets—that is, budgets that take into account women's concerns across all expenditures (health, pensions, public utilities, tariffs) rather than segregating funding for women's issues solely into one office or department (which can often marginalize women's concerns).[20] Gender mainstreaming is the latest iteration of a development philosophy that attempts to come to grips with the ways that women differ in their experiences of the social, economic, and political transformations wrought by economic development in a rapidly globalized world. In addition, women's issues were integrated into a number of other UN-sponsored conferences. While gender was not the organizing theme, it was often the implicit subtext. Global meetings, such as the International Conference on Population and Development, held in Cairo, Egypt, in 1994, or the World Summit on Social Development, held in 1995 in Copenhagen, inherently involved a discussion of women's rights and resulted in explicit calls for women's equality.

The UN is not a static organization, and it continues to respond to the changing needs of the world's women. For example, in 2010, the UN General Assembly created UN Women to work on gender equality and the empowerment of women. This office merges the work of four previous distinct UN agencies: the Division for the Advancement of Women (DAW); International Research and Training Institute for the Advancement of Women (INSTRAW); Office of the Special Advisor in Gender Issues and the Advancement of Women (OSAGI); and the UN Development Fund for Women (UNIFEM). Led by former Chilean President Michelle Bachelet, UN Women focuses on the following priority areas: violence against women, peace and security, leadership and participation, economic empowerment, and incorporating women's needs and priorities into national planning and budgeting.

Further, the UN has responded to some of the shifting gendered challenges in the global arena. For example, as we shall discuss in Chapter 11, war is not for men only; women engage in, are caught in the crossfire of, and are differently affected by the ravages of violent conflict. Yet, they are often treated as invisible; sexual crimes committed against them are ignored, they are shut out of the peace and reconciliation process, and little thought is given to their roles in maintaining and rebuilding the family economy in times of conflict and peace. The UN is trying to reverse this trend, and in October 2000, the UN Security Council unanimously passed Resolution 1325 on Women and Peace and Security. This resolution recognized the importance of women in resolving issues of peace and security by discussing their role in negotiating peace agreements, planning refugee camps and peacekeeping operations, and reconstructing war-torn societies.[21] And in 2008, 2009, and 2010, they passed a series of additional resolutions recognizing conflict-related sexual violence as a matter of international peace and security, as an issue relevant for peace negotiations and national recovery, and in need of international monitoring and reporting. Development agencies are also recognizing the gendered aspects of civil strife and warfare within developing nations by focusing more explicitly on issues such as rape as a war crime. As we move forward in the twenty-first century, development agencies will continue to grapple with how gender intersects with poverty, political instability, social inequality, and sustainable development.

In sum, development agencies themselves have moved through a variety of frameworks that can be used to improve women's lives. At first, they assumed that women would benefit from large-scale development efforts and that benefits would trickle down. They then moved to implementing a WID approach, which focused directly on programs designed to improve women's lives. After a decade or so, however, WID was replaced by a growing awareness—the GAD approach—that development policies needed to address the preexisting gender imbalances between men and women. The extension of this line of thinking has been gender mainstreaming, a set of policy prescriptions in which gender concerns need to be integrated into all programs rather than ghettoized into a separate portfolio. We have also seen that women's transnational activism has had an indelible impact. Increased international networking has helped foster greater public awareness of women's issues at the local level; transnational advocacy networks have teamed up with local activists to organize public information campaigns or stimulate greater levels of domestic activism. Also, international women's organizations increasingly have been active in lobbying development agencies, such as the UN, the World Bank, and the European Union, to devote more time, rhetoric, research, and money to advancing gender equality. They have been critical players in developing and filling spaces in women's policy machinery at the international level, which has had a strong influence on development policy.[22]

International Norms and Law

In addition to sponsoring development programs, conferences, and research related to fostering gender equality, the family of organizations under the UN umbrella has steadily constructed a body of international norms and law. International efforts to agree upon common standards to ensure gender equality started in the 1920s, when the International Labour Organization attempted to regulate the conditions under which women could be employed at night (a time, women's advocates argued, that women needed to be at home, caring for their families). International legislation rapidly evolved with the creation of the UN in 1945, and since then, almost 50 resolutions addressing gender equality have been passed by a variety of international organizations. Table 7.2 shows some of the landmark resolutions and

Table 7.2 Selected International Resolutions on Gender Equality

YEAR	DOCUMENT	SIGNIFICANCE
1948	Resolution on the Universal Declaration of Human Rights	A comprehensive statement of universal human rights; arguably the world's most translated document
1949	Convention for the Suppression of the Traffic in Persons and the Exploitation of the Prostitution of Others	Commits governments to take steps to prevent and punish the trafficking of women for sexual exploitation
1951	Convention concerning Equal Remuneration for Men and Women Workers for Work of Equal Value	Commits governments to ensure the application of the principle of equal remuneration for women and men for work of equal value
1962	Convention on Consent to Marriage, Minimum Age for Marriage and Registration of Marriage	Obligates governments to specify a minimum age for marriage, officially register all marriages, and prohibit marriages entered into without free and full consent of both parties
1979	Convention on the Elimination of All Forms of Discrimination Against Women (CEDAW)	The central women's rights convention outlining international legal obligations on governments to prevent discrimination against women

YEAR	RESOLUTION	ACTION
1981	Convention concerning Equal Opportunities and Equal Treatment for Men and Women Workers with Family Responsibilities	International Labour Organization (ILO) General Conference
1989	Convention on the Rights of the Child	United Nations General Assembly (UNGA); protection of children from early and forced marriage, recognition of adulthood as 18 years of age, rights to education
1993	Declaration on the Elimination of Violence Against Women	UNGA; to support and complement CEDAW
1994	International Conference on Population and Development Programme of Action	UN global conference; placed women's rights, health, and empowerment at the center of efforts for human rights and sustainable development
1995	Beijing Declaration and Platform for Action	UN Fourth World Conference on Women; international commitments to equality, development, and peace for women

Table 7.2 *(continued)*

YEAR	RESOLUTION	ACTION
1999	Resolution on Traditional or Customary Practices affecting the Health of Women and Girls	UNGA
2000	Resolution on Improvement of the Situation of Women in Rural Areas	UNGA
2000	Resolution on Violence Against Women Migrant Workers	UNGA
2000	UN Millennium Declaration	UNGA; set out an international development agenda—Goal 3 is to promote gender equality and empower women
2000	Security Council Resolution 1325 on Women, Peace and Security	UN Security Council; first Council resolution that specifically addresses the impact of war on women, as well as women's contributions to conflict resolution and sustainable peace
2002	Convention on Preventing and Combating Trafficking in Women and Children for Prostitution	South Asian Association for Regional Cooperation (SAARC)
2004	Resolution on Conflict Prevention and Resolution: The Role of Women	Council of Europe's Parliamentary Assembly
2005	Resolution on Trafficking in Women and Girls	UNGA
2005	Resolution in the Elimination of All Forms of Violence Against Women	UNGA

SOURCE: Condensed from Annex 6, "Selected Global Resolutions, Conventions and Agreements on Women's Rights," in UN Women, "In Pursuit of Gender Justice. Progress of the World's Women 2011–2012," pp. 142–143. Available at http://progress.unwomen.org/.

treaties (also known as conventions) in gender equality that have been passed by a range of international organizations in addition to the UN. Interests have changed over the decades regarding the core issues involved in promoting women's equality. Early resolutions focused on ensuring women's access to basic political, economic, and social rights. Starting in the 1970s, we can see increased attention given to issues that revolve around women as mothers. In the 1990s, violence against women emerged as an enduring international issue. In addition, acknowledging the diverse experiences of women around the world became a more important priority, with resolutions passed regarding older women in development and rural women, for example. The Commission on the Status of Women, housed within the UN, promotes, reports, and monitors the progress of the wide array of treaties that touch on women's equality.

What has been the effect of these international laws? A quick perusal of the language of many of these treaties reveals high-minded ideals and profuse commitments to equality. Turning commitment into policy, however, is a much stickier proposition. The following example illustrates the difficulties involved in transforming principle into action.

In 1979, the United Nations adopted the Convention on the Elimination of All Forms of Discrimination Against Women (CEDAW), an "international women's bill of rights that obligates governments to take actions to promote and protect the rights of women."[23] The convention defines what constitutes discrimination against women and sets up an agenda for national action to end such discrimination. This convention stretches beyond access to economic resources; it also contains provisions to confirm a woman's right "to decide freely and responsibly on the number and spacing of . . . children and to have access to the information, education and means to enable [exercise of] these rights."[24] By signing on to the convention, countries are agreeing to incorporate the principles of equality between men and women in their legal system, to establish tribunals and other public institutions to ensure the protection of women from discrimination, and to ensure elimination of all acts of discrimination against women. States that have agreed to the terms of the convention are legally bound to put its provisions into practice. In addition, they are committed to submitting national reports at least every 4 years on the measures they have taken to honor their treaty obligations.[25] In other words, CEDAW is an ambitious piece of international legislation that requires significant commitments from signatory nations if it is to be implemented effectively.

First, a large hurdle to surmount in drafting, passing, and implementing a convention such as CEDAW is finding treaty language that can inspire consensus among a very diverse array of countries. Countries often disagree on how compliance with convention terms should be monitored. Negotiations often continue for several years as members hammer out agreements. For example, how should countries interpret the phrase "full equality among men and women"? What does this require governments to do to ensure that this happens? For non-Western cultures in which there is a more rigid division between men and women's spheres of appropriate activity, how can treaty writers respect a diversity of cultural norms while at the same time upholding the general principle of equality? Thus, for example, the assembly voted to adopt CEDAW by a vote of 130–0 after a 5-year drafting and negotiating process. Yet, countries were also given the option of voting separately on several controversial paragraphs. Nearly 40 countries expressed reservations.[26] On the one hand, this practice helps hold together an often fragile and tenuous coalition of governments; on the other hand, it can decrease the legitimacy of the treaty by allowing countries to opt out of important principles and norms.

Also, what force do the treaties have? While 173 countries had ratified CEDAW as of 2012, the United States, arguably the most powerful country in the world, has not, along with countries such as North Korea and Iran.[27] While President Carter signed the convention on behalf of the United States in 1980, Congress has not ratified it. In fact, the Senate Foreign Relations Committee did not even hold a hearing on the treaty until 1990. Finally, in 1994, the committee forwarded CEDAW to the Senate for a floor vote, where it was blocked by a group of senators. In 2002, the Foreign Relations Committee once again sent CEDAW to the Senate for ratification, but the Senate was unable to vote on it before the end of the 107th Congress. The committee will have to vote once again in favor of sending the treaty forward for another vote in the Senate. Politicians have opposed the treaty for a variety of reasons, ranging from concerns about infringement on national sovereignty to beliefs that the treaty encourages abortion, interferes with the family, and will legalize prostitution (even though nothing in the treaty language indicates support for any of these concerns).[28] The U.S. decision to ignore the treaty hurts the legitimacy of CEDAW, despite the large number of signatories. When powerful and influential countries opt out of international agreements, it lessens the force of treaties because the authority of such treaties mostly resides in the power of widespread global agreement, particularly among the world's most powerful nations.

The legitimacy of international law is also hurt when nations commit to a treaty but then do not make efforts to implement its terms. Countries such as Haiti, Rwanda, and Iraq have ratified CEDAW, yet research on the position and status of women in these countries indicates that they have not done much to turn promise into proactive policy.[29] For example, a quick look at UN statistics for many of the countries that have signed on to CEDAW reveals that women live substandard lives, whether it is in terms of access to education, work, or adequate health care. This further erodes a treaty's legitimacy; passed but all but ignored, what use is international legislation? States have been more willing to promise to implement women's equality than to actually pass the legislation and commit the funds to do so.

On a positive note, international law can help to change norms slowly over time by putting pressure on governments to honor their commitments. While policy results are slow to catch up to policy ideal, nonetheless, many activists credit international law with setting the bar that nations must at least pay lip service to meeting. In other words, particularly for female activists in the developing world, the UN legislation has provided them with the tools by which to lobby, slowly and painstakingly, for change. When a nation professes to support the ideas of equality, this gives activists a foot in the door; they can critique leadership for not living up to its promises. In addition, this international legislation led many countries to establish Commissions on the Status of Women, relevant cabinet positions on women's issues, and other women's policy machineries within their own countries, thereby placing further pressure on governments to pass domestic legislation. Thus, even though international treaties are not, in practice, always implemented, international law is an important starting point from which local activists can build momentum for further change. This has been particularly important in places where domestic women's movements are often too weak to make significant policy gains on their own or where semi-democratic governments limit domestic organizations' access to the policymaking process. Further, some scholars argue that these international norms and networks can create change even when national governments are not responsive to local activists; the international arena is some-times the only means by which domestic actors can gain attention for their issues when government interest is lacking or weak. This is known as the "boomerang" effect: local activists team up with international networks, which in turn place pressure on domestic governments to respond to their own constituents.[30] In sum, while international legislation can be more difficult to craft and to enforce at the global level, at times, it can also push the evolution of norms, patterns of behavior, and domestic legislation in countries where it otherwise would not have passed. And it has helped show that, despite cultural differences among the many countries of the world, human rights are universal and international organizations can walk the often sticky line between respecting cultural diversity and simultaneously maintaining a commitment to the equality and dignity of all living beings.

CONCLUSION

Over 60 years after the passage of the UN Declaration of Human Rights, the foundation of the Commission on the Status of Women, and the passage of numerous resolutions, conventions, and treaties, the international community is still calling for women's equality. In addition, a plethora of international agencies have collected data, funded development programs, sponsored conferences, and worked for the passage of international law and the development of international norms in their efforts to acknowledge that women's rights are human rights. Increasingly, in response to grassroots mobilization by women from the global South, they have turned from viewing women as subjects of the development process to seeing them as agents responsible for important and dynamic social change. The Millennium Declaration of 2000 represents the latest (but we hope not the last) effort to systematically address women's secondary status in every country of the world. Throughout the document, gender equality is emphasized as an end in and of itself as well as a means to better standards of living for all the world's citizens. Over the decades, there has been a growing general awareness that women's issues are not marginal, segregated from more "strategic" issues of war, peace, and economic stability. And promoting the status of women is not just a moral imperative but a strategic one; women's equality is a critical component of a country's overall economic prosperity, and a cornerstone of global peace and security. The following chapters delve further into the position and status of women in developing countries by focusing on the issues of women in economic development, health, education, war, and physical autonomy. What is the nature and scope of the gender divides on these issues, and what have been the results of international efforts to bridge these divides? We hope that by the end of the book, you'll have a better sense.

What Will $1 a Day Buy?

The UN has placed the international poverty line at $1 a day. (The World Bank later recalibrated the line to $1.25.) Some of you may be thinking that $1 will go much further in Brazil, potentially, than in the United States. That's why the $1 figure has been adjusted to purchasing power parity (PPP). That is, the UN makes that $1 universal. So you, too, could experiment with living on less than $1 a day to get a sense of the challenges that one in five people around the world face on a daily basis. In the fall of 2008, a couple, both high school social studies teachers, decided to conduct their own experiment and live on $1 a day for food (the average American eats about $7 worth of food per day). Overnight, their diets, and lives, changed dramatically. Most store-bought foods—even bread and canned goods—became too expensive. Fresh fruits and vegetables were not an option. Instead, they relied primarily on buying foods in bulk, such as beans, rice, cornmeal, and oatmeal, and on making their own bread and tortillas. To get some vitamin C, they made room for Tang orange drink mix in their budget. Not only were their food choices and levels of consumption narrowed, but they also found they had to spend much more of their time on food preparation. Further, although they lost weight, they also lost significant stores of energy eating a diet rich in empty calories. They pursued their experiment for one month.[i]

One in five of the world's citizens lives below this international poverty line, and a majority of them are women. Unlike the couple cited here, those who live below the international poverty line must also find ways to feed, clothe, and house their families on $1 a day. Nor can they choose to return to their "normal" lives after a month, as the couple here did—malnutrition, lack of secure employment, and poor health are daily realities for them. Women are more likely to be poor, and in addition, because they are the caretakers of their families, they must deal with the logistics of feeding, clothing, and caring for their families on this figure. How long do you think you could subsist on $1 a day?

---

[i]Tara Parker-Pope, "Money Is Tight, and Junk Food Beckons," *New York Times*, November 4, 2008, p. D6.

FOR MORE INFORMATION

Video and Multimedia
Half the Sky documentary, http://www.pbs.org/independentlens/half-the-sky/

Readings
Joni Seager. *The Penguin Atlas of Women in the World,* 4th ed. (New York: Penguin, 2008).

UN Women, "Progress of the World's Women 2012: In Pursuit of Justice," United Nations Commission on the Status of Women, http://www.un.org/womenwatch/daw/csw/index.html

World Bank 2012 World Development Report on Gender Equality and Development, http://econ.worldbank.org/WBSITE/EXTERNAL/EXTDEC/EXTRESEARCH/EXTWDRS/EXTWDR2012/0,,menuPK:7778074~pagePK:7778278~piPK:7778320~theSitePK:7778063~contentMDK:22851055,00.html

Sheryl WuDunn and Nicholas Kristof, *Half the Sky: Turning Oppression into Opportunity for Women Worldwide* (New York: Knopf, 2010).

Organizations and Websites
Center for Women's Global Leadership, http://www.cwgl.rutgers.edu

Development Alternatives with Women for a New Era, http://www.dawnnet.org/

Gender and Development in the World Bank, http://web.worldbank.org/WBSITE/EXTERNAL/TOPICS/EXTGENDER/0,,menuPK:336874~pagePK:149018~piPK:149093~theSitePK:336868,00.html

Gender Inequality Index, http://hdr.undp.org/en/statistics/gii/

Half the Sky Movement, http://www.halftheskymovement.org/

Human Rights Watch, Women's Rights, http://www.hrw.org/topic/womens-rights

Millennium Development Goals, http://www.un.org/millenniumgoals

Siyanda, Online Database of Gender and Development materials from around the world, http://www.siyanda.org

Social Institutions and Gender Index, OECD, http://genderindex.org/

TrustLaw Women, http://www.trust.org/trustlaw/womens-rights/

UN Women, United Nations Entity for Gender Equality and the Empowerment of Women, http://www.unwomen.org/

United Nations Development Programme, http://www.undp.org

UNDP Millennium Development Goals, http://www.undp.org/content/undp/en/home/mdgoverview.html

United Nations Gender Equality News Feed, http://www.un.org/womenwatch/ungen/index.html

United Nations Inter-Agency Network on Women and Gender Equality (IANWGE), http://www.un.org/womenwatch/ianwge/

Women Watch, UN Internet Gateway to the Advancement and Empowerment of Women, http://www.un.org:80/womenwatch

Women's Economic Opportunity Index, The Economist Intelligence Unit, https://www.eiu.com/public/topical_report.aspx?campaignid=weoindex2012

Women's Environment and Development Organization, http://www.wedo.org

World Economic Forum, Global Gender Gap, http://www.weforum.org/issues/global-gender-gap/

8

Women and the Global Economy

Lufta, a mother of two, lives in a slum on the western edge of Dhaka, Bangla-desh's capital city. Lufta, however, is better off than many women raising a family in the slums of the city: during a good month, she can earn up to 3,000 takas (about $50) a month, working in Bangladesh's export-oriented garment industry, which is barely enough to feed her family. She is not the only woman turning to this occupation; out of the 180 million people employed in Bangladesh's garment industry, 80 percent are women.[1] Many of you reading this book are probably wearing an item made by a woman in a developing country. Roshinara Begum lives in rural Bangladesh, in the village of Kalimajani. Surrounded by paddy fields, dotted by huts made of corrugated iron, Kalimajani is isolated from the outside world; there are no roads or phone lines to connect villagers to the outside world. Like many rural women in poverty-stricken Bangladesh, Roshinara could have spent her life hovering just above or below the poverty line, working tirelessly (but without remuneration) to keep her family at the subsistence level for another day. Instead, Roshinara makes a good living, earning $60 to $70 a month selling calls on a cell phone she acquired through a microcredit loan from the Grameen Bank, a nonprofit organization that offers small loans to primarily women in an effort to change women's position and status in society, one loan at a time. Like Lufta and Roshinara, 19-year-old So-Young of North Korea was also searching for employ-ment and the opportunities that wages could bring, not only to her, but also to her struggling family. Illegally crossing the border into China, she was soon offered approximately $1.40 per day in exchange for "work." In reality, she was sold to a 40-year-old Chinese man. Although she escaped, traffickers kidnapped her once again, raping her multiple times before selling her to another man, who in turn repeatedly raped her before her escape.[2] So-Young remains in hiding, unwilling to return home to North Korea but unable to search out legal employment opportu-nities in China. These women's life stories illustrate the ways in which an increas-ingly globalized economy can offer both promises as well as increased dangers to often undereducated, disempowered women in search of better lives.

This chapter provides an overview of the economic position and status of women in the developing world. Economic development is important because it is often a means to enabling all citizens—male as well as female—to live the kinds of lives they value.[3] Access to income not only can help people to meet their basic needs but also ensures that they have greater latitude to make choices about the direction of their lives. Yet, economic development is not a gender-neutral process. Women participate in and benefit from the process of socioeconomic development in different and predominantly unequal ways, which have resulted in enormous gender gaps in access to and control of resources. This in turn has fueled women's disproportionate burden of poverty around the world.

In particular, this chapter addresses how globalization, the increasing integration of and rapid interaction between economies through production, trade, and financial transactions, has dramatically reshaped women's lives. We focus on a few critical trends. For example, we discuss how outsourcing, primarily in labor-intensive fields such as garment manufacturing, has led to increased employment opportunities for women, but also to the feminization of the flexible labor force. Is this an opportunity for further economic development, or is it the exploitation of cheap, predominantly female workers who have little choice in determining their own futures? We then turn to women's (and girls') migration; in search of better lives, not only for themselves but also for their families, women form the bulk of transnational migrants. On the one hand, employment overseas can offer opportunities not available to women in poverty-stricken, tradition-bound societies. On the other hand, demand for cheap unregulated labor from the North feeds a massive underground trafficking industry in bonded workers in which women are often targeted for the sex trade or domestic slavery. Can legal migration offer women better lives, or does it merely create a new global underclass? Third, we look at how globalization has impacted rural women. Women are responsible for approximately half the world's agricultural production, and as the primary cultivators and gatherers of food, water, and fuel for family consumption they are often the first to notice and feel the effects of environmental stress and unsustainable economic development practices. How are women differently impacted by unsustainable development, and how is their activism gendered? Finally, we turn to the embrace of free market principles at a global level; the rise of international financial institutions, such as the World Bank and the International Monetary Fund (IMF); and the increased vulnerability of Southern countries to global financial trends, such as the 2008 global financial crisis. In times of financial crisis, women often have to bear the social and financial costs of economic reform. Why is economic restructuring gendered, and how have women responded in gendered ways to economic downturns? In closing, we turn to how development agencies, non-governmental organizations (NGOs), and activists have worked to break the vicious cycle of poverty by increasing women's participation and equality in the labor market. While globalization has launched some alarming economic, social, and political trends, it has also opened up opportunities, both for women and for the transnational activists and organizations working to ameliorate the negative ramifications of globalization.

WOMEN AND WORK

Gro Harlem Brundtland, former prime minister of Norway, director general of the World Health Organization, and tireless advocate for women's equality, once commented, "In many countries, women own nothing, inherit nothing, and earn nothing."[4] As we shall see, this is changing somewhat; one of the most dramatic changes in developing countries has been the rapid influx of women into paid employment. However, the relatively recent increase in women's participation in the paid labor force does not mean that women previously didn't work. Women have always worked, throughout history and all over the world. For most of history, however, the bulk of this work has been and continues to be unpaid and, as a result, undervalued. That is because women's work is often seen as an extension of their "natural" roles as mothers, nurturers, and caretakers of hearth and home. Yet, in countries of the developed world, while tasks such as cooking, cleaning, and caring take up hours of women's lives, cost them income in terms of the ever-pervasive wage gap, and often diminish their status, women's unpaid workloads only increase as we travel to the South. Grinding poverty, lack of or low literacy skills, absence of labor-saving technologies, and a culture that reinforces a strict household division of labor all combine to make women's days filled with time-consuming, backbreaking feats of manual work. In an effort to convey the critical yet undervalued role that a "housewife" plays in a predominantly rural, poor country, the Food and Agricultural Organization profiled one woman's day in Sierra Leone, one of the world's poorest countries. Rising at 4 a.m., the woman fishes in the local pond for food for her family, returning to light the fire, heat the washing water, cook breakfast, clean the dishes, and sweep the compound. At 8 a.m., she straps her baby on her back and takes her 4-year-old son with her to work in the rice fields. After 3 hours, she returns home, collecting berries, leaves, and bark on her way to prepare for and clean up from the next meal. After washing clothes by hand, fetching more water, and cleaning and smoking the fish, she works for the rest of the afternoon in her small plot of land, which she uses to feed her family. She returns to fish in the pond before dinner, and then starts the 2-hour preparation and cleanup process again before cleaning the children and getting them ready for bed. For 2 hours, she may converse around the fire, shelling seeds and making fishnets before extinguishing the flames and going to sleep at around 11, only to get up 5 hours later to repeat the same process.[5] All of this is done without the benefit of modern conveniences such as running water, prepackaged food, fuel stoves, electricity, or modern plumbing. Try this schedule for a week, and you'll quickly discover how much of this "housework" is actually back-breaking labor! Certainly, not all women in the developing world live this way. According to the United Nations (UN) Human Development Report, Sierra Leone has one of the lowest levels of human development in the world: life expectancy at birth is less than 50 years, the average adult has had less than 3 years of schooling; and the country's Gross Domestic Product (GDP) per capita is $734, making it one of the world's poorest countries. Women in Sierra Leone are particularly disempowered; women are about half as likely as men to have at least a secondary education, and they face extreme danger during pregnancy and childbirth (Sierra Leone has the world's fifth highest maternal mortality ratio). Nor do they have significant levels of political representation; they make up less than 13 percent of the national legislature.[6] However, the example of this woman's day underscores that fact that in almost all countries, much of women's work is unpaid and physically punishing. Yet it is of tremendous importance to the well-being of families, communities, and countries.

Unfortunately, this unpaid labor is often to the detriment of the women performing the work. Particularly in very low-income countries, the long hours spent collecting fuel and water often cut into time that could be spent engaging in activities that could improve the quality of women's lives. This situation is particularly dire for young girls, who often have to lessen their time in or forgo school altogether to help with household work.[7] Further, performing women's work in the home can be a serious health hazard. More than half the world's households cook with wood, crop residues, or untreated coal. Because work in the home is often women's work, women and children are the primary targets of indoor air pollution, which can lead to a number of health problems, such as respiratory infections and blindness. It can, and often does, lead to death. In developing countries, nearly 2 million women and children die each year as a result of exposure to indoor air pollution.[8] In developing countries, performing ordinary "housework" is not only physically demanding and exhausting but can also be deadly.

Given the importance of this work, as well as the high costs it can impose on those performing it, what is its economic worth? We don't know for sure. Women's "housework" has typically been excluded from economic analysis because economists have tended to view women's work in maintaining the household as a "natural" aspect of women's roles and as not being "work" because it is so often unpaid. As a result, most of the economic data collected on countries (and presented in this book!), particularly in the developing world, misrepresent women's participation in and contribution to a country's economy. This is particularly true, given that women are much more likely to work within the informal sector, subsistence economies, and the unpaid work involved in reproduction and care of the household. In fact, the UN Development Programme has estimated that women's "invisible" output amounts to $11 billion. Expanding the definition of work to include women's full range of caretaking responsibilities adds up to the equivalent of an extra 48 percent of the world's gross domestic product.[9] That is a lot of unpaid hours. In addition, broadening our definition of what constitutes "labor" also causes us to reassess the level and nature of women's participation in workforces all over the world. For example, in the Dominican Republic census in 1981, the rural female labor force participation rate was 21 percent. However, one study included activities such as homestead cultivation and livestock care, an area of unpaid household labor traditionally assigned to women. This broadened definition raised women's participation rates to 84 percent. In India, narrow and extended definitions of labor place women's participation rates at 13 percent and 88 percent, respectively. And in Pakistan, a separate survey documented a 45.9 percent participation rate (as opposed to the official 13.9 percent rate) when labor was broadened to include such tasks as rearing livestock, collecting firewood, fetching water, making clothes, and undertaking domestic work on a paid basis.[10] In fact, if one factors in women's workloads outside of paid employment, women work longer hours than men.[11] In sum, it is critical to acknowledge both that we need to think broadly in terms of what constitutes "work" if we are to capture accurately the situation many women in the developing world face and that women work in many ways outside of the formal paid sector. However, as we shall see, gaining access to paid work can be a crucial step to advancing women's status.

Why should we worry about women's access to paid employment? From a human rights perspective, women's status should be a source of concern, particularly if women have unequal access to economic opportunities and benefits. There are also a number of practical arguments for improving the economic position and status of women, particularly in the developing world, where it is even more challenging for women to transform their labor into paid work and their paid work into better lives, not only for themselves but also for their families. For one, women's access to paid employment is important because it usually puts some money directly into their own hands, thus increasing their abilities to make more decisions about their own lives. Also, increasing a woman's access to paid work and income often increases her autonomy and power within the household, giving her a more equal status in decision making within the family. In addition, because women tend to be the primary caretakers of hearth and home, they also are more likely than men to reinvest their income into the well-being of their families, specifically their children. This finding holds across many countries; in Ghana, the share of assets and the share of land owned by women are positively correlated with higher food expenditures. In Brazil, women's income has a positive impact on the height of their daughters. In China, increasing adult female income increased the fraction of surviving girls as well as the years of schooling for both boys and girls. In India, a woman's increased income is accompanied by an increase in her children's years of schooling. Across countries, women are more likely to allocate their resources toward better nutrition, health care, and provisions for household members, while men tend to spend more of their income in leisure activities, cigarettes, and alcohol.[12] Finally, improving women's access to paid employment also contributes to larger national trends; large-scale entry of women into the workforce can help stimulate economic growth, which in turn is critical for reducing overall numbers of people living in poverty. For an economy to be functioning at its potential, women's skills and talents should be engaged in activities that make the best use of those abilities. Gender equality, according to the 2012 World Bank Development Report, is important in its own right, as well as "smart economics." As the report eloquently argues,

> When women's labor is underused or misallocated—because they face discrimination in markets or societal institutions that prevents them from completing their education, entering certain occupations, and earning the same income as men—economic losses are the result. When women farmers lack security of land tenure, as they do in many countries, especially in Africa, the result is lower access to credit and inputs and to inefficient land use, reducing yields. Discrimination in credit markets and other gender inequalities in access to productive

inputs also make it more difficult for female-headed firms to be as productive and profitable as male-headed ones. And, when women are excluded from management positions, managers are less skilled on average, reducing the pace of innovation and technology adaptation.

In contrast, the payoff to increasing women's access to markets is high; for example, equalizing women farmers' access to fertilizer and other agricultural inputs would increase maize yields by 11 to 16 percent in Malawi and by 17 percent in Ghana. Improving women's property rights in Burkina Faso would increase total household agricultural production by about 6 percent.[13] Many developing nations need to harness the full potential of all their citizens, not just predominantly their male ones, to turn economic growth into better lives for all, and, in fact, excluding women comes at a high price. Thus, while there are certainly many things that money can't buy, in some respects, particularly for poor women in poor countries, the ability to earn money can provide enormous tangible and intangible benefits.

So what is the economic status of women? On a positive note, during the 1980s and 1990s, women's paid labor force participation rates increased substantially in almost every region of the world; between 1980 and 2008, over 552 million women joined the labor force (although these growth rates have leveled off in the past decade). Women now represent more than 40 percent of the global labor force, 43 percent of the agricultural workforce, and more than half of the world's university students (potentially poised to shatter some glass ceilings). It is hoped that these gains will translate into lower levels of female poverty and higher levels of economic and social independence for women. Further, the gap between female and male participation rates has narrowed, although in every region of the world, women are still less likely to be employed than men are. Take a moment to look at Table 8.1 to learn more about the regional variations between labor participation rates. For example, why do you think the gap between male and female participation rates is

Table 8.1 Labor Force Participation Rate by Sex and Region (%)

	MALES	FEMALES
World	77.9	52.7
Developed economies and European Union	68.4	53.1
Central and Southeastern Europe (non-EU) and Commonwealth of Independent States	69.9	50.4
East Asia	79.7	66.5
Southeast Asia and the Pacific	81.7	57.6
South Asia	82.6	39.6
Latin America and the Caribbean	79.9	52.0
Middle East	73.7	24.8
North Africa	75.6	27.6
Sub-Saharan Africa	80.4	61.3

SOURCE: International Labor Organization (ILO), Global Employment Trends 2011 (Geneva, Switzerland: ILO, 2011).

so much larger in the Middle East, North Africa, and South Asia? Certainly, in all countries, while not all women of working age may wish to work, the more common scenario in many countries is that women face many barriers, cultural and institutional, to finding paid employment.

Particularly in the developing world, women face more barriers to entering the formal paid labor force. A complex web of social norms often reinforces the idea that women's main responsibilities should revolve around reproduction and care of the family. Particularly in countries in South Asia, the Middle East, and North Africa, norms of female seclusion seriously limit women's physical mobility outside of the home, which makes paid employment extremely difficult. Further, a pervasive culture that undervalues girls ensures that women, if they enter the labor force, do so in poorer health, with less education, and with fewer skills than their male counterparts. As a result, women are often segregated into low-paying, low-skilled jobs, and, despite women's increased economic activity, women worldwide make less than men; on average, women earn about 75 percent as much as men.[14] Of course, this average masks substantial differences; for example, while women in Sweden receive about 83 cents for every dollar that men make, these differences widen as one moves to developing countries. See Table 8.2 for further examples of the pay gap between men and women in countries around the world.

Table 8.2 The Income Gap: The World's Worst Offenders

COUNTRY	ESTIMATED RATIO OF MALE TO FEMALE INCOME	COUNTRY	ESTIMATED RATIO OF MALE TO FEMALE INCOME
Saudi Arabia	0.16	Georgia	0.33
Oman	0.19	Syria	0.34
Egypt	0.23	Algeria	0.34
Qatar	0.24	Paraguay	0.34
Morocco	0.25	Cape Verde	0.35
Sudan	0.25	Turkey	0.35
United Arab Emirates	0.25	Bahrain	0.35
Pakistan	0.29	Kuwait	0.35
Swaziland	0.29	Malaysia	0.36
Tunisia	0.29	Samoa	0.38
Sao Tome and Principe	0.3	Iran	0.39
Yemen	0.3	Mexico	0.39
Botswana	0.31	Korea	0.4
India	0.31	Chile	0.4
Lebanon	0.31	Belize	0.4
Jordan	0.31	Suriname	0.4
Nicaragua	0.32	El Salvador	0.4
Guatemala	0.32		

SOURCE: UN Human Development Programme, *UN Human Development Report 2007/2008*, pp. 330–333.

However, despite the previous discussion, it is difficult to quantify the value of women's activities within countries' economies because much of women's paid labor occurs in the informal sectors of the economy or involves women being hired illegally without notifying the proper authorities or paying the relevant taxes. In fact, in developing countries, a much higher percentage of women who are active wage earners are informally employed. Sixty percent or more of women workers in the developing world are in informal employment (outside agriculture).[15] This is a growing area of women's employment, and the proportion of women who are self-employed in nonagricultural work is increasing faster than men's share. Most women who turn to the informal sector for their livelihood are self-employed, for example, as street vendors rather than engaged in wage work, such as domestic work or day labor.[16] Their income for the day rests on their abilities to sell their skills, products, or other services for whatever fee they can negotiate. Some of these women are visible. They often line the streets of cities, towns, and villages in developing countries, selling their wares. Other times, they are busy at home, engaged in activities such as sewing, embroidery, or cigarette or incense rolling, and are paid usually per unit produced. Those who work for wages are visible in the developing as well as developed world as casual workers in hotels and restaurants, as piece-rate workers in sweatshops, as temporary office helpers or offsite data processors, and as maids, child-care providers, and sex workers.

Women are overrepresented in the informal sector in part because it is more flexible, which may help them balance paid employment with their caretaking responsibilities in the home. In addition, however, women have a much more difficult time gaining access to formal employment in developing countries because these jobs are coveted by and primarily filled by men, and so informal labor markets are often their only outlets for ensuring their economic survival. Another problem with the rising numbers of informal sector jobs is that the predominantly female workers that fill these positions are often denied all of the benefits—secure contracts, unemployment, disability, and maternity—that can accrue from a position in the formal economy. While this has opened doors for women, the absence of social safety nets makes it a short-term rather than a long-term solution for women's lack of economic independence. Yet, the globalized, export-led economy, as we shall see, is creating more jobs than ever that provide fewer labor rights and little social protection.

In sum, over the past few decades there has been some progress in that more women than ever are participating in the paid workforce, although the female labor participation rate has stopped growing in the past decade. However, women are more likely to work either in the informal sector or in low-paying jobs, such as agriculture and services. In the following sections, we will look more closely at some of the ways in which women increasingly participate, willingly and unwillingly, in the global economy.

GLOBALIZATION

Globalization broadly refers to the growing integration of economies and societies around the world. Although early forms of globalization have existed since the Roman Empire, the current debates that swirl around globalization refer to the massive changes in economic, social, and political interaction from the 1980s onward. As Thomas Friedman explained in his bestselling book *The Lexus and the Olive Tree*, globalization is "the inexorable integration of markets, nation-states, and technologies to a degree never witnessed before—in a way that is enabling individuals, corporations and nation-states to reach around the world farther, faster, deeper, and cheaper than ever before. . . . [It is] the spread of free-market capitalism to virtually every country in the world."[17] As you can imagine, globalization has wrought profound changes in the international system, domestic government policies, and our day-to-day lives. The founding of international organizations such as the North American Free Trade Agreement (NAFTA) and the World Trade Organization (WTO) and the expansion of the European Community into a much broader and more powerful European Union have further eroded trade barriers and tariffs and facilitated the movement of goods and services across borders. International financial institutions that lend money and provide technical assistance to primarily developing countries, such as the IMF and the World Bank, have become much more influential in designing domestic economic policies that, as we shall discuss later in this chapter, have directly impacted the lives of millions of citizens living in these countries, who must live with the consequences of these policies. Further, domestic economies have become increasingly vulnerable to stresses and strains in the global economy; economic crashes in Mexico (1994), Thailand (1998), and the United States (2008) had far-reaching consequences, not only for neighboring countries but also for the entire global financial system. Alternative ideologies to free market capitalism have collapsed; China has all but abandoned its communist economic principles, and the disintegration of communist economic and political systems in eastern Europe and the former Soviet Union prompted scholars such as Francis Fukuyama to posit that liberal democracies run on market economies were the only viable political and economic options. Consumers could hardly miss the impact of globalization, as manufacturing and even customer service went global, in search of lower labor and production costs.

The backlash against the economic, political, and social implications of globalization have been just as momentous. New movements focusing on fair trade, not free trade, increased awareness of the excesses of sweatshop labor, and increased activism at international conferences have arisen in response to globalization. On a much more ominous note, the rise of fundamentalist and extremist movements in reaction to the perception of a secularized, Western hegemony over diverse political and cultural environments was instrumental in fueling movements such as al Qaeda. In terms of government economic policy, pro-globalization views translated into significant shifts in downsizing the role that governments played in managing the economy; in the 1980s and 1990s, governments everywhere reduced trade barriers and focused more heavily on attracting foreign investment and encouraging export-led growth. As a result, globalization has also become one of the most charged issues of the past two decades, and debating aspects of this phenomenon, such as the merits of free trade, foreign direct investment, and multinational corporations, has become commonplace on TV, on the Internet, in corporate boardrooms, and at labor union meetings and has often become a divisive political issue, particularly during election years. Proponents promise that globalization has improved and will continue to improve people's lives around the world by providing numerous economic opportunities, jobs, and income that will inevitably reduce poverty rates. Opponents charge that globalization simply further impoverishes the world's poor, enriches the already rich, devastates the environment, and alienates already marginalized citizens around the world. We now turn to how this increasingly integrated economy has impacted women by looking at women's participation in the global assembly line, the issue of migration, women's role in sustainable development and women and economic crisis.

Women in the Global Assembly Line

In many developing countries, particularly ones that have focused on manufacturing and export-led growth, young women are often the unsung heroes behind the rapidly expanding economy. For example, China has emerged as a global economic power, fueled by its enormous workforce and low labor costs. Much of its rise can be attributed to the 130 million migrant workers who have moved from rural poverty to the cities to help build the new industrial skylines, fill the factories, and churn out cheap goods in rapidly multiplying quantities. Many of these migrants who staff the assembly lines are young women who move from the hinterland to new industrial cities like the Pearl River Delta of southern China (see photo 8.1). As Leslie Chang narrates in her book about these workers, they are the invisible but crucial drivers of China's economic boom, working tirelessly and often making great sacrifices to escape the poverty of their rural origins. The book

Young women are the unseen engines of China's thriving export-oriented economy. In this photograph, Chinese women at the Foxconn factory in Fengcheng, central China's Jiangxi province, work on an assembly line. SOURCE: Imaginechina via AP Images.

centers on Dongguan, a massive factory town where the economy has grown at 15 percent every year for two decades. Seventy percent of the population of the town is female. Life in the factories can be harsh; shifts last for 12 hours, fines are assessed for talking on the job, and bathroom breaks are allowed only every 4 hours. The young women make about $100 a month and usually must commit to a minimum of 6 months or forfeit their first 2 months' salary, which is withheld upfront. They live in spare dormitories, and their lives revolve around work. Yet, many women continue to work, either because it is better than the alternative of returning to a rural life of poverty or because they believe that through hard work, their current jobs will serve as temporary stopping places before they move into a management position or even a highly coveted white-collar job.[18] China, while perhaps the most dramatic example of a country harnessing its future to manufacturing and export-led growth, is not alone in pinning its hopes to joining the global assembly line. In the effort to attract foreign capital, the low cost of labor, especially cheaper female labor, combined with little to no regulation, is often one of the lures governments have to attract outside investment. This is especially true in the growing world of export processing zones (EPZs), special manufacturing enclaves that are exempt from environmental and labor regulations. The number of EPZs has increased dramatically in the past 30 years. While only 25 countries had EPZs in 1975, in 2006, 130 countries had established 3,500 zones that employ 66 million workers. While almost two thirds of these workers come from China alone, nonetheless EPZs are a phenomenon affecting workers in nearly every developing country.[19] The rise of these free trade zones is part of a massive increase in world trade flows, particularly in manufactured goods. Exports in labor-intensive manufacturing have been rapidly expanding, with electronic components and the garment industry as the fastest-growing industries. These manufacturing jobs grew first in East Asian "miracle" economies and Mexico but soon spread to other parts of Asia and Latin America. In particular, the garment industry has taken off in Bangladesh, as well as in Indonesia, Malaysia, Mauritius, the Philippines, Sri Lanka, and Thailand.[20] This growth marks a shift away from male-dominated heavy industrial production of the post–World War II era and toward the repetitive assembly line work in export-oriented "light" industry subsectors of garments, textiles, shoes, and electronics. Further, in the current era of open economies and market deregulation, governments have focused on creating a market environment designed to attract investors, which can often come into conflict with the goal of managing the market for social ends—that is, providing an adequate standard of living and a safe working environment for adults.

There is a gendered component to this economic growth; women tend to be ghettoized in these industries. While in the industrialized West much attention is paid to the "glass ceiling" that prevents women from being promoted to the highest echelons of power, we sometimes forget that there is also a "sticky floor" that keeps millions of women in developed and developing countries trapped in low-skilled, low-paying jobs in light manufacturing and service industries. For example, the garment industry in many countries in Latin America, the Caribbean, and Asia and the electronics industry in Asia are industries that rely on cheap, unskilled labor provided predominantly by women to fuel profits. Women comprise 65 percent of the garment industry in Honduras, 70 percent in Morocco, 85 percent in Bangladesh, and 90 percent in Cambodia.[21] The field of data entry and data processing is populated overwhelmingly by women; for example, in the Caribbean, they make up the entire labor force.[22] As we discussed in Chapter 4, women in the advanced industrialized countries are also often relegated to sex-segregated occupations that pay less and offer less job security. But this trend has been fostered by the increased globalization of trade, in which goods and services are outsourced to far-flung regions of the world where labor costs are lower. These jobs are increasingly offered to women with no accompanying contract or benefits. Is this an opportunity for further economic development, or is it the exploitation of cheap, predominantly female workers who have little choice in determining their own future? Not surprisingly, the answer can be found in both interpretations.

On the one hand, women often work under worse conditions than men do; they almost always work for lower pay than it would cost to employ a man. Yet, from an employer's perspective, they often provide better service than men; one study of the *maquiladora* industry in Mexico found that employers chose women employees over men because they were more dexterous and skilled at assembling small components at a rapid pace. In addition, employers prized women for their perceived submissiveness. Because fewer young women had had experience living on their own outside of the home, they rarely questioned the policies set down by management, often acquiescing rather than fighting decisions that would affect them adversely. Alternatively, older women who were the single providers for their small children recognized the nature of their poor working conditions but continued to work so that they could feed and clothe their families. Fighting for better working conditions threatened the livelihoods of their families, for whom they were responsible. For many, the costs of protesting were simply too high.[23] Further, it is difficult for women workers to implement reform from within; they are still overrepresented at the bottom rungs of specific careers and underrepresented in positions of power in the areas of management or administration. As a result, they often do not occupy positions in which they could have an impact on labor policy. For many laborers, women as well as men, all they have to offer is their cheap, predominantly unskilled labor, which often is not much of a bargaining chip for better conditions. There are often other people, desperate for paid employment, willing to take their places. Further, as previously mentioned, much of this employment is informal, has no benefits, is accompanied by pitiful working conditions, and comes as an additional work burden to women who are already overburdened with household and family responsibilities. And studies have shown that while these jobs do put money in women's hands, the salary is rarely enough to lift women out of poverty; it simply moves them up the economic ladder to the "working poor."

Yet, as the Chinese example illustrated, however bleak, many women perceive these conditions as an opening to increased opportunities. While the conditions under which they work often violate international labor standards, these employment options still offer an improvement on their precarious lives. Ana, a worker in a Honduran *maquila*, commented, "Even though the salaries are low, the *maquilas* give us employment—they help us to make ends meet."[24]

And this increasing economic power has implications for how women are treated in the family. According to one woman worker in a Bangladeshi factory, "in my mother's time . . . women had to tolerate more suffering because they did not have the means to become independent. They are better off now, they know about the world, they have been given education, they can work and stand on their own feet. They have more freedom."[25] A study of more than 30 Bangladeshi garment factories found that two out of three women had some control of their earnings. This translates into increased decision-making power in the household and, sometimes, a shift in gendered divisions of labor.[26] And for many women, the alternative of working in the global economy, however fraught with uncertainty, poor conditions, and unequal outcomes, is better than the offerings of the domestic economy, where high unemployment, poor government regulation, corruption, and weak government capacity further undermine women's opportunities to participate in the labor market. Conditions in these factories tend to be better than what the domestic economy can offer. Factors such as these have prompted *New York Times* op-ed columnist Nicholas Kristof to argue, "[T]he central challenge in the poorest countries is not that sweatshops exploit too many people, but that they don't exploit enough." Using the example of Cambodia, where 5-year-old children scour toxic garbage dumps for recyclable material to sell for 5 cents a pound, Kristof argues that manufacturing jobs offer a potential alternative route out of poverty, particularly for women.[27]

Perhaps the reality is that these jobs both exploit women and simultaneously open up new opportunities for greater levels of economic independence and autonomy in decision making in the household. Particularly for students living in a country in the developed world, it can be hard to see the benefits of working in a factory for little pay under little to no regulation. But most students aren't faced with the alternative of scouring a garbage dump, illiterate, barefoot, poorly nourished, for salvageable refuse. Sweatshops often are a symptom of poverty, not a cause, and, despite their shortcomings, they are still out of reach as a development option to the world's poorest countries, which are often hampered by unreliable governments, transportation, and energy systems. As we shall see in the next section, economic opportunities for women in the developing world are still scarce, and increasingly thousands of women journey to other countries in search of better opportunities. We now turn to the issue of women and international migration.

WOMEN AND MIGRATION

Saokham, a young woman who grew up in poverty in a mountain village in Myanmar, emigrated to neighboring Thailand to work at assembling costume jewelry for export to North America. She earns 140 Thai bhat a day—about U.S. $3.50; this is a respectable wage, particularly given the economic conditions of her village. If she had stayed in rural Myanmar, she would not have had many prospects. Although she completed 8 years of free schooling, she had to leave school because her parents could not afford to pay for any additional schooling. With few economic opportunities in sight in her home environment, at the age of 14 she set out for neighboring Thailand to join her older sister, who had left 2 years previously. She now lives with her husband in a community of fellow compatriots. Reflecting on her new life, she said, "Living in Thailand, we have money for food and to spend. Life is convenient. Back home we didn't have any work except farm work."[28] Increasingly, women from the developing world are migrating to richer, more developed countries in search of increased opportunities. They may move to marry, to rejoin migrant husbands and family, or to find work as domestic workers, cleaners, or caregivers. Some work in low-skilled jobs in the peripheral world of sweatshops; others work as migrant farm laborers, while those with skills come to fill the growing need for qualified teachers and health-care workers. In today's globalized economy, transnational migration is increasing, both among men and women. Almost 100 million or about half of the world's migrants are women.

This migration has had a significant impact, not only on the women themselves but also on the families they leave behind. For one, the economic impact of this global migration is significant; in 2004, the World Bank estimated that migrant workers sent $126 billion home to their families in developing countries. This is particularly impressive given that many of these workers are working in unskilled or low-skilled jobs, with annual incomes that can range between $1,500 and $4,000. These remittances add up to almost double the amount of Official Development Assistance and approximately 75 percent of total foreign direct investment.[29] In late 2007, the UN estimated this figure to be even higher ($300 billion) and argued that remittances represent "one of the world's largest poverty reduction efforts" that contributes to "grass-roots economic development."[30] According to one Ethiopian woman who migrated (undocumented) to Yemen, "There are very limited job opportunities in this country [Ethiopia]. . . . I remember how I suffered before securing a job in Yemen. . . . [T]hings would have been worse for me and my family had I not gone abroad to work."[31] Although we don't know how much of this money is being sent by women migrants, available data indicate that women send a higher proportion of their earnings back to their families and that women tend to invest the remittances, providing for daily needs, health care, and education for their families. In contrast, men tend to spend remittance income on consumer items such as cars and TVs or on investments such as property and livestock.[32] Although the data are spotty, nonetheless it is clear that the money that female migrants send back home (and that female caretakers receive) can make a substantial impact on the daily lives of families and sometimes entire communities.

The women themselves can benefit from the transnational move; it can expose them to new ideas and norms about their rights and enable them to participate more fully in society. Also, if and when they return to their home country, they take those new norms back with them, and these norms can directly improve the lives of their families. For example, a World Bank report found that female migrant workers from Guatemala, Mexico, and Morocco, as a result of the health education they received while working abroad, improved their children's health and had lower mortality rates. Migration can also redefine traditional gender norms of behavior between men and women. In particular, women who migrate alone (rather than as part of a family) are more likely to report a positive experience and may even be reluctant to return home and potentially relinquish some autonomy. Women earning income abroad report receiving greater levels of respect and household help from their husbands.[33] And many do live better lives in their new countries. One Venezuelan domestic worker living in the United States, who fled with her two children from an abusive husband, commented, "Here there were a lot of opportunities for my children, so they could have a different kind of life. For all the opportunities, all the good things that my children have, I love this country, I love it. I am very thankful."[34]

However, many women have also paid a high price for this decision to leave their family, spouses, and children in search of better economic opportunities. Particularly for women who are migrating illegally, they often face sexual harassment and abuse or may be forced to provide sexual favors in return for transport. Further, upon reaching their host country, they may face increased discrimination as migrants and as women, particularly if they are of a different race, class, or religion than the dominant culture of the host country. Particularly if they are there illegally, many have no recourse to social, legal, or health services and may be afraid to contact the police if they face violent or predatory conditions. And as we shall discuss in greater detail, many women, in leaving their families and children behind, usually pass on the task of care to other female relatives, thus reproducing, rather than changing, gendered household divisions of labor.

We now move to some of main reasons women are pushed and pulled into transnational migration. For each example, take a moment to think about the impact of these women's choices on their own lives and their communities. Whose lives are being improved most? Are these situations "win–wins" for everyone, or does the transaction primarily benefit the host community in the wealthier country? How free are these women to choose their own futures, given the often bleak economic and social conditions that they face back in their home countries? Certainly, there are no right answers to these questions, but they are issues to ponder as you learn more about women as domestic workers, skilled professionals, mail-order brides, and sex providers.

Demand for domestic work in the wealthier countries is one of the largest factors driving female migration. In many ways, this global migration is a result of the strides that feminist movements have made in the more developed economies of North America, Western Europe, and East Asia. As more women move into the workforce, they have had to contract out and pay for the labor that they once had performed for free, such as caring for their children and elderly and infirm relatives. For example, in the United States in 1950, only 15 percent of women with children under the age of 6 worked; that number has since soared to 65 percent. While many feminists advocated for a more equitable distribution of labor between spouses in the household, in reality, fathers and husbands have not fully compensated for this shift by assuming more responsibilities in the home. The result, as one scholar claims, is a gaping "care deficit," and many middle-class families pay poorer women to shoulder the burden of balancing work and family life.[35]

Thus, in some ways, women's abilities to advance in the industrialized Northern Hemisphere are dependent on their abilities to transfer gendered divisions of labor to poorer women in the Southern Hemisphere who are looking for better employment opportunities than those that their own countries can provide them.

This phenomenon tends to create what is termed a "global care chain"—a situation in which migrant women, having left their own homes to care for others abroad, pass their domestic caregiving responsibilities on to other female relatives or, sometimes, hire lower-income domestic workers. These women often end up running two households—their employers' as well as their own from abroad. Women who make the difficult decision to leave their families in order to sustain them also pay a significant psychological and emotional price for their decision. Often, they provide love and affection to their employer's children to earn enough money to improve the quality of the lives of their own children, whom they may not get to see for many years.

Some female migrants possess enough skills and education to parlay their strengths into relatively stable careers in the West. Increasing numbers of female professionals—particularly teachers and nurses—are choosing to emigrate to wealthier, more economically and politically stable countries. For example, since the early 2000s, about one quarter of employed migrant women in Finland, Sweden, and the United Kingdom have been working in either the health or the education sectors. Since 2001, the United States and United Kingdom have been recruiting Caribbean teachers directly out of high school and college. And the ever-increasing demand for nurses in the wealthier countries has fueled a significant migration of qualified women from Africa, Asia, and the West Indies. In fact, more than one in four nurses and aides working in major cities in the United States is foreign-born.[36]

While this influx of foreign workers may help relieve pent-up demand for more health care in the industrialized West, it has also created a huge "brain drain" from the poorer regions of the world, many of which are facing severe health crises with even fewer human resources. The World Health Organization recommends a minimum ratio of 100 nurses for every 100,000 people. Many developing countries, particularly those in sub-Saharan Africa, do not even come close to meeting that goal. For example, the ratio is less than 10 nurses per 100,000 people in countries such as Uganda, while there are more than 2,000 nurses per 100,000 people in wealthier countries such as Finland or Norway. The yearly migration of 20,000 trained nurses and doctors from Africa exacerbates what was already a dire situation. The lack of trained health professionals is particularly problematic given the skyrocketing incidences of malaria, HIV/AIDS, and maternal mortality. While nurses are in extremely short supply in the developing world, their reasons for emigrating are not: collapsed health systems, underfunding, chronic shortages of basic supplies, and poor pay are all common scenarios for nurses who stay behind. But who will take care of the population of the countries they have left? In 2003, an estimated 85 percent of employed Filipino nurses were working abroad, a factor that has made an indelible impact on the quality of care available to Filipino citizens.[37]

A third major motivation for female migration is marriage. Further, advances in technology, such as the rise of the Internet, have aided the rise of the mail-order bride and arranged and forced marriages. As we shall see in Chapter 9, the under-valuation of girls in some cultures, such as India and China, has led to millions of "missing girls," those who are aborted in favor of producing only sons. But this has also led to an unprecedented shortage of marriageable women and has fueled the growth of international marriages, as families comb regions such as Southeast Asia for brides.

Yet, given the futures they face in their home countries, women are often willing participants in this business. Whether it is based in a desire to find a sup-portive partner, economic security, or a means to gain legal entry into another country, thousands of women are choosing to market themselves to the increas-ingly international marriage market. In the United States alone, according to the Department of Justice, 80,000 Russian women have entered the United States in the past 10 years looking for companionship and a brighter economic future than they would have faced in Russia. At the same time, some women face such extremely circumscribed options that it is somewhat hard to view their decisions as freely made "choices." A 2005 study of Vietnamese migrant women who had once lived in China found that most entered into unions because of poverty or to provide for elderly parents back home. Would they have made the same choice if coming from a position of economic security, not only for themselves, but for their families as well?[38] And the growing mail-order brides industry sometimes serves as a front for the illegal sex industry, and thousands of women, who may expect (and accept) to exchange sex for marriage, end up providing sex against their will as unwilling participants in the sex trade.

Millions of people—men, women, boys, and girls—are caught up in the trans-national trafficking chain. U.S. law defines trafficking as "the recruitment, harbor-ing, transportation, provision, or obtaining of a person for labor or services, through the use of force, fraud, or coercion for the purpose of subjection to involuntary servitude, peonage, debt bondage, or slavery."[39] A fundamental element of this def-inition is that there is a substantial power differential; while the trafficker is aware of the exploitation, the victim has at best only partial information and at worst none at all. In sum, fundamentally, trafficking is not considered to be a consensual em-ployment agreement, given the imperfect information available to the victim.[40] This phenomenon is relatively widespread; the International Labour Organization (ILO), the UN agency that addresses labor standards, employment, and social protection issues, estimates that 12.3 million people are in forced, bonded labor. Further, every year, approximately 800,000 people are trafficked across borders, in addition to the millions trafficked within their own countries. Trafficking has a gendered component: 80 percent of transnational victims are women, and up to 50 percent are minors. Many of these women are trafficked into some form of the burgeoning and extremely profitable sex industry, although they are also trafficked into migrant labor, bonded labor, and domestic servitude (as opposed to consen-sual domestic service). This underground, highly illegal business is also highly profitable. Human trafficking is the third most profitable illicit business in the world, edged out only by arms and drug trafficking.[41] Conservative estimates place the money generated by sex trafficking alone at $7 billion per year, although

Interpol puts the estimate at $19 billion; the ILO argues that each victim generates, on average, $23,000 a year in profits.[42] About half of the victims end up in industrialized countries and almost one third in Asia.[43] The largest numbers of trafficked persons come out of Asia; an estimated 225,000 are taken out of Southeast Asia, while another 150,000 come from South Asia. More than 100,000 persons are trafficked from the former Soviet Union, and 75,000 come from eastern Europe.[44]

In reading through the testimony of rescued workers, a familiar narrative emerges. Most of the victims come from an entrenched environment of poverty and lack of opportunity, combined with a dearth of education or other tools to give them skills to compete in an already extremely underdeveloped job market in their countries of origin. Women's lack of economic and social rights and access to opportunities often serve as a root cause of their trafficking, and many are lured by promises of fabricated jobs as hostesses, waitresses, nannies, or entertainers. The experiences of Sylvia, a 19-year-old living in Ungheni, Bulgaria, illustrate an all-too-common narrative facing many young women searching for employment. Unemployed, broke, with no job prospects but a baby daughter to support single-handedly, Sylvia was thrilled when a neighbor told her he could help her find a good job as a salesgirl in Moscow. Sylvia first traveled to Chisinau, the capital of Moldova, to meet two men who would arrange for her travel to Russia. Instead, she was beaten, raped, and eventually smuggled with 11 others to Moscow, and straight into prostitution. Now living in a safe house, she reflected, "I thought all the stories about trafficked girls were fake, a scare tactic. But now I know better. . . . [I]t is real and can happen to anyone."[45] And even if victims do manage to escape, for many, the nightmare has not ended. Particularly for victims of sex trafficking, they are too ashamed to return home, often prompting their reentry into the sex industry. This is particularly true for young boys, who face even greater levels of stereotypes that entrench the idea that they cannot be exploited in prostitution.

It is important to acknowledge that not all women in the sex trafficking industry are victims; they also work the other side of the industry as recruiters, brothel operators, and "clients." For example, women often recruit other women in Europe and Central and South Asia. Frequently, they themselves were victims of the system, but through a system of physical and psychological pressure, as well as the offering of limited incentives, they become part of the system, recruiting fresh victims through stories of having had ideal experiences in legitimate jobs in the West or elsewhere. In addition, women serve as pimps and madams, and often broker the transactions. Some hypothesize that this has become a deliberate hiring strategy for the industry; criminal organizations may hire female traffickers because they believe that governments will exhibit greater leniency toward female criminals. Further, in some countries, particularly in Eurasia, female traffickers are released from serving prison time when they are pregnant or mothers of young children, and thus are actively recruited by organizers higher up in the trafficking industry as a way to minimize risk to their profits.[46]

As with mail-order brides, the trafficking of women, as well as the burgeoning underground industry of sex tourism, has been spurred by advances in technology. The Internet has been a critical force in facilitating foreign travel with the express purpose of purchasing sex, often with what are legally considered under-age girls. And the Internet is teeming with websites that provide potential sex tourists with accounts written by other tourists and that supply information on destinations, prices, and procurement. In 1995 alone, there were over 25 U.S. busi-nesses that offered and arranged sex tours; one business promised sex with two young Thai girls "for the price of a tank of gas." And although almost all countries have laws on the books outlawing prostitution and underage sex, lax government regulation, poor enforcement, and/or lack of resources to tackle the problem all conspire to make domestic laws in some developing countries relatively useless. Places such as Thailand, Indonesia, Malaysia, and the Philippines have become hubs of the sex tourism industry, and the profits represent 2 to 14 percent of the gross domestic product of these countries.[47] This encourages governments to turn a blind eye to the situation because of the profits generated by the tourists, given the paucity of other economic development strategies.

The other factor that drives the sex industry is the relentless demand. Sex tourists are typically male and come from all income brackets, usually from na-tions in Western Europe and North America. Many may even perversely justify their actions as "humanitarian." Thus, one retired U.S. schoolteacher, traveling with the express purpose of purchasing sex, commented, "On this trip, I've had sex with a 14-year-old girl in Mexico and a 15-year-old in Columbia. I'm helping them financially. If they don't have sex with me, they may not have enough food. If someone has a problem with me doing this, let UNICEF feed them."[48] Others con-vince themselves that children in foreign countries are less sexually inhibited and that culturally, the destination countries do not have the same taboos against what is considered underage sex in their home countries. Many simply rely on the ano-nymity that foreign travel provides, releasing them from the usual moral con-straints that may check their behavior back home.

In closing, millions of women migrate annually in search of better lives, often motivated to leave their home countries because of severe levels of gender inequality, whether in educational, economic, or social opportunities. The impact of the grow-ing feminization of migration is complex; on the one hand, migration can open up new vistas for women who otherwise might have faced a life of penury and social disempowerment if they had stayed behind. On the other hand, their secondary status can often continue in their new countries, and their situations can worsen if they are trafficked into labor against their will. Globalization has been and will con-tinue to be a critical force in shaping women's lives; the increased interconnectedness of national economies, advances in technology, and spread of cultural values have all pushed and pulled women to cross borders for better opportunities.

RURAL WOMEN, THE ENVIRONMENT, AND SUSTAINABLE DEVELOPMENT

Increasingly, international organizations, policymakers, and activists have rallied behind the concept of sustainable development, which the UN defines as "devel-opment that meets the needs of the present without compromising the ability of future generations to meet their own needs."[49] Yet, economic development, seen by these same agencies as the engine behind greater levels of human development, often has negative environmental consequences and can imperil both long-term human and ecological health and survival. Further, the environmental impact often disproportionately affects some regions of the world; poorer countries in the South pay the environmental and human costs of the richer Northern countries' incessant desire for cheaper goods in the context of a high-consumption lifestyle. For example, the housing boom of the previous decade in the United States fueled demand for lumber, much of which is harvested in developing countries. Deforestation often leads to soil erosion, which lowers agricultural yields, which in turn can prompt a series of suboptimal practices, such as the increased reliance on fertilizers, which can increase soil salinity, which can lead to desertification, polluted waterways, and shortages of drinkable water and edible fish. This has an enormous impact not only on the ecosystem but also on people's livelihoods, health, and life trajectories. Deforestation also contributes to global warming, as there are now fewer trees to absorb excess carbon dioxide. As you can see, consumer choice in the United States can have far-reaching implications for people living in the global South. Certainly, citizens in less-developed countries also play a role in perpetuating unsustainable development practices; however, the damage done in terms of exhausting local renewable resources such as water and land is often prompted by the quest to meet basic needs, not to sustain a consumer lifestyle. Many people in the developing world have constrained choices and thus contribute to resource depletion and pollution in their larger struggle for survival.[50]

Women are particularly impacted by the environmental impact of larger development processes because millions of women in the developing world live in rural areas and ensure their families' survival through paid and unpaid agricultural work in activities such as food production, animal husbandry, and fuel collection. Yet, globalization has penetrated to even the most rural of areas and has redefined, in both positive and negative ways, women's roles in the rural economy. Further, we shall see that women are particularly vulnerable to the impact of pollution, soil erosion, and environmental degradation and that their response to these problems has also been deeply gendered, often rooted in their roles as caretakers of "mother earth" (see the text box on Wangari Maathai to read more about women's activism on sustainable development).

Until 2005, agriculture was the main sector of employment for women worldwide. Although the service sector now provides most jobs for women (42.2 percent), 40.4 percent of working women around the world are employed in agriculture. This number increases substantially as one moves from developed to developing countries (61 percent), and then to the least developed (79 percent) countries in the world.[51] In fact, women have a higher share of agricultural employment than men in East Asia, South Asia, sub-Saharan Africa, and the Middle East and North Africa.

Women are critical to the sustainability of rural economies and communities, although their roles are rapidly shifting in response to the larger forces of globalization.

As caretakers of hearth and home, they are often responsible for growing the food, and some estimate that women agricultural workers produce half of the world's food. In particular, women are the main producers of staple crops such as rice, maize, and wheat, which form the basis of diets in most developing countries. And in the least-developed countries of sub-Saharan Africa, the UN estimates that about 60 to 70 percent of all food production is done by women.[52] In many developing countries, they also are responsible for caring for livestock; in sub-Saharan Africa, 50 percent of all animal husbandry is done by women. Women are also the main food producers in terms of preparation; as the caretakers of the household, women are primarily responsible for ensuring that their families get enough to eat. Further, to prepare the food, women spend hours a day collecting water, gathering fuel sources, and cooking and cleaning up, in addition to their care work in tending to children, the elderly, and the sick. As a result, they are critical to ensuring food security and fighting to keep their families out of poverty.

Yet, despite the fact that women are an essential part of rural economies and produce a significant amount of the world's food, many women are excluded from opportunities to capitalize on their roles. Despite the fact that women work the land, local custom and/or law can deny women equitable access to and control over land. Women often do not hold formal and clear land titles, and women own less than 2 percent of land in the developing world. This lack of ownership puts many of the women who work the land in an extremely vulnerable position because they can be evicted, or simply because they lack the ability to make long-term plans to maximize their economic options. And without a strong tradition of land ownership, and the ability to claim it as an asset, it is difficult for women to gain access to other essential resources, such as credit. As a result, many women, if they need to borrow, must resort to informal methods, which often are accompanied by higher interest rates. Further, women's unequal and constricted access to education can limit their abilities to learn new technologies to increase production. Nor have development projects consistently addressed these problems; a study of women in agriculture in Africa found that while women produce about 70 percent of Africa's food, only 20 percent of these women are the direct recipients of extension advice.[53] As we discussed earlier in the chapter, much of women's work goes unnoticed because it is considered "housework," and therefore is unpaid. This oversight is even more problematic for rural women in that rural residents in particular struggle for daily survival; 75 percent of the poor in developing countries live in rural areas, and rural women are particularly vulnerable.[54] In particular, indigenous women, widows, and female-headed households are even further marginalized in rural economies.

Globalization has significantly impacted domestic agrarian economies and women's roles in them. Consumer demands from industrialized nations, spurred by increased efficiency in communication and transportation, has led to the increasing reliance on large-scale plantation farming as well as a focus on non-traditional exports and high-value foods, compared with the traditional exports of coffee, tea, sugar, and cocoa. The rise of chains such as Whole Foods, where shoppers can buy blueberries, exotic fruits, boutique coffees, and fresh flowers at any time of the year, has dramatically shifted how things are grown and who cultivates them. For example, in Africa, there has been a shift in focus to produce goods such as cut flowers in Zimbabwe, tobacco in Mozambique, and vanilla in Uganda. Fruit and flower production has also become much more important for Latin American economies. In Asia, shrimp farming has become increasingly important, and former rice farms are being taken over by shrimp farms that export to Europe and the United States.

Women in Movement: Wangari Maathai

"The planting of trees is the planting of ideas. By starting with the simple act of planting a tree, we give home to ourselves and to future generations."[1]

Nobel laureate, activist, politician—Wangari Maathai, mother of three, has accumulated a long list of firsts in her remarkable quest to revive the connection between thriving ecosystems and health, justice, and peace. Raised in rural Kenya in the waning days of the British Empire, Maathai, with the support of her mother and older brother, was one of the few girls who attended school beyond the primary level. Marked early on as an exceptionally bright student, Maathai was selected as part of a U.S. program (known as the Kennedy Airlift) to send young Africans to American colleges for further education in the hopes that they would return to assume leadership positions in the soon-to-be independent African states. Combining her academic interest in science with her deep love for the lush rural environment of her girlhood in Kenya, Maathai returned with a master's degree in biology, to which she soon added a Ph.D. in veterinary medicine from the University of Nairobi. She was the first woman in East and Central Africa to receive her doctorate. She became professor of veterinary anatomy at the university and went on to chair her department. In 1977, Maathai founded Kenya's Green Belt Movement to mobilize thousands of women to plant trees in an effort to revive the country's forest lands, which had been transformed from the lush, green, fertile land of plenty of her childhood to a deforested nightmare in her adulthood. Since she founded this organization, the Green Belt Movement has planted more than 40 million trees across Africa. In addition, what began as a targeted program to address the challenges of deforestation, soil erosion, and lack of water developed into a means of female empowerment, supporting and nurturing women's roles as champions for sustainable development, equitable economic growth, and responsible political governance. Maathai underwent a political transformation as well, eventually connecting Kenya's environmental degradation with the irresponsible policies of a corrupt government, and her Green Belt Movement also became part of the broader campaign for democracy in Kenya. When a new government came to power in 2002, she was elected to parliament and appointed assistant minister in the Ministry for Environmental and Natural Resources. Although she lost her bid for reelection in 2007, until her death in 2011, she continued to be an impassioned advocate for environmental conservation, democratic governance, and human rights for women and men.

As a woman, Maathai often had to fight against gender discrimination, sometimes within her own family. In the 1980s, her husband, a politician whom she had married in 1969, divorced her, maintaining that she was too strong-minded for a woman and that he was unable to control her. The judge agreed with the husband

and eventually jailed Maathai for speaking out. Her willingness to speak out also prompted political enmity; President Moi denounced her as a "wayward" woman and jailed her several times for her pro-democracy activities.

'Wangari Maathai, *Unbowed* (New York: Knopf, 2006). As quoted in the Green Belt Movement, http://www.greenbeltmovement.org.

On the one hand, globalization has helped diversify rural livelihoods and increase labor mobility. Women increasingly make up the bulk of migrant labor in the fresh-produce global supply chain, comprising 65 percent of the labor force in Colombia, 75 percent in Kenya, and 87 percent in Zimbabwe.[55] These jobs in the global food-production chain offer paid employment and the opportunity to work for waged labor, as opposed to what is often the norm—unpaid labor in service to the family. Research on female employment in the flower plantations in Ecuador, where two thirds of all workers are women, for example, showed that the presence of the industry did increase incomes and, indirectly, led to important changes in gender roles within the household. Some of the trends noted were changes in spending patterns, the division of work, and decision making regarding education and health. Men tended to increase their contributions to housework after women began work. In addition, the marriage rate among women working on the plantation dropped, as marriage became less an economic necessity and potentially more of a choice.

However, the study found that the entry of women, specifically mothers, into the paid labor force had a negative impact on their daughters, who often took on increased workloads at home, particularly with regard to caring for younger siblings. This often harmed their educational prospects. Second, because women are hired and are willing to work as temporary workers, many did not qualify for social benefits, such as health care, or fair labor practices, such as regulated work shifts. In turn, employers point out that the demands of the increasingly globalized economy mean that they must continue to find ways to slash production costs. As one South African apple farmer, who exports to the United Kingdom's biggest supermarket, Tesco, explained, "The only ham left in the sandwich is our labour costs. If they squeeze us, it's the only place where we can squeeze." Thus, hiring women on temporary contracts, with few to no benefits, is the only way they feel they can compete.[56] While the globalized economy enables women's employment, it is often on the punishing terms of free trade rather than fair trade. However, women themselves prefer the work to the alternative—work as a domestic or seasonal worker—which potentially requires moving away from their families in search of better opportunities.[57]

In addition, liberalization policies, which are an essential element of the free trade argument of globalization advocates, eliminate trade and market barriers as well as reducing government-funded price supports for basic agricultural commodities. The adoption of these policies has encouraged the prioritization of large-scale farming in support of cash and export crops over food crops for household and local consumption. This means that commercialized agriculture is squeezing out subsistence agriculture and that preference is given to export-oriented crops rather than domestic markets. This shift also requires greater investments in expensive inputs such as fertilizers, seeds, and farming equipment.

This has had a profound effect on domestic livelihoods, and also on women specifically. The shift away from producing food for individual consumption has created a food shortage for those living in the developing world. For example, the shift toward shrimp production for export in much of Asia has led to decreased availability of fish for low-income consumers, diminished availability of land for local food production, and increased levels of soil salinity, which has led to decreased food crop yields.[58] This problem of falling levels of local food production is not isolated to a few Asian countries. In 1960, developing countries had an overall agricultural trade surplus of almost $7 billion per year, but by 2001, the surplus had reversed into a deficit of more than $11 billion. This has created a serious food security issue, particularly for women, who are primarily responsible for cultivating, buying, and cooking food for their families.

Further, the increasing scarcity and degradation of land, water, and other property resources have affected women's caring work. Women have to spend more time coaxing smaller plots of overtaxed, overfarmed land to produce food. They also have to spend more time and energy searching for fuel, water, and other essentials that keep their families alive, given that deforestation and water contamination are increasingly common. Women, who had maybe once spent 1 hour gathering local firewood or fetching water from the local pump, may now need to walk several miles to find the same resources. Such searches often diminish the time they can spend on farming and caring for livestock, which simply increases the vicious cycle of food insecurity. Further, women's health, and the health of their families, may deteriorate, as women must carry heavier loads for longer distances; cook, drink, and wash with polluted water; and burn increasingly toxic fuel sources.

WOMEN AND ECONOMIC CRISIS

Women's role as caretakers is also called upon (and stretched to the limit) in times of economic crisis. Further, women respond differently to and are affected differently by economic downturns. This was particularly so in the 1980s and 1990s, when many countries began to implement what are known as structural adjustment programs (SAPs). Initially pushed by international lending agencies such as the IMF, SAPs were the expression of a neoliberal, pro-market approach that emphasizes making internal economic and political reforms to help the domestic economy to become more competitive in the global marketplace. In particular, lending institutions such as the IMF advanced loans to countries only when they could meet certain conditions that theoretically would reduce trade barriers and stimulate economic growth. Some of these conditions were reduced social expenditures, increased focus on export-led growth and resource extraction, currency devaluation against the dollar, removal of import and export restrictions, opening of domestic markets to foreign investment, balancing budgets, privatization of critical state-owned industries, and removing price controls and state subsidies. In sum, SAPs called for decreased government intervention in the economy, decreased government spending in favor of balanced budgets, and an embrace of global free market forces.

The results of these reforms for many countries were devastating and caused many to go more deeply into debt without reaping the rewards of economic growth. Many countries' increased focus on export-led growth reaped few rewards, given that prices for commodities and raw materials on the global marketplace were falling rather than rising. Devaluation often severely weakened domestic currencies, and domestic prices spiraled in turn, leading to rampant inflation. Privatization often resulted in a net loss of jobs, as new owners in the private sector laid off workers to try to reduce costs. And cuts on government expenditures slashed services to the citizens often most in need. Finally, corrupt governments squandered or embezzled the loans, ensuring that future generations would be held hostage to crippling debt loads.

Women were particularly vulnerable to these reforms, which increased their workload, not only in terms of their paid work responsibilities but also their unpaid responsibilities in the home. Women tried to increase their paid work to compensate for rising male unemployment and increased cost of living. In addition, women's unpaid labor increased to compensate for cutbacks in public services. For example, women assumed the responsibility of caring for sick relatives, who previously might have received care from a doctor or hospital. In addition, women had to find ways to substitute for the food and clothing the household could no longer afford.[59] In sum, the financial backlash when fragile economies in newly opened societies fail creates new stresses and strains for women, who must often bear the brunt of financial dislocation.

As the global recession continues, it looks as if women will once again bear the brunt of the social costs of financial collapse. Rising food prices, spiraling unemployment, and slashed social services are just a few of the manifestations of a larger economic meltdown. Yet, because women have been primarily affected by trends such as the dramatic rise in food prices, they have also been at the forefront of protests. In April 2008, more than 1,000 women protested the lack of accountability and action from their government regarding the food crisis by banging empty pots and pans. Similarly, women in Haiti protested by making biscuits out of mud, salt, and vegetable shortening. These protests were not isolated phenomena; in the first months of 2008, there were protests in over 34 countries over the spiraling costs of food.[60] As the implications of the U.S.-led recession deepen, so too will the gendered impact, as well as the response to the crisis.

ADVANCING WOMEN'S EQUALITY

Women's economic status in the developing world is slowly improving, in that a higher percentage of women have access to the paid labor force, and thus to the advantages that income can bring to their personal well-being and their families. Yet, women are also more likely to be trapped in low-paying, unstable, and insecure jobs, leaving them mired in poverty. It is harder for them to translate their labor into paid work, and their paid work into secure, living-wage incomes. Development agencies are aware of the gendered nature of these economic inequalities; however, it is often easier to recognize the problem than to design an effective solution. A good place to start is identifying the reasons why women's inequalities exist; if we can address some of these underlying factors, then perhaps it will be possible to change employment patterns. However, there is no single reason why women often come out as second-class citizens with regard to economic development. Depressingly, the World Bank estimates that only about one fifth of the wage gap can be explained by gender differences in education, work experience, or job characteristics; rather, they argue, the pervasive power of prejudice and discrimination against women accounts for much of women's second-class economic status.[61] Other issues, such as the unequal division of labor in the household, further impact women's abilities to gain equality in the workforce. This suggests that the target of development policy needs to be focused on society at large, rather than solely on women.

However, education still is a factor in explaining women's unequal access to economic resources, and according to the World Bank's World Development Report 2000/2001, closing the gender gap in education would significantly increase and, in some instances, double economic growth in sub-Saharan Africa, South Asia, the Middle East, and North Africa.[62] As a result, as we will discuss in greater detail in Chapter 10, development agencies have focused on increasing women's access to education, which is still quite low.

Another factor that inhibits gender equality is access to the appropriate resources, such as land and credit. In particular, land titling is particularly problematic. Women are often barred from owning the title to land, even when they are its primary users. This means that they cannot use the land as collateral for credit, a strategy available to many male farmers trying to expand their business. In addition, women's access to land is often based on their marital status; as a result, unmarried and divorced women are rarely named on title deeds. The World Bank has begun to address this issue by sponsoring a pilot project in north central Vietnam that gives both women and men rights to use land. In two rural communities in Nghe An province, land tenure certificates for households are being reissued with the names of both the wife and the husband, allowing both to take advantage of the opportunities that such property rights can bring to the well-being of the rural economy.[63]

In addition, women are barred from other forms of borrowing and thus cannot start small businesses that would help stimulate economic growth, not only for them, but also for their country's economy. One popular solution to this issue has been the funding of microcredit programs, which give very small loans primarily to women who are too poor, and thus lack collateral or traditional risk indicators, to qualify for traditional bank loans. Microcredit programs have shown some impressive results; many programs not only demonstrated that the poor were creditworthy in that they could repay their loans but also showed that the loans can catalyze wider impacts, such as female empowerment, increased use of contraceptives by women, and better health outcomes for children of borrowers. In addition, the ideological premise of microcredit—that the poor have underutilized skills that, if fostered with small amounts of funding, can be used to lift them out of poverty—appealed to a wide range of development specialists and political actors on the left and the right. As a result, microcredit has become extremely popular with development agencies as a poverty reduction strategy, and organizations such as the World Bank, the UN, and the U.S. Agency for International Development have devoted millions of dollars to funding microcredit projects as a way to reduce not only women's economic vulnerability but also their higher levels of social exclusion. Despite some impressive results, microcredit is no panacea, however. Critics warn that alone it is not sufficient to overcome the many social, political, and economic obstacles that the poorest confront on a daily basis. In addition, others warn that the focus on women, although important, may not be as empowering as supporters claim; men sometimes force their wives to take out loans only so that they can take control of the money themselves. Further, in some cases, a rise in household income was accompanied by the abandonment of more nutritious foods in favor of more prestigious, but less nourishing, prepackaged Western foods, which hold higher status in many communities.[64] Nonetheless, microcredit remains an inspirational example of the implementation of an idea that was once deemed unrealistic, unworkable, and untranslatable as a widely used development strategy. The accompanying text box on Muhammad Yunus and the Grameen Bank describes one of the best-known examples of microcredit.

Men in Movement: Muhammad Yunus and the Grameen Bank

Muhammad Yunus, founder of the Grameen Bank and co-winner of the 2006 Nobel Peace Prize, became an unlikely banker in 1976. Born to a middle-class family in Bangladesh and educated in the United States, Yunus returned to Bangladesh in 1972, where he soon became head of the Economics Department at Chittagong University. Increasingly aware of the gap between the lofty economic theories he taught in the classroom and the impoverished status of millions of citizens of his own country, Yunus became involved in local community efforts to stimulate economic development. But his plans soon changed when he interviewed an impoverished woman in a rural village in Bangladesh and learned that she lacked the 22 cents she needed to buy bamboo to weave stools. As a result, she was caught in a cycle of continuous poverty; she had to borrow the cash from a moneylender to buy her own raw materials. She would then sell her bamboo stool back to the moneylender, for a profit of about 2 cents, ensuring that she could never escape the vicious cycle of poverty. Yet, women such as her, desperate for credit at a fair price, could never get it from traditional banks, who saw poor people, with their lack of assets, as loan risks. Professor Yunus responded by loaning $27 from his own pocket to a group of 42 villagers, who repaid their loans. Realizing that serving as a personal banker to the local village was not a long-term solution, Professor Yunus set out to design a banking system that could loan small amounts of money to the poor. In 1977, he founded the Grameen Bank to make loans to poor, primarily female Bangladeshis. By the end of 2008, the Grameen Bank had grown from a pilot project to meet the needs of local villagers to a bank with 2,535 branches, working in 83,343 villages, providing services to 7.61 million borrowers, 97 percent of them women. Since its inception, the bank has loaned out over $7 billion, with a repayment rate of over 98 percent. Yunus proved that one could make very small loans (as of 2008, the average loan size was just under $350) to the very poor, the same group that traditional banks had deemed not creditworthy.

What makes Grameen Bank distinctive? One of the main things is its creative use of incentives to encourage repayment, given the absence of traditional sources of leverage, such as collateral. Yunus devised a system whereby borrowers were divided into support groups of five members. Each group is loaned money, but the whole group is denied further credit if one person defaults. Social pressure from one's peers replaces the monetary pressure of forfeiting on assets in this system. And small repayments are made on a weekly, rather than monthly or quarterly, basis to encourage clients to keep up a steady, incremental habit of repayment. Another distinctive feature is the bank's focus on women, they comprise 97 percent of the Bank's clientele. Yunus made a conscious decision to focus on women; not only are they in greater need of assistance, he reasoned, because of their secondary status in society, but they also are more likely to repay their loans. And finally, the bank is more than a financial program; it also asks that members abide by what are known as the "Sixteen Decisions," a set of principles designed to advance overall levels of well-being among women and their families. For example, women must promise to strive to keep their families small, to grow nutritious food, to educate their children, and to decline to participate in the dowry system. While the bank does not enforce these decisions, nonetheless it sees its loans as a small part of a larger process of changing the way that women and men live their lives in Bangladesh.

Yunus also helped expand the bank's activities, creating a number of other socially conscious enterprises under the Grameen name. For example, Grameen Bank established a program, discussed in the opening of this chapter, to bring telephones to distant villages, loaning money to almost 139,000 poor women in rural areas to pay for the phones. The bank also established Grameenphone, the leading telecommunications service provider in the country. Grameen has also expanded the reach of its clientele, starting a program for beggars.

The tireless work of Yunus and the Grameen Bank was recognized by the Nobel Prize Committee, who awarded them the Nobel Peace Prize in recognition for "their efforts to create economic and social development from below. Lasting peace cannot be achieved unless large population groups find ways in which to break out of poverty." And the larger idea of microcredit, or very small loans to the poor, has become a popular poverty-fighting strategy, funded by development agencies and other nonprofit organizations in over 130 countries around the world. And it all started with the effort to figure out a solution for one disempowered female basket weaver in the village of Jobra, Bangladesh, in 1972.

The Self-Employed Women's Association (SEWA) of India is another example of an organization that works to improve the lives of poor, self-employed women workers, who, as mentioned previously in the chapter, work without the stability of salaries, benefits, insurance, or, in most cases, representation. Founded as an independent trade union in 1972, SEWA emerged when a small group of migrant women working as cart-pullers in India's vast textile industry approached the women's wing of the Textile Labour Association, India's largest and oldest union of textile workers, to ask for help in finding housing. At the time, they were living in the streets without shelter. Ela Bhatt, the head of the Women's Wing with the union, went with the women to the areas where they were living to assess the situation, and there she met with another group of women who were working as head-loaders, carrying loads of clothes between the wholesale and retail markets. Collectively, they discussed their jobs, their low and erratic wages, and their larger problems with translating their capacity for work into stable, wage-paying employment. The ensuing proposal to form an association of their own was a novel idea at the time, for the self-employed had no real history of organizing, because unlike other unions, they had no recognized employer. SEWA argued that a union was necessary to promote the unity of workers, rather than fight against an employer. In April 1972, the union was born. In addition to its efforts to improve the working conditions of its members, SEWA has expanded to provide services to its members such as savings and credit, health care, child care, insurance, legal aid, capacity building, and communication services. Like the Grameen Bank and its Sixteen Decisions, which emphasize the need to reinvest higher incomes into better life decisions for the borrowers and their families, SEWA emphasizes the importance of its members' abilities to answer positively to 11 questions that assess women's abilities to lead secure lives, not only for themselves, but also for their families. The questions ask whether the women's income has increased and whether they have obtained food and nutrition, are safeguarding their health, are obtaining child care, are improving their housing, or are increasing their literacy, for example. Like the Grameen Bank, SEWA sees increased employment opportunities for women as a means to a healthier, more autonomous life, rather than an end expressed solely in higher income.

As we discussed earlier in this chapter, many women, desperate for increased earning opportunities, are either pushed or pulled, often against their will, into the sex industry. While poverty and lack of opportunity help create a supply of sex workers, ever-increasing levels of demand (often from the industrialized world), combined with lax local laws and corrupt officials, seriously compound the problem.

And finally, women have been at the forefront of organizing to protest the negative human impact of environmental degradation. For example, the Chipko (literally "embrace") movement was started by Indian villagers, primarily women, in the 1970s and 1980s to protest the impact of deforestation on their livelihoods. The work of activists such as Wangari Maathai, featured in a previous textbox, also demonstrates how environmental protection can go hand in hand with social and economic progress, for women as well as men.

CONCLUSION

Even though women are entering the labor force in increasing numbers, they are paid less than men and are segregated into low-skill, low-paying jobs. The reasons for women's differing status in the economy are varied; persistent cultural values, discriminatory practices, and undereducation are just a few reasons women are underutilized in some areas of economic production and overutilized in others. As the global economy becomes increasingly interdependent, women have become the lynchpin of the economy. As wage laborers, they fuel the global economy by working primarily in low-skilled, low-wage jobs outsourced from the West. Alternatively, they travel to Western industrialized nations, willing to work for low pay, in search of better lives. In their traditional roles as wives and mothers, they hold the family together in times of economic crises. While women have improved their economic status, they have yet to reach any form of gender parity with men. Yet, we know that there are enormous dividends to be reaped from increasing women's participation in the labor force. It can enable women to provide food, clothing, shelter, and educational opportunities, not only for themselves but also for their families. And it can also engender increased social status, influence, and a heightened personal sense of empowerment and can ultimately shift and redefine the division of labor in traditional households.

FOR MORE INFORMATION

Video and Multimedia

EIU Women's Economic Opportunity Index. (2011). http://ideas.economist.com/video/we-did-it. Presented at The Economist's World in 2011 event, this animation provides key data from The Economist Intelligence Unit's Women's Economic Opportunity Index, the first of its kind.

G. Ferraro. (2000). *Sixteen Decisions*, http://www.aerial-productions.com/16d_syn.html. *Sixteen Decisions* is a documentary film that explores the impact of the Grameen Bank on impoverished women in Bangladesh.

Ross Kauffman and Zana Briski. (2004). *Born into Brothels*, http://www.kids-with-cameras .org/bornintobrothels. This film won the 77th annual Academy Award for Best Documentary Feature. A tribute to the resiliency of childhood and the restorative power of art, *Born into Brothels* is a portrait of several unforgettable children who live in the red-light district of Calcutta, where their mothers work as prostitutes. Zana Briski, a New York-based photographer, gave each one of the children a camera and taught him or her to look at the world with new eyes.

Leslie Chang. (2008). *Factory Girls*. Google@Authors. http://www.youtube.com/watch?v= NhcqoxNhrSY&feature=youtube_gdata_player. Leslie T. Chang, a former correspondent for the *Wall Street Journal* in Beijing, tells the story of these workers primarily through the lives of two young women, whom she follows over the course of 3 years as they attempt to rise from the assembly lines of Dongguan, an industrial city in China's Pearl River Delta.

Sharmeen Obaid. (2011). *Saving Face*. http://sharmeenobaidfilms.com/2011/08/saving-face-film/. *Saving Face* tells the stories of two acid-attack survivors, Zakia and Rukhsana, their arduous attempts to bring their assailants to justice, and the charitable work of London-based, Pakistani-born plastic surgeon Dr. Mohammad Jawad, who strives to help these women put this horrific act behind them and move on with their lives.

Readings

Franck and A. Spehar. (2010). *Women's Labour Migration* (2010). http://www.ilo.org/public/libdoc/jobcrisis/download/Womens%20labour%20migration,%20WIDE,%20Oct%202010.pdf. The report *Women's Labour Migration in the Context of Globalisation* offers an introduction to important contemporary political analysis on the influence of globalization on women's work, mobility, and empowerment.

International Labour Organization. (2010). *Women in Labour Markets: Measuring Progress and Identifying Challenges.* http://www.ilo.org/empelm/pubs/WCMS_123835/lang--en/index.htm. The report focuses on the relationship of women to labor markets and compares employment outcomes for men and women to the best degree possible, given the latest available labor market indicators from the ILO Key Indicators of the Labour Market. The main findings highlight a continuing gender disparity in terms of both opportunities and quality of employment.

International Labour Organization. (2012). *Global Unemployment Outlook.* http://www.ilo.org/global/publications/books/global-employment-trends/lang--en/index.htm. According to the 2012 ILO report on global employment trends, the world faces the "urgent challenge" of creating 600 million productive jobs over the next decade in order to generate sustainable growth and maintain social cohesion. The link offers a video clip, an interactive website, and a report on the latest global and regional information and projections on several indicators of the labor market, including unemployment, gender, youth employment, and working poverty.

International Poverty Center, Report on Gender Equality, www.ipc-undp.org/pub/IPCPovertyInFocus13.pdf. This collection of articles should contribute to a better understanding of the importance of recognizing the crucial role of gender inequalities as barriers to economic and social development, and thus of undertaking policy and institutional reforms that will more effectively reduce poverty and social injustice.

United Nations Development Programme. *Corruption, Accountability and Gender: Understanding the Connection.* http://www.undp.org/content/undp/en/home/librarypage/democratic-governance/anti-corruption/corruption-accountability-and-gender-understanding-the-connection.html. Understanding corruption's linkages to gender equality issues and how it impacts women's empowerment is part of the process of advancing women's rights and understanding gender dimensions of democratic governance. This report from UNDP and UNIFEM aims to enhance the effectiveness of women and men, particularly those in public office, when advancing a gender equality agenda.

United Nations. (2009). *2009 World Survey on the Role of Women in Development.* http://www.un.org/womenwatch/daw/ws2009/. The World Survey on the Role of Women in Development, presented every 5 years, is the flagship publication of the UN's Division for the Advancement of Women. The 2009 theme was "Women's Control Over Economic Resources and Access to Financial Resources, Including Microfinance."

United Nations. (2012). *Global Women's Submission for the Rio+20 Zero-Draft Document.* http://www.uncsd2012.org/rio20/index.php?page=view&nr=574&type=230&menu=38. The Women's Major Group was developed by over 70 women's organizations from over 40 countries worldwide. It participated in Rio+20, the UN Conference on Sustainable Development in Rio de Janeiro, Brazil, in June 2012.

United Nations. (2011). *Prevent, Combat, Protect: Human Trafficking.* http://www.unwomen.org/publications/prevent-combat-protect-human-trafficking/. This is a joint UNHCR, OHCHR, UNICEF, UNODC, ILO, and UN Women commentary on selected articles of the EU Directive on preventing and combating trafficking in human beings and protecting victims.

U.S. Department of State. (2011). *Trafficking in Persons Report 2011.* http://www.state.gov/j/tip/rls/tiprpt/2011/. This is the U.S. Government's principal diplomatic tool to engage foreign governments on human trafficking. The 2011 report calls for "a Decade of Delivery," building on the progress of the last 10 years and fulfilling country commitments to and implement legal, policy, and programmatic obligations.

World Bank Group. (2011). *Gender Action Plan Four-Year Progress Report.* http://web.worldbank.org/WBSITE/EXTERNAL/TOPICS/EXTGENDER/0,,contentMDK:22148542~pagePK:210058~piPK:210062~theSitePK:336868,00.html. From 2007 to 2011, the World Bank Group launched an action plan to improve women's economic opportunity. The 4-year plan, Gender Equality as Smart Economics, invested in the improvement of women's access to jobs, land rights, financial services, agricultural inputs, and infrastructure.

Organizations and Websites

Association for Women's Rights in Development (AWID), http://www.awid.org. This international feminist membership organization is committed to achieving gender equality, sustainable development, and women's human rights.

Coalition Against Trafficking in Women, http://www.catwinternational.org. This NGO promotes women's human rights. It works internationally to combat sexual exploitation in all its forms, especially prostitution and trafficking in women and children, in particular girls.

Global Alliance Against Traffic in Women, http://www.gaatw.org. This is an alliance of 106 NGOs from Africa, Asia, Europe, Latin American countries, and North America. The Secretariat is based in Bangkok, Thailand, and coordinates the activities of the Alliance, collects and disseminates information, and advocates on behalf of the Alliance at regional and international levels.

Grameen Bank, http://www.grameen-info.org. Grameen Bank has reversed conventional banking practice by removing the need for collateral and has created a banking system based on mutual trust, accountability, participation, and creativity. It provides credit to the poorest of the poor in rural Bangladesh, without any collateral. Credit is used as a cost-effective weapon to fight poverty, and it serves as a catalyst in the overall improvement of socioeconomic conditions of the poor, who have been kept outside the banking orbit on the grounds that they are poor and hence not bankable.

Green Belt Movement, http://greenbeltmovement.org. The Green Belt Movement was founded by Professor Wangari Maathai in 1977 under the auspices of the National Council of Women of Kenya to respond to the needs of rural Kenyan women who reported that their streams were drying up, their food supply was less secure, and they had to walk further and further to obtain firewood for fuel and fencing. The Green Belt Movement encouraged the women to work together to grow seedlings and plant trees to bind the soil, store rainwater, provide food and firewood, and receive a small monetary token for their work.

International Labour Organization, Bureau for Gender Equality, http://www.ilo.org/gender/lang--en/index.htm. The Bureau for Gender Equality coordinates the global ILO Gender Network, which brings together gender specialists and gender focal points at headquarters and in the field offices.

International Labour Organization, Women's Entrepreneurship Development Program, http://www.ilo.org/empent/areas/womens-entrepreneurship-development-wed/lang--en/index.htm. This program works on enhancing economic opportunities for women by carrying out affirmative actions in support of women starting, formalizing, and growing their enterprises, and by mainstreaming gender equality issues into the ILO's work in enterprise development.

Self-Employed Women's Association, http://www.sewa.org. SEWA, a trade union registered in 1972, supports poor, self-employed female workers who earn a living through their own labor or small businesses.

UN Statistics Division, Demographic and Social Statistics, http://unstats.un.org/unsd/demographic/products/Worldswomen/Gender%20statistics%20sources.htm. This site provides links to gender statistics sources.

UN Development Programme, Gender and Poverty Reduction, http://www.undp.org/poverty/genpov.htm

Women Rio+20. *Women's Priorities for Sustainable Development.* http://www.womenrio20.org/. This website belongs to the Women's Major Group for the Rio+20 Conference and covers their key issues.

9

Women and Health

Abeba Zerehun lives in Ethiopia. She got married at the age of 15 to a man whom her parents chose for her, and whom she met for the first time on her wedding day. She left school in the seventh grade to start her new life as a married woman, and she became pregnant within a year. When it came time to deliver, she labored unsuccessfully for many hours at home in her village with her mother and husband by her side, until she was eventually taken to a hospital, where they removed her baby, which had already died. But Abeba's pain was not over; she soon discovered that during her long and difficult labor, she had developed a fistula, or hole between her birth passage and one or more of her internal organs. Left incontinent and unable to bear more children, her husband, who married another woman, abandoned Abeba; after that, she faced a future of physical disability, shame, and destitution. However, she traveled from her village in southern Ethiopia to the Addis Ababa Fistula Hospital in the capital, which provides free fistula repair surgery to about 1,200 women every year. When she returns home, she hopes to resume her education so she can someday become a doctor to help girls, such as her, who have developed fistulas.[1]

Abeba's story is, unfortunately, not unique. Fistulas, which rarely happen any longer in the industrialized West, afflict approximately 100,000 women in Ethiopia alone and approximately 2 million untreated women in the developing world. They occur when women are in difficult labor; the baby becomes lodged in the narrow birth canal, and the resulting pressure cuts off blood to vital tissues. As a result, a hole forms between two areas of the body that should normally be separated, such as between the vagina and bladder or sometimes between the rectum and vagina. Not only do the babies die during labor, but the women become incontinent for life and are unable to bear more children. The women often become societal outcasts because they are perceived by their communities to be unfit to fulfill their traditional roles as wives and mothers. In addition, they are shunned because they are often severely disabled from the injuries they sustained during labor and are unclean as a result of their incontinence. Many live the rest of their lives sequestered in their huts, with rags stuffed between their legs to catch their urine and feces. But fistulas are also entirely treatable, which is why they disappeared as a medical issue in the wealthy, industrialized West nearly a hundred years ago. Access to trained medical staff who can perform cesarean sections, or even the $300 operation to repair fistulas, would dramatically improve women's lives. Yet, despite the estimated 2 million women living with fistulas throughout the developing world, the world capacity to treat them is estimated at 6,500 fistula repair surgeries annually.[2] At the end of the chapter, you'll read about the inspiring work of Dr. Catherine Hamlin and the work she has done to increase this capacity.

This high incidence of fistulas points to the larger problems that women such as Abeba face. For example, the life expectancy for a girl born in Ethiopia is expected to be 59 years. Although we don't have sex-segregated data, she might be one of the 20 percent of babies born with a low birthweight. By the time she reaches age 5, it is probable (51 percent) that she will be suffering from moderate to severe stunting as a result of undernourishment. Thanks to the Millennium Development Goals, one of which targets sex parity in primary education, she is increasingly likely to be in school. Nonetheless, the effects of this are slow to trickle down. While school enrollments are up, female literacy still lags behind male literacy: literacy rates for girls are 33 percent (compared to 56 percent for boys) and men are more than twice as likely to be literate as women. The transitions to adulthood come early for girls in Ethiopia. One in four girls is married by the age of 15, and one in two girls is married by 18. A woman can expect to give birth to four children, not counting the ones who will die during pregnancy or will not survive the first 5 years of life (although this rate is lower than it was a decade ago), perhaps because an estimated 15 percent of women use contraception. A woman's lifetime risk of dying from childbirth is one in forty. In part, this is because of the chronic undervaluation of girls in society; underfed from birth, their growth is stunted and they will have difficulty, particularly if they start bearing children at a young age, pushing them down and out of the birth canal. Also, only about 6 percent of births are accompanied by a skilled attendant. Even worse, Ethiopian women have internalized their lesser status; according to surveys from UNICEF, women are more likely than men (81 percent vs. 52 percent) to think that a husband is justified in hitting or beating his wife under certain circumstances.[3] In sum, the combination of poverty; early marriage; a lack of rights, independence, education, and access to resources; and a generally low standing within society robs women of the ability to make decisions about how to live long and healthy lives.

Women around the world face serious impediments to good health and bodily well-being. In this chapter, we will focus on several issues that threaten women's health: inadequate access to family planning, maternal care, and other reproductive health services; societal preferences for boy children; and the spread of HIV/AIDS and its impact on women. In closing, we look at international efforts to improve women's quality of life.

THE STATUS OF WOMEN'S HEALTH

Living a long and healthy life is now seen as an integral component of human development; the United Nations (UN) uses longevity as one of its three measurements (along with literacy/enrollment figures and gross domestic product) to rank countries in its Human Development Index. This index, combined with many other measurements and statistics relating to women's health, indicates that men and women live different lives. In some ways, women are biologically built to survive. Women outlive men in almost every country in the world and, on average, live about 3 years longer than men. In countries and cultures where children's access to resources such as food and medical care does not differ greatly by sex, males are more vulnerable both before and after birth. Worldwide, more girls are born and more boys die in the early years of life. Women are hardier and more resilient to external crises. However, while women on average live longer lives, they are less healthy. This, in part, is because culturally, females are often undervalued in society. As a result, they are often poorly fed, nourished, and nurtured, whether as mothers or as daughters (see photo 8.1).

Why should we be concerned about women's health? From a human rights perspective, women's unequal status should be a source of concern. In addition, however, improving women's health is important, not only because women, like all citizens of the world, deserve to live long and healthy lives, but also because healthy

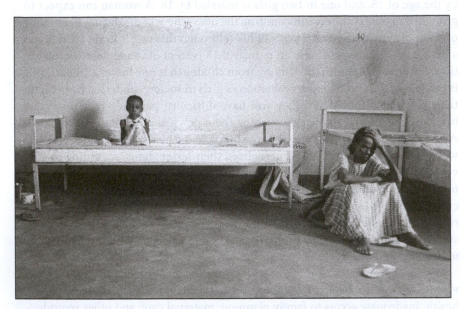

Although women live longer lives than men, they are often less healthy, usually because they have been malnourished since childhood. Nor do they have access to adequate medical treatment and facilities in many developing countries. Here, a little girl is treated in the hospital of the Ethiopian city of Kabridahar for malnutrition and tuberculosis.
SOURCE: JOEL ROBINE/AFP/Getty Images.

women have a significant impact on the world around them. Because women often form the heart of the family by cooking the food, caring for sick relatives, and maintaining the household, healthy women are critical for raising healthy children. In particular, when women die in childbirth, from AIDS, or from other health complications, the children left behind are more likely to suffer health problems, fall into poverty, or even die. The story of Fatima, a mother of nine from Afghanistan, illustrates how a mother's death usually has dire consequences for her family and her community. When Fatima became pregnant with her tenth child, family resources were stretched to the breaking point; the family was already barely surviving on the husband's salary as a security guard. The family's stability and health plummeted precipitously when Fatima died giving birth to twin boys, a not uncommon fate for women giving birth in Afghanistan, where a shattered health-care system multiplies women's risks to astronomical levels. Fatima's hospital expenses put her husband deeper in debt, so he took their 13-year-old son out of school to work. The twins, who survived, were sickly, often ill with diarrhea or acute respiratory infections, the most common killers of infants worldwide. As a result, their 11-year-old daughter was taken out of school to care for them. Nonetheless, the smaller twin died at 7 months of a respiratory infection. The father, still mired in debt and poverty, married off his oldest daughter when she turned 13. Pregnant by the age of 15, her body struggled to deliver her baby successfully; her baby was born brain-damaged, and she was left with a fistula (described at the beginning of the chapter). Her husband abandoned her, and she had to return to her father's home.[4] Unfortunately, this story, while harrowing, is all too common in the developing world. Why do so many women like Fatima have so few options in terms of determining their own health? Let's now turn to looking at the issue of women and reproductive health.

Women and Reproductive Health

Carrying, delivering, and nurturing a baby should be a joyous event in any woman's life. Yet, for millions of women around the world, the time from conception to the month following the birth of a child can be the most dangerous period of a woman's life. Maternal mortality, defined as the death of a pregnant woman during her pregnancy or within 4 days of pregnancy termination, remains a leading cause of death for women in the countries of the developing world. Every day, approximately 800 women die from preventable causes related to pregnancy and childbirth; in 2010, this added up to 287,000 women around the world. Almost all of these deaths occurred in the developing world, with over half in sub-Saharan Africa and almost one third in South Asia. Because women in developing countries have, on average, many more pregnancies than women in developed countries, their lifetime risk of death due to pregnancy is higher. For example, in the countries of sub-Saharan Africa, a woman might spend two thirds of her time between the ages of 17 and 35 pregnant or lactating. Thus, maternal mortality is an ever-present possibility for women, who, if they had been born in a wealthier country, would likely be enjoying the healthiest years of their lives. Instead, persistent malnutrition, early marriage and pregnancy, inadequate education, and lack of access

to resources ensure that women in the developing world have a profoundly different experience of birth. This difference is stark; a woman's lifetime risk of maternal
death—the probability that a 15-year-old girl will eventually die from a maternal
cause—is 1 in 3,800 in developed countries versus 1 in 150 in developing countries. Girls under 15 are particularly at risk, and in most developing countries,
complications of pregnancy and childbirth are the leading cause of death among
adolescent girls.[5] As we discussed, their bodies, already stunted from years of malnutrition, are not sufficiently developed to consistently push the baby through a
small birth canal. Depressingly, in the Sudan, a war-torn country, a 15-year-old
girl has a better chance of dying in childbirth than of finishing school. Even these
brutal statistics and examples mask the more far-reaching health risks associated
with pregnancy for millions of the world's women; for each woman who dies as a
result of complications, many more women survive but suffer from serious disability or physical damage, as the opening narrative of this chapter illustrated. The
UN has made reducing maternal mortality a key element of the Millennium Development Goals discussed in Chapter 7, but as we shall discuss toward the end of
the chapter, while progress has been made, it has been at a much slower rate than
some of the other Millennium Goals. Table 9.1 shows how women in different
countries fare in terms of maternal mortality.

A variety of factors influence the quality of women's reproductive health.
Family planning is a critical first step in ensuring safe motherhood. Ideally, families, and women in particular, should be able to plan how many children they want
and when they want them. There are compelling reasons for why family planning,
when centered on women and their needs, benefits not only women but also their
families and communities. For one, maternal health improves when women can

Table 9.1 Estimates of Lifetime Risk of Maternal Death*

REGION	LIFETIME RISK 1 IN:
Arab States	220
Asia and the Pacific	270
Eastern Europe and Central Asia	1,700
Latin America and the Caribbean	520
Sub-Saharan Africa	40
More developed countries	3,800
Less developed countries	150
Least developed countries	52
World	180

*IN 2007, A JOINT UN AGENCY WORKING GROUP BEGAN USING A NEW METHOD
OF CALCULATING AND ESTIMATING MATERNAL MORTALITY WORLDWIDE. THIS
METHODOLOGY TAKES INTO ACCOUNT BOTH THE PROBABILITY OF GETTING PREG-
NANT AND THE PROBABILITY OF DYING AS A RESULT OF PREGNANCY, CUMULATED
ACROSS A WOMAN'S REPRODUCTIVE YEARS. THIS IS CALLED THE LIFETIME RISK OF
MATERNAL MORTALITY.

SOURCE: WHO, UNICEF, UNFPA, and the World Bank. "Trends in Maternal
Mortality: 1990–2010. World Health Organization, 2012."

control the timing, spacing, and total number of their children. High-risk pregnancies are often those that come too early, too frequently, or too late in life, and maternal mortality drops significantly when births are spaced out to at least 15 months. Also, increased family planning reduces women's recourse to abortion, particularly in the developing world, where abortions are largely illegal and/or unsafe. As a result, almost all abortion-related deaths occur in developing countries. Further, better timing and spacing of births reduces the risks posed to the millions of women who face illness or disability from pregnancy-related complications every year. Focusing on better timing and spacing of births also has dramatic effects on child health and survival. In some countries, infants born less than 2 years apart have almost twice the risk of dying than those born farther apart. In fact, if women in developing countries could space their births 3 years apart, mortality rates for infants and for children under 5 would fall by 24 percent and 35 percent, respectively. Imagine if something as simple as family planning could reduce the deaths of more than 3 million newborns every year, and the stillbirths of an additional 2.6 million babies![6] Better spacing could also improve perennial problems such as stunting and underweight children, since parents have longer to focus on the nutritional needs of each child. Because families with more children have a risk of falling into poverty, having fewer children allows parents to invest in adequate nutrition, housing, and education for the whole family.

And finally, empowering women to make choices about their own fertility is an important step in raising their status in society. Women who have the ability to decide the timing and number of children they want are also in a stronger position to negotiate other decisions in their households as well as ones that involve how they want to lead their lives.[7] This right, not just for women but also for all couples, has been affirmed numerous times at the international level. In 1968, the UN International Human Rights Conference declared family planning to be a human right, and this declaration has been revisited and reemphasized at numerous international conferences, such as the UN-sponsored 1994 International Conference on Population and Development in Cairo, Egypt. As we will discuss later, one of the biggest shifts in international family planning efforts has been to place women and their choices at the center of family planning, rather than as objects that need to have their fertility "controlled."

Worldwide, women, when they are able to choose, are choosing to have fewer children; women in the developing world are currently having half as many children as they did in the 1960s.[8] Modern contraceptive use by married women aged 15 to 49 in the developing world also rose from nearly nonexistent levels in the 1960s to roughly 55 percent in 2009. Yet millions of women and families still lack access to all of the goods and services associated with family planning and reproductive health; an estimated 222 million women who want to delay or cease childbearing (about one in six women of reproductive age) are in need of effective contraception (methods such as withdrawal and periodic abstinence are not considered effective). This overall figure is spread unevenly throughout the world; unmet need in the 69 poorest countries accounts for 73 percent of all unmet need in the developing world. Also, unmet need is much higher in Africa and Western Asia.

Overall, the impact of this unmet need is significant; the UN Population Fund (UNFPA) estimates that in 2012 80 million unintended pregnancies will occur in the developing world. These unintended pregnancies will result in 30 million unplanned births, 40 million abortions, and 10 million miscarriages.[9] Many of these abortions end up in death for women, as they are often illegal and unsafe.

Women's limited access to family planning services is in part the result of undersupply and underfunding of family planning services in the developing world. There is also still a dearth of family planning information in many countries; many women in the developing world who do not want more children but are not using contraception report that it is because they believe they are not at risk of getting pregnant. They believe they are too young, are too old, are nursing, or are practicing what they believe to be an effective form of birth control (such as early withdrawal). In addition, women may not be presented with a full range of contraceptive options, so that they may match a method with their needs. And despite the label "family planning," this is still primarily women's work; fewer than 5 percent of couples in the majority of developing countries use male methods of birth control, such as the condom, withdrawal (which is already ineffective), or vasectomy.[10]

In addition, women's limited access to family planning services is symptomatic of a much larger problem—women's lack of power and choice within the household. Although a woman's role as a reproducer has been a source of status, it has also largely been a reason for her disempowerment, and in truth, despite much of the rhetoric about the essential importance of mothers to society, millions of women around the world lack the freedom to control whether, when, how many, and under what circumstances they will bear children. In some parts of the world, women's bodies are still perceived, and in some circumstances legally recognized, as being the property or under the jurisdiction of their husbands.

Women may need to get their husband's permission to use contraceptives, pursue sterilization, or receive an abortion. Even if women are legally free to pursue their own reproductive choices, cultural norms, which place decision-making power in the hands of the male head of the household, may prohibit this. As one woman in Pakistan stated, "In our home, the household head decides about the attainment of healthcare. If he is not home, we have to wait." And in some countries, such as Taliban-controlled Afghanistan, women may have extremely limited freedom of movement, which hinders their ability to seek medical help. Thus, often it is the husband who ultimately decides whether the woman will gain access to family planning services, or when and how the couple will have sexual relations. This is particularly problematic for many girls who are married off at a young age and are unable to exercise choice over these issues. Further, male partners often resist the adoption of contraceptive methods because of the fear that access to birth control will lead to the woman's promiscuity and potentially will encourage her to have sex for pleasure with other men as opposed to for procreation with her husband. Other cultures equate multiple offspring with male virility, or with impotence if multiple pregnancies in as many years is not the result. The pervasive belief that women should remain virgins until marriage also inhibits the spread of information about various family planning methods, since girls are often sheltered from this information under the fear, again, that it will lead to promiscuity. In sum, lack of power over making decisions about reproductive choice is also embedded in larger patterns in which women have little control over making decisions about their lives, whether it involves the timing and spacing of their own children, going to the doctor, purchasing medication, buying better food for their families, or making other decisions about the household's economic resources. And gendered inequalities in other areas of their lives limit their abilities to make choices about their health. For example, women are less likely to be literate than men; educated women generally have more access to information about family planning.

Once women become pregnant, many lack access to adequate medical care through the pregnancy and birth and in the immediate weeks following the birth. It is encouraging that more women in the developing world have at least one visit with a doctor, nurse, or midwife during their pregnancy, but that number is still only 80 percent. Further, a significant proportion of women deliver without trained medical attendants. As of 2010, only 65 percent of women in developing countries deliver with the assistance of a trained midwife or doctor, and even less do so in a hospital or other medical facility.[11] In fact, five complications, which are largely medically preventable, account for 70 percent of maternal deaths: hemorrhage (25 percent), infection (15 percent), unsafe abortions (13 percent), eclampsia (a condition resulting from high blood pressure; 12 percent), and obstructed labor (8 percent). In addition, over 20 percent of women die as a result of diseases that are aggravated by pregnancy, such as malaria, anemia, tuberculosis, and HIV/AIDS.[12]

In part, women lack access to medical care because there are few trained medical staff and facilities in the developing world. For example, there is a global shortage of 4 million health-care workers, which is most severe in rural parts of developing countries.[13] But a variety of other issues impede women's abilities to obtain medical services and care before, during, and after delivery, even if that care is available. For example, maternal survival rates often depend on the distance a woman must travel, and the time it takes, to reach skilled emergency care. Yet, many women do not or cannot seek care because they may have to get permission from family members, may not recognize the emergency, or may fear hospital practices. For example, in Bolivia, indigenous traditions dictate that women give birth at home with only family members to help. When Albina Chambe, age 15, went into labor, her fiancé wanted to take her to a hospital. But Albina's mother had delivered 13 children at home, without medically trained birth attendants, and felt that Albina should follow tradition. After unsuccessful labor at home, Albina's fiancé helped her hike to the nearest dirt road, where they spent more than a day's pay on a taxi to the hospital. Fortunately, she eventually delivered a healthy baby and suffered no long-term consequences herself. A variety of factors associated with Albina's status as a woman limited her abilities to seek out the care that was available. Lack of knowledge, lack of decision-making power, and lack of economic resources all complicated her ability to deliver a healthy baby and emerge a healthy mother.

In sum, women's abilities to choose whether, when, and how many children to have, as well as the circumstances under which to bear them, are still extremely constrained. Their access to family planning services, as well as to prenatal and postnatal care, is still extremely limited. Part of the problem is undersupply, but this constrained access is also a symptom of a larger problem—women's social, political, and economically disadvantaged position in society. As we shall discuss later in the chapter, improving women's reproductive rights will require a multi-pronged approach that addresses the short-term and long-term reasons for women's disempowerment.

The Problem of Boy Preference

Mothers are not the only women at risk in the developing world; their daughters are also at risk. Often girls are systematically undervalued and, at times, unwanted; traditional cultural values often put a premium on sons. Sons are traditionally expected to take over the family livelihood and care for their parents when they reach old age, and, given the wide and pervasive employment participation and income gaps between men and women, it is true that men are usually financially in a better situation to care for their parents, particularly in poorer countries where state-funded social security systems are nonexistent or poorly funded. In contrast, girls are seen as a financial burden on families in countries such as Bangladesh or India, where a dowry system, although illegal, still flourishes. While sons, when they are grown and married, bring a woman into the household to help with running the family, girls traditionally join their husband's family, bringing a dowry that can be a cash settlement or a pre-agreed list of valuables to contribute to the household. Thus, traditionally, sons grow up to add to the household economy, and girls are perceived to be a financial drain. A few proverbs illustrate this traditional preference for boys. A Hindu proverb claims, "They who are full of sin beget only daughters" a Chinese proverb states, "A stupid son is better than a crafty daughter" and a Sanskrit proverb declares, "A virtuous son is the sun of his family."[14] In contrast, as an Indian proverb states, raising a daughter is like watering the neighbor's garden—an activity that produces no gain for the family. These sayings still express deep-seated beliefs about ideal family structures and the roles that women play in them.

These cultural norms of strong preferences for sons can endanger the lives of millions of unborn girls every year. Because girls are often unwanted, parents resort to infanticide or sex-selective abortions in the hopes of having a boy. Around the world, there are an estimated 100 million "missing" women; China and India together account for more than 85 million of them.[15] The larger cumulative impact of these individual choices is significant: in some societies, men outnumber women. A "natural" ratio is about 105 girls born for every 100 boys, and this is the figure that predominates in areas such as Europe and North America, where sex-selective abortion is relatively uncommon. However, in the Middle East, the northern areas of Africa, the Indian subcontinent, and China, there are more than 105 boys born for every 100 girls.[16] In fact, in China, the figures rose to 120 boys born for every 100 girls, and as high as 130 in some provinces. In India, where figures are calculated a little differently, there are only 914 girls below the age of 7 for every 1,000 boys.[17] These figures are particularly disheartening given that, as discussed at the beginning of this chapter, girls are biologically built with stronger survival abilities. Girls' unequal and lesser status in family hierarchies is literally a matter of life and death. Nor are the problems of boy preference lessening: Vietnam and Nepal are following in India and China's footsteps, with similar demographic patterns emerging. Although the problem is most severe in East Asia, it is by no means a problem specific only to this region, and sex-selective abortion is becoming increasingly common in countries all over the world. Let's now take a closer look at sex-selective abortion and the problem of boy preference in India, where strongly embedded cultural practices of dowry devalue girls, and China, where coercive government policy, along with traditional values of boy preference, create tragic results.

"Spend 3,000 [rupees] now and save 300,000 later": before sex-selective abortion was outlawed in India in 1994, this type of advertisement was displayed at clinics to entice parents to find out the sex of their baby in utero. While these overt advertisements have all but disappeared, the problem of sex-selective abortion in India has not, despite the fact that it is also now illegal in India to tell parents the sex of their fetus. Yet, two journalists working for an Indian TV channel found 100 doctors, in both private and government hospitals, who were willing to perform illegal abortions of female fetuses. Although the TV images, shot from hidden cameras, were somewhat grainy, the information captured on them was indisputable: doctors willingly agreed to help parents terminate their pregnancies, even advising them about where to deposit the remains. Although the doctors were caught on tape, the police were slow to act on the report, and a year later, only seven doctors were suspended. Nor was the report an isolated incident: the following year, police officers recovered almost 400 tiny bones believed to be from newborn girls or fetuses. And parents resort to other options as well; when girls are born, they are much more likely to be dropped off at an orphanage by parents unwilling to incur the perceived costs of raising girls. For example, of the 40 children at Mother Theresa's Missionary Sisters of Charity, 37 are girls.[18] Confirming the data discussed earlier, daughters are not wanted in many Indian families.

Women who bear girls are also at risk, and the inability to produce sons may increase the incidence of what has been termed "dowry death," murder or induced suicide as a result of continual harassment by husbands and in-laws disappointed with the short-term and long-term gains of the marriage settlement. For example, when Varsha Hitkari failed to produce sons after bearing two daughters, the husband's family demanded additional dowry, and eventually beat her unconscious before trying to hang her by a noose from a shower head. Women face other forms of physical abuse for bearing daughters; one husband poured hot coals on his wife's abdomen after she bore a daughter, and another tortured his wife with cigarette burns. Still other mothers are discouraged from feeding or educating their daughters, under the belief that such investments are wastes of time and money. Although it's the man, not the woman, who contributes the Y chromosome that determines the baby's sex, women are often the ones blamed for being unable to produce the invaluable son.[19] Those who hoped that India's economic boom over the previous 15 years would usher in more egalitarian attitudes and practices have been sadly disappointed. While economic growth rates have skyrocketed, so have the costs of traditional, but now illegal, customs such as dowry, which is estimated to be about five times the average annual salary in India.[20] And the increased availability of technology, such as early sonograms, as well as parents' abilities to pay for them, has simply accelerated the rate of sex-selective abortion. Depressingly, the data indicate that wealthier and better-educated Indians—the ones predicted to shun "traditional" cultural values—still want sons. In fact, a study found that the rate of sex-selective abortion was highest among women with university degrees.

While China does not practice the custom of dowry, cultural traditions value boys over girls. Sons are particularly valued in China because they are seen as the ones who will care for the parents when they become old, particularly in a country that offers only minimal social safety nets for its elderly. As one farmer explained, "The worst situation to be in is to have no son and no money. That's when you have nothing at all."[21] Thus, while boy preference in India is more common among better-off urban families, in China it is much more of a rural phenomenon. And the government's strictly enforced one-child policy, enacted in 1980, has meant that, when faced with the possibility of having only one child, parents want to ensure that it is a boy. As a result, the problem of boy preference is even more severe in China than in India. As in India, using scanning technology such as sonograms to determine the sex of the child is illegal, and so are sex-selective abortions. But like in India, doctors, if caught, face only a fine and suspension, which has not stopped many doctors in search of making extra income in China's booming economy. Often, the interaction can be accomplished without even any verbal communication; to avoid getting caught for revealing the sex of the fetus, a doctor may resort to sign language, nodding his or her head to indicate a boy, and shaking the head to signal a girl. One report found that retired doctors would perform abortions for as little as $20.[22] And like in India, even when girls are born, they receive worse care. A study conducted in Shanxi province, where death rates for girls are higher, found that after birth, the environment was much more unfriendly for girls. Boys tended to be born in hospitals, where mother and child could receive care, while girls were born at home. Boys were fed better and more nutritious food than girls, and they were sent to the hospital more quickly when they became ill, while girls were cared for at home and expected to rely on their own resistance to illness.[23]

The tragic consequences of boy preference in both India and China are beginning to emerge. Many demographers warn of an impending social crisis due to too many men and not enough women to marry them. Not only will this shake the stability of the entire marriage system, they argue, but it will also create tides of social unrest, as men, particularly the poorest with the least options, will be unable to marry. In fact, in their book *Bare Branches: The Security Implications of Asia's Surplus Male Population*, Valerie Hudson and Andrea Den Boer argue that throughout history, men who were unable to marry and create families (called "bare branches" in China because they are branches of a family tree that will never bear fruit) have played a role in instigating societal instability, violent crime, and gang formation. The cumulative effect of this is increased levels of insecurity, violence, and internal threat. This threat is particularly severe for China and India, where "bare branches" are projected to comprise 12 to 15 percent of the young adult male population.[24] Further, demographers argue that the lack of women will simply drive up the demand for (and supply of) young girls for sexual trafficking, as well as the kidnapping and selling of women to provide brides for those who can pay the fee. In sum, boy preference is a problem that has significant repercussions not only for girls and women but also for overall levels of democracy, stability, and peace, and the low status of women in developing countries will reduce the health of not only those societies but potentially the world as well.

As girls move from infancy to young adulthood, their health continues to suffer because of the cultural norms of undervaluing females. While female infants have a biological advantage over male infants in the first year of life, that advantage disappears as cultural norms of discrimination result in less healthy lives for girls. Even malnutrition among children is gendered. Women and girls are more affected by hunger than men and boys because females often eat last, as well as least, in households.[25] As girls grow older and begin to bear children, the cycle of ill health begins anew; poorly fed mothers give birth to underweight children; low-birthweight children are three to four times more likely to die from diarrheal diseases, acute respiratory infections, and, if not immunized, measles. By the time they reach the age of 5, low-birthweight babies may have had more cyclic episodes of infection and malnutrition and may be severely stunted. This will be carried into adult life, potentially to be repeated on yet another generation of young girls.[26]

Women and HIV

Increasingly, the spread of HIV/AIDS has come to be perceived as the next looming health crisis that will require concentrated, coordinated, international attention. The global statistics are overwhelming; as of 2010, an estimated 34 million people were living with HIV, and over 95 percent of them were in developing countries. While these numbers are up 17 percent from 2001, this is mostly a reflection of the increased availability of successful antiretroviral therapy. Sub-Saharan Africa is most heavily affected by HIV; the region accounts for 70 percent of new infections in 2010, even though it represents just 12 percent of the global population. It would seem as if the virus was gender-blind; women account for about 50 percent of people living with HIV.[27] However, as we shall see, the transmission and impact of HIV are deeply gendered.

First, while infection rates seem to have stabilized, nonetheless transmission rates for women have risen, and in sub-Saharan Africa, women currently account for about 60 percent of people living with HIV.[28] Further, transmission is rising rapidly in people ages 15 to 24, particularly among girls and young women; in some countries, females ages 15 to 24 have infection rates that are six times higher than those of males of the same ages. There are several reasons why women are particularly vulnerable to HIV. For example, even transmission is not gender-neutral; for a variety of physiological reasons, the transmission of the virus through sexual contact is more efficient from men to women than vice versa. HIV transmission from male to female is seven times more likely than transmission from female to male.[29] But the rapid rise in women's transmission rates is not only an expression of biology; women's unequal social, economic, and legal status increases their vulnerability to AIDS. As Jonathan Mann, the former head of the UN global HIV and AIDS program, argued, "When women's human rights and dignity are not respected, society creates and favours their vulnerability to AIDS."[30] For example, women's lack of power in their relationships increases their risk of contracting AIDS. Cultural values often designate men as the initiators of sexual activity. Promiscuity is often condoned and even encouraged in men but condemned in women. In practice, this means that women lack the power in relationships to either refuse sex or negotiate protected sex. The high incidences of child marriages and forced marriages also contribute to women's lack of influence in negotiating their sexual relationships. Further, the traditional focus on preserving women's innocence with regard to sexual relations, in addition to women's lower levels of education, often means that they lack adequate knowledge about preventing the transmission of HIV and other sexually transmitted diseases. Across sub-Saharan Africa, women are much less likely than men to gain a comprehensive knowledge of HIV transmission. And in some cultures, the pervasive but patently untrue belief that sex with a virgin will cure AIDS has put many young women at risk for infection. As rape increasingly becomes used as a tool of war, women in conflict zones and refugee camps are also particularly vulnerable to the virus.[31]

Once women contract HIV, they often are further victimized by their families, who may turn them out of the house, deprive them of their property, and cut them off from loved ones. For example, the story of Rajni, a young Indian mother, illustrates the plight of many women in the developing world. She was married at 14 and became a widow at 20 when her husband, who ran a small business, died of AIDS. She, too, tested positive for HIV. Her son, now 12, is also HIV positive; her 9-year-old daughter, who is healthy, was given to her sister to raise so that she does not have to bear the social stigma of the disease. She and her extended family live in poverty, having been forced to sell their home to pay her husband's medical bills.[32] Widows of AIDS victims, even if they are not infected, often face a dire future; unable as women to inherit or own property or land in many countries, they often become destitute, many at a young age, given the high incidence of child marriages in many areas of the developing world.

But AIDS has a female face in other ways as well, in terms of how it impacts primarily women by adding to their already high levels of household responsibility. When AIDS arrives in a household, it is primarily the women who take on the added responsibilities of caring for the infected family members, particularly in developing countries where access to medical services is extremely limited. Yet, women are already overburdened in terms of their responsibilities in raising, feeding, and clothing their often extended household. Particularly in regions where women not only prepare the food but also grow it and care for the livestock, the arrival of AIDS, and the caring duties that come with it, adds to women's already overloaded days and takes them away from other critical household production tasks. And when they are pulled out of their work in household production, the whole household suffers, falling further into poverty, ill health, and potential star-vation. As students primarily located in wealthy developed nations, we easily forget how lack of basic amenities can quickly overwhelm already overextended women. For example, one rural woman from southern Africa estimated that it took 24 buckets of water a day to care for an AIDS patient in her household. This quantity of water was needed because the severe diarrhea that afflicted her relative required that she bathe the patient and wash the bedding and clothes five or six times a day. In the absence of washing machines, cooking stoves, running water, and potentially electricity, the work involved in this caring activity is intense—and remember that women must walk increasingly long distances to fetch water (every day in South Africa, the country's women walk the equivalent of going to the moon and back 16 times over to fetch water). In addition, this work keeps her from all the other life-sustaining tasks she must normally perform. And even if the patient is lucky enough to receive medical care in a hospital, women still spend countless hours bringing food and providing care, given the understaffed, over-taxed status of many of the medical facilities that serve severely ill patients.[33]

And when the women themselves become ill with HIV, the problem of the overtaxed caretaker worsens exponentially. As women succumb to the effects of the virus, many cannot perform their normal household activities, which, in turn, reduces the well-being of the entire family. One news story covered one woman's struggle to raise her family while coping with HIV. Often sick and exhausted, she must still somehow find a way to get out of bed to feed the children, fetch water, and keep house. In her weakened circumstances, she cannot feed her own family and depends on the help she gets from well-wishers.[34] Further, the loss of mothers can have drastic effects on the families they leave behind; the million children who are left motherless each year are three to ten times more likely to die within 2 years than are children with two living parents.[35] For those children who survive, life is still difficult; over 17 million children around the world (although 15 million of them are in sub-Saharan Africa) have lost one or both parents to AIDS.[36] Finally, as HIV shifts toward being a young person's affliction—an increasing number of 15- to 24-year-olds are living with AIDS or HIV—young women already infected are more likely to give birth to children who are HIV positive, thus compounding the infection rate. As of 2011, nearly 3.5 million children under the age of 15 were living with HIV.[37] Not only do these trends create new depths of human tragedy, but they also put new stresses and strains on governments with inadequate bud-gets to absorb the effects of these demographic changes. As we will discuss in our next section, it is only recently that the international community has mobilized around the issue of women's unequal caring burdens and the dramatic impact that this can have on families' livelihoods.

ADVANCING WOMEN'S EQUALITY

How have international development agencies, states, nongovernmental organiza-tions (NGOs), and individual activists addressed women's health, and what has been the impact of their work? In terms of reproductive health, ensuring women's right to decide the number, timing, and spacing of children is critical. This right was clarified and endorsed internationally in the Cairo Consensus that emerged from the 1994 International Conference on Population and Development. It was reaffirmed at the Beijing Conference and various international and regional agreements since, as well as in many national laws. There has been a significant shift in the attitudes and beliefs of development policymakers, state officials, and demographers that population growth rates cannot be dictated to women but that women and men have the right to choose the appropriate size of their own families and that when they do choose, everyone is better off. Many countries are turning away from the policies of forced population control to focus on larger strategies such as increasing girls' access to education, and eventually employment opportunities, as a more effective means of controlling population growth.

Numerous international organizations address issues of family planning and reproductive health. The UNFPA is the world's largest international source of funding for population and reproductive health programs. It works with governments and NGOs in 150 countries, at their request, to, in their words, ensure that "every pregnancy is wanted, every birth is safe, that every young person is free of HIV, and that every girl and woman is treated with dignity and respect."[38] The International Planned Parenthood Federation, the world's largest voluntary organization working on issues of family planning and sexual and reproductive health, links autonomous family planning agencies in over 180 countries.[39] The World Health Organization also promotes family planning by working to help improve the safety and effectiveness of contraceptive methods, widen the range of family planning methods available to women and men, and improve the quality of family planning service delivery.[40]

On a positive note, women's access to contraception has increased, particularly in the 1990s, and women are now choosing to have fewer children, spaced more widely apart. Thanks to women's increased access to contraception, education, and paid employment, families are half the size they were in 1960.[41] However, despite increasing international rhetorical support for a woman's right to control various aspects of her body and her health, international reproductive rights efforts often become mired in domestic political struggles between social conservatives and liberals, and funding for international family planning programs has been held hostage by governments with conservative agendas. "Family planning" covers a variety of practices and issues, such as contraception, abortion, and women's rights, that make many governments uncomfortable. The Catholic Church has been extremely active in trying to narrowly define "family planning," with a focus on abstinence as a form of birth control. In addition, religious organizations have successfully lobbied the U.S. government to attach conditions to international family planning funds. Since 1973, the Foreign Assistance Act has prohibited the use of U.S. funds for any abortion services overseas. President Reagan imposed further restrictions in 1984 when he issued an executive memorandum, which became informally known as the Global Gag Rule. Under these stipulations, family planning agencies may not receive U.S. assistance if they provide abortion services, which includes counseling and referrals on abortions. Nor can they lobby to make or keep abortion legal in their country. In effect, if they want U.S. assistance, they may not refer to, advocate for, or mention abortion as an option, regardless of the circumstances (such as to save the life or health of the mother or in instances of incest or rape). This rule was revoked by President Clinton in 1993 but reinstituted by President George W. Bush on Jan. 22, 2001.[42] Family planning advocates worried that this would increase the number of unplanned pregnancies and would drive women to resort to backstreet abortions in the absence of reliable medical information. When President Obama assumed office in January 2009, he promptly reversed the ban, once again freeing up funding for a variety of family planning NGOs around the world.

In addition to the gag rule, the U.S. president is authorized under the 1985 Kemp-Kasten Amendment to prohibit U.S. foreign aid for any organization that he or she determines "supports or participates in the management of a program of coercive abortion or involuntary sterilization." President Bush also wielded this power, and in July 2002, despite congressional approval, the Bush administration cut off funding for UNFPA's work, arguing (inaccurately) that the UNFPA supports China's coercive abortion policies (the UNFPA does work in China). The administration continued to withhold funding, totaling $235 million as of 2008, from the UNFPA.[43] The Obama administration resumed funding in 2009. This ambivalence about funding reproductive rights is not a solely American phenomenon; donors' share of funding for family planning has steadily fallen since 1995, in part to fund other critical initiatives such as the fight against the sexually transmitted diseases and HIV/AIDS.

Despite these financial concerns, or perhaps because of them, citizen activism has become a critical source of support. For example, Jane Roberts, a retired schoolteacher, and Lois Abraham, an attorney, cofounded the NGO 34 Million Friends of UNFPA in reaction to President Bush's withdrawal of $34 million in funding for the UNFPA in 2002. Both wrote to friends and the local paper, asking fellow citizens to send $1 and a message of support for the UNFPA's work. Soon, they started a website, www.34millionfriends.org. As of the end of October 2012, individuals, many donating just $1, had sent in over $4 million. While this represents just a fraction of what the U.S. government owed the UNFPA in withheld funding, in the words of Abraham and Roberts, it nonetheless demonstrates

> the growing power of citizen efforts in an information age that daily draws people
> and countries closer and closer together.... [W]e hope that our grassroots efforts
> will serve as an example for citizen action around the world on behalf of women's
> health, the environment and other common causes that serve the global good.[44]

What is the status of maternal health? Goal 5 of the Millennium Development Goals pledges to improve maternal health by working to reduce the maternal mortality ratio, increasing the proportion of births attended by skilled health personnel, and improving antenatal care coverage, among other things. The good news is that maternal mortality has been nearly halved since 1990. However, sub-Saharan Africa, the region with the highest maternal mortality rate (and, incidentally, the lowest contraception prevalence rate), has not reflected this global pace, and the region is not even close to meeting the goals.[45] And in some places, such as war-torn Afghanistan, the rates are truly abysmal: about 1 in 23 mothers will die from childbirth-related causes. Progress has been made in increasing the number of deliveries in the developing world that are attended by skilled health personnel (up from 55 percent in 1990 to 65 percent in 2010); again, however, this overall improvement masks little to no change in sub-Saharan Africa. Prenatal care has also increased: four out of five women in the developing world have at least one visit with a doctor, nurse, or midwife during their pregnancy. As you can imagine, however, while one visit is better than none, it is a far cry from the services that women in industrialized nations, particularly those with universal health care, are accustomed to. Reducing maternal mortality and improving maternal health can seem overwhelming. However, the international community has focused with renewed energy on several specific issues related to maternal health that have made a real difference in women's lives. The UNFPA has launched its Campaign to End Fistula in 30 countries in sub-Saharan Africa, South Asia, and some Arab states. Part of their funding supports the work of dedicated doctors and health professionals in Ethiopia. The accompanying text box entitled "Women in Action: Dr. Catherine Hamlin" describes the significant difference that the founders of the Addis Ababa Fistula Hospital have made in the lives of thousands of young women and their families. Numerous individual examples such as these demonstrate that, with determination and effort, institutions and individuals can make a difference in many people's lives, which isn't necessarily reflected in the aggregate data.

Women in Action: Dr. Catherine Hamlin

The narrative about fistula repair surgery that opened this chapter illustrates how a few dedicated individuals can effect substantial change. Responding to an advertisement in the British medical journal Lancet, Catherine and Reginald Hamlin traveled from Australia to Ethiopia to establish a school of midwifery in Addis Ababa in 1959. Originally planning on staying for 3 years, their plans changed when they saw the plight of so many young girls suffering from inadequate prenatal and postnatal care, as well as the sacrifices many had made to search for treatment. Many young women had walked for days through rough terrain, were carried by relatives, or had sold the one piece of family livestock crucial to the family economy to buy the bus fare in hopes of receiving treatment. Reflecting on her experiences, Catherine Hamlin said, "I had never seen injuries like that before. Our hearts broke at the sight of these women and what they were experiencing, and we knew we could not ignore it." Fifteen years later, deeply dedicated to their efforts to provide better medical care for women in Ethiopia, they decided to found the Addis Ababa Fistula Hospital. Speaking of her motivation to help, Catherine Hamlin noted that

> Childbirth should be a joyful occasion, but for these fistula girls it has developed into a nightmare and a horror—to suffer the agony of days of labour, with nobody but the village women to help and nothing to relieve the pain, to deliver their longed-for child as a stillbirth, and then to experience the awful

consequences of this ordeal. . . . The whole picture is an unimaginable plight, and one which no woman should be called on to endure, but one that is being repeated all over the developing world, where women have no access to any medical help.

Discussing her motivation to work in the face of what must be extremely difficult circumstances, Hamlin notes that

every day our hearts go out to them as they arrive at our hospital with nothing in this world except their faith and hope in us, and their urine-soaked clothes— young beautiful girls with a life shattered and in ruins. . . . Each one pulls at our heart strings and calls forth the utmost compassion.[ii]

The compassion of Dr. Hamlin and her staff has significantly changed the lives of thousands, and promises to continue to do so. Since opening, the hospital has treated over 32,000 women. All medical students specializing in obstetrics and gynecology in Ethiopia are required to train for 2 months at the hospital; in addition, staff train doctors from all over the developing world. They have also built Desta Mender (which means Village of Joy), a village of ten cottages and two common buildings, to house long-term care patients. The hospital is now building five smaller fistula hospitals throughout Ethiopia in the hope of reaching more rural patients, most of whom do not have the financial or personal resources to make the arduous journey, often alone, to the capital city for treatment. And to help staff them, Dr. Hamlin has opened the Hamlin Midwifery College, which accepted its first 12 students in 2008. The students will undergo a 3-year diploma program in midwifery before returning to their villages to provide medical care. With only 1,000 qualified midwives to serve a population of 80 million, investing in training is critical if Ethiopia is to reduce its high maternal mortality figures. Eventually, Dr. Hamlin hopes to train a midwife for every village in Ethiopia.

Dr. Hamlin ultimately traces the problem of fistulas to the pervasive undervaluation of girls in Ethiopia and many other areas of the developing world. Part of the problem, she feels, is the tradition of early marriage, in which girls are betrothed at 8 or 9 years old. At this point, the girl moves to the mother-in-law's house until she reaches puberty and is ready for marriage. In the meantime, she often works in the mother-in-law's household, performing extremely demanding labor, but often with few nutritional resources to fuel that labor because she is a girl, and thus the last one in the family to be fed. The result is that her growth is stunted, and her pelvis is too small to successfully deliver a baby. Dr. Hamlin would like to improve girls' access to education so that girls have alternative options to early marriage. The impact of the Hamlins' work is significant. Not only have they healed the physical scars of thousands of poor women from predominantly rural areas of Ethiopia, but they have also helped emotionally heal these young girls, who would have faced a life of social ostracism and severe physical disability. As one health worker commented, Dr. Hamlin "pulls these untouchables back into society."[iii]

---

[i]Kate Benson, "Australia's Mother Theresa," *Sydney Morning Herald,* March 29, 2008, http://www .smh.com.au/news/world/australias-mother-teresa/2008/03/28/1206207412966.html
[ii]Dr. Catherine Hamlin, "United Nations Population Award Acceptance Speech," July 6, 2004, http://www.fistulafoundation.org/pdf/UN%20pop%20award%20speech.pdf
[iii]Benson, "Australia's Mother Theresa."

In terms of changing the culture of boy preference, the Indian and Chinese governments have adopted a variety of policies, with mixed success. In India, although the government has tried to become more proactively involved in discouraging the practice, it also seems to condone the undervaluation of girls. Renuka Chowdhury, India's minister of state for women and child development, urged parents to give up their children to state-run orphanages instead of aborting them in the womb. In a public statement, she urged parents who "don't want a girl, [to] leave her to us." The government, she promised, "will bring up your children. Don't kill them."[46] Although this proposal was later abandoned, the Indian government has attempted to apply additional sanctions and incentives to encourage parents to shift their beliefs to value daughters. The government is proposing to stiffen the sentences against the doctors who perform sex-selective abortion. In the 14 years since the practice was outlawed, only two doctors had been convicted of the crime, a sign that various offices of the government did not take the existing law very seriously.[47] Certainly, laws are important, but they are not enough, particularly if, like this one, they are easy to evade. At the regional level, some state governments have offered free immunizations, no school fees, and free books for girls and an age allowance to take care of parents to lessen the financial burden on parents of having a daughter.[48] The Indian government has also liberalized inheritance laws, equalizing sons' and daughters' claims to land and other immovable property. However, designing policy to discourage powerful customs, such as dowry, continues to be a severe challenge to fostering gender equality in India.

The Chinese government has also begun to realize that its policy of population control, which essentially coerces parents into having one child (rather than persuading them to want fewer children), will have dramatic consequences. In 2003, the government launched a "Care for Girls" campaign to change the pervasive culture of boy preference. In addition to public education, the campaign includes a set of financial incentives to offset the costs of raising a girl. Families with only daughters can qualify for small loans to help them develop income-generating projects or support schooling for girls. Girls are offered additional medical examinations to ensure that they are receiving adequate care from their families. And the program has provided additional training to girls to help them find employment, and thus give them the ability to contribute to the family economy. Other measures include pension payments for parents of daughters to offset the pressure to produce a son as an informal social insurance mechanism.[49] Although China is pursuing this issue more aggressively than before, it's not necessarily out of concern for gender equality; rather, China's birth rate is well below replacement levels, and China is facing a massive demographic crisis as the elderly population continues to bulge. Nonetheless, both the Indian and the Chinese examples illustrate how governments can provide incentives to foster changing cultural values. At the same time, both examples illustrate how difficult it can be for governments to demonstrate the political will, and capacity, to truly effect a shift in deeply embedded values.

Finally, combating the spread of HIV/AIDS has become one of the most prominent campaigns waged by development agencies. The Joint UN Programme on HIV and AIDS, or UNAIDS, is the primary international effort to provide co-ordinated international action on the HIV epidemic. UNAIDS is a partnership between eight UN agencies: UNICEF, the UN Development Programme (UNDP), UNFPA, the UN Office on Drugs and Crime (UNODC), the International Labour Organization (ILO), the UN Educational, Scientific and Cultural Organization (UNESCO), the World Health Organization (WHO), and the World Bank. By taking collective action, these organizations hope to better coordinate their re-sponse to the AIDS crisis and avoid duplicating each others' work and projects. They focus primarily on sponsoring programs to prevent the transmission of HIV, offering care to these living with HIV by providing antiretroviral treatments, and reducing the negative impact of HIV on individuals and communities. UNAIDS has also launched a Global Coalition on Women and AIDS. Its efforts focus on preventing new HIV infections among women and girls, promoting equal access to HIV care and treatment, protecting women's property and inheritance rights, and eliminating violence against women.[50]

The impact of these efforts has been significant: the global percentage of adults living with HIV has leveled off since 2000. By the end of 2010, 6.5 million people were receiving antiretroviral treatment in developing countries—the largest 1-year increase ever. Nonetheless, the UN estimates that this is still meeting only an esti-mated 48 percent of global need. However, treatment coverage has been higher for women than men, and there has been particular progress in providing pregnant women living with HIV with antiretroviral treatment to prevent mother-to-child transmission. UNAIDS has also focused on the disproportionate burden of care that women shoulder in tending to people living with HIV, as well as the reduced circumstances that many widows face once their husbands succumb to AIDS. In particular, they have focused on providing microcredit, or small loans, to these women to increase their independent income-generating potential.[51]

Yet, similar to reproductive rights issues, the global AIDS campaign is also affected increasingly by conservative domestic agendas. In 2003, President Bush announced an "Emergency Plan for AIDS Relief" and pledged $15 billion over 5 years to the campaign. However, conservative groups in the United States that are interested in the issue of AIDS have also been hostile to AIDS-prevention strat-egies, such as comprehensive sex education and condom distribution. As a result, they have lobbied successfully for increased funding for abstinence promotion programs. When Congress passed the U.S. Leadership Against HIV/AIDS, Tuber-culosis, and Malaria Act of 2003, conservatives in the House were able to dedicate one third of the AIDS-prevention funding toward programs urging abstinence before marriage. They were, in part, inspired by the success of Uganda's ABC (Abstinence, Be Faithful, and Use Condoms) program. Uganda's HIV infection rate peaked at about 15 percent (30 percent among pregnant women in urban areas) in 1991, and then declined significantly through the mid-1990s and reached 5 percent (14 percent for pregnant urban women) by 2001.[52] However, aid workers on the Ugandan project attribute the success of the program primarily to the in-creased use of condoms and partner reduction, rather than solely to the abstinence component. Further, research on abstinence-only programs in the United States finds that they have little impact on the sexual behavior or contraceptive use among sexually active teenagers. Yet, despite little evidence supporting the effectiveness of abstinence-only programs, they are becoming a critical part of U.S. AIDS-prevention programs overseas.[53] However, with a change of administration came a change of rules, and the 2008 reauthorization of PEPFAR eliminated the requirement for abstinence programs. Finally, development agencies have become concerned increasingly with putting women's unequal health status in a broader context of larger gender inequalities. Thus, they have focused on larger themes, such as women's access to education, as a way of improving women's reproductive health. Women with less education are more likely to have children at a young age, when their risks for complications are particularly high. Further, studies have shown that low maternal levels of education often translate into malnutrition and poor quality of care for children. Demographic and health surveys from more than 40 developing countries show that the mortality rate for children under 5 is lower in households in which women have some primary schooling. This figure drops even lower in households in which mothers have benefited from secondary schooling.[54] Another study of 63 countries showed that gains in women's education accounted for 43 percent of the decline in malnutrition from 1970 to 1995, although food availability and the government's commitment to health were also important.[55] Thus, as we discussed in Chapter 7, gender mainstreaming, or focusing on the status of women in society across all development programs, has become an increasingly common approach.

CONCLUSION

Women have made strides in improving the quality of their health. With international support for various family planning initiatives, women have more choice over the timing and spacing of their children. Women are choosing to have fewer children, and fertility rates are steadily declining. However, some indicators have barely changed; women are still at risk at all stages of pregnancy, childbirth, and recovery. Nor do broader cultural values that place a premium on sons appear to be disappearing soon. And as international donors gain more experience in battling the AIDS crisis, they are beginning to recognize and address the gendered dimensions of the virus. We do know that educating women is central to improving not only their own health but also the health of their immediate family. In sum, addressing these issues requires multifaceted, multilateral action.

FOR MORE INFORMATION

Video and Multimedia

A Walk to Beautiful, http://www.pbs.org/wgbh/nova/beautiful/program.html. This documentary follows the recovery of five Ethiopian women who have traveled to the Addis Ababa Fistula Hospital to receive medical care.

In Silence, http://www.hrw.org/video/2009/10/06/silence-maternal-mortality-india. Photographer Susan Meiselas and reporter Dumeetha Luthra traveled to India for Human

Rights Watch to retrace the steps of one woman who died after giving birth to a son. *In Silence* received a 2010 Webby Award in the Online Film & Video Documentary: Individual Episode category.

The Edge of Joy. http://www.theedgeofjoy.com/index.html. This documentary explores the challenges and triumphs of maternal health care in Nigeria.

Organizations and Websites

Center for Health and Gender Equity (CHANGE), http://www.genderhealth.org

Eldis Gender and HIV/AIDS Resources, http://www.eldis.org/go/topics/resource-guides/hiv-and-aids/gender

The Fistula Foundation, http://www.fistulafoundation.org

Gender and Health Equity Network (GHEN), http://www2.ids.ac.uk/ghen

International Women's Health Coalition, http://www.iwhc.org

34 Million Friends of UNFPA, http://www.34millionfriends.org

UNIFEM Gender and HIV/AIDS Web Portal, http://www.genderandaids.org/index.php

United Nations Environment Program, Women and the Environment, http://www.unep.org/Documents.Multilingual/Default.asp?DocumentID=468&ArticleID=4488&l=en

Women, Health, and the Environment: At a Glance, http://www.ourplanet.com/imgversn/152/glance.html

Women Won't Wait (End HIV and Violence Against Women), http://www.womenwontwait.org

World Health Organization, Department of Gender, Women, and Health, http://www.who.int/gender/en

10

Women and Education

It was only the school fees that made it difficult for me to continue studying. When you don't pay your fees, the teacher in charge comes and calls out the names, and then you go home. He tells you to take home the message, that when you come back to school you must come with money.[1]

My parents feel that girls should be married; that they are not like boys who need education. Every month they plan my marriage. They don't help me. I can't talk about my ambitions with them.[2]

These quotations illustrate just two of the continuing barriers to women's education in the developing world—school fees and cultural views of appropriate roles for women. Development agencies emphasize that achieving parity in education, not only in primary school but at all levels, is critical if women are to engage fully in society. Yet, all too often girls are denied access to education and all of the benefits that accrue from formal schooling. Fifty-four percent of the estimated 72 million children who are out of school are girls.[3] Further, two thirds of the world's 774 million illiterate adults are women.[4] Despite the fact that the gap between boys' and girls' enrollment figures is narrowing, the problem is significant enough that the United Nations (UN) pledged as part of the Millennium Development Goals to eliminate gender disparities in primary and secondary education by 2005 and in all levels of education no later than 2015.[5] In this chapter, we will focus on the status of women's education, discussing several issues that threaten women's access to education as well as international efforts to reverse women's unequal status.

THE STATUS OF WOMEN AND EDUCATION

There are many reasons why women (and by using this term we also mean girls) should be educated. First, education is a fundamental human right. In 1948, the Universal Declaration of Human Rights became the international standard for human rights law. One of its tenets was that education is a human right and thus elementary education should be free and compulsory while higher education should be made accessible to all on the basis of merit. Since this declaration, numerous other treaties have reiterated this right. Most recently, the Convention on the Elimination of All Forms of Discrimination Against Women (CEDAW, 1979) and the Convention on the Rights of the Child (CRC, 1990) set forth "the most comprehensive set of legally enforceable commitments concerning both rights to education and to gender equality."[6] As of 2012, CEDAW had been ratified by 187 nations and the CRC had been ratified by all nations worldwide except Somalia and the United States. Thus, education is a legally sanctioned human right that applies equally to men and women.

Second, educated girls have more choices about their futures. If they work, they will be able to earn higher wages (even though those wages will be lower than those of their male counterparts with a similar level of education and experience). Not only does this add to their household income, thus reducing poverty, but it also increases their status in the family. Education also empowers women to participate more fully in public life; for instance, women in Bangladesh with a secondary education are more likely to attend a political meeting than are those with no education.[7] Education also enables women to make autonomous choices about their personal lives; educated girls marry later and have fewer children. This is a benefit not only to them and their health, but also to governments that are straining to provide adequate services to all of their citizens. In addition, educated girls and women have a dramatic impact on their families. Educated women have healthier, better-nourished children because while they are pregnant, lactating, and beyond, they have the ability to gain the knowledge required to care adequately for themselves and their children. They are more likely to send their children to school, especially their daughters, and their children are more likely to do well there. Thus, there are multiple compelling reasons to invest in the education of girls and women. As Greg Mortensen, founder of the Central Asia Institute, a nonprofit that builds schools in central Asia, argues, "If the girls aren't educated, nothing will change. . . . We can drop bombs, we can build roads, or we can put in electricity. But unless the girls are educated, the world won't change."[8]

There has been some clear progress in educating girls in the developing world over the past few decades. To begin with, since 1990, 44 million more girls are attending primary schools.[9] Further, the gender gap, particularly in access to primary education, is narrowing. By 2007 (the most recent date for which data are available), of countries with available data, 117 out of 163 had attained gender parity in education at the primary level.[10] "Gender parity" is the term used to describe how well a country is educating both girls and boys. To have attained gender parity means that boys and girls are attending schools at the same rate. It does not tell us anything about what percentage of a country's children are in school, it just tells us if boys and girls are in school at the same rate. Gender parity has been attained in Europe, Latin America and the Caribbean, North America, eastern and southeastern Asia, and Oceania, and the gap has narrowed even in Africa and south-central and western Asia. And, while the gaps are narrowing in all regions, even ones with historically large gaps, there still remain a few countries where the gender parity index is at or below 0.75 (Central African Republic, Chad, Guinea-Bissau, and Niger).[11] These gender disparities widen even further when combined with the urban/rural split in access to education: a girl living in a rural area is three times more likely to drop out of school than is a boy living in a city.[12]

Further, it is important to recognize that while increasing numbers of girls are gaining access to primary education, gender disparities tend to increase at higher levels of education. While in Latin America more girls than boys are enrolled in secondary school, this is the exception, not the rule. Girls in southern and western Asia and in sub-Saharan Africa are the least likely to advance beyond primary school. As we mentioned previously, while 117 countries have achieved gender parity in primary education, only 54 out of 144 countries with available data have done so in secondary education.[13] As Pape Snow, former director of planning and reform in the Senegalese Ministry of Education points out, parity in primary education was attainable, but the number of girls in secondary schools drops off dramatically as many leave school to become domestic workers—the government can remove fees, but it cannot control demand for education.[14] In addition, completion of primary education in many countries does not necessarily guarantee literacy or adequate educational skills needed to progress in life. On a positive note, gender parity in tertiary education is improving for women. While only 8 countries have parity and in 54 more men than women participate in tertiary education, in 92 countries, women represent the majority in tertiary education.[15] Thus, while this may seem obvious, when women make it through secondary school they are more likely to be able to access tertiary education, and often they are more likely to do so than men.

Why has it been so difficult for girls to gain access to primary and secondary education? As the quote at the beginning of chapter demonstrates, one barrier to educating children, boys as well as girls, is school fees, which can include tuition, cost of books, required school uniforms, and community contributions. Many governments that lack the budgetary resources to offer free universal primary education charge students fees to attend school, and since household income is often quite low in many developing countries, fees place education out of reach for many children. Parents who have multiple children and school fees often opt to send their sons to school instead of their daughters. Daughters are expected to perform household chores as well as care for the young, the elderly, and the sick. Thus school fees are a greater barrier to girls than to boys. The World Bank notes that the elimination of school fees benefits all children, but as shown in Uganda and Tanzania, the impact is greater for girls.[16] One nonprofit advocacy group argues that when school fees were eliminated in Kenya, enrollment shot up and gender disparities in education almost disappeared because families with financial difficulties no longer had to decide which children to educate.[17] Nonetheless, school fees persist in numerous countries despite the existence of human rights instruments that "commit states to free and compulsory education at [the] primary level."[18] Part of the reason for the persistence of school fees is that their removal is costly and difficult for countries that are struggling economically. Togo was able this past year to remove school fees because of an $80 million investment in the education system, but school administrators worried about how they would pay for supplies, cultural activities, sanitation, and assistants in the long term.[19]

While eliminating school fees will certainly help improve access to education, it will not eradicate it (see text box "Elizabeth Scharpf" for another financial barrier to female education and an attempt to overcome it). Many children must work, in addition to or instead of attending school, to supplement low family incomes. According to recent estimates by the UN, about 215 million children work, many full-time, and over half are girls.[20] While we do not know the exact percentage of these children who are unable to attend school, we do know that it certainly complicates their abilities to access an education. This is compounded by lack of government enforcement of compulsory education laws and labor laws.[21] On top of this, many children must perform unpaid domestic labor, and a much larger proportion of these children are girls.[22] When family incomes are limited, it is often the girls in the family who are kept back from school instead of the boys. And it is often the girls who must stay home to perform domestic labor and care for the younger children. Further, many girls, some as young as age 8, are given or sold by their families to others as domestic laborers, with no access to education. A recent report by Human Rights Watch concerning girl domestic workers in Guinea documents the numerous girl domestic laborers who work as many as 18 hours a day for no pay, are often raped by their employers, and suffer other forms of abuse.[23] Thus the problem is much greater than just school fees.

Further, cultural, social, religious, and political beliefs about women often keep girls at home. As a result of cultural and social norms, girls are often *expected* (no matter the household income) to stay at home and help with the household chores and with raising younger children. In addition, in many cultures girls are often forced to marry young; in Nepal, 40 percent of girls are married by the age of 15, and in Ethiopia and some countries of western Africa, some girls are married off as early as 7 or 8.[24] Many families do not want to invest in a daughter's education because they perceive it to be a wasted expense. Given that girls become part of the husband's family and household upon marriage, they are often treated as a financial drain, in comparison to boys, who bring in an extra pair of hands upon marriage to aid in maintaining the household economy. Religious beliefs about the appropriate role of education in girls' lives also complicate matters. Specifically, Islam has come under attack in recent years as a barrier to girls' education. Briefly stated, some followers of Islam argue that secular education is antithetical to the Islamic faith and that girls should not receive any education other than religious education, while other followers (the majority) argue that Allah, and thus Islam, supports both boys and girls receiving a secular education. One of the notable examples of the former school of thought is the Taliban. When the Taliban ruled Afghanistan, girls were forbidden to attend school, and even the curriculum for boys was tightly controlled and limited. In December 2008, one Taliban group (the Tehrik-i-Taliban Swat) in northwest Pakistan issued an order that girls are not to attend schools in the region, arguing that girls should receive only religious education (and see photo 10.1 regarding a recent shooting of a female student). But other, larger, Taliban groups in the area have refused to follow the order and argue that Islam is supportive of both boys and girls receiving a secular education.[25]

In June 2008, some followers of Islam destroyed two dozen girls' schools in Pakistan, and in November 2008, Islamic extremists sprayed acid on a group of schoolgirls in the Kandahar province. These are but a few examples of the various ways that some fringe elements of the Islamic faith have tried and are continuing to try to prevent girls from receiving a secular education. That said, the majority of the followers of Islam worldwide are supportive of girls having access to education and work hard to ensure girls' access to schools. One such example is Shoukat Ali, a former Kashmiri freedom fighter and member of the Taliban who is now a teacher. Ali teaches at a school built by the Central Asia Institute. He argues that education is crucial as a weapon to fight extremism (and misunderstandings of the true nature of Islam): "If you can't read, then you must believe what the Imam tells you. . . . If you cannot read the language, you can get the wrong idea. . . . If we invest, it will come back to us. We have to deal with problems of tradition and culture. But we can stop extremism. If people are educated, we can fight against poverty, cruelty and injustice."[26]

There are also a variety of problems related to infrastructure, both material and human, that limit girls' access to education. In particular, while inadequate roads and transportation are problematic for all children, this particularly impedes girls since many families refuse to send their daughters away from home for fear for their physical and sexual safety.[27] The Central Asia Institute lists proximity of schools to girls' homes as one of the six key ingredients to building successful girls' schools. When roads are poor, schools are far away, and there is not adequate public transportation to and from school, many families prefer to keep their daughters at home rather than risk their being raped, kidnapped, or killed while walking to school. Further, the lack of female teachers limits girls' access to education; in some Muslim states only female teachers are permitted to educate girls, and in all countries female teachers serve as role models to young girls and thus help them see the relevance of an education and help keep them interested and enrolled. A report by UNICEF on Yemen finds that

> The causal link between recruitment of female teachers and girls' enrollment and retention is direct and very significant. . . . Many Yemeni families would like to see their girls continue schooling beyond the age of 11, provided there are female teachers. From the family's point of view, female teachers offer a safe environment for girls' education. At the same time, from the girls' perspectives, the work of female teachers inspires them and the teachers become role models.[28]

Second, female teachers generally do not sexually harass their female students (or their male students), and so parents do not fear sending their daughters to school. The fear of sexual harassment and the attendant possibility of pregnancy is a real concern for many parents and is often enough to keep them from sending their daughters to school once they reach puberty. As the World Education Forum noted, "parents who willingly send their daughters to school remove her at puberty, for fear of an unwanted pregnancy, and marry her off early instead."[29] The presence of female teachers is another of the six key ingredients for success for girls' schools listed by the Central Asia Institute. A lack of female teachers results in many girls not receiving an education.

Nor are girls necessarily safe from their fellow students. Sexual harassment by male students is also a barrier to girls' education, and parents often do not trust the education system to protect their daughters from pregnancy and sexually transmitted diseases. The increased prevalence of HIV/AIDS has made girls' safety even more pressing; one report found that "In South Africa and the Caribbean, girls between 15 and 19 are infected by HIV/AIDS at rates four to seven times higher than boys, 'a disparity linked to widespread exploitation, sexual abuse and discriminatory practices.'"[30] A report done for USAID on the topic of school-based violence against women in developing countries sums up much of what we have discussed regarding the impact of sexual violence on girls in schools and the ways it serves as a barrier to girls' education. The quote is lengthy, but it hammers home the importance of safe learning environments for girls. The report finds:

> Many studies we reviewed have documented that SRGBV [school-related gender-based violence] is perpetrated on female students by their male peers and teachers in school. Outside of school, girls can fall prey to "sugar daddies," older men who can provide favors and financial assistance with school fees. Several studies point out that the consequences of SRGBV adversely affect girls' educational attainment. Girls report losing their concentration in class, feeling bad about themselves, missing school, and even dropping out. The health consequences in terms of increased exposure to sexually transmitted infections (STIs), including HIV/AIDS, and unwanted pregnancies are also devastating. Schools in many countries turn a deaf ear to the female students' complaints and many girls do not even complain because of a fear of reprisals, especially from teachers, but also because they believe that nothing will be done. In many countries SRGBV goes unchecked in the face of indifference from school administrators, the larger community, and the ministries of education.[31]

Until girls are safe in schools, they will often be kept home.

A final barrier to girls' (and boys') education is the increased prevalence of civil conflicts and international war. Girls are voluntarily or involuntarily swept up in violent conflicts as sex slaves, fighters, cooks, and so on, and as a result do not attend school (see Chapter 11 for more on the topic of girls during war). Further, violence often causes large segments of the population to flee the war-torn region, and women and girls disproportionately make up most refugees and internally displaced persons. One report published by UNESCO estimated that nearly 100,000 girls "directly participated in conflicts in at least 30 countries during the 1990s . . . and the vast majority of the world's estimated 25 million internally displaced persons are women and children."[32] Many of these children grow up in refugee camps, denied an education and thus all the lifelong benefits that can accrue from it. While in these refugee camps, they are often lured into the sex slave trade or into child labor scams. A report from Kenya suggests that many girls ages 12 to 18 who fled to camps for displaced persons after the recent postelection conflict in Kenya have been taken out of these camps by men offering to take them to lunch or the hairdresser—they then find themselves in brothels for the day.[33] Civil conflicts also result in the destruction of schools and the murder of teachers.

Indian students gather to pray in support of and for the recovery of 14-year-old Pakistani schoolgirl Malala Yousafzai, who was shot in the head by the Taliban for speaking out in support of education for girls. SOURCE: AP Photo/Ajit Solanki.

In Nepal, Maoist rebels targeted teachers and schools, killing an estimated 150 teachers and closing 187 schools and 15 district offices.[34] Thus, civil conflicts and international war are a grave barrier to girls' education.

While this is not an exhaustive discussion of the barriers to girls' education, it highlights many of the major barriers that still exist in many developing countries. These barriers certainly impact boys, too, but reports by international organizations repeatedly show that these barriers disproportionately impact girls. Next we turn to examine efforts to improve girls' access to education.

ADVANCING WOMEN'S EQUALITY

International organizations, nongovernmental organizations (NGOs), and national and local governments have worked for decades toward removing barriers to women's education, and their efforts range from international treaties and laws to community programs. One international organization committed to advancing women's equality is the UN. As we mentioned previously, in 2000, as part of the Millennium Development Goals, the UN targeted the elimination of gender disparities in primary and secondary education by 2015. As part of this goal, in April 2000, representatives from 164 countries met in Dakar, Senegal, at the World Education Forum to discuss the various problems they all confront regarding educating the children of their respective countries and to launch their Education for All—Fast Track Initiative.[35] The Fast Track Initiative is an organization that raises money from donor countries and then doles this money out to low-income countries "which demonstrate serious commitment" in attempting to meet the Millennium Development Goals of universal primary education.[36] The Fast Track Initiative, which changed its name to the Global Partnership for Education (GPE) in 2011, comprises about 30 major countries and donor agencies such as the United States, the European Commission, France, Greece, The Netherlands, Portugal, Spain, Russia, the World Bank, and UNICEF, to name just a few. Countries may apply for aid; if aid is offered, it is contingent on the country signing a memorandum of understanding that binds it to using the money only for specific actions and items. The GPE currently supports 46 countries around the world. Since 2003 it has "helped educate 19 million students, constructed 30,000 classrooms, trained nearly 350,000 teachers and distributed 200 million new textbooks in primary schools."[37]

The overall progress toward the Millennium Development Goals of universal primary and secondary education has been uneven. While the UN notes that enrollment in primary education has increased by 18 percentage points in sub-Saharan Africa and has reached 89 percent in the developing world in 2008, the pace is insufficient to attain universal education by 2015.[38]

Why has the goal of universal primary education been so hard to attain? Part of the problem lies with the countries themselves (discussed earlier when describing barriers to education). Some countries, like Malawi, have eliminated school fees but lack the funding or planning to provide quality education. To deal with the massive influx of students, new teachers had only 2 weeks of training and the pupil-to-teacher ratio climbed to 70 to 1.[39] But part of the problem also lies with donor countries who have promised funds but have not delivered: "Four of the richest nations—the U.S., Germany, Japan, and Italy—have been among the slowest to offer their share of the necessary funds."[40] Another problem is that donor countries and the World Bank are reluctant to provide funds for such important items as paying teacher's salaries; they would rather fund tangibles such as desks and chairs. But funding teacher's salaries is crucial to nations that are struggling economically. One report found that a large amount of the money the World Bank spent on education "from the early 1990s onwards had been wasted on building schools that were closed within a few years due to a lack of teachers."[41] Certainly, some states have trouble attracting teachers because of civil strife, but many have trouble recruiting teachers because salaries are so poor. Thus, donor countries and institutions need to reexamine their policies regarding use of funds. To build schools only to see them shut down for lack of teachers is problematic.

Despite these problems, the Millennium Development Goals and the GPE are important because they commit the participants to the goal of gender equality. And while compliance with the Goals is not mandatory, agencies like UNESCO use this as a yardstick by which to measure countries' progress. The embarrassment that may result from being shown to be lagging behind one's compatriots may be enough to prod countries into working harder to meet their international commitments.

Another program is the Girls Education Movement (GEM) launched in 2001 by UNICEF. This project recruits young women in school to encourage other girls to attend school, improve their study habits, and gain confidence.[42] The U.S. Agency for International Development (USAID) has established a Girls' and Women's Education Initiative. It "supports advocacy for girls' education and helps decision makers at the national, regional, and community levels identify the barriers and it strengthens the capacity of individuals and groups to finance and implement girls' education projects using their own resources."[43] The efforts of these development agencies are important in the struggle to improve women's access to education because they indicate support and commitment from the international community.

The World Bank is another player in attempting to advance women's equality. The World Bank has emphasized the importance of expanding education as a means of reducing overall levels of poverty. Toward this goal they have combined grants and interest-free loans with debt relief. Debt relief is the forgiveness of often billions of dollars of debt owed to international lending institutions, like the World Bank. For instance, in 2005, G8 finance ministers agreed to cancel up to $55 billion in debts owed to the World Bank and the African Development Bank by poor countries.[44] The intention of debt relief is to rid poor countries of crippling debt service payments, thereby freeing up large chunks of money for countries to redirect toward social services. Many argue that it is of great benefit to countries and has greatly enhanced access to education, especially for girls, in the countries receiving it. One of its biggest supporters is the Irish rock star Bono, from the band U2. Bono has been at the forefront of international efforts to raise awareness about debt relief. In 2002, Bono and former U.S. Treasury Secretary Paul O'Neill toured countries in Africa that had been recipients of debt relief. In Uganda they visited schools that were built from savings that arguably accrued to Uganda as a result of debt relief.[45] Bono's attention to the plight of poor countries has heightened public awareness of the problem of debt and poverty and the relationship between the two.

Uganda is an example of a country that has received grants, interest-free loans, and debt relief. In 1998, the World Bank approved a $155 million package of grants and interest-free loans to support universal primary education there. In particular, the World Bank emphasized securing education for girls, orphans, and children from poor or rural families. Recent debt relief in Uganda began in the late 1990s when $650 million in debt to external creditors was written off under the Initiative for Heavily Indebted Poor Countries (HIPCs). Uganda qualified for this debt relief after meeting stringent requirements for a poverty reduction plan set forth by the International Monetary Fund and the World Bank. In 2000, Uganda again benefited from another round of relief granted by the World Bank and the International Monetary Fund as a result of its efforts to reduce poverty. And in 2006, Uganda's $4.5 billion in foreign debt was reduced to $1 billion through a debt waiver granted by the World Bank.[46]

What has been the impact of these grants, interest-free loans, and debt forgiveness? Has it been used to reduce poverty, as was intended?

In 1997, Uganda was able to launch universal primary education (a requirement for receiving debt relief), and enrollment increased from 2.5 million to 6 million, the ratio of boys to girls narrowed drastically, and annual expenditures on education increased by 9 percent (secondary education was made free in 2007).[47] Net enrollment rates for primary schooling (the total number of children in school) in Uganda increased from a total 62.3 percent in 1992 to 96 percent of girls and 95 percent of boys in 2005.[48] And as of May 2012, the gender gap in primary and secondary schooling is nearly closed.[49] Uganda's finance minister, Ezra Suruma, has argued that because of the debt forgiveness, Uganda has been able to free up a lot of money that would have gone to debt repayment but instead has now been directed toward increased funding for universal primary and secondary education, as well as other social services.[50] A report written by a U.K.-based organization that watches G8 promises to Africa notes that Uganda has effectively utilized its debt relief savings, as evidenced by "doubling the school enrollment rate to 94 percent, which has contributed to Uganda's remarkable decline in HIV rates."[51] Elsewhere in Africa, Zambia and Tanzania have both used savings from debt relief to build schools, and Simon Maxwell, director of Britain's leading aid think tank, the Overseas Development Institute, argues that "Millions of children in Africa are now at school, because debt relief has given governments the resources to pay for teachers and school buildings."[52]

On the downside, while more children were going to school in Uganda, there are not enough resources to ensure that they are receiving a quality education. They face overcrowded classrooms, shortages of materials, and, most importantly, shortages of teachers.[53] The UN notes that while gender parity has almost been reached, there is uneven access across regions and levels of schooling and there is unequal treatment of boys and girls in terms of susceptibility to violence, teachers' attitudes, textbooks, and subject choices.[54] Recent estimates find that there are still approximately 94 to 100 students per classroom.[55] Many Ugandans echo these concerns. They argue that the lack of resources has led to students who are learning nothing.[56] Minister of Education Gerard Namirembe Bitamazire, when asked about these problems, replied that Uganda's priorities in education were "access, equity and quality," in that order, and that "What was the point of quality education for a proportion of the population if it left plenty of children out?"[57] Further, the Canadian International Development Agency notes that the enrollment numbers given here can be misleading because they hide huge discrepancies between those children living in war-torn northern Uganda and those in the South, with enrollment figures being much lower in the North.

There are other problems with debt relief. The auditor general notes that money saved from debt relief—over $2 trillion—is sitting in the state's coffers, not being utilized.[58] Other critics argue that previous debt relief to Uganda resulted in money being skimmed off the top by local governments that were given funds intended to be utilized for education. One report found that "only 13 percent of central government grants for nonsalary education spending in Uganda . . . actually made it to the local schools that were the intended beneficiaries."[59] Thus, the merits of universal primary education as well as the merits of debt relief in Uganda are more nuanced than one might expect.

There are also some general problems associated with debt relief. William Easterly of the World Bank's Development Research Group argues that debt forgiveness has a lot of pitfalls, one of which is that when a country's debt is forgiven, that country often goes out and borrows more money, thus beginning the cycle all over again. Easterly notes that "From 1989 to 1997, debt forgiveness for the 41 nations now designated as HIPCs reached $33 billion, while new borrowing for the same countries totaled $41 billion."[60] Creating new debt is not the point of providing debt relief, but when debt relief is offered to countries whose regimes may be corrupt or suffer from severe mismanagement, this may be one of the results. Easterly goes on to note that even in Uganda, where President Yoweri Museveni is a vast improvement over the dictatorial rule of Idi Amin, "Museveni's government continues to spend money on questionable military adventures in the Democratic Republic of Congo."[61] While debt relief offers promise and has clearly shown some positive results, it is not without its critics and is unlikely to be the sole answer to the problem of increasing access to education for girls.

Other efforts to improve girls' access to education are conducted at the domestic level by NGOs and by national and local governments. NGOs in several African countries have set up programs to educate people about sexual harassment, teach girls to resist unwanted sexual advances, and make male students sensitive to the rights of women and girls.[62] National and local initiatives to improve girls' access to education are numerous, so we will just highlight a few:

- In Chile, the Women's Institute "promotes educational activities to enable women to take an active public role and to deal with social and political issues."[63]
- Malawi has eliminated school fees and abolished compulsory school uniforms, thus making an education more affordable to many citizens.[64]
- In Mashan County in China, priority loans or development funds are awarded to villages and households that adopt successful measures to send girls to school.[65]
- Guinea has raised the marriage age, and it is now illegal for male teachers to harass female pupils; Benin is now offering some basic education opportunities to girls who drop out of school.[66]
- In Mali, a community-based project works to alter traditional beliefs about women and girls by involving women in literacy and income-generating activities, after which they usually support the education of their girls. The results are promising—daily visits were made to homes of girls who were absent from school, and the girls were accompanied to school. Enrollment in 18 villages doubled to 44 percent, and in just 3 years girls' enrollment rose to 33 percent from 18 percent.[67]
- In Senegal, via a partnership between UNESCO and Procter & Gamble, 100 literacy classes for girls and women have opened in seven regions of the country.[68]

Overall, NGOs, local and national governments, and international organizations are actively working toward improving the state of women's education. Yet, it is clear from the discussion that while important strides have been made in removing barriers to women's education in developing nations, international pledges, treaties, and increased legislation will not be sufficient to close the gap.

Elizabeth Scharpf

In 2007 Elizabeth Scharpf launched Sustainable Health Enterprises (SHE). Scharpf recognized that one of the reasons that girls missed school was because they could not afford imported sanitary pads, and thus when they had their period they stayed home. So Scharpf began to investigate ways to produce sanitary pads locally. The result are pads made from locally sourced materials, like banana leaves, that cost up to 30% less than imported pads. Currently working in Rwanda, the pads are made by local women who will ultimately own the businesses through microfinance loans. Scharpf hopes the project will ultimately move into other countries as well. The SHE initiative confronts multiple issues at once: it helps keep girls in school and improves women's economic status—a win–win situation!

Most of the discussion so far has focused on primary education. We noted earlier that gender parity in secondary education is still elusive: only 54 of 144 countries have gender parity in secondary education. Why do enrollment levels drop so significantly for girls once they enter secondary school? The reasons don't differ terribly from what has been discussed earlier. The key factors are school fees and families' beliefs that daughters should remain at home to help with chores, younger children, the sick, and the elderly. Families that may be willing to send young girls to primary school balk at sending older daughters, who can contribute to household chores and who will eventually be married off to another family. And, if the school is not free, then there really is no reason to send a daughter and waste the money. As long as these barriers exist, girls will not attend secondary school.

On a practical level, a number of specific proposals would help remove barriers to girls' education. First, increasing household income results in a huge benefit to girls. For example, in Ethiopia "increasing a household's wealth index by one unit enhances a boy's chances of attending school by 16%, against *41% for girls*"[69] (emphasis added). An increase in household income can reduce or remove the need for children to work. Further, a variety of improvements are needed in schools, such as increased teacher training on gender awareness, higher numbers of female teachers, and the elimination of school fees. Gendered classroom practices need to be altered; for example, girls in school are often more likely than boys to be sent to fetch water, sweep floors, and other such chores.[70]

A critical player in advancing all of these reforms is the government. Further, this requires coordinated commitment from a variety of agencies, given that "a massive expansion of basic education is required."[71] This can often require the redirection of the state's resources from some areas, like defense, to education, and also entails a crackdown on government corruption.

Finally, writing proactive legislation is often not sufficient; local practices, customs, and beliefs about girls' rights and abilities must also change. This can be accomplished through the use of campaigns, role models, and working directly with adolescent girls to strengthen their voice.[72] This also means that donors must be careful in making sure that they are not imposing overly Westernized visions of girls' equality and that the people and culture of each country also drive efforts for change. For example, one important lesson that USAID states that it has learned from its years of work in this area is that its programs are most effective when they are "owned" by the citizens of the country, not the donor community, and they must fit the country's economy, political system, culture, and such.[73] While the international community can stress the importance of improving girls' access to education, until local communities, NGOs, and domestic governments share this goal, gender parity in education will remain an elusive goal. However, judging from the improvements made in many areas of the world, improved access to education has been one of the more successful development campaigns with the UN's Millennium Development Goals.

CONCLUSION

Educated children, both girls and boys, will help many countries escape poverty. Educated girls have fewer children, have better nourished and healthier children, bring in more income to their families, are more likely to participate in the political process, value themselves more, and live longer and healthier lives. There are obvious and proven benefits to educating girls; however, for local communities and governments, improving access to girls' education is not always a priority in the face of multiple, competing needs. While the international community has successfully prodded governments to increase girls' access to primary education in many countries, ensuring that girls are integrated into the education system at all levels is still a target rather than a completed campaign.

FOR MORE INFORMATION

Interested in finding out what citizens in the United States are doing to let their voices be heard? Go to http://www.endpoverty2015.org and find out about the various actions taken by "regular people" to try to help end poverty in the developing world.

Global Partnership for Education, http://www.globalpartnership.org/

Sustainable Health Enterprises http://www.sheinnovates.com/ourteam.html

UNICEF, http://www.unicef.org/girlseducation/india_39596.html?q=printme; "Girl Stars" take their show on the road to highlight the importance of girls' education in India.

UNICEF, Gender Parity and Education, http://www.unicef.org/progressforchildren/2005n2/gender.php

United Nations, Progress Toward the Millennium Development Goals, Education, http://www.undp.org/mdg/basics_ontrack.shtml

World Bank, Information about Girls' education, http://web.worldbank.org/WBSITE/EXTERNAL/TOPICS/EXTEDUCATION/0,,contentMDK:20298916~menuPK:617572~pagePK:148956~piPK:216618~theSitePK:282386,00.html

The Debt Police—This documentary describes the role of debt relief in Uganda.

Educating Lucia—This documentary shows the life of three sisters in Zimbabwe and their hopes and aspirations.

Girls Can't Wait—This documentary looks at the status of girls' education in India.

The New Sudan—This documentary looks at girls and education in Sudan; http://nadusfilms.com/#new-sudan.

11

Women and Sexual Violence
During War

It was April 14th when we left our house and on the 15th we were walking near Djakovica. . . . We met Serb paramilitaries. . . . They approached my uncle and separated him. . . . They came up to me. . . . He took my hand and told me to get in his car. . . . He told me not to refuse or there would be lots of victims. . . . He told me not to scream and to take off my clothes. He took off his clothes and told me to suck his thing. I did not know what to do. He took my head and put it near him. He started to beat me. I lost consciousness. When I came to I saw him over me. I had great pain. . . . Another man came with a car and he got over me. . . . I was crying with pain and he was laughing the whole time. . . . He told me not to tell anyone or they would take me for good and shoot my family.[1]

They put us in a small barn with hay in it. Then the four men came into the barn and slammed the door and pointed machine guns at us. . . . Then they took me. I was pregnant. I was holding my son. They took him away from me and gave him to my mother. They told me to get up and follow them. I was crying and screaming, "Take me back to my child!" They took me to another room. It was so bad I almost fainted. I can't say the words they said. . . . Because I was pregnant, they asked me where my husband was. . . . One of them said to another soldier, "Kick her and make the baby abort." They did this to me four times—they took me outside to the other place. Three men took me one by one. Then they asked me, "Are you desperate for your husband?" and said, "Here we are instead of him."[2]

These graphic testimonies from Kosovar Albanian women illustrate the atrocities that women and girls have suffered and continue to suffer during times of war. And while such atrocities have been committed against women during wars for centuries, it is only recently that sexual violence against women during times of war and displacement has received any attention from the international community. In this chapter we will look at the issue of sexual violence against women during times of war and displacement. This will include examining sexual violence against women in their home countries and as refugees fleeing their countries (sometimes because of war, other times because of forcible expulsion). We will discuss the intent of sexual violence, examine varying manifestations of sexual violence in four countries, discuss the impact it has on women's lives, and analyze what is being done about it.

THE INTENT OF SEXUAL VIOLENCE

Sexual violence against women and girls during times of war generally takes the form of rape. Human rights organizations have documented cases of individual and gang rape of women and girls by soldiers and rebel groups and rape with objects such as firewood, weapons, and umbrellas. Females who have suffered sexual violence are often also forced to serve as slaves or "wives" to soldiers and are often subject to a life of permanent sexual slavery. Even females who become fighters report being forced to serve as sexual slaves and soldiers' "wives" in addition to fighting.[3] Such violence is often committed by government soldiers, rebel forces, and even government and international peacekeeping forces. It is also committed against women in refugee camps by locals of the country in which the refugee camp is located.

Why do soldiers and others commit this type of violence against women? First and foremost, it is not for sexual gratification. Rather, rape during war and in refugee camps is about the display of power and is a way of letting the enemy know who is in control. However, the reasons for needing to display this power are often varied. To this end, rape is often:

- Committed in homes in front of male relatives to humiliate the men. It is used to shame them because they are unable to protect their women.
- Committed while the woman is fleeing war-torn areas and in detention centers as a form of political terror and intimidation.
- Committed against women as a way of terrorizing communities into accepting the control of the aggressor or to punish a community for assisting opposing forces.
- Committed against women by their husbands and male relatives in refugee camps. Refugee life often leads to stressful situations that erupt into violence. Further, the extended network of family and friends is not present to act as a deterrent to sexual violence.
- Committed against women who had held positions of power prior to the war. These women are often raped by men who had felt inferior to them.
- Committed against women by their husbands when they return from war angry, confused, and armed.
- Used as a method of revenge, which is often inflicted on the women of the oppressor's ethnic group. Sometimes, media coverage of victimized women fuels the anger of the ethnic group that is being oppressed.
- Used as a method of "ethnic cleansing." Women are often forced to bear the children of the enemy that has raped them. Thus, the child will be the nationality of the man who impregnated the woman.

While power is the primary motivator for rape as a tool of war, the reasons for needing to display this power are varied.

Many women who have survived sexual violence have few options in seeking legal retribution. Some countries lack specific legislation that criminalizes rape and sexual assault; the legislation that does exist does not clearly articulate provisions regarding rape. Women often do not know how to pursue prosecution in criminal courts; as refugees, women are unfamiliar with the local legal system and may be wary of police and judicial authorities. For years, adjudicators rejected women's claims of being raped by soldiers and police; they treated these acts as "private moments" not open to public scrutiny.[4] Further, international groups are not always receptive to or experienced in addressing rape and sexual violence. For example, in Indonesia, women were sexually abused by Indonesian security forces. When some women decided to report this abuse, a human rights nongovernmental organization (NGO) agreed to bring the women to the provincial capital, where the case and their identities were widely publicized. As a result, when the women were taken into custody and questioned about the incidents of abuse, not surprisingly, they recanted their stories. In this instance, women essentially became pawns of the police as a result of the lack of protection for victims of sexual violence and the NGO's inexperience in dealing with the issue in such a politicized context.

There is also often a cultural taboo against speaking about rape, and so women keep silent after it has occurred. Many societies still function around an honor ethic in which a man's honor depends on female chastity. If a woman is raped and the rape becomes public knowledge, a man's honor is marred in multiple ways. It displays to the community that he was unable to protect the females in his family, and/or the man may see the raped woman as having "encouraged" the rape with her actions. Thus, many women who are raped but are not killed afterward or impregnated as a result die with their secret. And finally, when sexual violence has occurred during war, women often fear retaliation against their families if they tell others. This retaliation could come from soldiers (as the quote at the beginning of the chapter indicates), or it could even come from family and others in the refugee community. For example, Burundian refugees in Tanzania often rely on the *abashingatahe* system for dealing with internal matters. The *abashingatahe* is a group of respected, mostly male elders, who act as an arbiter of disputes. Fellow refugees expect women who have been raped by other refugees to take their complaints to the *abashingatahe*, even though this group is not supposed to deal with serious criminal matters like rape.[5] If women choose to take their cases to government authorities, they suffer at the hands of their own people. In sum, women who have been raped by soldiers, fellow refugees, or government or international actors have few resources for addressing the violence. The victims are wary of local police and judicial authorities, they fear retaliation by their aggressors and sometimes by their own people, and international agencies and NGOs have little experience in handling such crimes. Later we will address some recent efforts to change this situation.

INCIDENTS OF SEXUAL VIOLENCE

Let us now turn to some specific documented incidents of sexual violence against women refugees and during times of war. There are numerous cases, but we will focus on four: the former Yugoslavia (including the Kosovo and Bosnian conflicts), the Democratic Republic of Congo, Sierra Leone, and Tanzania. The first three cases focus mainly on sexual violence during wartime. The last case is an example of the sexual violence that women face in refugee camps when fleeing war-torn countries. These cases were chosen because they are some of the most horrific examples of sexual violence in recent decades and because of the extensive amount of documentation available.

The Former Yugoslavia

The republics of the former Yugoslavia erupted into violent conflict in the early 1990s, as the country quickly polarized along ethnic lines. Slovenia, Croatia, Macedonia, and Bosnia and Herzegovina were recognized as independent states in 1992, while the remaining republics of Serbia and Montenegro formed the Federal Republic of Yugoslavia (FRY) under President Slobodan Milosevic. Under his leadership, the army led various campaigns to unite ethnic Serbs (and destroy the Muslim population) in neighboring republics in the name of forming a "greater Serbia." Further, in 1989–99, FRY military and paramilitary forces launched massive expulsions of ethnic Albanians living in the Kosovo region of Serbia, which in turn prompted further NATO intervention and the stationing of NATO forces in Kosovo.[6]

Bosnian Serb soldiers drove 1.5 million non-Serbs (mainly Muslims) from their homes and villages in an egregious example of ethnic cleansing. In particular, women were targeted as pawns of war and were raped in their homes, while fleeing the conflict, and in detention centers as part of a "well-planned strategy of national humiliation," many experts claim.[7] Many women and girls were held in camps that were run like brothels, where Serb soldiers could come and rape women and girls as often as they liked. In the indictment filed with the War Crimes Tribunal for the former Yugoslavia in The Hague, a 15-year-old girl testified about her 8-month ordeal in such a camp. Raped and tortured by Bosnian Serb soldiers on a regular basis, she was finally sold by one of her captors to two Montenegro soldiers for 500 deutschmarks (about $280).[8] Further, one Serb leader, Dragoljub Kunarac, was reported to have "taunted one of his victims by telling her she would carry Serb babies and would not know who the father was because of the number of men who raped her."[9] A report by the European Commission (the executive arm of the European Union) estimated that "as many as 20,000 Bosnian women—including girls as young as six and women as old as 80—were raped by Bosnian Serbs during the war."[10] No woman or girl was immune or safe.

The use of rape in the Kosovo conflict several years later was similar in its form and intent. Serbian and Yugoslav forces used the rape of women as a way to terrorize the Albanian population (largely Muslim) and force them to flee the country in their campaign to "ethnically cleanse" Serbia. Women were raped in their homes in front of male relatives, on the road while fleeing, and in centers, often multiple times. Further, in this conflict the oppressed rape against the aggressor. As the testimonies at the beginning of th indicate, many Serbian, Albanian, and Roma women were raped Albanians, sometimes members of the Kosovo Liberation Army.[11] The Yugoslav case illustrates several of the reasons for sexual violence against women during war—to induce humiliation, intimidation, and terror as part of an overall project of ethnic cleansing. We will discuss this case further when we look at the role of the international community in addressing this problem.

The Congo

The next case we will examine is the war in the eastern Democratic Republic of Congo (Congo). The massive inflow of refugees in 1994 from neighboring Rwanda and Burundi sparked ethnic strife and civil war within Congo, as the aging dictator, Mobutu Sese Seiko, slowly lost his grip on power. In May 1997, Mobutu was toppled from power by a coalition of forces led by Laurent Kabila. Fifteen months later, his regime was in turn challenged when in August 1998 Rwandan- and Ugandan-backed forces invaded eastern Congo. Troops from Zimbabwe, Angola, Namibia, Chad, and Sudan entered the conflict on the side of Kabila's regime. Although a ceasefire among the relevant parties was signed in 1999, sporadic fighting continued, and the eastern Congo was in effect controlled by the Rwandan-financed Rassemblement congolais pour la democratie (RCD) from 1998 to October 2002.[12] The war went on, however, with fighting continuing "among dozens of militia groups—mostly consisting of poor young men who prey upon impoverished villagers—despite the presence of the largest [United Nations] peacekeeping mission in the world."[13] On Jan. 21, 2008, warring militia groups signed an agreement to end the fighting, which had claimed, by some estimates, more than 5.4 million people; the agreement was signed on January 23 by President Kabila and other militia leaders.[14] But in the fall of 2008 rebels advanced toward the eastern provincial capital; the United Nations (UN) estimated that more than 200,000 people were displaced from their homes in September and October 2008 alone.[15]

All groups involved in this war have used rape as a weapon. One NGO estimates that in the Northern Kivu province alone there have been 14,000 rapes since 2004.[16] In some instances rape has been used as part of a broader attack on a village, designed to terrorize local communities into accepting the aggressor's control, and in other instances it has been used to punish a village for allegedly supporting an opposing militia.[17] Dr. Denis Mukwege, director and founder of the Paniz General Referral Hospital in the eastern Congo town of Bukavu, argues that "Rape and sexual violence are now used as a war strategy. . . . It is a tactic of war. It is not rape as understood by many parts of the world, as a violation of the rights of a human being. It is rape used as a weapon of mass destruction. . . . It is sexual terrorism that seeks to destroy the identity of the individuals and their communities."[18] Women and girls are also assaulted as, in an attempt to feed their families, they

A ten-year-old girl who was raped twice during the war in the Congo sits under a bed and washes her hands in a clinic set up by an NGO for rape victims of the war. The girl was first raped by soldiers in her hometown and somehow made her way to the capital, Goma, where she wandered the streets and was raped again by soldiers. A woman found her and brought her to this clinic. SOURCE: ROBERTO SCHMIDT/AFP/Getty Images.

venture off to fields to cultivate produce, into forests to make charcoal, and to town to sell their wares (see photo 11.1). Further, many women have been raped as they fled, with other members of their villages, into the forests in hope of escaping the terrors of war, only to be met by another terror: abduction. Human Rights Watch, an interest group dedicated to documenting human rights abuses worldwide, found that these acts of sexual violence are often aggravated even further by additional acts of brutality, including shooting victims in the vagina or mutilating them with knives or razorblades.[19] One young woman reports how soldiers raped her with a pestle: "One of them restrained me, while another took my pili pili pestle and pushed it several times into my vagina, as if he was pounding. . . . For two weeks my vagina was discharging. . . . They also killed my husband and my son."[20]

Further, women who have been abducted are often kept as sexual slaves by members of the various militias. One survivor recounts her story:

Fifteen men with guns and bows and arrows surrounded us. We had to walk for three days through the jungle to the village that was the Mai Mai headquarters. I was there for three months—five men took me as their "wife" and their slave. I saw one woman killed because she refused; they cut off her breasts. My daughter died while we were there. We got home eventually. It's because of God that I'm alive. But no-one will want me now.[21]

This horrific tale documents only too well the horrors that women in this war-torn region face on a daily basis. These women have little recourse for the damage that has been done to them. A law on sexual violence was passed in 2006 by the parliament. The intent of the law was to speed up the prosecution of rape cases and to increase penalties against those found guilty. However, many NGOs argue that the law has had little effect—that it was a nice symbolic gesture, but that it has not made a difference in the lives of female rape victims. Dirk Deprez of Rejusco, a European-funded organization designed to help the justice system, argues that "It was an ambitious law in an understaffed and underequipped system. . . . [W]e don't see a lot happening in the field since the law came out."[22] Further, while local courts have punished rapes conducted by private citizens, soldiers and other combatants have historically not been tried. Police and judicial authorities do not take these rape cases seriously. As a result, few women come forward to charge their rapists; they fear that authorities will not act on the charges, and they fear the social stigma attached to having been raped.[23] Female rape victims also argue that they see no point in bringing their cases to court in a system that responds to the highest bidder and where there are few to no courts, police, or lawyers in the rural areas, where most rapes occur.[24] Later we will discuss what is being done to help these women and girls.

Sierra Leone

In 1991, a former army corporal, Foday Sankoh, and his Revolutionary United Front (RUF) informed the one-party government that if it did not institute multiparty politics within 90 days the RUF would take up arms to overthrow the government. The Lome peacekeeping agreement was agreed to by all sides in 1999 but was not terribly successful, as fighting continued, fueled in part by conflicts in neighboring countries like Liberia. In 2002 democratic elections were held and a government was elected, which brought a modicum of stability. Eighteen years and a few governments later, the war is essentially over, and UN peacekeeping forces are slowly withdrawing. Nonetheless, during the 12 years of conflict tens of thousands of citizens were killed and over 2 million people (about one third of the population) fled the country and are now refugees in surrounding states. This has been one of the bloodiest, most brutal wars of the twentieth century, and the gradual withdrawal of UN forces, poverty and ethnic and political tension within Sierra Leone, and the deteriorating conditions in surrounding countries present ongoing challenges to Sierra Leone's stability.[25]

Both government forces and the RUF used notoriously horrible tactics, usually upon the civilian population. The RUF specifically targeted civilians and terrorized the population of Sierra Leone through acts of bodily mutilation (such as the amputation of hands and arms) and forced recruitment of child soldiers. Given the brutality of this war, it is not surprising that sexual violence against women was one of the tools adopted by government and rebel forces.

Women and girls in Sierra Leone have reported grotesque abuses of their human rights by both government and rebel forces. Human Rights Watch collected testimonies from numerous girls and women who reported how they were rounded up by rebel forces, brought to their command centers, and subsequently subjected to individual and gang rape, in addition to rape with objects such as pestles, firewood, and weapons. Rapes were often accompanied by other physical abuses—including the hacking off of limbs. Physicians for Human Rights also conducted research in Sierra Leone into the use of sexual violence. One young woman they interviewed, Bola N. Bola, had been abducted four times by 2001. During her first abduction she and other villagers ran off into the bush when the soldiers attacked the village. The soldiers followed them and captured many of them. They held some of the villagers down, cut off some hands, killed some, and raped some. She reports her own rape in the following words, "We were taken to the bush where the sexual act was forced on us. . . . Nine men raped me. . . . After they had raped me to their satisfaction, they left me in the bush. I was beaten, bruises on my body, part of my body. Some around me were amputated. I was not well."[26]

These women and girls were also expected to serve as slaves to the rebel soldiers, performing housework and farm work.[27] Human Rights Watch comments that the point of this sexual violence was

> to dominate women and their communities by deliberately undermining cultural values and community relationships, destroying the ties that hold society together. Child combatants raped women who were old enough to be their grandmothers, rebels raped pregnant and breastfeeding mothers, and fathers were forced to watch their daughters being raped.[28]

Thus this sexual violence was a calculated tactic; rape was used as a means to destroy a population and overthrow a government. Later we will discuss what, if any, recourse these women and girls had after the war ended.

Tanzania

On Oct. 21, 1993, Melchior Ndadaye, Burundi's first democratically elected Hutu president, was assassinated by army officers after having served only 100 days in office. This launched a period of intense ethnic violence between Hutu and Tutsi factions. (The ethnic makeup of Burundi is similar to Rwanda, with approximately 85 percent of the population Hutu and 15 percent of the population Tutsi. Tutsis dominated the armed forces.) The violence has claimed over 200,000 Burundian lives; in addition, some 350,000 Burundians are living in exile in Tanzania alone. A new government (Tutsi-dominated), inaugurated in November 2001, signed a power-sharing agreement with the largest rebel faction (Hutus) in December 2003. A new constitution was ratified in 2005 and a Hutu-dominated government was democratically elected that same year. The president of the government, Pierre Nkurunziza, brokered a peace agreement, with the assistance of South Africa, with the country's last rebel group in 2006,[29] and in 2008, the final ceasefire agreement was signed. General elections were held in 2010, and while seen as credible, they were marked by violence. And Tanzania has said it will close the last of its refugee camps by the end of 2012.

The violence in Burundi resulted in a massive influx of refugees into neighboring Tanzania. These refugees were subject to horrid conditions, but in particular women were the victims of sexual violence. In 1997, Human Rights Watch received reports that many women refugees were suffering human rights abuses in the camps, primarily sexual violence, and that the response of the UN High Commissioner for Refugees (UNHCR) and that of the Tanzanian government was inadequate. Human Rights Watch and other human rights groups investigated these reports in 1998 and 1999. They found that Burundian women in Tanzanian refugee camps had suffered from a great deal of sexual violence at the hands of both Burundian male refugees as well as Tanzanian nationals, soldiers, policemen, husbands, and relatives.[30] The International Rescue Committee researched similar complaints about the refugee camps and determined that "Burundi refugees have suffered a high degree of sexual and gender violence. The initial results of the IRC assessment suggest that approximately 26% of the 3,803 Burundi refugee women between the ages of 12–49 in the established camp of Kanembwa have experienced sexual violence since becoming a refugee."[31]

These women, like those in the Congo, were often attacked while carrying out daily tasks, such as gathering firewood, harvesting vegetables, or looking for employment in nearby towns (see text box "A Typical Rape in Darfur"). They often did not report the attacks because they were either unfamiliar with the local legal system and/or were wary of local police and authorities. Human Rights Watch argues that the sexual violence that these women suffered is the consequence of the "absence of well-designed and concrete programs to protect women refugees from violence and to punish the perpetrators of such violence when it occurs."[32] We will examine the shortcomings of the UNHCR response to the problem a bit later in the chapter. No matter the shortcoming, this case illustrates the sexual dangers that female refugees face on top of their daily attempts to survive harsh circumstances far from home.

These four cases clearly illustrate the use of sexual violence against women and girls as a deliberate tool during war. Rape during war and in refugee situations is not random, nor is it a result of overly keyed-up men with weapons. It is a tactic that military leaders have chosen to use to attain their desired end—military victory and total submission of a defeated population. The main victims of modern warfare are the civilians of the countries at war, and no one is safe and no tactic is out of bounds, including mutilating a woman's vagina. How do women, assuming they survive, cope with such abuses? We now turn to discussing the impact of this sexual violence on the remainder of their lives.

THE IMPACT OF SEXUAL VIOLENCE ON WOMEN

The impact of sexual violence on women is far-reaching. Women who have been raped suffer physical, psychological, and social consequences. The physical impacts are many. Pregnancy is one obvious impact. Many rapes result in pregnancy, and rape victims are often forced, either by societal pressure or lack of access to health care, to carry the pregnancy to term. Many of these women end up as poor single mothers (if married, they are often cast off by their husbands), shunned by society because of the circumstances of their pregnancy. Sometimes these babies are given up for adoption, thus swelling the ranks of victims of these crimes. And even when an abortion is an option, the procedure still leaves emotional scars on its recipients.

Other physical impacts include sexually transmitted diseases (STDs) such as AIDS and salpingitis. In the Congo, it is estimated that upward of 60 percent of the military forces are infected with HIV, thus exposing their rape victims to this dreadful disease.[33] Salpingitis is a sexually transmitted disease that causes pain, infertility, and a foul-smelling discharge. Further, Médecins Sans Frontières (MSF), the international group of doctors who help in war-torn countries, notes that many women are so badly damaged by the sexual assaults that they will require surgery to repair them physically.[34] These women end up suffering incontinence because of a fistula between the anus and the vagina. According to one health worker interviewed by MSF, "There is no life for a woman with a fistula. They smell so bad, they will not be accepted by society; maybe, just maybe, their mother will stand by them. But no one will want to approach them."[35] There are often no facilities or money for these women to be treated, so they must live with this physical pain.

In addition to the physical scars are emotional and psychological impacts. The National Center for Post Traumatic Stress Disorder states that women who have been raped during war suffer permanently from shock, intense fear, tearfulness, anger, shame, helplessness, nervousness, numbness, confusion, disorientation, unwanted memories, decreased ability to concentrate, and self-blame.[36] They note that these symptoms were found in up to 75 percent of Bosnian female refugees, even among those who did not report being raped.[37] A recent study of fighters in Liberia exposed to sexual violence echoes these findings. Kirsten Johnson, MD, MPH, of the Harvard Humanitarian Initiative at Harvard University, found that "Seventy-four percent of female former combatants who experienced sexual violence had symptoms of [posttraumatic stress disorder], compared with 44 percent who did not experience sexual violence."[38] The emotional and psychological ramifications of sexual violence should not be ignored when analyzing its impact, since many of these scars do not heal easily, if at all.

Finally are the social impacts of rape during war. Rape survivors often are rejected by their families and their villages. Sometimes this rejection is because they are suspected of having been infected with AIDS or other STDs. MSF notes that in many African countries, a husband will often turn out his wife, and even if he lets her return home "it is normal for him to find a new wife, moving the old one into a different room and ignoring her. Fear of disease, real or perceived, is often given as the reason for this rejection."[39] Other times the rejection is just because of the stigma attached to having been raped. Jeanette, a young woman who was raped by a member of the local militia in her village in the Congo, reported to interviewers that her family had rejected her, saying that "she offered herself to her attacker."[40] Because of this, many women never report their rapes or seek medical attention.

We can see that the impacts of rape during war are far-reaching. Not only do these women suffer from the well-known horrors of war—the slaughter of family members, the destruction of villages, food scarcity, and refugee status—but they have also an additional, often not discussed, horror to face, that of being raped. The consequences are many, and thousands of women and girls live with these consequences every day. We now turn to international and domestic efforts to address the problem.

ADDRESSING SEXUAL VIOLENCE AGAINST WOMEN

International law increasingly has been used as a tool to combat and criminalize sexual violence against women. One of the more far-reaching developments in dealing with sexual violence against women was the verdict rendered against some of the Bosnian Serb leaders for their role in the rapes of women during the war in Yugoslavia. In February 2001, the International Criminal Tribunal for the Former Yugoslavia convicted Dragoljub Kunarac, Radomir Kovac, and Zoran Vukovic for their role in the rape, torture, and enslavement of women during the conflict in Bosnia. They received sentences of 28, 20, and 12 years, respectively. These three cases are the first time in history that an international tribunal has brought charges against military leaders solely for crimes of sexual violence against women. And it is the first time that an international tribunal has found rape and enslavement a crime against humanity. Building on this record, in 2007, the International Criminal Court (ICC) filed charges against men in two high-profile war crimes cases: that of two Sudanese suspected of mass rape and other war crimes and that of the leader of the Lord's Resistance Army in Uganda, who was charged with sexual enslavement and rape. Further, in 2008 the UN Security Council voted officially to recognize rape and sexual violence as war crimes and to prohibit postconflict agreements from granting amnesty to those perpetrators of sexual violence.

While the ICC has been criticized for a lack of emphasis on crimes of sexual violence against women (particularly in the Congo, where the case against warlord Thomas Lubanga did not include any charges of sexual violence), its record is improving. What follows is a brief history of the cases before the ICC that include charges of sexual violence. In November 2009, the ICC began its second trial (the first was the Lubanga case). This trial was against Germain Katanga, a leader of the Forces for Patriotic Resistance in the Congo. The case does include charges of sexual violence. As of July 2012, no verdict had been handed down. In November 2010, the trial against Jean-Pierre Bemba, a former vice-president of the Congo, began, and it too included charges of sexual violence used by troops under his command in the Central African Republic (this trial was ongoing as of July 2012). The former Chief Prosecutor, Luis Moreno-Ocampo, initiated an investigation in June 2011 into the alleged distribution of Viagra to Libyan troops as an official policy of rape. This investigation is ongoing and the ICC and Libya are at odds over who has the right to bring charges against former officials in Libya. At present, all situations before the ICC include charges of sexual violence or rape. And in June 2012, the ICC appointed its first-ever female Chief Prosecutor, Fatou Bensouda. Finally, on July 10, 2012, the ICC handed down its first-ever prison sentence to Lubanga, whom they sentenced to 14 years in jail for the use of child soldiers to build a rebel army that was accused of committing rape, murder, and ethnic cleansing. While the charges did not include specific charges of sexual violence, it is key that Lubanga was arrested, tried, and convicted for his part in the atrocities in the Congo.

In April 2012, the former President of Liberia, Charles Taylor, who was responsible for overseeing massive amounts of violence in neighboring Sierra Leone, was sentenced to 50 years in prison for war crimes by the Special Court for Sierra Leone. The war crimes included charges of rape.

The decision of the International Tribunal for the Former Yugoslavia, the ICC's actions, and the UN vote are important because they establish legal precedents for charging soldiers and combatants who use sexual violence against women during war. Nonetheless, they will not end the use of sexual violence against women during war. Nor will they necessarily eradicate the climate of indifference surrounding sexual violence against women during war. Further, women will still fear coming forward and reporting rape because of the anticipated reaction of their husbands, families, or communities.

Truth and reconciliation commissions (TRCs) have been popular ways to heal the wounds of civil conflicts, like the one in Sierra Leone. Women have testified before Sierra Leone's TRC about the multitude of abuses they suffered during the many years of conflict. Initially, investigators had a tough time getting women to speak up about sexual violence. As has been discussed elsewhere, women fear discussing sexual violence because of the stigma that will be attached to them. To aid the TRC in Sierra Leone, the UN Development Fund for Women provided support and training for TRC staff and for the women themselves.[41] As a result of this outreach and help from other NGOs, more women felt safe speaking up and a record of the abuses now exists. However, the Lome peace accord (which created the TRC) has an amnesty clause that granted immunity to the perpetrators of war crimes between 1991 and 1999. Such deals leave the victims of sexual violence with no recourse. Nonetheless, some perpetrators of sexual violence have been tried and convicted. In 2007, the Special Court for Sierra Leone found three senior members of the armed forces guilty of 11 out of 14 counts of war crimes and crimes against humanity, including sexual slavery and rape.[42] Many, however, have gone free and will never be tried.

International agencies such as the UNHCR also work on issues of sexual violence against women, although not always with great levels of success. Since 1950, the UNHCR has been charged with leading and coordinating "action to protect refugees and resolve refugee problems worldwide. Its primary purpose is to safeguard the rights and well-being of refugees."[43] In particular, it has written directives protecting women from gender-based violence in refugee camps. However, while the existence of this agency is useful, it also has its shortcomings. Human Rights Watch regularly monitors the actions of the agency and has found some serious problems. For instance, in 2002 some UNHCR refugee aid workers were charged with sexual exploitation of children in Nepal. UNHCR subsequently removed these workers; nonetheless, the very fact that some of its staff were guilty of the very crimes they were supposed to prevent is disconcerting. Further, Human Rights Watch has charged UNHCR with ineffectual enforcement of the guidelines concerning gender-based violence, in particular in Tanzania.[44] Thus, the UNHCR has the potential to be a useful tool for protecting women from gender-based violence in refugee camps, but it needs to monitor its staff more forcefully and strictly enforce its own directives.

A number of international groups work to assist women who have been sexually violated during war and in refugee situations. Three such groups are Human Rights Watch, Amnesty International, and MSF. The first two groups visit war-torn areas and refugee camps to document human rights abuses against women (and others). They, in turn, put pressure on the national government where the abuses have occurred to end the practices and to punish those who have committed them. They also urge other nations and individuals to put pressure on the country to end the abuses. The third group sends doctors into war-torn areas to administer medical aid to those in need. They have assisted numerous women with physical healing after being harmed by sexual violence. Local groups also have emerged to assist women who have been victims of sexual violence. In the Congo one such group is Amaldefea. This NGO supports mothers and children through such acts as teaching them skills so that they can be self-supporting. All of these organizations, international and local, are crucial in assisting women who have been victims of sexual violence. Through the work of such groups, perpetrators are charged with their crimes and women are assisted in their attempts to rebuild a life for themselves.

WOMEN AS COMBATANTS

Until recently it was assumed that women's and girls' only role in armed conflict was that of victim, but recent research has begun to dispel this myth.[45] As we discussed in Chapter 3 on women and revolutionary movements, women have played and do play a variety of roles in armed conflict. Research has begun to document the number of girls and young women who have played an active role in terrorizing and destroying their communities in armed conflicts in numerous countries, including Cambodia, Colombia, Chechnya, Israel, Sierra Leone, and Uganda. Peter Singer's work on child soldiers finds that "roughly thirty percent of the world's armed forces that employ child soldiers include girl soldiers. Underage girls have been present in the armed forces in fifty-five countries. In twenty-seven of these, girls were abducted to serve and in thirty-four they saw combat."[46] And one survey found that at least 25,000 women and girls participated in the fighting forces in the conflict in Liberia.[47] Girl soldiers have taken up arms; led forces on the frontlines; mutilated and killed friends, family, and civilians; and served in more expected roles such as cooks, cleaners, and wives to rebel soldiers.

While it might sound as if this role might be empowering for women and girls and a step toward being on equal footing with men, this assumption would be mistaken. As Singer's work reveals, most of these female fighters did not join voluntarily (they were abducted), especially the children, and most experienced sexual violence during their time as soldiers. Singer argues that "The fact that sexual abuse is often a common part of the child soldiering experience for these girls debunks any idea that their recruitment is somehow progressive."[48] And a survey conducted by the Liberian Coalition of NGOs in collaboration with Amnesty International found that female soldiers in Liberia often experienced rape and were used as sex slaves and cooks.[49] The survey corroborates Singer's findings that female soldiers often did not join "voluntarily," nor do they see it as a way to attain equality—rather, the "majority were forced to participate in the war, although some opted to take up arms to protect themselves against sexual violence and to avenge the death of family members."[50] Other females in Liberia joined because they were promised cash, education, or jobs (and would be willing to take up arms again to escape poverty).[51] The UN, in its research on the conflict in Sierra Leone, found that while some women joined the armed forces voluntarily, most were forced to join and almost all were forced to take drugs. Many of them remain addicted today. The UN argues that these women bear a triple burden because they were forced to fight and then when the war was over they were ostracized by society for having been combatants and were marginalized for having been sexually violated.[52] A young woman who was recruited as a child soldier into the Lord's Resistance Army in Uganda told the international child aid agency Plan that the war followed her home: "People say we have ghosts attached to us because we have killed."[53] And another young woman, Bintu from Liberia, told Plan that she was abducted by soldiers when she was a child and raped repeatedly during her captivity and "service" as a child soldier.[54]

Finally, because girls are seen as victims, not as combatants, these girl soldiers are being ignored in the disarmament, demobilization, and reintegration (DDR) plans being conducted by the international community at the end of a conflict. For instance, in Sierra Leone, 6,052 boys went through DDR, while only 506 girls did.[55] The result of this is that these girls, who have been socialized to kill, have seen untold horrors, and are ostracized by their community after the war, are not receiving any assistance in reintegrating back into life after war. Boys, because they are assumed to be the vast majority of combatants (although this isn't always the case), are receiving most of the training, schooling, and reintegration efforts (discussed in the next section), while girls are left to fend for themselves and the children they often bore during the conflict. While the presence of female combatants in armed conflicts forces us to rethink women's roles in armed conflicts; they clearly are not solely victims, nor do they all think of themselves as such, but it would be a mistake to see this new role as one on a path toward liberation.

What Happens to the Boys?

While this chapter is primarily focused on the sexual violence experienced by women and girls during war, we find it important to discuss the boys and men who have been trained to commit this violence. What happens to them when the armed conflicts are over? How can we expect sexual violence (and violence in general) to end when wars are over if generations of men and boys have been taught that violence is acceptable? While this topic alone could be a book, we will attempt to highlight a few of the key concerns and issues with child soldiers and with reintegrating back into society boys and men who have been trained to rape, mutilate, and kill.

Child soldiers are a fairly recent phenomenon. For most of history a general rule of warfare was that children would not be conscripted, especially for combat.[56] The reasons for this were based on both principle and pragmatism. Most cultures believed that it was not appropriate for children to carry weapons and engage in warfare and, in reality, most children could not physically carry premodern weapons.[57] There are some exceptions to this rule, but as Singer notes, "while there were isolated instances where children did serve in armies or other groups at war, a general norm held against child soldiers across the last four millennia of warfare."[58] In the late twentieth century this all began to change as nonstate militias began to recruit (often via abduction) child soldiers, usually boys. One of the best-known examples of the use of child soldiers is in Sierra Leone. It is estimated that 80 percent of the forces of the Revolutionary United Front, the militia that instigated the violence, were children ages 7 to 14.[59] The RUF was not the only group to use child soldiers in this conflict; all sides did, and it is estimated that close to 10,000 of the fighters in Sierra Leone were children.[60] Sierra Leone is but one place where child soldiers have been used extensively. Other countries that have made use of child soldiers span the globe and include, among others, Algeria, Angola, Bosnia, Cambodia, the Central African Republic (the Congo), Chechnya, Colombia, Lebanon, Liberia, Kosovo, Nepal, Rwanda, and Turkey (in the Kurdish Worker's Party). Child soldiers are used extensively by nonstate actors (rebel groups, militias, ethnic groups), with one study finding that 60 percent of nonstate armed forces (77 of 129) use child soldiers (the UN estimates this to be about 300,000 child soldiers).[61] But they are also used by state military and paramilitary forces that are currently at peace (the UN estimates this number to be around half a million).[62] Finally, it is important to note that the ranks of child soldiers do not comprise just children on the verge of adulthood; they include vast numbers of children age 15 and under. In his seminal work on child soldiers, Singer finds that "Twenty-three percent of the armed organizations in the world (84 total) use children age fifteen and under in combat roles. Eighteen percent (64) use children twelve and under."[63] Child soldiers are becoming the norm and are presenting the world with new challenges.

Child soldiers have normally been abducted or have "chosen" to join because their parents have been killed and they have no other recourse. While surveys have shown that many children are joining voluntarily, Singer argues that to phrase their joining as voluntary is misleading—children are defined as children because they are deemed to be unable to make mature decisions (like the decision to go to war and risk one's life).[64] Many child soldiers are given alcohol and drugs and often are victims of sexual abuse (both girls and boys, although the number of girls is higher). One boy in Sierra Leone, Abu, reports that he and 30 other young boys were kidnapped in 1991, forced to join rebel forces backed by Liberia's Charles Taylor, and given alcohol and drugs while being trained to kill. He tells his story like this:

> People were fleeing from the fighting. They raided the place. They took all the young men. I was about 13. . . . First of all, they made us carry loads, things that were stolen when they raided. If you did not do it, they would kill you. . . . That was the first killing I saw. That made me silent and made me obey orders.[65]

Another young man in Guatemala reports:

> They killed my parents in front of me, my uncle's hands were cut off and my sister was raped in front of us by their commander called "Spare no Soul." After all this happened, they told us, the younger boys, to join them. If not, they were going to kill us.[66]

These stories highlight many of the key themes that surround the recruitment of child soldiers in armed conflict. Recruitment is often forced, and if they are not abducted, the children may see no option to joining aside from death.

Child soldiers do not just fetch water and clean weapons—they are trained to mutilate and kill. Many have been forced to kill their parents and family members, have mutilated citizens, have cut unborn fetuses out of pregnant women, and have disemboweled victims and eaten their organs. We discussed women and girl soldiers earlier and the difficulties in reintegrating them back into society; now we will look at the problems associated with reintegrating into society those boys who have been trained to live a life of violence.

Most efforts to reintegrate boys and men back into society have focused on providing psychological help as well as education. The psychological problems faced by former boy soldiers are great. One study found that "as many as 97 percent of child soldiers may suffer from [posttraumatic stress disorder], regardless of the time they spent in violence."[67] In Bukavu, Congo, one facility is staffed with counselors who strive to help the boys "discharge negative energy, teach them respect for women, find out and encourage their aspirations, and eventually place them with relatives or foster parents."[68] The counselors note that the boys have been severely traumatized and that they, the counselors, end up traumatized as well.[69] The extreme trauma suffered by former combatants is a pervasive theme in all reports of efforts to reintegrate boy and adult male soldiers back into society. It is a challenge that will remain for years to come. And for male combatants who suffered sexual violence, the road to recovery is even tougher. Recent research done by the Harvard Humanitarian Initiative at Harvard University indicates that male combatants who suffered sexual violence have worse mental health outcomes than the general population and than other combatants. This finding, the authors argue, compels the international community to rework its gender-based programs to deal with males who have suffered sexual violence as combatants during war.[70] Trauma is compounded for children who lost their parents or whose parents do not wish to be reunited with them. Thus, the psychological trauma suffered by male combatants (as well as females, discussed earlier) is far-reaching and unimaginable, and the timeline for recovery is lengthy, and possibly never-ending.[71]

Education and vocational training is also seen as key to helping former combatants, and many efforts have focused on providing this education. The challenges are extensive, as many of these children have missed years of schooling and lack a basic primary education (they are often illiterate and have no basic math skills). In Liberia, demobilized fighters were given money ($300) and scholarships that could be used for either vocational training or 3 years of formal education.[72] And Sierra Leone has implemented a fairly successful education program aimed at former soldiers who need to catch up. The program provides intensive 6-month schooling designed to get former fighters up to par with students in their age cohort, so that they are not going to school with children years younger than them. A problem that schools are facing, however, is that parents do not wish to send their children to a school that has former combatants in it. In Liberia, one school, St. Peter's Episcopal School, struggles to overcome its bad reputation. St. Peter's principal, Edward Fayia, notes that

"Other schools refused to accept (ex-combatant) students because they threatened to burn the building. . . . [I]f you saw what they did to this country—small, small children. Some parents were very skeptical about sending ordinary children here."[73] Another problem is that many of the programs instituted at the end of armed conflicts have directed most of their funding and efforts toward adults. It is not clear yet, and may not be for years to come, what the impact of these reintegration efforts will be. But in countries with struggling economies and few employment options after school, the outlook is not bright. One boy who fought in Sierra Leone and received some schooling through a UN program left school because he "missed the fighter's life, 'we used to be free, go to the clubs, get money, get women.'"[74]

CONCLUSION

Sexual violence against women and girls has been a tool of warfare for centuries and will likely continue to be used in the future. However, rape and sexual enslavement are now considered crimes against humanity, and thus perpetrators can be tried in international courts and potentially convicted. Further, international groups like Human Rights Watch and Amnesty International are working diligently to pressure governments to prosecute incidents of sexual violence during war and in refugee camps and are working to educate the public at large about these crimes. These groups also are monitoring and pressuring international organizations, like UNHCR, to enforce their regulations on gender-based violence strictly. These efforts provide some relief to women seeking to rebuild their lives after living through the horrors of war and refugee status. The use of child soldiers in recent conflicts has added to the horrors of war and has presented new challenges to the international community. The success of its response remains to be seen.

A Typical Rape in Darfur

In March 2004, a 16-year-old young woman in West Darfur was out collecting firewood for her family when three armed men on camels surrounded her. Two men held her down and tied her hands while the other raped her; they then took turns raping her. When the rapes were over, the young girl returned home and told her family what had just taken place. Her family kicked her out of the house, instructing her that she had to build her own hut away from them. This young girl was also engaged to be married, but upon finding out about the rapes her fiancé ended the engagement, saying that she was no longer clean and that she was disgraced. The rapes resulted in a pregnancy; when she was 8 months pregnant the police came to her home and forcibly brought her to the police station, where they questioned her about her pregnancy. She told them she had been raped, but they did not care. They told her that since she was not married she would be delivering the baby illegally; they then beat her with whips and put her in jail. While in jail she met many other women in her situation. Her time in jail was spent cooking and cleaning for the policemen. She and the other women had to walk to a well four times a day to fetch water; their only food was whatever they could find during the day, and their only water was what they could drink at the well. The young girl spent 10 days in jail and still was required to pay a fine of 20,000 Sudanese dinars ($65). She gave birth to her child soon after.[i]

This story was told by a young woman to interviewers with MSF, which has been working extensively in Darfur to help all victims of the violence there. Her story is, unfortunately, not unique. It painfully illustrates the multiple horrors that women victims of sexual violence must endure: the rape itself, rejection by family, impossibility of marriage, lack of recourse with the state (and abuse by state actors), mental anguish, malnourishment, and rejection by society as a whole. On top of these horrors, many victims suffer physical wounds such as fistulas. Groups like MSF are working hard to assist these victims in Sudan, but unfortunately some of their work has recently been halted. The International Criminal Court in The Hague issued a war crimes warrant in March 2009 for President Bashir of Sudan. The Sudanese government seemed unfazed by the warrant, saying that they would pay it no heed. But MSF said it was told by the Sudanese government to shut down its operations and get out of the country shortly after the warrant was issued.

[1]Médecins Sans Frontières, "The Crushing Burden of Rape: Sexual Violence in Darfur," A Briefing Paper, Amsterdam, March 8, 2005.

FOR MORE INFORMATION

Amnesty International, http://www.amnestyusa.org/violence-against-women/sexual-violence/page.do?id=1108442

Human Rights Education Associates: Crimes of War; Educator's Guide: Sexual Violence, http://www.hrea.org/index.php?base_id=126

Migrant Women and Children in Somalia. International Organization for Migration, http://www.youtube.com/watch?v=fFhdQL0GIbs&feature=plcp&context=C33a0ddeUPOEgs ToPDskJN-C81kJgn-0WGSuCCYSHE. This short video depicts the status of women in refugee camps.

Women's Refugee Commission: Video Gallery. http://womensrefugeecommission.org/resources/video-gallery.

Outreach program on the Rwanda genocide by the United Nations: http://www.un.org/en/preventgenocide/rwanda/about/bgsexualviolence.shtml

Stop Rape Now: United Nations Action Against Sexual Violence in Conflict, http://www.stoprapenow.org

United Nations Development Fund: Facts and Figures on Violence Against Women, http://www.unifem.org/gender_issues/violence_against_women/facts_figures.php

WomenWarPeace.org, a portal on women, peace, and security, http://www.womenwarpeace.org/issues/violence

At the End of a Gun: Women and War—This film looks at the impact of the separatist war in Sri Lanka on women's lives.

All Different, All Equal—This documentary examines the global progress toward ending violence against women both during war and in general.

Lumo—One Young Woman's Struggle to Heal in a Nation Beset by War—This documentary film follows Lumo, a 20-year-old woman in Eastern Congo who was raped by soldiers. As a result of the rape she develops a fistula, her fiancé abandons her, and she makes her way to a hospital for rape survivors on the border with Rwanda.

Women in War Zones: Sexual Violence in the Congo—This documentary looks at the sexual violence committed against women during the war in Eastern Congo.

12

Women and Physical Autonomy

"I was taken to a very dark room and undressed. I was blindfolded and stripped naked. . . . I was forced to lie flat on my back by four strong women, two holding tight to each leg. Another woman sat on my chest to prevent my upper body from moving. . . . I was genitally mutilated with a blunt penknife. After the operation no one was allowed to aid me to walk. . . . These were terrible times for me. Each time I wanted to urinate I was forced to stand upright. The urine would spread over the wound and would cause fresh pain all over again. . . . Afterwards I haemorrhaged and became anaemic. This was attributed to witchcraft. I suffered for a long time from acute vaginal infections."[1]

"Increasing reports of parents beating daughters who flunk the exams have given some virginity testing supporters pause and opponents new ammunition. Publicly labeling girls virgins is also not without danger. An African folk belief that sex with a virgin can cure AIDS puts virgins here at risk of rape. Already, a few certified virgins in KwaZulu-Natal Province have been attacked by HIV-positive men hoping for the spurious cure. The girls managed to escape."[2]

"On June 22, during a Mastoi tribal council meeting . . . four men, including one of the tribal council members, allegedly raped Mukhtaran Bibi, a thirty-year-old member of the Gujjar tribe. The rape, which occurred in the presence of a large number of villagers, was intended as 'punishment' for the conduct of her brother . . . who had been seen with an unchaperoned woman from the Mastoi tribe."[3]

These three quotes all relate different tales: one is about female genital cutting, one is about virginity testing, and the third is about a woman being raped as punishment for her brother's indiscretions. So what could they all share in common? They all share the fact that women and girls often have no say regarding what is done with their bodies. Women often lack physical autonomy, a basic human right that is enshrined in many international treaties and declarations. Women's bodies are used as scapegoats for the indiscretions of male relatives, are mutilated to control their sexuality, are stoned or flogged for breaking laws that do not apply to men, and are forcibly examined to ensure their chastity. In this chapter we will examine three practices that violate women's physical autonomy: female genital cutting, virginity tests, and physical violence against women either as a form of punishment for their own or their family's actions or as domestic violence. We conclude with a discussion of international and domestic efforts to address these problems.

FEMALE GENITAL CUTTING

Female genital cutting (FGC), also known as female circumcision, is the removal of all or part of the female genitalia. There are different types of FGC. The most common form is excision of the clitoris accompanied by partial or total excision of the labia minora. It is estimated that about 85 percent of genital cuttings are of this type.[4] The most severe form of genital cutting, and the least widely practiced (about 15 percent of all), is infibulation, which "consists of a clitoridectomy (where all, or part of, the clitoris is removed), excision (removal of all, or part of, the labia minora), and cutting of the labia majora to create raw surfaces, which are then stitched or held together in order to form a cover over the vagina when they heal. A small hole is left to allow urine and menstrual blood to escape."[5] No matter which form of FGC is done, the procedure is extremely invasive.

The age at which the procedure is performed, which procedure is performed, and exactly how it is performed depend on what country the girl lives in, which ethnic group she belongs to, her family's socioeconomic status, and whether she lives in a rural or urban setting. The procedure can be done anytime after birth through a woman's first pregnancy but is most commonly performed in prepubescence, between the ages of 4 and 8. The procedure can be done in a girl's home, at a neighbor's home, or at a site with some special significance like a tree or river. Very occasionally it is done at a hospital or health clinic. FGC is usually done to a group of girls of the same age at the same time, although occasionally it is done to a girl alone. The procedure is generally performed by women, most of whom have no medical training. They are village elders, healers, and occasionally trained midwives or doctors. Girls often have little information beforehand regarding what is going to happen to them, and the procedure is often carried out with some type of cutting instrument, ranging from a razorblade or a penknife to broken glass and tin can lids. Very seldom is there any kind of anesthesia to numb the area or any type of antibiotics to prevent infection afterward.

The World Health Organization estimates that as of 2012, 140 million women had undergone the procedure worldwide.[6] FGC is most prevalent in Africa (it is done in at least 28 African nations), and it is also prevalent in some countries in the Middle East and Asia. Its usage varies widely from a low of 5 percent in Ghana and Niger to highs of 92 percent and 97 percent in Mali and North Sudan, respectively. In Europe, the United States, and Latin America it occurs primarily in immigrant communities. Further, the United Nations (UN) Population Fund estimates that every year another 3 million girls are at risk.[7]

Why is FGC practiced? What could be the reason for performing such a grisly procedure on young girls? The most common explanation for why FGC is conducted is tradition; it is part of a community's culture and custom (see photo 12.1).

As one Egyptian woman commented about her own daughters, "Of course I shall have them circumcised, exactly as their parents, grandparents, and sisters were circumcised. This is our custom."[8] Further, it is often argued that it is an initiation rite into adulthood and that women who are not circumcised will not be considered adults in the village and will not be allowed to perform tasks like cooking, fetching water, or participating in certain dances because they will not be seen as "clean." Further, uncircumcised women are often not considered fit for marriage or, if married, will be ostracized by their husbands. On top of this there is concern that uncircumcised women will be too sexual and mentally unbalanced. As Lukman Hakim, chairman of the Assalaam Foundation in Indonesia, an Islamic educational and social services organization, stated, "One, it will stabilize her libido. . . . Two, it will make a woman look more beautiful in the eyes of her husband. And three, it will balance her psychology."[9] While there is no evidence to support the first and third points, educating people about these issues is a slow process. Later we will discuss efforts, many successful, by groups such as Tostan (see the text box "Tostan") to educate communities about the impact of FGC on women's bodies.

Some of the other rationalizations for FGC are grounded in inaccurate understanding of the female genitalia or of how the female reproductive system works. In some cultures, parts of the female genitalia are considered male and thus must be removed. As one Egyptian woman stated, "We are circumcised and insist on circumcising our daughters so that there is no mixing between male and female. . . . An uncircumcised woman is put to shame by her husband, who calls her 'you with

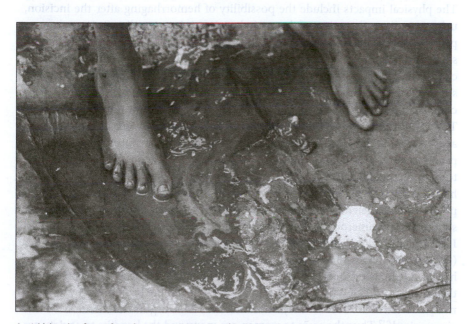

A girl bleeds after a female circumcision ritual in Kenya. SOURCE: Photo by Stephanie Welsh/ Getty Images.

clitoris.' People say she is like a man. Her organ would prick the man."[10] Others believe that FGC enhances fertility, that an unmutilated woman cannot get pregnant, and that it makes childbirth safer.[11] As noted earlier, education to eradicate these misunderstandings is integral. But it is crucial to remember that people tend to believe information that fits into their cultural worldview, so change may be slow in coming in some areas.

Fundamentally, FGC is also about control over women's sexuality. FGC allows a man to know that his bride is a virgin at the time of marriage. Many societies believe that FGC decreases a woman's desire for sex, thus decreasing the likelihood that she will be promiscuous before or after marriage. In some societies women are sewn up again after intercourse. And, in many societies it is argued that their religion dictates that it be done to keep women chaste until marriage. Yet, although FGC is often practiced in Muslim and some Christian communities, neither the Quran nor the Bible say that women should be circumcised. And numerous Muslim leaders are now speaking out against its connection to Islam and are condemning the practice. In Egypt and Kenya, many Muslim leaders have publicly stated that FGC is a cultural tradition that has no ties to (and actually predates) the teachings of Islam.[12] This is a crucial step to eradicating FGC. Where people feel a deep connection to their religious and cultural belief systems they are likely to listen to those they respect and look up to. The role of religious leaders in ending FGC will be quite important if we truly wish to see this practice eliminated.

The impacts of FGC on women range from physical to emotional to social. The physical impacts include the possibility of hemorrhaging after the incision, urine retention, ulceration of the genital region, injury to adjacent tissue, severe pain and shock, and damage to the urethra that can result in urinary incontinence, sexual dysfunction, urinary tract infection, infertility, and complications during childbirth.[13] The procedure also increases the risk of contracting AIDS when unsterilized instruments are used on multiple girls. Statistics on how often these complications occur are scarce because these complications are not often reported. Thus, opponents of FGC say these complications are frequent and proponents argue that they are rare. Emotional and psychological scars also result from the procedure and may include shock and an increased tendency for girls afterward to be more docile and calm. Women also report feelings of anxiety and terror, humiliation, and betrayal.[14] Some women also note that they feel shame and a physical incompleteness after the procedure. Princess Euphrasia Etta Ojong from southwestern Cameroon, who now campaigns to end the practice, states, "Today, I feel ashamed when I am with other women. I do not feel like a complete woman."[15] (Conversely, some women report feeling accepted by society once the procedure has been completed and they have survived.[16]) Finally, there are some social scars that result from FGC. As Princess Ojong notes, "Even the boys from my area are not interested in me because they think that the sexual urge is not there since I was circumcised."[17] Thus the scars to women are many and the benefits to society are primarily the maintenance of a tradition grounded largely in inaccurate religious interpretations or beliefs about the female reproductive system.

Tostan

In 1974, Molly Melching traveled to Senegal as an exchange student and when her studies were completed she stayed on as a Peace Corps volunteer and settled in Senegal. Ms. Melching had a vision of a different type of development program, one that understood the culture in which it was situated and "respectfully engaged communities in the process by working in their own language and using traditional methods of learning."[i] As a result of her vision, Tostan was born in 1991, and today it operates in 10 countries and 17 languages. While Tostan focuses on many aspects of community empowerment, one issue it has had great success with is ending FGC. Tostan offers communities a basic education program about human rights and health, and as a result of the information that participants learn, many communities have decided of their own accord to abandon FGC. The first to do so was the community of Malicounda Bambara in Senegal. In 1997, a group of women from this village came to a decision to end FGC. The women had participated in one of Tostan's basic education programs and afterward decided to abandon the centuries-old tradition. To date, 5,000 communities from eight countries have abandoned FGC. Tostan believes that its approach works because it is respectful of local cultures, allows participants to decide for themselves what, if any, changes they wish to implement, and hires culturally competent and knowledgeable local staff; classes are taught in a participatory manner and emphasize skills valued in African society like dialogue and consensus building.[ii]

---

[i] Tostan, "History," http://www.tostan.org, July 23, 2012.
[ii] Ibid.

VIRGINITY TESTS

Virginity tests are tests where a girl's hymen is examined to see if it is intact. If it is intact, then the girl is deemed to be a virgin. The test administrators make no allowances for the fact that the hymen can be torn in ways other than intercourse, and some girls are not born with one at all. The practice is used in some African and Asian nations such as South Africa and India, has been used in the past in Turkey (and continues to generate political discussion), and was also proposed in Jamaica and Indonesia. Recently it made the news again when an Egyptian protestor, Samira Ibrahim, accused a military doctor of conducting a virginity test on her when she was detained in Tahrir Square in February 2011.

Why are virginity tests conducted? Like FGC, virginity tests are a way to limit women's physical autonomy and to control their sexuality. The rationale for using them, however, is often the claim that it is in women's best interests to abstain from intercourse because of the risk of AIDS. This is the claim that is being used in many African nations such as South Africa, which conducted these tests on both girls and boys as young as 6 (although most forms of virginity testing were banned by the parliament in 2005). In 2004, President Zuma of South Africa spoke out in favor of virginity tests as a way to curb the spread of AIDS/HIV and decrease teenage pregnancy. He further argued, in what has become a controversial statement, that if girls valued their family's honor, then they would abstain from sex: "Girls knew that their virginity was their family's treasure. . . . They would only have sex when permitted to do so by their families after marriage."[18] But, while the practice has been essentially outlawed in South Africa, Zulus actively defy the ban and continue to do testing and issue certificates to girls who pass.[19] Some Zulu girls appear to be in favor of the testing and the celebrations that take place for the girls who have passed. One girl commented, "They [the South Africans] didn't come up with it [virginity testing]. . . . So why should they stop it? It could just be that they don't give the Zulu culture dignity."[20] But when pressed about how she would feel if she had failed the test, one said, regarding the usefulness of virginity testing, that "I really don't know what to believe."[21] And another 14-year-old girl who failed her test was devastated and told reporters, "I feel very bad because I haven't done anything."[22] But Zulu leaders state that they will continue to practice the tradition of virginity testing because it is an important part of their culture, one that the state has no right to try to end.

In Zimbabwe, a country with one of the highest rates of AIDS/HIV infection in the world, voluntary virginity tests were recently imposed by Chief Naboth Makoni in the Makoni district in a controversial attempt to combat AIDS. His order also includes men providing documented proof that they are HIV-negative if they wish to marry a "documented" virgin.[23] Chief Makoni argues, in response to critiques of his policy, that "it is unfair to allow a marriage between a person living with the virus and a virgin who has tested negative. . . . So far 3,500 girls have been tested, on their own insistence, and some have been awarded certificates. . . . That's why we're demanding proof of a man's HIV status if he wants to marry any of these angels."[24] The district also holds a "feast for the virgins" once a month that is designed to honor those girls who have passed the test. People complain that anyone can forge a document and so there really is no proof that the men who claim to be HIV-free truly are. Thus the men are on the winning end, so to speak, but the girls who fail the tests, even if they are virgins, must suffer the public humiliation and stigma that result from the failure.

Virginity tests were also recently proposed in Jamaica by two legislators who felt that the tests (as well as sterilizing women with three or more children) would help curb the growing number of unwanted pregnancies and thus the welfare burden on the government.[25] And in Turkey, where the tests were proposed again in 2001 after their use had been banned, advocates claimed that they would protect minors from prostitution and underage sex.[26] In March 2011, in Egypt, Samira Ibrahim and 17 other women were arrested during protests in Tahrir Square. They were transferred to a military facility and seven of them were allegedly subjected to virginity tests. Ms. Ibrahim initially brought charges against the military officers who ordered the tests, but ultimately she could bring charges against only the doctor, who was declared innocent in March 2012. Ms. Ibrahim says she will take this case to an international court. Finally, in Iraq, women are still subject to virginity tests, often immediately after they have been married. Their husbands bring them to facilities like the Medical Legal Institute in Baghdad and ask that the test be performed if they suspect their new bride was not a virgin.[27] The reason for requesting a virginity test may be rooted in a lack of sexual education/knowledge. For instance, Iraqi men may believe that a woman should bleed upon intercourse if she is a virgin, and lack of bleeding implies she is not a virgin. Or the request may be made by the husband to avoid the shame of such conditions like male erectile dysfunction, says Dr. Munjid al-Rezali, the Director of the Medical Legal Institute.[28] No matter the cause and no matter the result of the test, the procedure is shaming and frightening for women and the test is no indicator of anything.

While the prevention of AIDS, prostitution, and unwanted pregnancies is generally viewed as a positive end, the method is reprehensible. Virginity tests affect girls in a few ways. First, in African nations now using them there is some evidence that rape is on the rise since it is believed that having sex with a virgin will cure AIDS. Thus many girls are not safe on their way to and from school or doing other daily chores. Public celebrations of the girls who have passed their tests is akin to advertising which girls would be good to rape. There are also reports of parents beating children who failed the test and girls feeling isolated and outcast by their community if they fail (and it must be noted that there is no foolproof way to prove that a girl is a virgin).[29] Second, teaching girls to remain virgins is just that, teaching them to be virgins; it does nothing to teach them how to prevent AIDS, which is arguably a crucial step in curbing the spread of the AIDS epidemic.

Given that AIDS is often spread to married women by their husbands who do not remain faithful or who come to the marriage already infected, virginity testing is going to do little to truly curb the spread of AIDS. Chief Makoni did not have a very good answer when asked about this. He could only say that failed marriages are usually the result of women who come to the marriage not a virgin, that "if a young woman is not a virgin she is considered to have less value. This often leads to her being abused by her husband, and sometimes results in divorce."[30] Virginity testing as a way to combat AIDS puts the onus on women and girls and absolves men of any responsibility for the spread of AIDS. As Netsai Mushonga of the Harare-based Women Coalition of Zimbabwe (a nongovernmental organization) pointed out, "Virginity testing leaves a man free to roam, without enforcing any similar checks and balance on his, while it strips girls of their dignity."[31]

In Turkey, the tests were going to be used as part of the admissions procedure for nursing school, and girls who failed the tests would be denied admittance. Thus girls' education was going to be held captive by the state. And, some girls attempted suicide when they thought they would be subjected to the tests.[32] When death is seen as preferable to the method used to protect girls from supposed evils, then it becomes necessary to examine the method closely. In Egypt the test was used as a shaming mechanism and in Iraq as a way for men to avoid their own physical problems or get out of a marriage with impunity. Finally, it affects girls in that their bodies, and hence their futures, are subject to regulation by the state. While some boys have been subject to these virginity tests, no one is suggesting that castration be used as a method to curb unwanted pregnancies or that male virginity be required for admission to university. Although these tests are no longer being used in Turkey and the proposal in Jamaica appears to have foundered, they are still used in India, Iraq, and countries in Africa (as the case of Egypt exemplifies).

WOMEN'S BODIES AS WHIPPING POSTS

Women's bodies are also often used, literally, as whipping posts for their partner's anger or for their family's actions or their own. Stoning and flogging, rape, domestic abuse, and honor killings are inflicted on women on a daily basis. Here will we address stonings and honor killings and attempt to understand why they are used.

Stoning, or lapidation, is a method of execution where a group of people throw stones at an individual until he or she is dead. Stoning as a method of execution is an ancient one: there are records of it across cultures and across religions. The practice was used by the ancient Greeks to execute adulterers, prostitutes, and murderers. Discussion of stoning can be found in the Jewish tradition in the Torah and the Talmud and in the Old Testament of the Bible, which both Christians and Jews follow. There is no mention of stoning in the Quran, but the practice of stoning has increasingly become associated with Islam, primarily because of its use in Iran (to be discussed later). Stoning is a controversial topic among Muslim clerics. Some argue that it should not be used because it is not prescribed in the Quran, and they add that any action that reflects poorly upon Islam should not be practiced. Others, however, cite passages of the Hadith, the acts and sayings of the Prophet Mohammed, as evidence that stoning is a legitimate punishment for certain acts. The Hadith prescribes stoning specifically for Jews found guilty of adultery, and others add that Mohammed had both men and women stoned in his time, so he must have intended it to be used.[33] Stoning is used today as a "legal" form of punishment for the crime of adultery in Afghanistan, Iran, Nigeria, Pakistan, Sudan, and the United Arab Emirates. The states of Iraq and Pakistan have never officially carried out a stoning decree, but there is evidence that local communities have done so on their own. Stoning violates a number of international treaties, including the International Convention of Civil and Political Rights (ICCPR; 1966), which states that in states that have not abolished the death penalty, the death penalty may be used for only the most serious crimes, of which adultery is not one. The ICCPR goes on to state that no state shall use cruel and unusual punishments. Iran, Iraq, Sudan, and Afghanistan are all signatories to the ICCPR. The other international treaty that addresses the issue of stoning is the Convention Against Torture and Other Cruel, Inhuman, or Degrading Treatment or Punishment (1987). Over 50 countries are signatories to this convention, including numerous Muslim nations. But as you will read, the use of stoning continues despite these international conventions and even in light of the laws in some states that ban it.

In December 2001, the criminal court in Nyala, southern Darfur, Sudan, sentenced Abok Alfau Akok (a Christian) to death by stoning for having engaged in sex outside of marriage. She was pregnant at the time of the sentence. An appeals court later overturned this sentence and "reduced" the punishment to 75 lashes. The lashings were carried out immediately upon the decision being handed down.

At the time of the lashings she had already given birth. No action was taken against the man with whom she allegedly had sexual relations. In March 2002, a Shari'a (Islamic) court in the state of Katsina in northern Nigeria sentenced Amina Lawal to death by stoning for having committed adultery. Amina Lawal was pregnant at the time of the sentence and her pregnancy was taken as evidence of her having committed adultery. Amina Lawal gave birth more than 9 months after she had obtained a divorce from her husband. In August 2002, an appeals court upheld the sentence. In September 2003, another appeals court finally overturned the stoning sentence, arguing that the conviction was invalid because she was pregnant at the time the conviction was handed down. One can assume that had she not been pregnant then the conviction would not have been considered invalid by the appeals court. The alleged father repeatedly asserted that the baby was not his. Three men testified that he had not had sexual relations with Lawal, and under Shari'a law this was enough to corroborate his story and free him.

Lawal's stoning sentence is the second in Nigeria since 2000, when more than 12 of Nigeria's 36 states adopted strict Islamic Shari'a law. The sentence of Safiya Hussaini Tungar Tudu was reversed by an appeals court in March 2002 after a great deal of international grassroots pressure and a warning from the president of Nigeria, Olusegun Obasanjo, that Nigeria faced international isolation as a result of the case.[34] And while stoning sentences have thus far not been carried out, flogging (whipping) sentences for charges of having sex outside of marriage have been. In September 2000 in Nigeria, Bariya Ibrahim Magazu was charged with having sex outside of marriage and received 100 lashes in January 2001, even though an appeal was pending.[35]

In December 2008, two men convicted of adultery were stoned to death in Iran despite a moratorium on the use of stoning handed down by the state's judiciary chief, Ayatollah Mahmoud Hashemi-Shahroudi, in 2002. As per Iranian law, they were buried up to their waist in a pit, and then people hurled rocks at them (rocks that, according to the law, must not be large enough to kill them immediately) until they died. If they could escape the pit, then they were free. A spokesman for Iran's judiciary said the moratorium on stoning was purely advisory and not an edict: "Judges can't act based simply on advisories by the head of the judiciary, since judges are independent," he said.[36] Human rights activists, like those with Amnesty International, argue that 12 women and 3 men are still awaiting stoning in Iran, despite Iran's commutation of stoning sentences for 4 people (instead of stoning 2 received 300 lashes each and the other 2 were sentenced to 10 years in jail).[37] Amnesty International notes that, while both men and women receive stoning sentences, stoning disproportionately affects women. They note that the majority of those awaiting stoning are women and that the court system does not treat women the same as men. Women often have unfair trials, largely as a result of their higher rates of illiteracy, which lead them to be more likely to sign confessions for crimes they did not commit.[38] Further, the way stoning is implemented is different for men and women. In Iran, a woman who is stoned to death is buried up to her neck, whereas a man is buried only up to his waist, thus giving him a greater ability to escape.

In 2008, in Kismayo, Somalia, a 13-year-old girl who had been raped was stoned to death. A witness to the stoning told the BBC that she first pleaded for her life, crying, "Don't kill me, don't kill me."[39] She was then forcibly placed in a hole and buried up to her neck; 50 people stoned her until she died. Amnesty International reports that while she was initially reported to be 23 years old, she was in actuality 13.[40] According to the girl's family, she was raped by three men; when her family tried to report the rape, the girl was accused of adultery and detained. The port of Kismayo is not under government control but rather under the control of forces loyal to the country's main radical Islamist insurgent organization. Thus, while stoning a 13-year-old to death is illegal under Islamic law, these forces have no regard for the law. And while it is reported that the citizens present at the stoning were mortified at the action, they did nothing to stop it, fearing for their lives. One boy who ran forward was shot by armed forces. As we can see, punishments that have been deemed cruel and inhumane by the international community continue to be imposed on women in numerous locales.

Recently, Iran made the news with the stoning sentence handed down for Sakineh Mohammadi Ashtiani. Ashtiani's case is full of twists and turns. She was originally convicted of having an "illicit relationship" with two men in 2006 after the death of her husband. She was given 99 lashes. Then, her case was reopened during the murder trial of her husband, and she was charged with adultery based on allegations that she committed adultery before her husband died. In yet another bizarre twist, she "confessed" to murdering her husband and then quickly retracted this confession, saying it was forced under duress (further, she never actually admits to murder in the taped confession). A concerted international outcry over her case erupted, including a statement by Secretary of State Clinton and an offer of amnesty by the Brazilian government (with whom Iran has warm relations), and the Iranian government commuted her sentence to hanging, which has yet to be done. Finally, she has also received another 99 lashes for purportedly having a picture of herself without a headscarf published in a British paper, but her son claims it is not her, and two German reporters were sentenced to 20 months in jail for entering Iran illegally to interview her. After discussions between the German foreign minister and the Iranian government, their sentences were commuted to fines in February 2011, and they quickly returned home.

Another punishment occasionally inflicted upon women who defy their family's code of honor is an honor killing. Honor killings occur when women behave in ways that are unacceptable to their family or as a way to deal with the alleged indiscretions of their male relatives who have brought dishonor to the family. As the story at the beginning of the chapter relates, women's bodies are used as literal whipping posts for the actions of their male relatives. In honor killings, a woman may be killed (or severely maimed) by a relative or a hired hit man, as was the case with Samia Sarwar, who was gunned down in her attorney's office in April 1999 in Pakistan because she was seeking a divorce from her estranged husband.[41] More recently in 2006, a 16-year-old Turkish girl was shot by her family for the perceived dishonor she brought to them from a pregnancy and birth that resulted from a rape. She had tried to hide the rape but it was discovered when she was hospitalized for a severe headache. Because of threats made by the family to try to get her out of the hospital, the hospital decided to keep her and let her go home after the birth only when her father promised that no harm would come to her. She was shot dead by her brother shortly after she returned home.[42] In a rare occurrence, the entire family was convicted, three of them receiving life sentences (including the brother who shot her). Normally these killings are not dealt with in the judicial system since they are seen as family matters. Or often the family member chosen to do the killing is the youngest male, since male youths often receive much lighter sentences (sometimes as little as 3 months in jail) than adult family members do. Finally, in 2007, a Kurdish Muslim woman was killed by her father and uncle in Great Britain. Both were arrested and convicted, which is not generally the case in countries in the developing world. Women may also be maimed by male relatives because of actions the men deem as having brought dishonor to the family. Specifically, in Southeast Asia male relatives often throw acid on women who have allegedly brought dishonor to the family. The resulting injuries are gruesome.

According to reports submitted to the UN Commission on Human Rights, honor killings have been documented in Bangladesh, Great Britain, Brazil, Ecuador, Egypt, India, Israel, Italy, Jordan, Pakistan, Morocco, Sweden, Turkey, and Uganda.[43] In Pakistan alone it has been estimated that every day three women, including victims of rape, are killed via honor killings.[44] Among countries that do not submit reports to the UN, honor killings were condoned in Afghanistan under the Taliban and have been reported in Iraq and Iran. Honor killings have even been alleged in the United States, as the case of Yaser Abdel Said, discussed in the text box "Honor Killings Come to the United States," indicates. Honor killings typically occur in countries where the notion of women as property and as a vessel of the family still dominates, and their use travels across cultures and religions. In some places they are referred to as honor killings, but in other places they may be called a dowry death (when a bride is murdered because her dowry is seen as insufficient), as in India, or a crime of passion, as in Latin America. According to UNICEF, more than 5,000 brides in India are killed annually because their dowries are not big enough, according to their fiancés.[45] These acts are condoned by family and friends, including female relatives, which is part of the reason they are so hard to eradicate. As Zaynab Nawaz, a program assistant for Amnesty International, points out, "Females in the family—mothers, mothers-in-law, sisters and cousins—frequently support the attacks. It's a community mentality."[46] The presence of this community mentality exacerbates the notion that women are property and that these acts should be dealt with via the family and not via the judicial system. When women are viewed as the property of the men in their family they have no autonomy whatsoever. Further, the very idea that a human is a piece of property makes it easier to think about exterminating her—people can do with their property as they wish. Thus, it is crucial that laws that perpetuate women's status as the property of the men in their life are removed and that women are educated about and assisted in securing employment, because we know that when women have an independent source of income, they have more autonomy in the household. Until then, women who engage in sex outside of marriage or defy their family's moral code (something that men are allowed to do) may receive the ultimate punishment for their actions—death.

Why are all of these practices (FGC, virginity tests, stoning, and honor killings) committed upon women? While each abuse is different, a common thread that unites them is control. These physical abuses are all ways to control women's actions, whether sexual or otherwise. Stoning, flogging, and honor killings are generally used to punish women for having sex outside of marriage (or being accused of it) or for attempting to end a marriage. It is hoped that the possibility of such punishments will deter women from acting in an independent fashion. When men control women's bodies, women lack the most basic of human rights.

Honor Killings Come to the United States

On Jan. 1, 2008, Yaser Abdel Said, a taxi driver, took his two teenage daughters for a drive. He drove them to Irving, Texas, where he is alleged to have murdered them. The girls' aunt and close friends argue that he was angry with them for wanting to wear Western dress and for dating non-Muslim boys. In Jonesboro, Georgia, in July 2008, Chaudhry Rashid allegedly strangled his daughter, Sandeela, with a bungee cord for filing for a divorce from her husband (their arranged marriage had been conducted in Pakistan). In upstate New York in summer 2008, Waheed Allah Mohammad was charged with the attempted murder of his sister, who, he argued, had angered him because she was going out dancing, was wearing Western clothing, and was planning on moving to New York City. All of these murders took place on U.S. soil and arguably fit the definition of honor killings put forth in this chapter. While these murders appear to have been fairly actively discussed in the blogosphere, their coverage in mainstream U.S. newspapers was minimal. The little coverage there was focused on whether or not labeling them as honor killings was useful or not. The arguments against labeling them as such focused on the fact that the term distracts from the larger issues of patriarchy, male control, and domestic violence and that the term is inherently racist (because these killings are covered as a "Muslim" phenomenon, which they are not, as we have discussed in this chapter). Proponents of the term argue that if we classify honor killings as a form of domestic violence then we end up lumping crimes together that are not the same. The circumstances surrounding domestic violence are often different from those surrounding an honor killing. A man who beats his wife or kills his wife because she is having an affair may look similar to a father killing his married adult daughter who is having an affair, but the two cases are not the same. In an honor killing a woman is killed because she has disgraced her family's honor; this murder is not generally done by her husband but, rather, by her own blood family. Proponents of using the term "honor killings" argue that we need to look at these crimes as different from other killings because they have different motivations. Whatever the merits and demerits of the term, the fact is that honor killings, once seen as a phenomenon that occurred outside the United States, are now a U.S. phenomenon, too.

The impacts of these actions on women are many. At the extreme end is death. But in instances where death is not the result, the impact of FGC is physical, emotional, and psychological. Physically, flogging and the like leave women's bodies battered and bruised and, at times, permanently damaged. Emotionally and psychologically, these abuses leave women permanently scarred. The trauma of experiencing such abuses cannot be forgotten. And when death is the result, the impact is obvious—a human being has been denied her life to preserve the alleged honor of a family. The acceptance of these acts by all family members and by the community means that many women will continue to suffer similar fates in the future. We next discuss efforts to improve women's physical autonomy.

ADDRESSING WOMEN'S PHYSICAL AUTONOMY

A number of international conferences have been held in recent years regarding women's human rights. Further, a few international treaties ban violence against women and require signatories to respect the civil rights of all of their citizens. A few important declarations and treaties are the Universal Declaration of Human Rights, which is seen as the bedrock of the human rights system because it protects people from being subject to cruel and inhumane or degrading treatment; the UN Convention on the Elimination of All Forms of Violence Against Women (CEDAW), which provides specific steps for signatories to take to eliminate violence against women; the International Covenant on Civil and Political Rights, another important treaty in international law; and the 1993 UN World Conference on Human Rights, which called for the "elimination of violence against women in public and private life . . . and the eradication of any conflicts which may arise between the rights of women and the harmful effects of certain traditional or customary practices."[47] While there are other declarations, covenants, and treaties, these are among the most applicable to the issues addressed in this chapter.

These important works require nations (signatories) to protect women from the type of abuses that have been discussed in this chapter, but unfortunately many nations do not adhere to the terms of the treaties. In the absence of an international police force to enforce international law obligations, it is difficult to ensure compliance. Compliance, if it happens, often comes only after human rights organizations make public the violations and conduct a grassroots campaign. Even then, there is no guarantee that the violation will not occur again. This is largely because the nation, assuming it wishes to end the practice, has a difficult time changing old cultural practices like FGC, honor killings, and even domestic violence, which are culturally accepted in many places, particularly in small towns and villages far from the capital. Even in the major cities, many people, including those in positions of power, still ascribe to views of women that permit the continuation of such actions. For instance, Human Rights Watch interviewed a policeman in Pakistan who believed that "in practically all cases of alleged rape, women had consented to the act of intercourse and then lied to incriminate their male partners."[48] And in Russia a judge recently threw out one of the first sexual harassment cases to be brought to court because he argued that sexual harassment was necessary to the survival of the human race, that the employer had acted gallantly rather than criminally and that "If we had no sexual harassment we would have no children."[49] Until societal views regarding women's rights change, international treaties and similar efforts will make little headway in eradicating the actions discussed in this chapter.

Possibly more promising than international treaties, declarations, and similar efforts are bans initiated by the state and/or local communities and individuals. For instance, at least 17 countries in Africa have banned FGC, and many communities have replaced the act with a coming-of-age ceremony. Further, in 2003, the Pan African Committee on Traditional Practices met in Addis Ababa, Ethiopia. Delegates from 30 African countries attended and declared February 6 the international day on zero tolerance for FGC. And this day has been celebrated every year since. The African Union has adopted the Maputo Protocol, which condemns FGC. And, in southwestern Cameroon, and as mentioned above, a local princess works to end the practice of FGC in her ethnic group, the Ejagam. Efforts like these may bear more fruit in the long run because they are less likely to be seen as imposed by the West. The numbers are supportive of this notion as rates of FGC are lower among younger women than older women.

Other efforts to end the practices discussed in this chapter are often initiated by human rights groups like Human Rights Watch and Amnesty International. Both groups monitor nations for abuses of international human rights treaties, write extensive reports detailing any abuses found, and then conduct campaigns to end the abuses. The campaigns often consist of writing letters to the leaders of nations found in violation, issuing press releases regarding the violations, and conducting grassroots campaigns in which citizens from around the world are educated about the issue and urged to write a letter to the nation in violation. Such efforts have arguably assisted in overturning the stoning sentences we discussed earlier and Turkey's efforts to reinstate virginity tests, but they are not as likely to be successful in eradicating FGC, domestic violence, and honor killings. This is largely because stoning and virginity tests are actions often initiated by or at least under the control of the government. Actions by international groups that publicly humiliate a government in front of the international community may be effective. However, FGC, domestic violence, and honor killings are cultural practices over which the state often has little control. Certainly the state can pass laws outlawing them, educate police and doctors on how to handle domestic violence and other reports of violence against women, and conduct campaigns to educate the public about the inhumanity of such acts, but these efforts, while necessary steps, may be very slow in effecting change. And the efforts of human rights groups to pressure governments to do something about such practices may be of limited use. Nonetheless, their efforts are worthwhile since they educate people about the abuses, bring attention to the issue, and, in some instances, effect change.

CONCLUSION

In sum, there is a solid basis in international law for protecting women from the practices discussed in this chapter. Further, local efforts in many nations have sprung up to end the various practices discussed, and international human rights groups continue to work to educate the public about abuses and to urge nations to comply with international law. All of these efforts have met with varying levels of success. Arguably, local efforts will ultimately prove the most successful since they will not be seen by locals as attempts by the West to eradicate their culture. Ultimately, success will be attained only when citizens view such practices not only as unacceptable but also as unnecessary parts of their culture.

FOR MORE INFORMATION

CARE, http://www.care.org/newsroom/specialreports/fgc/index.asp; the site contains information on the work they do to end FGC.

Death by Stoning: Justice, Punishment, and Human Rights—This ABC news program discusses the stoning case of Amina Lawal in Nigeria. http://ffh.films.com/id/5969/Death_by_Stoning_Justice_Punishment_and_Human_Rights.htm

The Female Genital Cutting Education and Networking Project, http://www.fgmnetwork.org/intro/fgmintro.html

Human Rights Watch, http://www.hrw.org

International Campaign Against Honour Killings, http://www.wluml.org/contact/wrrc/content/international-campaign-against-honor-killings.com

Ayse Onal. *Honour Killing: Stories of Men Who Killed* (London: Saqi Books, 2008). This book provides interviews with Turkish men who killed women in the name of honor.

Karen Tintori. *Unto the Daughters: The Legacy of an Honor Killing in a Sicilian-American Family* (New York: St. Martin's Press, 2007). Tintori tells the story of the honor killing of her great-aunt.

Saving Face, http://savingfacefilm.com. This documentary looks at acid attacks against women in Pakistan.

"Study to map the current situation and trends of female genital mutilation." *European Institute for Gender Equality.* http://www.eige.europa.eu/content/news-article/study-to-map-the-current-situation-and-trends-of-female-genital-mutilation

Tostan, Community-Led Development, http://www.tostan.org; organization that works to end FGC

United Nations Development Fund for Women, http://www.unifem.org/gender_issues/violence_against_women/facts_figures.php; facts and figures on violence against women

UNFPA. *Annual Report 2011 for the UNFPA/UNICEF Joint Programme on Female Genital Mutilation/Cutting.* http://www.unfpa.org/public/home/publications/pid/10418

Notes

PREFACE

1. Najma Chowdury and Barbara J. Nelson, with Kathryn A. Carver, Nancy Johnson, and Paula L. O'Loughlin, "Redefining Politics: Patterns of Women's Engagement from a Global Perspective," in *Women and Politics Worldwide*, ed. Barbara J. Nelson and Najma Chowdury (New Haven, CT: Yale University Press, 1994), 10–15.
2. Maxine Molyneux as quoted in Ibid., 18.
3. For example, see Sonia E. Alvarez, *Engendering Democracy in Brazil: Women's Movements in Transition Politics* (Princeton, NJ: Princeton University Press, 1990).
4. See Ronald Inglehart, *The Silent Revolution: Changing Values and Political Styles Among Western Publics* (Princeton, NJ: Princeton University Press, 1977); Ronald Inglehart, *Culture Shift in Advanced Industrial Society* (Princeton, NJ: Princeton University Press, 1990); Ronald Inglehart, *Modernization and Postmodernization: Cultural, Economic and Political Change in 43 Societies* (Princeton, NJ: Princeton University Press, 1997).
5. Ronald Inglehart and Pippa Norris, *Rising Tide: Gender Equality and Cultural Change Around the World* (New York: Cambridge University Press, 2003), 36.
6. Ibid., 21.
7. "Beijing Declaration and Platform for Action. Fourth World Conference on Women," September 15, 1995, http://www.un.org/womenwatch/daw/beijing/platform/(Feb. 15, 2013).
8. Nancy F. Cott, *The Grounding of Modern Feminism* (New Haven, CT: Yale University Press, 1987), 4–5.
9. Lynne E. Ford, *Women and Politics: The Pursuit of Equality* (New York: Houghton Mifflin, 2002), 20–27.
10. Mayra Buvinic, "Promoting Gender Equality," *International Social Science Journal* 162 (1999): 573.
11. Ford, *Women and Politics*, 8.
12. Ibid., xiii.

CHAPTER 1

1. Frederick Nzwili, "Women Candidates in Kenya Assaulted, Under-Funded," December 27, 2002, Women's eNews, www.womensenews.org (Dec. 27, 2002).
2. Ibid., 1.
3. Ibid., 1.
4. Ibid., 1.
5. "Women in National Parliaments," http://www.ipu.org/wmn-e/classif.htm (May 29, 2012).
6. "Michelle Bachelet Highlights Quotas to Accelerate Women's Political Participation," http://www.unwomen.org/2012/03/michelle-bachelet-highlights-quotas-to-accelerate-womens-political-participation/ (May 29, 2012).
7. "Women in National Parliaments."
8. Ibid.
9. Ibid.
10. Jane Jaquette, "Women in Power: From Tokenism to Critical Mass," *Foreign Policy* 108 (Fall 1997): 23–38.
11. Ibid.
12. "Women in National Parliaments."
13. "Voters in United Arab Emirates Set to Vote in Historic Elections," http://www.dubaicity.com/news/historic-elections12–16.htm (Oct. 14, 2008).
14. Pippa Norris, *Electoral Engineering: Voting Rules and Political Behavior* (New York: Cambridge University Press, 2004), 180.
15. United Nations Development Programme, *Human Development Report 2004* (New York: Oxford University Press, 2004), 234–237.
16. Ibid., 234–237.
17. Diana Elias, "Kuwait Appoints Its First Woman Cabinet Member," The Associated Press, June 12, 2005.
18. Susan Welch, "Women as Political Animals? A Test of Some Explanations for Male–Female Political Participation Differences," *American Journal of Political Science* 21 (1977): 711–730.
19. Laurent Belsie, "Men Lag Women at the Voting Booth," *Christian Science Monitor,* February 28, 2002, p. 4.
20. Center for American Women and Politics, "The Gender Gap and the 2004 Women's Vote: Setting the Record Straight," October 28, 2004.
21. Belsie, "Men Lag Women at the Voting Booth," p. 4.
22. U.S. Census Bureau, "Voter Turnout increases by 5 million in 2008 Presidential Election, U.S. Census Bureau Reports," July 20, 2009, http://www.census.gov/newsroom/releases/archives/voting/cb09-110.html (May 29, 2012).
23. *World Almanac and Book of Facts 2001* (New York: World Almanac Books, 2000), 40.
24. *World Almanac and Book of Facts 2004* (New York: World Almana Books, 2004), 47.
25. M. Margaret Conway, Gertrude Steuernagel, and David W. Ahern, *Women and Political Participation* (Washington, DC: Congressional Quarterly Press, 1997), 81–82.
26. Ibid., 83.
27. Ibid., 91.

28. As cited in Ronald Inglehart and Pippa Norris, *Rising Tide: Gender Equality and Cultural Change Around the World* (New York: Cambridge University Press, 2003), 105.

29. International Institute for Democracy and Electoral Assistance, "Gender and Political Participation: Voter Turnout by Gender," http://www.idea.int/vt/survey/by_gender.cfm (May 29, 2012).

30. Yael Yishai, *Between the Flag and the Banner: Women in Israeli Politics* (Albany: SUNY Press Albany, 1997).

31. Hir Joseph, "WRAPA Prepares Women for Voting," April 11, 2003, http://allAfrica.com/stories/printable/200304120067.html (April 21, 2003).

32. Gehan Abu-Zayd, "In Search of Political Power—Women in Parliament in Egypt, Jordan, and Lebanon," 2002 update of case study originally published in *Women in Parliament: Beyond Numbers* (Stockholm: International IDEA, 1998), http://www.idea.int.

33. As quoted in Inglehart and Norris, *Rising Tide,* 77.

34. Ibid., 99–100.

35. Sidney Verba, Norman Nie, and Jae-on Kim, *Participation and Social Equality* (Cambridge, MA: Harvard University Press, 1978).

36. See Carol Christy, *Sex Differences in Political Participation: Processes of Change in Fourteen Nations* (New York: Praeger, 1987); Conway, Steuernagel, and Ahern, *Women and Political Participation;* David DeVaus and Ian McAllister, "The Changing Politics of Women: Gender and Political Alignments in Eleven Nations," *European Journal of Political Research* 17 (1989): 241–262; and Sidney Verba, Kay Schlozman, and Henry E. Brady, *Voice and Equality* (Cambridge, MA: Harvard University Press, 1995).

37. Inglehart and Norris, *Rising Tide,* 123–126.

38. Pippa Norris, "Women's Power at the Ballot Box," paper written for International Institute for Democracy and Electoral Assistance, *Voter Turnout from 1945-2000: A Global Report on Political Participation.*

39. Ibid.

40. Saleh al-Shaibani, "No Women Elected in Omani Vote," Reuters, October 28, 2007, http://uk.reuters.com/articlePrint?articleId=UKL2808041220071028 (October 14, 2008).

41. Andrew Reynolds, "Women in the Legislatures and Executives of the World: Knocking at the Highest Glass Ceiling," *World Politics* 51, no. 4 (1999): 547–572.

42. Ibid., 547–572.

43. Ali Mari Tripp, *Women and Politics in Uganda* (Madison: The University of Wisconsin Press, 2000), 230.

44. For example, see Inglehart and Norris, *Rising Tide,* 130–131; Wilma Rule, "Electoral Systems, Contextual Factors and Women's Opportunities for Parliament in 23 Democracies," *Western Political Quarterly* 40 (1987): 477–498; Wilma Rule, "Why Women Don't Run: The Critical Contextual Factors in Women's Legislative Recruitment," *Western Political Quarterly* 34 (1988): 60–77.

45. "Quick Takes, Women in the Law in the United States," April 2012 http://www.catalyst.org/publication/246/women-in-law-in-the-us (May 29, 2012)

46. Inglehart and Norris, *Rising Tide,* 130–131.

47. Pippa Norris, *Electoral Engineering: Voting Rules and Political Behavior* (New York: Cambridge University Press, 2004), 187.

48. Inter-Parliamentary Union, *Women in Parliament in 2007: The Year in Perspective* (Switzerland: IPU, 2007), 5.

49. Miki Caul, "Women's Representation in Parliament: The Role of Political Parties" (Irvine: Center for the Study of Democracy, UC Irvine, 1997): 6.

50. Norris, *Electoral Engineering*, 201–202.

51. Ibid., 202.

52. International IDEA and Stockholm University, "Global Database of Quotas for Women," http://www.quotaproject.org/system.cfm (June 3, 2012)

53. Ibid.

54. Inglehart and Norris, *Rising Tide*, 145.

55. Norris, *Electoral Engineering*, 193.

56. Ibid., 191–192.

57. International IDEA and Stockholm University, "Global Database of Quotas for Women," http://www.quotaproject.org/system.cfm (June 4, 2012)

58. Eileen McDonagh, "Assimilated Leaders: Democratization, Political Inclusion and Female Leadership," *Harvard International Review* 21 (Fall 1999): 3.

59. Pamela Paxton and Sheri Kunovich, "Women's Political Representation: The Importance of Ideology," *Social Forces* 82 (September 2003): 90.

60. Ibid., 87–114.

61. Inglehart and Norris, *Rising Tide*, 144.

62. Tripp, *Women and Politics in Uganda*, 230.

63. Saleh al-Shaibani, "No Women Elected in Omani Vote."

64. Inglehart and Norris, *Rising Tide*, 144.

65. International IDEA, "Gender and Political Participation: Gender Facts," http://www.idea.int.gender/facts.htm (April 23, 2003).

66. Adventure Divas, "Helen Clark," http://www.adventuredivas.com/divas/article.view?page5245 (May 1, 2003).

67. See Barbara Burrell, *A Woman's Place Is in the House: Campaigning for Congress in the Feminist Era* (Ann Arbor: University of Michigan Press, 1994); Janet Clark, "Women at the National Level: An Update on Roll Call Voting Behavior," in *Women and Elective Office: Past, Present, and Future*, ed. Sue Thomas and Clyde Wilcox (New York: Oxford University Press, 1998); Freida Gehlen, "Women Members of Congress: A Distinctive Role," in *A Portrait of Marginality: The Political Behavior of the American Woman*, ed. Marianne Githens and Jewell Prestage (New York: McKay Co., 1977); Susan Welch, "Are Women More Liberal Than Men in the U.S. Congress?" *Legislative Studies Quarterly* 10 (1985): 125–134.

68. Karin L. Tamerius, "Sex, Gender, and Leadership in the Representation of Women," in *Gender, Power, Leadership, and Governance*, ed. Georgia Duerst–Lahti and Rita Mae Kelly (Ann Arbor: University of Michigan Press, 1993).

69. See Clara Bingham, *Challenging the Culture of Congress* (New York: Times Books, 1997); Barbara Boxer, *Strangers in the Senate* (Bethesda, MD: National Press Books, 1994); Karen Foerstal and Herbert Foerstal, *Climbing the Hill: Gender Conflict in Congress* (Westport, CT: Praeger, 1996); Irwin Gertzog, *Congressional Women: Their Recruitment, Integration and Behavior*, 2nd ed. (Westport, CT: Praeger, 1995); Marjorie Margolies-Mezvinsky, *A Woman's Place: The Freshman Who Changed the Face of Congress* (New York: Crown, 1994).

70. See Edith Barrett, "The Policy Priorities of African-American Women in State Legislatures," *Legislative Studies Quarterly* 20 (1995): 223–247; Tamerius, "Sex, Gender, and Leadership in the Representation of Women."

71. Michelle Swers, "Are Congresswomen More Likely to Vote for Women's Issues Bills Than Their Male Colleagues?" *Legislative Studies Quarterly* 23 (1998): 445; and Michelle Swers, *The Difference Women Make: The Policy Impact of Women in Congress* (Chicago: University of Chicago Press, 2002).

72. Ibid., 445.

73. Brian Frederick, "Gender Turnover and Roll Call Voting in the US Senate," *Journal of Women, Politics, and Policy* 32 (2011): 193–210.

74. Debra L. Dodson and Susan Carroll, *Reshaping the Agenda: Women in State Legislatures* (New Brunswick: Center for American Women and Politics, Rutgers, The State University of New Jersey, 1991).

75. See Deborah Dodson, "Representing Women's Interests in the U.S. House of Representatives," in *Women and Elective Office: Past, Present, and Future*, ed. Sue Thomas and Clyde Wilcox (New York: Oxford University Press, 1998); Dodson and Carroll, *Reshaping the Agenda*; and Sue Thomas, *How Women Legislate* (New York: Oxford University Press, 1994).

76. Sue Thomas and Susan Welch, "The Impact of Gender on Activities and Priorities of State Legislators," *Western Political Quarterly* 44 (1991): 454–455.

77. See Barrett, "The Policy Priorities of African-American Women in State Legislatures"; Dodson, "Representing Women's Interests in the U.S. House of Representatives"; Dodson and Carroll, *Reshaping the Agenda*; and Thomas, *How Women Legislate*.

78. Michael B. Berkman and Robert E. O'Connor, "Do Women Legislators Matter? Female Legislators and State Abortion Policy," *American Politics Quarterly* 21 (January 1993): 102–124.

79. See Malcolm Jewell and Marcia Lynn Wicker, *Legislative Leadership in the American States* (Ann Arbor: University of Michigan Press, 1994); Cindy Simon Rosenthal, *When Women Lead: Integrative Leadership in State Legislatures* (New York and Oxford: Oxford University Press, 1998).

80. Carol Gilligan, *In a Different Voice: Psychological Theory and Women's Development* (Cambridge, MA; Harvard University Press, 1982).

81. Rosenthal, *When Women Lead*.

82. Burrell, *A Woman's Place Is in the House*, 153.

83. Jewell and Whicker, *Legislative Leadership in American States*, 177.

84. Rosenthal, *When Women Lead*, 76.

85. Dodson and Carroll, *Reshaping the Agenda*.

86. For an excellent discussion and overview of the gendered nature of legislatures, see Rosenthal, *When Women Lead*.

87. Alana Jeydel and Andy Taylor, "Are Women Legislators Less Effective? Evidence from the U.S. House in the 103d–105th Congress," *Political Research Quarterly* 56 (March 2003): 19–28.

88. Jill M. Bystydzienski, *Women in Electoral Politics: Lessons from Norway* (Westport, CT, and London: Praeger, 1995), 21.

89. Kathleen Bratton and Leonard Ray, "Descriptive Representation, Policy Outcomes, and Municipal Day-Care Coverage in Norway," *American Journal of Political Science* 46 (2002): 428–437.

90. Bystydzienski, *Women in Electoral Politics*.

91. Ibid.

92. Ibid., 54–56.

93. Ibid., 110.

94. Ibid., 109–110.

95. Sarah Childs, "In Their Own Words: New Labour MPs and the Substantive Representation of Women," *British Journal of Politics and International Relations* (June 2001): 173–190.

96. Sarah Childs, "Hitting the Target: Are Labour Women MPs 'Acting for' Women?" Paper for the 51st Political Studies Association Conference, April 10–12, 2001, Manchester, United Kingdom, 3–4.

97. Pippa Norris and Joni Lovenduski, "Blair's Babes: Critical Mass Theory, Gender, and Legislative Life," John F. Kennedy School of Government, Harvard University, Faculty Research Working Paper Series (September 2001).

98. Sandra Grey, "Does Size Matter? Critical Mass and New Zealand Women MPs," *Parliamentary Affairs* 55 (2002): 19–29.

99. A critical mass is generally considered to be 14 percent or more.

100. Nikki Craske, *Women and Politics in Latin America* (New Brunswick, NJ: Rutgers University Press, 1999), 56.

101. Ilja A. Lluciak, *After the Revolution: Gender and Democracy in El Salvador, Nicaragua, and Guatemala* (Baltimore, MD: Johns Hopkins University Press, 2001), 198.

102. Lluciak, *After the Revolution*, 201.

103. Karen Olsen de Figueres, "The Road to Equality—Women in Parliament in Costa Rica," 2002 update of case study originally published in *Women in Parliament: Beyond Numbers* (Stockholm, International IDEA, 1998): 3, http://www.idea.int.

104. Ibid., 3.

105. Maryam Poya, *Women, Work and Islamism: Ideology and Resistance in Iran* (London and New York: Zed Books, 1999), 144.

106. Ibid., 146.

107. Interparliamentarian Union, "Women in Parliaments: World Classification," http://www.ipu.org/wmn-e/classif.htm (June 5, 2012).

108. Poya, *Women, Work and Islamism*, 145.

109. Ibid., 145.

110. Azadeh Kian–Thiebaut, "Women and the Making of Civil Society in Post-Islamist Iran," in *Twenty Years of Islamic Revolution: Political and Social Transition in Iran Since 1979*, ed. Eric Hooglund (Syracuse, NY: Syracuse University Press, 2002), 58.

111. British Broadcasting Corporation, "Guide to Iran's Presidential Poll," June 16, 2005, http://news.bbc.co.uk/1/hi/world/middle_east/4086944.stm (Aug. 17, 2005).

112. Yishai, *Between the Flag and the Banner.*

113. Ibid., 100.

114. Peroshni Govender, "56 Female Candidates up for Election in Israel," January 28, 2003, Women's eNews, http://womensenews.org (Jan. 28, 2003).

115. Shirin Rai, "Class, Caste and Gender—Women in Parliament in India," 2002 update of case study originally published in *Women in Parliament: Beyond Numbers* (Stockholm, International IDEA, 1998), http://www.idea.int.

116. The Inter-Parliamentary Union, *Women in National Parliaments*, September 30, 2008, http://ipu.org/wmn-e/classif.htm (June 5, 2012).

117. The British Broadcasting Corporation, "Indian Parliament Refuses Women Quotas," July 14, 1998.

118. Anuradha Sengupta, "Kashmiris Look to a Woman for Resolution of Strife," www.womensenews.org, January 24, 2003, p. 1.

119. Ibid.

120. The Inter-Parliamentary Union, *Women in National Parliaments.*

121. Ibid.

122. Ibid.

123. Mavivi Myakayaka–Manzini, "Women Empowered—Women in Parliament in South Africa," 2002 update of case study originally published in *Women in Parliament: Beyond Numbers* (Stockholm, International IDEA, 1998), http://www.idea.int.

124. Ibid., 1.

125. Ibid.

126. International Institute for Democracy and Electoral Assistance, "Global Database of Quotas for Women," http://www.quotaproject.org/displayCountry.cfm?CountryCode5ZA (Aug. 18, 2005).

127. Government of South Africa, http://www.genderismyagenda.com/country_reports/states_reports_eng/south_africa_report.pdf (Feb. 15, 2013)

128. Myakayaka–Manzini, "Women Empowered."

129. Shirin Rai, "Class, Caste and Gender," 1.

130. Joni Saeger, *The State of the Women in the World Atlas* (Penguin Books, 1997). These countries are Sweden (50 percent), Norway (42 percent), Finland (41 percent), Seychelles (41 percent), Barbados (39 percent), Denmark (35 percent), Sri Lanka (29 percent), Gambia (25 percent), Netherlands (24 percent), Austria (22 percent), Luxemburg (21 percent), Bahamas, Bhutan, Fidischi, and the United States (all 20 percent).

131. United Nations Development Programme, *Human Development Report 2004* (New York: Oxford University Press, 2004), 234–237.

132. Inter-Parliamentary Union Quarterly Review, "The World of Parliaments," March 2010, no. 37, 18.

133. Carlos Lozada, "Colombia Gets Tough with a Woman's Touch," *Christian Science Monitor,* October 28, 2002.

134. International Women's Democracy Center, "Resources: Fact Sheet: Women's Political Participation," June 2008, http://www.iwdc.org/resources/fact_sheet.htm (Oct. 22, 2008).

135. See Craske, *Women and Politics in Latin America;* de Figueres, "The Road to Equality"; Yishai, *Between the Flag and the Banner.*

136. Craske, *Women and Politics in Latin America,* 75.

137. Ibid., 67–68.

138. Myakayaka–Manzini, "Women Empowered."

139. Craske, *Women and Politics in Latin America,* 68.

140. Tripp, *Women and Politics in Uganda,* 219.

141. Ibid., 219.

142. David S. Meyer, "Restating the Woman Question: Women's Movements and State Restructuring," in *Women's Movements Facing the Reconfigured State,* ed. Lee Ann Banaszak, Karen Beckwith, and Dieter Rucht (New York: Cambridge University Press, 2003), 279.

143. International Institute for Democracy and Electoral Assistance and Stockholm University, "Global Database of Quotas for Women," http://www.quotaproject.org (August 19, 2005).

144. Craske, *Women and Politics in Latin America,* 73.

145. Caroline Lambert, "French Women in Politics: The Long Road to Parity," The Brookings Institution, May 2001, http://www.brookings.edu/research/articles/2001/05/france-lambert (April 23, 2003).

146. Ibid.

147. Ibid.

148. Wilma Rule and Matthew Shugart, "The Preference Vote and Election of Women," Center for Voting and Democracy, 1995, http://www.fairvote.org/reports/1995/chp7/rule.html (April 21, 2003).

149. Kira Sanbonmatsu, Susan J. Carroll, and Debbie Walsh, "*Poised to Run: Women's Pathways to State Legislatures*," Center for American Women and Politics (2009): 3.

150. Inglehart and Norris, *Rising Tide*, 144–146.

151. Sophi Arie, "Elisa Carrio in Lead to Be Argentina's President," Women's eNews, July 18, 2002, http://www.womensenews.org (July 18, 2002).

CHAPTER 2

1. British Broadcasting Company News, "Talks to End Nigerian Oil Siege," July 11, 2002, http://news.bbc.co.uk/1/hi/world/africa/2119872.stm (Feb. 5, 2003).

2. British Broadcasting Company News, " 'Deal Reached' in Nigerian Oil Protest," July 16, 2002, http://news.bbc.co.uk/1/hi/africa/2129281.stm (Feb. 5, 2003).

3. See Karen Beckwith for a longer discussion of definitions of women's movement. Karen Beckwith, "Beyond Compare? Women's Movements in Comparative Perspective," *European Journal of Political Research* 37 (2000): 431–468.

4. Jeffrey M. Berry, *Interest Group Society*, 3rd ed. (New York: Longman, 1997), 4–5.

5. Karen Beckwith, "Lancashire Women Against Pit Closures: Women's Standing in a Men's Movement," *Signs* 21, no. 4 (2000): 1034–1068.

6. Beckwith, "Beyond Compare?," 431–468.

7. Amrita Basu, "Introduction," in *The Challenge of Local Feminisms: Women's Movements in Global Perspective*, ed. Amrita Basu (Boulder, CO: Westview Press, 1995), 11.

8. See William Kornhauser, *The Politics of Mass Society* (Glencoe, IL: The Free Press, 1959); Neil Smelser, *Theory of Collective Behavior* (New York: The Free Press, 1962); Ralph H. Turner and Lewis Killian, *Collective Behavior* (Englewood Cliffs, NJ: Prentice Hall, 1957).

9. See Jo Freeman, *The Politics of Women's Liberation* (New York: McKay, 1975); J. Craig Jenkins, *The Politics of Insurgency* (New York: Columbia University Press, 1985); John D. McCarthy and Meyer Zald, eds., *Social Movements in an Organizational Society* (New Brunswick, NJ, and Oxford: Transaction Books, 1987).

10. See Anne Costain, *Inviting Women's Rebellion* (Baltimore, MD: Johns Hopkins University Press, 1992); Peter K. Eisenger, "The Conditions of Protest Behavior in American Cities," *American Political Science Review* 67 (1973): 11–28; J. Craig Jenkins and Charles Perrow, "Insurgency of the Powerless: Farm Workers Movements," *American Sociological Review* 42 (1977): 249–267; Mary Fainsod Katzenstein and Carol M. Mueller, *The Women's Movements of the United States and Western Europe* (Philadelphia: Temple University Press, 1987);

Herbert P. Kitschelt, "Political Opportunity Structures and Political Protest: Anti-Nuclear Movements in Four Democracies," *British Journal of Political Science* 16, no. 1 (1986): 57–85; Doug McAdam, *Political Process and the Development of Black Insurgency 1930-1970* (Chicago and London: University of Chicago Press, 1985); David Meyer, "Institutionalizing Dissent: The United States Structure of Political Opportunity and the End of the Nuclear Freeze Movement," *Sociological Forum* 8, no. 2 (1993): 157–179; Francis Fox Piven and Richard Cloward, *Poor People's Movements* (New York: Vintage Books, 1979); Sidney Tarrow, *Power in Movement* (Cambridge, UK: Cambridge University Press, 1994).

11. Nancy McGlen and Karen O'Connor, *Women's Rights* (New York: Praeger, 1983).

12. Betty Friedan, *The Feminine Mystique* (New York: W.W. Norton & Co., 2001).

13. McGlen and O'Connor, *Women's Rights.*

14. British Broadcasting Company News, "Oil Deal 'Off,' Nigerian Women Say," July 16, 2002, http://news.bbc.co.uk/1/hi/world/africa/2132494.stm (Feb. 5, 2003).

15. British Broadcasting Company News, "Nigerian Women Leave Oil Plant," July 18, 2002, http://news.bbc.co.uk/1/hi/world/africa/2136509.stm (Feb. 5, 2003).

16. British Broadcasting Company News, " 'Deal Reached' in Nigerian Oil Protest."

17. Jennifer Schirmer, "The Seeking of Truth and the Gendering of Consciousness," in *Viva: Women and Political Protest in Latin America*, ed. Sarah A. Radcliffe and Sallie Westwood (New York and London: Routledge, 1993), 32.

18. Aili Mari Tripp, *Women and Politics in Uganda* (Madison: The University of Wisconsin Press, 2000), 108.

19. Schirmer, "The Seeking of Truth," 48–49.

20. Sheila Rowbotham and Stephanie Linkogle, eds., *Women Resist Globalization: Mobilizing for Livelihood and Rights* (London and New York: Zed Books, 2001), 2.

21. Tripp, *Women and Politics in Uganda*, 107–108.

22. Maxine Molyneux, "Mobilization Without Emancipation? Women's Interests, the State and Revolution in Nicaragua," *Feminist Studies* 11(1985): 227–254.

23. Temma Kaplan, "Uncommon Women and the Common Good," in *Women Resist Globalization*, 29.

24. Nikki Craske, *Women and Politics in Latin America* (New Brunswick, NJ: Rutgers University Press, 1999); Tripp, *Women and Politics in Uganda.*

25. UNESCO, "Baseline Definitions of Key Concepts and Terms," http://www.unesco.org/new/fileadmin/MULTIMEDIA/HQ/BSP/GENDER/PDF/1.%20 Baseline%20Definitions%20of%20key%20gender-related%20concepts.pdf

26. Craske, *Women and Politics in Latin America*, 119.

27. Jacqueline Adams, "Art in Social Movements: Shantytown Women's Protest in Pinochet's Chile," *Sociological Forum* 17 (2002): 30.

28. Tripp, *Women and Politics in Uganda*, 110.

29. Craske, *Women and Politics in Latin America*, 2–3.

30. Ibid., 112–113.

31. Helen I. Safa and Cornelia Butler Flora, "Production, Reproduction, and the Polity: Women's Strategic and Practical Gender Issues," in *Americas: New Interpretive Essays*, ed. Alfred Stepan (New York and Oxford: Oxford University Press, 1992), 127.

32. Schirmer, "The Seeking of Truth," 32–33.

33. Ibid., 39–41.

34. Anne Costain and Doug Costain, "Strategy and Tactics of the Women's Movement in the U.S.: The Role of Political Parties," in *The Women's Movements of the United States and Western Europe: Consciousness, Political Opportunity and Public Policy,* ed. Mary F. Katzenstein and Carol M. Mueller (Philadelphia: Temple University Press, 1987), 197.

35. Ibid.

36. Lee Ann Banaszak, Karen Beckwith, and Dieter Rucht, "When Power Relocates: Interactive Changes in Women's Movements and States," in *Women's Movements Facing the Reconfigured State,* ed. Lee Ann Banaszak, Karen Beckwith, and Dieter Rucht (New York: Cambridge University Press, 2003), 1–6.

37. Louise Krasniewicz, *Nuclear Summer: The Clash of Communities at the Seneca Women's Peace Encampment* (Ithaca, NY: Cornell University Press, 1992).

38. Maren Klawiter, "Racing for the Cure, Walking Women and Toxic Touring: Mapping Cultures of Action Within the Bay Area Terrain of Breast Cancer," *Social Problems* 46 (1999): 105.

39. Kaplan, "Uncommon Women," 37.

40. Myra Marx Ferree, "Equality and Autonomy: Feminist Politics in the United States and West Germany," in *The Women's Movements of the United States and Western Europe,* ed. Mary Fainsod Katzenstein and Carol McClurg Mueller (Philadelphia: Temple University Press, 1987), 172–177.

41. Paul Burstein, "Legal Mobilization as a Social Movement Tactic: The Struggle for Equal Employment Opportunity," *American Journal of Sociology* 96 (1991): 1201–1225.

42. Amy G. Mazur, *Theorizing Feminist Policy* (New York: Oxford University Press, 2002), 48.

43. Beckwith, "Beyond Compare?," 439–440.

44. As quoted in Dorothy McBride Stetson and Amy G. Mazur, "Introduction," in *Comparative State Feminism,* ed. Dorothy McBride Stetson and Amy G. Mazur (Thousand Oaks, CA: Sage Publications, 1995), 10.

45. Stetson and Mazur, "Introduction," in *Comparative State Feminism,* 1.

46. United Nations, "Fact Sheet No. 8: Institutional Mechanisms for the Advancement of Women," http://www.un.org/womenwatch/daw/followup/session/presskit/fs8.htm (Sept. 14, 2005).

47. Cynthia Enloe, "Closing Remarks," *International Peacekeeping* 8 (Summer 2001): 111.

48. Costain, *Inventing Women's Rebellion,* xv.

49. Sarah L. Henderson, "Women in a Changing Context," in *Contemporary Russian Politics,* ed. Michael Bressler (Boulder, CO: Lynne Rienner Press, forthcoming).

50. Amy G. Mazur, *Gender Bias and the State: Symbolic Reform at Work in Fifth Republic France* (Pittsburgh: University of Pittsburgh Press, 1995), 1–4.

51. Tripp, *Women and Politics in Uganda,* 12.

52. Haya al-Mughni, "Women's Organizations in Kuwait," in *Women and Politics in the Middle East,* ed. Saud Joseph and Susan Slyomovics (Philadelphia: University of Pennsylvania Press, 2001), 176–182.

53. Banaszak, Beckwith, and Rucht, "When Power Relocates," 2.

54. Craske, *Women and Politics in Latin America,* 131.

55. Ibid., 131; Tripp, *Women and Politics in Uganda,* 110.

56. Nikki Craske, "Women's Political Participation in Colonias Populares in Guadelajara, Mexico," in *Viva: Women and Popular Protest in Latin America,* ed. Sarah Radcliffe and Sallie Westwood (London and New York: Routledge, 1993), 134.

57. David Meyer and Nancy Whittier, "Social Movement Spillover," *Social Problems* 41 (1994): 277.

58. Ronald Inglehart and Pippa Norris, *Rising Tide: Gender Equality and Cultural Change Around the World* (New York: Cambridge University Press, 2003), 29–48.

59. "Women's Studies Programs Worldwide," http://userpages.umbc.edu/~korenman/wmst/programs.html (Sept. 15, 2005).

60. As quoted in Nonna Mayer and Mariette Sineau, "France: The Front National," in *Rechtsextreme Parteien,* ed. Helga Amsberger and Brigitte Halbmayr (Opladen: Leske & Budrich, 2002), 80–81.

61. Ibid., 65.

62. Ibid., 68.

63. Ibid., 73.

64. Valentine M. Moghadam and Margot Badran, *Causes and Gender Implications of Islamist Movements in the Middle East* (Helsinki: World Institute of Development Economic Research, United Nations University, 1991).

65. al-Mughni, "Women's Organizations in Kuwait," 179.

66. Burcak Keskin, "Confronting Double Patriarchy: Islamist Women in Turkey," in *Right-Wing Women: From Conservatives to Extremists Around the World,* ed. Paola Bacchetta and Margaret Power (New York: Routledge, 2002), 245–247.

67. Nilufer Narli, "The Rise of the Islamist Movement in Turkey," *Middle Eastern Review of International Affairs* 3, no. 3 (1999).

68. Mayer and Sineau, "France," 70.

69. Ibid., 72.

70. Keskin, "Confronting Double Patriarchy," 251.

71. Henri Astier, "Le Pen's Voters," BBC News Online, April 23, 2002, http://news.bbc.co.uk/1/hi/world/europe/1946764.stm (Sept. 30, 2005).

72. Mayer and Sineau, "France," 57.

73. Merve Kavakci, "Headscarf Heresy: For One Muslim Woman, the Headscarf Is a Matter of Choice and Dignity," *Foreign Policy* (May/June 2004): 66–67.

74. Marge Berer and T. K. Sundari Ravindran, "Fundamentalism, Women's Empowerment and Reproductive Rights," *Reproductive Health Matters* 4, no. 8 (1996): 10–15.

75. Rowbothom and Linkogle, *Women Resist Globalization,* 3.

76. David S. Meyer, "Restating the Woman Question: Women's Movements and State Restructuring," in *Women's Movements Facing the Reconfigured State,* 275–294.

CHAPTER 3

1. Dina Zayed, "Attack on Egyptian Women Protesters Spark Uproar," Thomson Reuters, Dec. 21, 2011, http://www.reuters.com/article/2011/12/21/us-egypt-protests-women-idUSTRE7BK1BX20111221.

2. Associated Press, "Egyptian Women Protesters Sexually Assaulted in Tahrir Square," *The Guardian,* June 8, 2012, http://www.guardian.co.uk/world/2012/jun/09/egyptian-women-protesters-sexually-assaulted.

3. Zayed, "Attack on Egyptian Women Protesters Spark Uproar."

4. Samuel P. Huntington, *Political Order in Changing Societies* (New Haven, CT: Yale University Press, 1968).

5. T. R. Gurr, *Why Men Rebel* (Princeton, NJ: Princeton University Press, 1970).

6. Theda Skocpol, *States and Social Revolutions* (Cambridge: Cambridge University Press, 1979).

7. Jack A. Goldstone, *Revolution and Rebellion in the Early Modern World* (Berkeley: University of California Press, 1991).

8. The dates listed refer to the year of regime change; the actual revolutionary movement started earlier and often continued to implement changes for several years afterward.

9. British Broadcasting Corporation News, "Country Profile: Algeria," http://news.bbc.co.uk/1/hi/world/middle_east/country_profiles/790556.stm (Aug. 4, 2005).

10. Jack A. Goldstone, "Toward a Fourth Generation of Revolutionary Theory," *Annual Review of Political Science* 4 (2001): 142.

11. It is difficult to come up with an exact figure. Jane Jacquette estimated that about 30 percent of Salvadoran guerrillas were women. In her study of Nicaraguan guerrillas, Chinchilla estimated that women represented about 20 percent of armed combatants. Norma Stoltz Chinchilla, "Feminism, Revolution, and Democratic Transitions in Nicaragua" in *The Women's Movement in Latin America: Participation and Democracy* (2nd ed). Ed. Jane S. Jaquette. (Boulder: Westview Press, 1994), 177–196. Karen Kampwirth estimated that perhaps a third of the combatants in the FSLN (Nicaragua), FMLN (El Salvador), and FZLN (Zapatistas) were women, in contrast to the Cuban case, in which women made up 5 percent of armed combatants. Karen Kampwirth, *Feminism and the Legacy of Revolution: Nicaragua, El Salvador, Chiapas* (Athens: Center for International Studies at Ohio University Press, 2004), x.

12. As quoted in Christine Sylvester, "Simultaneous Revolutions and Exits: A Semi-Skeptical Comment," in *Women and Revolution in Africa, Asia, and the New World*, ed. Mary Ann Tetrault (Columbia: University of South Carolina Press, 1994), 38–39.

13. Nelson Mandela, *Long Walk to Freedom: The Autobiography of Nelson Mandela* (Boston: Back Bay Books, 1995).

14. Linda M. Lobao, "Women in Revolutionary Movements: Changing Patterns of Latin American Guerilla Study," in *Women and Revolution: Global Expressions*, ed. M. J. Diamond (Boston: Kluwer Academic Publishers, 1998), 260–265.

15. Beryl Williams, "Kollantai and After: Women in the Russian Revolution," in *Women, State and Revolution: Essays in Power and Gender in Europe Since 1789*, ed. Sian Reynolds (Amherst: University of Massachusetts Press, 1987), 68.

16. Michael Lynch, *Mao* (New York, Routledge Press, 2004), 209.

17. Kampwirth, *Feminism and the Legacy of Revolution*, 113.

18. Luisa Maria Dietrich Ortega, "Gendered Patterns of Mobilisation and Recruitment for Political Violence: Lessons Learned from Three Latin American Countries," Centre for Research on Inequality, Human Security and Ethnicity, Oxford, England, 2009.

19. Vladimir Ilyich Lenin, "Speech at the First All-Russia Congress of Working Women," November 19, 1918, http://www.marxists.org/archive/lenin/works/1918/nov/19.htm (April 21, 2006).

20. Lynch, *Mao*, 208.

21. Lois M. Smith and Alfred Padula, *Sex and Revolution: Women in Socialist Cuba* (New York: Oxford University Press, 1996), 4.

22. Margaret Randall, *Gathering Rage: The Failure of Twentieth Century Revolutions to Develop a Feminist Agenda* (New York: Monthly Review Press, 1992), 49.

23. As quoted in Kampwirth, *Feminism and the Legacy of Revolution,* 112.

24. As quoted in Karen Kampwirth, *Women and Guerilla Movements: Nicaragua, El Salvador, Chiapas, Cuba* (University Park: Penn State University Press, 2002), 114.

25. M. J. Diamond, "Olympe de Gouges and the French Revolution: The Construction of Gender as Critique," in *Women and Revolution: Global Expressions,* ed. M. J. Diamond (Boston: Kluwer Academic Publishers, 1998).

26. Valentine M. Moghadam, "Gender and Revolutions," in *Theorizing Revolutions,* ed. John Foran (New York: Routledge Press, 1997), 144.

27. Shana Penn, *Solidarity's Secret: The Women Who Defeated Communism in Poland* (Ann Arbor: University of Michigan Press, 2005), xiii.

28. Ibid., 23.

29. Sarah L. Henderson, "Women in a Changing Context," in *Understanding Contemporary Russia,* ed. Michael L. Bressler (Boulder, CO: Lynne Rienner Press, 2008).

30. As quoted in Penn, *Solidarity's Secret,* 332–333.

31. See Chapter 1 in Valentine M. Moghadam, *Modernizing Women: Gender and Social Change in the Middle East* (Boulder, CO: Lynne Rienner Publishers, 2003), 1–32.

32. Azadeh Kian-Thiebaut, "Women and the Making of Civil Society in Post-Islamist Iran," in *Twenty Years of Islamic Revolution: Political and Social Transition in Iran Since 1979,* ed. Eric Hooglund (Syracuse, NY: Syracuse University Press, 2002), 60.

33. British Broadcasting Corporation News, "Iran: Country Profile," August 3, 2005, http://news.bbc.co.uk/1/hi/world/middle_east/country_profiles/790877.stm (Aug. 24, 2005).

34. As quoted in Kian-Thiebaut, "Women and the Making of Civil Society in Post-Islamist Iran," 60.

35. Roksana Bahramitash, "Revolution, Islamization, and Women's Employment in Iran," *The Brown Journal of World Affairs* 9 (Winter/Spring 2003): 233.

36. Moghadam, "Gender and Revolutions," 137–167.

37. Moghadam, *Modernizing Women,* 98.

38. Julia Shayne, *The Revolution Question: Feminisms in El Salvador, Chile, and Cuba* (New Brunswick, NJ: Rutgers University Press, 2004), 5.

39. Kampwirth, *Women and Guerilla Movements,* 6.

40. Kampwirth, *Feminism and the Legacy of Revolution,* 8.

41. British Broadcasting Corporation News, "Transcripts: The Guerilla's Story," January 1, 2001, http://news.bbc.co.uk/1/hi/in_depth/uk/2000/uk_confidential/1090986.stm (April 21, 2006).

42. Ilya Llukiak, *After the Revolution: Gender and Democracy in El Salvador, Nicaragua, and Guatemala* (Baltimore: Johns Hopkins University Press, 2001), 70.

43. Kampwirth estimated that up to a third of combatants of FSLN, FMLN, and FZLN were female. Kampwirth, *Feminism and the Legacy of Revolution,* x.

44. Juan Lazaro, "Women and Political Violence in Contemporary Peru," in *Women and Revolution: Global Expressions,* ed. M. J. Diamond (Boston: Kluwer Academic Publishers, 1998), 305.

45. Timothy Wickham-Crowley, *Guerillas and Revolution in Latin America: A Comparative Study of Insurgents and Regimes Since 1956* (Princeton, NJ: Princeton University Press, 1992), 216.

46. Lukiak, *After the Revolution.*

47. Kampwirth, *Feminism and the Legacy of Revolution,* xi.

48. Diamond, "Olympe de Gouges and the French Revolution."

49. Vera Figner, *Memoirs of a Revolutionist,* introduction by Richard Stites (DeKalb: Northern Illinois Press, 1991).

50. As quoted in Smith and Padula, *Sex and Revolution,* 46.

51. Sandra C. Taylor, *Vietnamese Women at War: Fighting for Ho Chi Minh and the Revolution* (Lawrence: University of Kansas Press, 1999).

52. Ibid., 127.

53. Smith and Padula, *Sex and Revolution,* 27.

54. As quoted in Ibid., 24.

55. Nikki Craske, *Women and Politics in Latin America* (New Brunswick, NJ: Rutgers University Press, 1999), 142.

56. Penn, *Solidarity's Secret,* 9.

57. Kampwirth, *Feminism and the Legacy of Revolution,* 175.

58. Roksana Bahramitash, "Revolution, Islamization, and Women's Employment in Iran," *The Brown Journal of World Affairs* 9 (Winter/Spring 2003), 232–233.

59. Mia Bloom, "Bombshells: Women and Terror," *Gendered Issues* (2011), 28:1–21.

60. Mary Ann Tetrault, "Women and Revolution in Vietnam," in *Global Feminisms Since 1945,* ed. Bonnie G. Smith (New York: Routledge, 2000), 56.

61. Taylor, *Vietnamese Women at War,* 125.

62. As quoted in Smith and Padula, *Sex and Revolution,* 28.

63. Ibid., 30.

64. As quoted in Francesca Miller, *Latin American Women and the Search for Social Justice* (Hanover, NH: University of New England Press, 1991), 146–147.

65. Shayne, *The Revolution Question,* 164.

66. Craske, *Women and Politics in Latin America,* 142.

67. Randall, *Gathering Rage,* 44.

68. Ibid., 30.

69. Tom Heyden, "FARC's Female Guerillas Submitted to Sexual Slavery: Police Report," *Columbia Reports,* June 13, 2011, http://colombiareports.com/colombia-news/news/16935-colombian-police-report-details-sexual-atrocities-within-farc.html.

70. As quoted in Molyneux, "Mobilization Without Emancipation? Women's Interests, the State and Revolution in Nicaragua," *Feminist Studies* 11 (1985): 227–254, footnote 19.

71. Kampwirth, *Feminism and the Legacy of Revolution,* 12.

72. Ibid., 14.

73. Sue Ellen M. Charlton, Jana Everett, and Kathleen Staudt, "Women, the State, and Development," in *Women, the State, and Development,* ed. Sue Ellen M. Charlton, Jana Everett, and Kathleen Staudt (Albany: SUNY Press, 1989), 10.

74. Barbara Wolfe Jancar, *Women Under Communism* (Baltimore: Johns Hopkins University Press, 1978), 113–114.

75. Craske, *Women and Politics in Latin America,* 139–140.

76. Beryl Williams, "Kollantai and After: Women in the Russian Revolution," in *Women, State and Revolution: Essays on Power and Gender in Europe Since*

1789, ed. Sian Reynolds (Amherst: The University of Massachusetts Press, 1987), 60.

77. Smith and Padula, *Sex and Revolution*, 32.

78. Craske, *Women and Politics in Latin America*, 145.

79. Karen Beckwith, "Beyond Compare? Women's Movements in Comparative Perspective," *European Journal of Policy Research* 37 (2000): 444.

80. Craske, *Women and Politics in Latin America*, 147.

81. Charlton, Everett, and Staudt, "Women, the State and Development," 11.

82. Craske, *Women and Politics in Latin America*, 146.

83. Ziva Galili, "Women and the Russian Revolution," in *Women and Revolution: Global Expressions*, ed. M. J. Diamond (Boston: Kluwer Academic Publishers, 1998), 63–77.

84. Marilyn B. Young, "Reflections in Women in the Chinese Revolution," in *Women and Revolution: Global Expressions*, ed. M. J. Diamond (Boston: Kluwer Academic Publishers, 1998), 357–361.

85. Taylor, *Vietnamese Women at War*, 31.

86. Kampwirth, *Feminism and the Legacy of Revolution*, 5–14.

87. As quoted in Shayne, *The Revolution Question*, 1.

88. Craske, *Women and Politics in Latin America*, 140.

89. Kampwirth, *Feminism and the Legacy of Revolution*, 176.

90. Penn, *Solidarity's Secret*, 199.

91. Marilyn Rueschemeyer, ed., *Women in the Politics of Postcommunist Eastern Europe* (Armonk, NY: M. E. Sharpe, 1994).

92. Sarah L. Henderson, "Women in a Changing Context," in *Understanding Contemporary Russia*, ed. Michael L. Bressler (Boulder, CO: Lynne Rienner Press, 2008).

93. Valentine Moghadam, ed., *Democratic Reform and the Position of Women in Transitional Economies* (Oxford: Clarendon Press, 1993).

94. Human Development Unit, Eastern Europe and Central Asia Region, World Bank, "Gender in Transition" (Washington, DC: World Bank, May 21, 2002).

95. Diamond, "Olympe de Gouges and the French Revolution."

96. Penn, *Solidarity's Secret*, 28.

97. Azadeh Kain, "Women and Politics in Post-Islamist Iran: The Gender Conscious Drive to Change," *British Journal of Middle Eastern Studies* 24, no. 1 (1997): 75–97.

98. As quoted in Ibid., 75–97.

99. Nahid Siamdoust, "A Woman as President: Iran's Impossible Dream?" *Time*, May 20, 2009, http://www.time.com/time/world/article/0,8599,1899763,00.html.

100. "Women and the Vote," Tehran Bureau, Frontline, May 12, 2009, http://www.pbs.org/wgbh/pages/frontline/tehranbureau/2009/05/women-and-the-vote.html.

101. Kian-Thiebaut, "Women and the Making of Civil Society," 65–67.

102. Homa Hoodfar, "Bargaining with Fundamentalism: Women and the Politics of Population Control in Iran," *Reproductive Health Matters* 4, no. 8 (1996): 30–40.

103. Ibid.

104. Kian-Thiebaut, "Women and the Making of Civil Society," 60.

105. Hoodfar, "Bargaining with Fundamentalism."

106. Kian-Thiebaut, "Women and the Making of Civil Society," 63.

107. Robert Tait, "Anger as Iran Bans Women from Universities," *The Telegraph*, August 20, 2012, http://www.telegraph.co.uk/news/worldnews/middleeast/iran/9487761/Anger-as-Iran-bans-women-from-universities.html.

108. BBC News, "Arab Uprising–Country by Country. http://www.bbc.co.uk/news/world-12482315

109. Chris McGreal, "Arab Women Fight to Keep Gains Won on the Street," *The Guardian*, June 13, 2012, http://www.guardian.co.uk/world/2012/jun/13/arab-women-egypt-laws-parliament.

110. Isobel Coleman, "Is the Arab Spring Bad for Women?" *Foreign Policy*, December 20, 2011, http://www.foreignpolicy.com/articles/2011/12/20/arab_spring_women.

PART II INTRODUCTION

1. Amy G. Mazur and Susanne Zwingel, "Comparing Feminist Policy in Politics and at Work in France and Germany: Shared European Union Setting, Divergent National Contexts," *Review of Policy Research* 20, no. 3 (2003): 365–383.

2. For example, see Dorothy McBride Stetson and Amy G. Mazur, eds., *Comparative State Feminism* (Thousand Oaks, CA: Sage Publications, 1995); Amy G. Mazur, *Theorizing Feminist Policy* (New York: Oxford University Press, 2002).

CHAPTER 4

1. The Economist, "Special Report: Women and Work: Closing the Gap," November 26, 2011: 2. http://www.economist.com/node/21539928 (June 21, 2012).

2. Kim Campbell, "Women Seek Solutions to Pension-System Bias," *Christian Science Monitor,* May 9, 1996, vol. 88, p. 9.

3. Diane Nicol, "Employers Face Rise in Equal Pay Claims," *The Scotsman*, April 19, 2003, p. 23.

4. Fiona Davidson, "Male Workers Say It's Unfair That Dress Rules Don't Apply to Women; Men Shirty About Ties," *The Express,* July 16, 2003, p. 7.

5. OECD Work on Gender, " 8 Key Figures on Gender Equality," May 2012, http://www.oecd.org/gender (June 19, 2012).

6. United Nations Development Programme, *Human Development Report 2004* (New York: Oxford University Press, 2004), 221–224.

7. Ronnie Steinberg-Ratner, "The Policy and Problem: Overview of Seven Countries," in *Equal Employment Policy for Women,* ed. Ronnie Steinberg-Ratner (Philadelphia: Temple University Press, 1980), 41–42.

8. Amy G. Mazur and Susanne Zwingel, "Comparing Feminist Policy in Politics and at Work in France and Germany: Shared European Union Setting, Divergent National Contexts," *Review of Policy Research* 20, no. 3 (2003): 370.

9. Organization for Economic Co-operation and Development, http://stats.oecd .org/OECDStat_Metadata (June 15, 2012).

10. European Commission, "Gender Mainstreaming," http://europa.eu.int/comm/employment_social/gender_equality/gender_mainstreaming/employment/employment_labour_market_en.html (Oct. 5, 2003).

11. Amy G. Mazur, *Theorizing Feminist Policy* (New York: Cambridge University Press, 2002), 80–87.

12. United Nations, "The World's Women 2010: Trends and Statistics," http://unstats.un.org/unsd/demographic/products/Worldswomen/WW2010pub.htm (June 20, 2012).

13. Bnet.com, "Labour Market Trends: Advancing Women in the Workplace," http://findarticles.com/p/articles/mi_qa3999/is_200408/ai_n9448236 (Dec. 9, 2008).

14. United States Department of Labor, "Quick Statistics on Women Working, 2010," http://www.dol.gov/wb/factsheets/QS-womenswork2010.htm (June 18, 2012).

15. Lynne E. Ford, *Women and Politics: The Pursuit of Equality* (New York: Houghton Mifflin Company, 2002), 199.

16. Suvendini Kakuchi, "Rights-Japan: Not All Working Women are Equal," Inter Press Service News Agence, August 17, 2010, http://www.ipsnews.net/2010/08/rights-japan-not-all-working-women-are-equal/ (June 18, 2012).

17. Katrin Bennhold, "Working (Part-Time) in the 21st Century," *The New York Times,* December 29, 2010, http://www.nytimes.com/2010/12/30/world/europe/30iht-dutch30.html?pagewanted=all (June 18, 2012).

18. The World's Women 2010: 94.

19. Catalyst, "Quick Takes," April 2012, http://www.catalyst.org/publication/433/women-on-boards (June 18, 2012); Catalyst, "Women CEOs of the Fortune 1000s," June 2012, http://www.catalyst.org/publication/271/women-ceos-of-the-fortune-1000" (June 18, 2012).

20. "Helping Women Get to the Top," *Economist,* July 23, 2005.

21. Ibid.

22. World Bank, *Engendering Development: Through Gender Equality in Rights, Resources, and Voice* (New York: Oxford University Press, 2001), 1.

23. Carol Gilligan, *In a Different Voice* (Cambridge, MA: Harvard University Press, 1982).

24. Joyce Gelb, "The Equal Employment Opportunity Law: A Decade of Change for Japanese Women?" *Law & Policy* 22 (October 2000): 386.

25. M. Grazia Rossilli, "The European Union's Policy on the Equality of Women," *Feminist Studies* 25 (Spring 1999): 178–180.

26. Suzanne Burri and Sacha Prechal, *EU Gender Equality Law: Update 2010,* European Commission, December 2010: 19.

27. National Organization for Women, "Facts About Pay Equity," http://www.now.org/issues/economic/factsheet.html (Oct. 6, 2003).

28. Louise Nousratpour, "Hit out over Pay Injustice: Unions Urge Government to Confront Poverty," *Morning Star,* September 18, 2003, p. 1.

29. Hiromi Tanaka, "Equal Employment in Contemporary Japan: A Structural Approach," *Political Science* (January 2004): 66.

30. Suvendrini Kakuchi, "Rights-Japan: Not All Working Women are Equal," Inter Press Service News Agency, August 17, 2010, http://www.ipsnews.net/2010/08/rights-japan-not-all-working-women-are-equal (June 18, 2012).

31. Ibid.

32. M. Margaret Conway, David W. Ahern, and Gertrude A. Steuernagel, *Women and Public Policy: A Revolution in Progress* (Washington, DC: Congressional Quarterly Press, 1999), 74.

33. See Eileen Applebaum et al., "Shared Work, Valued Care: New Norms for Organizing Market Work and Unpaid Care Work," Economic Policy Institute, June 2002.

34. Kia Franklin, "A Vote in Favor of Fairness; the Candidates' Opinions on Pay Discrimination Case Offers a Glimpse into Judicial Philosophy," *Newsday,* October 21, 2008, p. A35.

35. "Treaty Establishing the European Community," http://www.hri.org/docs/Rome57/Part3Title08.html#Art119 (April 22, 2006).

36. "European Parliament Fact Sheet 4.8.7. Equality for Men and Women," http://www.europarl.eu.int/factsheets/4_8_7_en.htm (Sept. 30, 2003).

37. M. Grazia Rossilli, "The European Union's Policy on the Equality of Women," *Feminist Studies* 25, no.1 (1999): 173.

38. European Union, "Equal Pay," http://europa.eu.int/scadplus/leg/en/cha/c10905.htm (April 22, 2006).

39. Ilona Ostern, "From Equal Pay to Equal Employment: Four Decades of European Gender Politics," in *Gender Policies in the European Union,* ed. Mariagrazia Rossilli (New York: Peter Lang, 2000), 28.

40. Catherine Hoskyns, "Four Action Programmes on Equal Opportunities," in *Gender Policies in the European Union,* 43–47.

41. Scottish Labour, "Women and the Changing European Union," November 4, 2002, http://www.scottishlabour.org.uk/helenliddell (Sept. 30, 2003).

42. International Federation of Business and Professional Women, "About: Policy Based Initiatives: Equal Pay Day," http://www.bpw-international.org/about-bpw/policy-based-initiatives/equal-pay-day (June 20, 2012).

43. U.S. General Accounting Office, "A New Look Through the Glass Ceiling: Where Are the Women?" January 2002.

44. American Association of University Women, "The Simple Truth About the Gender Pay Gap," 2012 Edition, http://www.aauw.org/learn/research/upload/simpletruthaboutpaygap1.pdf (June 20, 2012).

45. European Commission, "Gender Pay Gap," http://ec.europa.eu/justice/gender-equality/gender-pay-gap/index_en.htm (June 20, 2012).

46. Commission of the European Communities, "Gender Pay Gaps in European Labour Markets—Measurement, Analysis, and Policy Implications," Brussels, 4.9.2003 SEC(2003)937: 10.

47. AAUW:8.

48. Ibid.

49. Sarah Jane Glynn and Audrey Powers, "The Top 10 Facts About the Wage Gap," Center for American Progress, April 16, 2012, http://www.americanprogress.org/issues/2012/04/wage_gap_facts.html (June 21, 2012).

50. The Economist, "Special Report: Women and Work: Closing the Gap," November 26, 2011: 6. http://www.economist.com/node/21539928 (June 21, 2012).

51. CEC, "Gender Pay Gaps in European Labour Markets," 11–17.

52. "Harman Pledges to Reduce the Widening Gender Wage Gap," *Birmingham Post,* September 6, 2007, p. 4.

53. CEC, "Gender Pay Gaps in European Labour Markets," 15.

54. "Japan's Salary Gap," *The Japan Times,* March 24, 2008.

55. James Graff et al., "Help Wanted for Europe," *Time,* June 19, 2000, vol. 155, issue 25, p. 18.

56. Ilse Lenz, "Globalization, Gender, and Work: Perspectives on Global Regulation," *Review of Policy Research* 20 (Spring 2003): 35–38.

57. Dongxiao Liu and Elizabeth Heger Boyle, "Making the Case: The Women's Convention and Equal Employment Opportunity in Japan," *International Journal of Comparative Sociology* 42 (2001): 389–390.

58. Tadashi Hanami, "Equal Employment Revisited," *Japan Labour Bulletin,* The Japan Institute of Labour 39 (January 1, 2000).

59. Joyce Gelb, "Japan's Equal Employment Opportunity Law: A Decade of Change for Japanese Women?" *Law and Policy* 22 (October 2000): 387.

60. M. Margaret Conway, David W. Ahern, and Gertrude A. Steuernagel, *Women and Public Policy: A Revolution in Progress* (Washington, DC: CQ Press, 2004), 95.

61. As quoted in Lynne E. Ford, *Women and Politics: The Pursuit of Equality* (New York: Houghton Mifflin, 2002), 211.

62. As quoted in Ibid., 213.

63. Executive Order 11246, 3 C.F.R. 169, 1974.

64. "The ERA: A Brief Introduction," http://www.equalrightsamendment.org/ overview.htm (April 22, 2006).

65. Ostner, "From Equal Pay to Equal Employability," 28.

66. British Broadcasting Corporation, "Amsterdam Treaty," April 30, 2001, http:// news.bbc.co.uk/1/hi/in_depth/europe/euro-glossary/1216210.stm.

67. Grazia Rossilli, "The European Union's Policy on the Equality of Women," *Feminist Studies* 25, no. 1 (1999): 171–172.

68. European Commission, Directorate-General for Education and Culture, *European Employment and Social Policy: A Policy for People* (Luxembourg: European Communities, 2000): 26.

69. Rossilli, "The European Union's Policy on the Equality of Women," 175.

70. Grant Thorton, "Proportion of Women in Senior Management Falls to 2004 Levels," http://www.internationalbusinessreport.com/Press-room/2011/ women_in-senior_management.asp (June 21, 2012).

71. Gelb, "Japan's Equal Employment Opportunity Law," 390–391.

72. Tanaka, "Equal Employment in Contemporary Japan," 66.

73. Fackler, "Career Women in Japan," A1.

74. Gelb, "Japan's Equal Employment Opportunity Law," 394.

75. Ibid., 396–397.

76. Akemi Nakamura, "Four Women Await Outcome of 10-Year Quest for Equal Pay," *The Japan Times,* March 27, 2005; "Four Women Win 63 Million Yen Ruling: Sumitomo Metal Guilty of Gender Bias," *The Japan Times,* March 29, 2005.

77. Ibid.

78. "Only 8.9% of Managerial Positions Taken by Women in Japan," *Deutsche Press-Agentur,* September 13, 2003, Miscellaneous section.

79. Takahashi, "Working Women in Japan," p. 11 of 12.

80. Ibid., p. 11 of 12.

81. WomenOf.com, "Non-Profits Improve Numbers of Women CEOs," http:// www.womenof.com/News/cn092500.asp (Oct. 6, 2003).

82. Catalyst, "Women CEOs of the Fortune 1000s," June 2012, http://www.catalyst .org/publication/271/women-ceos-of-the-fortune-1000 (June 21, 2012).

83. National Organization for Women, "Pay Equity Still a Dream Worth Pursuing: New Report Shows Glass Ceiling Intact," Summer 2002, http://www.now.org/ nnt/ summer-2002/payequity.html (Oct. 6, 2003).

84. "The European Parliament Takes Stock," *Women's International Network News* 26, issue 4 (Autumn 2000), p. 59.

85. The World's Women 2010: 92.

86. "Women and Work: European Situation," http://www.etuc.org.EQUALPAY/
    UK/women_and_work/European-Union/default.cfm (Nov. 11, 2003).
87. European Commission, "European Employment and Social Policy," 24.
88. PR Newswire, " European Quotas for Women CEOs Help Crack Boardroom
    Glass Ceilings," November 16, 2011, http://www.thestreet.com/print/story/
    11312710.html (June 21, 2012).
89. *Christian Science Monitor,* August 8, 1997, vol. 89, issue 178, p. 10.
90. As cited in Heidi Gottfried and Laura Reese, "Gender, Policy, Politics, and
    Work: Feminist Comparative and Transnational Research," *Review of Policy
    Research* 20, no. 1 (2003): 10.
91. Conway, Ahern, and Steuernagel, *Women and Public Policy,* 82.
92. Christopher Uggen and Chika Shinohara, "Sexual Harassment Comes of Age:
    A Comparative Analysis of the United States and Japan," *Sociological Quarterly*
    50 (2009): 203.
93. Ibid.
94. Ibid.
95. U.S. Department of State, Bureau of Democracy, Human Rights, and Labor,
    "Japan: Country Reports on Human Rights Practices—2000," February 23, 2001,
    http://www.state.gov/g/drl/rls/hrrpt/2000/eap/709pf.htm (Nov. 19, 2003).
96. Christopher Uggen, "Sexual Harassment: The Emergence of Legal Councious-
    ness in Japan and the US," *The Asia-Pacific Journal: Japan Focus* http://www
    .japanfocus.org/-christopher-uggen/3199 (June 25, 2012).
97. As quoted in Ford, *Women and Politics,* 218.
98. Jeanne Gregory, "Sexual Harassment: The Impact of EU Law in the Member
    States," in *Gender Policies in the European Union,* 175–189.
99. Commission of the European Communities, "Report from the Commission to
    the Council, the European Parliament, the European Economic and Social
    Committee and the Committee of Regions: Annual Report on Equal Opportu-
    nities for Women and Men in the European Union 2002," Brussels, March 5,
    2003, COM (2003) 98.
100. U.S. Department of State, Bureau of Democracy, Human Rights, and Labor,
    "Japan."
101. Ibid.
102. Ibid.
103. "Sexual Harassment," encyclopedia article from Encarta, http://www.encarta
    .msn.com/encyclopedia_761579949 (Nov. 19, 2003).
104. "EU Tightens Sex Harassment Law," CNN.com, April 18, 2002, http://articles.
    cnn.com/2002-04-18/world/eu.harassment_1_sexual-harassment-harass
    ment-law-sexual-remarks?_s=PM:WORLD (Nov. 20, 2003).
105. Ibid.
106. Commission of the European Communities, "Report from the Commission to
    the Council, the European Parliament, the European Economic and Social
    Committee and the Committee of Regions."
107. Social Security Administration, "Social Security is Important to Women,"
    January 2012, http://www.ssa.gov/pressoffice/factsheets/women.htm (July 2,
    2012).
108. "Women in Europe Towards Healthy Ageing," European Institute of Women's
    Health (1997), http://www.eurohealth.ie/report/index.htm, Introduction, p. 4
    of 5 (Sept. 29, 2003).

109. Ross Clare, "Women and Superannuation," The University of New South Wales, School of Economics and Actuarial Studies, paper presented at the Ninth Annual Colloquium of Superannuation Researchers, July 2001, p. 2.

110. Ayako Doi, "In Other Words," Foreign Policy: The Magazine of Global Politics, Economics and Ideas (November/December 2003), http://www.foreignpolicy .com/story/story.php?storyID=13976 (Nov. 20, 2003).

111. "Women in Europe Towards Healthy Ageing," Introduction, p. 4 of 5.

112. Social Security Administration, "Social Security is Important to Women," January 2012, http://www.ssa.gov/pressoffice/factsheets/women.htm (June 2, 2012).

113. "1 in 5 Women Relying on Partner's Pension," The Financial Times, August 16, 2003, Money section, p. 23.

114. "Women Given Unfair Choice of Babies or a Good Pension," The Western Mail, July 7, 2003, p. 1.

115. "Women in Europe Towards Healthy Ageing," European Institute of Women's Health, Introduction, p. 4 of 5.

116. Campbell, "Women Seek Solutions to Pension-System Bias," p. 9.

CHAPTER 5

1. Elissa Gootman and Catherine Saint Louis, "Maternity Leave? It's More Like a Pause," New York Times, July 20, 2012, http://www.nytimes.com/2012/07/22/ fashion/for-executive-women-is-maternity-leave-necessary.html? pagewanted=all

2. Meghan Casserly, "Sheryl Sandberg's 'Lean In' More Aspirational than Inspirational," Forbes, August 31, 2012, http://www.forbes.com/sites/meghancasserly/ 2012/08/31/sheryl-sandberg-lean-in-more-aspirational-than-inspirational/

3. Anne-Marie Slaughter, "Why Women Still Can't Have it All," The Atlantic, July 2012, http://www.theatlantic.com/magazine/archive/2012/07/why-women-still- cant-have-it-all/309020/

4. For example, see Nancy Fraser, "After the Family Wage: Gender Equity and the Welfare State," Political Theory 22, no. 4 (1994): 591–618.

5. Diane Sainsbury, "Introduction," in Gender and Welfare State Regimes, ed. Diane Sainsbury (Oxford: Oxford University Press, 1999), 7.

6. The original delineation of welfare states into liberal, social capitalist, and social democratic welfare states was put forth by G. Esping Andersen, The Three Worlds of Welfare Capitalism (Cambridge: Cambridge University Press, 1990).

7. This framework is taken from Sainsbury, ed., Gender and Welfare State Regimes.

8. Sheila Kamerman and Shirley Gatenio, "Tax Day: How Do America's Child Benefits Compare?" Columbia University, the Clearinghouse on International Developments in Child, Youth, and Family Policies, Issue brief, Spring 2002.

9. International Labor Organization, Maternity at Work: A Review of National Legislation, 2nd edition, 2010.

10. OECD, Overview of Gender Differences in OECD Countries, http://www .oecd.org/els/familiesandchildren/overviewofgenderdifferencesinoecdcoun tries.htm

11. J. O'Connor, "Gender, Class and Citizenship in the Comparative Analysis of Welfare State Regimes: Theoretical and Methodological Issues," *British Journal of Sociology* 44, no. 3 (1993): 501–518.
12. Wisensale, *Family Leave Policy,* 110.
13. Christopher J. Ruhm, "Policies to Assist Parents with Young Children," *Work and Family,* vol. 21, no. 2, Fall 2011: 37–58.
14. ILO, *Maternity at Work: A Review of National Legislation,* 2nd edition, 2010.
15. The Clearinghouse on International Developments in Child, Youth, and Family Policies, "Section 18: Child and Family Allowances," Table 1: Child and Family Cash and Tax Benefits in Select Industrialized Countries, http://www.childpolicyintl.org (April 22, 2006).
16. Rebecca Ray, Janet C. Gornick, and John Schmitt, "Parental Leave Policies in 21 Countries: Assessing Generosity and Gender Equality," Center for Economic and Policy Research, Washington, D.C., September 2008.
17. Amy Mazur, *Theorizing Feminist Policy* (New York: Oxford University Press, 2002), 112.
18. Wisensale, *Family Leave Policy,* 109.
19. Kamerman and Gatenio, "Tax Day."
20. Institute for Women's Policy Research, "Fact Sheet" May 2011, http://www.iwpr.org/publications/pubs/maternity-paternity-and-adoption-leave-in-the-united-states/
21. Erin Kelly and Frank Dobbin, "Civil Rights Law at Work: Sex Discrimination and the Rise of Maternity Leave Policies," *American Journal of Sociology* 105, no. 2 (1999): 455–492.
22. Institute for Women's Policy Research, "Fact Sheet" May 2011, http://www.iwpr.org/publications/pubs/maternity-paternity-and-adoption-leave-in-the-united-states/
23. Amy Mazur, *Theorizing Feminist Policy* (New York: Oxford University Press, 2002), 112.
24. Wisensale, *Family Leave Policy,* 141
25. Kelly and Dobbin, "Civil Rights at Work."
26. George Bush, "The President's Veto Message," *Congressional Digest,* January 1993, p. 12.
27. Kelly and Dobbin, "Civil Rights Law at Work."
28. Wisensale, *Family Leave Policy,* 109.
29. The Clearinghouse on International Developments in Child, Youth, and Family Policies at Columbia University, "Germany," http://www.childpolicyintl.org (Aug. 9, 2005).
30. OECD, *OECD in Figures.*
31. Katrin Bennhold, "In Germany, a Tradition Falls, and Women Rise," *New York Times,* January 17, 2010.
32. Karin Gottschall and Katherine Bird, "Family Leave Policies and Labor Market Segregation in Germany: Reinvention or Reform of the Male Breadwinner Model?" *Review of Policy Research* 20, no. 1 (2003): 115–135.
33. Katrin Bennhold, "In Sweden, Men Can Have it All," *New York Times,* June 9, 2010.
34. http://nordsoc.is/Sweden/Family-benefits/
35. Katrin Bennhold, "Paternity Leave Law Helps to Redefine Masculity in Sweden," *New York Times,* June 15, 2010, 6.

36. Wisensale, *Family Leave Policy*, 227.

37. Ibid., 218.

38. Ruhm, "Policies to Assist Parents with Young Children."

39. ILO, "Maternity at Work: A Review of National Legislation," 2nd edition, 2010.

40. Kamerman and Gatenio.

41. OECD, "Child Care in OECD Countries," in *Employment Outlook 1990* (Paris: OECD, 1990).

42. Sheila B. Kamerman, "Early Childhood Education and Care (ECEC): An Overview of Developments in the OECD Countries," unpublished paper, 3–6.

43. Sheila B. Kamerman, "Early Childhood Education and Care (ECEC)," 23–31.

44. Ruhm, 49.

45. Abby J. Cohen, "A Brief History of Federal Financing for Child Care in the United States," *Financing Child Care* 6 (Summer/Fall 1996): 29.

46. Emilie Stoltzfus, *Citizen, Mother, Worker: Debating Public Responsibility for Child Care After the Second World War* (Chapel Hill: University of North Carolina Press, 2003), 8–10.

47. Gwendolyn Mink, *Welfare's End* (Ithaca, NY: Cornell University Press, 1998).

48. As quoted in Cohen, "A Brief History of Federal Financing for Child Care in the United States," 32.

49. Stoltzfus, *Citizen, Mother, Worker*, 14.

50. Henneck, "Family Policy in the US, Japan, Germany, Italy, and France."

51. Ibid.

52. Gottschall and Bird, "Family Leave Policies and Labor Market Segregation in Germany," 115–135.

53. German Federal Ministry of Health and Social Security, "Child Benefit, Child Raising Allowance, Parental Leave, Maintenance Advance and Supplementary Child Allowance," January 2005, http://www.bmgs.bund.de/downloads/ Child_benefit-Kindergeld.pdf (April 22, 2006).

54. The Clearinghouse on International Developments in Child, Youth, and Family Policies at Columbia University, "Germany," http://www.childpolicy intl.org (Sept. 8, 2005).

55. Ingela K. Naumann, "Child Care and Feminism in West Germany and Sweden in the 1960s and 1970s," *Journal of European Social Policy* 15, no. 1 (2005): 51–54.

56. Ibid., 51–54.

57. Ibid., 56–57.

58. "Germany to Bolster Child Care," *Deutsche Welle*, October 28, 2004.

59. The Clearinghouse on International Developments in Child, Youth, and Family Policies at Columbia University, "Germany," http://www.childpolicy intl.org (March 16, 2009).

60. Katrin Bennhold, "In Germany a Tradition Falls, and Women Rise," *New York Times*, January 17, 2010, http://www.nytimes.com/2010/01/18/world/europe/ 18iht-women.html?_r=1&pagewanted=all

61. Gottschall and Bird, "Family Leave Policies and Labor Market Segregation in Germany," 115–135.

62. Ibid., 115–135.

63. Marcia K. Meyers, Janet C. Gornick, and Katherin E. Ross, "Public Childcare, Parental Leave, and Employment," in *Gender and Welfare State Regimes*, ed. Sainsbury, 126.

64. The Swedish Institute, "Childcare in Sweden," September 2004, http://www .sweden.se/templates/cs/BasicFactsheet (April 22, 2006).

65. Ibid.

66. Ibid.

67. Naumann, "Child Care and Feminism in West Germany and Sweden in the 1960s and 1970s," 54–58.

68. The Swedish Institute, "Childcare in Sweden."

69. The Clearinghouse on International Developments in Child, Youth, and Family Policy at Columbia University, Table 1.32, "Family and Child Allowance Programs: Coverage, Qualifying Conditions, Benefit Levels and other Related Allowances," http://www.childpolicyintl.org (April 22, 2006).

70. Naumann, "Child Care and Feminism in West Germany and Sweden in the 1960s and 1970s," 58–60.

71. U.S. Bureau of the Census, Income, Poverty, and Health Insurance Coverage in the United States: 2010, Report P60, n. 238, Table B-2, pp. 68–73.

72. OECD, Social Policies and Data, http://www.oecd.org/els/socialpoliciesand data/

73. Kamerman et al., "Social Policies, Family Types and Child Outcomes in Selected OECD Countries," 25.

74. OECD, Social Policies and Data, http://www.oecd.org/els/socialpoliciesand data/

75. Wisensale, Family Leave Policy, 219.

76. Diane Sainsbury, "Gender, Policy Regimes, and Politics," in Gender and Welfare State Regimes, ed. Sainsbury, 266–267.

77. Ibid., 267–268.

78. Wisensale, Family Leave Policy, 185–212.

79. Shorto, Russel "No Babies?," The New York Times Magazine, June 28, 2008, http://www.nytimes.com/2008/06/29/magazine/29Birth-t.html?page wanted=all&_r=0 (Feb. 15, 2013).

80. http://europa.eu.int/scadplus/printversion/en/cha/c10916.htm (April 22, 2006).

81. Arnlaug Leira, Working Parents and the Welfare State: Family Change and Policy Reform in Scandinavia (Cambridge: Cambridge University Press, 2002), 146.

82. Jet Bussemaker and Kees van Kinsbergen, "Contemporary Social Capitalist Welfare State and Gender Inequality," in Gender and Welfare State Regimes, ed. Sainsbury, 15–47.

CHAPTER 6

1. Guttmacher Institute, "State Policies in Brief: Counseling and Waiting Periods for Abortion as of September 1, 2012," http://www.guttmacher.org/statecenter/ spibs/spib_MWPA.pdf

2. Terry Baynes, "U.S. Judge Allows Enforcement of Texas Abortion Law," Thomson Reuters, Februrary 7, 2012, http://www.reuters.com/article/2012/02/07/ us-texas-abortion-idUSTRE81605220120207

3. Guttmacher Institute, "Spurious Science Triumphs as U.S. Court Upholds South Dakota 'Suicide Advisory' Law, July 27, 2012, http://www.guttmacher .org/media/inthenews/2012/07/27/index.html

4. Kristin Luker, Abortion and the Politics of Motherhood (Berkeley: University of California Press, 1984), 1–1

5. Susheela Singh, Stanley K. Henshaw, and Kathleen Berentsen, "Abortion: A World-wide Overview," in *The Sociocultural and Political Aspects of Abortion: Global Perspectives,* ed. Alaka Malwade Basu (Westport, CT: Praeger, 2003), 15–16.

6. Marina Calloni, "Debates and Controversies on Abortion in Italy," in *Abortion Politics, Women's Movements, and the Democratic State,* 181–203.

7. The United Nations, *Abortion Policies: A Global Review* (New York: United Nations Press, 2002), http://www.un.org/esa/population/publications/abortion (August 10, 2005).

8. Luker, *Abortion and the Politics of Motherhood,* 16.

9. Guttmacher Institute, "Facts on Induced Abortion Worldwide," January 2012, http://www.guttmacher.org/pubs/fb_IAW.html

10. Law Students for Reproductive Justice, "Access to Abortion Around the World, 2012, http://lsrj.org/documents/factsheets/12_Abortion%20Around%20the%20World.pdf

11. Ibid.

12. As cited in Caldwell and Caldwell, "Introduction," 2.

13. Ibid., 3.

14. Evelyn Mahon, "Abortion Debates in Ireland: An Ongoing Issue," in *Abortion Politics, Women's Movements, and the Democratic State,* 157.

15. Ibid., 159.

16. United Nations Population Division, Department of Economic and Social Affairs, "Ireland," in *Abortion Policies: A Global Review* (New York: United Nations Press, 2002).

17. For information about abortion in Great Britain, see Dorothy McBride Stetson, "Women's Movements' Defense of Legal Abortion in Great Britain," in *Abortion Politics, Women's Movements, and the Democratic State,* 135–156.

18. United Nations Population Division, Department of Economic and Social Affairs, "Ireland."

19. Mahon, "Abortion Debates in Ireland," 161.

20. Shawn Pogatchnik, "Irish Bishops Reject Pregnancy Pamphlet," Associated Press, June 16, 2005.

21. Mahon, "Abortion Debates in Ireland," 162–163.

22. United Nations Population Division, Department of Economic and Social Affairs, "Ireland."

23. Mahon, "Abortion Debates in Ireland," 167.

24. Ibid., 165.

25. United Nations Population Division, Department of Economic and Social Affairs, "Ireland."

26. "Abortion Will Pop up Again on Political Radar Screen," *Irish Independent,* March 8, 2005.

27. "Rights Group Says Law Must Be Changed to Allow for Abortions," *Irish Independent,* March 8, 2005.

28. Mahon, "Abortion Debates in Ireland," 169.

29. "Voters in Ireland Reject Change in Abortion Law," *USA Today,* March 8, 2002, p. 7a.

30. Pogatchnik, "Irish Bishops Reject Pregnancy Pamphlet."

31. "Rights Group Says Law Must Be Changed to Allow for Abortions."

32. Irish Family Planning Association, "Statistics," http://www.ifpa.ie/Hot-Topics/Abortion/Statistics

33. CNN World News, "Abortion Ship Arrives in Ireland," June 15, 2001, http://articles.cnn.com/2001-06-15/world/ireland.ship02_1_surgical-abortions-medical-abortions-abortion-pill?_s=PM:WORLD (April 22, 2006).

34. "Abortion Will Pop up Again on Political Radar Screen."

35. Center for Reproductive Rights, "Fact Sheet: A, B and C v. Ireland," http://reproductiverights.org/en/document/fact-sheet-a-b-and-c-v-ireland.

36. Mahon, "Abortion Debates in Ireland," 170.

37. Richard Oakley, "Irish Faith on Wane but Tolerance Rises," *The Times*, April 10, 2005.

38. As quoted in Lee Ann Banaszak, "The Women's Movement Policy Successes and the Constraints of State Reconfiguration: Abortion and Equal Pay in Differing Eras," in *Women's Movements Facing the Reconfigured State*, ed. Lee Ann Banaszak, Karen Beckwith, and Dieter Rucht (New York: Cambridge University Press, 2003), 154.

39. Irish Medical Council, *A Guide to Ethical Conduct and Behavior*, 6th ed. (Dublin, Ireland: Irish Medical Council, 2004), 44.

40. Oakley, "Irish Faith on Wane but Tolerance Rises."

41. Claire McCormack, "Abortion Law Decisions Coming to Catholic England," *Forbes*, August 27, 2012, http://www.forbes.com/sites/womensenews/2012/08/27/abortion-law-decisions-coming-to-catholic-ireland/.

42. Banaszak, "The Women's Movement Policy Successes and the Constraints of State Reconfiguration," 148–155.

43. Dorothy McBride Stetson, "US Abortion Debates: 1959–1998: The Women's Movement Holds On," in *Abortion Politics, Women's Movements, and the Democratic State: A Comparative Study of State Feminism*, ed. Dorothy McBride Stetson (Oxford: Oxford University Press, 2001), 247.

44. Stetson, "US Abortion Debates 1959–1998," 247.

45. Luker, *Abortion and the Politics of Motherhood*, 11–39.

46. United Nations Population Division, Department of Economic and Social Affairs, "United States of America," in *Abortion Policies: A Global Review* (New York: United Nations Press, 2002).

47. As quoted in Center for Reproductive Rights, *Roe v. Wade and the Right to Privacy* (2003), http://www.reproductiverights.org/pdf/roeprivacy.pdf (April 22, 2006), 30.

48. United Nations Population Division, Department of Economic and Social Affairs, "United States of America."

49. As quoted in Center for Reproductive Rights, *Roe v. Wade and the Right to Privacy*, 44.

50. United Nations Population Division, Department of Economic and Social Affairs, "United States of America."

51. Guttmacher Institute, "State Policies in Brief as of September 1, 2012," www.guttmacher.org.

52. Ibid.

53. As quoted in Find Law for Professionals, http://caselaw.lp.findlaw.com/scripts/getcase.pl?court=tx&vol=/sc/010061&invol=1.

54. United Nations Population Division, Department of Economic and Social Affairs, "United States of America."

55. Ibid.

56. The White House, "President Bush Signs Partial Birth Abortion Ban Act 2003," Nov 5, 2003, http://www.whitehouse.gov/news/releases/2003/11/print/20031105-1.html (April 22, 2006).

57. The Alan Guttmacher Institute, "State Policies in Brief as of August 1, 2005," http://www.guttmacher.org/statecenter/spibs/spib_BPBA.pdf (August 10, 2005).

58. The Alan Guttmacher Institute, "State Policies in Brief as of September 1, 2012," http://www.guttmacher.org/statecenter/spibs/spib_OAL.pdf

59. United Nations Population Division, Department of Economic and Social Affairs, "United States of America."

60. Physicians for Reproductive Choice and Health and The Alan Guttmacher Institute, "An Overview of Abortion in the United States."

61. Joe Stumpe and Monica Davey, "Abortion Doctor Shot to Death in Kansas Church," New York Times, June 1, 2009. http://www.nytimes.com/2009/06/01/us/01tiller.html

62. Physicians for Reproductive Choice and Health and The Alan Guttmacher Institute, "An Overview of Abortion in the United States."

63. Ibid.

64. The Alan Guttmacher Institute, "State Policies in Brief as of September 1, 2012," http://www.guttmacher.org/statecenter/spibs/spib_OAL.pdf

65. Physicians for Reproductive Choice and Health and The Alan Guttmacher Institute, "An Overview of Abortion in the United States."

66. Evert Kettering, "Netherlands," in Abortion in the New Europe: A Comparative Handbook, ed. Bill Roston and Anna Eggert (Westport, CT: Greenwood Press, 1994), 173–186.

67. United Nations Population Division, Department of Economic and Social Affairs, "Netherlands," in Abortion Policies: A Global Review (New York: United Nations: 2002), http://www.un.org/esa/population/publications/abortion (August 10, 2005).

68. Kettering, "Netherlands," 173–174.

69. Ibid., 174–175.

70. Joyce Outshoorn, "Policy-Making on Abortion: Arenas, Actors, and Arguments in the Netherlands," in Abortion Politics, Women's Movements and the Democratic State, ed. Dorothy McBride Stetson (New York: Oxford University Press, 2001), 207.

71. Kettering, "Netherlands," 175; Outshoorn, "Policy-Making on Abortion," 209–213.

72. Kettering, "Netherlands," 175–176.

73. United Nations Population Division, Department of Economic and Social Affairs, "Netherlands."

74. Agence France Presse, "Dutch Women Go Abroad for Late-Term Abortions," April 12, 2005.

75. Trees A. M. Te Braake, "Late Termination of Pregnancy Because of Severe Foetal Abnormalities: Legal Acceptability, Notification and Review in the Netherlands," European Journal of Health Law 7 (2000): 387–403.

76. Statistics Netherlands, "Annual Number of Abortions Stable over the Past Decade," 22 February 2011, http://www.cbs.nl/en-GB/menu/themas/bevolking/publicaties/artikelen/archief/2011/2011-3322-wm.htm

77. The Guttmacher Institute, "Facts on Induced Abortion in the United States."

78. Agence France Presse, "Dutch Women Go Abroad for Late-Term Abortions."

79. Netherlands Ministry of Foreign Affairs, "Questions and Answers on Dutch Policy on Abortion—2003."

80. World Values Survey, "1999–2002 World Values Survey Questionnaire," http://www.worldvaluessurvey.org/statistics/index.html.

81. Ronnee Schreiber, "Injecting a Woman's Voice: Conservative Women's Organizations, Gender Consciousness, and the Expression of Women's Policy Preferences," *Sex Roles* 47 (October 2002): 337–339.

PART III INTRODUCTION

1. United Nations Department of Public Information, "1.5 Billion People Living in Absolute Poverty Makes its Eradication Humankind's," October 17, 2011, http://www.un.org/News/Press/docs/2011/gaef3313.doc.htm.

2. Amartya Sen, *Development as Freedom* (New York: Anchor Books, 2000).

CHAPTER 7

1. TrustLaw, "Factsheet—The World's Most Dangerous Countries for Women," June 15, 2011, http://www.trust.org/trustlaw/news/factsheet-the-worlds-most-dangerous-countries-for-women.

2. UNIFEM, "Who Answers to Women? Gender and Accountability," *Progress of the World's Women 2008/09* (New York: UNIFEM, 2009), 117–133.

3. United Nations Development Program, *Human Development Report 2007/2008* (New York: UNDP, 2008), 337.

4. World Bank, *Engendering Development: Through Gender Equality in Rights, Resources, and Voice* (New York: Oxford University Press, 2001), 8–14.

5. Ibid, 1.

6. Ricardo Hausmann, Laura D. Tyson, and Saadia Zahidi, *Global Gender Gap Report 2011* (Geneva: World Economic Forum, 2011).

7. OECD Development Centre, *2012 SIGI (Social Institutions and Gender Index): Understanding the Drivers of Gender Inequality* (Paris, 2012).

8. The Economist Intelligence Unit, "Women's Economic Opportunity Index 2012" (London, 2012).

9. For example, see Gender Equality and Statistics, at http://datatopics.worldbank.org/gender/

10. United Nations, *The Millennium Development Goals Report 2012* (New York, 2012).

11. Irene Tinker, "Empowerment Just Happened: The Unexpected Expansion of Women's Organizations," in Jane S. Jaquette and Gale Summerfield, eds., *Women and Gender Equity in Development Theory and Practice: Institutions, Resources, and Mobilization* (Durham, NC: Duke University Press, 2006), 268.

12. Ester Boserup, *Women's Role in Economic Development* (New York: St. Martin's Press, 1970).

13. Janet Henshall Momsen, *Gender and Development* (New York: Routledge, 2004), 11.

14. As quoted in Jane S. Jaquette and Kathleen Staudt, "Women, Gender, and Development," in Jaquette and Summerfield, eds., *Women and Gender Equity in Development Theory and Practice*, 21.

15. United Nations, "United Nations International Decades Designated by the General Assembly," September 27, 2001, http://www.nalis.gov.tt/National-UN-Days/UN_INTERNATIONALDECADES.html (Oct. 13, 2005).

16. Tinker, "Empowerment Just Happened," 277.

17. Valentine M. Moghadam, *Globalizing Women: Transnational Feminist Networks* (Baltimore: The Johns Hopkins University Press, 2005), 1–9.

18. Maxine Molyneux, "Mobilization Without Emancipation: Women's Interests, State, and Revolution in Nicaragua," *Feminist Studies* 11, no. 2 (1985): 227–254; Janet Henshall Momsen, *Gender and Development* (London: Routledge, 2004), 14.

19. United Nations, *Gender Mainstreaming: An Overview* (New York: United Nations, January 2002), v.

20. United Nations Development Fund for Women (UNIFEM), "Gender-Responsive Budgets," http://www.unifem.org/gender_issues/women_poverty_economics/gender_budgets.php (Aug. 12, 2005).

21. Elisabeth Rehn and Ellen Johnson Sirleaf, "Women War Peace," *Progress of the World's Women 2002*, vol. 1, Executive Summary (New York: UNIFEM, 2002), 3.

22. Moghadam, *Globalizing Women*, 13–17.

23. United Nations, "UN Action for Women," http://www.un.org/ecosocdev/geninfo/women/dpi1796e.htm (Oct. 13, 2005), 3.

24. United Nations, Division for the Advancement of Women, "Convention on the Elimination of All Forms of Discrimination Against Women," http://www.un.org/womenwatch/daw/cedaw (Oct. 13, 2005).

25. Ibid.

26. United Nations, Division for the Advancement of Women, *Women Go Global* (New York: UN Press, 2003).

27. Center for Reproductive Rights, "CEDAW: The Importance of U.S. Ratification," http://www.crlp.org/pub_fac_cedaw.html (Oct. 13, 2005).

28. Human Rights Watch, "CEDAW: The Women's Treaty," January 31, 2005, http://hrw.org/campaigns/cedaw (Oct. 13, 2005).

29. For example, see *Human Development Report 2005*, Table 28: Status of Major International Human Rights in the United Nations Development Program (New York: Oxford University Press, 2005), 311–314.

30. Margaret E. Keck and Kathryn Sikkink, *Activists Beyond Borders: Advocacy Networks in International Politics* (Ithaca, NY: Cornell University Press, 1998), 12–13.

CHAPTER 8

1. Qurratul Ain Tahmina, "South Asia: Working Women Get Poor Health Services," Inter Press Service, June 3, 2003.

2. U.S. State Department, *Trafficking in Persons Report* (Washington, D.C.: June 2008), 24.

3. Amartya Sen, *Development as Freedom* (New York: Anchor Books, 2000).

4. http://www.worldmapper.org/display.php?selected=181.

5. Food and Agricultural Organization, *Gender and Food Security: Division of Labor* (Rome, Italy: Food and Agricultural Organization, 2003).

6. http://hdrstats.undp.org/en/countries/profiles/SLE.html.

7. World Bank, Gender and Development Group, *Gender Equality and the Millennium Development Goals* (New York: April 4, 2003), 19.

8. http://www.who.int/mediacentre/factsheets/fs292/en/index.html#

9. Naila Kabeer, *Gender Mainstreaming in Poverty Eradication and the Millennium Development Goals: A Handbook for Policy-Makers and Other Stakeholders* (London: Commonwealth Secretariat, 2003), 35.

10. Ibid., 31.
11. United Nations Development Programme, *Human Development Report 2004* (New York: Oxford University Press, 2004), 233.
12. World Bank, "World Development Report 2012: Gender Equality and Development," p. 5.
13. Ibid., 4–5.
14. United Nations Development Programme, *Human Development Report 2002* (New York: Oxford University Press, 2002), 23.
15. International Labour Office, *Women and Men in the Informal Economy: A Statistical Picture* (Geneva: ILO, 2002), 8.
16. Diane Elson and Hende Keklik, UNIFEM, *Progress of the World's Women 2002*, vol. 2, 37.
17. Thomas L. Friedman, *The Lexus and the Olive Tree: Understanding Globalization* (New York: Farrar, Straus and Giroux, 2000), 7–8.
18. Leslie T. Chang, *Factory Girls: From Village to City in a Changing China* (Spiegel & Grau, 2008).
19. Jean-Pierre Singa Boyenge, *ILO Database on Export Processing Zones* (revised), Working Paper 251 (Geneva: ILO, April 2007). http://www.ilo.org/public/english/dialogue/sector/themes/epz/epz-db.pdf.
20. Kabeer, *Gender Mainstreaming in Poverty Eradication*, 69.
21. Oxfam International, *Trading Away Our Rights: Women Working in Global Supply Chains* (Oxford: Oxfam International, 2004), 17.
22. Kabeer, *Gender Mainstreaming in Poverty Eradication*, 70.
23. Norma Iglesias Prieto, *Beautiful Flowers of the Maquiladora: Life Histories of Women Workers in Tijuana* (Austin: University of Texas Press, 1997).
24. As quoted in Oxfam International, *Trading Away Our Rights*, 16.
25. Ibid.
26. Ibid.
27. Nicholas D. Kristof, "Where Sweatshops Are a Dream," *New York Times*, January 14, 2009.
28. United Nations Population Fund (UNFPA), *State of the World Population 2006. A Passage to Hope. Women and International Migration*, www.unfpa.org/swp/2006/english/chapter_2/print/chapter_2.html, Chapter 2, p. 2.
29. As cited in UNIFEM (2008), 58.
30. As quoted in U.S. State Department, *Trafficking in Persons Report*, 22.
31. UNFPA, *State of the World Population 2006*, 2.
32. Ibid., 11.
33. Ibid., 13–14.
34. Ibid., 8.
35. Arlie Russell Hochschild and Barbara Ehrenreich, eds., *Global Woman: Nannies, Maids, and Sex Workers in the New Economy* (New York: Metropolitan Books, 2004).
36. UNFPA, *State of the World Population 2006*, 8–9.
37. Ibid., 9–10.
38. Ibid., 5–6.
39. U.S. State Department, *Trafficking in Persons Report*, 6.
40. Vidyamali Samarasinghe, "Confronting Globalization in Anti-Trafficking Strategies in Asia," *Brown Journal of World Affairs* 10, no. 1 (2003): 91.
41. UNFPA, *State of the World Population 2006*, Chapter 3, 2.
42. U.S. State Department, *Trafficking in Persons Report*, 34.

43. UNFPA, *State of the World Population 2006*, Chapter 3, 2.

44. Ibid., Chapter 3, 3.

45. Ibid., Chapter 3, 1–2.

46. U.S. State Department, *Trafficking in Persons Report*, 11.

47. U.S. Department of Justice.

48. As quoted in U.S. Department of Justice, *Child Sex Tourism* (Washington, D.C.: n.d.), www.usdoj.gov/criminal/ceos/sextour.html.

49. UN Department of Economic and Social Affairs, Division for Sustainable Development, http://www.un.org/esa/sustdev.

50. Shawn Meghan Burn, *Women Across Cultures: A Global Perspective*, 2nd ed. (New York: McGraw-Hill, 2005), 153–156.

51. ILO, Global Employment Trends, 2011, Annex 1, Table A10, p. 67.

52. Howard Handelman, *The Challenge of Third World Development*, 3rd ed. (Upper Saddle River, NJ: Prentice Hall, 2003), 121.

53. World Bank, "Women Dairy Farmers in Africa," http://www.worldbank.org/html/cgiar/newsletter/june97/9dairy.html (April 22, 2006).

54. Women Watch, "International Day of Rural Women," October 15, 2008, www.un.org/womenwatch/feature/idrw/index.html.

55. Oxfam International, *Trading Away Our Rights*, 17.

56. Ibid., 7.

57. As described in United Nations, *Rural Women in a Changing World*, 10–11.

58. United Nations, *Rural Women in a Changing World*, 7–9.

59. Kabeer, *Gender Mainstreaming in Poverty Eradication*, 31.

60. UNIFEM, *Who Answers to Women? Gender and Accountability* (New York, 2009), 60.

61. World Bank, Gender and Development Group, *Gender Equality and the Millennium Development Goals*, 4.

62. As cited in Denis Dreshsler, Johannes Jutting, and Carina Lindberg, "Gender, Institutions, and Development: Better Data, Better Politics," in *Poverty in Focus: Gender Equality*, no. 13, ed. International Poverty Centre (Brasilia, Brazil: ICP-UNDP, January 2008), no pagination.

63. World Bank, "Land Use Rights and Gender Equality in Vietnam," in *Promising Approaches to Engendering Development*, no. 1 (New York, September 2002), 1–2.

64. Emily Kearney, "Reaching the Poorest with Microfinance: The Importance of Innovation in Program Design," unpublished thesis, Oregon State University, 2009.

CHAPTER 9

1. Abeba Zerehun, "One Woman's Story," Fistula Foundation, http://www.fistula foundation.org/press/archives/0501ows.html

2. Hamlin Fistula International, "Fast Facts and FAQs," http://www.hamlinfis tula.org/what-is-a-fistula/fast-facts-and-faqs.html

3. UNICEF, Ethiopia: Statistics. http://www.unicef.org/infobycountry/ethiopia_statistics.html

4. Women Deliver, "Real Stories About Women and Girls: Putting a Face on Women Deliver," Women Deliver Global Conference, October 18–20, 2007, London. http://www.womendeliver.org/assets/Real_Faces_Real_Stories__factsheet_(A4).pdf

5. World Health Organization, "Maternal Mortality: Fact Sheet no. 348," http://www.who.int/mediacentre/factsheets/fs348/en/index.html#.

6. Ibid.

7. Sneha Barot, "Back to Basics: The Rationale for Increased Funds for International Family Planning," *Guttmacher Policy Review* 11, no. 3 (2008), www.gutmacher.org/pubs/gpr/11/3/gpr110313.html.

8. United Nations Population Fund (UNFPA), "Population Issues Overview," http://www.unfpa.org/issues/index.htm (October 13, 2004).

9. Susheela Singh and Lacqueline E. Darroch, "Adding it Up: Costs and Benefits of Contraceptive Services—Estimates for 2012," Guttmacher Institute, June 2012.

10. UNFPA, "Reducing Risks by Offering Contraceptive Services."

11. World Bank, *World Development Indicators 2012* (New York: World Bank, 2012).

12. WHO, "Making Pregnancy Safer."

13. Women Deliver, "Saving Women's Lives: Leading Killers and Practical Solutions," http://www.womendeliver.org/assets/WD_Killers-Solutions_(SP).pdf

14. http://www.snowcrest.net/freemanl/world/women/sons.htm.

15. United Nations Development Programme, "The State and Progress of Human Development," in *Human Development Report 2002* (New York: Oxford University Press, 2002), 23.

16. Naila Kabeer, *Gender Mainstreaming in Poverty Eradication and the Millennium Development Goals* (London: Commonwealth Secretariat, The International Development Research Center/CIDA 2003), 92.

17. Sneha Barot, "A Problem-and-Solution Mismatch: Son Preference and Sex-Selective Abortion Bans." *Guttmacher Policy Review*, Spring 2012 (15.2): 18–22.

18. Julia Duin, "Brides Bound by Traditions; Indian Women, Families Carry Costly Commitment of Dowry," *Washington Times*, February 27, 2007, A1.

19. Ibid.

20. Janet Bagnall, "When Women Become a Burden; Selective-Sex Abortions Threaten to Turn India into a Land Full of Angry, Lonely Young Men," *The Gazette (Montreal)*, May 16, 2008, p. A15.

21. "Scans for Baby's Sex Illegal—but Rampant," *Straits Times (Singapore)*, July 14, 2007. http://justwoman.asiaone.com/Just%2BWoman/Motherhood/Stories/Story/A1Story20070720-19064.html

22. Ibid.

23. "'Care for Girls' Gaining Momentum," *China Daily*, July 8, 2004, http://www.chinadaily.com.cn/english/doc/2004–07/08/content_346700.htm.

24. Valerie M. Hudson and Andrea M. Den Boer, *Bare Branches: The Security Implications of Asia's Surplus Male Population* (Cambridge, MA: MIT Press, 2004).

25. World Bank, Gender and Development Group, *Gender Equality & the Millennium Development Goals* (New York: World Bank, 2003), 9.

26. WHO, "Women's Health in South-East Asia," February 2001, http://www.ncbi.nlm.nih.gov/pubmed/11036908

27. United Nations, Millennium Development Goals Report 2012. http://mdgs.un.org/unsd/mdg/Resources/Static/Products/Progress2012/English2012.pdf

28. Ibid.

29. Michael Kelly, "Hasten the Day When AIDS No Longer Has a Female Face," *Irish Times,* March 13, 2007, p. 16.

30. Ibid., 16.

31. Noeleen Heyzer, "To Fight AIDS, Empower Women," *Chicago Sun-Times,* July 10, 2003, p. 35.

32. Aishwarya Rai, *Our Planet* (Nairobi, Kenya: United Nations Environmental Programme), volume 15, no. 2, p. 18.

33. Noeleen Heyzer, "Peace of Mind, Piece of Land," *Our Planet,* volume 15, no. 2, pp. 11–12.

34. Michael Fleshman, "Women: The Face of AIDS in Africa," *Africa Renewal* volume 18, no. 3 (October 2004): 6, http://allafrica.com/stories/printable/200410120768.html (Oct. 13, 2004).

35. UNFPA, "Fast Fact—Maternal Mortality and Reproductive Health," www.unfpa.org/mothers/fact.htm (Oct. 13, 2004).

36. UN, MDG Report 2012.

37. http://www.globalhealthfacts.org/data/topic/map.aspx?ind=6

38. UNFPA, "Who We Are," http://www.unfpa.org/publications/detail.cfm?ID=384& filterListType=.

39. International Planned Parenthood Federation, "About IPPF," http://www.ippf.org/about/what.htm (Oct. 13, 2005).

40. WHO, "Family Planning," http://www.who.int/reproductive-health/family_planning/ index.html (Jan. 30, 2004).

41. Nafis Sadik, "Practical Consensus," *Our Planet,* volume 15, no. 2, p. 6.

42. http://www.plannedparenthood.org/global/education/viewer.asp?ID=238.

43. Guttmacher Institute, "Bush Administration Withholds UNFPA Funding for Seventh Year," June 27, 2008, http://www.guttmacher.org/media/inthenews/2008/06/27/index.html.

44. Lois Abraham and Jane Roberts, "Citizen Engagement," *Our Planet,* volume 15, no. 2, p. 29. See also http://www.34millionfriends.org.

45. Kirrin Gill, Rohini Pande, and Anju Malhotra, "Women Deliver for Development," October 2007, http://www.womendeliver.org.

46. Raekha Prasad and Randeep Ramesh, "India's Missing Girls: Daughters Aren't Wanted in India," *The Guardian,* February 28, 2007, 4.

47. Randeep Ramesh, "India to Crack Down on Doctors Aborting Girls," *The Guardian,* April 25, 2008, 24.

48. Ibid.

49. "'Care for Girls' Gaining Momentum," *China Daily,* July 8, 2004, http://www.chinadaily.com.cn/english/doc/2004–07/08/content_346700.htm

50. UNAIDS, *A Joint Response to HIV/AIDS,* (Geneva: UNAIDS, 2004), 9.

51. UNAIDS, *Report on the Global Aids Epidemic: Executive Summary.*

52. The Alan Guttmacher Institute, "Beyond Slogans: Lessons from Uganda's ABC Experience," http://www.guttmacher.org/pubs/tgr/06/5/gr060501.html.

53. Holly Burkhalter, "The Politics of AIDS: Engaging Conservative Activists," *Foreign Affairs* (January/February 2004).

54. World Bank, *Engendering Development: Through Gender Equality in Rights, Resources, and Voice* (New York: Oxford University Press, 2001).

55. Lisa C. Smith and Lawrence Haddad, *Explaining Child Malnutrition in Developing Countries: A Cross-Country Analysis* (Washington, DC: International Food Policy Research Institute, 2000).

CHAPTER 10

1. Global Campaign for Education, "Must Try Harder: A School Report on 22 Rich Countries' Aid to Basic Education in Developing Countries," November 2003, http://www.campaignforeducation.org (Nov. 25, 2003).

2. Ibid.

3. United Nations Department of Economic and Social Affairs, "The World's Women 2010: Trends and Statistics," http://unstats.un.org/unsd/demographic/products/Worldswomen/WW2010pub (June 12, 2012).

4. Ibid.

5. United Nations, *The Millennium Development Goals Report 2005* (New York: United Nations, 2005), 14.

6. Global Campaign for Education, "Must Try Harder."

7. World Education Forum, "Women and Girls: Education, Not Discrimination!," April 26–28, 2000, http://www2.unesco.org/wef/en-docs/press-kit/wome.pdf (April 23, 2006).

8. Karin Ronnow, "Journey of Hope: An In-Depth Report, Educate Girls, Change the World" (Central Asia Institute, 2008), 25.

9. World Education Forum, "Women and Girls."

10. United Nations Department of Economic and Social Affairs, "The World's Women 2010: Trends and Statistics," http://unstats.un.org/unsd/demographic/products/Worldswomen/WW2010pub.htm (June 12, 2012).

11. United Nations Department of Economic and Social Affairs, "The World's Women 2010: Trends and Statistics," http://unstats.un.org/unsd/demographic/products/Worldswomen/WW2010pub.htm (June 12, 2012).

12. United Nations Educational, Scientific and Cultural Organization (UNESCO), "Girls Continue to Face Sharp Discrimination in Access to School," June 11, 2003 press release no. 2003–91, http://portal.unesco.org/en/ev.php-URL_ID=17039&URL_DO=DO_TOPIC&URL_SECTION=201.html (Nov. 25, 2003).

13. United Nations Department of Economic and Social Affairs, "The World's Women 2010: Trends and Statistics," http://unstats.un.org/unsd/demographic/products/Worldswomen/WW2010pub.htm (June 12, 2012).

14. UN Integrated Regional Information Networks, "Togo; School Year Reopens with Free Primary Schools," *Africa News*, October 6, 2008.

15. United Nations Department of Economic and Social Affairs, "The World's Women 2010: Trends and Statistics," http://unstats.un.org/unsd/demographic/products/Worldswomen/WW2010pub.htm (June 12, 2012).

16. The World Bank, "Girls' Education—Key United Nations Department of Economic and Social Affairs Issues," 2009, http://go.worldbank.org/SP3Y3AHK10 (Jan. 7, 2009).

17. Results, "2007 Basics: Global Education for All," 2007, http://www.results.org/website/article.asp?id=2566 (Jan. 7, 2009).

18. UNESCO, "Girls Continue to Face Sharp Discrimination in Access to School."

19. UN Integrated Regional Information Networks, "Togo."

20. United Nations, "World Day Against Child Labour," June 12, 2012, http://www.un.org/en/events/childlabourday/background.shtml (July 5, 2012).

21. United States Agency for International Development (USAID), Office of Women and Development, "Girls' and Women's Education: A USAID Initiative," Fact Sheet (April 1998).

22. UNESCO, "Girls Continue to Face Sharp Discrimination in Access to School."

23. Human Rights Watch, "Guinea; Thousands of Girls Face Abuse as Domestic Workers," *Africa News,* June 15, 2007.

24. Global Campaign for Education, "Must Try Harder."

25. Aamir Latif, IslamOnline.net, "Taliban Divided on Girls Education," December 26, 2008, http://www.islamonline.net (Jan. 8, 2009).

26. Karin Ronnow, "Journey of Hope: An In-Depth Report, Keeping Hope Alive" (Central Asia Institute, 2008), 7.

27. USAID, Office of Women and Development, "Girls' and Women's Education."

28. Abdul Alim, Ben Abdallah, Solofo Ramaruson, Maman Sidikou, and Lieke Van de Wiel, "Accelerating Girl's Education in Yemen: Rethinking Policies in Teachers' Recruitment and School Distribution," February 2007, http://www.ungei.org/resources/files/Policy-Paper-Girls-education-Yemen.pdf (January 8, 2009).

29. World Education Forum, "Women and Girls."

30. UNESCO, "Girls Continue to Face Sharp Discrimination in Access to School."

31. Wellesley Centers for Research on Women and Development and Training Services, Inc., for USAID, September 2003, "Unsafe Schools: A Literature Review of School-Related Gender-Based Violence in Developing Countries," http://pdf.usaid.gov/pdf_docs/PNACU253.pdf (Jan. 8, 2009).

32. UNESCO, "Girls Continue to Face Sharp Discrimination in Access to School."

33. "Kenya; Teenage Girls Targetted for Sexual Exploitation," *East African Standard,* Africa News, February 7, 2008.

34. UNICEF, *Gender Achievements and Prospects in Education: The GAP Report,* Part One, "South Asia Yawning Chasm," http://www.ungei.org/gap/ (Jan. 8, 2009).

35. UNESCO, *EFA Global Monitoring Report 2003/4, Gender and Education for All, the Leap to Equality* (Paris: UNESCO Publishing, 2003), http://www.efareport.unesco.org (November 25, 2003).

36. The Global Partnership for Education http://www.globalpartnership.org/ (Feb. 15, 2013).

37. Global Partnership for Education, "All Children Learning Report Shows Bold Vision to Help Millions of Poor Kids Learn and Grow," June 27, 2012, http://www.globalpartnership.org/news/338/762/All-Children-Learning-Report/ (July 5, 2012).

38. United Nations, "We Can End Poverty 2015 Millenium Development Goals," Fact Sheet, September 2010.

39. Michael Fleshman, "Abolishing Fees Boosts African Schooling," *Africa Renewal,* January 2010, p 16, http://www.un.org/africarenewal/magazine/january-2010/abolishing-fees-boosts-african-schooling (July 5, 2012).

40. Brendan O'Malley, "The Global Classroom," *South China Morning Post,* June 16, 2007, Education section, p. 6.

41. Ibid., 6.

42. UN News Service, "With UNICEF Help, Teens Show Girls in Uganda, Pakistan the Way to School," December 11, 2001, http://www.un.org/apps/news/story.asp?NewsID=9178&Cr=unicef&Cr1= (December 15, 2003).

43. USAID, Office of Women and Development, "Girls' and Women's Education."

44. Department for International Development, "DFID and the G8 Presidency 2005: Progress on Debt Relief," http://www.dfid.gov.uk/g8/debtrelief.asp (Jan. 15, 2009).

45. Associated Press, "The Debt Relief Tour," May 28, 2002, http://www.cbsnews.com/stories/2003/07/08/world/main562166.shtml (January 15, 2009).

46. "Uganda; Country's Debt Drops to $1 Billion," *The Monitor,* Africa News, February 28, 2007.

47. KatineChronicles, "Debate: The State of Education in Uganda," *The Guardian,* May 2008, http://www.guardian.co.uk/society/katineblog/2008/may/23/uganda willachieveitsmillen (Jan. 15, 2009).

48. Canadian International Development Agency, "Uganda," http://www.acdi-cida.gc.ca/uganda (Jan. 12, 2009).

49. United Nations Girls' Education Initiative, "Formative Evaluation of The United Nations Girls' Education Initiative: Uganda Report," April 2012, p.16.

50. "Uganda; Country's Debt Drops to $1 Billion," *The Monitor,* Africa News, February 28, 2007.

51. Ibid.

52. James Button, "Rich Are Failing to Keep Their Word to Africa," *Sydney Morning Herald (Australia),* June 2, 2007, International News, p. 15.

53. World Bank, "World Bank's First-Ever Combination Grant-Credit Will Support Uganda Education, March 24, 1998, http://web.worldbank.org/WBSITE/EXTERNAL/NEWS/0,,contentMDK:20012678~menuPK:34466~pagePK:640 03015~piPK:64003012~theSitePK:4607,00.html (Oct. 15, 2005).

54. United Nations Girls' Education Initiative, "Formative Evaluation of The United Nations Girls' Education Initiative: Uganda Report," April 2012, p.16.

55. The World Bank, "Independent Evaluation Group," http://www.worldbank.org/ieg/education/findings.html (Jan. 12, 2009).

56. "Uganda; Country's Debt Drops to $1 Billion."

57. KatineChronicles, "Debate: The State of Education in Uganda."

58. Ibid.

59. William Easterly, "Think Again: Debt Relief," *Foreign Policy,* November/December, 2001, p. 3.

60. Ibid.

61. Ibid., p.2 .

62. Global Campaign for Education, "Must Try Harder."

63. World Education Forum, "Women and Girls."

64. Ibid.

65. Ibid.

66. Ibid.

67. Ibid.

68. United Nations Girls' Education Initiative, "100 Literacy Classes for Girls and Women Open in Senegal," http://www.ungei.org/senegal_3086.html?q=printme (July 5, 2012).

69. Global Campaign for Education, "Must Try Harder."

70. Ibid.

71. Ibid.

72. Ibid.

73. USAID, Office of Women and Development, "Girls' and Women's Education."

CHAPTER 11

1. Human Rights Watch, testimony from the press release "Serb Gang-Rapes in Kosovo Exposed," March 21, 2000, http://www.hrw.org/press/2000/03/kosrape.htm (Nov. 7, 2003).
2. Ibid.
3. Peter W. Singer, 2006, *Children at War* (Berkeley: University of California Press), 33–34.
4. Human Rights Watch, "Refugee and Internally Displaced Women; Gender-Based Asylum Claims," 2003, http://www.hrw.org/topic/womens-rights/refugee-and-internally-displaced-women (Nov. 7, 2003).
5. Human Rights Watch, "Seeking Protection: Addressing Sexual and Domestic Violence in Tanzania's Refugee Camps," October 2000, http://www.hrw.org/reports/2000/tanzania (Nov. 17, 2003).
6. Central Intelligence Agency, "Montenegro," and "Serbia" in *The World Factbook,* October 4, 2005, https://www.cia.gov/library/publications/the-world-factbook/geos/mj.html and https://www.cia.gov/library/publications/the-world-factbook/geos/ri.htmland (Oct. 15, 2005).
7. Kitty McKinsey, "Yugoslavia: Crimes Against Women Become Focus of Tribunals," Radio Free Europe, May 13, 1998, http://www.rferl.org/nca/features/1998/05/ F.RU.980513135425.html (Dec. 3, 2003).
8. Ibid.
9. CNN.com, "Historic War Crime Verdict Vindicates Women," February 23, 2001, http://edition.cnn.com/2001/fyi/news/02/23/war.crime.verdict/ (Dec. 2, 2003).
10. McKinsey, "Yugoslavia."
11. Human Rights Watch, testimony from the press release "Serb Gang-Rapes in Kosovo Exposed."
12. Central Intelligence Agency, "Congo, Democratic Republic of the," in *The World Factbook,* October 4, 2005, https://www.cia.gov/library/publications/the-world-factbook/geos/cg.html (Oct. 15, 2005).
13. Stephanie McCrummen, "Groups Sign Deal to End Long Fight in E. Congo; Accord Portrayed as Key Initial Step," *Washington Post,* January 24, 2008, p. A13.
14. Ibid., p. A13.
15. Omar El Akkad, "Civil War: Canada on Sidelines of Aims for Peace in Congo," *The Globe and Mail,* October 29, 2008, p. A13.
16. Institute for War and Peace Reporting, "Congo-Kinshasa; Rape a 'Weapon of War' in Eastern Congo," *Africa News,* December 23, 2007.
17. Human Rights Watch, "The War Within the War: Sexual Violence Against Women and Girls in Eastern Congo," June 2002, http://www.hrw.org/reports/2002/drc/index.htm (Dec. 4, 2003).
18. Peter Goodspeed, "Rape Now War Strategy in Congo, Doctor Says; Sexual Terrorism," *National Post,* December 1, 2008, p A7.
19. Reseau des Femmes Pour un Developpement Associatif, "Women's Bodies as a Battleground: Sexual Violence Against Women and Girls During the War in the Democratic Republic of Congo, South Kivu (1996–2003)," *International Alert* 2005, p. 34.

20. Human Rights Watch, "The War Within the War."
21. Polly Markandya and Fionna Lloyd-Davis, "DRC: A Plaster on a Gaping Wound," Medecins Sans Frontieres, April 16, 2002, http://www.msf.org/countries/page.cfm (December 4, 2003).
22. Institute for War and Peace Reporting, "Congo-Kinshasa."
23. Human Rights Watch, "The War Within the War."
24. Institute for War and Peace Reporting, "Congo-Kinshasa."
25. Central Intelligence Agency, "Sierra Leone," in *The World Factbook,* October 4, 2005, https://www.cia.gov/library/publications/the-world-factbook/geos/sl.html (October 15, 2005).
26. Physicians for Human Rights, "War-Related Sexual Violence in Sierra Leone: A Population-Based Assessment" January 23, 2002, p. 7, http://physiciansforhumanrights.org/library/reports/war-related-sexual-violence-sierra-leone-2002.html.
27. Human Rights Watch, "Sierra Leone: Sexual Violence Widespread in War," January 16, 2003, http://www.hrw.org/press/2003/01/s10116.htm (Nov. 17, 2003); Human Rights Watch, "Shocking War Crimes in Sierra Leone," June 24, 1999, http://www.hrw.org/press/1999/jun/s10624.htm (Nov. 7, 2003).
28. Human Rights Watch, "Sierra Leone."
29. Central Intelligence Agency, "Burundi," in *The World Factbook,* October 4, 2005, https://www.cia.gov/library/publications/the-world-factbook/geos/by.html (October 15, 2005).
30. Human Rights Watch, "Seeking Protection."
31. Sydia Nduna and Lorelei Goodyear, "Pain Too Deep for Tears: Assessing the Prevalence of Sexual and Gender Violence Among Burundi Refugees in Tanzania," International Rescue Committee, revised 1997, http://www.rescue.org/sites/default/files/migrated/resources/sgbv_1.pdf (Jan. 23, 2009).
32. Human Rights Watch, "Seeking Protection."
33. Human Rights Watch, "The War Within the War."
34. Markandya and Lloyd-Davis, "DRC."
35. Ibid.
36. National Center for Post Traumatic Stress Disorder, "Rape of Women in a War Zone: a National Center for PTSD Fact Sheet," May 14, 2003, http://www.ptsd.va.gov/public/pages/rape-women-war-zone.asp (Dec. 2, 2003).
37. National Center for Post Traumatic Stress Disorder, "Rape of Women in a War Zone."
38. The Analyst, "Liberia; Fighters Exposed to Sexual Violence Have More Mental Health Disorders After War," *Africa News,* August 14, 2008.
39. Markandya and Lloyd-Davis, "DRC."
40. Institute for War and Peace Reporting, "Congo-Kinshasa."
41. Nirit Ben-Ari and Ernest Harsch, "Sexual Violence, an 'Invisible War Crime,'" *Africa Renewal* 18, no. 4 (January 2005): 1, http://allafrica.com/stories/200501060580.html (January 23, 2009).
42. Louise Arbour, "War Crimes Against Women Go on with Impunity," *The Toronto Star* (March 11, 2007), p. A15.
43. UN High Commissioner for Refugees, "Basic Facts," http://www.unhcr.org (December 9, 2003).
44. Human Rights Watch, "Seeking Protection."

45. Susan McKay, "Girls as 'Weapons of Terror' in Northern Uganda and Sierra Leoneon Rebel Fighting Forces," *Studies in Conflict and Terrorism* (April 2005): 385–397.

46. Singer, *Children at War*, 32.

47. The News, "Liberia; Survey—Commanders Took Away Weapons from Ex-Female Fighters," *Africa News*, June 26, 2008.

48. Singer, *Children at War*, 33.

49. The News, "Liberia."

50. Ibid.

51. UN Integrated Regional Information Networks, "Liberia; Some Women Ready to Fight Again," *Africa News*, October 14, 2008.

52. Ben-Ari and Harsch, "Sexual Violence."

53. Dewi Cooke, "Women and the Hell of War: Justice," *The Age (Melbourne, Australia)*, June 28, 2008, p. 8.

54. Ibid.

55. McKay, "Girls as 'Weapons of Terror.'"

56. Singer, *Children at War*, 15.

57. Singer, pp. 9–15.

58. Ibid., 15.

59. Ibid., 15.

60. Ibid., 16.

61. Ibid., 30.

62. Ibid., 31.

63. Ibid., 29.

64. Ibid., 62.

65. Nick Tattersall, "Savage Life of Boy Soldiers Made to Kill," *The Advertiser*, June 9, 2007, p. 76.

66. Singer, *Children at War*, 61.

67. Ibid., 194.

68. Michael Gerson, "Thorns in the Congo," *The Washington Post*, November 30, 2007: A23.

69. Ibid.

70. The Analyst, "Liberia."

71. Singer, *Children at War*, 195.

72. Vanessa Gezari, "Killing Our Fathers, Raising Our Sons," *St. Petersburg Times*, August 5, 2007, p. 1.

73. Ibid.

74. Tattersall, "Savage Life of Boy Soldiers Made to Kill."

CHAPTER 12

1. Testimony of Hannah Koroma, Sierra Leone, as quoted in Amnesty International, "Section One: What Is Female Genital Mutilation," http://www.amnesty.org/en/library/info/ACT77/006/1997 (Dec. 15, 2003).

2. Rena Singer, "Chastity Tests: Unusual Tool for Public Health," *The Christian Science Monitor*, June 2, 2000, http://www.csmonitor.com/2000/0602/p1s4.html (Dec. 18, 2003).

3. Human Rights Watch, "Pakistan: Tribal Councils Source of Abuse," July 12, 2002, http://www.hrw.org/press/2002/pak0712.htm (Nov. 7, 2003).

4. Amnesty International, "Section One: What Is Female Genital Mutilation."
5. Ibid.
6. World Health Organization, "Female Genital Mutilation," Fact Sheet no. 241, February 2012, http://www.who.int/mediacentre/factsheets/fs241/en/print .html (July 12, 2012).
7. United Nations Population Fund, "2,000 More African Communities End Female Genital Mutilation/Cutting in 2011," February 6, 2012, http://www .unfpa.org/public/home/news/pid/9976 (July 12, 2012).
8. Sara Corbett, "A Cutting Tradition," *New York Times Magazine,* January 20, 2008, p. 44.
9. Amnesty International, "Section One: What Is Female Genital Mutilation."
10. Ibid.
11. Ibid.
12. Wakabi, "Africa Battles to Make Female Genital Mutilation History."
13. BBC News, "Senegal Village Rejects FGM," http://news.bbc.co.uk/2/hi/africa/ 3132350.stm (Dec. 15, 2003).
14. Amnesty International, "Section One: What Is Female Genital Mutilation."
15. Omer Songwe, "Cameroon Princess Fights Mutilation," BBC News, December 9, 2002, http://news.bbc.co.uk/1/hi/world/africa/2547503.stm (Dec. 15, 2003).
16. Amnesty International, "Section One: What Is Female Genital Mutilation."
17. Songwe, "Cameroon Princess Fights Mutilation."
18. BBC News, "South Africa Leader Urges Virginity Tests," http://news.bbc.co.uk/ go/pr/fr/-/2/hi/africa/3683210.stm (Feb. 3, 2009).
19. Karin Brulliard, "Zulus Eagerly Defy Ban on Virginity Test," Washingtonpost .com, September 26, 2008, http://www.washingtonpost.com (Feb. 2, 2009).
20. Ibid.
21. Ibid.
22. Ibid.
23. Stanley Karombo, "Rights-Zimbabwe: Virginity Testing Strips Girls of Their Dignity—Groups," Inter Press Service News Agency, February 2, 2009, http:// ipsnews.net (Feb. 2, 2009).
24. Ibid.
25. Stevenson Jacobs, "Jamaica: MPs Recommend Virginity Tests, Sterilization for Young Women," Associated Press, July 30, 2003, http://www.highbeam.com/ doc/1P1-76469704.html (Dec. 18, 2003).
26. Associated Press, "Turkey Bans Forced Virginity Tests," January 6, 1999, http:// www.apnewsarchive.com/1999/Turkey-Bans-Forced-Virginity-Tests/id-edfebb5b30e8f95307a8b24cdb8f6c38 (Dec. 18, 2003).
27. Agence France-Presse, "Iraqi Women Face Court-Ordered Virginity Tests," July 1, 2012, http://www.rawstory.com/rs/2012/07/01/iraqi-women-face-court-ordered-virginity-tests/ (July 12, 2012).
28. Ibid.
29. Singer, "Chastity Tests."
30. Karombo, "Rights-Zimbabwe."
31. Ibid.
32. Associated Press, "Virginity Tests Protested in Turkey."
33. The Global Campaign to Stop Killing and Stoning, "Frequently Asked Questions About Stoning," http://www.violenceisnotourculture.org/faq_stoning (Feb. 6, 2009).

34. Jeff Koinange, "Woman Sentenced to Stoning Freed," CNN, September 26, 2003, http://www.cnn.com/2003/WORLD/africa/09/25/nigeria.stoning (Dec. 18, 2003).

35. Human Rights Watch, "Nigeria: Teenage Mother Whipped," January 23, 2001, http://www.hrw.org/press/2001/01/nigeria0123.htm (Nov. 17, 2003).

36. Thomas Erdbrink, "Iran Stones 2 Men to Death; 3d Flees; Sentences Carried Out Despite Judicial Moratorium in 2002," *Washington Post Foreign Service,* January 14, 2009, p. A14.

37. Saeed Kamali Dehghan and Ian Black, "Iranians Still Facing Death by Stoning Despite 'Reprieve,'" July 8, 2010, http://www.guardian.co.uk/world/2010/jul/08/iran-death-stoning-adultery (July 12, 2012).

38. Amnesty International, "Campaigning to End Stoning in Iran," January 15, 2008, http://www.amnesty.org (Feb. 2, 2009).

39. "Stoning Victim 'Begged for Mercy,'" *BBC News,* November 4, 2008, http://news.bbc.co.uk/2/hi/7708169.stm (Feb. 2, 2009).

40. Ibid.

41. Human Rights Watch, "Crime or Custom? Violence Against Women in Pakistan," August 1999, http://www.hrw.org/reports/1999/pakistan (Nov. 7, 2003).

42. "Family Guilty in 'Honour Killing'; Turkish Clan Gets Life for Killing Rape Victim, 16," *The National Post,* January 13, 2009, p. A14.

43. Hillary Mayell, "Thousands of Women Killed for Family Honor," *National Geographic News* February 12, 2002, http://news.nationalgeographic.com/news/pf/15061734.html (Feb. 2, 2009).

44. Ibid.

45. Ibid.

46. Ibid.

47. As quoted in Amnesty International, "Female Genital Mutilation—A Human Rights Information Pack," in Section Four, "A Human Rights Issue," http://www.amnesty.org/en/library/info/ACT77/006/1997 (Dec. 15, 2003).

48. Human Rights Watch, "Crime or Custom?"

49. Huffington Post, "Russian Judge Rules Sexual Harassment is Okay as it Ensures Survival of Human Race," August 13, 2008, http://www.huffingtonpost.com/2008/08/05/russian-judge-rules-sexua_n_117071.html (July 16, 2012).

Bibliography

"1 in 5 Women Relying on Partner's Pension." *The Financial Times*. August 16, 2003, Money section.

"Abortion Will Pop up Again on Political Radar Screen." *Irish Independent*. March 8, 2005.

Abraham, Lois, and Jane Roberts. "Citizen Engagement." Our Planet, United Nations Environmental Program, Nairobi Kenya vol. 15, no. 2, (2004), p. 29. http://www.34millionfriends.org.

Abu-Zayd, Gehan. "In Search of Political Power—Women in Parliament in Egypt, Jordan, and Lebanon." 2002 update of case study originally published in *Women in Parliament: Beyond Numbers*. Stockholm: International IDEA, 1998. http://www.idea.int.

Adams, Jacqueline. "Art in Social Movements: Shantytown Women' Protest in Pinochet's Chile." *Sociological Forum* 17 (2002): 21–56.

Adventure Divas. "Helen Clark." http://www.adventuredivas.com/divas/article.view?page=245 (May 1, 2003).

Agence France Presse. "Dutch Women Go Abroad for Late-Term Abortions." April 12, 2005.

Aishwarya, Rai. *Our Planet*. United Nations Environmental Programme, vol. 15, no. 2, (2004), p. 18.

Alan Guttmacher Institute. "State Policies in Brief as of August 1, 2005." http://www.guttmacher.org/statecenter/spibs/spib_BPBA.pdf (Aug. 10, 2005).

Alim, Abdul, Ben Abdallah, Solofo Ramaruson, Maman Sidikou, and Lieke Van de Wiel. "Accelerating Girl's Education in Yemen: Rethinking Policies in Teachers' Recruitment and School Distribution," February 2007, http://www.ungei.org/resources/files/Policy-Paper-Girls-education-Yemen.pdf (Jan. 8, 2009).

al-Mughni, Haya. "Women's Organizations in Kuwait." In *Women and Politics in the Middle East*, ed. Saud Joseph and Susan Slyomovics. Philadelphia: University of Pennsylvania Press, 2001.

al-Shaibani, Saleh. "No Women Elected in Omani Vote," Reuters, October 28, 2007, http://uk.reuters.com/articlePrint?articleId=UKL2808041220071028 (Oct. 14, 2008).

Alvarez, Sonia E. *Engendering Democracy in Brazil: Women's Movements in Transition Politics*. Princeton, NJ: Princeton University Press, 1990.

Amnesty International. "Female Genital Mutilation—a Human Rights Information Pack," in Section Four, "A Human Rights Issue," http://www.amnesty.org/ailib/intcam/femgen/fgm4.htm (Dec. 15, 2003).

———. "Campaigning to End Stoning in Iran." January 15, 2008. http://www.amnesty.org (Feb. 2, 2009).

———. "Section One: What Is Female Genital Mutilation." http://www.amnesty.org/ailib/intcam/femgen/fgm1.htm (Dec. 15, 2003).

Amsberger, Helga, and Brigitte Halbmayr, eds. *Rechtsextreme Parteien.* Opladen: Leske & Budrich, 2002.

Analyst. "Liberia; Fighters Exposed to Sexual Violence Have More Mental Health Disorders After War." *Africa News.* August 14, 2008.

Andersen, G. Esping. *The Three Worlds of Welfare Capitalism.* Cambridge: Cambridge University Press, 1990.

Applebaum, Eileen, Thomas Bailey, Peter Berg, and Arne L. Kalleberg. *Shared Work, Valued Care: New Norms for Organizing Market Work and Unpaid Care Work.* Washington, DC: Economic Policy Institute, June 2002.

Arbour, Louise. "War Crimes Against Women Go on with Impunity." *Toronto Star.* March 11, 2007, p. A15.

Arie, Sophi. "Elisa Carrio in Lead to Be Argentina's President." *Women's eNews.* July 18, 2002. http://www.womensenews.org (July 18, 2002).

Associated Press. "The Debt Relief Tour," May 28, 2002, http://www.cbsnews.com/stories/2003/07/08/world/main562166.shtml (Jan. 15, 2009).

———. "Egyptian Women Protesters Sexually Assaulted in Tahrir Square," *The Guardian,* June 8, 2012, http://www.guardian.co.uk/world/2012/jun/09/egyptian-women-protesters-sexually-assaulted.

———. "Virginity Tests Protested in Turkey," July 17, 2001. http://www.jsonline.com/news/intl/ap/ju101/ap-turkey-virginit071701.asp?fomrat=print (Dec. 18, 2003).

Babb, Florence E. *After Revolution: Mapping Gender and Cultural Politics in Neoliberal Nicaragua.* Austin: University of Texas Press, 2001.

Bacchetta, Paola, and Margaret Power, eds. *Right-Wing Women: From Conservatives to Extremists Around the World.* New York: Routledge Press, 2002.

Bagnall, Janet. "When Women Become a Burden; Selective-Sex Abortions Threaten to Turn India into a Land Full of Angry, Lonely Young Men." *The Montreal Gazette.* May 16, 2008, p. A15.

Bahramitash, Roksana. "Revolution, Islamization, and Women's Employment in Iran." *Brown Journal of World Affairs* 9 (Winter/Spring 2003).

Baker, Maureen. *Canadian Family Policies: Cross National Comparisons.* Toronto: University of Toronto Press, 1995.

Banaszak, Lee Ann. "The Women's Movement Policy Successes and the Constraints of State Reconfiguration: Abortion and Equal Pay in Differing Eras." In *Women's Movements Facing the Reconfigured State,* ed. Lee Ann Banaszak, Karen Beckwith, and Dieter Rucht. New York: Cambridge University Press, 2003.

Banaszak, Lee Ann, Karen Beckwith, and Dieter Rucht. "When Power Relocates: Interactive Changes in Women's Movements and States." In *Women's Movements Facing the Reconfigured State,* ed. Lee Ann Banaszak, Karen Beckwith, and Dieter Rucht. New York: Cambridge University Press, 2003.

———, eds. *Women's Movements Facing the Reconfigured State.* New York: Cambridge University Press, 2003.

Barot, Sneha. "Back to Basics: The Rationale for Increased Funds for International Family Planning." *Guttmacher Policy Review* 11, no. 3 (2008). http://www.gutmacher.org/pubs/gpr/11/3/gpr110313.html.

Barrett, Edith. "The Policy Priorities of African-American Women in State Legislatures." *Legislative Studies Quarterly* 20 (1995): 223–247.

Basu, Alaka Malwade, ed. *The Sociocultural and Political Aspects of Abortion: Global Perspectives.* Westport, CT: Praeger, 2003.

Basu, Amrita. "Introduction." In *The Challenge of Local Feminisms: Women's Movements in Global Perspective,* ed. Amrita Basu. Boulder, CO: Westview Press, 1995.

——, ed. *The Challenge of Local Feminisms: Women's Movements in Global Perspective.* Boulder, CO: Westview Press, 1995.

Baynes, Terry. "U.S. Judge Allows Enforcement of Texas Abortion Law," Thomson Reuters. February 7, 2012, http://www.reuters.com/article/2012/02/07/us-texas-abortion-idUSTRE81605220120207

BBC News, "Arab Uprising – Country by Country." http://www.bbc.co.uk/news/world-12482315

Beckwith, Karen. "Beyond Compare? Women's Movements in Comparative Perspective." *European Journal of Political Research* 37 (2000): 431–468.

——. "Lancashire Women Against Pit Closures: Women's Standing in a Men's Movement." *Signs* 21, no. 4 (2000): 1034–1068.

Belsie, Laurent. "Men Lag Women at the Voting Booth." *Christian Science Monitor.* February 28, 2002.

Ben-Ari, Nirit, and Ernest Harsch. "Sexual Violence, an 'Invisible War Crime.'" *Africa Renewal* 18, no.4 (January 2005): 1. http://allafrica.com/stories/200501060580.html (Jan. 23, 2009).

Bennhold, Katrin. "In Germany a Tradition Falls, and Women Rise." *New York Times,* January 17, 2010, http://www.nytimes.com/2010/01/18/world/europe/18iht-women .html?_r=1&pagewanted=all.

——. "In Sweden, Men Can Have it All." *New York Times,* June 9, 2010.

——. "Paternity Leave Law Helps to Redefine Masculity in Sweden." *New York Times,* June 15, 2010, 6.

——. "Working (Part-Time) in the 21st Century." *New York Times.* December 29, 2010. http://www.nytimes.com/2010/12/30/world/europe/30iht-dutch30.html? pagewanted=all (June 18, 2012).

Berkman, Michael B., and Robert E. O'Connor. "Do Women Legislators Matter? Female Legislators and State Abortion Policy." *American Politics Quarterly* 21 (January 1993): 102–124.

Berry, Jeffrey. *Interest Group Society.* 3rd ed. New York: Longman, 1997.

Bingham, Clara. *Challenging the Culture of Congress.* New York: Times Books, 1997.

"Blair Puts Focus on Family-Friendly Reforms." *Guardian,* February 28, 2005.

Bloom, Mia. "Bombshells: Women and Terror." *Gendered Issues* (2011): 28:1–21.

Bnet.com. "Labour Market Trends: Advancing Women in the Workplace." http://findarticles .com/p/articles/mi_qa3999/is_200408/ai_n9448236 (Dec. 9, 2008).

Boserup, Ester. *Women's Role in Economic Development.* New York: St. Martin's Press, 1970.

Boxer, Barbara. *Strangers in the Senate.* Bethesda, MD: National Press Books, 1994.

Boyenge, Jean-Pierre Singa. ILO Database on Export Processing Zones (revised). Working Paper 251, International Labour Office, Geneva, April 2007. http://www.ilo.org/ public/english/dialogue/sector/themes/epz/epz-db.pdf.

Bratton, Kathleen, and Leonard Ray. "Descriptive Representation, Policy Outcomes, and Municipal Day-Care Coverage in Norway." *American Journal of Political Science* 46 (2003): 428–437.

British Broadcasting Corporation News. "Amsterdam Treaty." April 30, 2001. http://news .bbc.co.uk/1/hi/in_depth/europe/euro-glossary/1216210.stm (April 30, 2006).

——. "Talks to End Nigerian Oil Siege." July 11, 2002. http://news.bbc.co.uk/1/hi/world/ africa/2119872.stm (Feb. 5, 2003).

——. "'Deal Reached' in Nigerian Oil Protest." July 16, 2002. http://news.bbc.co.uk/1/hi/africa/2129281.stm (Feb. 5, 2003).

——. "Oil Deal 'Off', Nigerian Women Say." July 16, 2002. http://news.bbc.co.uk/1/hi/world/africa/2132494.stm (Feb. 5, 2003).

——. "Nigerian Women Leave Oil Plant." July 18, 2002. http://news.bbc.co.uk/1/hi/world/africa/2136509.stm (Feb. 5, 2003).

——. "Wal-Mart Battles Huge Sexism Claim." September 25, 2003. http://news.bbc.co.uk/1/hi/business/3138188.stm (Aug. 8, 2005).

——. "Stoning Victim 'Begged for Mercy.'" November 4, 2008. http://news/bbc.co.uk/go/pr/fr//2/hi/africa/7708169.stm (Feb. 2, 2009).

——. "South Africa Leader Urges Virginity Tests." http://news.bbc.co.uk/go/pr/fr//2/hi/africa/3683210.stm (Feb. 3, 2009).

Brulliard, Karin. "Zulus Eagerly Defy Ban on Virginity Test." September 26, 2008. http://www.washingtopost.com (Feb. 2, 2009).

Burkhalter, Holly. "The Politics of AIDS: Engaging Conservative Activists." *Foreign Affairs* (January/February 2004), pp. 8–14.

Burn, Shawn Meghan. *Women Across Cultures: A Global Perspective*. 2d ed. New York: McGraw-Hill, 2005, pp. 153–156.

Burrell, Barbara. *A Woman's Place Is in the House: Campaigning for Congress in the Feminist Era*. Ann Arbor: University of Michigan Press, 1994.

Burri, Suzanne, and Sacha Prechal. "EU Gender Equality Law: Update 2010." European Commission. December 2010, p. 19.

Burstein, Paul. "Legal Mobilization as a Social Movement Tactic: The Struggle for Equal Employment Opportunity." *American Journal of Sociology* 96 (1991): 1201–1225.

Bush, George. "The President's Veto Message." *Congressional Digest*, January 1993.

Bussemaker, Jet, and Kees van Kinsbergen. "Contemporary Social Capitalist Welfare State and Gender Inequality." In *Gender and Welfare State Regimes*, ed. Diane Sainsbury. Oxford: Oxford University Press, 1999.

Button, James. "Rich Are Failing to Keep Their Word to Africa." *Sydney Morning Herald (Australia)*. June 2, 2007, International News, p. 15.

Buvinic, Mayra. "Promising Gender Equality." *International Social Science Journal* 162 (1999): 567–574.

Bystydzienski, Jill M. *Women in Electoral Politics: Lessons from Norway*. Westport, CT, and London: Praeger, 1995.

Caldwell, John C., and Pat Caldwell. "Introduction: Induced Abortion in a Changing World." In *The Sociocultural and Political Aspects of Abortion: Global Perspectives*, ed. Alaka Malwade Basu. Westport, CT: Praeger, 2003.

Calloni, Marina. "Debates and Controversies on Abortion in Italy." In *Abortion Politics, Women's Movements, and the Democratic State: A Comparative Study of State Feminism*, ed. Dorothy McBride Stetson. Oxford: Oxford University Press, 2001.

Campbell, Kim. "Women Seek Solutions to Pension-System Bias." *Christian Science Monitor*, May 9, 1996, p. 9.

Canadian International Development Agency. "Uganda." http://www.acdi-cida.gc.ca/uganda (Jan. 12, 2009).

"Care for Girls' Gaining Momentum." *China Daily*. July 8, 2004. http://www.chinadaily.com.cn/english/doc/2004–07/08/content_346700.htm.

Casserly, Meghan. "Sheryl Sandberg's 'Lean In' More Aspirational than Inspirational." *Forbes*, August 31, 2012.

Catalyst. "Quick Takes, Women in the Law in the United States." April 2012. http://www
.catalyst.org/publication/246/women-in-law-in-the-us. (May 29, 2012).

———. "Quick Takes, Women on Boards." April 2012. http://www.catalyst.org/publication/
433/women-on-boards (June 18, 2012).

———. "Women CEOs of the Fortune 1000s." June 2012. http://www.catalyst.org/publica
tions/271/women-ceos-of-the-fortune-1000 (June 18, 2012).

Caul, Miki. *Women's Representation in Parliament: The Role of Political Parties.* Irvine:
Center for the Study of Democracy, UC Irvine, 1997.

Center for American Women and Politics. "The Gender Gap and the 2004 Women's Vote:
Setting the Record Straight." Advisory of October 28, 2004.

Center for Reproductive Rights. "CEDAW: The Importance of U.S. Ratification." http://
www.crlp.org/pub_fac_cedaw.html (Oct. 13, 2005).

———. "The World's Abortion Laws." www.crlp.org/pub_fac_abortion_laws.html (April 26,
2006).

Central Intelligence Agency. "Serbia and Montenegro," in *The World Factbook,* October 4,
2005. https://www.cia.gov/library/publications/the-world-factbook/geos/ri.html https://
www.cia.gov/library/publications/the-world-factbook/geos/mj.html (Oct. 15, 2005).

Chang, Leslie T. *Factory Girls: From Village to City in a Changing China.* New York:
Spiegel & Grau, 2008.

Charlton, Sue Ellen M., Jana Everett, and Kathleen Staudt. "Women, the State, and Development." In *Women, the State, and Development,* ed. Charlton, Everett, and Staudt.
Albany: SUNY Press, 1989.

Childs, Sarah. "Hitting the Target: Are Labour Women MPs 'Acting for' Women?" Paper for
the 51st Political Studies Association Conference. April 10–12, 2001. Manchester,
United Kingdom, pp. 3–4.

———. "In Their Own Words: New Labour MPs and the Substantive Representation of
Women." *British Journal of Politics and International Relations* (June 2001): 173–190.

Chowdury, Najma, and Barbara J. Nelson with Kathryn A. Carver, Nancy Johnson, and
Paula L. O'Loughlin. "Redefining Politics: Patterns of Women's Engagement from a
Global Perspective." In *Women and Politics Worldwide,* ed. Barbara J. Nelson and
Najma Chowdury. New Haven, CT: Yale University Press, 1994.

Christy, Carol. *Sex Differences in Political Participation: Processes of Change in Fourteen
Nations.* New York: Praeger, 1987.

Clare, Ross. "Women and Superannuation." The University of New South Wales, School of
Economics and Actuarial Studies, paper presented at the Ninth Annual Colloquium of
Superannuation Researchers, July 2001, p. 2.

Clark, Janet. "Women at the National Level: An Update on Roll Call Voting Behavior." In
Women and Elective Office: Past, Present, and Future, ed. Sue Thomas and Clyde
Wilcox. New York: Oxford University Press, 1998.

Clearing House on International Developments in Child, Youth and Family Policies at
Columbia University. "France." http://www.childpolicyintl.org (Sept. 8, 2005).

———. "Germany." http://www.childpolicyintl.org (Aug. 9, 2005).

———. "Sweden." http://www.childpolicyintl.org (Sept. 8, 2005).

CNN.com. "EU Tightens Sex Harassment Law." April 18, 2002. http://cnn.worldnews.print
this.clickability.com (Nov. 20, 2003).

CNN World News. "Abortion Ship Arrives in Ireland." June 15, 2001. http://articles.cnn
.com/2001-06-15/world/ireland.ship02_1_surgical-abortions-medical-abortions-
abortion-pill?_s=PM:WORLD (April 22, 2006).

Cohen, Abby J. "A Brief History of Federal Financing for Child Care in the United States." *Financing Child Care* vol. 6, no. 2 (Summer/Fall 1996), pp. 26–40.

Coleman, Isobel. "Is the Arab Spring Bad for Women?" *Foreign Policy*, December 20, 2011, http://www.foreignpolicy.com/articles/2011/12/20/arab_spring_women.

Commission of the European Communities. "Report from the Commission to the Council, the European Parliament, the European Economic and Social Committee and the Committee of Regions: Annual Report on Equal Opportunities for Women and Men in the European Union 2002." Brussels, March 5, 2003.

———. "Gender Pay Gaps in European Labour Markets—Measurement, Analysis and Policy Implications." Brussels, September 4, 2003.

Conway, Margaret, Gertrude Steuernagel, and David Ahern. *Women and Political Participation*. Washington, DC: CQ Press, 1997.

Cooke, Dewi. "Women and the Hell of War: Justice." *The Age (Melbourne, Australia)*. June 28, 2008, p. 8.

Corbett, Sarah. "A Cutting Tradition." *New York Times Magazine*. January 20, 2008, p. 44.

Costain, Anne. *Inviting Women's Rebellion*. Baltimore, MD: Johns Hopkins University Press, 1992.

Costain, Anne, and Doug Costain. "Strategy and Tactics of the Women's Movement in the U.S.: The Role of Political Parties." In *The Women's Movements of the United States and Western Europe: Consciousness, Political Opportunity and Public Policy*, ed. Mary F. Katzenstein and Carol M. Mueller. Philadelphia: Temple University Press, 1987.

Cott, Nancy F. *The Grounding of Modern Feminism*. New Haven, CT: Yale University Press, 1987.

Coven, Martha. "An Introduction to TANF." Center on Budget and Policy Priorities, October 24, 2003.

Craske, Nikki. "Women's Political Participation in Colonias Populares in Guadalajara, Mexico." In *Viva: Women and Popular Protest in Latin America*, ed. Sarah Radcliffe and Sallie Westwood. London and New York: Routledge, 1993.

———. *Women and Politics in Latin America*. New Brunswick, NJ: Rutgers University Press, 1999.

Craske, Nikki, and Maxine Molyneux, eds. *Gender and the Politics of Rights and Democracy in Latin America*. New York: Palgrave, 2002.

Cronin, Stephanie, ed. *Reformers and Revolutionaries in Modern Iran: New Perspectives on the Iranian Left*. New York: Routledge Curzon, 2004.

Davidson, Fiona. "Male Workers Say It's Unfair That Dress Rules Don't Apply to Women: Men Shirty About Ties." *The Express*. July 16, 2003, p. 7.

de Figueres, Karen Olsen. "The Road to Equality—Women in Parliament in Costa Rica." 2002 update of case study originally published in *Women in Parliament: Beyond Numbers*, vol. 3. Stockholm: International IDEA, 1998. http://www.idea.int.

Dehghan, Saeed Kamali and Ian Black. "Iranians Still Facing Death by Stoning Despite 'Reprieve.'" July 8, 2010. http://www.guardian.co.uk/world/2010/jul/08/iran-death-by-stoning-adultry/print (July 12, 2012).

Department for International Development. "DFID and the G8 Presidency 2005: Progress on Debt Relief." http://www.dfid.gov.uk/g8/debtrelief.asp (Jan. 15, 2009).

DeVaus, David, and Ian McAllister. "The Changing Politics of Women: Gender and Political Alignments in Eleven Nations." *European Journal of Political Research* 17 (1989): 241–262.

Diamond, M. J. "Olympe de Gouges and the French Revolution: The Construction of Gender as Critique." In *Women and Revolution: Global Expressions*, ed. M. J. Diamond. Boston: Kluwer Academic Publishers, 1998.

———, ed. *Women and Revolution: Global Expressions.* Boston: Kluwer Academic Publishers, 1998.

Dodson, Debra L. "Representing Women's Interests in the U.S. House of Representatives." In *Women and Elective Office: Past, Present, and Future,* ed. Sue Thomas and Clyde Wilcox (New York: Oxford University Press, 1998).

Dodson, Debra L., and Susan Carroll. *Reshaping the Agenda: Women in State Legislatures.* New Brunswick: Center for American Women and Politics, Rutgers, The State University of New Jersey, 1991.

Doi, Ayako. "In Other Words." *Foreign Policy: The Magazine of Global Politics, Economics and Ideas.* November/December 2003. http://www.foreignpolicy.com/story/story .php?storyID=13976 (Nov. 20, 2003).

Dore, Elizabeth, and Maxine Molyneux, eds. *Hidden Histories of Gender and the State in Latin America.* Durham, NC: Duke University Press, 2000.

Dreshsler, Denis, Johannes Jutting, and Carina Lindberg. "Gender, Institutions, and Development: Better Data, Better Politics." International Poverty Centre. *Poverty in Focus: Gender Equality,* no. 13. January 2008 (no pagination).

Duin, Julia. "Brides Bound by Traditions; Indian Women, Families Carry Costly Commitment of Dowry." *The Washington Times.* February 27, 2007, p. A1.

Easterly, William. "Think Again: Debt Relief." *Foreign Policy* 3 (Nov./Dec. 2001): 20–26.

The Economist, "Special Report: Women and Work: Closing the Gap," November 26, 2011: 2. http://www.economist.com/node/21539928 (June 21, 2012).

The Economist Intelligence Unit, Women's Economic Opportunity Index 2012, London, England, 2012.

Education for All—Fast Track Initiative. "About FTI." http://www.education-fast-track.org (Jan. 13, 2009).

Einhorn, Barbara. *Cinderella Goes to Market: Citizenship, Gender, and Women's Movements in Eastern Central Europe.* New York: Verso Press, 1993.

Eisenger, Peter K. "The Conditions of Protest Behavior in American Cities." *American Political Science Review* 67 (1973): 11–28.

El Akkad, Omar. "Civil War: Canada on Sidelines of Aims for Peace in Congo." *The Globe and Mail.* October 29, 2008, p. A13.

Elias, Diana. "Kuwait Appoints Its First Woman Cabinet Member." The Associated Press, June 12, 2005.

Enloe, Cynthia. "Closing Remarks." *International Peacekeeping* 8 (2001): 111–114.

Erdbrink, Thomas. "Iran Stones 2 Men to Death; 3d Flees; Sentences Carried Out Despite Judicial Moratorium in 2002." *Washington Post,* January 14, 2009, p. A14.

European Commission. "Gender Mainstreaming." http://europa.eu.int/comm/employ ment_social/gender_equality/gender_mainstreaming/employment/employment_ labour_market_en.html (April 30, 2006).

"European Parliament Fact Sheet 4.8.7. Equality for Men and Women." http://www .europarl.eu.int/factsheets/4_8_7_en.htm (Sept. 30, 2003).

"The European Parliament Takes Stock." *Women's International Network News* 26, no. 4 (Autumn 2000): 59.

"European Quotas for Women CEOs Help Crack Boardroom Glass Ceilings." *PR Newswire.* November 16, 2011. http://www.thestreet.com/print/story/11312710.html (June 21, 2012).

European Union. "Equal Pay." http://europa.eu.int/scadplus/leg/en/cha/c10905.htm (April 30, 2006).

Eurostat News Release. "The Life of Women and Men in Europe: A Statistical Portrait of Men and Women in All Stages of Life." October 8, 2002.

Fackler, Martin. "Career Women in Japan Find a Blocked Path, Despite Equal Opportunity Law," *New York Times.* August 6, 2007, p. A1.

"Family Guilty in 'Honour Killing'; Turkish Clan Gets Life for Killing Rape Victim, 16." *National Post.* January 13, 2009, p. A14.

Farole, Thomas and Gokhan Akinci, eds. *Special Economic Zones: Progress, Emerging Challenges, and Future Directions* (Washington, D.C.: The World Bank, 2011).

Ferree, Myra Marx. "Equality and Autonomy: Feminist Politics in the United States and West Germany." In *The Women's Movements of the United States and Western Europe,* ed. Mary Fainsod Katzenstein and Carol McClurg Mueller. Philadelphia: Temple University Press, 1987.

Figner, Vera. *Memoirs of a Revolutionist,* introduction by Richard Stites. Dekalb: Northern Illinois Press, 1991.

Fleshman, Michael. "Women: The Face of AIDS in Africa." *Africa Renewal* 18, no. 3 (October 2004): 6. http://allafrica.com/stories/printable/200410120768.html (Oct. 13, 2004).

_____. "Abolishing Fees Boosts African Schooling." *Africa Renewal.* (January 2010): 16. http://www.un.org/africarerenewal/magazine/january-2010/abolishing-fees-boosts-african-schooling (July 5, 2012).

Foerstal, Karen, and Herbert Foerstal. *Climbing the Hill: Gender Conflict in Congress.* Westport, CT: Praeger, 1996.

Food and Agricultural Organization. *Gender and Food Security: Division of Labor.* Rome: Food and Agricultural Organization, 2003.

Foran, John, ed. *Theorizing Revolutions.* New York: Routledge Press, 1997.

Ford, Lynne E. *Women and Politics: The Pursuit of Equality.* Boston: Houghton Mifflin Company, 2002.

"Four Women Win 63 Million Yen Ruling: Sumitomo Metal Guilty of Gender Bias." *Japan Times. Tokyo and Osaka,* March 29, 2005.

Franklin, Kia. "A Vote in Favor of Fairness; the Candidates' Opinions on Pay Discrimination Case Offers a Glimpse into Judicial Philosophy." *Newsday, Melville.* October 21, 2008, p. A35.

Fraser, Nancy. "After the Family Wage: Gender Equity and the Welfare State." *Political Theory* 22, no. 4 (1994): 591–618.

Frederick, Brian. "Gender Turnover and Roll Call Voting in the US Senate." *Journal of Women, Politics, and Policy.* 32 (2011): 193–210.

Freeman, Jo. *The Politics of Women's Liberation.* New York: McKay, 1975.

Friedan, Betty. *The Feminine Mystique.* New York: W. W. Norton & Co., 2001.

Friedman, Thomas L. *The Lexus and the Olive Tree.* New York: Farrar, Straus & Giroux, 1999.

Galili, Ziva. "Women and the Russian Revolution." In *Women and Revolution: Global Expressions,* ed. M. J. Diamond. Boston: Kluwer Academic Publishers, 1998.

Gehlen, Freida. "Women Members of Congress: A Distinctive Role." In *A Portrait of Marginality: The Political Behavior of the American Woman,* ed. Marianne Githens and Jewell Prestage. New York: McKay Co., 1977.

Gelb, Joyce. "The Equal Employment Opportunity Law: A Decade of Change for Japanese Women?" *Law & Policy* 22 (October 2000): 385–408.

"Gender Gap in Government." http://www.gendergap.com/governme.htm (April 21, 2003).

GenderStats. http://web.worldbank.org.

German Federal Ministry of Health and Social Security. "Child Benefit, Child Raising Allowance, Parental Leave, Maintenance Advance and Supplementary Child Allowance." January 2005. http://www.bmgs.bund.de/downloads/Child_benefit-Kindergeld .pdf (April 30, 2006).

"Germany to Bolster Child Care." *Deutsche Welle.* October 28, 2004.

Gerson, Michael. "Thorns in the Congo." *Washington Post.* November 30, 2007, p. A23.

Gertzog, Irwin. *Congressional Women: Their Recruitment, Integration and Behavior.* 2d ed. Westport, CT: Praeger, 1995.

Gezari, Vanessa. "Killing Our Fathers, Raising Our Sons." *St. Petersburg Times.* August 5, 2007, p. 1.

Gill, Kirrin, Rohini Pande, and Anju Malhotra. "Women Deliver for Development." Family Care International and the International Center for Research on Women. 2008, 2007. http://www.womendeliver.org.

Gilligan, Carol. *In a Different Voice: Psychological Theory and Women's Development.* Cambridge, MA: Harvard University Press, 1982.

Global Campaign for Education. "Must Try Harder: A School Report on 22 Rich Countries' Aid to Basic Education in Developing Countries." November 2003. http://www.campaignforeducation.org (Nov. 25, 2003).

Global Campaign to Stop Killing and Stoning. "Frequently Asked Questions About Stoning." http://www.stop-stoning.org/faq_stoning (Feb. 6, 2009).

Global Partnership for Education. "All Children Learning Report Shows Bold Vision to Help Millions of Poor Kids Learn and Grow." June 27, 2012. http://www.globalpartnership.org/news/338/22/All-Children-Learning-Report/d,WhatsNew/ (July 5, 2012).

Glynn, Sarah Jane, and Audrey Powers. "The Top 10 Facts About the Wage Gap." Center for American Progress. April 16, 2012. http://www.americanprogress.org/issues/2012/04/wage_gap_facts.html (June 21, 2012).

Goldstone, Jack. *Revolution and Rebellion in the Early Modern World.* Berkeley: University of California Press, 1991.

———. "Toward a Fourth Generation of Revolutionary Theory." *Annual Review of Political Science* 4 (2001): 139–187.

———, ed. *Revolutions: Theoretical, Comparative and Historical Studies.* 3rd ed. Belmont, CA: Thompson Wadsworth, 2003.

Goodspeed, Peter. "Rape Now War Strategy in Congo, Doctor Says; Sexual Terrorism." *National Post.* December 1, 2008, p. A7.

Gootman, Elissa and Catherine Saint Louis, "Maternity Leave? It's More Like a Pause," *New York Times,* July 20, 2012, http://www.nytimes.com/2012/07/22/fashion/for-executive-women-is-maternity-leave-necessary.html?pagewanted=all.

Gornick, Janet C., Marcia K. Meyers, and Katherin E. Ross. "Public Policies and the Employment of Mothers: A Cross-National Study." *Social Science Quarterly* 79, no. 1 (1998): 35–54.

Gottfried, Heidi, and Laura Reese. "Gender, Policy, Politics, and Work: Feminist Comparative and Transnational Research." *Review of Policy Research* 20, no. 1 (2003).

Gottschall, Karin, and Katherine Bird. "Family Leave Policies and Labor Market Segregation in Germany: Reinvention or Reform of the Male Breadwinner Model?" *Review of Policy Research* 20, no. 1 (2003): 115–135.

Govender, Peroshni. "56 Female Candidates up for Election in Israel." January 28, 2003. Women's eNews. http://womensenews.org (Jan. 28, 2003).

Graff, James, et al. "Help Wanted for Europe." *Time,* vol. 155, issue 25 (June 19, 2000).

Graham-Brown, Sarah. "Women and Power in the Middle East." In *Women and Politics in the Middle East,* ed. Suad Joseph and Susan Slyomovics. Philadelphia: University of Pennsylvania Press, 2001.

Gregory, Jeanne. "Sexual Harassment: The Impact of EU Law in the Member States." In *Gender Policies in the European Union,* ed. Mariagrazia Rossilli. New York: Peter Lang, 2000.

Grey, Sandra. "Does Size Matter? Critical Mass and New Zealand Women MPs." *Parliamentary Affairs* 55 (2002): 19–29.

Gurr, T. R. *Why Men Rebel.* Princeton, NJ: Princeton University Press, 1968.

Guttmacher Institute. "Bush Administration Withholds UNFPA Funding for Seventh Year." June 27, 2008. http://www.guttmacher.org/media/inthenews/2008/06/27/index.html.

———. "Spurious Science Triumphs as U.S. Court Upholds South Dakota 'Suicide Advisory' Law. July 27, 2012, http://www.guttmacher.org/media/inthenews/2012/07/27/index .html

———. "State Policies in Brief: Counseling and Waiting Periods for Abortion as of September 1, 2012."

Hamlin Fistula International, "Fast Facts and FAQs." http://www.hamlinfistula.org/what-is-a-fistula/fast-facts-and-faqs.html

Hanami, Tadashi. "Equal Employment Revisited." *Japan Labour Bulletin,* The Japan Institute of Labour 39 (Jan. 1, 2000).

Handelman, Howard. *The Challenge of Third World Development.* Upper Saddle River, NJ: Prentice Hall, 2003.

"Harman Pledges to Reduce the Widening Gender Wage Gap." *Birmingham Post.* September 6, 2007, p. 4.

Hassim, Shireen. "'A Conspiracy of Women': The Women's Movement in South Africa's Transition to Democracy." *Social Research* 69 (Fall 2002): 693–732.

Hausmann, Ricardo, Laura D. Tyson, and Saadia Zahidi. *Global Gender Gap Report 2011,* World Economic Forum, Geneva, Switzerland, 2011.

Henderson, Sarah L. "Women in a Changing Context." In *Understanding Contemporary Russia,* ed. Michael Bressler. Boulder, CO: Lynne Rienner Press, 2008.

Henneck, Rachel. "Family Policy in the US, Japan, Germany, Italy, and France: Parental Leave, Child Benefits/Family Allowances, Child Care, Marriage/Cohabitation, and Divorce." Unpublished paper, May 2003.

Heyden, Tom. "FARC's Female Guerillas Submitted to Sexual Slavery: Police Report." *Columbia Reports,* June 13, 2011, http://colombiareports.com/colombia-news/news/16935-colombian-police-report-details-sexual-atrocities-within-farc.html.

Heyzer, Noeleen. "Peace of Mind, Piece of Land." *Our Planet,* United Nations Environmental Program, Nairobi Kenya *vol.* 15, no. 2, 2004, pp. 11–12.

Hochschild, Arlie Russell, and Barbara Ehrenreich, eds. *Global Woman: Nannies, Maids, and Sex Workers in the New Economy.* New York: Metropolitan Books, 2004.

Hoodfar, Homa. "Bargaining with Fundamentalism: Women and the Politics of Population Control in Iran." *Reproductive Health Matters* 4, no. 8 (1996), pp. 30–40.

Hooglund, Eric, ed. *Twenty Years of Islamic Revolution: Political and Social Transition in Iran Since 1979.* Syracuse, NY: Syracuse University Press, 2002.

Hoskyns, Catherine. "A Study of Four Action Programmes on Equal Opportunities." In *Gender Policies in the European Union,* ed. Mariagrazia Rossilli (New York: Peter Lang, 2000).

Hudson, Valerie M., and Andrea M. Den Boer. *Bare Branches: The Security Implications of Asia's Surplus Male Population.* Cambridge, MA: MIT Press, 2004.

Human Rights Watch. "Guinea; Thousands of Girls Face Abuse as Domestic Workers." *Africa News.* June 15, 2007.

———. "Crime or Custom? Violence Against Women in Pakistan." August 1999. http://www.hrw.org/reports/1999/pakistan (Nov. 7, 2003).

———. Testimony from the press release "Serb Gang-Rapes in Kosovo Exposed." March 21, 2000. http://www.hrw.org/press/2000/03/kosrape.htm (Nov. 7, 2003).

——. "Seeking Protection: Addressing Sexual and Domestic Violence in Tanzania's Refugee Camps." October 2000. http://www.hrw.org/reports/2000/tanzania (Nov. 17, 2003).

——. "Nigeria: Teenage Mother Whipped." January 23, 2001. http://www.hrw.org/press/2001/01/nigeria0123.htm (Nov. 17, 2003).

——. "The War Within the War: Sexual Violence Against Women and Girls in Eastern Congo." June 2002. http://www.hrw.org/reports/2002/drc/index.htm (Dec. 4, 2003).

——. "Pakistan: Tribal Councils Source of Abuse." July 12, 2002. http://www.hrw.org/press/2002/pak0712.htm (Nov. 7, 2003).

——. "Refugee and Internally Displaced Women; Gender-Based Asylum Claims." 2003. http://www.hrw.org/women/refugees.html (Nov. 7, 2003).

Huntington, Samuel P. *Political Order in Changing Societies.* New Haven, CT: Yale University Press, 1970.

Inglehart, Ronald. *The Silent Revolution: Changing Values and Political Styles Among Western Publics.* Princeton, NJ: Princeton University Press, 1977.

——. *Culture Shift in Advanced Industrial Society.* Princeton, NJ: Princeton University Press, 1990.

——. *Modernization and Postmodernization: Cultural, Economic and Political Change in 43 Societies.* Princeton, NJ: Princeton University Press, 1997.

Inglehart, Ronald, and Pippa Norris. *Rising Tide: Gender Equality and Cultural Change Around the World.* New York: Cambridge University Press, 2003.

Institute for War and Peace Reporting. "Congo-Kinshasa; Rape a 'Weapon of War' in Eastern Congo." *Africa News.* December 23, 2007.

Institute for Women's Policy Research, "Fact Sheet" May 2011, http://www.iwpr.org/publications/pubs/maternity-paternity-and-adoption-leave-in-the-united-states/.

International Institute for Democracy and Electoral Assistance. "Gender and Political Participation: Gender Facts." http://www.idea.int/vt/survey/by_gender.cfm (May 29, 2012).

——. "Gender and Political Participation: Voter Turnout by Gender." www.idea.int/gender/turnout (April 23, 2003).

International Labour Organization. "Global Employment Trends for Women Brief." March 2007. http://www.ilo.org/public/english/employment/strat/download/getw07.pdf.

——. *Condition of Work Digest 1994: Volume 13 Maternity and Work.* Geneva: ILO, 1994.

——. *Maternity at Work: A Review of National Legislation,* 2nd ed., 2010.

——. *Women and Men in the Informal Economy: A Statistical Picture.* Geneva: ILO, 2002.

——. *Time for Equality at Work: Global Report Under the Follow-up to the ILO Declaration on Fundamental Principles and Rights at Work.* Geneva: ILO, 2003.

International Women's Democracy Center. "Resources: Fact Sheet: Women's Political Participation." http://www.iwdc.org/factsheet.htm (May 1, 2003).

Inter-Parliamentary Union. "Women in National Parliaments." May 29, 2012. http://www.ipu.org/wmn-e/classif.htm (May 29, 2012).

——. *Women in Parliament in 2007: The Year in Perspective* (Switzerland: IPU, 2007), p. 5.

——. *Quarterly Review.* "The World of Parliaments." March 2010, no. 37, p. 18.

"Iraqi Women Face Court-Ordered Virginity Tests." *Agence France-Presse.* July 1, 2012. http://www.rawstory.com/rs/2012/07/01/iraqi-women-face-court-ordered-virginity-tests/ (July 12, 2012).

Irish Medical Council. *A Guide to Ethical Conduct and Behavior.* 6th ed. Dublin: Irish Medical Council, 2004.

Jackson, Maggie. "Study: Part Time Work Is Widespread but Undervalued." The Associated Press, November 20, 1997.

Jacobs, Stevenson. "Jamaica: MPs Recommend Virginity Tests, Sterilization for Young Women." The Associated Press, July 30, 2003. http://www.imdiversity.com/villages/global/article_detail.asp?Article_ID=18541 (Dec. 18, 2003).

Jancar, Barbara Wolfe. Women Under Communism. Baltimore, MD: Johns Hopkins University Press, 1978.

Jancar-Webster, Barbara. Women and Revolution in Yugoslavia. Denver, CO: Arden Press, 1990.

"Japan's Salary Gap." The Japan Times. March 24, 2008.

Jaquette, Jane. "Women in Power: From Tokenism to Critical Mass." Foreign Policy 108 (Fall 1997): 23–38.

Jaquette, Jane S., and Kathleen Staudt. "Women, Gender, and Development." In Women and Gender Equity in Development Theory and Practice: Institutions, Resources, and Mobilization, ed. Jane S. Jaquette and Gale Summerfield. Durham, NC: Duke University Press, 2006, p. 21.

Jehl, Douglas, and Michael R. Gordon. "American Forces Reach Cease-Fire with Terror Group." New York Times, April 29, 2003.

Jenkins, J. Craig. The Politics of Insurgency. New York: Columbia University Press, 1985.

Jenkins, J. Craig, and Charles Perrow. "Insurgency of the Powerless: Farm Workers Movements." American Sociological Review 42 (1977): 249–267.

Jewell, Malcolm, and Marcia Lynn Whicker. Legislative Leadership in American States. Ann Arbor: University of Michigan Press, 1994.

Jeydel, Alana, and Andrew Taylor. "Are Women Legislators Less Effective? Evidence from the U.S. House in the 103d–105th Congress." Political Research Quarterly 56 (March 2003): 19–28.

Joint United Nations Programme on HIV/AIDS (UNAIDS). A Joint Response to HIV/AIDS. Geneva: UNAIDS, 2004.

Jones, Del. "Few Women Hold Top Executive Jobs, Even When CEOs Are Female." USA Today. January 27, 2003. http://www.usatoday.com/money/jobcenter/2003-01-26-womenceos_x.htm (Oct. 6, 2003).

Joseph, Hir. "WRAPA Prepares Women for Voting." April 11, 2003. http://allAfrica.com/stories/printable/200304120067.html (April 21, 2003).

Joseph, Saud. "Women and Politics in the Middle East." In Women and Politics in the Middle East, ed. Saud Joseph and Susan Slyomovics. Philadelphia: University of Pennsylvania Press, 2001.

Kabeer, Naila. Gender Mainstreaming in Poverty Eradication and the Millennium Development Goals: A Handbook for Policy-makers and Other Stakeholders. London: Commonwealth Secretariat, 2003.

Kain, Azadeh. "Women and Politics in Post-Islamist Iran: The Gender Conscious Drive to Change." British Journal of Middle Eastern Studies 24, no. 1 (1997): 75–97.

Kakuchi, Suvendini. "Rights-Japan: Not All Working Women are Equal." Inter Press Service News Agence. August 17, 2010. http://www.ipsnews.net/2010/08/rights-japan-not-all-working-women-are-equal/ (June 18, 2012).

Kamerman, Sheila B. "Early Childhood Education and Care (ECEC): An Overview of Developments in the OECD Countries." Unpublished paper.

Kamerman, Sheila, and Shirley Gatenio. "Mother's Day: More Than Candy and Flowers, Working Parents Need Paid Time-Off." Columbia University, the Clearing House on International Developments in Child, Youth, and Family Policies. Issue Brief, Spring 2002.

———. "Tax Day: How Do America's Child Benefits Compare?" Columbia University, the Clearing House on International Developments in Child, Youth, and Family Policies. Issue Brief, Spring 2002.

Kamerman, Sheila B., Michelle Neuman, Jane Waldfogel, and Jeanne Brooks-Gunn. *Social Policies, Family Types and Child Outcomes in Selected OECD Countries.* Paris: OECD, 2003.

Kampwirth, Karen. *Women and Guerilla Movements: Nicaragua, El Salvador, Chiapas, Cuba.* University Park: The Pennsylvania State University Press, 2002.

———. *Feminism and the Legacy of Revolution: Nicaragua, El Salvador, Chiapas.* Athens: Ohio University Press, 2004.

Kaplan, Temma. "Uncommon Women and the Common Good." In *Women Resist Globalization,* ed. Sheila Rowbotham and Stephanie Linkogle. London and New York: Zed Books, 2001.

Karombo, Stanley. "Rights-Zimbabwe: Virginity Testing Strips Girls of their Dignity—Groups." Inter Press Service News Agency. February 2, 2009. http://ipsnews.net (Feb. 2, 2009).

KatineChronicles. "Debate: The State of Education in Uganda." *The Guardian.* May 2008. http://www.guardian.co.uk/society/katineblog/2008/May/23/ugandawillachieve itsmillen (Jan. 15, 2009).

Katzenstein, Mary Fainsod, and Carol M. Mueller, eds. *The Women's Movements of the United States and Western Europe.* Philadelphia: Temple University Press, 1987.

Kavakci, Merve. "Headscarf Heresy: For One Muslim Woman, the Headscarf Is a Matter of Choice and Dignity." *Foreign Policy* (May/June 2004): 66–67.

Kearney, Emily. "Reaching the Poorest with Microfinance: The Importance of Innovation in Program Design." Unpublished thesis, Oregon State University, 2009.

Keck, Margaret E., and Kathryn Sikkinkh. *Activists Beyond Borders: Advocacy Networks in International Politics.* Ithaca, NY: Cornell University Press, 1998.

Kelly, Erin, and Frank Dobbin. "Civil Rights Law at Work: Sex Discrimination and the Rise of Maternity Leave Policies." *American Journal of Sociology* 105, no. 2 (1999): 455–492.

Kelly, Michael. "Hasten the Day When AIDS No Longer Has a Female Face." *The Irish Times.* March 13, 2007, p. 16.

"Kenya; Teenage Girls Targeted for Sexual Exploitation." *East African Standard,* Africa News. February 7, 2008.

Keskin, Burcak. "Confronting Double Patriarchy: Islamist Women in Turkey." In *Right Wing Women: From Conservatives to Extremists around the World,* ed. Paola Bacchetta and Margaret Power. New York: Routledge, 2002.

Kettering, Evert. "Netherlands." In *Abortion in the New Europe: A Comparative Handbook,* ed. Bill Roston and Anna Eggert. Westport, CT: Greenwood Press, 1994.

Kian-Kian-Thiébaut, Azadeh. "Women and the Making of Civil Society in Post-Islamist Iran." In *Twenty Years of Islamic Revolution: Political and Social Transition in Iran Since 1979,* ed. Eric Hoogland. Syracuse, NY: Syracuse University Press, 2002.

Kitschelt, Herbert P. "Political Opportunity Structures and Political Protest: Anti-Nuclear Movements in Four Democracies." *British Journal of Political Science* 16, no. 1 (1986): 57–85.

Klawiter, Maren. "Racing for the Cure, Walking Women and Toxic Touring: Mapping Cultures of Action Within the Bay Area Terrain of Breast Cancer." *Social Problems* 46, no. 1 (1999): 104–126.

Koinange, Jeff. "Woman Sentenced to Stoning Freed." CNN, September 26, 2003. http://www.cnn.com/2003/WORLD/africa/09/25/nigeria.stoning (Dec. 18, 2003).

Kornhauser, William. *The Politics of Mass Society.* Glencoe, IL: The Free Press, 1959.

Krasniewicz, Louise. *Nuclear Summer: The Clash of Communities at the Seneca Women's Peace Encampment.* Ithaca, NY: Cornell University Press, 1992.

Kristof, Nicholas D. "Where Sweatshops Are a Dream." *New York Times,* January 14, 2009.

La Franiere, Sharon. "Nightmare for African Women: Birthing Injury and Little Help." *New York Times,* September 28, 2005.

Lambert, Caroline. "French Women in Politics: The Long Road to Parity." The Brookings Institution. May 2001. http://www.brookings.edu/research/articles/2001/05/france-lambert (April 23, 2003).

Latif, Aamir. "Taliban Divided on Girls Education." December 26, 2008. http://www.islamonline.net (Jan. 8, 2009).

Law Students for Reproductive Justice, "Access to Abortion Around the World, 2012." http://lsrj.org/documents/factsheets/12_Abortion%20Around%20the%20World.pdf.

Lazaro, Juan. "Women and Political Violence in Contemporary Peru." In *Women and Revolution: Global Expressions,* ed. M. J. Diamond. Boston: Kluwer Academic Publishers, 1998.

Leira, Arnlaug. *Working Parents and the Welfare State: Family Change and Policy Reform in Scandinavia.* Cambridge: Cambridge University Press, 2002.

Lenz, Ilse. "Globalization, Gender, and Work: Perspectives on Global Regulation." *Review of Policy Research* 20 (Spring 2003).

"Liberia; Survey—Commanders Took Away Weapons from Ex-Female Fighters." *Africa News.* June 26, 2008.

"The List: The Worst Places to Be a Woman." May 2008. http://www.foreignpolicy.com/story/cms.php?story_id=4319&print=1.

Liu, Dongxiao, and Elizabeth Heger Boyle. "Making the Case: The Women's Convention and Equal Employment Opportunity in Japan." *International Journal of Comparative Sociology* 42 (2001).

Lluciak, Ilja A. *After the Revolution: Gender and Democracy in El Salvador, Nicaragua, and Guatemala.* Baltimore, MD: Johns Hopkins University Press, 2001.

Lobao, Linda M. "Women in Revolutionary Movements: Changing Patterns of Latin American Guerilla Study." In *Women and Revolution: Global Expressions,* ed. M. J. Diamond. Boston: Kluwer Academic Publishers, 1998.

Lovenduski, Joni, and Pippa Norris, eds. *Women in Politics.* New York: Oxford University Press, 1996.

Luker, Kristin. *Abortion and the Politics of Motherhood.* Berkeley: University of California Press, 1984.

Lynch, Michael. *Mao.* New York: Routledge, 2004.

Mahon, Evelyn. "Abortion Debates in Ireland: An Ongoing Issue." In *Abortion Politics, Women's Movements, and the Democratic State,* ed. Dorothy McBride Stetson. Oxford: Oxford University Press, 2001.

Mandela, Nelson. *Long Walk to Freedom: The Autobiography of Nelson Mandela.* United Kingdom: Back Bay Books, 1995.

Margolies-Mezvinsky, Marjorie. *A Woman's Place: The Freshman Who Changed the Face of Congress.* New York: Crown, 1994.

Markandya, Polly, and Fionna Lloyd-Davis. "DRC: A Plaster on a Gaping Wound." April 16, 2002. http://www.msf.org/countries/page.cfm (Dec. 4, 2003).

Mayell, Hillary. "Thousands of Women Killed for Family Honor." February 12, 2002. http://news.nationalgeographic.com/news/pf/15061734.html (Feb. 2, 2009).

Mayer, Nonna, and Mariette Sineau. "France: The Front National." In *Rechtsextreme Parteien*, ed. Helga Amsberger and Brigitte Halbmayr. Opladen: Leske & Budrich, 2002.

Mazur, Amy G. *Gender Bias and the State: Symbolic Reform at Work in Fifth Republic France.* Pittsburgh: University of Pittsburgh Press, 1995.

———. *Theorizing Feminist Policy.* New York: Oxford University Press, 2002.

Mazur, Amy G., and Suzanne Zwingel. "Comparing Feminist Policy in Politics and at Work in France and Germany: Shared European Union Setting, Divergent National Contexts." *Review of Policy Research* 20, vol. 1 (2003): 365–383.

McAdam, Doug. *Political Process and the Development of Black Insurgency 1930–1970.* Chicago and London: University of Chicago Press, 1985.

McCarthy, John D., and Meyer Zald, eds. *Social Movements in an Organizational Society.* New Brunswick, NJ, and Oxford: Transaction Books, 1987.

McCormack, Claire. "Abortion Law Decisions Coming to Catholic Ireland" *Forbes*, August 27, 2012, http://www.forbes.com/sites/womensenews/2012/08/27/abortion-law-decisions-coming-to-catholic-ireland/.

McCrummen, Stephanie. "Groups Sign Deal to End Long Fight in E. Congo; Accord Portrayed as Key Initial Step." *The Washington Post.* January 24, 2008, p. A13.

McDonagh, Eileen. "Assimilated Leaders: Democratization, Political Inclusion and Female Leadership." *Harvard International Review* 21 (Fall 1999): 64–69.

McDonald, Dearbhail. "Abortion—It's Back to Court." *Sunday Times of London.* August 14, 2005.

McGlen, Nancy, and Karen O'Connor. *Women's Rights.* New York: Praeger, 1983.

McGreal, Chris. "Arab Women Fight to Keep Gains Won on the Street." *The Guardian*, June 13, 2012, http://www.guardian.co.uk/world/2012/jun/13/arab-women-egypt-laws-parliament.

McKay, Susan. "Girls as 'Weapons of Terror' in Northern Uganda and Sierra Leoneon Rebel Fighting Forces." *Studies in Conflict and Terrorism* (April 2005): 385–397.

McKinsey, Kitty. "Yugoslavia: Crimes Against Women Become Focus of Tribunals." May 13, 1998. http://www.rferl.org/nca/features/1998/05/F.RU.980513135425.html (Dec. 3, 2003).

Medecins Sans Frontieres. "The Crushing Burden of Rape: Sexual Violence in Darfur." A Briefing Paper. Amsterdam. March 8, 2005.

Meyer, David. "Institutionalizing Dissent: The United States Structure of Political Opportunity and the End of the Nuclear Freeze Movement." *Sociological Forum* 8, no. 2 (1993): 157–179.

———. "Restating the Woman Question: Women's Movements and State Restructuring." In *Women's Movements Facing the Reconfigured State,* ed. Lee Ann Banaszak, Karen Beckwith, and Dieter Rucht. New York: Cambridge University Press, 2003.

Meyer, David, and Nancy Whittier. "Social Movement Spillover." *Social Problems* 41 (1994): 277–298.

Meyers, Marcia K., Janet C. Gornick, and Katherin E. Ross. "Public Childcare, Parental Leave, and Employment." In *Gender and Welfare State Regimes,* ed. Diane Sainsbury. Oxford: Oxford University Press, 1999.

"Michelle Bachelet Highlights Quotas to Accelerate Women's Political Participation." http://www.unwomen.org/2012/03/michelle-bachelet-highlights-quotas-to-accelerate-womens-political-participation/ (May 29, 2012).

Migration Policy Institute, "The Global Remittances Guide," http://www.migrationinformation.org/datahub/remittances.cfm.

Miles, Alice. "Maybe Baby's Best with Dad." *The Times (London)*. March 2, 2005.

Mink, Gwendolyn. *Welfare's End*. Ithaca, NY: Cornell University Press, 1998.

Moghadam, Valentine, ed. *Democratic Reform and the Position of Women in Transitional Economies*. Oxford: Clarendon Press, 1993.

——. "Gender and Revolutions." In *Theorizing Revolutions*, ed. John Foran. New York: Routledge Press, 1997.

——. "Revolution, Religion, and Gender Politics: Iran and Afghanistan Compared." *Journal of Women's History* 10 (Winter 1999): 172–195.

——. *Modernizing Women: Gender and Social Change in the Middle East*. 2d ed. Boulder, CO: Lynne Rienner Press, 2003.

——. *Globalizing Women: Transnational Feminist Networks*. Baltimore, MD: The Johns Hopkins University Press, 2005.

Moghadam, Valentine M., and Margot Badran. *Causes and Gender Implications of Islamist Movements in the Middle East*. Helsinki: World Institute of Development Economic Research, United Nations University, 1991.

Molyneux, M. "Mobilization Without Emancipation? Women's Interests, the State and Revolution in Nicaragua." *Feminist Studies* 11 (1985): 227–254.

Momsen, Janet Henshall. *Gender and Development*. London: Routledge, 2004.

Myakayaka-Manzini, Mavivi. "Women Empowered—Women in Parliament in South Africa." 2002 update of case study originally published in *Women in Parliament: Beyond Numbers*, vol. 1. Stockholm: International IDEA, 1998. http://www.idea.int (April 30, 2006).

Nakamura, Akemi. "Four Women Await Outcome of 10-Year Quest for Equal Pay." *The Japan Times*. March 27, 2005.

Narli, Nilufer. "The Rise of the Islamist Movement in Turkey." *Middle Eastern Review of International Affairs* 3, no. 3 (1999).

National Center for Post Traumatic Stress Disorder. "Rape of Women in a War Zone: A National Center for PTSD Fact Sheet." May 14, 2003. http://www.ptsd.va.gov/public/pages/rape-women-war-zone.asp (Dec. 2, 2003).

National Organization for Women. "Facts About Pay Equity." http://www.now.org/issues/economic/factsheet.html (Oct. 6, 2003).

——. "Pay Equity Still a Dream Worth Pursuing: New Report Shows Glass Ceiling Intact." Summer 2002. http://www.now.org/nnt/summer-2002/payequity.html (Oct. 6, 2003).

National Women's Law Center. "The Paycheck Fairness Act: Helping to Close the Women's Wage Gap." May 2003. http://www.nwlc.org (Oct. 6, 2003), p. 1.

Naumann, Ingela K. "Child Care and Feminism in West Germany and Sweden in the 1960s and 1970s." *Journal of European Social Policy* 15, no. 1 (2005).

Nduna, Sydia, and Lorelei Goodyear. "Pain Too Deep for Tears: Assessing the Prevalence of Sexual and Gender Violence Among Burundi Refugees in Tanzania." Revised 1997. http://www.rescue.org/sites/default/files/migrated/resources/sgbv_1.pdf (Jan. 23, 2009).

Nelson, Barbara J., and Najma Chowdury, eds. *Women and Politics Worldwide*. New Haven, CT: Yale University Press, 1994.

Netherlands Ministry of Foreign Affairs. "Questions and Answers on Dutch Policy on Abortion—2003." http://www.minvws.nl/en/themes/abortion/default.asp (Aug. 10, 2005).

Nicol, Diane. "Employers Face Rise in Equal Pay Claims." *The Scotsman*. April 19, 2003, p. 23.

Norris, Pippa. "Women's Power at the Ballot Box." Paper written for International Institute for Democracy and Electoral Assistance, Voter Turnout from 1945–2000: A Global Report on Political Participation.

———. *Electoral Engineering: Voting Rules and Political Behavior.* New York: Cambridge University Press, 2004.

Norris, Pippa, and Joni Lovenduski. "Blair's Babes: Critical Mass Theory, Gender, and Legislative Life." John F. Kennedy School of Government, Harvard University, Faculty Research Working Paper Series (September 2001).

Nousratpour, Louise. "Hit out Over Pay Injustice: Unions Urge Government to Confront Poverty." *Morning Star.* September 18, 2003, p. 1.

Nzwili, Frederick. "Women Candidates in Kenya Assaulted, Under-Funded." December 27, 2002. www.womensenews.org (Dec. 27, 2002).

Oakley, Richard. "Irish Faith on Wane but Tolerance Rises." *The Times.* April 10, 2005.

O'Connor, J. "Gender, Class and Citizenship in the Comparative Analysis of Welfare State Regimes: Theoretical and Methodological Issues." *British Journal of Sociology* 44, no. 3 (1993): 501–518.

O'Malley, Brendan. "The Global Classroom." *South China Morning Post.* June 16, 2007, Education, p. 6.

"Only 8.9% of Managerial Positions Taken by Women in Japan." *Deutsche Press-Agentur.* September 13, 2003, Miscellaneous section.

OECD Development Centre, 2012 SIGI (Social Institutions and Gender Index): Understanding the Drivers of Gender Inequality, Paris, 2012.

Organization for Economic Co-operation and Development. "Child Care in OECD Countries," in *Employment Outlook 1990.* Paris: OECD, 1990.

———. *OECD in Figures: Statistics for the Member Countries.* Paris: OECD, 2002.

———. Overview of Gender Differences in OECD Countries, http://www.oecd.org/els/familiesandchildren/overviewofgenderdifferencesinoecdcountries.htm.

Organization for Economic Co-operation and Development Economics Department. "Female Labour Force Participation: Past Trends and Main Determinants in OECD Countries," May 2004. http://www.oecd.org/dataoecd/25/5/31743836.pdf (April 30, 2006).

Ortega, Luisa Maria Dietrich. "Gendered Patterms of Mobilisation and Recruitment for Political Violence: Lessons Learned from Three Latin American Countries." Centre for Research on Inequality, Human Security and Ethnicity, Oxford, England, 2009.

Ostner, Ilona. "From Equal Pay to Equal Employability: Four Decades of European Gender Policies." In *Gender Policies in the European Union,* ed. Mariagrazia Rossilli (New York: Peter Lang, 2000).

Outshoorn, Joyce. "Policy-making on Abortion: Arenas, Actors, and Arguments in the Netherlands." In *Abortion Politics, Women's Movements and the Democratic State,* ed. Dorothy McBride Stetson. New York: Oxford University Press, 2001.

Oxfam International. *Trading Away Our Rights: Women Working in Global Supply Chains.* Oxford: Oxfam International, 2004.

Paxton, Pamela, and Sheri Kunovich. "Women's Political Representation: The Importance of Ideology." *Social Forces* 82 (2003): 87–114.

Penn, Shana. *Solidarity's Secret: The Women Who Defeated Communism in Poland.* Ann Arbor: University of Michigan Press, 2005.

Physicians for Human Rights. "War-Related Sexual Violence in Sierra Leone: A Population-Based Assessment." Cambridge: Physicians for Human Rights, 2000.

Piven, Francis Fox, and Richard Cloward. *Poor People's Movements.* New York: Vintage Books, 1979.

Pogatchnik, Shawn. "Irish Bishops Reject Pregnancy Pamphlet." Associated Press, June 16, 2005.

Pope, Charles. "Social Security Must Protect Women, Bush Told." *Seattle Post-Intelligencer.* June 13, 2001. http://seattlepi.nwsource.com/national/27227_socsec13.shtml (Sept. 29, 2003).

Poya, Maryam. *Women, Work and Islamism: Ideology and Resistance in Iran.* London and New York: Zed Books, 1999.

Prasad, Raekha. and Randeep Ramesh. "India's Missing Girls: Daughters Aren't Wanted in India." *The Guardian.* February 28, 2007, p. 4.

Prieto, Norma Iglesias. *Beautiful Flowers of the Maquiladora: Life Histories of Women Workers in Tijuana.* Austin: University of Texas Press, 1997.

Rai, Shirin. "Class, Caste and Gender—Women in Parliament in India." 2002 update of case study originally published in *Women in Parliament: Beyond Numbers,* vol. 1. Stockholm: International IDEA, 1998. http://www.idea.int (April 30, 2006).

Ramesh, Randeep. "India to Crack Down in Doctors Aborting Girls." *The Guardian.* April 25, 2008, p. 24.

Randall, Margaret. *Gathering Rage: The Failure of Twentieth Century Revolutions to Develop a Feminist Agenda.* New York: Monthly Review Press, 1992.

Ray, Rebecca, Janet C. Gornick, and John Schmitt, "Parental Leave Policies in 21 countries: Assessing Generosity and Gender Equality," Center for Economic and Policy Research, Washington, D.C., September 2008.

Rehn, Elisabeth, and Ellen Johnson Sirleaf. "Women War Peace." In *Progress of the World's Women 2002,* vol. 1. New York: UNIFEM, 2003.

Reseau des Femmes Pour un Developpement Associatif. "Women's Bodies as a Battleground: Sexual Violence Against Women and Girls During the War in the Democratic Republic of Congo, South Kivu (1996–2003)." *International Alert* (2005): 34.

Results, "2007 Basics: Global Education for All." 2007. http://www.results.org/website/article.asp?id=2566 (Jan. 7, 2009).

Reuters. "Women Paid 16% Less Than Men, Report Says; Gap Widest in Asia, Americas." *The Gazette (Montreal).* March 7, 2008.

Reynolds, Andrew. "Women in Legislatures and Executives of the World: Knocking at the Highest Glass Ceiling." *World Politics* 51, no. 4 (1999): 547–572.

Reynolds, Sian, ed. *Women, State and Revolution: Essays on Power and Gender in Europe Since 1789.* Amherst: University of Massachusetts Press, 1987.

"Rights Group Says Law Must Be Changed to Allow for Abortions." *Irish Independent.* March 8, 2005.

Ronnow, Karin. "Journey of Hope: An In-Depth Report, Keeping Hope Alive." *Bozeman Daily Chronicle,* 2008, p. 7 (Central Asia Institute).

Rosenthal, Cindy Simon. *When Women Lead: Integrative Leadership in State Legislatures.* New York: Oxford University Press, 1998.

Rossilli, M. Grazia. "The European Union's Policy on the Equality of Women." *Feminist Studies* 25 (Spring 1999): 171–182.

———, ed. *Gender Policies in the European Union* (New York: Peter Lang, 2000).

Roston, Bill, and Anna Eggert. *Abortion in the New Europe: A Comparative Handbook.* Westport, CT: Greenwood Press, 1994.

Rowbotham, Sheila, and Stephanie Linkogle, eds. *Women Resist Globalization: Mobilizing for Livelihood and Rights.* London and New York: Zed Books, 2001.

Rueschemeyer, Marilyn, ed. *Women in the Politics of Postcommunist Eastern Europe* (Armonk, NY: M.E. Sharpe, 1994).

Ruhn, Christopher J. "Policies to Assist Parents with Young Children," *Work and Family,* vol. 21, no. 2, Fall 2011: 37–58.

Rule, Wilma. "Electoral Systems, Contextual Factors and Women's Opportunities for Parliament in 23 Democracies." *Western Political Quarterly* 40 (1987): 477–498.

———. "Why Women Don't Run: The Critical Contextual Factors in Women's Legislative Recruitment." *Western Political Quarterly* 34 (1988): 60–77.

Rule, Wilma, and Matthew Shugart. "The Preference Vote and Election of Women." Center for Voting and Democracy. 1995. http://www.fairvote.org/reports/1995/chp7/rule.html (May 6, 2003).

"Russian Judge Rules Sexual Harassment is Okay as it Ensures Survival of Human Race." *Huffington Post.* August 13, 2008. http://www.huffingtonpost.com/2008/08/05/russian-judge-rules-sexua_n_11707.html (July 16, 2012).

Sadik, Nafis, "Practical Consensus." *Our Planet.* United Nations Environmental Program, Nairobi Kenya, vol. 15, no. 2 (2004) p. 6.

Saeger, Joni. *The State of the Women in the World Atlas.* New York: Penguin Books, 1997.

Safa, Helen I., and Cornelia Butler Flora. "Production, Reproduction, and the Polity: Women's Strategic and Practical Gender Issues." In *Americas: New Interpretive Essays,* ed. Alfred Stepan. New York and Oxford: Oxford University Press, 1992.

Sainsbury, Diane. "Introduction." In *Gender and Welfare State Regimes,* ed. Diane Sainsbury. Oxford: Oxford University Press, 1999.

———, ed. *Gender and Welfare State Regimes.* Oxford: Oxford University Press, 1999.

Samarasinghe, Vidyamali. "Confronting Globalization in Anti-trafficking Strategies in Asia." *Brown Journal of World Affairs* 10, no. 1 (2003): 91.

Sanbonmatsu, Kira, Susan J. Carroll, and Debbie Walsh. "Poised to Run: Women's Pathways to State Legislatures." Center for American Women and Politics, (2009): 3

"Scans for Baby's Sex Illegal—but Rampant." *The Straights Times (Singapore).* July 14, 2007. http://justwoman.asiaone.com/Just%2BWoman/Motherhood/Stories/Story/AlStory20070720-19064.html

Schirmer, Jennifer. "The Seeking of Truth and the Gendering of Consciousness." In *Viva: Women and Political Protest in Latin America,* ed. Sarah A. Radcliffe and Sallie Westwood. New York and London: Routledge, 1993.

Schreiber, Ronnee. "Injecting a Woman's Voice: Conservative Women's Organizations, Gender Consciousness, and the Expression of Women Policy Preferences." *Sex Roles* 47 (October 2002).

Scottish Labour. "Women and the Changing European Union." November 4, 2002. http://www.scottishlabour.org.uk/helenliddell (Sept. 30, 2003).

Sen, Amartya. *Development as Freedom.* New York: Anchor Books, 2000.

Sengupta, Anuradha. "Kashmiris Look to a Woman for Resolution of Strife," January 24, 2003. http://www.womensenews.org/article.cfm?aid=1195 (Jan. 24, 2003).

Shayne, Julie D. *The Revolution Question: Feminisms in El Salvador, Chile, and Cuba.* New Brunswick, NJ: Rutgers University Press, 2004.

Siamdoust, Nahid. "A Woman as President: Iran's Impossible Dream?" *Time,* May 20, 2009, http://www.time.com/time/world/article/0,8599,1899763,00.html.

Singer, Peter W. *Children at War.* Berkeley: University of California Press, 2006.

Singer, Rena. "Chastity Tests: Unusual Tool for Public Health." *The Christian Science Monitor.* June 2, 2000. http://www.csmonitor.com/ 2000/06/02/pls4.html (Dec. 18, 2003).

Singh, Susheela, and Lacqueline E. Darroch, "Adding it Up: Costs and Benefits of Contraceptive Services – Estimates for 2012." Guttmacher Institute, June 2012.

Singh, Susheela, Stanley K. Henshaw, and Kathleen Berentsen. "Abortion: A Worldwide Overview." In *The Sociocultural and Political Aspects of Abortion: Global Perspectives,* ed. Alaka Malwade Basu. Westport, CT: Praeger, 2003.

Skocpol, Theda. *States and Social Revolutions.* New York: Cambridge University Press, 1979.

Slaughter, Anne-Marie. "Why Women Still Can't Have it All," *The Atlantic,* July 2012, http://www.theatlantic.com/magazine/archive/2012/07/why-women-still-cant-have-it-all/309020/.

Smelser, Neil. *Theory of Collective Behavior.* New York: The Free Press, 1962.

Smith, Bonnie G., ed. *Global Feminisms Since 1945.* New York: Routledge, 2000.

Smith, Lisa C., and Lawrence Haddad. *Explaining Child Malnutrition in Developing Countries: A Cross-Country Analysis.* Washington, DC: International Food Policy Research Institute, 2000.

Smith, Lois M., and Alfred Padula. *Sex and Revolution: Women in Socialist Cuba.* New York: Oxford University Press, 1996.

Social Security Administration. "Women and Social Security," October 3, 2005. http://www.ssa.gov/pressoffice/factsheets/women.htm (April 30, 2006).

Social Security Network. "Issue Brief #6: Social Security: A Women's Issue." http://www.socsec.org/facts/Issue_Briefs/women.htm (Oct. 3, 2003).

Songwe, Omer. "Cameroon Princess Fights Mutilation." December 9, 2002. http://news.bbc.co.uk/1/hi/world/africa/2547503.stm (Dec. 15, 2003).

"Special Report: Women and Work: Closing the Gap." *The Economist.* November 26, 2011. http://www.economist.com/node/21539928 (June 21, 2012).

"Statement by Congresswoman Carolyn B. Maloney: Women's Equality Amendment—11/14/2002." *Women's International Network News* (Winter 2003): 29–31.

Statistics Netherlands, "Annual Number of Abortions Stable over the Past Decade," 22 February 2011, http://www.cbs.nl/en-GB/menu/themas/bevolking/publicaties/artikelen/archief/2011/2011-3322-wm.htm

Steinberg-Ratner, Ronnie. "The Policy and Problem: Overview of Seven Countries." In *Equal Employment Policy for Women,* ed. Ronnie Steinberg-Ratner. Philadelphia: Temple University Press, 1980.

Stephen, Lynn. 1997. *Women and Social Movements in Latin America: Power from Below.* Austin: University of Texas Press.

Stern, Andrew. "US Pharmacist Sues, Refusing to Sell Contraceptive." Reuters News Service. June 10, 2005.

Stetson, Dorothy McBride. "US Abortion Debates: 1959–1998: The Women's Movement Holds On." In *Abortion Politics, Women's Movements, and the Democratic State: A Comparative Study of State Feminism,* ed. Dorothy McBride Stetson. Oxford: Oxford University Press, 2001.

———, ed. *Abortion Politics, Women's Movements, and the Democratic State: A Comparative Study of State Feminism.* New York: Oxford University Press, 2001.

Stetson, Dorothy McBride, and Amy G. Mazur. "Introduction." In *Comparative State Feminism,* ed. Dorothy McBride Stetson and Amy G. Mazur. Thousand Oaks, CA: Sage Publications, 1995.

———, eds. *Comparative State Feminism.* Thousand Oaks, CA: Sage Publications, 1995.

Stoltzfus, Emilie. *Citizen, Mother, Worker: Debating Responsibility for Child Care after the Second World War.* Chapel Hill: University of North Carolina Press, 2003.

Swedish Institute. "Childcare in Sweden." September 2004. http://www.sweden.se/templates/cs/BasicFactsheet (April 22, 2006).

Swers, Michelle. "Are Congresswomen More Likely to Vote for Women's Issues Bills Than Their Male Colleagues?" *Legislative Studies Quarterly* 23 (1998): 435–448.

———. *The Difference Women Make: The Policy Impact of Women in Congress.* Chicago: University of Chicago Press, 2002.

Sylvester, Christine. "Simultaneous Revolutions and Exists: A Semi-Skeptical Comment." In *Women and Revolution in Africa, Asia, and the New World*, ed. Mary Ann Tetrault. Columbia: University of South Carolina Press, 1994.

Tahmina, Qurratul Ain. "South Asia: Working Women Get Poor Health Services." Inter Press Service, June 3, 2003.

Tait, Robert. "Anger as Iran Bans Women from Universities," *The Telegraph*, August 20, 2012, http://www.telegraph.co.uk/news/worldnews/middleeast/iran/9487761/Anger-as-Iran-bans-women-from-universities.html.

Takahashi, Hiroyuki. "Working Women in Japan: A Look at Historical Trends and Legal Reform." Japan Economic Institute, no. 42. November 6, 1998. http://www.jei.org/Archive/JEIR98/9842f.html (Nov. 13, 2003).

Tamerius, Karin L. "Sex, Gender, and Leadership in the Representation of Women." In *Gender, Power, Leadership, and Governance*, ed. Georgia Duerst-Lahti and Rita Mae Kelly. Ann Arbor: University of Michigan Press, 1993.

Tanaka, Hiromi. "Equal Employment in Contemporary Japan: A Structural Approach." *Political Science and Politics*, (January 2004), pp. 66–66.

Tarrow, Sidney. *Power in Movement*. Cambridge: Cambridge University Press, 1994.

Tattersall, Nick. "Savage Life of Boy Soldiers Made to Kill." *The Advertiser*. June 9, 2007, p. 76.

Taylor, Sandra C. *Vietnamese Women at War: Fighting for Ho Chi Minh and the Revolution*. Lawrence: University Press of Kansas, 1999.

Te Braake, Trees A. M. "Late Termination of Pregnancy Because of Severe Foetal Abnormalities: Legal Acceptability, Notification and Review in the Netherlands." *European Journal of Health Law* 7 (2000): 387–403.

Tetrault, Mary Ann. "Women and Revolution: A Framework for Analysis." In *Women and Revolution in Africa, Asia, and the New World*, ed. Mary Ann Tetrault. Columbia: University of South Carolina Press, 1994.

———. "Women and Revolution: What Have We Learned?" In *Women and Revolution in Africa, Asia, and the New World*, ed. Mary Ann Tetrault. Columbia: University of South Carolina Press, 1994.

———. "Women and Revolution in Vietnam." In *Global Feminisms Since 1945*, ed. Bonnie G. Smith. New York: Routledge, 2000.

Thomas, Sue. *How Women Legislate*. New York: Oxford University Press, 1994.

Thomas, Sue, and Susan Welch. "The Impact of Gender on Activities and Priorities of State Legislators." *Western Political Quarterly* 44 (1991): pp. 454–455.

Thorton, Grant. "Proportion of Women in Senior Management Falls to 2004 Levels." http://www.internationalbusinessreport.com/Press-room/2011/women_in-senior_magagement.asp (June 21, 2012).

Tinker, Irene. "Empowerment Just Happened: The Unexpected Expansion of Women's Organizations." In *Women and Gender Equity in Development Theory and Practice: Institutions, Resources, and Mobilization*, ed. Jane S. Jaquette and Gale Summerfield. Durham, NC: Duke University Press, 2006, p. 268.

Tostan. "History." http://www.tostan.org (July 23, 2012).

"Treaty Establishing the European Community," http://www.hri.org/docs/Rome57/Part3 Title08.html#Art119 (April 30, 2006).

Tripp, Aili Mari. *Women and Politics in Uganda*. Madison: The University of Wisconsin Press, 2000.

Turner, Ralph H., and Lewis Killian. *Collective Behavior*. Englewood Cliffs, NJ: Prentice Hall, 1957.

"Uganda; Country's Debt Drops to $1 Billion." *Monitor,* Africa News. February 28, 2007.

Uggen, Christopher. "Sexual Harassment: The Emergence of Legal Conciousness in Japan and the US." *The Asia-Pacific Journal: Japan Focus.* http://www.japanfocus.org/-christopher-uggen/3199 (June 25, 2012).

Uggen, Christopher and Chika Shinohara. "Sexual Harassment Comes of Age: A Comparative Analysis of the United States and Japan." *The Sociological Quarterly* 50 (2009): 203.

UNAIDS. *Report on the Global Aids Epidemic Executive Summary.* Geneva, Switzerland: UNAIDS, July 2008, p. 8.

"The Unfortunate Facts of Life in 2007." Women Deliver Global Conference 2007.

UNIFEM. "Gender Equality Now. Accelerating the Achievement of the Millennium Development Goals." Part II of Progress 2008/2009, New York: UNIFEM, 2008/2009.

———. "Who Answers to Women? Gender and Accountability." Progress of the World's Women 2008/09. New York, UNIFEM, 2008/2009, pp. 117–133.

United Nations. "Charter of the United Nations." http://www.un.org/aboutun/charter (Oct. 12, 2005).

———. *The United Nations and the Advancement of Women, 1945–1996.* New York: United Nations, Department of Public Information, 1996.

———. *Human Development Report 2007/2008,* New York: United Nations Development Programme, p. 337.

———. "United Nations International Decades Designated by the General Assembly." September 27, 2001. http://www.nalis.gov.tt/National-UN-Days/UN_INTERNATIONALDECADES.html (Oct. 13, 2005).

———. "We Can End Poverty 2015 Millenium Development Goals, Fact Sheet." September 2010.

———. *Women Go Global: The United Nations and the International Women's Movement, 1945–2000.* New York: United Nations, 2003.

———. *The Millennium Development Goals Report.* New York: United Nations, 2005.

———. "The Millennium Development Goals Report 2008." September 2008. http://www.undp.org/publications/MDG_Report_2008_EN.pdf (Jan. 13, 2009), p. 4.

———. *Rural Women in a Changing World: Opportunities and Challenges.* New York: United Nations, October 2008.

———. "The World's Women 2010: Trends and Statistics." http://unstats.un.org/unsd/demographic/products/Worldswomen/WW2010pub.htm (June 20, 2012).

United Nations Children's Fund (UNICEF). "Domestic Violence Against Women and Girls." Florence, Italy: Innocenti Research Centre, June 2000.

———. Ethiopia: Statistics. http://www.unicef.org/infobycountry/ethiopia_statistics.html

———. "Gender Achievements and Prospects in Education: The GAP Report, Part One, South Asia Yawning Chasm." http://www.ungei.org/gap/reportSasia.php (Jan. 8, 2009).

United Nations Department of Economic and Social Affairs, Division for Sustainable Development. http://www.un.org/esa/sustdev.

———. *Annual Report 2003.* New York: UNICEF, 2004.

———. "The World's Women 2010: Trends and Statistics." http://unstats.un.org/unsd/demographic/products/Worldswomen/WW2010pub.htm

United Nations Development Fund for Women. *Progress of the World's Women 2002: Gender Equality and the Millennium Development Goals.* New York: UNIFEM, 2002.

United Nations Development Programme. *Human Development Report 2002.* New York: Oxford University Press, 2002.

———. *Human Development Report 2003.* New York: Oxford University Press, 2003.

———. *Human Development Report 2004.* New York: Oxford University Press, 2004.

———. *Human Development Report 2005.* New York: Oxford University Press, 2005.

———. *Human Development Report 2007/2008.* New York: Oxford University Press, 2007/2008.

United Nations, Division for the Advancement of Women. "Convention on the Elimination of All Forms of Discrimination Against Women." http://www.un.org/womenwatch/daw/cedaw (Oct. 13, 2005).

United Nations Educational, Scientific and Cultural Organization (UNESCO). "Girls Continue to Face Sharp Discrimination in Access to School." June 11, 2003. Press release No 2003–91. http://portal.unesco.org/en/ev.php-URL_ID=17039&URL_DO=DO_TOPIC&URL_SECTION=201.html (Nov. 25, 2003).

United Nations Girls' Education Initiative. "Formative Evaluation of the United Nations Girls' Education Initiative: Uganda Report." (April 2012): 16.

———. "100 Literacy Classes for Girls and Women Open in Senegal." http://www.ungei.org/senegal_3086.html?q=printme (July 5, 2012).

United Nations High Commissioner for Refugees. "Basic Facts." http://www.unhcr.org (Dec. 9, 2003).

United Nations Integrated Regional Information Networks. "Liberia; Some Women Ready to Fight Again." *Africa News.* October 14, 2008.

———. "Togo; School Year Reopens with Free Primary Schools." *Africa News,* October 6, 2008.

United Nations Population Division, Department of Economic and Social Affairs. *Abortion Policies: A Global Review.* New York: United Nations Press, 2002.

United Nations Population Division. "Ireland." In *Abortion Policies: A Global Review.* New York: United Nations Press, 2002.

———. "Netherlands." In *Abortion Policies: A Global Review.* New York: United Nations: 2002. http://www.un.org/esa/population/publications/abortion/ (Aug. 10, 2005).

———. "United States of America." In *Abortion Policies: A Global Review.* New York: United Nations Press, 2002.

United Nations Population Fund (UNFPA). "UNFPA: United Nations Population Fund." http://www.unfpa.org/about/index.htm (Oct. 13, 2004).

———. "State of the World Population 2006. A Passage to Hope. Women and International Migration." http://www.unfpa.org/swp/2006/english/chapter_2/print/chapter_2.html.

———. "Selling Hope and Stealing Dreams: Trafficking in Women and the Exploitation of Domestic Workers." *State of World Population 2006,* New York: UNFPA, 2006.

———. "Who We Are." http://www.unfpa.org/publications/detail.cfm?ID=384& filterList-Type=.

U.S. Agency for International Development (USAID), Office of Women and Development. "Girls' and Women's Education: A USAID Initiative." Fact Sheet (April 1998).

U.S. Census Bureau. Income, Poverty, and Health Insurance Coverage in the United States: 2010, Report P60, n. 238, Table B-2, pp. 68–73.

———. Statistical Abstract of the United States: 2011, p. 858.

———. "Voter Turnout Increases by 5 Million in 2008 Presidential Election, U.S. Census Bureau Reports." July 20, 2009. http://www.census.gov/newsroom.releases/archives/voting/cb09-110.html (May 29, 2012).

U.S. Department of Justice. "Child Sex Tourism." http//www.usdoj.gov/criminal/ceos/sextour.html.

U.S. Department of Labor. "Quick Statistics on Women Working, 2010." http://www.dol .gov/wb/factsheets/QS-womenswork2010.htm (June 18, 2012).

U.S. Department of State. *Trafficking in Persons Report.* Washington, DC: U.S. Department of State, June 2008, p. 24.

U.S. Department of State, Bureau of Democracy, Human Rights, and Labor. "Japan: Country Reports on Human Rights Practices—2000." February 23, 2001, http://www.state .gov/g/drl/rls/hrrpt/2000/eap/709pf.htm (Nov. 19, 2003).

U.S. General Accounting Office. "A New Look Through the Glass Ceiling: Where Are the Women?" Washington, DC: U.S. General Accounting Office, January 2002, pp. 1–13.

Varnon, Rob. "Census Report on Earning: Struggling to Bridge the Wage Gap." *Connecticut Post.* August 17, 2003, Your Money section.

Verba, Sidney, Norman Nie, and Jae-on Kim. *Participation and Social Equality.* Cambridge, MA: Harvard University Press, 1978.

Verba, Sidney, Kay Schlozman, and Henry E. Brady. *Voice and Equality.* Cambridge, MA: Harvard University Press, 1995.

"Voters in Ireland Reject Change in Abortion Law." *USA Today.* March 8, 2002, p. 7A.

"Voters in United Arab Emirates Set to Vote in Historic Elections," http://www.dubaicity .com/news/historic-elections12–16.htm (Oct. 14, 2008).

Wakabi, Wairagala. "Africa Battles to Make Female Genital Mutilation History." *The Lancet* 369 (March 31, 2007–April 6, 2007): 1069.

Wasserstrom, Jeffrey N. "Gender and Revolution in Europe and Asia, Part 2: Recent Works and Frameworks for Comparative Analysis." *Journal of Women's History* 6 (Spring 1994): 109–120.

Welch, Susan. "Women as Political Animals? A Test of Some Explanations for Male-Female Political Participation Differences." *American Journal of Political Science* 21 (1977): 711–730.

———. "Are Women More Liberal Than Men in the U.S. Congress?" *Legislative Studies Quarterly* 10 (1985): 125–134.

Wellesley Centers for Research on Women and Development and Training Services, Inc., for USAID. "Unsafe Schools: A Literature Review of School-Related Gender-Based Violence in Developing Countries." September 2003. http://pdf.usaid.gov/pdf_docs/ PNACU253.pdf (Jan. 8, 2009).

White House. "President Bush Signs Partial Birth Abortion Ban Act 2003." http://www .whitehouse.gov/news/releases/2003/11/print/20031105–1.html (April 22, 2006).

Wickham-Crowley, Timothy. *Guerillas and Revolution in Latin America: A Comparative Study of Insurgents and Regimes Since 1956.* Princeton, NJ: Princeton University Press, 1992.

Williams, Beryl. "Kollantai and After: Women in the Russian Revolution." In *Women, State and Revolution: Essays on Power and Gender in Europe Since 1789,* ed. Sian Reynolds. Amherst: The University of Massachusetts Press, 1987.

Wisensale, Steven K. *Family Leave Policy: The Political Economy of Work and Family in America.* Armonk, NY: M.E. Sharpe, 2001.

Woloch, Nancy. *Women and the American Experience.* New York: Alfred A. Knopf, 1984.

Women Deliver. "Saving Women's Lives: Leading Killers and Practical Solutions." www .womendeliver.org/assets/WD_Killers-Solutions_(SP).pdf/.

"Women and the Vote," Tehran Bureau, *Frontline,* May 12 2009, http://www.pbs.org/wgbh/ pages/frontline/tehranbureau/2009/05/women-and-the-vote.html.

"Women and Work: European Situation." http://www.etuc.org.EQUALPAY/UK/women_ and_work/European-Union/default.cfm (Nov. 11, 2003).

"Women Given Unfair Choice of Babies or a Good Pension." *The Western Mail.* July 7, 2003, p. 1.

"Women in Europe Towards Healthy Ageing." European Institute of Women's Health. 1997) http://www.eurohealth.ie/report/index.htm (Sept. 29, 2003), Introduction, p. 4 of 5.

WomenOf.com. "Non-Profits Improve Numbers of Women CEOs." http://www.womenof .com/News/cn092500.asp (Oct. 6, 2003).

Women Watch. "International Day of Rural Women." October 15, 2008. www.un.org/ womenwatch/feature/idrw/index.html.

World Bank. *Engendering Development: Through Gender Equality in Rights, Resources, and Voice.* New York: Oxford University Press, 2001.

———. "Girls Education—Key Issues." 2009. http://go.worldbank.org/SP3Y3AHK10 (Jan. 7, 2009).

———. "World Bank's First-Ever Combination Grant-Credit Will Support Uganda Education, March 24, 1998. http://web.worldbank.org/WBSITE/EXTERNAL/NEWS/0,,cont entMDK:20012678~menuPK:34466~pagePK:64003015~piPK:64003012~ theSitePK:4607,00.html (Oct. 15, 2005).

———. "Uganda: Development Results." http://web.worldbank.org/WBSITE/EXTERNAL/ COUNTRIES/AFRICAEXT/UGANDAEXTN/0,,menuPK:374871~pagePK:141159~ piPK:141110~theSitePK:374864,00.html (Oct. 15, 2005).

———. *Engendering Development: Through Gender Equality in Rights, Resources, and Voice.* New York: Oxford University Press, 2001.

———. *World Development Indicators 2001.* New York: World Bank, 2001.

———. *World Development Indicators 2002.* New York: World Bank, 2002.

———. *World Development Report 2012: Gender Equality and Development*

———. "Land Use Rights and Gender Equality in Vietnam." *Promising Approaches to Engendering Development* 1 (September 2002): 1–2.

World Bank, Gender and Development Group. *Gender Equality and the Millennium Development Goals.* New York: World Bank, April 4, 2003.

World Bank, Independent Evaluation Group. http://www.worldbank.org/ieg/education/ findings.html (January 12, 2009).

World Health Organization. *Abortion: A Tabulation of Available Data on the Frequency and Mortality of Unsafe Abortion.* 2d ed. Geneva: Maternal Health and Safe Motherhood Program, Division of Family Health, World Heath Organization, 1994.

———. "Female Genital Mutilation," Fact Sheet no. 241, May 2008, http://www.who.int/ mediacentre/factsheets/fs241/en/print.html (Feb. 3, 2009).

———. *Unsafe Abortion: Global and Regional Estimates of Incidence of and Mortality Due to Unsafe Abortion.* 3d ed. Geneva: World Health Organization, 1998.

———. "Making Pregnancy Safer," February 2004. http://www.who.int/mediacentre/ factsheets/fs276/en/print.html (Oct. 13, 2004).

———. "Reproductive Health," http://www.who.int/topics/reproductive_health/en/.

World Health Organization, UNICEF and United Nations Population Fund. *Maternal Mortality in 2000: Estimates Developed by WHO, UNICEF, and UNFPA.* Geneva: World Health Organization, 2004.

Worldmapper. http://www.worldmapper.org/display.php?selected=181.

World Values Survey. "1999–2002 World Values Survey Questionnaire." http://www.world valuessurvey.org/statistics/index.html (April 22, 2006).

Yishai, Yael. *Between the Flag and the Banner: Women in Israeli Politics.* Albany: SUNY Press Albany, 1997.

Young, Marilyn B. "Reflections on Women in the Chinese Revolution." In *Women and Revolution: Global Expressions,* ed. M. J. Diamond. Boston: Kluwer Academic Publishers, 1998.

Zayed, Dina. "Attack on Egyptian Women Protesters Spark Uproar." Thomson Reuters, December 21, 2011, http://www.reuters.com/article/2011/12/21/us-egypt-protests-women-idUS TRE7BK1BX20111221.

Zerehun, Abeba. "One Woman's Story." Fistula Foundation, http://www.fistulafoundation org/press/archives/0501ows.html.

INDEX

Note: Page numbers in italics indicate figures; page numbers followed by "*t*" indicate tables.

417

Printed in the USA/Agawam, MA
December 17, 2018

693316.062